Globalisation Growth and Poverty

GLOBALISATION GROWTH AND POVERTY

Edited By

V.B. Jugale, *Ph.D.*
Professor & Head, Department of Economics
Shivaji University,
Kolhapur–416 004 (India)

SERIALS PUBLICATIONS
NEW DELHI

First Published–2004

ISBN: 81-86771-31-X

Published by

Head Office : **SERIALS PUBLICATIONS**
4, B.S.S. Hall, Khyber Pass Market,
Civil Lines, Delhi–110054 (India)
Fax: 91-11-23272135
Phone: 23245225
e-mail: serials@satyam.net.in

Branch Office : *4830/24, Prahlad Street, Ansari Road,*
Darya Ganj, New Delhi-110002 (India)

Printed at :

PRINTED IN INDIA

PREFACE

Development has no end in itself; it is a continuous process of eradication of the mental and physical discomforts in the life of a human being. However, development can only be understood better when we come to know, what is development? Backwardness is an incentive to the development. Degree of discomforts in the given social and economic system confines the urge of development. Creation of fearless society with aesthetic values is the main thrust of the development; hence the degree of freedom, moral values and ethical code of conduct became the elements of the development processes. Majority of the development models are replicable. But, in practice the domain idea of comforts leads to happiness and satisfaction compared to the imported idea. In fact, if followed, it requires some time to acclimatize in the given system. Development, in fact, proceeds through utpati, sthithi and laya i.e. birth, life and death of a community as a whole. To guard or to uphold the attained level of development is the level playing field for the development activities in a given social and economic system. HRD plays a significant role in extending the happiness, while the ignorance takes the life near to the death.

Welfare is the rich men's idea against the poverty. Poverty is not a problem to the poor people; but, it is a problem to others. Any welfare activity should not allow begging forever. It should help to develop in at least few cases; so as to restore the meaning of comforts and happiness. The myth of the modern development programmes did not ascertain a compete freedom from backwardness. Backwardness indeed makes a person to proceed towards the development. A worker works in the fields and factories for his family, so, the family or the population is the main attraction of the development activities. Provision of favourable atmosphere is the fundamental duty of the governments. Job (any activity) satisfaction should be an indicator of development. So a state intervention is essential in development activities. State intervention means not to impose a control or to support with some incentives. State support is not required for the poor and small enterprises, but the big push is required to the large enterprises. Support should not be the hangmen's rope supports the hanged. Subsidy to poor is based on the wrong footing of the state support.

The articles in this volume can be classified in to three main themes viz. an idea of globalization as a new development paradigm, its challenges and effects on various segments of the economy, globalization and the state of some regions and Indian states and the poverty eradication programmes since the introduction of the liberalisation model of growth in India.

A discursive debate on neo-globalization has been made by P. Jagadish Gandhi. He expressed the need of humanized globalization rather than WC led globalization. N. Narayan has discussed the long term prospects for developing countries, but it is a challenge to the developing countries. He emphasized the need of sustainable effects of globalization. The economic myths of globalization have been explored by M. Lakshmi Narasaiah. He thought, lots of demands have to be fulfilled by the government to promise for the globalization. A.P. Birader-Patil urges for the domestic liberalisation before the external led globalization for the future development of India. S.K. Mitra and I.D. Singh looks into the whole issues within the framework of feminist perspectives. Their observation reveals that the globalization has deteriorated the quality of life and the work of women disappointed. G.L. Bhong explained the passing dangers of the globalization on the small-scale industries in India. However the gradual process of globalization will help to prepare, proper mind setting for SSIs in India. Similarly R.G.Desai has also acknowledged the impact of reforms on the banking sector in India. The CAR of banks has improved the capital base of the sector but the deregulation of interest rates did not work effectively; while the NPAs also did not meet the desired success in the economy. S.K. Gandhe explained the excellence, equity and competitiveness of education within the global system of education. S. Indrakant accounts for the post-reform nutritional level in his study area and the role of NGOs in Nutritional Security Programme. He concluded that, the NGOs should be accountable to the Government. V.B. Kakade and A.S. Nalawade are not happy with the reforms on labour. They feel that the concept of safety net and human face is lacking in the reforms. The issues and remedies of the WTO and human rights have been discussed by P. Bhuvaneshwari. Observance of all human rights in the development activities should be the integral part of globalization. Kavita Bhatnager has explored the vital impact of globalization on growth and poverty. B.K. Mohanty has raised some issues of trade labialization and IPRs, in which he stressed the need of having legislative measures, constituting proper administrative machinery and evolving the judicial mechanism. Sectoral fluctuations of the economy during the reform regime have been estimated by Doddangouda Patil. The effects of globalization on the FDI have been measured by Sandeepa Malhotra. Satya Prema accounts for the impact of globalization on the export-imports of the agro-products and suggested numerous measures to improve the trade conditions. D. Rudrappan has identified globalization process as an opportunity to correct anti-agriculture biasness in India. S. Murthy believes that, the multinational enterprises bring not only blessings but also woes to the development process of the Third World economies. But a careful intervention of the government is thought essential. D.H. Munjappa and M.R. Vinay have very exhaustively accounted for the behaviours of the automobile industry during the regime of globalization. The implications of information revolution during globalization on the women have been discussed by Sushila Jain.

The intensity and spread of development depends upon the region and the people to whom it is meant for. Globalization as a development strategy deals with the improvements vis-à-vis adversities over the state's performance in various macro economic variables. The implications basically visualized by some of the studies in the Volume, examines the effects of reforms on various aspects of the region and the states. V.B. Jugale's paper deals with the state's struggle for growth even with adversities in the Maharashtra's economy. He has made some important policy suggestions for improving the state's economic conditions. K.V. Rao and B.S. Rao have attempted to study the fiscal reforms in the state of Andhra Pradesh. The present IT revolution in the state is not receiving proper attention for taking the state economy on sound financial lines. Vinod Singh has analyzed the major recommendations of the Kelkar Committee Report on direct taxation. Unlike the state's studies, an attempt has been made by the M. Rathedi to explore the challenges of globalization on the developing countries. He believes that the existing driver for sustainable development, globalization is currently viewed by many is contributing to the marginalization of developing countries and weakening of their capacity to improve the livelihood of their people in a sustainable way. R.S.Gadage has examined the changing social dimensions and economic development due to liberalisation with the help of some indicators of the selected countries of the world. Similarly, Mokhtar M. Metwally has also attempted to study the status of employment of expatriates' vis-à-vis nationals in the private sector in the GCC (Gulf Co-operation Council) group of countries. Nicholas Apergis and Dimitrios Kyrkills have made an attempt to examine the relationship among output exchange rate, inflation and monetary dynamics in transitional Southeast European economies (Bulgaria, Romania,

Croatia and Slovenia) from 1990 to 2002. Radhika Lobo and Vinayak Deshpande have very exhaustively explained the experiences of the Southeast Asian countries with the help of some macro economic variables as a lesson to India. They consider that, unlike the goods markets, the liberalisation of the financial markets is a complex affair. G.R. Motlaleng deem in achieving the goals of globalization through regional economic integration in Southern Africa. The things are not so positive to integrate due to varieties of reasons. On the contrary the EU's trading arrangements are likely to have a fragmentary impact on the existing integration and regionalism in Southern Africa. Multinational marketing risk and opportunities available around the operational landscape of MNCs has been discussed by P.P. Ekerete. The product differentiation and development characteristically offers much to achieve the marketing objectives of the MNCs.

During 1960s poverty eradication programmes has been accepted as one of the indicators of development. But it was intended to make it possible in controlled economies. Globalization, of late, intends to make the economies open and competitive for eradication of poverty in developing countries; which has rendered adverse impact on the development of developing countries. Paramjit Nanda and P.S. Raikhy have made it clear that unless the developing countries try to achieve international development goals set by the international communities by pulling up their own boot straps to alleviate poverty, respectable position at international flora may not be possible for the developing countries. S. Chinnammi considers that the economic reforms without clear rules and policies may not have any impact on the economy as a whole. The role of government at the advent of crisis is immense. Ajit Kumar Sinha has developed a model of participatory monitoring of the process of social mobilization for poverty alleviation for economic development. P. Srinivas Subbarao deems WTO has serious implications on the SSIs in India. Target oriented poverty alleviation programmes have a separate entity with wide range of effects on the poor people. The role of micro credits by the SHGs has created a special image in the poverty eradication programmes. Debnarayan Sarker' study of SHGs is based on the SIPRD, Kalyani (W. Bengal). Such other studies have been made by Laxmi R. Kulshrestha and Archana Gupta; in which they have built three paradigms of linkage models for combating poverty. Awadhesh Kr. Singh has identified the fact that, SHGs are not linked with viable micro-enterprises for sustaining the resources and their effective utilization for poverty eradication. Falendra K. Sudan has also emphasized for revitalizing the micro-income generating activities through SHGs and other micro credit programmes for the rural women. An integrated approach with a new institutional framework for ensuring the poor to get reed of poverty is thought off by the author. Probodhita Pande has also reiterated the need of women empowerment through collective efforts. Silvia Maria de Mendonca Naronha attempted to study the changing pattern of employment in the primary sector of the Goain economy. D. Rudraappan and Suresh Kumar Jha have made an attempt to study the ways and means of empowerment of weaker section in the society. Multiple issues have been addressed by the authors to overcome the poverty. A macro view has been narrated by Talwar Sabanna in respect of growth, poverty and economic reforms in India. The jobless growth during the reform period is not tenable, if poverty has to be ameliorated. The extent of poverty during the reform period has been analyzed by Ravi M. Tirlapur. Unlike the experiences of other countries, growth is necessary but not an essential condition for poverty eradication. C.K. Renukarya and B. Gopalsingh have made an attempt to account for the poverty alleviation programmes by way of waste land development in Karnataka state. B. Shyamala, in her study, an alternative paradigm of human development has been suggested for poverty eradication in India. The readers have varieties of issues related to globalization to feed for their interest. Suggestions are most welcomed.

V.B. Jugale

CONTENTS

1

Poverty Alleviation for Development

Ajit Kumar Sinha*

The process of sustainable development must bring the degree of abject poverty to a minimum level as far as possible. The relative poverty is a universal fact and has existed in every society at all times. The matter of serious contemporary concern is, a maintained level of abject poverty of the exposed poor masses, deprived of basic human needs under the Glass Curtain Economy. The process of sustainable development is badly obstructed by the Neo Vicious Circle of Poverty which implies a circular constellation of forces tending to act and react upon one another in such a way as to keep a poor country in a State of poverty. It is a humiliating reality before the civil society and world's greatest challenge of the 21st century.

South Asia has been the centre of poverty. Out of 1.2 billion developing world's poor (20% of the total population living on less than $1 a day), 43.5 per cent live in South Asia (India, Pakistan, Bangladesh, Nepal, Bhutan, Maldives, Srilanka and Afghanistan), 24.3 per cent in Sub-Saharan Africa, 23.2 per cent in East Asia and Pacific, 6.5 per cent in Latin America and Caribbean, 2.0 per cent in Europe and Central Asia and 0.5 per cent in the Middle East and North Africa (Sinha 2002).

The poverty has resulted into low survival rate, low adult literacy rate; population without access to safe water, health services and sanitation and under weight children below the age of five amongst poor in the developing world.

* Former President, Indian Economic Association, Pro Vice-Chancellor, T.M. Bhagalpur University.

Poverty has been historically identified as the main persistent malady of the Indian Economy. Calculations of poverty indices for the Indian economy including Head-Court Index (HCI), Poverty Gap Index (PGI) and Squared Poverty Gap Index (SPGI) from August 1951 to December 1997 have clearly revealed that poverty had persisted in our system in a chequered way and the absolute number of poor has risen (Table 1).

State Wise variation in poverty level is an added dimension of the problem. Undivided Bihar had the highest poverty level from all the three poverty estimates i.e. HCI, PGT and SPGI. The classified estimation for rural and urban poverty indicate that rural poverty was the highest in Bihar, but this place was occupied by Madhya Pradesh in case of urban poverty (Table 2) Since 74.29% & 86.89% poor live in rural areas in India and Bihar respectively, the rural setting has a predominant impact on the poverty situation.

Reduction in poverty and unemployment and improvement in the quality of life have the basic goals of our plans which have remained unchanged since the beginning of the plan era. The earlier Indian plan models had visualised that the Trickle Down effect would result in higher income opportunities for the poor sector and significant dent on the incidence of poverty. But the average annual growth rate was around 3.5 per cent against the desired growth rate of 5.0 per cent during the first three decades of planning and the growth rate of population could not be brought down which jointly resulted extremely low per capita income growth and exposed the trickle down hypothesis.

A distinct change in the strategy of poverty alleviation was visualised since later part of 1970s. Instead of relying on growth to percolate, efforts were initiated to directly attack the problem of poverty by endowing the poor with productive assets/skill to employ themselves to earn larger income. Policy initiatives were also taken to create additional opportunities for wage employment essentially as a supplement to fill the gaps of unemployment in lean seasons. A number of poverty alleviation measures were introduced in the Sixth Five Year Plan and the subsequent plans followed suit. The Tenth Five Year Plan has also introduced a number of poverty alleviation measures.

The poverty alleviation programmes have not made significant dent on the problem of poverty. Poverty of poverty alleviation programmes jointly with anti development institutional frame work have successfully kept the poverty intact. The object poverty is prevalent over the system in tune with the global counterparts with the following characteristics:

Table 1: Poverty in India 1951-97 (with coefficient for (CPIAL).

(Poverty line = Rs. 49 per capita per month at Oct. 1973-Jun. 1974 rural prices)

NSS Survey Period		*Headcount Index*			*Poverty Gap Index*			*Squared Poverty Gap Index*		
round		*Rural*	*Urban*	*National*	*Rural*	*Urban*	*National*	*Rural*	*Urban*	*National*
3	Aug. 1951-Nov. 1952	47.37	35.46	45.31	16.05	11.14	15.2	7.53	4.82	7.06
4	Apr. 1952-Sept. 1952	43.87	36.71	42.63	14.64	10.91	13.99	6.71	4.41	6.31
5	Dec. 1952-Mar. 1953	48.21	40.14	46.80	16.29	13.25	15.76	7.56	5.96	7.28
6	May 1953-Sept.1953	54.13	42.77	52.15	19.03	13.83	18.12	9.12	6.29	8.62
7	Oct. 1953-Mar. 1954	61.29	49.92	59.30	21.95	17.24	21.12	10.26	7.74	9.82
8	Jul. 1954-Mar. 1955	64.24	46.19	61.07	25.04	15.76	23.41	12.5	7.02	11.54
9	May 1955-Nov. 1955	51.83	43.92	50.44	18.44	14.65	17.78	8.80	6.40	8.38
10	Dec. 1955-May 1956	48.34	43.15	47.43	15.65	13.34	15.24	6.71	5.41	6.48
11	Aug. 1956-Feb. 1957	58.86	51.45	57.55	19.45	18.16	19.22	8.50	8.51	8.50
12	Mar. 1957-Aug. 1957	61.11	48.88	59.77	21.69	16.31	20.73	10.01	7.25	9.52
13	Sep. 1957-May 1958	55.16	47.75	53.84	19.01	15.95	18.47	8.78	7.00	8.46
14	Jul. 1958-Jan. 1959	53.26	44.76	51.75	17.74	13.75	17.03	7.88	5.87	7.52
15	July. 1959-Jan. 1960	50.89	49.17	50.58	15.29	15.83	15.39	6.13	6.75	6.24
16	Jul. 1960-Aug. 1961	45.40	44.65	45.27	13.6	13.84	13.64	5.33	5.83	5.59
17	Sept. 1961-Jul. 1962	47.20	43.55	46.54	13.6	13.79	13.64	5.31	6.05	5.45
18	Feb. 1963-Jan. 1964	48.53	44.83	47.85	13.88	13.29	13.77	5.49	5.17	5.43
19	Jul. 1964-Jun. 1965	53.66	48.78	52.75	16.08	15.24	15.93	6.60	6.38	6.00
20	Jul. 1965-Jun. 1966	57.6	52.9	56.71	17.97	16.82	17.75	7.60	6.98	7.49
21	Jul. 1966-Jun. 1967	64.3	52.24	62	22.01	16.81	21.02	10.01	7.19	9.47
22	Jul. 1967-Jun. 1968	63.67	52.91	61.6	21.8	16.93	20.86	9.85	7.22	9.35

(Table Contd...)

Table 1: (Contd...)

NSS Survey Period		*Headcount Index*			*Poverty Gap Index*			*Squared Poverty Gap Index*		
round		*Rural*	*Urban*	*National*	*Rural*	*Urban*	*National*	*Rural*	*Urban*	*National*
23	Jul. 1968-Jun. 1969	59.0	49.29	57.11	18.96	15.54	18.29	8.17	6.54	7.85
24	Jul. 1969-Jun. 1970	57.61	47.16	55.56	18.24	14.32	17.47	7.73	5.86	7.36
25	Jul. 1970-Jun. 1971	54.84	44.98	52.88	16.55	13.35	15.91	6.80	5.35	6.51
27	Oct. 1972-Sept. 1973	55.36	45.67	53.37	17.35	13.46	16.55	7.33	5.26	6.90
28	Oct. 1973-Jun. 1974	55.72	47.96	54.1	17.18	13.60	16.43	7.13	5.22	6.73
32	Jul. 1977-Jun. 1978	50.6	40.5	48.36	15.03	11.69	14.28	6.06	4.53	5.72
38	Jan. 1983-Dec. 1983	45.31	35.65	43	12.65	9.52	11.9	4.84	3.56	4.53
42	Jul. 1986-Jun. 1987	38.81	34.29	37.69	10.01	9.10	9.79	3.70	3.40	3.63
43	Jul. 1987-Jun. 1988	39.23	36.2	38.47	9.28	9.12	7.24	2.98	3.06	3.00
44	Jul. 1988-Jun. 1989	39.06	36.6	38.44	9.50	9.54	9.51	3.29	3.29	3.29
45	Jul. 1989-Jun. 1990	34.3	33.4	34.07	7.80	8.51	7.98	2.56	3.04	2.69
46	Jul. 1990-Jun. 1991	36.43	32.76	35.49	8.64	8.51	8.61	2.93	3.12	2.98
47	Jul. 1991-Dec. 1991	37.42	33.23	36.34	8.29	8.24	8.28	2.68	2.90	2.74
48	Jan. 1991-Dec. 1992	43.47	33.73	40.93	10.88	8.82	10.35	3.81	3.19	3.65
50	July 1993-Jun. 1994	36.66	30.51	35.04	8.39	7.41	8.13	2.79	2.42	2.69
51	July. 1994-Jun. 1995	39.75	33.5	38.4	8.89	8.38	-	2.90	2.8	-
52	Jul. 1995-Jun. 1996	37.46	28.04	35	8.31	6.78	-	2.64	2.22	-
53	Jan. 1997-Dec. 1997	35.69	29.99	34.4	8.39	7.77	-	2.83	2.73	-

Source: World Bank, India-Reducing Poverty Accelerating Development, Oxford University Press, New Delhi, 2000.

Table 2: State Poverty Rates.

State	*Total*			*Rural*			*Urban*		
	HCI	*PGI*	*SGPI*	*HCI*	*PGI*	*SPGI*	*HCI*	*PGI*	*SPGI*
Punjab	11.46	1.84	0.46	11.69	1.90	0.48	10.90	1.69	0.40
Andhra Pradesh	21.87	4.54	1.48	15.89	2.88	0.86	38.82	9.27	3.20
Gujarat	24.15	4.77	1.42	22.16	4.07	1.16	28.28	6.22	1.96
Kerala	25.12	5.59	1.86	25.38	5.61	1.84	24.31	5.53	1.88
Haryana	25.22	4.94	1.51	28.26	5.60	1.74	16.47	3.05	0.85
Rajasthan	27.46	5.62	1.72	26.40	5.21	1.55	31.02	7.00	2.24
Himachal Pradesh	28.58	5.19	1.50	30.36	5.55	1.61	9.26	1.25	0.26
Karnataka	32.91	7.73	2.69	30.11	6.27	2.01	39.90	11.36	4.36
Tamil Nadu	35.40	8.33	3.00	32.95	7.30	2.49	39.92	10.23	3.92
Maharashtra	36.82	9.61	3.65	37.91	9.28	3.34	34.99	10.15	4.15
West Bengal	36.94	7.42	2.21	41.18	8.29	2.45	22.95	4.55	1.41
Assam	41.09	7.46	2.00	44.19	8.21	2.20	7.93	0.92	0.22
Uttar Pradesh	41.55	10.23	3.50	42.32	10.37	3.53	35.10	9.03	3.26
Madhya Pradesh	42.46	10.40	3.68	40.75	9.48	3.26	48.08	13.43	5.05
Orissa	48.64	11.89	4.10	49.81	11.96	4.07	40.64	11.41	4.29
Bihar	55.15	13.83	4.77	57.95	14.66	5.06	34.84	7.86	2.63
All India	36.13	8.42	2.86	37.07	8.43	2.80	33.06	8.38	3.07

Note: HCI: Headcount Index; PGI: Poverty Gap Index; SPGI: Squared Poverty Gap Index.

Source: World Bank, Reducing Poverty in India, Report No. 1788-in, June 29, 1998.

1. Lack of income and assets to attain basic necessities-food, shelter clothing and acceptable level of health and education.
2. Sense of voicelessness and powerlessness in the institutions of State and society.
3. Vulnerability to adverse shocks, linked to an inability to cope with them (World Bank 2000/2001).

Challenges Ahead

Development is growth plus change. Change Indicates the structural transformation of the system. Developing nations cannot be satisfied on the achievement of positive growth. But structural transformation cannot be possible with abject poverty of common masses. Alleviation of abject poverty is the primary condition for development of the countries like India.

Democracy is the best alternative from development point of view also. This was the reason of economic transformation of the Socialist economies to market economies. They have transformed their system due to international scrutiny and without any external pressure. Even the economic development of Punjab and human development index of Kerala is better placed and without any coercion in comparison to China in respective areas. But for overall development of the system it is essentially needed to salvage the system from the traps of Crime Syndicates functioning in perfect nexus with Bureaucracy, Police, Politicians and Mafias to siphon off any type of resources with chikenery methods (Sinha 2000).

For alleviation of poverty, as a precondition of development, the recommendation of the Independent South Asian Commission on poverty Alleviation should be implemented in the form of 'Sociogram'.

The criteria in the sociogram are all interrelated and mutually reinforcing. However, they deserve to be presented separately not only for their own sake but more importantly, because they contribute to each other's growth and thereby to the total process. If one element in the process is not

Participatory Monitoring of the Process of Social Mobilisation for poverty Alleviation Sociogram.

moving forward it can easily be identified and strengthened. The three major planks that deepen social consciousness and lead to the empowerment of the poor are attitudinal change, the capacity for self-management and the economic and social base of the poor. It is axiomatic that the economic base of the poor has to be improved over a period of time through a dual process of savings investment and asset creation and the emancipation of the poor from economic and social bondage, to enable them not only to be more productive and keep the surplus in their own hands. The establishment of a self-reliant activity base will mutually reinforce the process of promoting positive attitudinal values. Conscious attempts to diagnose, assess and mutually stimulate such values will bring them to the fore and will contribute to turning them into a driving force for further action, contributing to a deepening expansion of the process itself. Ultimately the process as a whole, which starts with the release of the creativity of the poor, has to be judged by the increase in their social consciousness, empowerment and self-respect. It would have the way to break the Neo-Vicious Circle of Poverty (Vicious Circle of Poverty under institutional framework) and initiate the virtuous circle of development.

REFERENCES

1. Sinha, Ajit Kumar 2000, Organised Crime and Development, Forum of Free Enterprise, Bombay.
2. Sinha, Ajit Kumar 2002, Dynamics of Poverty Alleviation Programmes, Deep & Deep Publications, New Delhi, World Bank 2000, India, Reducing Poverty Accelerating Development, Export University Press, New Delhi World Bank.
3. World Bank, 1998, Reducing Poverty in India, Report No. 1788.

2

WTO and its Implications for Small Industry

Dr. P. Srinivas Subbarao*

The World around us is changing and changing very fast. The changes are visible in multiple forms and form multiple directions. Starting from economic reforms with emphasis on liberalisation, privatisation, and globalisation, the World has witnessed emergence of World Trade Organisation (WTO) and its conditionalties which have altered the basic principles of trade, regional grouping, barrier free movements, mergers and acquisitions, foreign direct investments, bilateral and multilateral agreements etc., which have become the order of the day. Labour standards and environmental situation in our country affect the cost of production and competitiveness of products in other countries. Marketing strategy has changed, but more than that there has been a major change in consumer tastes and preferences. Their pressure for better quality and hygienic product has once again proved that consumer is king. The World is in grip of technological changes and revolution in the field of information technology. Organisations, where big or small, are compelled to upgrade technology, cut costs, improve quality and adopt innovative management strategies.

The role played by small-scale industry (SSI) in the process of economic development is no doubt significant. It is contributing about 36% GDP, 35% to India's exports and employing 18.56 millions (2000-2001).

The emergence of World Trade Organisation (WTO) and its conditionalties, small-scale industries will have to complete on their own to find a place for

* Assistant Professor, Department of Management Studies P.G. Courses, M.R. College, Viziannagaram. (A.P)

themselves in the domestic as well as international markets. The WTO agreement does not discriminate on the basis of size of industries or enterprises. Hardly there is single agreement of WTO, which is directly dealing with SSIs. Under the WTO scenario, Indian SSIs might face competition both from MNC's and from Indian large-scale companies. The market access agreements encompassing TRIPS & TRIMS means that import of goods will increase in all product categories including reserved items of SSIs. Reduced tariff rates would effect the Indian SSIs depending upon the level of import intensity of exportable items and demand for importable products.

Role of Small Scale Industry

The recent years have witnessed a dramatic expansion in the small scale sector in almost all parts of the world. It is not only in developing countries that have experienced such a phenomenon but a similar experience has also been gathered by a large number of industrially developed countries like Japan, U.K, Germany, U.S.A, Switzerland, etc.

Japan for instance, achieved rapid industrialisation through the small-scale sector in the latter half of the 19th century. The small-scale sector in this country plays a catalytic and predominant role in the accelerated growth of the economy.

Even in the developed countries of Western Europe, United kingdom and United States of America there is recognition that small and rural industries play a significant role in complimenting the large industry and in providing opportunities for creative energies of the skilled people. The watch industry in Switzerland-the largest in the World-is based on the work of a multitude of small, almost cottage industry, units. So important were small firms considered in United Kingdom that a report (Boiton Committee, 1971) parodised the famous saying of Voltaire that "if small business does not exist, it would be necessary to invent it." In the United States of America small business administration, more than 30 years old, had been placed on a statutory footing reporting directly to the president.

Small Scale Sector-Indian Economy

India's vision of emerging as an economic power in the 21st century can be realised through the promotion and development of the small enterprises. In fact the small-scale enterprises is the sector of the millennium. The small-scale is the hub of many economic activities in a developing country like India. The socio-economic transformation of India cannot be achieved without paying adequate attention to the development of this labour intensive and capital sparing sector.

The Small-Scale sector has emerged over four decades as a highly vibrant and dynamic sector of the Indian economy. Today, this sector accourt for about 95 per cent of the industrial units and is contributing more than 40 per cent of value addition in the manufacturing sector and about 35 per cent of export (both direct and indirect). More than 33.70 lakh units are spread all over the country producing over 7500 items. Next to agriculture, this sector's contribution to employment is magnificent. It is an excellent sector in the country's economy.

One of the most significant features of the planned economic development in India has been the development of Village, Tiny and Small Scale Enterprises. The country accorded a high priority to this sector on account of its employment potential, comparatively low requirement of capital, short gestation period, use of traditional skills, useful links with the medium and large sectors, wide geographical dispersal, promotion of balanced regional development, low per unit cost of employment, utilisation of local resources, suitability of production of goods for mass consumption, mobilisation of small savings, provision of part time working arrangements and production of exportable products etc.

Small Scale Industry-Credit Dispensation

Credit is an essential input for the working for small-scale industries. Any delay in inadequate supply of credit is determined to growth of the SSI units. Therefore, timely and adequate availability of credit is of crucial importance for setting up and for expanding the existing SSI units. We are fully conscious of the fact that the SSI sector needs a credit delivery system, which is effective, simple and efficient to administer. The financial sector consisting of scheduled commercial banks and other financial institutions like SIDBI, SFCs, NSIC, KVIC, SIDCs/SIICs play a significant role in the growth and development of the small-scale sector. The issue of credit dispension is especially important for SSIs because of their greater dependence on borrowed capital in their day to day operations.

A major segment of the Indian Financial system consists of commercial banks and they are the most important source of finance for their working capital and term loans to the SSI sector. The SSI sector, as a part of the priority sector for banks lending, has been receiving direct assistance from commercial banks as well. The outstanding credit to SSI by public sector banks by the end of March, 2001 is Rs. 484.45 billion, contributing about 14.2% of the net bank credit. The private sector banks deployed Rs. 85.18 billion to SSI, contributing to 14.4% of their net bank Credit and Foreign banks advances to SSIs aggregated to Rs. 37.16 billion, accounting for 11.0 per cent of net bank credit as on the last Friday of March 2001. Besides the commercial banks SIDBIs contribution to the SSI sector is Rs. 145.71 billion, SFCs contribution to SSI is Rs. 16.17 billion, KVIC contribution is 11.80 million, to SSIs in the nation. The banks are suffering with the enormous increase of the NPAs in the SSI sector year by year. As at end-March 2000, the outstanding balance in respect of 304, 235 sick/weak SSI units amounted to Rs. 46.08 billion.

The Government has identified that finance is the main reason for sickness in small Industry after several studies conducted by various committees and institutions. To provide finance to the SSI sector the Government have implemented the recommendations of Nayak Committee, 1991, Abid Hussain Committee on Small Enterprises-1997, Kapur Committee-1998, Dr. S. P. Gupta Committee through RBI to commercial banks and State Finance Corporations, treating SSI finance as the priority sector finance for banks. Establishing SIDBI as a refinance agency for free flow of credit, Creation of separate ministry for SSI & ARI from the previous department of SSI & ARI. Introduction of various financial schemes like Credit Guarantee Scheme, Credit linked capital subsidy scheme, creation of National Equity Fund, establishing specialised SSI-commercial branches, besides introducing new credit facilities like factoring services, venture capital, Technology & Modernisation Fund, change in the scope of SSI definition and special schemes like cluster development, market development assistance, providing finance for quality standardisation (ISO-9000) like these encouraging aspects relating to SSI on one side, and strict credit norms, Huge NPAs, tightening the credit delivery system by RBI through various rules, competition among the financial sector internally and globally, availability of other less risk lending areas (Housing, vehicle finance, etc.), unhealthy competition among the SSI products in domestic and international market, free flow of capital and goods, impact of liberalisation and WTO agreements on SSI products are on one side influencing the small industry financial institutions.

Facing the Challenge of WTO Agreement

The World Trade Agreements and negotiations have a direct impact on all economic activities including the development and promotion of the small-scale sector. WTO Agreement are likely to affect the SSI sector in the following ways:

- Removal of QRS will allow free and cheap imports and will result in stiff competition to the SSIs.

- In view of the Agreement of TRIPS, it would be difficult for the SSI sector to continue with the reverse engineering and manufacture many items without paying royalty to the patent holders.
- In terms of Sanitary and Phyto-sanitary measures, SSIs will have to adopt international standards with regard to quality, health and hygiene.

The Small Scale Industry (SSI) Sector has emerged over four decades as a highly vibrant and dynamic sector for the Indian economy. Today, this sector accounts for about 95 per cent of the industrial units and is contributing more than 40 per cent of value addition in the manufacturing sector and about 35 per cent of exports (both direct and indirect). More than 31 lakhs units are spread all over the country producing over 7,500 items.

Small Enterprises, i.e., small scale units, not only play a crucial role in providing large scale employment opportunities at lower capital cost than large scale industries, but also help in industrialisation of rural and backward areas, thereby reducing regional imbalance, assuring more equitable distribution of national income and wealth. SSI units are also supplementary and complementary to large and medium scale units as ancillary units.

Though this sector has shown substantial progress, its major problems like inadequate credit flow from banks and financial Institutions, inadequate infrastructure facilities, low quality standard of products, use of obsolete technology, plant, machinery and equipment, inefficient management techniques, etc., are still inhabiting the sector. Beside, this sector has to face challenges of competition from opening up of economy to globalisation, need for increasing exports and meet WTO commitments.

WTO-Its Impact on Indian SSI

The emerging regime of liberalisation of international trade and deregulation and privatisation of internal economy, in the light of WTO has rendered the small-scale industry (SSI) sector highly vulnerable. The umbrella of WTO is likely to create some far reaching implications on the SSI sector in India, specifically with regard to their competitive ability and integration with the global markets. Most of the problems arise due to the unorganised nature of this sector, lack of date and information, use of low technology sometimes absolute technology and poor infrastructure in the country. WTO will affect all types of SSI units whether producing for the domestic market or for the international market.

Over two lakh units are sick and on the verge of dying because of the WTO. The growth of Indian SSI at a shade of 7 per cent is the lowest in has ever been in the last 10 years. As per the SIDBI report on SSI sector-2002 identifies that the food processing is the first sector which is adversely affected by the WTO.

The foreign exchange earning leather industry due to entry of China out of 330 units 300 factories going to be shut down as a result our exports will be decreased from 20 per cent to 5 per cent.

The Glass industry-in Firozabad half of the glass factories will shut down with in a year because of Chinese, Indonesian, Thais, make better quality machine made glass at cheaper price. Share of Firozabad's contribution to the country which is reducing 80 to 30 per cent.

Chemical industry-which manufacture inorganic fine chemicals which is used in laboratories as intermediate. Because of entry of Chinese products the Indian products will not be preferred due to cost of raw material of India is Rs. 35/- per Kg and finished product is Rs. 45/- per kg, where as the selling price the same product from China is Rs. 25/- per Kg. So this industry is adversely effected and it is opportunity to consumers and challenge to the producers.

The SSI sector which produces over 8,000 items will have to be aware of the patents of products including even of the technological patterns, trade marks, industrial designs, etc., 95 per cent of the SSI units are in the nature of tiny micro enterprises and are weak. Many of them are one man shows. They are bargaining power is low and do not have access to information and modern management practices. They constitute most vulnerable segment of the SSI sector. Hence, they will be needed to be guided and supported since they are also employment generators for the economy. Balance 5 per cent of SSI units are in the category of modern SSIs and have already established global links. Indian small enterprises have certain inherent strengths, which helped them raise their shape in total exports to 35% even in the face of tough global competition. The sector possesses the advantage of immovableness and flexibility. Their inventories are low and have weathered many adverse situations successfully and boldly. Indian SSIs have also advantage of local raw material and world class till besides cheap labour, which could be harnessed to the advantage. At the same time, it is an essential to note their vulnerability in the context of emerging global environment.

The Indians, small enterprises find themselves handicapped and at disadvantageous position. Hence they will need to be guided. The provisions or agreements, which are likely to affect Indian SSI sector, are outlined in the following points.

Quantitative restrictions and SSI reservation Policy.

- Tariff reduction and reduced protection.
- Anti dumping practices.
- Subsidies and countervailing measures.
- Technical barriers in trade and investment bases SSI definition.
- Trade related investment measures.
- Trade related intellectually property rights (TRIPS)
- Trade and investment.
- Government procurement.
- AARC commitments.
- Sustainability of export obligation.

REFERENCES

1. SIDBI Report on Small Scale Industries Sector-2000 (2000) Published by Small Industries Development Bank of India, Lucknow.
2. SIDBI Report on Small Scale Industries Sector-2001 (2001) Published by Small Industries Development Bank of India, Lucknow.
3. D. Pandhrangrarao, (2001) WTO and Competitiveness, Excel Books, New Delhi.
4. Dr. D.D. Sharma and Dr. S.K. Dhameja, (2002), Indian Entrepreneurship, Abhishek Publications, Chandigarh.
5. Francis Cherunilam, International Economics, Third Edition, Tata Edition, Tata McGraw-Hill Publishing Company Ltd., New Delhi.

3

Profiles of Women Employment in Unorganised Sector

A Case Study of Domestic Women Workers In Urban Areas of Uttaranchal

Mrs. Prabodhita Pande*

Economic Participation of Women

Women in search of better status, social dignity, higher self-earned income, and greater influence and party with those of male counterparts have shown impressive results of their performance in recent decades. They seem to miss no opportunity in proving their worthiness and capacity. The examination results often place them far superior to the male examinees. In training courses, service selections, as professionals and employees, and as well informed alert mothers the women are tending to indicate their performance orientation. Women leadership in the period of our freedom struggle had established very high ideals and motivated quite a vast part of Indian educated women. In the post Independence regime they lost their hold in political affairs and could not wield any substantial impact of their presence towards significant betterment in the socio-economic status of the women folk largely due to illiteracy and lack of opportunities for them. The western women 'Liberation' movements had considerable impact on the educated women. Educational growth as well as the economic betterment paved the path of progress in this direction. Family Planning Movement and the reduced fertility alongwith the falling infant mortality helped women to participate effectively in public affairs. Reservation for women in political participation

* Author is deeply grateful to Prof. G.C. Pandey, Prof. Emeritus, Kumaun University, Nainital for provocative discussion and guidance on this paper.

encouraged them to come forward inspite of revengeful outlook of the contesting male counterparts. Though the feeble law and order situations insecurity, and staunch opposition by conservatives have checked their path all along, yet Indian women took the challenge and proved their capabilities in every sphere of life. It is more impressive in the technological spheres and economic spheres. Their fate being tied with child bearing and baby care besides the household responsibilities, their freedom of participation at other much status oriented and remunerative areas can be assured by the assistance of helping hands in domestic front. Without Aayas, Maharees, Lady Cooks, etc. it is indeed difficult to spare women for participation in higher assignments. Domestic servants were being employed by upper and lower middle class households in good olden days of 'Economic Depression' when the rural labour was very cheap and the cost of maintenance was only little due to low standards, low wages, and unemployment. In post Independence period the wage rates picked up and prices were soaring up. Salaried class was hit hard so that the employment of domestic servants got unpopular at least in the lower middle class. The alternate avenues opened to employ the male labour and daily wages grew up in urban areas. The shortages of sugar, kerosene, food grains etc. discouraged the whole time employment and gave birth to a new tendency of employment of part time workers for every day domestic work. The officials used to take work from menial class Government employees now known as 'class Four! The outgoing jobs and official employment of women led to a sort of new division of labour. The urban areas developed a class of 'domestic workers' as in case of Bombay. Infect, these were the women workers of poverty stricken households who serve the relatively better off in household functions like washing, cooking, cleaning and wiping, caretaking, child care, baby feeding, taking children to distant schools as escourts, water collection and storage, fuel collection and so on. These services are important for relieving the working women for their places of work. Generally there are three categories of women who work as the domestic workers; (a) Widows or divorcees or other less fortunate women who have none other to depend on; (b) Those women from poorer sections of society who have several children to feed but the total income of the household is only meagre. (c) Those rural migrants who find their cash income far below to live better and they maintain better life by supplementing income by working part time in domestic jobs.

The young generation of the females has considerable educational equipment and training to fetch jobs in offices as clerks, typists, computer assistants, sales, marketing, factories and assembling operations, and the high grade supervisory jobs of the organised sector. A vast number of the educated girls and even the senior ladies opt to work as Teachers at primary, secondary or senior levels. Health, sanitation and related fields are also employing women for various cadres. Even in the sphere of self employed men women organise manufacturing and sales of various types wherein the women labour finds ready bread. These earn good wages and out of these earnings, a small part is paid to the domestic women workers working at home and other part is spent on transport, entertainment's and presents for the kids the grudging old, and the male counterparts. The growing educational costs of children in the urban areas have a big role in pressing the young mothers to go for more paying jobs leaving the domestic responsibilities in hands of domestic women workers. The prohibitive costs of prevalent dowry system push the educated young girls to official and private jobs so that they are able to save some thing towards their marriage. The gender bias was against the employment of women in offices, companies, sales, institutions and in other places in almost every country till the Twentieth Century. Abel Folhers (H.K. 1989) reported such bias even in United States. Blumberg (R.L. 1979) reported that the roles of women in human society are separate and it was a common view till recently that women have no place in serious employments involving higher intellect, technology, calculations, and staff governance. In Europe, the women were treated fit for secretarial jobs and typing. This misunderstanding withered away as the women proved their worthiness. Kumar (S. 1991) analysed at length the roles of women in various types of employments and reported that they function with high efficiency and equal ease and grace. Lady officers and assistants are less corrupt than the male counterparts. Women participation has enundated the labour market now and as Mincer and Polacheck (M.J. and S.W. 1974) found, it has brought the wages down even in highly specialised and technical fields of activity. This makes the output competitive in process of globalisation. There is a well demarcated trend of continued shifting of women labour forces from the household activities to technological spheres of organised sector.

Technological innovations and cultural change have considerable impact on freedom of women labour force from the tiresome drudgery and the continued irksome business of several hours in cooking, fuel-collection, storing water, washing, brooming, wiping, and sanitary cleanliness. The new inventions like refrigerators, cookers, cooking range, water filters and piped gas, etc have made it possible to free women from domestic work. They have been able to join various assignments of white collar and use their time for better level of remuneration. But women also have three distinct categories of workers; (a)

Highly skilled and managerial cadre of women and women political leaders who share the top rank privileges and are free from all economic worries (b) Women workers of educated class who discharge various functions as 'class two' and 'class three' employees or work for any technical wing of services or industry. (c) The third category is of the 'class four' women employees, domestic part time workers, full time private sector jobs, etc. The second category is the bulkiest of all because women serving in official class three jobs like clerks, typists, secretaries, personal assistants, computer operators, field workers of various departments in villages and outskirts, teachers of all kinds, health assistants, nurses, etc are in very big numbers. Contribution of the top level women to the social management, social engineering, administration, and organisational functions is well recognised now.

Women Under Pressure & Excessive Strain

A girl child begins her life with a deeper sense of fear, scaring challenges, insecurity, a feeling of neglect in hands of parents, harsh and crude treatment in hands of the elders and mother. She is supposed to be extra humble, mannerly, tolerant, thrifty, diligent, and always prepared to assist mother, brothers, sisters and others. No body expects this from a male child. At the stage of schooling she gets the last priority and her educational effort receives the least accommodation. While brothers are free and worriless after school hours, she is supposed to assist mother in the day today household work. A girl is always over conscious of her being a female and unwanted. This has been realised now that an educated mother is a real social asset and girls must be accorded priority in education. "Women seek jobs is distress" is an old saying. In the present references, there in demand for jobs by womenworkers not for their distress but for the use of their acquired skills, making substantial incomes for their own expenses, gaining the status of productivity employed class which is now treated prestigious. Developing economies do not create enough jobs to employ all educated girls and boys at high wages due to the fact that these seek only white collar jobs and investment level is much less to employ all.

Oppression and Exploitation due to Excess Supply

Women often seek white collar jobs to get a respite from the drudgery of household work for temporary periods and have to drop down due to their more urgent preoccupations at household levels. They get in their family way, go for delivery, devote to baby care, they have to accompany their husbands and elderly for other stations, and are constrained to leave job. Employers have a great advantage in employing such candidates because these do not accumulate annual increments, claim no seniority, are available at nominal wages and can be overloaded with work assignment without any addition to liabilities like Provident Fund Contributions, pensions, or pay for the period of leaves. Their salaries are subjected a number of illegal deductions and contributions to the benefit of the employers. The salaries paid to these are often far less than the prescribed pay scales. Though the department of labour is supposed to regulate this but these officials are neither supervised nor are ever punished for so common illegal gratifications from the private employers. Women employers are more cruel and crafty as is commonly seen in private schools, missionary schools, English medium schools, and other establishments. Women workers are put to excessive work in their assignments and they have to attend to their domestic work after the return from their job. The total work load on each exceeds even 16 hours a day which is inhuman by any standard. Women workers are not motivated by career potentiability, non wage perks of jobs, or by other allurements, but they seek recognition and status even at very low wages. They prefer part-time work.

Women workers prefer piece wages. Electronics related industrial work provided a good field of activity to women workers with moderate training in work-skills. In precision tools, watch factories, television, electric goods, gazettes, and assembling operations women proved to be good workers with far less labour disputes. Routinised work is good for them but the new trend is towards innovative works and computerised technologies, where women workers are making space for male workers in making the multi-function combinations of the new products.

Employers often complain that there are several hazards in keeping women workers. They go for maternity leaves, sick leaves, can't devote till late hours as per need, are'nt prepared to pick up new work, demand too many half day leaves to attend to the domestic contingencies. Women need escourts very off and on and can not be deputed anywhere as is possible in case of male workers. Chauhan (P.S. 1995) analysed the impact of the technological innovations on labour process and reported that new technology disfavours employment of women. In constructions, kilns, factories, sanitation domestic helping services, etc a very vast work force of women workers is engaged but no protection is so far provided to such labour against ruthless exploitation. In carpet making, woollen textiles, hoseries, food industries, Dal and Rice mills, floor mills, in cleaning and drying operations of food stuffs, the women workers are paid far less than the male counterparts.

Domestic Women Workers of Uttaranchal

The present study refers to a household survey held in 1998-99 in townships of Dehradun, Nainital, Haldwani and Rishikesh wherein the domestic women workers at household level were identified in urban areas. Out of 660 identified domestic women workers (274 in Dehradun, 184 in Nainital, 105 in Haldwani and 97 in Rishikesh) only 412 workers could be contacted for field interviews in these towns. Data on family background, biodata, work hours, wages, total family income, family size, marital status, child education husband's occupation, health conditon of worker, and caste belonging etc were collected from the workers. Distribution of workers by their family background is shown below.

Table 1: Distribution of Workers by Origin.

Town under study	*Under Background*	*%*	*Rural Background*	*%*	*Suburban Workers*	*%*	*Total*	*%*
Dehradun	42	41	113	48	29	40	184	45
Nainital	17	16	68	29	25	34	110	27
Haldwani	32	30	28	12	16	22	76	18
Rishikesh	14	13	25	11	3	4	42	10
Total	**105**	**100**	**234**	**100**	**73**	**100**	**412**	**100**

Caste belonging of the lady domestic workers shows that 39 per cent of them are from the scheduled castes and nearly 38 per cent are from upper caste groups and 22.8 per cent are from various subgroups of backward communities. Town wise distribution shows wide variation. Precise figures can be read from the following table.

Table 2: Caste Status of Women.

Name of Town	*Caste-Status of the Women Workes in Domestic Work*							
	Upper Caste		*Backward Community*		*Scheduled Caste*		*Total*	
	Nos.	*%*	*Nos.*	*%*	*Nos.*	*%*	*Nos.*	*%*
Dehradun	69	37.5	47	25.5	68	37.0	184	100
Nainital	33	30.0	28	16.5	49	44.5	110	100
Haldwani	36	47.4	11	14.4	29	38.2	76	100
Rishikesh	18	42.9	8	19.0	16	38.1	42	100
Total	**156**	**37.9**	**94**	**22.8**	**162**	**39.3**	**412**	**100**

Occupational status of the households to which these workers belonged shows that 24.3 per cent of them belonged to the disintegrated crafts, wood sellers, stone and slate workers. One fifth of them were rickshaw pullers, transporters of various kinds, and household load carriers. 17.7 per cent of them had family occupation of vendors, hawkers, fruit sellers, vegetable sellers, etc. 16 per cent of them were working as labourers in constructions and as Mali in Household gardens besides selling flowers for Pooja. 13.8 per cent were from outskirts devoting to cropping and animal husbandry. 8 per cent of them belonged to families of washermen and matress weavers. There were notable town wise variations in occupations. The following table shows the profiles.

Table 3. Occupational Structure.

Towns	*Occupational Belonging by family origin*						
	Agri. & allied	*Crafts & Wood collectors etc*	*Vendors Hawkers sellers*	*Dhobi & matress weavers*	*Transport horsemen boatmen*	*Labour coolie*	*Total*
Dehradun	36 (19.7)	51 (27.7)	24 (13.0)	14 (7.6)	42 (22.8)	17 (9.2)	184
Nainital	14 (12.7)	30 (27.3)	16 (14.5)	8 (7.3)	16 (14.6)	26 (23.6)	110
Haldwani	7 (9.2)	16 (21.0)	23 (30.4)	3 (3.9)	12 (15 8)	15 (19.7)	76
Rishikesh	-	3 (7.2)	10 (13.8)	8 (19.0)	13 (31.0)	8 (19.0)	42
Total	**57 (13.8)**	**100 (24.3)**	**73 (17.7)**	**33 (8.0)**	**83 (20.2)**	**66 (16.0)**	**412**

Marital status of the domestic women workers can explain the reasons of poverty and helplessness of the women workers. Nearly 36 per cent of these were widows or the divorcees. The percentage of the married women was greater. They constituted 39 per cent of the total workers. Nearly one fourth of these were unmarried girls who supplemented the domestic low earnings of the parents. These workers were sending children as substitutes when otherwise busy or ailing. The following table shows the distribution of workers by their marital status.

Table 4: Marital Status.

Towns under study	*Unmarried*	*%*	*Married*	*%*	*Widow / Divorced*	*%*	*Total*	*%*
Dehradun	26	14.1	64	34.8	94	51.1	184	100
Nainital	39	35.4	43	39.1	28	25.5	110	100
Haldwani	13	17.0	38	50.0	25	33.0	76	100
Rishikesh	22	52.4	17	40.5	3	7.1	42	100
Total	**100**	**24.3**	**162**	**39.3**	**150**	**36.4**	**412**	**100**

Earnings of Domestic Women Workers

The 412 workers covered by this study actually worked in 1523 households for the same functions but the work and wage agreed varied by paying capacity of the employer and size of the employee's family. It also varied by the area of accommodation and the time devoted to work. Some where the work was only of baby sitting and guarding the house in absence of the working house lady. In others utensil cleaning, wiping the floor, washing, or preparing food etc involved more care. The overall wage per worker per month inclusive of the kind payment was Rs. 843.00 from all the houses. The highest wage was Rs. 1200 and the lowest was Rs. 400 per month. For the goods they supplied to households like milk, fuel, eggs, etc., separate payments were charged. Per worker earned wage was greater in Haldwani and least was Rs. 783 in Rishikesh. The following table shows details.

Table 5: Working Hours & Wages.

Towns under study	*Workers covered*	*Houses served P.W.*	*Hours P.W. Per day*	*monthly cash wages Rs.*	*Monthly wages kind Rs.*	*Total Monthly earning*
Dehradun	184	3.8	8.09	684.0	120.0	804.0
Nainital	110	3.4	6.70	731.0	114.0	845.0
Haldwani	76	4.2	9.20	834.2	106.0	940.0
Rishikesh	42	3.2	8.84	665.0	118.0	783.0
Total	**412**	**3.6**	**8.21**	**728.6**	**114.5**	**843.0**

Analysis of data indicates that 27 per cent of the women workers were in the age group of 11-15 years most of which are from the backward social communities and the Scheduled castes. 44 per cent were between 16-45 years. In Upper and backward communities more than 60 per cent of such workers were in this age groups while among the Scheduled Castes these were hardly 16 per cent. Most of these S.C. women were going for daily wage earning in constructions and other labour. Domestic women labourers were either teenagers (39.5%) or were between 46-60 age group. Only 2.7 per cent of these workers were beyond 60 years of age. The details may be checked from the following table.

Table 6: Classification of Caste.

Age Groups of workers	*Caste group wise distribution of workers*							
	Upper Caste		*Backward*		*Scheduled*		*Total*	
	Nos.	*%*	*Nos.*	*%*	*Nos.*	*%*	*Nos.*	*%*
11-15	18	11.4	26	30.9	68	39.5	112	27.2
16-25	42	26.9	33	39.3	10	5.8	85	20.6
26-45	62	40.0	18	21.4	18	10.5	98	23.8
46-60	23	14.7	7	8.4	76	44.2	106	25.7
60+	11	7.0	-	-	-	_	11	2.7
Total	**156**	**100.0**	**84**	**100.0**	**172**	**100.0**	**412**	**100.0**

Generally the earnings of domestic women workers constitute supplementary income to the family income. If we see them as a part of the total family income of the workers, it is notable that in 47.3 per cent cases the domestic services add 10 to 20 per cent share. In 25.5 per cent cases these incomes make 20 to 30 per cent share. These are relatively poorer groups. In still poor cases domestic services add 30 to 50 per cent share. Among the extremely poor Scheduled caste workers this income makes 50 to 90 per cent of income. In still worseoff cases domestic services contribute 100 per cent and it is the sole source of income. Caste wise details of lady servants in various age groups contributing different parts of family income are shown below:

Table 7: Source of Family Income.

Categories	*Number of cases*							
	Upper caste	*%*	*Backward communities*	*%*	*Scheduled caste*	*%*	*Total cases*	*%*
Sole source	1	0.7	-	-	3	1.7	4	0.9
50-90 per cent	-	-	-	-	9	5.2	9	2.3
30-50 per cent	-	-	4	4.8	7	4.1	11	2.7
20-30 per cent	40	25.6	13	15.5	52	30.2	105	25.5
10-20 per cent	87	55.8	31	36.9	77	44.8	195	47.3
Below 10 per cent	-	-	-	-	9	5.2	9	2.3
Total	**156**	**100.0**	**84**	**100.0**	**172**	**100.0**	**412**	**100.0**

Large size of the household is the primary cause of poverty which pushes the women to search for household work assignments and earn little more income to supplement the meagre household income. In some cases the male partners are heavy drink-addicts and spare only little income for meeting the domestic expenses. Cost of maintenance of children is increasing day by

Table 8: Number of Workers Interviewed (Women).

Size of the Households	*Number of women workers interviewed*									
	Dehradun		*Nainital*		*Haldwani*		*Rishikesh*		*Total*	
	Nos.	*%*	*Nos.*	*%*	*Nos.*	*%*	*Nos.*	*%*	*Nos.*	*%*
1-3	15	8.1	7	6.4	11	14.5	5	11.9	38	9.2
4-7	44	24.0	17	15.4	27	35.5	11	26.2	99	24.0
8-10	76	41.3	68	61.8	30	39.5	16	38.1	190	46.2
10+	49	26.6	18	16.4	8	10.5	10	23.8	85	20.6
Total	**184**	**100.0**	**110**	**100.0**	**76**	**100.0**	**42**	**100.0**	**412**	**100**

day and schooling of children has become so costly. Hardly 9 per cent households from which domestic women workers come, have a size below 3 members. 24 per cent of these have 4-7 members while 46.2 per cent have 8-10 members to feed. 20.6 per cent households have even more than 10 members. The following table shows women domestic workers in various towns categorised by size of their households.

Conclusions

Employment of women for domestic services has emerged as the natural consequence of growing specialisation of labour in a growing economy. It has closer interrelationship with growing employment of women in organised sector of private and public enterprises. The office going women employ the domestic women workers as helpers. There is considerable exploitation and oppression of women labour in educational institutions under private managements. It has three forms generally interlocked with each other; (a) Low remuneration and job privileges and harsh treatment; (b) Unending work load of women workers (c) Illegal collections and deductions from already low salaries. Even the social security provisions compulsory by law are openly shirked by the private employers. The domestic constraints and social customs (like dowry) drive the women to go for jobs. In sophisticated areas of employment involving innovations and higher skills, male labour is substituting women workers. Women employment is avoided because only males can render extra time work, organisational tasks, and over time managements and entertainments. The status of domestic women workers is the weakest link in Indian Labour market. Their wages are embarrassingly low. The wages do not grow commensurate to price-rise. There are no off-days in domestic services. Greater fertility and social demands of upkeep of the old and invalids, are the causes why women go for domestic services in extremely poor wages. Alcoholism among the male earners also constitutes a reason. The scheduled caste women send young children for these works which darkens the future of these children in so far as they do not go to Schools. The earnings of domestic workers are education of the workers. Mincer and Polacheck (1974) found earnings related to education of worker in organised sector. Parsarthy (1987) reported that earnings of domestic attendants depend on the sincerity of work, hours devoted and much on dependability. Greater the helplessness of worker lesser is the wage rate. Banerjea (1981) found that if these are well organised, as in Bombay, they have an upper hand in fixing wages and conditions of work. Swapna (1988) reported on the pitiable state of women in construction industry. Avasthy (1982) reported the pitiable state of the women agricultural labourers who devote for strenuous work for prolonged hours without commensurate return and surety of getting two meals a day. Joyce Lebra (1984) found that women labour is overburdened everywhere and this trend has a continuity. Majid (1986) illustrated the case of Punjab agricultural labour to show how women supplement domestic income besides looking after the household work at home as well. Maria Mies (1987) explains that the participation of women in agricultural work is largely a matter of their subsistence. The struggle of the female labour force for finding a respectable status and reasonale return on their work effort goes on waiting for some state intervention to ensure at least the least the minimum wage. The case of domestic woman workers so far is waiting for legislative support and social security provision for such workers. Legal provisions and enactments for gender justice are not lacking as Remka Dagar (1998) analysed but social support needs be encouraged. The Beijing conference (1995) adopted a historical landmark resolution yet the problems of women remain unresolved. Bandhyopadhya (1989) very aptly explained that much of the gap lies between governance and promises. Women's impoverishment and status of social disregard needs attention and exceptionally strong legal as well as judicial measures.

Note: Presently the author is Asst. Manager, NABARD, Mumbai, Maharashtra.

REFERENCES

1. Avasthy, Indira, 1982, "Rural Women in India; Jammu Women; Book Publishing Corproation, Delhi, 1982.
2. Bandhyopadhya, M.J., 1989, Gender & Governance in India, E.P.W. 35, No. 31, July 1989.
3. Folhers, Abel, H.K., 1989, *"Social Research,"* Vol. 56, No. 3, 545-69.
4. Blumberg, R.L., 1979, Predicting the position of women: Implications & Problems; Ed. in Lipman, B., & J. Bemerd; *Sex Roles And Social Policy*; ASA, p. 113-42.
5. Banerjea, N., 1981, *"Women Workers in Unorganised Sector;* Sangam Publishers, New Delhi, 1981.
6. Chauhan, P.S., 1995, "Impact of Technological Innovation on Women in Economic Sphere", *Women & Development*, Vol. 1, No. 1, 1995.
7. Dagar, Renuka, 1998, "Intervening for Gender Justice IJSW, 59, No. 4, 1998.
8. Gold Stein, N.; 1989, "Women's Employment in Semi Conductor Industry. Ed. Elson D. and R. Pearson", *Women Employment and Multinationals in Europe*; Macmillan, London, 1989.
9. Joyce, Lebra et. al.; 1984, *"Women & Work: Continuity & Change;* Promilla & Company, New Delhi, 1984.
10. Kumar, S., 1991, *"Urban Labour Market & Female Work Force In Tertiary Sector;* Ph.D. Thesis, J.N.U.; School of Social Sciences; New Delhi, 1991.

11. Majid, A., 1986, "*Women's Contribution to Household Income:* Agricultural Labour of Punjab; A.E.R. Centre; University of Delhi, 1986.

12. Maria, Mies; 1987, "*Indian Women in Subsistence and Agricultural Labour;* VISTAR, New Delhi, 1987.

13. Mincer, J. & Polacheck S.W.; 1974, Family Investments in Human Capital; Earnigns of women; *Journal of Political Economy;* Vol. 82, p. 76-111.

14. Mukhopadhyaya, Swapna; 1988, "*Women Workers in Construction Sector;* Institute Rep., Institute of Economic Growth; N.C.S.E.W.; New Delhi, 1988.

15. Munshi, Mitra, 1987, "*Impact of Operation Flood*"*;* Rural Dairy Producers National Council Social Education, New Delhi, 1987.

16. Ratra Mahila, 2000, Fourth World Confr. on Women, (Beijing) 1995. Vol. No. 3, Issue-16, 2000.

17. Rao Meena, B & S. Uma Devi, 2001, Gender Justice, Policy Approaches; I.J.S.D., Vol. I, No. 2, 2001, (243-263).

4

Globalisation and Decentralised Development

A Feminist Perspective

Dr. S.K. Mishra*
Dr. I.D. Singh**

In the 1960s the state played major role in promoting the well being of the majority of people in developing countries. Poverty reduction was at the centre of development planning and there was an emphasis on an approach to development which was broad-based and integrated. All of this changed from the decade of 1980s onwards in the context of the debt crisis and the steep rise in the cost of living in industrialised countries, which made inflation and deficit reduction major preoccupation of the governments of those countries. Within a policy framework set by Washington, 'the Washington Consensus' the role of status to promote broad-based socio-economic development was severely eroded. In many countries macro economic policies and structural adjustment programmes took precedence over socio-economic development planning; and economic growth privileged over social development. In the decade of 1980s, the World Bank and the I.M.E. set the policy framework through a strategy of policy dialogue. From the beginning of 1990s, trade replaced development as the central policy issue. WTO now sets the policy framework based on epistemology that liberalisation of markets for goods and finance, small government and fiscal discipline in best for capturing the benefits of globalisation.

* Reader in Economics, P.G. College, Sakaldiha, Chandauli, U.P.
** Senior Lecturer in Economics, P.G. College, Sakaldiha, Chaudauli, U.P.

However, international environment is for from enabling and those of us are committed to the goals of sustainable human development have to fight disillusionment, despair and worst of all, cynicism in form of deteriorating quality of life of poor in general and of women in particular.

Thus, the dramatic changes in power relations brought about by the globalisation of financial and labour markets and by critical reinterpretations of modernity provide fertile ground for rethinking changing gender relations and development practice in the third world (Feldman, 1998).

The present paper aims at examining the impact of globalisation on women in form of its influences on women's awareness (literacy), physical capability (health) and autonomy (employment status). The paper also discusses the role played by feminists in countering the ill-effects of globalisation on women.

A Brief Account of Debate on Globalisation and Women's Status

Globalisation is touted as the panacea for the economic ills of the world. The free flow of capital, labour, goods and information without state and other forms of intervention is claimed to be the only path towards world prosperity promoted by various regional organisations like EU, NAFTA, APEC and world organisations such as GATT, WTO and financially aided by IMF and IBRD, economic liberalism is sweeping the globe as it leaves millions of skeletons behind. Capital has become free to pursue the greatest profit wherever it may lead. Out flows often cause closures of plants and ouster of workers from job. Capital inflows lead either to greater exploitation of workers and plunder of natural resources, or to destroy nascent local industries and traditional enterprises due to serve competition. Both situations, while creating opportunities for some, drive more to destitution (Lucie Cheng, 1999).

UK governments' white paper on Globalisation of December, 2000-Making Globalisation Work for the Poor—recognizes that "Globalisation creates new opportunities for sustainable development and poverty reduction" and therefore opines that "There is no alternative to globalisation and we should learn to live with it". But, the paper also admits that globalisation poses great threats to employment and livelihoods, to the environment and to human security in general—and so it argues finally that "making globalisation work for the world's poor is the greatest moral challenge facing our generation. The paper, however, does advocate intervention of the governments in the interests of equity and justice, for benefits of globalisation will not automatically reach poor people (John Harriss, 2001). Therefore, remedy to this challenge was perceived in decentralisation, local development, and gross root initiatives that focused attention on the plight of the excluded—the rural landless, the urban poor, and women—and shift in development discourse to "meeting basic needs".

Boserup (1970), described the institutional barriers that limit women's productive capacity and competitive position in the market. To her, traditional values victimising women, were associated with subsistence—based production. Rogers shared Boserup's commitment to market competition as the means for increasing gender equity. Though, Boserup and Rogers sought to improve women's status through participation in market-based exchange relations, they under estimated women's reproductive responsibility in status production.

Studies of women's resistance and intra household bargaining have more recently been elaborated (Sen, 1990). However, patriarchal familiar relations between women and household limited women's voice and opportunity. Therefore, the policy goal was to free women from backward oppressive households and patriarchal relations which prohibited their participation in labour market. Hence, becoming wage labourers and self reliant individuals then became the criteria for measuring women's status, mobility and achievement. It was further thought that the availability of credit, in combination of new skills and training would transform subsistence and non-wage relations into marketable skills, enabling women to similar to those of men.

In the last decade, the recent tide of globalisation compelled countries to renegotiate their approach to development, a process that shifted national economic planning from import substitution and agricultural self-sufficiency to strategies of comparative advantage and export led growth. In the mean-time, it was felt that the negative effects could be medicated by special programmes for women and children until economic equilibrium could once again be realised (Cornia etal, 1987). Despite the problems entailed in this analysis, the discussions nonetheless linked the costs of economic reorganisation directly to poverty, motherhood, and the privatisation of welfare institutions (Cornia etal, 1987; Bakkar, 1994).

This all led to a significant departure in 1990s from earlier researches with regards to women's development—Earlier, women's unequal status was attributed to their lack of access to resources, their limited skills, traditional cultural practices and their relationship to patriarchal household structures. In the 1990s, scholars recognised that women bear the unequal burden of reduction in social expenditure caused by introduced economic restructuring and social dislocation and concluded that these costs are not temporary (Elson 1990, 1992; Feldman, 1992; Bakkar, 1994).

Globalisation and Women's Status in other Asian Countries

It is a general perception that women tend to bear the brunt of globalisation. On the one hand, the general deterioration of living conditions and traditional patriarchal attitudes meant that they have had to take care of their families while generating an income. On the other hand, women are often the victims of plant closures.

In both Taiwan (China) and the Republic of Korea as the 'economic miracle' abated, a large number of textile, shoe, and garment plants, the labour-intensive manufacturing industries, closed leaving millions of women workers jobless overnight, for these industries lost their competitiveness. These women struggled for compensation and the right to work.

In Masan, announcement of Japanese Sumida Company's withdrawal of capital caused loss of joy by 300 women workers in 1990. In response to a long protest and struggle of the workers, the company promised a significant amount of economic compensation (Lim, 1998).

In Taiwan (China), textile, garment, shoe and electronic plants, women comprising more than 50 per cent of their labour force, began to shut down one by one in the 1980s. To the report of Ministry of Economics more than 174000 companies and plants ceased to operate between 1993 and 1995, many leaving their workers without jobs, severance pay, or even back wages (Huang, 1998). Prevalence of low wages in Taiwan, compelled women in their 30s and 40s to seek employment—to supplement their women in their 30s and 40s to seek employment—to supplement their family income. Most of them could not find comparable work for age-sex discrimination and had to take on food service or janitorial jobs, part-time, temporary contract, and other flxible work or suffer unemployment.

Likewise, many women workers in Philippines have also been victims of globalisation. Development of a more sophisticated resistance movement, the organisation like Gabriela in Philippines has gained an international reputation and is spear heading a transterritorial anti-globalisation movement in the Asia-Pacific. In view of women in Philippines, the problem they face are related to their long colonial past as well as to the globalisation of international capital (Hsia, 1998).

Committee for Asian Women Workers started in 1981 (CAW) with its head quarter at Hong Kong is an example of transnational labour activist group which arose to meet with the problem of brutal exploitation of women due to globalisation. The CAW convenes conferences and workshops of Asian women labour organisers and also brings out a newsletter, carrying stories on women's labour conditions and their struggles in almost all Asian countries. Globalisation and its impact on women workers in Asia have been a frequent topic since 1991.

Globalisation and Women in South Africa

To South African Women, most government budgets are gender-biased, overlooking the ways in which programmes and policies either fail to address women's oppression, or exacerbate it (Joanna Kerr, 1999). They therefore take initiative to ensure that every government department annually draws up its own 'women's budget', analysing every line item for its impact on women. The success of the South African model is inspiring women elsewhere to create women's budgets as transformative tools for equality.

Women need a greater voice with this vision in mind, Gender and Economic Reforms in Africa (GERA) have been created to develop alternative and transformative economic policies and programmes that ensure gender equity and economic justice with the help of feminist economists, critical feminist researchers and activists who are able to analyse and influence economic policies and institutions—who can speak the language of economics.

Analysis of Indian Empirical Evidences

Public expenditure on health and education and state of women's health, education and work during pre and post reform period in India and in developing countries on the whole have been demonstrated to evaluate the effect of globalisation.

Table 1: Public Expenditure on Social Sector as Percentage of GDP in Pre and Post Reform Period.

Countries	*Expenditure on Health*			*Expenditure on Education*		
	1990	*1998*	*Change*	*1990*	*1998*	*Change*
India	0.9	0.6	–0.3	3.9	3.2	–0.7
Developing Countries	1.9	3.8	+1.9	3.5	3.8	+0.3
Difference	–1.0	–3.2	–	+0.4	0.6	–

Source: UNDP HDR-1992, HDR-2000 & HDR-2001.

Public expenditure on health and education in India is not only less in comparison to other countries but also shrinking influences of economic restructuring. The table shows that public expenditure on health and education as percentage of GDP reduced by 0.3 and 0.7 per cent respectively in India whereas it increased in developing countries in the post reform period.

The difference in expenditures on health and education between India and developing countries increased sharply during this period. It clearly shows that the neglect of social sector in India is for more than that in developing countries.

Social Development Indicators

Literacy

It is supposed to be a significant indicator of social development Indian position in literacy is shown in the following table.

Table 2: Adult Literacy in Pre and Post Reform Period in India.

Countries	*Adult Literacy (In Per cent)*							
	1990			*1998*			*TDL*	
	M	*F*	*GDL*	*M*	*F*	*GDL*	*M*	*F*
India	62	34	28	67.1	43.5	23.6	5.1	+9.5
Developing Countries	74	54	20	80.3	64.5	15.8	6.3	+10.5
SDL	12	20	8	13.2	21.0	7.8	1.2	1.0

Source: UNDP, HDR-1992, and HDR-2000.

GDL = Gender Difference in Literacy.

TDL = Temporal Difference in Literacy.

SDL = Spatial Difference in Literacy.

The above table throws light on situation of literacy in population above 15 years of age. The female literacy has improved in post reform period faster than that of males. However, India has much less than half literate adult females in comparison to nearly two third of that in developing countries. Moreover, the gap in female literacy between India and other developing countries. Moreover, the gap in female literacy between India and other developing countries was 20 percentage point in pre reform period which rose to 21 percentage point after economic reforms. Thus, India has not appropriate taken care of a very significant indicator of social development like female literacy.

Health

Availability of health facilities to the women may be measured by Maternal Mortality Ratio, Expectation of Life at birth and also by sex ratio.

Maternal Mortality Ratio for India in 1998 was almost same as it was for overall average all developing countries a decade ago.

Life expectancy at birth for women in India has made substantial increase and now it is greater than that for men by 0.8 years (1998). However, the same figure of difference for overall developing countries is noted to be 3.2 years.

Sex Ratio, i.e., number of females per thousand males is a significant indicator of attitude of society towards females and the facility of health and nutritions given to them.

Table 3: Sex Ratio in Pre and Post Reform Period in India.

Sex Ratio	*Census*		*Change over*
	1991	*2001*	*1991*
General	927	933	+6
Child Population age 0-6 years	945	927	-18
Population aged 7+	923	935	+12

Source: M.K. Premi, The Missing Girl Child, EPW, May 2001, p. 1875.

Increase in sex ratio in general population seems to be a matter of satisfaction. But, it conceals more significant facts than what it reveals. Increase in sex ratio is a result of tremendous rise in survivorship of elderly women. A sharp decline in sex ratio among the children of upto age six from 945 to 927 shows mass growth of foeticide and infanticide of girl child. This may be attributed to the realisation of social attitude against the girl child into practice through foetus sex test. This action may not be considered that much immoral under the influence of globalisation of thought at the social and individual level.

Status of Employment

Earning and workforce participation of women have been considered by UNDP as important factors to workout Gender Development Index. Globalisation has significantly influenced women's WFPR.

Table 4: Women's (15+) Work Force Participation Rate in Pre and Post Reform Period in India.

Country	*WFPR of Women (In Percentage)*		
	Year		
	1988-90	*1998*	*TDE*
India	25.6	41.8	16.2
Developing Countries	32.5	55.6	23.1
SDE	6.9	13.8	6.9

Source: UNDP, HDR-1992 & HDR-2000.
TDE = Temporal Difference in Employment.
SDE = Spatial Difference in Employment.

The table shows that Women's Work Force Participation Rate increased by 16.2 percentage point during the last decade which is far less than 23.1 percentage point, the rate of increase for overall developing countries. Likewise, Work Force Participation Rate for developing countries was higher than that for India by 6.9 percentage in 1990 which rose by double, i.e., to 13.8 percentage point in 1998.

One of the very disturbing features of growth pattern in the post liberalisation period is very low employment generating potential of growth in the secondary and the tertiary sectors. The result is concentration of work force in agriculture and a persistent deterioration of relative productivity and income of both male and female workers engaged in the primary sector (G.S. Bhalla, 2001).

In the wake of globalisation, there has also been causalisation and informalisation of labour market both for males and females (Jeemol Unni, 2001). However, this was comparatively more for females than that for males. Increase in percentage of casual employee has been by 2.4 and 3.3 percentage points for males and females respectively whereas there was reduction in percentage of regular employee by 1.7 and 1.1 percentage point for males and females respectively.

Remedial Measures

The decade of ninetees has been of paramount significance as regards to feminist research, strategy and advocacy. Attempts made by feminists to promote equality and women's empowerment have begun to bring fruition. Act of devoting an entire issue of the prestigious journal 'World Development' to gender and macro economics in 1995 clearly indicates interest and seriousness of main stream economists in feminist economic theory. Other remedial measures and their impacts are as follows:

Influencing Corporate Behaviour

Corporation are the biggest players in the global economy and also the biggest winners. Foreign private investment in developing countries alone has grown five-fold and translates into investments of almost US$1 trillion (Sutherland and Sewell, 1998:2). In comparison, the investment in development cooperation is a drop in the bucket.

Campaigns to make corporations more responsible have been waged for decades for environmental protection, better working conditions for labour, ban on child labour etc. Now, Southern Women's groups have become active on behalf of women factory workers. As a result of external pressure, some corporations are introducing voluntary codes of conduct covering ethical, environmental, and labour practices in all their operations, both domestic and abroad (Hibler and Beamish, 1998). However, enforcement of voluntary codes of conduct needs independent monitoring. Moreover, most importantly, codes of conduct can not ultimately influence a global production system dependent on cheap and flexible female labour.

UN Endeavours

Institutions like the World Bank are increasingly seeing women as active agents of social, political and economic change instead of passive recipients of development. The 1995 UN World Conference on Women was probably the most visible and international focus on governments and their responsibilities. More than thirty five thousand women from all over the world went to Beizing, many of them to share their experiences of working conditions, inadequate health care, or lack of access to technology in the context of globalisation. Non-governmental organisations had unprecedented access to government delegates attending the numerous preparatory meetings and Beizing summit, and they lobbied intensely for substantive changes in the final document—The Platform for Action. However, the Beizing summit does not seem to have gained ground. Firstly, sectoral approach adopted by UN denies any strategising about the structural causes of gender discrimination. Secondly, the participants attending the summit mostly represented the 'minor' government ministries. Lastly, most of the Beizing recommendations addressing problem of globalisation are vague.

Pressure on Governments

The observations reveal that the globalisation, well supported and strengthened by the government policies, has deteriorated the quality of life and work of women and disappointed to all those who are committed to the goals of sustainable human development. Nelson (1994), rightly says that it is women who have had to be the shock absorbers of the Structural Adjustment Programme (SAP). Therefore, government policies must have to pay due attention to the plight of those who are expected to be worsened by the globalisation by extending some sort of safety net to them. For this, government need to be pressured and held accountable to these international commitments by the women's organisations, researchers and activists. Governments can be influenced to address the structural causes of poverty, or restructure the allocation of public expenditures—but unless feminist leaders show them how, it is unlikely to happen.

REFERENCE

1. Bakkar, I. (ed.), 1994, "The Strategic Silence: Gender an Economic Policy", London: Zed.

2. Bhalla, G.S., 2001, "Political Economy of Indian Development in the 20th Century," Presidential address at 83rd Annual Conference of IEA, University of Jammu, Dec. 30, 2000 to Jan. 1, 2001.

3. Boserup, E. 1970, "Women's Role in Economic Development, New York, St. Martin's.

4. Cornia, G.A. etal. (eds.), 1987, "Adjustment with a Human Face," Vol. I, New York, UNICEF/Clarendon.

5. Elson, D. (1990), "Male Bias in Macro Economics: The Case of Structural Adjustment". In Diana Elson (ed.), Male Bias in Development Process, Manchester, Manchester University Press, pp. 164-190.

6. Elson, D. 1992, "From Survival Strategies to Transformation Strategies: Women's Needs and Structural Adjustment". In Lourdes Beneria and Shelley Feldman (eds.) Unequal Burden: Economic Crises, Persistent Poverty and Women's work, Boulder: West View, pp. 26-48.

7. Feldman, S. 1992, "Crises, Poverty and Gender Inequality: Current Themes and Issues". In Lourdes Beneria and Shelly Feldman (eds.), op. cit., pp. 1-25.

8. Feldman, S. 1998, "Conceptualising Change and Equality in the Third World Context". In Nelly P. Stromquist (ed.), Women in the Third World, New York: Garland.

9. Harriss, John 2001, Globalisation and World's Poor, EPW, Bombay, India, June 9, pp. 2035.

10. Hsia, H.C. 1998, 'Awaking the Women who nourished the earth', Taiwan Lihpao, April 1, p. 11.

11. Hunag, C.H. 1998, 'Economic Liberalism and Fate of Women Workers', Article presented at the globalisation and Asia Workshop, Taichung, July.

12. Kerr, Joanna (1999), 'Responding to Globalisation', In Marilyu Porter and Ellen Judd (Eds.) Feminists Doing Development, London: Zed Books.

13. Lim, Y.I. 1998, 'Han Young Cases viewed from Korean experiences, Article presented at the Labour Rights and Labour Organising in the Pacific Rim Conference, May 22, 1998, University of California, Los Angeles.

14. Lucie, C. 1999, Globalisation and Women's Paid Labour in Asia, International Social Science Journal, UNESCO: Blackwell, June, p. 225.

15. Rogers, B. 1980, The Domistication of Women: Discrimination in Developing Societies, New York: St. Martin's.

16. Sen, A.K. 1990, "Gender and Cooperative Conflicts", In Irine Tinker (ed.), Persistent Inequalities: Women and World Development, New York: Oxford, pp. 123-149.

17. Sutherland and Sewell, 1998, Quoted in Kerr. Joanna, 1999, op. cit.
18. Unni, Jeemol, 2001, Gender and Informality in Labour Market in South Asia, EPW, June 30.

Suggestions

So, if development is to expand people's choices and guarantee their human rights, two things are necessary. First, global economic system must change and secondly, processes of change have to recognize gender imbalances to ensure that all people benefit from development. For this, feminist research and activism has to deepen its impact, expand its approach, and strengthen its alliances.

Deepening of impact means exposing and challenging vested interests and power structures—the historically rooted culture, principles, rules and procedures that underlie an organisation. Simply adding women into existing structures is not going to serve the purpose.

Expanding of approach denotes our need to be more multidisciplinary and holistic. Development objectives need to be informed by human rights, ecology, cultural studies, political science and so on. Economic growth will always supersede human welfare as long there is dominance of economics over other disciplines in defining development.

Finally, alliances need to be strengthened between women—North and South, East and West, rich and poor. We must be respectful to one another, taking care not to misrepresent the diverse positions of different women. The tensions that exist within international feminism need to be acknowledged and tackled. Global sisterhood can be replaced by a form of sisterhood which is both strategic and effective.

5

Foreign Investment and Economic Growth Through Multinational Corporations and Their Multiple Impacts

Dr. S. Murty*

Introduction

New development are occurring in the international Trading and Financial Systems as a consequence of which the study of the behaviour of Multinational Corporations (MNCs) has become crucial. The impact of MNCs on the economy of a developing country is enormous in the sense that they affect the industrial sector of economy to a great extent. There has been numerous studies aiming to elucidate the economic theory of the MNCs. Prominent among these are Caves (1982); Casson (1987); Bhagwati, J. (1991, 1994); Feldstein (1994); and Montiel (1993), Mrs. S. Murty (1998). These theoretical as well as empirical studies attempts to combine the theory of the firm, industrial systems (organisation), international trade theories and international finance to be able to answer a variety of doubts about MNCs.

In most of the industries, all over the world, the MNCs have become dominant. An important question is: What are these MNCs and why they are becoming so important in the present day world?

What is a Multinational Corporation?

An MNC is one which undertakes foreign direct investment. It owns or controls income generation assets in more than one country and in so doing produces goods or service outside its country of origin. Its managerial

* Professor of Economics, Vikram University, Ujjain (M.P.).

headquarters are located in the country referred to as the "home country" while the enterprise carries out operations in a number of other countries known as host countries. Thus it has the character of giant size, international operations, oligopolistic structure, spontaneous evolution and collective transfer of resources.

In short, Multinational Corporations (MNCs) are giant firms with their head quarters located in one country, and with a variety of business operations in several other countries. They are also referred to as Trans National Corporations (TNCs) which implies that their operations extend beyond the boundaries of nation in which they are originally envisaged.

The phenomenon of MNCs is nothing new, they were characteristic form of the mercantilistic period. Some of the important examples of the period were Hudson's Bay Co., The Royal African Co. and the East India Company which went out of their lands in search of markets for the products produced at home and to secure raw materials from distant lands.

Background of Multinational Corporations in India

With planned economy in 1951, India started with a mixed blend of public and private sectors. Individual private companies did not have enough resources required for major infrastructural investment and this part came to public sector along with basic industries and security sector. Besides mixed economy, in sixties we started to believe in closed economy and started raising tariff walls. Our export orientation was also limited and being suspicious of foreign investment, we were not prepared to invite foreign capital inspite of the fact that we were continuously feeling capital crunch. As regards technology, we were neither able to develop our own technology nor prepared to import technology because we were not willing to pay high royalties or high fees. On the other hand the strict industrial licensing policy was making the economic system all the more protected.

In seventies, inspite of all the restricted foreign trade policy, stringent imports and liberal exports, our balance of payments was getting upset and we had to borrow a massive loan of 2½ billion dollars from the IMF and we got trapped to liberalize and deregulate our economy. Besides, in the 1950's, 60's 70's we were getting soft, low interest loans from IDA and world bank. But things started changing in 1980s because we were on a lower priority of the international institutions and the loans started getting costlier.

MNCs have a strong hold over Indian economy since 1970s; when these corporations controlled 53.7 per cent of the assets of the industrial sector in India. According to Industrial Licensing Policy Inquiry Committee, there were

112 companies in India with assets of worth 10 crores in 1966, out of these 48 were either foreign branches or Indian subsidiaries of foreign companies. 14 Indian companies had extremely heavy loans and equity capital and, therefore, were virtually foreign controlled. These 62 companies and Rs. 1370 crores worth of assets which constituted 54 per cent of the total assets of India's giant sector. Dalip S. Swamy, in his book, "The Political Economy of Industrialisation". From Self-Reliance of Globalisation (New Delhi, 1994), p. 114, said that "Western foreign capital dominated the country's big business and controlled the apex of India's industrial pyramid in the mid sixties and further argues forcefully that Globalisation is bound to lead to debt explosion and massive unemployment. Several others like John Martinkussen (1988); Sudip Chaudhari (1979) and B. B. Bhattacharya (1992) recommend to adopt a cautious and suspicious approach regarding the growth of multinational in India's industrial sector.

Growth of multinationals through collaboration with Indian industries has been fast during 1980s, trends of liberalisation gave a substantial spurt to foreign collaboration. Out of the total 12760 foreign collaboration agreements approved in 40 years between 1948-88; as many as 6165 (i.e. 48% approx.) were approved during the period 1981-88.

In eighties, with the coming up of Rajeev Gandhi, liberalisation and deregulation started getting up into the economy but actually it started getting strength in nineties. In 1990-91, there was gulf war. Mandir and Mandal issues frightened investors who were lending money to India and we had no alternative but to enter the era of liberalisation and opening up of our economy.

Politicians, Economists, Civil Servants and others are scared of the dangers of multinationals on the pretext of CIA and American administration. Some are against multinationals in consumer goods because they bring in elitist products and increase social inequalities. Some think that the multinationals lobbying for their interests will get interested in trying to influence the country's politics and this is dangerous.

Actually, before reaching to any conclusion, it is necessary to assess and evaluate the impact of multinational corporations on the economy, on industry, on cross national flows, on capital investment, on economic development, on economic growth, on employment generation, on technology transfer, on balance of payments and so on.

This paper aims at to look into these impacts of FDI and MNCs in the economy.

Impacts of Multinational Companies

Impact on Industrial Development

The impact of MNCs on the industrial development of India during 1980s reveals that during the period 1990-92, the index of industrial production has increased from 47.6 in 1970 to 155.8 in 1992. The increase has been more distinct and substantial during 1980s which implies that the policies of Globalisation and liberalisation pursued by the government had a positive impact on industrial development. The contribution of manufacturing sector also went up from 7928 thousand U.S. dollars in 1970 to 41558 thousand U.S. dollars in 1992. The average annual growth rate of manufacturing earnings in India was 0.4 per cent during 1970-80 which rose to 2.5 per cent during 1980-92. The index of these earnings rose to 134 in 1990 (1980=100) from 83 in 1970 which increased to 217 in 1992. This desirable change during the period 1970-92, can be attributed to industrial policy changes and the rising flows of capital of MNCs in recent times. On the whole, it can be said that the growth of MNCs has a positive impact on the industrial development in India during this period. With regards to the harmful effects of these MNCs, we suggest that government as well as industrialist in the country should have better terms and conditions, depending on their bargaining power.

The announcement of Industrial Policy of July 24, 1991 has contributed significantly in the rise of multinationals in the Indian economy. The main features of Industrial Policy, 1991 are:

1. To accelerate the pace of industrial growth by providing greater freedom in investment decisions, keeping in view the objectives of increasing exports, efficiency and competitiveness of the industry. The policy encourages foreign investment and provides enhanced access to the state-of-the-art technology to enable advances in production techniques and to help attain international competitiveness.

2. Industrial licensing has been abolished for all industries other than 6 industries reserved for the public sector, those reserved for small scale and a list of 15 industries that are compulsorily licensed.

3. In order to attract foreign investment in high priority industries involving large investments and advanced technologies, direct investment upto 51 per cent foreign equity is being freely permitted.

4. A system of automatic approvals has been introduced for speedy clearance of proposals.

5. The use of foreign brand names and/or trade mark of goods is also now being permitted freely.

As a consequence of this Industrial Policy (1991), the approval of FDI in India has reached upto Rs. 39870.80 crores in 1995. The countries with FDI approvals of more than Rs. 1000 crores are USA (11,935.90); U.K. (3766.70); Japan (1514.50); Switzerland (1336.70) and Germany (1049.00). The flow of foreign direct investments (FDIs) has not been very high in case of India. Region-wise, East Asia and the Pacific had 52 per cent of the total global capital flows in 1995. The share of other regions is: Latin America (29%); Eastern Europe and Central Asia (9%); Middle East and North Africa (4 percent); Sub-Saharan Africa (4 percent); and South Asia (2%). The data on foreign-approvals in India indicate that despite best efforts by the government during 1991-95 period the FDIs have not responded to expected level, when compared to other countries.

Effect on Cross National Flows

Multinational Enterprises (MNEs) play a pivotal role in the cross-national flow of goods, capital and technology. As such, they play a key role in evolving international political economy characterised by rising globalisation of production process, interdependence of national product markets, interlocking of holdings of financial assets, and diffusion of manufacturing technology, it is estimated that multinationals now account for foreign sales worth some US$ 5.5 trillion. Foreign direct investment (FDI) by these firms has recently gained further importance through their market channels and communication media as many developing countries, beset by the huge debt crisis of the 1980s and beyond, have begun to seek this investment as an alternative source of external finance. With the waning of socialism, the turn towards market economies by the former socialist countries and their reinsertion into the capitalist world economy have also increased the salience of FDI. This salience has moreover been accentuated by the declining amount of assistance by the United States and Russia to many developing countries. Finally, because intra-firm trade among the majority-owned subsidiaries of MNCs has consisted a major source of surplus or deficit in international trade, FDI has become a new focus for analysing the industrial competitiveness and commercial rivalry among developed countries. Hence it is arguable that the impact of transnational actors on the economy of under-developed countries are top-heavy and there is an intimate relationship between MNCs and developing countries. But the nature of the relationships between MNEs and developing countries and the implications of this relationship for growth and development remain highly controversial when viewed from the perspectives of international economy. For several decades as such, the debate occurred primarily in the dialogue of the deaf between modernisation theory (which saw MNEs as promoting growth in the periphery) and dependency theory (which argued that MNEs prevented or distorted growth or, simply, they are the Trojen Horses of Neo-colonialism).

More recently, statist theory has tried to resolve this conundrum by bringing the state back in. In particular this approach argues that strong and autonomous states can regulate MNEs, thereby making them contribute to national economic development. However, this approach is a partial and biased approach if we analyse the interactions among state-society relations, MNEs access, economic growth as well as the historical experience of these cases which challenge some of the basic prepositions of dependency, modernisations and statist perspectives regarding the impact of MNEs on the economic performance of LDCs. We have before us Northeast Asian countries and Southeast capitalist Asian economies and Latin American countries where the strategic interactions between MNEs and governments have produced vastly different developmental outcomes on growth, employment and other economic activities.

Effect on Capital Movement

After World War-II, we observed that FDI became increasingly associated with the expansion of very large firms, mostly, but not entirely from the United States and this phenomenon was attracting considerable political criticism.

Free flow of capital transfers the savings to investors world-wise so as to maximise the incremental productivity of investment. Capital-rich countries can earn better rate of return of their savings through Foreign Direct Investment when they are transferred to the developing countries where high yielding projects have to be shelved due to shortage of funds. Therefore, it (free flow of capital) provides funds to the developing countries.

Secondly, International Capital flows help the people to achieve a smoother consumption profile. Overall welfare would be greater with cross-border capital flows.

The most important vehicle for cross border capital flows have been Foreign Direct Investment (FDI). Direct investment have played a crucial role in the world economy since the Second World War. The main determinant of Direct Investment is superior technology or skill which primarily takes place under monopolistic or oligopolistic market conditions. With the emergence of the Multinational Corporations (MNCs), and other contractual arrangements, production and distribution of goods and services has been globalised during the last four decades.

In regard to net inflows of private capital including FDI, to developing countries there has been a dramatic improvement. The flow of FDI in developing countries has increased from $4 billion in 1970 to about $25 billion in 1980. Though portfolio flows declined in 1995 owing to the turbulence in the world market following the Mexican Crisis of December 1994, FDI continued its steady upward trend, rising to $ 90.3 billion in 1995 from US $ 78.0 billion in 1994. The South Asia, including India accounted for a mere 1 percent of total direct investment. Among these, the share of FDI in gross capital formation was the lowest for India among all developing countries (only 0.2 per cent as against an average of about 6 per cent for all developing countries). Thus FDI has so far played a minor role in providing capital formation for India. It is a matter of hope that in recent years there has been an upward trend of FDI in India as it is evident from the table below:

Item	*1995-96*	*1994-95*	*1993-94*	*1992-93*	*1991-92*
A. Direct Investment	2133	1314	586	341	150
B. Portfolio Investment	2214	3581	3649	92	8
Total (A+B)	**4347**	**4895**	**4235**	**433**	**158**

Source: Economic Survey, 1995-96 and Annual Report, RBI, 1995-96.

From US $586 million in 1993-94 FDIs became more than doubled to US$ 1314 million in 1994-95. During 1995-96, FDIs were US$ 2133 million. The ratios of foreign investment to exports and GDP which increased during 1991-96 also tell that there has been a growing integration of the Indian economy with the global economy over such a short time. This has been made possible due to a more liberal policy, towards foreign investment announced by the government of India in July 1991 and onwards as compared to highly restrictive policy announced from time-to-time during the 1980s. Both the proponents and opponents of foreign investment done by MNEs would now seem to agree that FDI in the 1980s failed to function well in India as the economy earlier to reform episode was highly protected and FDI took place behind high tariff walls.

Impact on Economic Development

Some early economists as Alfred Marshall, J.B. Clark, Frank Knight and D.H. Robertson paid little attention to the growth of the MNEs. They concentrated as they were on the look out for the theory of prices and the allocation of resources. They continued to treat FDI within the traditional framework of the pricing system and thus simply as capital flows determined by international differences in the rate of return on capital. The role of the firm did not come within the purview of economic theory except as an aspect of imperfect (monopolist) competition. With Hymer's (1960) work the floodgates of theoretical and empirical studies of MNEs were opened and economies began to enquire into what difference it made when FDI took place in a variety of fields and areas under the co-ordinating umbrella of a large administrative organisation. Economists began to think that this type of investment was not to be regarded as simply an international movement of capital but as the movement of a bundle of resources. The investment was undertaken by firms that were not international in ownership but usually national firms operating in a number of countries through separately incorporated enterprises connected with and responsible to a central headquarters, and, above all, was administratively organised on such a scale as to displace the "market" over wide and varied types of activity. By the early 1980s many such firms were increasingly referred to as "global" corporations forming and implementing competitive strategies on a "global" scale. In effect, it is recognised that the emergence and growth of MNEs, can be regarded as the growth of firms (defined as administrative organisations) through investment abroad. And in a world where competition in technological innovation and in the ability to influence consumer demand are often more prevalent than price competition, these MNEs expand their ability to manage growth efficiently with minimal interference with on-going operations. This becomes possible when production, marketing, R&D, financial management, development link form into a coherent network of activities guided by a coherent administrative organisation with the objective of capitalising the rents generated at each level.

The effects of FDI on the LDCs host economy run from the microeconomic to aggregative economics (savings, investment, growth of real income), to the political and social system. As an instrument of foreign domination, they come to dominate not only the important industries ranging from mineral and oil, to pharmaceutical, electric and other high-technology industries but at times the entire economy of small countries depend on a narrow range of exports. In some sectors, the entry of MNEs (indeed, of modern industry) has brought the demise of artisans and small scale local producers. This is displacement of a less efficient technology by a more efficient one. In some industries MNEs hold decisive advantages, so local entrepreneurs either imitate them or are expelled; this pattern applies especially to advertising intensive industries.

The political as well as economic power MNEs possess undoubtedly at times is used to the disadvantage of host countries. It seems that a regime of multinational corporations would offer LDCs neither national independence nor equality. It would tend instead to inhibit the attainment of these goals. It would turn the LDCs into branch-plant countries, not only with reference to their economic functions but throughout the whole gamut of social, political and cultural roles. The top executives of the subsidiaries of MNEs play an influential role in the political, social and cultural life of the host country. For example, in Bangladesh by easy crossing of the international boundaries they pull and tear at the social and political fabric and erode the cohesiveness of national milieu. So the expectation that an underdeveloped country will bring forth the creative imagination needed to apply science and technology to the problem of degrading poverty seems rather spurious. And the fear that large scale foreign ownership of industrial assets might pose a threat to national sovereignty or mortgage the national interest to foreigners looms large on LCDs.

Impact on Economic Growth

FDI has a positive impact on the growth of the host economy. Researchers have found a negative association between the inflow of foreign resources and domestic savings. The degree of MNE penetration (defined as the ratio of capital stock controlled by MNEs to the local capital stock of the host country) is negatively associated with the subsequent pace of income growth in the host country. This relationship is particularly strong in LCDs with a large modernised sector. In other words, the higher the level of MNE investment/involvement in an LDC in a given year, the less probable that the country will achieve high rates of growth in subsequent years. In fact, MNE operations reduce the supply of funds available for investment, transferring resources out of the host economy by repatriating declared profits or by over pricing production inputs. This drain of investment resources leads to an inevitable reduction in subsequent growth. The possible negative relationship between MNE penetration and the growth in the host country can be explained in terms of its impact on the domestic industrial structure. An extensive MNE presence is associated with high levels of industrial concentration that contribute to income inequalities and a rapid depletion of investment funds in agriculture. For example, the strategic interactions between MNEs and Latin American Governments have produced the lacklustre performance in those countries which give rise to the "empty box problem", so-called because none of the Latin American Countries has been able to achieve growth with equity. The reason is not far to seek. In such a case domestic demand fails to rise sufficiently, import substitution possibilities becomes increasingly difficult and foreign trade opportunities are limited by protectionist policies of trading partners and the reluctance of MNE-subsidiaries to encroach upon the market for sister companies. Hence, profit rate falls, investment levels are reduced and the high growth rates associated with high level of domestic and foreign investment do not pertain.

India is now endowed with a relatively mature domestic industrial economy and she is infrastructually rich over other developing countries. FDI will find a suitable destination here. Though on the basis of empirical research on the past performance of MNEs in India, it has been suggested that their net contribution to India has often been welfare retarding, still considering the recent changes in Indian economy as well as changes in the nature of FDI as most of the FDI proposals are in the form of joint ventures with Indian partners, managed and stuffed by Indian nationals or persons of Indian partners effects of such investment so as to create jobs and accelerate growth in line with the country's dynamic comparative advantage, if tariff and trade policies along with other suitable policies are turned to maximise the benefits towards that direction. It is upto the country to take advantages of the new opportunities provided by FDI, lest the advantage should take over by other industrialising countries in terms of development of technology, managerial expertise, integration with the world economy, exports and higher growth.

Effect on Employment Generation

The wealth of a nation, wrote Adam Smith two hundred years ago, is determined by "First, thc skill, dexerity and judgement with which the labour is generally applied, and secondly, by the proportion between the number of those who are employed in useful labour, and those who are not employed". Capitalist enterprises has come a long way from his day, but it has never been able to bring more than a fraction of the world's population into useful or highly productive employment. Available data from the past reveal that direct employment provided by MNEs range from 13 to 30 million. Even if the most liberal estimates are accepted, the proportion of total global employment accounted for by MNEs was only 1.3 per cent. In terms of industrial employment, MNEs contributed 4.8 per cent of the job total. In the Third World, MNEs were credited with the creation of 2 to 4 million jobs representing 0.3 per cent of total employment and 2 per cent of total industrial employment. Employment generated by MNEs was mainly concentrated in Western countries and as regards creation of direct employment generated by MNEs remained a small percentage of total employment. Unlike in the past, a strikingly new development is that most of the employment created by MNEs now a days are in the developing countries. As many as 5 million out of 8 million direct and indirect employment through forward/direct linkages and distribution associated with foreign investment as triggered off by MNEs are located in the developing countries. But, still now, productive and massive employment, however, is very illusory from the side of MNEs.

The investor's choice of techniques is another important determinant of the investment employment relationship. Stewart (1974) has argued that technologies imported to the Third world are fairly 'rigid' since they tend to predominate in modern complex industries with continuous production process and highly capital-intensive and in turn, generates little employment within the host economies. And MNEs subsidiaries have been induced to deploy relatively labour-intensive technologies in various Asian and Latin American countries and in fact, they have not played a major role in the employment and export expansion drives of the rapidly industrialising countries.

Most of the critics of the MNEs opine that in coming years, as MNCs gain increasing control over industries and use high technology, many workers are likely to be displaced. But this is contrary to the international experience. According to World Development Report (1995) which is on "Wonders in an Integrating world", the multinational corporations being an agent of change, created 5 million of the total 8 million jobs in the developing countries between 1985-1992. The number of workers employed by the multinationals in developing countries stands at 12 million, but the true number who owe their livelihood to multinationals may be twice that given the prevalence of sub contractual.

The 'balanced outlook' in this context suggests that the capital flows (MNCs, being the carrier of these flows) will have greater impact on the workers in developing countries as compared to developed countries. These flows imply a boost to GDP growth of 0.5 to 1 per cent a year. The future of the workers in the developing countries including India, will be brighter if their governments manage to strike the right balance between fiscal prudence, reliance on markets and stabilising social policies.

Effect on Technology Transfer

The growth and development of both the developed and developing countries depend on the extent and efficacy of technology transfer. Product-life-cycle theory as formulated by Vernon showing a fairly definite sequence in the relationship between international technology transfer and trade, explained the trend of events in many industries. This concept was, however, in vogue during the 1960s and the 1970s, but with time, situation rather drastically changed. Foreign subsidiaries, not exports, dominated the field and through these subsidiaries new technologies are exploited abroad. Technology frontier is now becoming increasingly internationalised by continuously shifting outward as a result of the effort of MNEs aimed at innovation. The higher the MNEs initial proportion of sales made abroad through both exports and subsidiary sales, the quicker are innovations transferred for production abroad. In this game, the experiences of India,

Taiwan and South Korea, for example, would seem to indicate difficulty for labour abundant nations in claiming a comparative advantage in labour intensive goods such as textiles. Even in this sector, catching up to the technological frontier is essential to international competitiveness. Otherwise, the technology which is transferred to such developing nations by the MNEs endowed with extensive overseas manufacturing facilities as well as substantial R & D activities will not run parallel in the context of the developed countries.

Effect on Balance of Payments

Government's concern with the balance of payments was the chief policy issue to bear on MNEs financial behaviours in the 1960s, when almost all the industries chose to maintain exchange rate arrangements. To fix an exchange rate at an officially declared value is to forgo using the price of foreign exchange as an adjustment device. Although many prices other than the exchange rate can respond to payments imbalances, the inability of the exchange rate to adjust make governments more likely to be facing imbalances. In the short run, deficits prove harder to manage than surpluses, and therefore governments with fixed exchange rates often found themselves bending every policy instrument to ward off payments deficits.

In the short run, when a MNE transfers one dollar from home to foreign, real spending is likely to expand in foreign and fall at home. Extra real spending in foreign falls on all goods concerned, and so Home's exports rise. The reduced spending in home comes partly out of imports, and so Home's imports fall. Home's balance of trade improves, and indeed could improve enough to require the capital outflow so that it involves no short-run deterioration of Home's overall balance of payments. This is nothing but the transfer process. The transfer process helps us to investigate the short-run consequences of FDI for the balance of payments. Just as one dollar of foreign investment is expected to earn a flow of profits for the MNE, it is expected to bring a reflux of foreign exchange earnings into the nation's balance of payments. An investment outflow could either support or replace Home's exports-the former effect favouring, the latter harming, Home's balance of payments.

Miscellaneous Effects

Multinationals add a tremendous amount of managerial know how...when one is employed with a MNC for some years, one learns a great deal. If one leaves the MNC and sets up one's own business, one is not starting a new, not with a clean slate, but with experience of entrepreneurship and management.

Some people are afraid that foreign things may destroy Indian culture, traditions and values, but we should remember that culture is not a static thing. India had changed over centuries with our capacity and capability to absorb.

Today, our GDP consists of 28% of agricultural product, 32% industrial contribution and 40% services. The growth rate of GDP in 1996-97 has been 7%, of which 4% can be attributed to industry and this industrial growth has come about mainly because of industrial delicencing, liberalisation and opening up of the economy to multinationals.

Actually, it all depends on our security, confidence in self, our political leadership. Our honest media and our transparency. MNCs bring in technologies, machines and most important, they bring in ideas. In many products of MNCs, we have created a detailed retail distribution system where the products reach the remotest villages of the economy within a short time, where the goods can go by trucks instead of trains if the rail is not there, where the goods can go in cardboard boxes instead of wooden boxes which are heavier, costlier and dangerous to our forests and ecological equilibrium. Above all these MNCs have respect for the law, environmental issues and taxes. Today, large multinationals realise that they have to be the citizens of the country, they are in and they have to honour the country, if they want to succeed.

Opening up means easier access to multinational corporations and joint ventures, which can play a major role in developing a nation as it did in U.S.A. We now live in the world, where the distinction of Swadeshi and foreign becomes almost irrelevant as a thing which is foreign branded that is produced in our own country through a multinational company, absorbs our topmen as managers, gives employment to our people, uses our raw materials and land, uses our packing material, develops our marketing and gives business to our whole-sellers and retailers. Above all is satisfies the needs of our people. In short, the MNCs are solving to a great extent our problems of shortage of goods. Many people think that joint ventures are better in so far as local partners know local conditions and ways and how to get through the maze of bureaucracy, red tape etc. Besides when you go for a joint venture, you have to think very carefully about what are you in it for? What do you bring to the table? What is your partner looking for? What happens if something goes wrong? So you have to work-out a plan of action before going in for a joint venture.

Conclusion

It is clear from the above discourse that the multinational enterprises bring not only blessings but also woes to the development process of the third world economies. Their involvement often transcends beyond economic sphere and this warrants selective and careful intervention by the state to monitor their functioning, to minimize the costs and maximise the benefits. In the present world of globalisation and market integration across nation, the role of transnational enterprises are likely to expand further, and unless the host country governments device suitable checks and balances for regulation of these enterprises, it would be difficult to extract benefit and diffuse the modern knowledge that MNEs bring together with their investments. The success or failure of the states of these LDCs to effectively monitor the investment programs of these enterprises will determine the long run growth prospects of these economies in the coming century.

6

The Truth about Global Competition

The Economic Myths Behind Globalisation

Prof. M. Lakshmi Marasaiah*

Local communities everywhere are on the front lines of what might well be characterised as World War III. It is not the nuclear confrontation between East and West-between the Soviet Union and the United States—that we once feared. It is a very different kind of conflict. There is no clash of competing military forces and the struggle is not defined by national borders. But it does involve an often violent struggle for control of physical resources and territory that is destroying lives and communities at every hand. It is a struggle between the forces and institutions of economic globalisation and the communities that are trying to reclaim control of their economic lives. It is a conflict between competing goals—economic growth to maximize profits for absentee owners versus creating healthy communities that are good places for people to live. It is a competition for the control of markets and resources between global corporations and financial markets on the one hand and locally owned businesses serving local markets on the other.

Two things of fundamental importance to each and every one of us are now very much at stake.

- Will people and communities control their local resources and economies and be able to set their own goals and priorities based on their own values and aspiration? Or will these decisions be left to global financial markets and corporations that are blind to all values save one—instant financial returns?

* Professor and Head, Department of Economics, S.K.U.P.G. Centre, Karnool-518 002.

- Will the life sustaining resources produced by the regenerative capacities of our planet's ecosystem be equitably shared to provide for the material needs of all of us who inhabit this bountiful planet, as well as for our children and their children unto the seventh generation and beyond? Or will we allow a global economic system that is now functioning on auto-pilot beyond conscious human control to consume and destroy the ecosystem and our social fabric in its insatiable quest for money?

Economists, politicians, cooperate spokespersons and the media have for years been touting the benefits of the global economy. They have called on us to support trade agreements such as the North American Free Trade Agreement (NAFTA) and the World Trade Organisation (WTO) to remove the constraints of economic borders and open to everyone the opportunities of growth and prosperity in the global economy. They have promised rich rewards for those workers and communities that become successful global competitors.

Many of the most ardent boosters of economic globalisation met earlier in the year at the annual meeting of the World Economic Forum. This Forum has for years brought together top industrialists and political figures from around the world to advance the proposition that removing tariffs and other restrictions on the free international flow of trade and money is a key to creating new economic opportunity and prosperity. It thus caused quite a stir when the Forum publicly announced that economic globalisation is producing disastrious consequences that threaten the political stability of the Wesern democracies. Their warning bears close examination for being one of the most honest and accurate assessments of other consequences of economic globalisation yet produced by leading advocates of that process. The observation is that:

- Economic globalisation is causing severe economic dislocation and social instability.
- The technological changes of the past few years have eliminated more jobs than they have created.
- The global competition "that is part and parcel of Globalisation leads to winner-take-all situations; those who come out on top win big, and the losers lose even bigger."
- Higher profits no longer mean more job security and better wages. "Globalisation tends to delink the fate of the corporation from the fate of its employees."

- Unless serious corrective action is taken soon, the backlash could destabilize the Western democracies.

We don't have to go far to find examples of what they are talking about and why people are getting a bit upset as they wake up to the realities of who is winning in the ruthless competition of the global economy. The disparities between the winners and losers in the global competition are becoming more obscene with each passing day.

We are coming to realize that the extravagant promises of the advocates of the global economy are based on a number of myths that have become so deeply embedded in Western industrial culture that we have grown to accept them without examination.

- The myth that growth in GNP is a valid measure of human well-being and progress.
- The myth that free unregulated markets efficiently allocate a society's resources.
- The myth that growth in trade benefits ordinary people.
- The myth that global corporations are benevolent institutions that if freed from governmental interference will provide a clean environment for all and good jobs for the poor.
- The myth that absentee investors create local prosperity.

The Growth Myth

Our measures of growth are deeply flawed in that they are purely measures of activity in the monetised economy. Expanded use of cigarettes and alcohol increases economic output both as a direct consequence of their consumption and because of the related increase in health care needs. The need to clean up oil spills generates economic activity. Gun sales to minors generate economic activity. A divorce generates both lawyers fees and the need to buy or rent and outfit a new home increasing real estate brokerage fees and retail sales. It is now well documented that in number of other countries the quality of living of ordinary people has been declining as aggregate economic output increases.

The growth myth has another serious flaw. Since 1950, the world's economic output has increased 5 to 7 times. That growth has already increased the human burden on the planet's regenerative systems-its soils, air water, fisheries, and forestry systems-beyond what the planet can sustain. Continuing to press for economic growth beyond the planet's sustainable limits does two things. It accelerates the rate of breakdown of the earth's regenerative systems-as we see so dramatically demonstrated in the case of many ocean fisheries, and it intensifies the competition between rich and poor for the resource base that remains.

This is vividly illustrated by many of the development projects in India many funded with loans from the World Bank and other multilateral development banks-that displace the poor so that the lands and waters on which they depend for their livelihood can be converted to uses that generate higher economic returns—meaning converted to use by people who can pay more than those who are displaced.

The Myth of Free Unregulated Markets

It is almost inherent in the nature of markets that their efficient function depends on the presence of a strong government to set a framework of rules for their operation. We know that free markets create monopolies, which government must break up to maintain the conditions of competition on which market function depends.

We also know that markets only allocate efficiently when prices reflect the full and true costs of production. Yet in the absence of governmental regulations, market incentives persistently push firms to cut corners on safety, pay workers less than a living wages, and dump untreated toxic discharges into a convenient river. In our present competitive context if management does not take such measures, they are likely to be replaced by the owners or bought out by someone with less scruples who will.

The Myth of Free Trade

Many so-called trade agreements, such as the North American Free Trade Agreement (NAFTA) and the World Trade Organisation (WTO) are not really trade agreements at all. They are economic integration agreements intended to guarantee the rights of global corporations to move both goods and investments where ever they wish—free from public interference and accountability. WTO is best described as a bill of rights for global corporations.

The Myth that Economic Globalisation is Inevitable

Many of the people who claim globalisation is a consequence of inevitable historical forces are paid to promote that message by the same global corporations that have invested millions of dollars in advancing the globalisation policy agenda.

The Myth that Corporations are Benevolent Institutions

The corporation is an institutional invention specifically and internationally created to concentrate control over economic resources while shielding those who hold the resulting power from liability for the consequences of its use. The more national economies become integrated into a seamless global economy, the further corporate power extends beyond the reach of any state and the less accountable it becomes to any human interest or institution other than a global financial system that is now best described as a gigantic legal gambling casino.

All over the world people are indeed waking up to the truth about economic globalisation and are taking steps to reclaim and rebuild their local economies. Such communities face basic choices as to how they will divide their efforts between competing for a share of the declining pool of good jobs that global corporations offer and working to create locally owned enterprises that sustainably harvest and process local resources to produce the jobs and the goods and services that local people need to live healthy, happy, and fulfilling lives in balance with the environment.

Our experience with the real consequences of economic globalisation is pointing to many important lessons. One such lesson is that economies should be local, rooting power in the people and communities who realize their well-being depends on the health and vitality of their local ecosystem. If it is protectionist to favour local firms and workers who pay local taxes, live by local rules, respect and nurture the local ecosystems, compete fairly in local markets, and contribute to community life then let us all proudly proclaim ourselves to be protectionist.

Such choices are not isolationist, To the contrary, they create a foundation for creative cooperation with our neighbours—whether they be in the United States or in other countries—to share experience, ideas, and technology—and to join in international solidarity in rewriting the rules of the global economy to favour local over global businesses, and to encourage cooperative relations among people and committees. It is our consciousness—our ways of thinking and our sense of membership in a larger community-not our economies-that should be global.

Millions of people are also making an important discovery—that life is about living-not consuming. A life of material sufficiency can be filled with social, cultural, intellectual, and spiritual abundance that place no burden on the planet.

It is time to assume responsibility for creating a new human future of just and sustainable communities freed from the myth that greed, competition, and mindless consumption are paths to individual and collective fulfilment. It will take millions of people around the world-linked together into a powerful political coalition aimed at radical political and economic-reform to win the war that global capital is waging against us.

Globalisation gives rise in some quarters to fears that can lead to suspicion, protectionism, and policies that are ultimately self-destructive. Such fears cannot be allowed to frustrate the great potential of a world in which countries drawing closer together. We believe that countries can face the challenges of globalisation positively, demanding as those challenges may be.

All countries can benefit from full participation in the world's markets, including its financial markets. Protectionist pressures must be resisted and reversed, and the principles of openness and multilaterism promoted by the World Trade Organisation, the IMF, and the World Bank must be honoured. And financial market integration should be seen as a positive force: it offers access to global financial intermediation and a stimulus for more competitive and efficient domestic financial sectors; and it promotes efficiency and growth worldwide.

How encouraging it is, therefore, to see that so many developing countries in transition have been freeing up white trade and exchange systems within the framework of our structural adjustment programs.

No country can afford to forgo the benefits of integration into global market: the alternative is marginalisation and stagnation. But all countries must take the steps to minimise the associated risks. More than ever before, countries need tightly disciplined macro economic policies to maintain a stable environment for investors, whether domestic or foreign. And while foreign capital can be a useful—and sometimes vital complement to domestic saving, it is not a substitute for it: domestic saving remains the key to investment and sustainable growth. It is also clear that strong financial institutions are essential to avoid market disturbances at home and to secure an effective defence against external resources. Competitive banking and financial systems that are found, well regulated, and properly supervised are indispensable for countries to be able to expose their economies safely to the pressures that can arise in global markets.

The challenges to globalisation therefore add to the need for the developing and transition countries to press ahead with their adjustment and reform efforts. For many, this means creating conditions to attract foreign financing and use it effectively. But a growing number of countries, have been facing a different problem: how to cope with large-scale capital inflows. Such inflows, especially when they are easily reversible, provide no grounds for relaxation of adjustment and reform.

They should not be used to finance domestic consumption. In many cases, they call for stronger fiscal discipline; and in some cases, exchange rates should be allowed to take part of the strain. Many developing countries and countries in transition also, of course, need to do more to depend and widen the role of market forces and to foster more competitive market environments, in order to promote transparent and efficient mechanism for resource allocation.

Is globalisation any less demanding for the industrial countries? Not at all! It adds to the urgency of the task of taking full advantage of the current expansion to tackle the deep-rooted problems that are limiting the pace, the quality, and perhaps, the sustainability of their growth.

All has to applaud the increased efforts and commitments to reduce fiscal deficits, but in most cases underlying imbalances remain large and the pace of consolidation too slow. More must be done not only to redress present imbalances but also to meet the growing demands of the future.

Another deep-rooted problem—structure unemployment-must also be tackled sooner, rather than later. Budget laxity and high unemployment tend to feed on each other. While cyclical conditions provide the opportunity, governments must not flinch from the task of improving the functioning of labour markets. How? It is not an easy task: by reforming regulations and policies that impete employment creation and job search.

Monetary stability, macroeconomic discipline, sound financial systems, and efficiently working market mechanisms are essential for all countries that embrace globalisation. But they are not sufficient for any. To fight the fears that globalisation sometimes inspires, countries need policies that promote not just economic efficiency, financial stability, and growth but also equity and high-quality growth. In too many countries, the quality of growth suffers from widening distributional inequalities related partly to high unemployment but also stagnating wages of unskilled workers. And too many countries continue to suffer from poor governance, corruption and increasing crime.

Of course, economic policy can provide only part of what is needed to rid the world of these blights. But it is a vital part. To promote equity, efficiency, and sustainable growth, governments carry an inspectable responsibility for investment in human capital—through education, health care, and well-targeted social safety nets—and also for establishing and maintaining honest and effective systems of public administration, law, order and justice. If these essential services are to be affordable, there is certainly no room for unproductive expenditures—military or otherwise—and wasteful subsidies: they must bear the brunt of fiscal consolidation. So Globalisation demands a lot from governments if it is to deliver its promise of stronger and high-quality growth.

7

The Impact of Reform Measures on Banking Sector in India—An Analysis

*R.G. Desai**

In India, as in many developing countries, the commercial banking sector has the dominant element in the countries' financial system. The sector has performed the key function of providing liquidity and payment services to the real sector, and has accounted for the bulk of the financial intermediation process. It has contributed to the process of economic development by serving as a major source of credit to house holds, Government, business and to weaker sectors of the economy. However over a period of time some maladies have crept into the system. In order to overcome those, Narasimham Committee recommendations were implemented by the Govt. since 1991.

Objectives

Main objectives of this paper is to assess the impact of reform measures in Banking sector in India. Accordingly an attempt is made to find out the impact of selected three variables mentioned below.

1. De-regualtion of interest rate, its impact on the type of deposits and on the lending pattern over a period 20 years.
2. Capital Adequacy norms, NAPs its impact on working of different commercial banks during the same period, and
3. Non performing assets, its different ramifications in the banking sector of the Indian economy.

* Professor and Fellow K.K. Birla Foundation, Dept. of Economics Bangalore University, Bangalore-56.

Interest Rate Deregulation

Prior to the reforms, the interest rates on both deposits and loans were fully administered by the RBI and were highly rigid under regulated environment. Following the recommendations of the Chakravarthy Committee (1985), a gradual process of deregulation was initiated. This gained momentum in the 1990s with recommendations of Narasimham Committee (1991).

Currently the structure of interest rates in India has become reasonably flexible, as most of the interest rates relating to banks and financial institutions and debt market have been deregulated. The first step in deregulating lending rates was taken in October 1994, when rates were deregulated for advances greater than Rs. 2,00,000/. As against the earlier regulations under which interest on credit limits up to Rs. 25,000/- was prescribed at 12 per cent and for credit limits between 25000 and Rs. 2,00,000 the rate was not to exceed 13.5 per cent per annum. Under current regulations Interests on all loans below Rs. 2,00,000 should not exceed the PLR (prime lending rates) which is available to the best borrowers of the concerned Bank.

Major objectives of deregulation of interest rate regimes were to improve functioning of the money market, facilitate better liquidity management of the bank, improve function of the secondary market and to increase the supply of long term funds for investment, facilitate better management of the Government debt, eliminate distortions in the flow of funds better, ensure sufficient financial intermediation process, and increase the scope for effective central bank control, strengthen the competitiveness, viability and vitality of the financial institutions to enable them to make better interest rate risk management. Facilitate better allocation of financial resources in the economy.

The process of deregulating deposit rates in phases began in April 1992 and has gathered momentum in recent years. Deregulation of term deposit rates first took the form of the RBI switching form prescribing a single rate for each category of term deposit (determined by maturity period) to announcing a ceiling rate below which banks were free to fix their deposits rates.

In July 1996, the RBI abolished the ceiling for deposits of different maturity and in April 1998, interest rates on deposits beyond fifteen days have been freed. Banks can now charge differential rates on deposits of similar maturity but different sizes. Currently, the interest rate on saving.

Analysis and Results

In order to assess the impact of deregulation of interest rates on the deposits and lending of the Bank credit the data pertaining to a period of 1981-

Table 1: Structure of Interest Rates 1994-2000.

Rates	*1994*	*1995*	*1996*	*1997*	*1998*	*1999*	*2000*
Lending Rates size of the credit limit							
(i) upto & 25000	12.0	12.0	12.0	12.0	Not exceeding PLR	Not exceeding PLR	Not exceeding PLR
(ii) Above Rs. 25000-200000	13.5	13.5	13.5		Not exceeding PLR	Not exceeding PLR	Not exceeding PLR
(iii) Over Rs. 200,000	Free	Free	Free	Free	Free	Free	Free
Deposit Rates							
1. Current	0	0	0	0	0	0	0
2. Savings	5.0	4.5	4.5	4.5	4.5	4.5	4.0
3. Term							
1-3 years	10.00	11.00	12.00	11-12*	10.50-11*	9-11*	8.50-9.50*
Over 3 years upto 5 years	10.00	11.00	13.00*	12-13*	11.50-12*	10.50-11.50*	10-10.50*
Above 5 years	10.00	11.00	13.00*	12.50-13*	11.50-12*	10.50-11.50*	10-10.50*

Source: RBI, Annual Report, Several Issues, RBI Busy season credit policy, CMIE, Monthly Review several Issues.

Note: 1. Free means banks are free to charge interest rates decided by them.
2. *Refers to deposit rates of major public sector bank as at end March.

2000 were collected. In order to obtain the results the period is divided into pre reform period of 10 years and post reform period of 10 years. With in the several parameters, the selected parameters are compared and analysis is drawn.

1. During the pre-reform period of 1989-90, there is uneven growth of demand deposits varying from 9.2% to 33.17%. However time deposits have grown consistently from 14.9% to 42.2%. There is less fluctuations in time deposits. Accordingly the aggregate deposits also grown consistently from 13.7% to 25.8% over a period.

2. If we compare these figures to the post-reform (1991-2000) period (Table 3), there is not only high fluctuations in demand deposits varying from 1.3% to as high as 27.6% and but also average growth is less than pre-reform period. The same trend is noticed even in time deposits as well as in aggregate deposits. The average growth rate for Pre-reform period for all types of deposits are higher than the Post-reform period. It indicates that deregulation of interest rates by government has not helped banks to mobilize more funds during Post-reform period compared to Pre-reform period.

Table 2: Annual Growth Rate of Selected Items of Scheduled Commercial Banks During Post-Reform Period.

Year	*Demand deposit*	*Annual growth rate (%)*	*Time deposit*	*Annual Growth rate (%)*	*Aggregate deposit*	*Annual growth rate (%)*	*Bank Credit*	*Annual growth rate (%)*	*Investment in govt. securities*	*Annual growth rate (%)*	*Initial investment in approved securities*	*Annual growth rate (%)*
1981	8290		32259		40549		25371		9219		3697	
1982	9055	9.2	37073	14.9	46128	13.7	29681	16.9	10619	15.1	5113	38.3
1983	10201	12.6	43838	18.2	54039	17.7	35493	19.5	12028	13.2	6368	24.5
1984	12195	19.5	52425	19.5	64620	19.5	37272	5.0	13474	12.0	7725	21.3
1985	15039	23.3	62036	18.3	77075	19.2	43854	17.6	17473	29.6	9435	22.1
1986	16993	12.9	74835	20.6	91828	19.1	56067	27.8	19045	8.9	11509	21.9
1988	21936	13.7	10438	17.7	126323	37.4	70536	11.4	30517	23.1	15987	38.90
1989	25108	14.4	112746	980.14	137854	9.1	84719	20.1	35815	17.3	18847	17.8
1990	33437	33.17	140078	24.2	173515	25.8	101453	19.7	42292	18.08	22078	17.1
Total	171537		654343		919829		547747		215263		113761	
Average		16.9		17.7		17.6		16.7		18.5		22.1

Source: RBI Annual Report Various issues.

Table 3: Annual Growth Rate of Selected Items of Scheduled Commercial Banks During Post-Reform Period.

Year	*Demand deposit*	*Annual growth rate (%)*	*Time deposit*	*Annual Growth rate (%)*	*Aggregate deposit*	*Annual growth rate (%)*	*Bank Credit*	*Annual growth rate (%)*	*Investment in govt. securities*	*Annual growth rate (%)*	*Initial investment in approved securities*	*Annual growth rate (%)*
1991	38300		162398		200698		116301		19998		25067	
1992	48893	27.6	188872	16.1	237565	18.3	125592	7.9	62727	213.6	27469	9.5
1993	49541	1.3	225397	19.4	274938	15.7	151982	21	75945	21	29711	8.1
1994	60700	22.5	262932	16.6	323632	17.7	161980	6.5	94872	24.9	30641	3.1
1995	76903	26.6	309956	17.8	386859	19.5	211560	30	117685	24	31568	3
1996	80614	4.8	353205	13.9	433819	12.1	254011	20	132227	12.3	32555	3.1
1997	101519	25.9	523001	48.1	624520	43.9	278401	9.6	158890	20	31624	-2.8
1998	118435	16.6	558167	6.7	676602	8.3	323619	16.2	186957	17.6	31748	0.3
1999	135117	14.1	663890	18.9	799007	18	368837	13.9	247047	32.1	31669	0.2
2000	127366	5.7	685978	3.3		17.9	435958	18.1	278456	12.7	30488	-3.7
Total	837388		3933596		4770984		2428241		1374804		302540	
Average		16.1		17.8		19.1		15.9		42.1		2.3

Source: RBI, Annual Report Various Issues.

3. With regards to Bank Credit, the Pre-reform period average growth was 16.7% as against 15.9% in the post reform period. It indicates that banks have not been benefited by the deregulation of interest rates. Perhaps only the competition among themselves has emerged.
4. In case of investment in government securities, banks were forced to invest more (42%) than in the approved securities (2.5%) during post reform period as against 18% and 22% in Pre-reform period. This indicates that banks were cautious about their risky investment in securities.
5. The important conclusion that can be derived is that the scheduled commercial banks might have either preferred government securities or forced by the government to invest in government securities. As a result of which the profitability of the scheduled commercial banks has been eroded.

Capital Adequacy Norm

One of the notable development in the banking regulatory framework in the recent years to the stipulation of capital requirements. Banking supervisions world over have unanimously agreed on the method of assessing adequacy of capital as also on the need to harmonize such requirement at the international level, at least in respect of internationally active banks. The agreement is known technically as the 'internationally convergence of capital measurement and capital standards, and popularly a 'The Base Accord'. The Accord has become the reference point for policy action among nations. In India, the committee on the financial system under the chairmanship of Sri. M. Narasimham has not only recommended the adoption of the Base Accord but also laid down a time frame for compliance.

Concept of capital adequacy: capital adequacy has been defined as the ration of capital to the risk weighted assets. Capital has been divided into:

1. Tier I—called are capital comprises fully paid up capital disclosed reserves and corresponds to the traditional measure of capital and
2. Tier II—which includes undisclosed reserves, revaluation of reserves general provisions, hybrid debt capital instruments and subordinated term debt.

Besides the national authorities on left with the discretion to include/exclude any items in the light of their national accounting and supervising regulations. This is an improvement over the conventional definition of capital.

However Tier I capital is granted greater importance due to certain well-recognised facts. This is the only element common to the banking system the world over, it is wholly visible in the published account; and it has a crucial bearing on the profit margins and the banks' ability to compete. Also, the strengthening of the core capital would facilitate a progressive enhancement in the quality of well as the level of the total capital resources maintained by the banks.

Thus the norms stipulated that Tier II should not exceed Tier I, in 1995 the Base Committee introduced the concept of Tier III capital to allow banks at the discretion of national regulations to address part of their market risks by issuing short term subordinated debt. Tier-III capital is therefore only permitted to cover market risks including those that derive from foreign exchange and commodities.

There are two ways in which the capital has been routed to banks balance sheets.

1. The budget allocation on for recapitalisation. Of late banks are made available in the form of two years Government of India bonds known as special securities 2006 at 10% interest to banks in need for additional capital after write-offs and provisioning. Thus there is no cash in flow. On the liabilities rule equity (i.e. Tier I capital) gets boosted by creating an equivalent investment (Govt. bonds) asset side since investment carries zero risk weight and earns 10% interest. There is no strain on capital adequacy & no loss too banks. The bonds are non risk securities and non transferable.
2. Under the World Bank's financial sector development projects, the rupee equipment of $35 million loaned to the government of India & in turn to banks.

Analysis & Results

1. From the table 4 it can be observed that SBI and its subsidiaries have striven hard consistently in maintaining capital adequacy norms consistently over a period of 8 years and now reached the stipulated requirement. However among nationalised banks some have succeeded and some have not reached the stipulated norms. Among those banks, the least capital is maintained by the Indian Bank. Government has to bail out by the budgetary support to this Bank.
2. Some of the Nationalised Banks namely Central Bank of India, United Bank of India, UCO Bank and Sindh Bank has the average percentage below the requirement of 9 per cent as on 31st March

2000. These banks are unable to maintain the capital adequacy norm. Therefore, the selected nationalised banks will have to make more efforts to maintain capital adequacy norms. Even after 9 years of stipulation they could not reach the norm.

Table 4: Comparison of Capital Adequacy Norm Among SBI and its subsidiaries vis-a-vis Nationalised Banks During the period 1994-2001.

Banks	*Total Percentage for 8 Years*	*Average Annual Percentage*
SBI	102.11	12.76
SBI Subsidiaries	69.57	9.93
Nationalised Banks	163.90	8.62

Source: Computed from the various Reports of RBI.

From Table 4 it can be observed that 8 years Average capital adequacy for the SBI is highest with 12.76 per cent followed by its subsidiaries 9.93 per cent and nationalised bank 8.62 per cent.

If one observes capital adequacy within the nationalised banks it may be concluded that some banks have reached the norms, some are nearer to the norms and some are below the norms. But on the whole, if grouped together nationalised banks as such have reached the capital adequacy norm with 8.62 per cent. It is a welcome trend.

Non-Performing Assets

Banks play an important role in economic development of a country in mobilisation of communities savings and deployment of funds to the productive sectors of the economy. Loans and advances are assets of the bank as they play an important part in gross earnings and net profits of banks. The share of advances in the total assets of the banks forms more than 60 per cent and such it is the back bone of banking structure. Bank lending is very crucial for it makes possible the financing of agricultural industrial and commercial activities of the country. The strength and soundness of the banking system primarily depends upon health of the advances. In other words improvement in assets quality in fundamental to strengthening the working of banks and improving their financial liability. It should be noted that (a) while advances to priority sectors by scheduled commercial banks got momentum after nationalisation of public sector banks effected in July 1969 and later on in December 1980.

The Narasimham Committee in its two reports (1991 and 1998) pointed out the glaring deficiencies of directed credit lending viz., deterioration in Asset quality to the tune of 47 per cent of NPAs alone in priority sector on account of wilful defaulters. No other single indicator amply reflects the status of quality of assets and its impact on banks liability than the figure of Net NPAs.

Gross NPAs and Net NPAs

The gross NPA and Net NPA are always expressed as a percentage of advances. The percentage of gross NPA to advances includes interest suspense account where the bank is following the accounting practice in debiting NPA to the customer account and crediting interest suspense account. Net NPAs are derived from gross NPA by excluding (i) balance in Interest suspense account (ii) DICGC/ECGC claims received and kept in suspense account pending adjustment (for final settlement), (iii) part payment received and kept in suspense account and (iv) total provision held.

Norms for Treating Different Advances as Non Performing

The following norms are adopted for treating different advances as non performing. An account will be treated as NPA whose status has to be worked out from the date the irregularity is stabilised after adding a period of seven months in the case of instalments.

Table 5: Norms for Treating Different Advances as non-performing.

Type of loan	*Condition*	*Period*
Term loan	Instalments & or interest Remain past due for	Two quarters/six months
Cash credit/ Over draft	A/c remains out of order for	-do-
Agricultural loans	Instalments/or interest Remains past due	Two harvest seasons not exceeding two half years
Bills purchased & Discounted	Bill remains over due & unpaid for	Two quarters/six months
Other accounts	Facility remain 'past due ' for	-do-

The NPAs have to be provided for in the banks profit and loss accounts. The RBI has adopted the four category classification suggested by the NC for provisions purposes, all borrowal accounts (loan assets) are to be classified on the criteria of well defined credit weaknesses and the value of entire available securities for realisation of bank dues. The four categories are:

1. **Standard assets.** The assets which do not disclose any problem and which do not carry more than normal risk attached to the business. These are performing assets. Further, advances against term

deposits, national savings certificates, Indira Vikas Patra, Kisan Vikas Patra and life insurance policies are to be classified as standard assets as no provision is required in these accounts. The government guaranteed advances are exception in the sense that even when they are classified as NPA for the purpose of income recognition, for the purpose of asset classification they must be treated as standard assets.

2. **Substandard Assets.** These assets are those which have been classified as NPA for a period not exceeding two years. In such cases the current net worth of the borrower/guarantor or the current marked value of the security charged to the Bank is not enough to ensure recovery of the dues in full such an assets will have well defined credit weaknesses that may jeopardize the recovery of the debt in full and these are distinct chances that the bank will sustain some loss, if deficiencies are not corrected. The classification of asset should not be upgraded merely as a result of rescheduling, unless there is satisfactory compliance of the above condition.

3. **Doubtful Assets.** These assets which have remained NPA for a period exceeding two years. The loans of this category have all the weaknesses inherent in those classified as substandard with the added characteristic that the weaknesses make collection or liquidation in full, on the basis of currently know facts, conditions and values, highly questionable and improbable.

4. **Loss Assets.** The loss asset is one where loss has been identified by the bank or internal or external auditors or the RBI inspectors, but the amount has not been written off, wholly or partly. The loss asset requires cent per cent provisioning as the realizable value of the security is negligible or near zero.

The most critical condition for bringing about an improvement in the profitability of banks is a reduction in the level of NPAs. In fact it is a precondition for the stability of the financial system. Although the level of NPAs has declined significantly in recent years, it is still considered relatively high by international standards. There are of course, varying country practices for provisioning.

Analysis and Results

1. From Table 6 the NPAs over a period of 1993-2000 has been consistently rising from Rs. 392 billion in 1993 to 530.3 billion in 2000. It indicate that NPAs are pertinent problem for the banking

sector. In spite of the effort of the government there is a wide gap between the Gross NPAs and Net NPAs. The gross NPAs as per cent of advances slowly declining but as net NPA as per cent of Advances is hovering around 8 to 9 per cent in all the 6 years under consideration.

Table 6: Non-performing Assets of Public Sector Banks.

End of March	*NPAs (Rs. billion)*	*Gross NPAs or percentage to Advances*	*Gross NPAs as percentage of Assets*	*Net NPAs percentage of Advances*	*Net NPAs percentage of Assets*
1993	392.5	23.2	11.8	N.A.	N.A.
1994	410.4	24.8	10.8	N.A.	N.A.
1995	383.8	19.5	8.7	10.7	4.0
1996	416.6	18.0	8.2	8.9	3.6
1997	435.8	17.8	7.8	9.2	3.6
1998	456.5	16.0	7.0	8.2	3.3
1999	517.1	15.9	6.7	8.1	3.1
2000	530.3	14.0	6.0	7.4	2.9

Soruce: Reports on Trend and Progress of Banking in India, RBI various Issues.

2. However, gross NPAs as percentage to assets is declining sharply from 11.8 per cent in 1993 to 6 per cent in 2000 year. The same trend is noticed in Net NPAs as per cent of assets., It is hovering around 3 to 3.5 per cent. It is some what satisfactory trend where we compare NPAs to the assets.

According to a study made by a Nambirajan of particular interest is the loss assets in NPA accounts which according to definition have no realizable securities and there is little prospects of realisation and 100% provisions are made for such accounts. As on 31.030.2000 the loss assets in NPA stood at Rs. 6,398 crores forming 17 per cent of total advances of public sector banks. However, as already mentioned, public sector banks have accumulated provisions to the extent of Rs. 21,137 crores.

Sector wise Analysis of NPA of Public Sector Banks

1. Sector wise NPAs of public sector banks gives a different picture for SBI group as well as nationalised bank groups towards priority and non priority sector. It is said that the total NPAs, in priority sector is being continuously reduced from 50 per cent in 1995 to 44.5 per cent in 2000. On the other hand non priority sector NPAs have increased from 46.5 per cent to 53.5 per cent. It indicate that villain

Table 8: Loan Asset Quality of Public Sector Bank Group. (Per cent)

Sl. No.	*Category*	*1994*	*1995*	*1996*	*1997*	*1998*	*1999*	*2000*
1.	Standard Assets	75.2	80.6	82	82.2	84	84.11	86.00
2.	Sub-Standard Assets	7.4	3.9	4.0	5.1	5.1	4.9	4.3
3.	Doubtful Assets	14.1	11.6	5.0	10.6	9.1	9.0	8.0
4.	Loss Assets	2.4	1.9	1.9	2.1	1.9	2.0	1.7
5.	NPA in advance with O/s of <Rs. 25000	0.9	2.0	1.4	*	*	*	*
6.	Total NPA's (2 to 5)	24.8	19.4	18.0	17.8	16.0	15.9	14.0
7.	Total Advance (1+6)	100	100	100	100	100	100	100

Soruce: Reports on Trend and Progress of Banking in India, RBI various Issues.

of the NPAs problem is in the non priority sector not much in the priority sector. Therefore the general feeling that NPA is due to agriculture small scale industry etc is not tenable. Therefore, NPA has to be attacked vigorously on all the sectors of the economy.

2. If we compare the NPA of SBI & its subsidiary vis-a-vis nationalised banks an important conclusion is nationalised banks NPA in priority sector is comparatively less than the SBI's NPAs in the priority sector. Therefore the nationalised bank were more to non priority sector NPAs than priority sector NPAs. It indicates that if SBI are suffered due to priority sector lending to agriculture and SSI. The nationalised banks have suffered mostly due to non-priority lending to industrial houses, trade and business sector.

3. At disegregate level the RBI data revealed that the private sector bank's total NPA stood at Rs. 6410.34 crores in which share of the non priority sector was 69.45 per cent or Rs. 4452.26 crores. The 23 old private sector banks had a small Rs. 1591.48 crores NPAs towards the priority sector, of which the highest Rs. 800.14 crores was towards small scale sector. Small sector accounted for maximum Rs. 11340.14 crores in NPA after non priority sector in the case of both the public sector banks (Rs. 10339.41 crores) as well as private sector banks (Rs. 1000.73 crores).

4. An interesting feature that the data revealed was the fact that within six days of beginning operations, eight new private sector banks— Bank of Punjab, Centurian Bank, Global Trust Bank, HDFC Bank, ICICI Bank, IDBI Bank, Industrial Bank and UTI Bank had generated NPA of Rs. 1599.52 crores, and the maximum (Rs. 1356.29)

came from the non priority sector lending as their exposure to the priority sector was negligible.

Conclusion

The measures discussed above in Banking Sector have different impact on the economy depending the type of measure adopted. In case of capital adequacy measure, the Banks are strengthened in terms of capital Base, while Deregulation of interest rates did not succeed so much in increasing the lending due to unfavourable investment climate. Similarly the reduction in NPAs also did not meet the desired success & this measure has only little impact on the economy. Therefore over all impact of these measures have only put the Banking sector on right track.

REFERENCES

1. A.K. Gupta, "Deregulation Issues in Credit Approval" PNB Monthly Review-September 1999.
2. A.K. Misra, "Interest Rate Swaps: Recent Developments Can Bank Quarterly Review, July-Sept. 2002, p. 24.
3. Editor's column: "Capital (In) Adequacy in Indian banks" PNB Monthly Review. Vol. 22, No. 9, Sept. 2000 p. 1.
4. RBI Study: "Some aspects & issues relating to NPAs in Commercial Banks". Published in PNB monthly Review. July 99.
5. RBI Report—Trend and progress of Indian Banking-various issues.
6. RBI Report on "Currency & Finance—various issues.

8

Growth Under the Fiscal Crisis of Maharashtra State

In Search of Resource

Dr. V.B. Jugale*

Introduction

Since 1980s, most of the State Governments in India are facing the financial imbalances at the different degrees. The financial imbalance or ill health of the state causes two types of problems, viz. (a) the problem of macro economic stability, and (b) the problem of micro economic allocative efficiency (M. Govind Rao 2002). The macro economic instability, as reflected on the macro economic variables, causes the political and social instabilities. Its reinstatement becomes very difficult due to social and political disorders. Thus a vicious circle of crises clasps the veins and nerves of the body economy. Hence, macro economic stability has to bid honourably at almost every cost. The micro economic allocative efficiency gets weakened due to the crisis. The allocation of the funds gets evaporated, if the dose is not properly affirmed for fulfilling the micro economic needs of the societies.

The Eleventh Finance Commission, Para 4 of the Terms of References encountered the need to check the financial health of the State Governments. The Planning Commission, in its Tenth Plan Approach Paper has also rightly pointed out, the seriousness financial crises of the stages and suggested to declare financial emergency in a few states. Due to political instability in the states, the problem becomes much serious due to unproductive priorities of the investments. The State may not have a perspective thought on the

*Professor and Head, Department of Economics, Shivaji University, Kolhapur-416 004.

financial issues. It generally prefers not to do anything or do only for a temporary plastering on the pains. The RBI's meeting held on 9th Jan. 2003 has indicated the seriousness of the Court battles between 24 State Governments and the financial institutions. The outstanding of the 24 States had gone to Rs. 1,69,562 crores as on Dec. 2002.

Measures Adopted

To tackle the problem of financial imbalances, following measures have been implementing since 1990s.

1. Compelling on the State Governments for following the financial responsibilities with some financial codes and disciplines. The Central Govt. has thought of this.
2. The limits of auctioning the State Development Loans have been extended from 5 per cent to 35 per cent in Nov. 1997.
3. The Ways and Means Advances to the state governments has been extended from Rs. 5,283 crores to Rs. 6,035 crores from April 01, 2002. The WMA is basically based on revenue receipts, capital expenditure and the investment in Government's Treasury Bills and Securities. The minimum WMA is limited to Rs. 50 crores.
4. The RBI for the State Govts. to tackle the temporary problem of financial imbalances notifies Twelve Days Overdraft facility.
5. The additional incentives based on bailouts in the areas of power and irrigation are provided by the Central Government by agreeing upon the MoU with the state governments.
6. The recommendations of the Ramachandran Committee regarding the WMA have been accepted by the RBI. They are brought under implementation from March 2003.

Under it;

(a) A State can draw advances at the rate of bank rate, equal to the aggregate revenue of last three years collected by the State Government.

(b) After 3 months of borrowing, additional penalty of one per cent interest is charged along with extension of the period of repayment for the loans borrowed, rather than a fresh borrowing.

(c) Aggregation of 3 year's revenue can be accounted for every year.

(*d*) The period of overdraft has been extended from 12 days to 14 days. If a state borrows beyond the limit, it has to pay additional 3 per cent interest on the loans borrowed so far.

(*e*) RBI has to supplement the information of States' borrowing position every week.

7. The 100 per cent compensation (100%, 75% and 50% in the 1st, 2nd and 3rd year respectively) on the VAT to the states, who are switching over to VAT in the ensuing fiscal regime is announced by the Central Government (The deadline was 1st April 2003). This facility is also applicable for the revenue losses incurred due to the Central Sales Taxes in the first two years (i.e. 2003-04 and 2004-05). The revenue realisation from sales tax and Central Sales Tax for all the States put together is at Rs. 79,715.05 crores and 10,780.69 crores respectively for 2002-03. The budgeted revenues from sales tax for Maharasthra, which has enacted its VAT legislation, is Rs. 14,680 crores in 2002-03. Another Rs. 2080 crores is projected from Central Sales Tax. The State is entitled to claim full compensation under the scheme.

8. The States can borrow from the market or in the form of negotiated borrowings under Special Purpose Vehicle floated by them. Special guidelines have been issued by the Govt. of India under article 293(3) and (4). The guidelines announced so far include:

(*a*) States cannot borrow without Center's okay.

(*b*) States have been floating SPVs to raise funds.

(*c*) Guarantees constitute contingent liabilities.

(*d*) Center wants to curb borrowing via SPVs. The liabilities of the States have gone up to 8 per cent of the GDP (Rs. 166712 crores) by the end of March 2001.

Intensity of the Financial Imbalances

1. The outstanding of liabilities to the NSDP of the State Govt. has gone up aggregately from 18.5 per cent in 1998 to 26 per cent in 2002. In the case of Maharashtra State, the revenue deficit as per cent to NSDP was 0.09 per cent in 1998, which went to 0.43 per cent in 1995-96 and 4.11 per cent in 1999-00 as per cent to NSDP. An alarming hike is seen within a period of a few years. The fiscal deficit during the same period has also gone from 2.65 per cent in 1990-00 as per cent to NSDP. An alarming hike is seen within a period of a few years. The fiscal deficit during the same period has

also gone from 2.65 per cent in 1990-91, 2.93 per cent in 1995-96 and 6.03 per cent in 1999-2000.

2. The outstanding liabilities of the State Govt. as percentage of NSDP were 15.9 per cent in 1999-2000 and ratio of own tax revenue to NSDP was 7.2 per cent during the same period.
3. The average annual growth rates of State's own tax revenue was 15.77 per cent during the period 1980-81 to 1989-90, which has come down to 14.16 per cent during 1990-91 to 1999-2000.
4. The average annual growth rates of State's own revenue have declined from 15.44 per cent in 1980-81 to 1989-90 to 13.13 per cent in 1990-91 to 1999-2000.
5. The average annual growth rate of State's revenue expenditure has come down from 16.67 per cent in 1990-81 to 1989-90 to 15.45 per cent during 1990-91 to 1999-2000.
6. The average annual growth rates of State's interest payment has also declined from 24.31 per cent during the period from 1980-81 to 1989-90 to 18.87 per cent during the period 1990-91 to 1999-2000.
7. The average annual growth rate of State's capital expenditure has increased from 9.13 per cent during 1980-81 to 1989-90 to 13.66 per cent in 1990-91 to 1999-2000.
8. The percentage of revenue to fiscal deficit was 62.3 per cent in 2000-01. The percentage of non-development expenditure to total expenditure was 34.6 during the same year and the percentage of own tax revenue to revenue expenditure was 56.9 in the same year.
9. The ratio of per capita consumption expenditure to per capita income of the State had remained the same at 0.37 during 1993-94 and 1999-2000. (CSO and NHD Report).
10. Maharasthra State ranks first in infrastructure investment (CMIE data) with an index growth of 112.80 per cent (Tenth Plan Report).

Causes of Imbalance

Compared to the other leading States, the position of the Maharastra State is quite good, but not satisfactory. The reasons are as under:

1. Low capacity to generate resources due to coalition Government. No sound measures are inducted due to coalition government.
2. Huge amount of investment on infrastructure sector, particularly, on social and development infrastructure consisting of more than 60 per cent of the total infrastructure funds prolonged the returns.

3. Revenue deficit is caused by interest payments and pension. More than 60 per cent of revenue comes from sales tax. The interest payment + administrative expenses as percentage of total revenue expenditure was 31.4 per cent in 2000-01, which was 20.4 per cent in 1994-95. One tenth of the revenue is harnessed by pension.
4. Poor health of the public sector units and enterprises.
5. The State finances are in a mess and under assessed of the revenue receipts The CAG has referred to them in the 2000-01 audits. A few states have accepted the complete assessment. The Maharashtra State has 1,380 notified under assessed cases, (second rank) of which the State has accepted only 17 cases. The West Bengal has the highest (90.38) accepted cases.

Policy Measures for Paradigm Shift

1. For maintaining the macro-economic perspectives, the political stability without party coalition or coalition without power conflict on the states development issues or coalition without power politics is essential. But it seems very difficult to attain all feasible levels required for development. People are important rather than a Party.
2. This is an era of state level reforms. The states should initiate in restructuring their economies prospectively. Long-term vision is essential for all the states. Now the state govts have realised this and have started to think on this direction. The irrelevant and counter productive laws, rules and procedures have to be amended. There is no accounting of laws in India. It is estimated that there are around 3,279 central statutes, and 25,000 to 30,000 state statues. There are around 38 million cases pending with the Courts, for which 320 years will be required to dispose. Kerala Govt. has started to revise some laws and rules. Thus legal reforms have to be undertaken soon.
3. There is nothing wrong in reserving some sectors to the private sector. Limited entry may be allowed to check the inefficiency lying with the PSUs. Several archaic details can be earmarked with the public consent rather than bureaucratic advice. There is ample scope to develop the physical infrastructure. One per cent increase in infrastructure stock helps to grow one per cent of GDP. (World Bank, Infrastructure Development Report. 1994). Rakesh Mohan Committee as well, pointed out the role of infrastructure in overall

development of the economy. But, what is required, is giving an appropriate fillip to the State's real growth engines. Power, ports, roads, aviation are the main areas of physical infrastructure.

4. The Maharasthra Economic Development Council (Vision 2005) has indicated the significance of repositioning the Mumbai's role in gearing up the WTO challenges in agriculture and industry. The State should get the benefit of Mumbai (as an international trading center) for the development of agricultural and industrial development in the State.

5. Tourism, finance and information technology are the service sector areas in which the State can initiate in developing these areas through Mumbai's standing role in the international trade. WTO related challenges in services sector could also be identified and designed in that direction. Additional services like biotechnology, entertainment, and export services are some of the additional areas, where the State can do better as before.

6. For improving the export performances, the Govt. of Maharashtra must insist on:

   (a) Export of SSI products, which constitute 60% of the total exports. Recommendation of the Kanade Committee Report should be taken into account.

   (b) Star fruits have to be identified for enhancing the export. Horticulture products along with, Carambola or Karvandah, Ayurvedic and Herbal Medicines can be given priorities.

   (c) Single window clearance on the line of Singapore can be encouraged.

   (d) Counter trade or barter trade can be explored for export development.

   (e) Level playing field with overseas business can be developed.

   (f) Media and publicity can be highlighted widely.

   (g) Effective presentations are required to be made to the overseas counterparts.

   (h) Intellectual infrastructure should be strengthened.

   (i) Co-ordination of existing trade promotions are required to be designed.

7. The share of manufacturing sector is slowly decelerating, while the service sector accelerating in the State's economy. Obviously, the State has to insist upon the growth of service sector for employment generation. The basic infrastructure is required to be developed and spread over the service sector.
8. The per capita income of Mumbai is around Rs. 48,000/- (or $1,000) compared to State's PCI in general of Rs. 25,000/- and India's PCI to Rs. 18000/-. This can be enhanced to rise by Rs. 1,00,000/- as is proposed to rise by the end of the decade. Developing through tourism, IT, entertainment, biotechnology and fanancial services can attain this. The tourism alone can provide 20,000 new jobs annually (MEDC, 2001) along without revenue of Rs. 1000 crore in 360 foreign flights coming to Mumbai. Around 25 per cent of top 500 IT companies is located in the State. The State accounts for 28 per cent of software export, which can be developed on priority. Around 50 per cent of Internet users are in Maharashtra. This can be looked into as the income and employment generation sector in the State. Film industry in the State, no doubt is the main hub in India. Financial services through Mumbai based institutes can serve all over the world. And this is much required to develop for spinning over the foreign currency along with consultancy and employment generation. Biotechnology can be developed in collaboration with vertical and horizontal links with various sectors.
9. The MEDC has planned to develop the Mumbai as a mega service center in the world by developing financial services market and as an export center.

Conclusions

Compared to other States, the financial position of the Maharasthra is better in various respects. The potentialities of growth should better be understood and should get reflected in the State's policies or reforms. There should be a complete change in the mind setting of the policy makers. The experience of small nation's ideology in the world can be taken into account by considering the ground realities. The weaknesses in the budget should be proved and worsened. Non-tax revenues have to be tapped.

Micro enterprises should be developed with effective institutional and state support. The institutional and state reforms in this direction will help to improve the economy. Legal reforms should timely be introduced. Growth indicators of Mumbai, Pune and Thane are more favourable. Inter-regional disparities should not be the issue raised in the economy. Growth is not philanthropic in liberalisation process. The intellectuals must enter into the State's politics for improving State's position in almost all levels. Hard and harsh decisions are essential. The economist can point out but politicians have to activate it. A serious dent in solving the problem is not possible in a coalition govt. Political course is not properly developed at this system. Avoidance of undue concentration on wrong coined activities quizzes the socio-economic atmosphere.

The image of investment friendly state should be cultivated through legal reforms and by developing infrastructure facilities. The State should have better destination of FDI. The cost of doing business can be minimised through various measures.

Redefine the role of state. Every thing cannot be left to the private sector. Identify the role of cooperative sector in the place of public enterprises. The State has historical experience of replanning private sector by co-operative sector in various activities.

Going to the market and praying for the growth along with sustainable fiscal housing order will definitely take care of the State's competitiveness within the framework of liberalisation.

REFERENCES

1. Maharashtra Economic Development Council, 2002, "Maharashtra: Vision 2005 Fast-Track Development of Maharashtra—Strategy and Action—Review, Analysis and Recommendations.
2. Mahatrasthra Economic Development Council, 2000—Four decades of Maharasthra—A Profile.
3. Govt. of Maharasthra, 2002, "Human Development Report, Maharasthra, 2002.,
4. M. Govind Rao, 2002, "State Finances in India: Issues and Challenges, EPW, August 3.
5. Govt. of Maharashtra, 1999, "White Paper on Economic Conditions of Maharashtra, December.
6. Economic Times—Various Issues.
7. Reserve Bank of India, 2002, "State Finances in India."

9

State Level Fiscal Reforms
A Case Study of Andhra Pradesh

K.V. Rao*
B.S. Rao**

The decade of the 1990s has been a watershed in India's development in several ways. The initiation of economic reforms and the onset of the process of gloablisation have led to far reaching changes in the economy. This has had repercussions on the relationship between the Center and the States as well. Though economic reforms were initially implemented at the level of the Union Government, measures to restructure the fiscal system such as reduction in tax rates in which the State Governments had a substantial share, the pruning down of the grant component in central assistance to states and the consequent increase in reliance on market borrowings, and the hike in the rate of interest at which the state governments borrow funds from the Center have had their cascading effect on State governments' finances. The recommendations of the Fifth Pay Commission, and the substantial hike in salaries of employees had added to the woes of the State Governments.

Consequently, State Governments have been under considerable stress during the 1990s in stabilising their finances. This in turn necessitated the State governments to initiate reforms, particularly since they have been facing the problems of rising expectations from the people with respect to better

* Prof. K.V. Rao, Department of Commerce & Business Administration, Nagarjuna University, Nagarjunanagar-522 510, A.P., India.

** Dr. B. Sambasiva Rao, Department of Economics, Nagarjuna University, Nagarjunanagar-522 510, A.P., India.

governance and ensuring a minimum quality of life. The developmental agenda has become increasingly important both on political grounds and for demonstrating that the Government is progressive and responsive to people's aspirations. As per the revised estimates for the year 2000-2001, the consolidated gross fiscal deficits of the states are estimated at Rs. 95,277 crore as against 91,480 crore during 1999-2000, showing an increase of 4.2 per cent. In terms of GDP, the overall resource gap is placed at 4.4 per cent. The other fiscal indicators such as revenue deficit and primary deficit are also high, warranting a serious action by the states. The revenue deficit is accounting for 2.3 per cent of the GDP during 2000-2001 and that of the primary deficit stood at 1.9 per cent. What is more worrying is the fact that both of them have recorded deterioration over the proceeding years. Turning to the position of Andhra Pradesh the fiscal deficit was put at 7306 crores for the year 2000-2001 which accounts for 5.41 per cent of GDP. As a matter of fact, the fiscal deficit was only 2,445 crores during 1995-96 accounting for 3.06 per cent. Similar trends could be observed in the other two indicators, namely revenue deficit and primary deficit.

Revenue Mobilisation

In respect of resource mobilisation, Andhra Pradesh's performance is quite disappointing. Between 1965-66 and 1996-97, its total receipts registered and increase of 47 times, from the annual average of Rs. 298 crores to Rs. 14,050 crores, as against 60 times for all states together. The relative share of Andhra Pradesh in the aggregate for all states declined from 8.7 per cent to 6.9 per cent over the above period. The per capital total receipts stood at only Rs. 1,962 during 1996-97, which was lowest among the southern states, and substantially lower than the all states average, being Rs. 2,255 (see Table 2).

It is evident from the figures given in Table 1, the total revenue of the state has improved further and stood at Rs. 19,475 crores during 2000-2001, which accounts for 14.41 per cent of the states' GDP. The states own revenue constituted 68.21 per cent in 2000-2001. The revenue mobilisation effort of the state has not been fruitful due to the decline in central transfers over the years. For instance, the share of central transfers to the total revenue of the state has declined from 45.1 per cent in 1995-96 to 31.7 per cent in 2000-2001.

Compared to the neighbouring states, the position of Andhra Pradesh is relatively discouraging. While the revenue deficit as a percentage of revenue receipts stood at 18.5 per cent in Andhra Pradesh, it was only 14.6 per cent in Karnataka for the year 2000-2001. Further, the rate of growth in the revenues of the state was around 14 per cent, where as the expenditure was

Table 1: Fiscal Trends of Andhra Pradesh 1995-96 to 2000-01.

	1995-96	*1996-97*	*1997-98*	*1998-99*	*1999-00*	*2000-01*
			Absolute figures in crores			
Total Revenue	9197	10498	13080	13622	15843	19475
Own Revenue	5048	5811	8141	9171	10489	13295
From Center	4149	4687	4939	4451	5354	6180
Total Expenditure	11642	13261	16380	19327	20819	26781
Revenue	9964	11386	13783	16306	17076	23070
Capital	1678	1875	2597	3021	3743	3711
Revenue Deficit	767	888	703	2684	1233	3595
Fiscal Deficit	2445	2763	2428	5705	4976	7306
Interest Payment	1529	1839	2153	2644	3101	3793
Primary Deficit	916	924	275	3061	1875	3513
Total Debt	15137	16894	19970	23905	29114	35246
GSDP	79854	90147	95782	113091	121703	135107
			As % of GSDP			
Total Revenue	11.52	11.65	13.66	12.05	13.02	14.41
Own Revenue	6.32	6.45	8.50	8.11	8.62	9.84
From Center	5.20	5.20	5.16	3.94	4.40	4.57
Total Expenditure	14.48	14.71	17.10	17.09	17.11	19.82
Revenue	12.48	12.63	14.39	14.42	14.03	17.08
Capital	2.10	2.08	2.71	2.67	3.08	2.75
Revenue Deficit	0.96	0.99	0.73	2.37	1.01	2.66
Fiscal Deficit	3.06	3.06	2.53	5.04	4.09	5.41
Interest Payment	1.91	2.04	2.25	2.34	2.55	2.81
Primary Deficit	1.15	1.02	0.29	2.71	1.54	2.60
Total Debt	18.96	18.74	20.85	21.14	23.92	26.09

growing by 20 per cent. As a part of the resource mobilisation the government of Andhra Pradesh has been revising the tax and non-tax rates from time to time. The sales tax, stamp duty, and registration fee, were increased by 20 per cent. Similarly the revenue occurring from fee. As such, the state had reached position of saturation whereby it was not in a position to improve upon the revenues by means or any conventional method. Royalties, cess, has also improved considerably. Further, there are huge amounts of arrears of revenue due to the government. By March 2000, thee is an arrear of revenue to the extent of Rs. 2,264 crore, which is 21 per cent of its own revenue, and around 50 per cent of these are in arrear for over five years.

Table 2: Trends in Budgetary Receipts of Andhra Pradesh in Relation to Other Major States.

(Rs. in Crores)

States	*Total receipts*	*Revenue receipts*	*Total receipts*	*Revenue receipts*	*Total receipts*	*Revenue receipts*
	1965-68 (a.a.)		*1975-78 (a.a.)*		*1994-97 (a.a.)*	
Andhra Pradesh	298	166 (55.7)	910	713 (78.4)	14050	9952 (70.8)
Assam	122	74 (60.7)	288	223 (77.4)	4711	3398 (72.1)
Bihar	229	136 (59.4)	781	537 (68.8)	5824	7404 (127.1)
Gujarat	175	129 (73.7)	702	528 (75.2)	11080	8673 (78.3)
Haryana	59	40 (67.8)	340	261 (76.8)	7845	5648 (69.7)
Karnataka	207	133 (64.3)	788	611 (77.5)	10442	8378 (80.2)
Kerala	146	103 (70.5)	505	389 (77.0)	7103	5412 (76.2)
Madhya Pradesh	237	137 (57.8)	784	614 (78.3)	11133	8762 (83.8)
Maharashtra	395	275 (69.6)	1544	1196 (77.5)	22351	16968 (75.9)
Orissa	160	97 (60.6)	435	327 (75.2)	5553	3918 (70.6)
Punjab	174	111 (63.8)	488	365 (74.8)	749	5352 (72.2)
Rajasthan	203	106 (52.2)	581	444 (76.4)	9895	.7171 (72.5)
Tamil Nadu	289	186 (64.4)	844	615 (72.9)	13414	10593 (79.0)
Uttar Pradesh	427	255 (59.7)	1479	1061 (71.7)	22279	14879 (66.8)
West Bengal	246	182 (74.0)	916	653(71.3)	11022	7489 (69.8)
All States	3429		11939	8969 (75.1)	180727	137308 (76.0)

aa: anual average a: average for 1966-68
b: revenue receipts as percentage to total receipts.

The over all debts stock of the state stood at Rs. 35,246 crore at the end of 2000-2001 constituting 26.10 per cent of GSDP. In comparison with neighbouring states, Andhra Pradesh has higher debt leading to considerable amount of interest payments. The interest payments are accounting for 28.5 per cent of its own revenues.

As a measure of toning up the total performance, the state government has formulated a Medium Term Fiscal Frame Work (MTFF) covering the period 2001-2007. It has conceived of a reform network covering some of the major sectors of the state Economy. The Andhra Pradesh government has already implemented uniform floor rates and streamlined the major revenue earning departments in enabling them to achieve higher targets and augment state resources. In fact, Government of Andhra Pradesh has not levied any new taxes during the last three years and has mainly focused in improving the revenues through better tax compliance and administration. The single most important reform is the introduction of the value-added tax (VAT). Government of Andhra Pradesh has made a great effort to prepare itself or launching of the VAT by April 2003 and is the first best prepared state for this exercise. The Centre has transferred powers to states to contain in taxing services. Beyond this, the main scope for revenue mobilisation lies in improving compliance, and reducing evasion of taxes. The introduction of VAT is intended to herald a major improvements in the tax administration, including the introduction of self-assessment and risk-based audit. Reforms of the other taxes are also, in the direction of improving enforcement and compliance. The Government of Andhra Pradesh has targeting an improvement in total state's own revenue mobilisation from 8.8 per cent of GSDP by the current Year to at least 9.5 per cent of GSDP by 2005—0.6. To help in developing an overall strategy for enhacing revenue mobilisation, while minimising negative distortions and compliance costs of the revenue system, Government of Andhra Pradesh has constituted a Revenue Reforms Committee to guide and develop concrete plans for further tax policy reform. Power sector reform is considered a key complement to fiscal reform because of the sector's major demand on budgetary resources. The gross budgetary support to the sector, including interest payments on outstanding power sector liabilities, totals over 2 per cent of GSDP. As a result, reform of the sector is considered key to achieving Government's fiscal reform objectives. Andhra Pradesh power sector reforms have made the state a leader in India with the achievement of major milestones: (i) the unbundling of the state Board into six new corporate companies (ii) Formation of the Electricity Regulatory Commission (ERS) in 1999 to provide independent oversight of the power sector reform process and its development (two tariff orders of APERS have been fully implemented), and (iii) Launching of a major drive in 2000 to regularize two million residential customers in one month, and prosecuting cases of theft with specially constituted tribunals.

Expenditure Control

The growth in budgetary expenditures of Andhra Pradesh has been relatively low over the entire period of three decades, 1965-68 to 1994-97. It multiplied 48 times from the annual average of Rs. 301 crores to Rs. 14,342 crores as against 52 times for all the states together. The per capita expenditure of Andhra Pradesh increased 26.5 times in this period from Rs. 75 to Rs. 2000 as against 28.2 times for all states from Rs. 72 to Rs. 1972. During the period, 1995-96 to 2000-2001, the total expenditure has increased from Rs. 11,642 crores to Rs. 26,781 crores. (Table 1). The ratio of revenue expenditure to capital expenditure stood at 86.2:13.8 and much of the revenue expenditure towards establishment of the government. As per cent of states own revenue, establishment expenditure stood at 74.8 per cent in 2000-2001. (See Table 3).

Table 3: Trends in Establishment Expenditure.

Year	*Pay and allowances and travelling allowances*	*Wages*	*Grant-in-Aid for salaries*	*Pensions*	*Total Expenditure Including pensions*	*Establishment Cost as % of States own Revenue*
1984-85	574	14	375	117	1080	76.9
1987-88	882	17	580	132	1611	73.2
1988-89	1036	11	716	213	1975	80.1
1989-90	1152	9	96	269	1525	86.5
1990-91	1231	12	1056	358	2657	85.7
1991-92	1418	13	1177	441	3049	82.6
1992-93	1633	14	1225	474	3347	81.8
1993-94	1890	14	1345	545	3794	79.9
1994-95	2197	14	1588	780	4580	88.5
1995-96	2351	14	1553	928	4845	95.6
1996-97	2575	7	1812	1004	5398	94.5
1997-98	2911	7	2021	1139	6078	75.7
1998-99	3218	8	2402	1373	7000	78.4
1999-00 (RE)	4173	20	2788	1805	8786	84.2
2000-01 (BE)	4470	10	3620	2179	10279	74.8

The other major commitment of the Government has been towards interest payments. Since there is no major change in the borrowing program of the governments interest payments constitute a significant item of expenditure in the years to come. The worrying fact is that the Government of Andhra Pradesh has been contemplating off-budget borrowings since 1997-98 through its public sector undertakings.

The third major item of expenditure to the Government has been the power and rice subsidies. The government has been spending around Rs. 3000 crores towards these two subsides. In order to contain the expenditure, the government has initiated measures towards reducing the establishment expenditure by swapping the departments, making the public sector organisations liable for their own commitments and reducing the subsides. The major development in this area has been the constitution of Andhra Pradesh Electricity Regulation Commission (APERS) for rationalising the power tariffs. The government has also been contemplating to spend the limited resources on priority areas like capital expenditure for new infrastructure creation, non-salary O&M for asset maintenance, and social sector investments in primary health and education. In this direction, the government has created an "Infrastructure Development fund" with an outlay of Rs. 82 crores to meet those critical counterpart investments, which would be necessary to attract private investors in infrastructure projects. Another important feature of the reform process of the government has been the restructuring of the public enterprises. The government is proposing to examine the options of privatisation, restructuring or even enclosure.

In addition, the Government of Andhra Pradesh has been providing guarantees to the loans taken by private sector and public sector enterprises. The amount of guarantee accounted for about Rs. 15,715 crores by the end of March 31, 2001. This is expected to reach the level of Rs. 20,000 crore by the next year. There is an inherent risk in these guarantee. To tackle this problem, the government has created a "Contigent Risk Fund" with one per cent contribution from each borrower.

Impact of Reforms

Having realised the gravity of the situation, the Government of Andhra Pradesh has started initiating serious measures only recently. It has contemplated an open discussion on the financial situation of the state at the time of proposing its budget for the year 2002-03. This was considered an attempt of the last resort. After allowing the situation to drift for many years, it is not known how people can remedy the same. It accounts for only the shortage of ideas with the government.

As per the statistics released, the GSDP of the state is Rs. 1,35,107 crore in 2000-01. It has recorded an increase at the rate of 11.2 per cent during the past five years. In terms of 1993-94 prices, the rate of growth turned out to be only 7 per cent. More so, there were wide fluctuations in the rate of growth in GSDP. In terms of sectoral contribution, the relative share of agriculture, industry and services was in the order of 28 per cent, 25 per cent and 47 per cent respectively. During the period of 1995-96 to 1999-2000, there had been a decline in the contribution of agriculture, where as the share of industry remained constant. For many years, the rate of growth of agriculture was negative. There is no effective contingent plan for the state government, if there is to be a failure of the monsoon (as it has happened this year).

Further, the reforms initiated in the individual sectors like power and transport have only yielded limited results. The division of APSEB into APGENC and APTRANSCO has streamlined organisational setup to some extent. But there is little improvement in the performance. The power generation has not increased, nor the losses in transmission could be checked up effectively. Even the unauthorised use of power could be controlled properly. In the transport sector, reforms need to focus more on the laying of village—link roads, conversion of riverbanks as link roads and the development of inland waterways in certain of the parts as in Kerala state. Further, the public sector reform also could not clear the debris. The disinvestments programme is going on at snail's pace in the state.

As a measure of clarification on the working of the government, it is essential to refer to the audit reports of the CAG. The Accountant General (Audit), Andhra Pradesh arranges to conduct periodical inspection of the Government departments concerned with tax revenue of the state to test check the transactions and verify the maintenances of important accounting and other records as per prescribed rules and procedures. These inspections are followed up with Inspection Reports. When important irregularities are detected during inspection, these IRs are issued to the heads of offices for necessary action. The heads are required to ensure compliance and take appropriate action. The department wise break-up of IRs and audit observations pending as on 30th June 2000 was given in Table-4. This indicates the failure of the government in taking appropriate action to check the pilferage of revenue.

Suggestions on The Future Reforms Agenda

A review of the situation prevailing in the state on the fiscal front makes one to believe that it is leading to a state of financial emergency. What could be the policy programme of the Government of Andhra Pradesh, if article 360 of the constitution is invoked, has to be decided by the Government. The present focus of the government on Information Technology (I.T.) will not place the state on sound financial lines. It should think of initiating certain concrete and realistic measures of the following type:

1. In view of the fact that the scope for mobilising revenues through taxes has dwindled, it is better for the state Government to explore possibilities in the direction on improving non-tax revenues. Incidence that have occurred in the state call for a realistic policy on the leasing of state's natural, mineral and other resources. The state has a particular advantage in exploiting the long coastline it has.

2. Strengthening the institutional framework and the link between Government policy and implementation to achieve consistency between financial allocations and economic and social goals. As has been pointed out by the CAG the government has to activate the

Table 4: Statement obtains Audit Observations Pending References by the Government as on 30.6.2000.

Sl. No.	Department	Inspection Reports	Audit Observations	Amount Involved (Rupees in lakh)	Year to Which observations Relate	No. of To which evenfirst replies have not been received
1.	Sales tax	2251	6595	63212.69	1992-93 to 1999-2000	131
2.	Land Revenue	1752	4824	2400.18	1992-93 to 1999-2000	359
3.	Taxes on Vehicles	254	904	14698.26	1987-88 to 1999-2000	12
4.	Entertainment Tax	566	772	775.18	1994-95 to 1999-2000	49
5.	Stamp Duty And Registration Changes	281	479	6794.99	1987-88 to 1999-2000	59
6.	Co-operation	190	449	—	1992-93 to 1999-2000	9
7.	Mines and Minerals	128	317	21094.14	1992-93 to 1999-2000	4
8.	Agriculture	222	315	—	1992-93 to 1999-2000	7
9.	Civil Supplies	124	303	787.43	1992-93 to 1999-2000	10
10.	State Excise	123	218	2516.81	1991-92 to 1999-2000	53
11.	Forest Receipts	113	143	2399.72	1990-91 to 1999-2000	25
12.	Purchase tax On Sugarcane	72	122	10273.13	1992-93 to 1999-2000	2
13.	Electricity Duty	29	40	5653.14	1992-93 to 1999-2000	—
14.	Betting Tax	8	8	77.24	1998-99 to 1999-2000	—
15.	Finance and Planning	—	1	15670.28	1997-98	—
	Total	**6113**	**15490**	**146353.28**		**720**

major revenue centres to plug the loopholes, limiting resources mobilisation.

3. Though the state government, like many other states has been boasting of initiating measures for containing expenditure, the out

come has been dismal. The ratio of administrative expenditure to total expenditure has not improved much. While the center and many other states have been very active in disinvestments process, there is low key of operations in the State.

4. The Government should be cautious and draft a comprehensive policy in imposing user charges and granting freedom to the private players in charging their prices. Review of the power purchase agreements is a case in point.

5. To the extent cross subsidisation is deemed necessary, it should be self balancing with no burden on the government. This is a valid strategy irrespective of public or mixed or private ownership of the concerned commercial and financial entitles. This approach would also be a precondition to adopt other compelling strategies.

6. In other to improve the fiscal situation of the state on a solid foundation, the Government of Andhra Pradesh has no other option but to focus the development of Agricultural sector. As it has formulated a Medium Term Fiscal Framework, (MTFF) the government of Andhra Pradesh, should formulate a comprehensive and realistic "Agricultural Policy". The policy should focus on the issues, such as cropping pattern, public and private investment in agriculture, regualtion of the use of the seeds, fertilizers, and pesticides; creation and regulation of employment in agriculture. If necessary, the Government should take immediate action to make or amend necessary legislation. In this regard, a contingent Agricultural plans covering a brief period of one or two years is an immediate task.

7. There is a need to pass legislation concerning fiscal responsibilities and budget management. This will provide a policy framework within which the performance of a Government can be assessed. It is gratifying to note in this context, that the central government has attempted to introduce a legislation of this kind in the name of "Fiscal Responsibility and Budget Management Bill-2000". This bill was intended to cast an obligation on the Government itself to strengthen the institutional framework for conduct of prudent and accountable fiscal policy and pave the way for promoting greater macro-economic stability. The proposed Fiscal Responsibility and Budget Management legislation will provide a legal and institutional framework to bring down the fiscal deficit contain the growth of public debt and stabilize debt as a proportion of GDP over the

medium term. It binds future governments to a pre-specified path of fiscal consolidation. This covers only the finances of the Central Governments. Unfortunately, the bill has not yet been passed and the parliamentary standing committee has recommended considerable toning down of the bill leading to much flexibility in the management of finances in the Government. Taking cue from the Central Government, the government of Andhra Pradesh shall consider adopting such a bill in its original form.

8. Modernisation of financial management system and use of Information Technology (I.T.).
9. Public participation in Budget formulation and implementation.

10

Kelkar's Recommendations on Reforms in Direct Taxes

Some Observations

Dr. Vinod Singh*

The existing tax system in India is quite complex. It distorts the market efficiency and provides arbitrage opportunities resulting in misallocation of resources. This calls for reforms. In view of this, Vijay Kelkar was entrusted with the job of drawing a blueprint of India's future tax system. Acting with lighting speed Kelkar submitted the report of the Task Force on Direct and Indirect Taxes on 27 December 2002. The report visualizes simple, transparent and efficient tax structure. However, now much depends on the Government to operaionalise these recommendations made by Kelkar. The focus of this paper is on a critical review of the recommendations on Direct Taxes. Also, the paper points out some basic issues left and offers suggestions.

Personal Income Tax

At present, the maximum marginal rate of income tax on individuals is 30% and applies to an income of over Rs. 1.5 lakh. The tax rate would be 31.5% inclusive of surcharge in case of individual income over Rs. 1.5 lakh. The other two-tax rate structures are 10% for the income group of Rs. 50,000 to Rs. 60,000 and 20% for the income group of Rs. 60,000 to Rs. 1,50,000 along with a 5% surcharge on tax. Currently for individuals, income upto Rs. 50,000 is exempt from tax. The Kelkar Task Force has suggested that

* Faculty Member, Department of Economics, Lucknow University, Lucknow.

the exemption limit of Rs. 50,000 should be raised to Rs. 100,000. It has also recommended that the current three rate structures should be reduced to two-rates-20% for taxable income above Rs. 1,00,000 and upto Rs. 4,00,000, and 30% for income above Rs. 4,00,000.

On criterion of equity this two-rate tax structures does not sound well. In lieu of this, three rate tax structures should be continued, 10% for taxable income above Rs. 100,000 and up to Rs. 2,00,000, 20% for taxable income above Rs. 2,00,000 and up to Rs. 3,00,000 and 30% for income above Rs. 3,00,000 because this structure fulfils the concept of progressive taxation.

However, the recommendation of raising exemption limit up to Rs. 1,00,000 is quite logical. This also helps to reduce the tax burden on individuals and particularly low-income groups. This is because unlike other countries, Indian families with less than Rs. 1,00,000 in annual income pay much higher quantum of indirect taxes on goods and services that they consume.

Standard Deduction for Employees

At present the Government has divided standard deduction into four categories viz. income upto Rs. 1.5 lakh, between 1.5 lakh to Rs. 3 lakh, between Rs. 3 lakh to Rs. 5 lakh and above 5 lakh. In addition to the above, salaried employees are also eligible for a deduction up to a maximum of Rs. 9,600 towards conveyance allowance received from their employer.

The Kelkar Task Force recommends that standard deduction should be eliminated. However, the exemption of conveyance allowance subject to a ceiling of Rs. 9,600/- should be continued.

This recommendation is not reasonable. The logic given by task force is that self-employed taxpayer has opportunities to evade tax and a salaried employee does not have opportunities to evade tax is not admissible. Therefore, the standard deduction should be seen as compensating for loss of such 'privilege'.

It may be suggested that the standard deduction should be allowed uniformly to all employees without any reference of the salary limit earned by them. The amount of standard deduction should be Rs. 25000. The basic philosophy behind giving deduction by way of standard deduction is that standard deduction is given to salary taxpayers not as a bounty but in lieu of expenses, which they incur in earning salary incomes. It is a simplified way of compensating for expenses. My suggestion is that the exemption of conveyance allowance should be eliminated or provide to all those taxpayers who do not receive conveyance allowance from their employer as per their income slab.

Treatment of Housing

Currently, up to Rs. 1,50,000 of interest payments are allowed as deductible in taxable income, which implies a subsidy of Rs. 45,000 per year for individuals who are living in their own house costing Rs. 20 lakhs or more. This violates both vertical and horizontal equity.

In order to protect low-income groups, the Task Force suggests an interest subsidy of 2% for housing loans up to Rs. 5,00,000 to all borrowers. This will help prospective homebuilders whose income is less than Rs. 1 lakh. This subsidy should be granted by the Government through the National Housing Bank.

However, the tax incentives have a strong positive impact on investment in housing and so far on investment in housing has strong multiplier impact on income. The increased investment in housing will not only generate higher revenue in terms of stamp duty, property tax, but also through multiplier impact lead to increased income through backward and forward linkages. So, Government should take care of this aspect of housing at the time of implementation of Task Force recommendation and compensate on housing sector through subsidies rate of interest on housing loans not only up to Rs. 5 lakh but to all housing loan up to Rs. 15 lakh.

Tax Incentives for Saving

Under the existing income tax provisions, section 88 allows tax rebate of 20% or 15% of contribution up to Rs. 70,000 under specified savings instruments with additional slot of up to Rs. 30,000 allowed exclusively for infrastructure investment. Further, the Government may also consider providing a separate window of Rs. 100000 for pension funds under Section 80CCC.

The Task Force recommends the elimination of the tax incentive for savings under Section 88 with immediate effect and not through the sunset clause.

The Task Force recommends the continuation of the deduction under Section 80 CCC for contribution to the pension fund of LIC or any other insurance company. The ceiling on the deduction should, however, be increased from the existing levels of Rs. 10000 to Rs. 20000 and converted to a tax rebate at the minimum marginal rate of 20%. There is no disagreement with the said recommendation because in another recommendation, the Task Force provides exemption from taxation on the earnings on certain types of investment, which compensate the taxable liability. However, it may be argued here that regarding the saving proposals of the Task Force. Gross domestic savings rate has averaged at around 23.2% of the GDP over the last nine years up to 2000-2001 while gross domestic investment rates has averaged at 24.4% of the GDP over the period.

Thus, targeting on 8% growth rate during the Tenth Plan period would require that the domestic savings rate is increased to 29% to 30% of the GDP and investment rates, be increased to 32.6% of the GDP. According to the Approach Paper to Tenth Plan, increasing the level of domestic savings would require. If Government will accept this recommendation related with the elimination of the tax incentives for savings then saving rate would be affected adversely. Therefore, I suggest that Government should implement this recommendation in a phased manner to maintain the saving rate as required the Approach Paper to Tenth Plan.

Treatment of Senior Citizens, Widows and Women below 65 years of age

The existing provision of Income Tax Act under Section 88B provides for a tax rebate of Rs. 15000/- to a senior citizen (aged 65 years or more). The Task Force recommends that the basic exemption limit for senior citizens should be Rs. 50,000/- more than the exemption limit for the general class of individual taxpayers i.e. Rs. 1,50,000/-. The Task Force recommends that this benefit of higher exemption limit should also be extended to widows. The rebate under Section 88B of Rs. 15,000 to senior citizens should be deleted. The Task Force recommends eliminating the tax rebate of Rs. 5000 to women taxpayers below 65 years of age due to increase in the exemption limit to Rs. 100000/-.

This recommendation regarding senior citizens, widows and women below the age of 65 years deserves all applause, as it is meritorious by virtue of its own cause.

Agricultural Taxation

Agricultural income was taxed for the first time in the Indian Income Tax Act, 1860. It was withdrawn in 1865. However, in 1869, income tax was again levied on all incomes including agricultural income. This tax on agricultural income was again withdrawn in 1873-74. Eventually, the Indian Income Tax Act, 1886 (Act No. 2 of 1886), exempted agricultural income from the levy of income tax. The reason was that the landlords paid land revenue to the Government and should not therefore be asked to contribute to the exchequer more than once.

Given the low collection of direct tax revenue, the issue of taxing agricultural income has come up time and again in the last three decades.

The taxation Enquiry Committee (Wanchoo Committee) devoted considerable attention to taxation of agricultural income, and observed that "agricultural income, which is at present outside the Central tax net, offers plenty of scope for camouflaging black money."

The Tax Reform Committee (Chelliah Committee) with an implied suggestion for the amendment of the Constitution to this effect, recommended that non-agriculturists (both individuals and others) should pay tax on agricultural incomes exceeding Rs. 25,000 and income from plantations subjected to taxation by States should be avoided. For this purpose, tax should be levied on the aggregate of both agricultural and non-agricultural income. The proceeds so earned by the Central Government from agricultural incomes should be distributed among States.

In this context, Kelkar Committee recommends the followings:

(a) A tax rental arrangement should be designed whereby States should pass a resolution under Article 252 of the Constitution authorising the Central Government to impose income tax on agricultural income. The taxes collected by the Centre would however be assigned to States.

(b) Tax from agricultural income for the purposes of allocation between States will be the difference between the tax of total income (including agricultural income) and the tax on total income net of agricultural income.

(c) Where a taxpayer derives agricultural income from different States, the revenues attributable to a State will be in the ratio of the income derived from a particular State to the total agricultural income.

(d) A separate tax return form should be prescribed for taxpayers deriving income from agriculture.

In totality, the Government should not accept this recommendation because it is a most impractical and ill-contrived proposal. Farming should not be equated with luxurious farmhouses located around the National Capital and other urban centres of the country. For all practical purposes, they are appendages of industry and business houses and have nothing to do with farming owner-cultivator is generally engaged in farming on fragmented and small holdings which is fast becoming economically unviable. Agriculture is not an industry. How could the cost of inputs, family labour and other variables be computed for ascertaining the income for tax purposes? No doubt, income generation from agricultural activities should be taxable. Here, the recommendation given by Chelliah Committee is more appropriate than Kelkar Task Force. Tax should be imposed on that agricultural income which is earned by the non-agriculturist taxpayers. The whole agricultural income of non-agriculturist taxpayers should be taxable and should be distributed among States as suggested by the Kelkar Task Force.

It may be observed here that agricultural income tax could be imposed on those rural rich who involve in a large number of commercial operations under agriculture, e.g. horticulture, sericulture, floriculture, orchards, sandal wood exports, plantation of teak which generate substantial income. After implementation of agricultural income tax land revenue (land holding tax) should be eliminated by the States.

Corporate Tax

Kelkar Task Force recommends the reform of corporate income tax as under:

(a) Reduction in corporate tax rate from the existing levels of 36.75% to 30% for domestic companies and to 35% for foreign companies from 40%.

(b) No tax on dividend in the hands of the shareholders. There will also be no tax on distribution of dividends by a company (At present this is 10%).

(c) No tax on long terms capital gains on listed equity.

(d) Elimination of Minimum Alternate Tax under Section 115JB.

(e) Removal of the distinction between unobserved depreciation and unobserved business loss. In other words, unobserved depreciation would be merged with business loss and loose it's separate identity. Further, business loss would be allowed to be carried forward indefinitely.

(f) Depreciation rates for the purposes of depreciation allowance under Section 32 should be reduced to 15% from existing 25%.

Government should implement the recommendation given by task Force regarding corporate tax reforms in a phased manner.

Other Recommendations

Wealth Tax

Under the existing scheme a tax at the rate of 1% is levied if the aggregate value of the selected assets exceeds Rs. 15 lakh. The selected assets are mostly unproductive assets in nature and at current prices, the revenues have almost stagnated at the measly level of approximately Rs. 135 crores, in real terms there has been a sharp decline. Task Force recommends the abolition of wealth tax. Due to the smartness of revenue and large-scale problems of administration and compliance this tax should be abolished.

Enlarging the Tax Base

Presently, the total number of income tax assesses is much smaller than the middle class population in India. This shows that a large chunk of India's population continue to remain out of the tax net. It is expected that the total number of tax assesses in the country is expected to touch five crore by 2003-04 from the present three crores. The one-by-six criterion has improved the portion but the introduction of presumptive tax has not proved quite successful.

The task Force is of the opinion that the key question should be the total income that is being brought into the tax net, and not the number of taxpayers. However, most taxpayers with income of up to Rs. 1 lakh will continue to file returns on account of the one-by-six scheme and therefore the concern they "drop-out" of the tax net is misplaced. By removal of the various exemptions, the Task Force in fact purports to enhance transparency as well as increasing the quantum of income-corporate and personal-that will attract taxes, albeit at lower rates. It is abundantly clear from the above analysis that The Committee proposals to tax agriculture income, there was considerable support as it promotes horizontal equity and captures agricultural income of non-agriculturists.

In our considered opinion, the one-by-six scheme has increased the number of 'return filers' as the persons satisfying the prescribed conditions are necessarily required to file the returns despite the fact that they may not be having any taxable income. This has increased a lot of infructuous paperwork for the Income Tax Department as well as taxpayers, and hence the Government should emphasise on the total income that is being brought under the tax net, and not the number of taxpayers.

Neglected Aspect of the Report

Kelkar Task Force on Direct Taxes, undoubtedly, made a bold attempt to discuss various aspects of direct taxation i.e. Approach to Tax Reforms, Reform of Tax Administration, Personal Income Tax Reforms, Corporate Tax Reforms etc. Report focuses on transparency, tax administration and tax compliance. However, it assiduously neglect the most pertinent issue i.e. Tax Evasion in its report. Not a single remedial recommendation regarding hardcore tax evaders' has been recommended by the Task Force. Since 1947, till date Government emphasised on taxpayer friendly programmes, tax awareness programmes, VDSs etc. But now time has come when Government should take hard measures for checking tax evasion and tax avoidance. Government should make adequate provisions of tough punishment, like imprisonment against those hardcore tax evaders who knowingly violate the Income Tax law and do not pay tax to the Government. Tax evaders should be treated as common criminals of the society. Provision for their punishment should be incorporated in IPC and CrPC.

Kelkar Report is still being debated time alone will tell us how the Government manages to reach consensus across party lines to bring about desired changes in the tax system. The irresistible conclusion that emerge from the present note is that a complex and archaic tax structure is giving way to a simplified transparent and reformed tax system of the modern age. It is always matter of real pleasure to welcome noble changes at all levels of public life.

REFERENCES

1. Report of the Task Force on Direct Taxes (December 2002), Ministry of Finance and Company Affairs, GOI, New Delhi.
2. Tax Reforms Committee—Final Report (August 1992), Ministry of Finance, Department of Revenue, New Delhi.
3. Thimmaiah; G. "How strong is the case for Agricultural Income Tax?" Journal of Fiscal Economics. Vol. 1, No. 1, July 1993.
4. Rangarajan, C.S. Jadhav, Narendra: "Issues in Financial Sector Reforms" The Indian Economy-problems and prospects Ed. by Bimal Jalan, 1992.
5. Wadhwa, K., Housing friendly Budgets, Economic and Politcal Weekly, Vol. XXXVIII No. 2 (Jan 11-17, 2003).

11

Micro Finance in India

Emerging Lessons and Challenges

Dr. Awadhesh Kr. Singh*

Micro-finance interventions are well-recognised world over as an effective tool for poverty alleviation and improving socio-economic conditions of poor. In India too, micro-finance is making headway in its effort for reducing poverty and empowering women. Micro-finance through the network of cooperatives, commercial banks, regional rural banks, NABARD and NGO's has been largely supply driven and recent approach. Interestingly, provision of credit to poor has been one of the main concerns of policy planners in India since Independence and cooperatives were strengthened to provide credit to the poor. To augment the credit flow to the priority sector, commercial banks, regional rural banks, cooperative banks etc. were promoted and loan melas were organised on a large scale. However, credit accessibility to poor from financial institutions is still limited and poor are depend on non-formal agencies for their credit needs. Thus, micro finance insuitutions (MFI's) are institutions other than banks now are engaged in providing financial services to the poor. India is also fast becoming one of the largest micro-finance markets in the world, especially with the growth of women's SHG's and encouraging Government Policy. However, micro-financial services as an instrument of development urgently require system wide attention and a policy framework for building of capabilities to ensure successful operation of viable micro enterprises for sustainable livelihoods. Moreover, the present

* Faculty, Institute of Development Studies, Lucknow University, Lucknow.

gap between demand and supply of micro financial services has to be narrowed down. Against this backdrop, present paper purports to review the status of micro finance in India, evaluating the performance of Indian microfinance and growing challenges in micro-finance sector. The policy implications of micro-finance in India are analysed with the view to assess the credit needs of poor and providing a policy framework to extend the micro-financial services.

Introduction

Micro-finance sector in India is relatively new and there is considerable scope for its development. The shift of NGO's to micro-finance operations on commercial lines, increase in the volumes of financial transactions, number of MFI's venturing into direct lending and savings, etc calls for immediate attention and need for bringing their operations under appropriate legislation as the present legislation does not explicitly permit them to undertake such activities. Interestingly, there are 3 types of lending technology (Nagpur, 2002).

1. The document based and asset based conventional technology which is followed by almost all existing banks;
2. The group lending technology which comes in various shapes and forms. It has its own advantages as well as drawbacks:
3. Individual based lending technology is one where the MFI's has to be very careful in assessing the repayment capacity of the borrowers.

The above technologies are focussed on micro-finance through SHG's, however, credit accessibility to poor through SHG's has enhanced tremendously and recovery is comparatively higher. Importantly, the provision of financial services dealing with small loans and savings has been increasingly acclaimed as an effective means of poverty reduction.

Since Independence, Government of India has made concerted efforts to provide financial services to the poor through the formal financial institutions. It has created an extensive banking network, much of which is state owned and controlled. Yet, these institutions have not been able to effectively provide financial services to the poor both in terms of outreach and sustainability. This was mainly due to the assumptions on which these lending programmes were pursued such (SIDBI, 2000).

- The poor have no capacity to save and are not bankable; and
- Their condition could only be improved through subsidy linked poverty alleviation credit programmes.

All this led to focussing on capital subsidies, low rate of interest on loans, soft lending terms with longer maturity etc. In order to cope up with the low interest margins and high transaction costs, banks reduced their appraisal and monetary costs, which seriously affected the recovery, rates. Despite the efforts made through the financial system and the Government programmes, the access of institutional credit to the poor remained limited being reached by less than 20 per cent rural poor (less than 10% the women). The poor continued to remit overwhelmingly dependent on the informal sector for their credit and related needs. As a result of the inadequate flow of funds from the formal financial institutions to meet the credit needs of the poor, micro-financial institutions emerged with a wide range of NGO's initiatives to extend financial services to poor. The movement initiated by these institutions has been encouraged by the various development financial institutions including SIDBI, NABARD, HUDCO, HDFC, RMK, and NGO's PRADAN, ASA, SHARE, MYRADA, SEWA, etc.

The Indian micro-finance sector is characterised by a variety of micro-finance service providers. These include various apex financial institutions like SIDBI and NABARD, Government owned societies like Rastriya Mahila Kosh, formal sector financial institutions, Commercial banks, Regional Rural Banks, in addition to member based institutions like Cooperatives, Mutually Aided Cooperative Societies, SHG Federations, Private sector companies like specialize NBFC's, Societies, Trusts, etc. Interestingly, micro finance institutions in India today offer a variety of products, follow different pricing strategies, adopt varied credit legal forms an organisational structure. The following approaches to micro-finance are commonly prevalent in India:

- The Basic Self Help Group Model and its minor variations (PRADAN, NBJK, LEAD and others).
- Grameen Replicator Approach (SHARE, ASA, CASHPOR India etc.).
- Cooperative-Grameen Hybrid Model (Mahila Vikasa).
- NBFC Approach (BASIX and Sanghamitra).
- Federated SHG Approach (Dhan Foundation).
- Rural Industries Promotion (SHG) Framework (MYRADA).
- Urban Cooperative Banking Model (Sewa Bank).
- Multistage Cooperative Solidarity Group Model (ICNW).
- Enabling cooperative networking framework (CDF and MACS).

Performance of Micro-Finance in India

According to NABARD Report, 1999-2000, the number of SHG's availing credit has increased from 3841 in 1997 to 81,780 in 2000. The total number of SHG's linked to the banks stand at 1,14,755 in March 2000. About 85 per cent of them are women groups. The number of financial institutions extending credit to the SHG's has increased from 120 in 1997 to 266 in 2000. Out of the 266 financial institutions majority of them are Regional Rural Banks. These SHG's are operating in 362 districts of 24 states and union territories. The number of NGO's dealing with the SHG's has increased from 220 in 1997 to 718 in 2000. Bank loans to these groups have also increased from Rs. 110 million in 1997 to Rs. 1930 million in 2000. The number of families assisted increased from 0.15 million in 1997 to 1.90 million in 2000 (Dasgupta, 2001). The cumulative number of SHG's credit linked as on December 2002 were reported to be 3.64 lakhs while cumulative number of SHG's refinance linked as on December 2002 were found to be 3.12 lakh. Out of total SHG's formed and financed, majority of the groups were covering members of disadvantaged classes (Table 1).

Table 1: Details of Swaranjayanti Gram Swarojgar Yojna. (SGSY)

(As on December, 2000)

Sl. No.	*Particulars*	
1.	Self Help Group	
	Groups Formed	292426
	Activity Taken up	29017
2.	Members covered Under SHG's	347912
3.	Individual Swarojgar's Assisted	585956
4.	Total Swarojgars Assisted	933868
5.	Credit Distursed to SHG's (Rs. Lakh)	9343.23
6.	Subsidies Disbursed to SHG's (Rs. lakh)	6858.61
7.	Cumulative No. of SHG's Credit linked as on December 2002	364964
8.	Cumulative No. of SHG's Refinance linked as on December 2002	312494
9.	Coverage of Disadvantaged Groups	
	Scheduled Castes	278938 (29.87)
	Scheduled Tribes	134644 (14.45)
	Women	416690 (44.62)
	Handicapped	8529 (0.91)
10.	Average Members Per Group	11.99

As the 1990's progressed, a fast growing number of savings and credit groups (SHG's), predominantly with women members, also emerged, as well as a range of specialised MFI's. By April 2001, 2,85,000 SHG's had taken loans from 41 Commercial Banks, 166 RRB's, and 111 Cooperative Banks, with an average loan per group of Rs. 18,000. During the year 2000-2001 alone, 171,000 SHG's took loans from banks, of which 149,000 were first time borrowers, suggesting a rapid acceleration of this process towards NABARD's target of ensuring bank loans are extended to 1 million SHG's by 2008 (Fisher and Sriram, 2002). With an average membership of 17, this would mean banks reach out to some 17 million members, the vast majority of whom will be women.

The impact of financial sector reforms has in many ways made things worse for poor. There has been a drastic fall in the share of cooperatives in rural credit (Karmakar, 1999). The share of rural credit in the total credit disturbed by Commercial Banks, which grew from 3.5 to 15 per cent from 1971 to 1991, has now declined to 11 per cent in 1998. (Sa-Dhan, 2001). During 1990's, the banks could not in fact meet their agricultural credit target of 18 per cent of net bank credit. Even the restructuring of RRB's also resulted in a fall in the availability of credit, leaving scope for informal sources as well as MFI's to fill the credit gaps.

Increasing Demand for Micro-financial Services

India is perhaps the largest emerging market for micro-financial services in the world. In the emerging micro finance sector, SHG's and mutually aided cooperatives have mobilised micro savings through sustained efforts. Even micro credit to the poor has widened the scope for promotion and development of viable micro-enterprises and economic activities for sustainable employment or livelihoods. India has nearly 400 million people living below or just above poverty line. About 75 million households therefore need micro-finance. Of these, nearly 60 million households are in rural India and remaining 15 million are urban slum dwellers. The current annual credit usage by these householders as estimated in 1998 to be Rs. 465,000 million or US$ 10 billion (Mahajan and Nagasri, 1999). It is estimated that the number of small loan accounts from banks covered some 40 million households are perhaps meeting their credit needs from the informal sector. Micro-finance institutions have given a rise because of this increasing gap between demand and supply. Melcom Harper has also estimated that the targets for the outreach of SHG's and of MFO's are, by 2009 a quarter of all poor households will have access to micro-financial services through such intermediaries. (Harper, 2002) NABARD has estimated in early 2001 that by 2008 about one million SHG's would be taking loans from banks, with a total membership of around 17 million people. Thus, it is clear from the estimation that a majority of the poor will be using SHG system for access to micro-credit. (Table 2). It is clear from the rapid growth of self help groups (SHG's) and other community based intermediaries that if credit were more readily available, credit usage would only go up, suggesting that much demand for credit among poor households is also not being met (Mathew, 2002). Importantly, the supply of insurance services to poor people is increasing, including low premium schemes, covering health, accidents, natural calamities, loss of assets, etc. However, attributes of these products are often non-appropriate and poor people, therefore, face significant risks in purchasing insurance. Not only is the total current demand for micro-financial services not being met, but also there is likely to be significant additional latent demand. Market imperfections and market distortions mean that many poor households will not express their demand for micro-financial services until such market imperfections and distortions are overcome or removed (Mathew, 2002). The total outreach of specialised providers of micro-financial services is expected to fall (Mahajan and Nagasri, 1999). Therefore, Mahajan and Nagasri have suggested a three track approach:

- Incentive existing mainstream financial service providers;
- Encourage new MFO's with a supportive policy and regulating framework and financial resources to enlarge and expand their services; and

Table 2: Credit Related Features of MFIs.

Sl. No.	*Name of MFI's*	*Period of operation (Year)*	*Average Loan size (Rs.)*	*Lending (Rate (%)*	*Cumulative Borrowers*	*Estimates Credit Demand (Rs. million)*
1.	SEWA Bank	25	10,000	18	200,000	—
2.	BASIX	3	7,000	24	20,000	100
3.	SHARE	7	3,000	15	14,000	100
4.	Mahila Kosh	10	5,000	14	100,000	30
5.	PREM	17	2,000	10-34	29,000	5
6.	ASA	10	4,500	15	6,000	60
7.	LUPIN	11	4,000	12	2,000	5
8.	FWWB	17	400,000	13.5	146	30
9.	YCO	13	5,000	FLEXIBLE	6,300	4
10.	ADITHI	11	5,000	12	5,000	15
11.	ASSIST	14	3,000	12	4,000	20
12.	UPBSN	3	9,000	12	40,000	NA
13.	JAMMUNA Grameen Bank	2	6,000	12	852	—

Source: IFAD Study, (1999).

- To build from the grassroots up, a network of community based financial intermediaries.

All of these clearly require better regulations and policy to create the appropriate enabling environment. The transformation of repayment culture is required which needs policy initiative. Financial institutions have to change their attitude towards small loans to poor people from seeing them a social obligation to treating them as potential business opportunities. Similarly, policy makers need to consider the potential of micro-financial services to support investment and growth in key sectors of development. It is to be noted that rural non-farm sector has the most potential to grow (Fisher and Mahajan, 1997). And especially services, which now contribute significant share in GDP. However, it requires accelerating the growth in agriculture sector through extending credit and farm inputs. Importantly, regulation of micro-financial services is also necessary (Fisher etal, 2001), since it helps in long term sustainability.

Emerging Challenges

Micro-financial services must be used as an instrument of development and social change, NGO's have a distinct role-play in formation, strengthening of SHG's and capacity building among SHG's members for developing and promotion of micro-enterprises. However, designing development micro-financial services can not be done without proper attention and adaptation to the environment in which those services will operate (Fisher, 2002). Targeting micro-financial services at the proper and more disadvantaged groups may be appropriate in many contexts. Supporting small enterprises can provide employment to poor people and will have wider impact on local economy. The challenges of the organisation of micro-finance provision and of capacity building for it become all the more acute in the context of developmental goals and changing paradigms of development. This is often conceived in terms of staff, product design, cost control, pricing strategy, systems, incentives, access to capital and governance through people's centered and democratic decentralisation. Importantly, Micro-finance organisations/institutions face the following constraints: (Mathew, 2002).

- In most states, Registrar of Societies has not recognised micro-finance as a permitted activity for societies.
- The Income Tax Act [Section 2(15)] does not define micro-finance as a charitable activity, thus NGO's engaged in micro-finance are loosing their charitable status.
- The Income Tax Act [Section 11(5)] does not allow NGO's to promote mutual benefit or commercial MFO's as they are not allowed to invest in equity.

- The Foreign contributors Regulation act is ambiguous about receiving funds for micro-finance, whether the foreign funds are used as grants or loans.
- Non-Profit MFO's have difficulty in raising deposits without contravening the RBI Act.

Conclusions and Policy Recommendations

With the massive expansion, the performance of SHG's also becomes even more critical, especially as many SHG's are being formed, strengthened and promoted by Government, international funding agencies and financial institutions, however, these SHG's are not linked with viable micro-enterprises for sustaining the resources and their effective utilisation for poverty alleviation. Importantly, the vast majority of resources are channelised through public agencies but no concrete attempt has been made to build more independent organisation for out-sourcing and extending support for service providers. Since Government is one of the most powerful stockholders, with overall responsibility for policy instruments, specific measures should be introduced by the Govt. The Government needs to establish an enabling environment for a diverse range of services providers to remove market distortions and irregularities. Moreover, Government needs to pay more attention on micro-finance, considering its potential to support poverty alleviation, empowerment and socio-economic development. Importantly, local resources are to be assessed for promotion of micro-enterprises. More budgetary resources should be allocated for promotion of SHG's system in India as an instruction of development and social change. Interestingly, micro-finance sector continues to be buffected by regulatory changes to be introduced to address the emerging needs of financial sector. Significantly, appropriate policy and support for sustainable livelihoods, micro-enterprises and community-based organisations are important for promotion and development of micro-financial services.

REFERENCES

1. Fisher, Thomas and M.S. Sriram, Beyond Micro-credit, Vistar Pub., Delhi, 2002.
2. Fisher, et al., Regulating micro-finance: Global perspective, New Economics Foundations, London, 2001.
3. Fisher, Thomas, Emerging lessons and challenges in Beyond Micro credit by Fisher & Sriram, Vistar Pub, Delhi, 2002.
4. Harper, M. 'Self help groups and Grameen Bank groups: What are the differences?' in Beyond Micro-credit by Fisher and Sriram, Vistar Pub, Delhi; 2002.

5. Harper, Malcom, Empowerment through Enterprise, OUP, Delhi, 1996.
6. Harper, Malcom, Profit for the poor: cases in micro-finance, OUP, New Delhi, 1998.
7. Kanitkar, A., 'Exploring Empowerment and Leadership at the Grassroot: Social Enterpreneurship in the Movement in India' in Beyond Micro Credit by Fisher & Sriram, Vistar Pub, Delhi, 2002.
8. Karmarker, K.G., Rural Credits and Self help Groups: Micro-finance Needs and Concepts in India, Sage Pub, New Delhi, 1999.
9. Mahajan, Vijai and G. Nagasri, Building Sustainable micro-finance institutions in India, paper presented in seminar on New Development Finance, Frankfurt, Sept. 1999.
10. Mathew, T., Rising to the Challenge of Scale in India: Growing the Micro Finance sector' in Beyond Micro credit by Fisher & Sriram, Virtar Pub, Delhi, 2002.
11. Mathew, T., Costs in Micro Finance: what do self help groups 'tell us' in Beyond Micro credit by Fisher & Sriram, Vistar Pub, Delhi, 2002.
12. Nagar, I.C., Impact of Micro-credit on Socio-Economic Empowerment of Rural Women; Ph.D. Thesis, Lucknow University; 2002.
13. Sa-Dhan, Micro-finance Regulation in India, Sa-Dhan, New Delhi, 2001.
14. Dasgupta, R., An Informal Journey through SHG's, Indian Journal of Agricultural Economics, Vol. 56(3) July-Sept, 2001.
15. SIDBI, SIDBI Report on Small Scale Industries Sector, 2000, Lucknow.

12

Globalisation of Education
Excellence, Equity and Competitiveness

S.K. Gandhe*

Economic Globalisation

The term globalisation implies a more comprehensive interaction between the nation-states than hithertofore. The national borders are gradually losing importance and social and economic identities are stretched beyond countries or regions. The flip side of globalisation is that local happenings are shaped by events, actions and decisions taking place far away, often without the knowledge of the affected people. Such effects are more often than not harmful to the developing countries.

Globalisation is viewed differently by different groups and interests. Some consider it as a new industrial revolution deeply rooted in the new and powerful information and communication technologies. Globalisation with its concomitants, namely liberalisation and privatisation, effected free international flow of products, capital, labour and human resources from one end of the world to the other, engulfing in the process both developed as well as developing nations. Unfortunately, thus far, inspite of the tall claims of its protagonists towards equity and fair distribution, it is only the developed countries which have derived real benefits of globalisation. These countries have welcomed globalisation with all eagerness and positiveness, for it is seen as an opportunity to become wealthier. On the other hand the developing

* Dr. S.K. Gandhe is Director-General of the Indian Institute of Education, Pune.
This paper is presented in ICSSR sponsored social Dimensions of Economic Reforms held in Department of Economics, Shivaji University, Kolhapur during 29-30 Jan. 2003.

countries, by and large, are afraid of the whole phenomena. There is a lurking fear that the marginal and poor countries may be rendered poorer because of the all-pervading effect of globalisation. These southern nations are in no condition to participate in globalisation because of uncompetitive products, unskilled labour and inefficient if not inhibitive governments and administrative machinery. Exclusion is harmful but inclusion is also very difficult. In many developing countries, unemployment increased, and the trained and highly skilled manpower migrated in search of better work opportunities and better returns leading to heavy brain-drain. Globalisation has created crises in many developing countries because of their inability to compete with the industrialised countries supported by highly skilled manpower.

The last two decades have witnessed a surge of liberalisation in the developing countries all over the world. This is considered to be a natural sequel to the policies adopted by these very countries immediately after their freedom from the colonies rule in the forties, fifties and sixties. The hall-marks of these policies were economic self-reliance and industrialisation which will lead to import substitution.

The developing world had experienced long spells of economic deprivation at the hands of the colonial powers when the natural resources and raw materials were exploited for the industrialisation in the ruling countries and export of the industrial products back to the colonies. In the process, colonies remained primary, mostly agricultural, economies with very little industrialisation. The natural aspirations of the local populace immediately after attaining freedom were protection from economic exploitation by the industrially powerful nations, through self-reliance and import substitution. This in turn led to an era of controls, licensing regulations, quotas, tariffs and duties, and social control of various types of production units. Socialisation which began with the basic or mother industries finally entered into various other units of production and services. The consequences were inevitable. Industrial inefficiency, labour-unrest, top-heavy management, poor quality of products and services and corruption and exploitation became the order of the day. Export incompetitiveness, both costwise and quality-wise, became all pervading. Economic stagnation was the net result. Need for liberalisation of economies of the developing countries was realised by the countries themselves and was also emphasised by the international organisations and the world community at large.

India launched the process of economic reforms in 1991. The first generation reforms involved fiscal discipline, deregulation and reduction of physical and tariff barriers relating to imports and exports. The second generation reforms recently initiated continued the first generation reforms and reinforced the process through disinvestment in public enterprises and opening of the economy to the multinational and other enterprises in the developed countries. India, like other developing countries, is attempting to give effect to the stipulations of the World Trade Organisation (WTO). In brief the reforms introduced in India were as under:

(a) Devaluation of Indian currency in July, 1991 to provide a substantial stimulus to exports.

(b) Introduction of freely tradeable Eximscrips.

(c) The advance licensing system for exports was simplified so as to improve exporters' access to imported inputs at duty-free rates.

(d) Export and Trading Houses and Star Trading Houses were permitted a larger range of imports. 51 per cent foreign equity was also now allowed in Trading Houses.

(e) Industrial licensing was abolished for all projects except in 18 industries where strategic or environmental concerns are paramount or where industries produce goods with exceptionally high import content.

(f) The MRTP Act was amended which enabled Indian firms to become large enough to compete effectively in global markets.

(g) Government clearance for the location of projects was dispensed with except in the case of 23 cities with a population of more than one million.

(h) Small scale enterprises were given the option to offer upto 24 per cent of their shareholding to large scale and other industrial undertakings which provide them with greater access to capital and technology.

(i) The limit of foreign equity holdings was raised from 40 to 51 per cent in a wide range of priority industries.

(j) Technology imports for priority industries are automatically approved for royalty payments upto 5 per cent of domestic sales and 8 per cent of export sales or for lumpsum payment of Rs. 1 crore.

India has completed a decade of economic reforms. A mixed impression prevails about the impact of these reforms on India's economic life. According to the Ninth Five Year Plan, the reforms have yielded good results thus far—the growth rate has risen from 5.8% in the Seventh Plan to 6.8 per cent in the Eight Plan. There are, however, many dimensions in which performance has lagged behind. Faster growth rate has not reduced poverty as much as it should have, nor has it created a number of high quality jobs we need to satisfy the aspirations of our increasingly educated youth. Growth has not been as regionally balanced as it should have been. The deficiencies in social development indicators have also continued and our level of social development is a major constraint for reaching a growth rate of 8 per cent, which is our target for the Tenth Plan. It must, however, be recognised that 'economic reforms' is a reality which cannot be denied, and hence should not be avoided. It needs to be managed. To do this, the Government strategy is to continue the process of opening up of the economy to international competition, while making parallel efforts to strength the potential of Indian industry to compete effectively in the world markets.

Liberalisation, privatisation and globalisation (LPG) are the important planks of the economic policy reforms. It must however be noted that while the first two are within the powers of national governments, the third is not. Globalisation is expected to be the result of a judicious combination of liberalisation and privatisation. India has brought about economic reforms leading to a great deal of liberalisation and privatisation. But has there been a Globalisation of Indian economy in the real sense consequent to its economic reforms? This is a moot question that needs to be examined in some details.

How do we measure globalisation? A common measure would be the proportion of a country's share in the international trade. From this angle Indian economy is hardly globalised. India's participation in the world trade is just insignificant; it is a meagre 0.7 per cent. It is less than the that of even the tiny countries of East Asia like, for example, Singapore. On the test of country's participation in international capital flow also, India is nowhere near the minimal expectation. The annual Foreign Direct Investment (FDI) flow into India is less than half a per cent. Same is true of the international institutional investments also. Thus, India sharing 16 per cent of world population, can hardly be considered globalised. There is one aspect, however, which has opened up the gates of globalisation for India. It is the death of distance and the services revolution. India has made tremendous progress in the field of information-technology based service sector. It must also be conceded that transition from a closed to a vibrant open and a more globally dominant economy is bound to take time. In the case of India, in particular with unlimited and ever-expanding domestic consumption market, globalisation is bound to be slow in coming. If the present national policy of economic reforms is sustained over the next couple of decades, India can hope to be a real participant in the world economy.

Globalisation and Human Resource Development

Need for excellence

In order that the developing nations are able to successfully grapple with globalisation, qualitative development of its human resource is an important—if not more—as its economic reforms. Globalisation essentially entails international competition in production and distribution of economic goods and services. The developed nations have derived full benefits of globalisation because of their highly qualified manpower and use of improved, modern technology. The latter is indeed dependent on the former to a large extent. Unfortunately, the present educational systems in the developing countries is beset with several restrictions and lacunae. India's educational system is in shambles and the quality of education has been the first casualty. Out of more than 270 or odd universities, not more than 8 to 10 can be identified as really top class educational institutions providing really good quality education and whose products can be compared with any university in the developed world. The affiliating system coupled with steady rise in population has resulted in a mushrooming growth of colleges. These institutions largely owned and operated by private societies or trusts and often controlled by local politicians, have very poor infrastructural facilities, libraries, laboratories, playgrounds; attendance requirements are not strictly insisted upon; teachers' quality and interest in teaching are below expectation; examination results are manipulated, and battalions of unemployable young men and women are produced every year from the portals of Indian universities. This type of manpower cannot compete with the high well-qualified and skilled manpower of the developed world and hence Indian products will always be at a disadvantage. India cannot globalize its trade in this situation.

Qualitative development of India's vast human resources is the urgent need. Indian youth must be equipped with modern high-tech skills, new knowledge and training so that they can develop new ideas and thoughts. This also calls for a great diversification of the higher education system.

What is impregnated in the above analysis is the need to create a real quality education system in India. This, in other words, calls for setting up of a large number of Educational Centres of Excellence. This is, however, easier said than done. Today, there are more than 270 Universities and 13,000 colleges. The total enrollment exceeds seven million students which is about 7 per cent of the relevant age-group population. The demand for higher education is steadily increasing year by year. A Centre of Excellence will call for a very heavy investment in infrastructure, tools and equipment, teaching-learning aids and of course, learned and techno-professionally qualified teachers. This is not easy to come by. There are several constraints, not the least of which is finance. Many State Government treasuries have reached their bottoms and have already drawn to the maximum-possible, on the out side resources like loans and overdrafts. The RBI has been from time to time reminding the States to reduce their debts, but to no avail. The Central Government is not in a much better position, either. With the decision of the Central Government (as a part of the Economic Reforms) to down-size the non-plan budgetary commitment, social services like education and health are hard hit. It is futile to expect additional public finance support for creation of a large number of educational centres of excellence to meet the challenges of globalisation.

Privatisation

Can, then, privatisation of the educational system be a solution? Present governmental thinking seems to be highly supportive of such an idea. It seems at the request of the Government of India a two-man committee (Mukesh Ambani and K. Birla—both foreign-educated young industrialists as members), has produced a report on the policy-framework for educational reforms which suggests, *inter alia,* that the State should undertake full responsibility for the priority sector in education (i.e. from pre-primary to secondary), but abandon University education fully and hand it over to the corporate sector. (S. Sikidav and G. Nath, 2001). The present policy makers seem to think that higher education is a *'non-merit'* good for the production of which public funds need not be invested.

Privatisation especially at the higher-education level is not new to India. In the wake of the freedom movement several private colleges were set up almost from the last couple of decades of the 19th century by nationalist organisations. Side by side religions organisations (especially the church) also set up private colleges. These proved to be equally efficient in comparison with the colleges set up and run by the then provincial governments. Some of the best Indian teachers worked in these (private) Colleges and served the student-community well. This trend continued in the first half of the 20th century also. After Independence, the higher education system witnessed an unprecedent growth, supported by spread of primary/secondary schools to all the nooks and corners of the country. However, the demand also increased steadily so much so that it actually out-stripped the supply. It was not possible for the state to meet the fast growing demand and they had no alternative but to adopt a very liberal policy of permitting "unaided" higher educational institutions including those in highly technical and professional fields. The result was that in the last two decades hundreds of non-grant colleges in practically all fields of higher education sprung up in even state.

Equity

The natural consequence of the above policy was that higher education became a *commercial enterprise* which only the richer sections of the population could take benefit of. The old nationalist fervour of private institutions has all gone. These new private colleges survive on capitation fees, donations and high tuition and other fees. *Social Equity* is conspicuously wanting in this new phase in higher education. Students of even the middle class, leave apart the poorer sections, can hardly afford to join these private institutions of higher education. If the state's accepted mandate is to ensure equitable welfare and development of its population, the principle of *social equity* cannot be neglected. The state can of course provide some checks and balances to mitigate the hardships faced by poor students, but these measures cannot go a long way.

Quality Improvement

Whether privatisation will lead to quality improvement is yet a myth, atleast in the Indian scenario. In fact with the mushrooming growth of private institutes of higher education, there is already a severe shortage of well-qualified and experienced teachers. These private institutes, as a measure of economy, are not inclined to appoint teachers on a regular basis with prescribed scales of pay and other perks. Instead the trend is to appoint "visiting faculty" on hourly basis. There is neither adequate interest in teaching on the part of these part-time teachers now adequate enthusiasm on the part of the students to learn from these teachers who don't have much rapport with the students.

With the exception of some well established technical or professional institutions (IITs, IIMs etc.) which have liberal financial support from the state, most of the others are not well equipped in respect of infrastructure, tools and equipment libraries, laboratories etc. use of electronic media and satellite based telecommunication as teaching aid is still a far cry. Thus it is difficult to support the claim that privatisation leads to quality improvement.

Curriculum Upgradation and Diversification

Once we accept the premise that education is not bound to any specific time-period in human life but is a life-long learning process, the need for a thorough revision and periodic upgradation cannot be over-emphasised. In the Indian Universities a large part of University curricula is still patterned on the old British University courses of study, though in Britain itself these are thoroughly revised. India cannot effectively benefit from globalisation, unless productivity and service-efficiency are enhanced. This also in turn calls for upgradation and diversification of course curricula. There cannot be a predetermined curriculum; anything that is necessary to study, any skill that is necessary to be acquired and discovery/invention that is necessary for globalisation of productivity should form basis of curriculum revision. This may mean discarding or down-sizing in content and importance some of the present-day social/physical science curricula. Benefit must be taken of the modern advances in the information technology which have revolutionised the content of knowledge and process of educational transaction. Electronic media can virtually bring new knowledge to the door-steps of the learner. IT and satellite communications through their planned educational programmes can replace the present-day educational systems in many countries, if planned and managed properly knowledge production, distribution and consumption can be globally planned and distributed. The role and relevance of the present educational institutions will in due course, be minimised if not totally eradicated. The gigantic potential of the IT and satellite, technology will be the foundation of the futural educational system. This cannot be effectively tapped by the developing nations unless the course-curricula is properly upgraded and fully diversified.

Care needs must, however be taken that there is no "Mc Donaldisation" of higher education by the spread of single formula and copy of the western model. With the increasing competition, and demand for productivity oriented skill-acquisition universities in developing countries may be tempted to invest in subjects that are going to be most profitable for them, to the detriment of less profitable ones like human sciences. Even the university-level research activity may be adjusted to suit the needs of the funding agencies. Care needs must also be taken to ensure that globalisation of education is not at the cost of teaching-learning of human values like ethics, equity, human security, sustainability, and reduction of poverty of the masses, especially the rural masses.

Conclusion

It may be stated by way of conclusion that globalisation has come to stay in India. Its effect will not be limited to the economic life of the country, but will also spread to various social sectors including education. India launched the process of economic reforms in 1991. But, the impact of these reforms has so far not been noticed in a big way. Though the growth rate has risen by about one per cent, there has been no reduction in poverty nor has it created high quality jobs. India has, however, made tremendous progress in the field of information-technology based service sector. This has certainly reduced distances and paved way for faster globalisation.

Education is one social sector which is being steadily impacted by the process of globalisation. If India is to derive full benefit of globalisation, it is imperative that it produces a very high quality manpower. Globalisation essentially entails international competition in production and distribution of economic goods and services. The developed nations could take full advantage of globalisation because of their high quality manpower and extensive use of modern technology. What India urgently needs is the creation of a large number of Educational Centres of Excellence. Because of the financial limitations, this is bound to lead to a great deal of privatisation of education. In fact the process has already begun in many parts of the country. The present policy-makers seem to support privatisation as, in their view, education is a non-merit good and hence investment of public funds in the production of this good is not considered a social need. While privatisation may enlarge intake capacities at the higher education level, also the danger of commercialisation of education. If this aspect is not taken care of, it may lead to social inequality and even social unrest. Another important prerequisite is quality improvement of the educational system. High quality norms must be insisted upon to ensure that whatever is delivered is of international standard, if not better. In this context need for curriculum upgradation and diversification of course-curricula cannot be over-emphasised.

BIBLIOGRAPHY

1. Ambatkar Sanjay; *India and Asean in the 21st Century;* 2002; Anmol Publications Pvt. Ltd., New Delhi.
2. Batra G.S.; Dangwal R.C.; *"Globalisation and Liberalisation;* 2001, Elegant Printers, New Delhi.
3. ICSSR, New Delhi: *Identity, Locality and Globalisation;* 2001, Indian Council of Social Science Research, New Delhi.
4. Jalan Bimal; *India's Economy in the New Millennium;* 2002; UBS Publishers' Distributors Pvt. Ltd., New Delhi.
5. Nayar Baldev Raj; *Globalisation and Nationalism; 2001, Sage Publications India Pvt. Ltd., New Delhi.*

13

Nutritional Security and Role of Voluntary Organisation in the Post-Reforms Period

S. Indrakant*

The adverse balance of payment, mounting fiscal deficit and double digit inflation rate experienced by the Indian Economy during late 80's forced the Government of India to initiate New Economic Program in 90's aimed at economic liberalisation, privatisation of public sector and globalisation by opening the Indian Economy. The new economic program consisted mostly of reduction in fiscal deficit, reduction in growth rate of money supply, correction of exchange rate of rupee and lowering of tariff rate. In the second phase of reforms, the pace of reforms has been accelerated by speeding the process of privatisation of public sector, reduction of interest rate at regular interval, opening-up the Indian economy in confirmity with World Trade Organisation Agreement.

The short-run impact of economic reforms on macro-economic variable appear to be favourable. However, their long-run impact on the economy is not clear. The improvement in the balance of payment may be at the expense of reduction in development expenditure. Planning would reduce to indicative planning and doubts have been expressed in some quarters about the ability of Government with limited policy instruments to guide the economy on desired lines.

* Professor, Department of Economic, Osmania University, Hyderabad.

This paper was presented in the ICSSR sponsored National Seminor on Social Dimensions of Economic Reforms held in Dept of Economics, Shivaji University, Kolhapur during 29-30 Jan 2003.

One of the major issue concerning social scientist is the impact of economic reforms on social security in a country like India where there is need for a strong and extensive social security system. According to National Family Health Survey – 2 data in 1998-99 almost half of the children under three years of age (47%) were under-weight and a similar percentage of children (46%) were stunted. The proportion of severely under nourished children was notable – 18% according to weight-for-age and 23% according to height-for-age. The survey data reveals that the girls are more likely than boys to be underweight and stunted whereas boys are more likely to be wasted. Further, undernutrition seems to be substantially higher in rural areas than in urban areas.

With economic reforms, the role of the Government has changed from an active player in development process to a facilitator. In this context, some issues need special attention. Do NGOs manage the ICDS Projects better? What are the problems faced by them? Is there a scope for increasing the participation of NGOs? If so, how? This Paper seeks to answer some of these questions?

Voluntary Organisations have grown in India over the years but their growth has been uneven and not uniform all over the country. The Voluntary Organisations have assumed tremendous importance in recent year in the task of ensuring national development, particularly in the area of welfare of women and children. In 1966, Government of India set up National Institute for Research and Training in Public Co-operation, later called as National Institute of Public Co-operation and Child Development (NIPCCD) to study, promote and strengthen voluntary action. Government created another autonomous institute called People's Action for Development India (PADI) to promote voluntary effort in rural development. In 1983, Council for Advancement of Rural Technology (CART) was set up to improve conditions in rural areas through diffusion and innovation of technology with the help of voluntary organisations. But in 1986, CART was merged with PADI to form the Council for Advancement of People's Action and Rural Technology (CAPART) to co-ordinate and catalyse the development work of voluntary agencies country wide.

A majority of voluntary organisations have concentrated in providing livelihood, employment and income generation activities. But very few organisations have concentrated on direct nutritional security program. In a study on working of voluntary organisations in Kamrup District of Assam (Bhatia 2000) it was found that the voluntary organisations had firm roots in their repective areas and had good rapport with local people which enabled them to organise women and mobilise community resources with relative case. However, some of the organisations were excessively depending upon government grants and had become complacent in mobilising their own resources. The dearth of trained personnel is another weakness. It is also felt that full potential of NGO's have not been realised.

Integrated Child Development Services (ICDS) program is direct nutrition program of the Government to feed the malnourished children and expectant and nursing mothers. The ICDS Program is mostly administered and implemented by a Government machinery. The Officials above the rank of Child Development Project Officer (CDPO) are burdened with paper work and they are busy in clearing files and attending meetings with higher Officials. Their interaction with ground level workers is very much limited. They lack initiative in taking new measures. The participating of voluntary organisations and Community is limited. CARE is participating in Supplementary Nutrition Programme by supplying Corn-Soya Beans and Oil, free of cost. Rayalsemma Seva Samithi (RASS), the only Voluntary Organisation, is managing ICDS Project at Tirupati in Andhra Pradesh.

Rayalseema Seva Samathi

Rayalseema Seva Samathi (RASS), established in 1981, through its various development activities is working for the welfare of women, children and aged persons. It is making a frontal attack on poverty simultaneously from various angles. The major activities of RASS include Pre-School Education through Day Care Centres and Early Childhood Centres, Non-Formal Education (NFE) for school drop-out children through NFE Centres, child development through sponsorship programs, Empowerment of women by forming Self Help Groups (SHGs) among women, up-gradation of skills in tailoring, embroidery, hosiery etc., among adolescent girls, Adult Literacy Programs, Homes and Day Care Centres for aged persons, Watershed Programs, Community Health and ICDS Programs.

The ICDS Project at Tirupati is a Urban Non-World Bank Assisted Project. It was started in 1984 with 100 AWCs. Even now there are 100 AWCs. However some of the AWCs have been shifted from their original location as it was felt that there was no need of AWCs in those places. Among the 100 AWCs,77 of them are located in Tirupati town and rest of them are adjacent to the town. The sanctioned posts are CDPO – 1, Supervisors – 4, AWWs – 100, Helpers – 100. Being a Urban Project additional posts: Medical Officer – 1 and ANMs – 4 are sanctioned. Generally, there is abnormal delay in grounding the scheme after its sanction. But RASS grounded the ICDS Project within 40 days. The staff is selected and appointed by RASS. Only CDPO post is vacant since 1991. The Medical Officer is discharging the duties of CDPO.

Coverage

The population in the Project area was estimated to be 112 thousand in March 1998. The number of beneficiaries in ICDS Project was estimated to be nearly 18 thousand, consisting of about 15 thousand children and 25 hundred expectant and nursing mothers. The composition of beneficiaries by caste and age-group is presented in Table – 1. About 20% of beneficiaries belong to SC/ST category while 40% of beneficiaries belong to backward class.

Table 1: Coverage of RASS ICDS Project.

Sl.		*Children*			*Women*		*Total*
No.	*Section*	*0-6**	*6m-3yrs.*	*3-6yrs.*	*Pregnant*	*Lactating*	
1.	Scheduled Caste	236 (18.20)	1179 (18.35)	1300 (17.08)	241 (19.85)	243 (18.20)	3199 (17.89)
2.	Scheduled Tribe	51 (3.93)	193 (3.00	248 (3.26)	35 (2.88)	51 (3.82)	578 (3.23)
3.	Backward Class	508 (39.17)	2533 (39.42)	3036 (39.89)	491 (40.44)	526 (39.40)	7094 (39.67)
4.	Others	502 (30.70)	2520 (39.22)	3026 (39.76)	447 (36.82)	515 (38.58)	7010 (39.20)
Total		**1297 (100)**	**6425 (100)**	**7620 (100)**	**1214 (100)**	**1335 (100)**	**17881 (100)**

Note: 1. * Usually, 0-6 months children are not considered as beneficiaries, but RASS has included them as beneficiaries.

2. Figures in the brackets represent percentage.

Source: RASS Office.

The number of total children as well as children below the age of 3 years per AWC is lower in Tirupati than Marepally (AP) and Bhubaneswar (Orissa) Project (See Table 2). The proportion of children in the age group 0-3 is also lower at Tirupati. However, the percentage of eligible children below 3 years enrolled in Tirupati Project is better than the other Projects.

Immunisation

RASS recognising the importance of immunisation, has taken up intensive Immunisation Program with the collaboration of Government Hospital and Municipality. The coverage of Immunisation at the time of inception of ICDS Project was very low. For instance, the coverage of B.C.G at the time of inception was less than 40%. Now the coverage is nearly 90%.

Table 2: Selected Indicators of Tirupati and Other Projects.

S.No.	*Particulars*	*Tirupati*	*Marepally*	*Bhubaneswar*
1.	No. of enrolled Children per AWC	54	80	93
2.	No. of enrolled Children in 0-3 Group per AWC	22	41	45
3.	% of 0-3 enrolled children in total enrolled children	40.70	51.00	48.00
4.	% of children enrolled in the age group of 0-3	100.00	82.00	81.00

Source: Monthly Progress Reports of Concerned Projects.

Similarly, the coverage under Polio Vaccination has increased from around 30% to about 90%. As a result of these activities the infant mortality rate (IMR) (per 1000) has steadily declined from 68 in 1984 – 85 to 40 in 1997-98 (see Table – 3).

Table 3: Coverage of Immunisation Under RASS ICDS Project.

(per 1000)

Sl. No.	*Year*	*B.C.G.*	*Polio*	*Measles*	*T.T.*	*IMR*
1.	At the time of Inception	39.9	31.9	–	2.2	–
2.	1984-85	40.1	69.8	–	67.8	–
3.	1985-86	50.4	71.3	85.9	89.0	68.1
4.	1986-87	82.9	87.0	85.9	89.0	52.0
5.	1987-88	83.5	93.6	83.3	96.0	65.0
6.	1988-89	86.6	98.5	84.0	96.0	52.0
7.	1989-90	84.0	87.3	84.0	92.5	44.5
8.	1990-91	81.0	86.6	80.0	89.0	37.5
9.	1991-92	88.0	95.5	83.1	98.7	31.5
10.	1992-93	89.0	98.0	92.0	98.0	30.0
11.	1993-94	88.0	87.0	87.0	83.0	54.0*
12.	1994-95	89.0	88.0	88.0	84.0	54.0
13.	1995-96	88.0	89.0	90.0	85.0	42.0
14.	1996-97	86.0	88.0	89.0	83.0	40.0
15.	1997-98	89.0	88.5	90.0	86.0	40.0

Source: RASS Office

Supplementary Nutrition Program

In the beginning CARE food was provided as supplementary food. At that time there was a central kitchen. Upma was prepared and distributed to all the 100 AWCs by Cycle Rickshaw. Due to strict supervision leakages in distribution was said to be negligible. As the off-loading of CARE food was changed from Chennai port to Vizag port, the CARE food was withdrawn. For about a year snacks, food and weaning diet was provided by the Government through its RTE Food Factory at Hyderabad. Presently, only RTE food is being served to children and mothers. The RTE food is sent to Tirupati by lorry. The RASS stores the food in its godown and distributes the same to the AWCs through its trucks and other vehicles. Unlike many Rural Projects, the Tirupati Project has never faced the problem of interruption in supply of food and consequently there is no interruption in distribution of food to AWCs. The leakages in the distribution of food is not a serious problem as children do not crave for food and many children go to English Medium Schools. According to the Monthly Progress Report of Dec'97 1291 mothers and 4579 children benefited by the Supplementary Feeding Program (see Table – 4). The number of children in Grade – III and Grade-IV was only 37. There seems to be no rigorous criterion for identifying the beneficiaries. While identifying eligible beneficiaries the general living level of the family is considered and relatively poor families are enrolled for the program.

Preschool Education

Both the parents as well as private schools management recognise the importance of training imparted to the children at AWCs. Most of the parents send their children to AWCs for one to two years and then shift them to English Medium Schools. Consequently, the percentage of children aged between 3 to 4 years seems to be more in AWCs of Tirupati Urban Project. Even the Private English Medium School Authorities recommend the parents to send their children for a year or so to the AWCs. To meet the competition from English Medium Schools, emphasis is laid on teaching alphabets and numerals in Pre-School Education Program. The enrollment in 100 AWCs has remained around 4000. The percentage of students attending has generally been above 95%.

Nutrition and Health Education

The Nutrition and Health Education is imparted, through house visits by AWWs, at Mahile Mandal Meetings, Co-ordination Committee Meeting, Film Shows, Exhibition and Group Discussions are also held. Some of the important topics covered under Nutrition and Health Education are breast feeding and its importance, weaning foods, pre-natal and post-natal care, personal hygiene etc. In addition to health check-up at AWCs on every Thursday, there is immunisation program and health check-up at the project office. They also have four sub-centres for health check-up. The accommodation at these sub-centres is relatively better. But, in respect of medicines there is an acute shortage. The compactness of geographical area is another conducive factor which has enabled the AWWs of Tirupati Urban Project to deliver better services than that of the AWWs of Government Managed Projects.

Health Check-up

In addition to normal Immunisation Programme, RASS conducts a Special Immunisation Program on every Thursday, at the Head Office of ICDS Project. Four Sub-Centres are started in ICDS Project area to provide Health Care to women at their door-step. A lady Medical Officer conducts Ante-natal Check-up, Immunisation and General Health Check-up, once in a week at the Sub-Centres. On account of periodical meetings with mothers and other services, the incidence to ailments like Respiratory infections, Diarrhea, Conjunctives, have considerably come down.

Additional Services

Non-formal Education Centres are functioning to help the school drop-out children. In order to improve the economic status of ICDS mothers, RASS has initiated Income Generating Program, by organising SHGs. Presently, there are 255 groups with a membership of 3000 women with a saving of Rs.3.2 million. RASS has taken up schemes for the up-gradation of skills in Tailoring, Embroidery, Hosiery etc., among the adolescent girls. RASS also has two Program to take care of aged and disable persons.

Convergence of Services

There is a view that the AWW in Government managed projects is not able to do full justice to her job because of too many responsibilities entrusted to her and hence there is a suggestion for provision of a second AWW. The story is different in the ICDS Project at Tirupati. The AWW performs her regular work at AWC, during 9 am to 12 noon. In the evening, she acts as a instructor at NFE Centre. Generally AWC and Non-Formal Education (NFE) Centre are at the same place. AWW also maintains the accounts of Self Help Group (SHGs). She has to devote one afternoon per week to maintain the accounts of one SHG. She generally maintains the accounts of four SHG. She is paid Rs.50 per month for maintaining the account of a Self Help Group. As an instructor at NFE Centre she receives an honorarium of Rs.300 per month. As a AWW she is paid a honorarium of Rs.400 to 500. Thus, an AWW earns about Rs.1000 per month. This has been made possible because of convergence of services.

Utilisation of Vehicles

In many projects, supervisors mobility is greatly restricted. However, in Tirupati Project here a novel scheme has been evolved in utilising the vehicle. All the supervisors share the AWCs on every route. Usually, the vehicle drops each Supervisor at the concerned AWC and picks them up in return journey. During their stay at the AWC they check the records of the AWC, conduct Nutrition and Health Education Program to the mothers and inspect the accounts of the SHG. Every day one route is selected and all the Supervisors travel in the same vehicle and get dropped at respective AWCs. In contrast, in other projects Jeep is exclusively at the disposal of CDPO. In RASS managed ICDS, CDPO as well as Supervisors make use of the vehicle. Supervisors reported that they never felt inconvenience of any sort in visiting their AWCs. As all the Supervisors are incharge of some AWS on all the routes and as they travel on all the routes, they have some acquaintance with all the AWWs and have an idea about the location of all the AWCs. This also facilitates supervision of some of the AWCs by another Supervisor, whenever the concerned Supervisor is on leave.

Problems of Tiripati Project

RASS is facing many problems, due to government attitude and other reasons, in managing the Tirupati Project.

Government Grants

The main problem faced by RASS is in regard to Government Grants. The Government grants given to RASS are insufficient and they are not released in time. The staff of Government managed ICDS Project are drawing the enhanced salaries, while there is a delay in releasing grants at old rates to the ICDS Project at Tirupati. The RASS has to go in for overdraft to pay the salaries of the staff. In this connection it has to bear the interest burden on the over-draft. RASS, out of its own funds, conducts 8-9 functions every year like Children Day, Women Day, Baby show etc.

RASS is willing to take up new ICDS Project, under certain conditions. The first and foremost condition is release of grants in time and a corpus fund to meet emergency situation. Secondly, there must not be any discrimination between the AWWs of NGO managed Project and Government managed Project. Thirdly, there must be adequate supply of medical kit. Fourthly, there must be a special grant from Government once in five years to meet non-recurring expenses.

Recruitment of Staff

Another problem faced by RASS is in the recruitment of staff. At the time of inception of the Project in 1984, a retired and experienced person was appointed as CDPO. But, the post has remained vacant since 1991 and the Medical Officer of the Project is discharging the functions of CDPO, RASS pays only honorarium to the staff. However, the honorarium more of less matches with the salaries drawn by the staff of the ICDS Projects run by the Government. The RASS cannot provide permanent job to the staff. Therefore, it is difficult to get suitable persons at the higher level. At the lower level, they get some candidates. But, the candidates complain that they will not be made permanent even if they serve for more than 10 years. They are also very unhappy about the Government's discriminating policy in not allowing the AWWs of ICDS Project of Tirupati to write the promotion test for promotion to supervisors' post. As a compensatory measure, RASS has adopted a plan of convergence of services, whereby an AWW earns about Rs.1000 per mounth.

Competition from English Medium Schools

The AWCs at Tirupati have to compete with the English Medium Convent Schools. Even the poor people prefer to send their children to English Medium Schools rather than to AWCs. Most of the parents send their children to AWCs for Pre-School education for 1 to 2 years and then shift them to English Medium Schools. To overcome this problem the AWCs start imparting Pre-School education to the children at the age of two and half years instead of 3 years. The emphasis is more on teaching alphabets and numerals. It is common scene to see children with slates and pencil in their hands at AWCs.

Accommodation

Non-availability of good accommodation for AWCs is one of the problem. The accommodation at AWCs very poor. It is difficult to get a good accommodation in a town like Tirupati with the allotted amount towards rent. It is out of good gesture, some people who are not commercially motivated allow a part of their front room for running AW class. The accommodation is just sufficient to cramp 25 children. There is no place to display charts and keep toys and other material. There is no question of playing ground for children. RASS, out of its own fund has constructed 6 AWCs on Government Land. The condition at these Centres appear to be far better in terms of accommodation, water facility etc. The AWCs are also used as Health Sub-Centre. RASS is willing to construct thatched huts out of its own fund, if Government provides five cents of land per AWC.

Growth Charts

Another problem faced by RASS is the non-availability of growth chart books. It seems growth chart books were supplied in 1987. Most of the AWCs have exhausted them by 1994. Therefore, they are recording the weights of children in registers and no growth charts are maintained.

For SNP ration is distributed based on the recorded weights of the children in the register. It is not clear who should supply growth chart books. RASS expects the Government to supply these books as supplied to other ICPS Projects. Government perhaps expects RASS to purchase out of Contingency Funds. RASS argues that contingency funds are inadequate.

Weighing Scales

Weighing scales with five trousers were supplied in 1984 to all the AWCs. Now most of the trousers are torn. It is not clear who should replace these trousers. Rass is contemplating to replace the torn trousers out of its own funds. RASS feels that Government should provide grants every five years to meet such non-recurring expenditure.

Medicines

Most of the AWCs do not have medicine and medical kit as they have already exhausted the medicine supplied earlier. The District Medical and Health Officer refuses to supply medicine as the project is managed by NGO and not by the Government.

Deccan Development Society

Deccan Development Society, a non-govermmental organisation is running Balwadies in about 30 villages in Zaheerabad Mandal of Medak District in Andhra Predesh. The Balwadies are managed by local Women Group. The Balwadies children are given ambali in the morning, roti or kichidi in the afternoon and guggilu (grams soaked in water) in the evening when the children leave for home (Deccan Development Society, 2000). Thus, children receive nutritious and sumptous food in Balwadies. In contrast, children in Anganwadi Centres of Government managed ICDS Projects in Medak are given upmas with the assistance of CARE. In two projects, there is no SNP component in ICDS program. The Deccan Development Society is motivating villagers and parents to contribute their mite to the feeding program. The response seems to be encouraging (Deccan Development Society 1998). The response to their community Grain Bank Program is also encouraging (Satheesh, 1998 and Raju, 1997). On the other hand, in most of ICDS Projects the cost of SNP component is borne by Government itself. It has been testimated that SNP component accounts for 80% of project cost in ICDS program (Radhakrishna etal, 1998). The Government is seriously contemplating to reduce the cost on this component by involving the community (villagers) in the program. Surprisingly, the response is poor. The Mid-day Meals Program under which 3 Kgs of rice per month is provided to the School-going children free of cost, has negative impact on ICDS program. The parents of anganwadi children expect Government to provide rice to their children and they feel it is unjust to ask them to contribute to the feeding program. Some parents are under the impression that funds are being misappropriated by the officials of ICDS Program.

Comparitive Study of Anganwadis and Balwadis

Medak District in Andhra Pradesh provides an interesting case study – some projects having supplementary feeding programme and others not having it. In a recent study (Indrakant 2002), two projects viz., Gajwel project having supplementary feeding programme and Zaheerabad project not having it, were selected. To enhance the utility of the Study, a few balwadi centres managed by the women self help groups were included in the study. In all, 20 anganwadi centres and 5 balwadi centres spread over 20 villages were selected.

The supplementary feeding accounts for a major share in the ICDS project cost. Hence, there is a need to reform supplementary feeding programme. The practice of contributing one kg of grains by the members of the women sangam and mothers of balwadi children indicate that parents can be motivated to contribute towards supplementary feeding programme. Nearly half of the parents in Gajwel project were willing to contribute Rs.10 per child per month. Elders in some villages, are ready to contribute, in kind, towards supplementary feeding programme. These evidences point out that there is a vast scope to involve people in the programme. No doubt, there are some counter- productive forces operating at the ground level. Therefore, the functionaries of anganwadi centres should motivate the parents/villagers to contribute to supplementary feeding programme. The possibility of involving mothers committee in this task must also be explored.

The practice of having supplementary feeding programme is one project and not having the same programme in the adjacent project without any consideration regarding nutritional status of children in the area leads to many complications and hence, has to be avoided. In short, there is a need and also vast scope for reforming supplementary feeding programme.

The pre-school education makes children active, bold, more social and upgrades their skill. However, the absence of formal education puts them in a disadvantage position. Gradually, the urban culture is being transmitted to rural areas. Nursery and kindergarten schools are coming up in small towns. The well-to-do families from the nearby villages send their children to towns and do not show interest in the functioning of anganwadi centres. Consequently, the strength in anganwadi centre is dwindling. In addition to this, the mid-day meals programme has a negative impact on the ICDS programme as some parents shift their children to primary school to avail the benefit of 3 kgs of free rice.

The introduction of the early child education programme during the afternoon in selected centres is a step in right direction to meet the competition from the private schools. This programme must be expended to all the centres in a phased manner. It also meets the aspiration of parents of children. There is an awareness even among the illiterate parents about the importance of the formal education. Nearly 42% of parents expressed their willingness to contribute on an average Rs.13 per month per child.

The parents gladly welcome the extension of working hours of anganwadi centres as their children would remain in the centre in the afternoon when most of the parents are away in the field. Therefore, early child education programme should be extended to all the centres.

The perception of women beneficiaries towards immunisation programme, supplementary feeding programme and nutritional and heath education programme is gradually undergoing a change. Almost all the pregnant women in the village are immunised. In the absence of government hospitals, they do not hesitate to go to the private doctors. In regard to the supplementary feeding programme, the women beneficiaries did not evince interest when they had to visit daily to the centre. The introduction of take home ration (for 15 days) has brought about a change. Now most of the beneficiaries avail the facilities.

The nutritional and health education programme indirectly benefits all the members of the household. This component has not received attention which it deserves. No doubt, it takes time for the impact of the programme to be felt. The attendance of women beneficiaries at nutritional and health education meeting needs to be improved.

Children evince more interest in playing with the indoor kits. The children learn more and faster through games. The expenditure on playing kits may be enhanced as it directly benefits the children.

A good accomodation is essential for the effective functioning of an anganwadi centre. The functioning of anganwadi centres with own accomodation is relatively better than those functioning in rented accomodation and hence attempts must be made in a phased manner to construct buildings for all the centres. Kitchen garden must be encouraged in centres functioning in own building with compound wall and having bore well facilities.

To protect children from sunstrokes, it is better to suspend pre-school education during summer and provide take-home ration to the children. This will provide some welcome relief to the anganwadi workers and the helpers.

Recent Evidence

The recent exposure of working of some of the NGOs highlight the need for strict vigilance on their working by the Government. Poor familes, who cannot bring up their children, in expectation of bright future for their children are willing to give their children to adoption houses run by NGO's. But some to the NGOs exploit the psycology of the parents to meet their selfish ends and use the children as commodity to be traded to make huge profits. Therefore, NGOs should be accountable to Government and to the people at large.

Scope for the Participation of Voluntary Organisations

The convergence of services will improve the performance of all the Programmes of Projects managed by voluntary organisations. It will make effective use of the existing infrastructure and provide better remuneration to the staff. The convergence of services can be achieved only when NGOs manage the Project. Convergence of services essentially requires dealing with various departments of Central and State Governments on one hand and various National and International Voluntary agencies on the other. It is possible for NGOs to approach the Government for one scheme and a private or voluntary agency for another scheme. The CDPO of Government run ICDS Project cannot approach any private or voluntary agency and it is difficult to interact on her own with other Government departments. On this count NGOs are in a better position to manage ICDS Project.

NGOs can reduce the cost of running ICDS Project by encouraging the preparation of food at local level. The expenses can also be reduced, by purchasing my locally made items like Cupboard, Playing Material etc.

Conclusion

Even today nearly half of the pre-school children in India are undernourished. The problem of malnutrition would continue to be severe during post-reforms period unless Government designs cost-effective nutritional program ICDS program aims to improve nutritional status of women and children. The government managed ICDS Projects cannot reduce their delivery cost due to rigid, and insufficient inter-departmental co-ordination. However, Projects managed by voluntary organisation can reduce their delivery cost and improve their performance on account of convergence of services. Therefore, Government should not hesitate to seek where ever possible the co-operation of voluntary organisations. However, NGOs must be accountable to Government and to the people at large. In short, there is a large scope for participation of voluntary organisations during post-reforms period in implementing cost-effective nutritional security program.

REFERENCES

1. Bhatia, A (2000): Women's Development and NGO's, Rawat Publication, Jaipur and New Delhi.
2. Deccan Development Society (1998): Balwadies or Children's Garden – Report for 1997 – 1998, Hyderabad (Mimeo).
3. Indrakant. S (2002): Efficacy of Integraded Child Development services Programme: A Household Study A Department of Economics Nizam college. Hyderabad (Mimeo).
4. National Family Health Survey (2000): National Family Health Survey – 2; Indiá 1998-99, International Institute for Population Sciences, Mumbai and ORC Macro International, Maryland U.S.A.
5. Radhakrishna, R, S.Indrakant and C.Ravi (1998): India's Integrated Child Devolopment Services Program – Assessment and Options for Reforms, Centre for Economic and Social Studies, Hyderabad (Mimeo).
6. Raju, K.N, K. Hanumanth Rao, K. Santhanam and B. Parameshwar (1997): Evaluation of Public Distribution System through Community Grain Fund, National Institute of Rural Development, Hyderabad (Mimeo).
7. Satheesh, P.V. (1998): How Can We Make PDS Work for poor, Paper presented at Seminar on Food Security Organised by Action-aid, Hyderabad.

14

Impact of Reforms on Labour

Dr. V. B. Kakade*
Nalawade A. S.**

The process of liberalisation, privatisation and globalisation has resulted in various social and economic costs to different sections of the society in different magnitude. The real brunt of the process is felt by the weaker factor in the chain. The experience of different countries implementing the package of structural reforms package shows that the reforms has created adverse impact on the poor and unorganised people. The New Economic Policy was launched in India on the background of foreign exchange crisis is now at the stage of launching second generation of reforms. The experience of the last 12 years can act as torch bearers in order to adopt proper alignment of the policy. The present paper examines the impact of economic reforms on workers in small scale industries with special reference to Kolhapur MIDC of Maharashtra. In the first section broad features of reforms having bearing on industry and labour are presented in a bird eye view manner followed by the methodology used for assessing the impact on the workers in SSI industries. The third section presents the findings of the survey and last section summarizes the impact of NEP on labour in SSI.

Section I: Reform Paradigm

The economic reforms coined as LPG are aimed at twin objectives of stabilisation in the macro economic parameters and restructuring for internal

* Reader, Department of Economics, Shivaji University, Kolhapur.
** Research student, Department of Economics, Shivaji University, Kolhapur.
This paper is presented in the ICSSR Sponsored National Seminar on Social Dimensions of Economic Reforms held in Department of Economics, Shivaji University, Kolhapur during 29-30 Jan 2003.

rigidities and imbalances reflected in growing fiscal deficit. The policy measures includes privatisation, liberalisation and globalisation and diametrically opposite to the earlier policies of control. Hence the NEP is termed as U turn in the policy. The new policy is based on market efficiency in the economic decision making. The market forces are supposed to be superior and efficient in the field of production and distribution. The role of state is also redefined and the private sector has been given the prime role in the economic growth. The term private sector includes both local as well as foreign too.

Stabilisation

- Devaluation of the currency to make exchange rate more realistic,
- Withdrawal of restrictions on imports,
- Reduction in fiscal and balance of payments deficits,
- Removal of all controls on prices, exchange and interest rate,
- Elimination/reduction of all subsidies,
- Introduction of financial structure reforms and free entry of foreign financial institutions,
- Complete autonomy of the central bank to pursue independent monetary policy.

Structural Adjustment

- Decontrol of industries,
- Privatisation of government-owned entities,
- Structural changes in the economy aimed at export-led growth,
- Free entry of foreign capital and technology without any let, hindrance or conditions,
- Free entry and exit of foreign firms including financial and services industries,
- Free cross border movement of capital and other funds,
- Legislative safeguards for protection of intellectual property rights,
- Creation of legal climate for enforcement of legal contracts, private property rights, and free entry and exit of business, industrial and financial firms

Section II

These measures have affected various sectors and sections of the Indian economy. The industry thought these measures as fulfilment of their demands as the policy measures aimed to provide more freedom to the industrial sector. But the industrial sector started demanding the level playing field as it experienced stiff competition from liberal imports. The burden of adjustment was shifted on the shoulders of the workers through wage reduction, casualisation of labour and retrenchment in various forms like VRS. The trade unions also adopted submissive attitude as they also realised that pressing the demands will aggravate the problem. This is reflected in reduction in the strikes. For the present study 300 workers working in Small Scale Industries in Kolhapur MIDC have been selected. These workers sample is drawn from skilled, semi-skilled and unskilled workers. For measuring the impact we observed the changes in wages, employment and nature of work and indebtedness of workers over the period of a decade (1990-91 to 2000-01)

Section III

The impact of reforms is felt by all categories of workers. However the burden of reforms is distributed in a regressive form. The study conducted in this regard covers workers in the small-scale sector will help to understand the impact of reforms on labour. The reform process has reduced the demand for local labour as result of imports of cheap goods and the recession in the industrial sector. The burden of recession is felt by all the sectors but borne by very few as these people are not in a position to shift the burden. The wages, employment, income and expenditure of the workers have been adversely affected. But whether the same trend holds true within the sub categories of workers is an important question. Following tables depict the economic position of workers during the last decade.

The reform process creates two types of impact on the demand for labour

(a) It reduces the total demand for labour as a result of restructuring of industrial sector. The recession and cheap imports also act to strengthen this trend.

Table 1: Nature of Job.

Type	*1990-91*	*% in total*	*95-96*	*% in total*	*00-01*	*% in total*
Skilled	209	14.62561	303	22.98938	333	29.10839
Semi Skilled	255	17.84465	282	21.39605	366	31.99301
Unskilled	965	67.52974	733	55.61457	445	38.8986
Total	1429	100	1318	100	1144	100
%change over period			-7.76767		-13.2018	

Source: Primary Data.

(*b*) Secondly within the total demand for labour the demand for unskilled labour is reduced and the demand foe skilled labour increases.

As result unskilled workers suffer more than skilled workers. These trends are observed in the case of SSI workers under study.

The demand for labour in total went down by 7.7% during 90-90 to 95-96 and the same trend was further accentuated as the demand went down by 13.2% in the next five years. The unemployment rate went up by 71.42% a whopping increase of 14% per annum.

As per the level of skill the demand for labour has shown different rates of changes. In the case of skilled labour the demand went down by 15% while the demand went down of the semi skilled labour by 17%. But the demand for unskilled labour went down by 68% during 1990-95. The fall in demand for skilled, semi skilled and unskilled went down by 21%, 32% and 39% respectively

The regularity of employment is another important factor which determines the income of the worker. The process of economic reforms has lead to increase in casual workers and tendency of outsourcing has increased in the large industries. In the case of SSI the proportion of permanent workers is very small. The reform process is expected to reduce the permanent workers to the possible extent. The trend regarding this tendency is presented in the following table.

Table 2: Regularity of Employment.

Type	*1990-91*	*% in total*	*95-96*	*% in total*	*00-01*	*% in total*
Regular	32	10.56106	35	11.55116	39	12.87129
Temporary	271	89.43894	268	88.44884	264	87.12871
Total	**303**	**100**	**303**	**100**	**303**	**100**

Source: As per table 1.

The SSI sector's labour composition shows that it employs only 10 to 12 % of labour in permanent form while the remaining is on the temporary basis having nearly 88 to 90%. The reform process has not made any significant change in this composition.

The working days determine the income of the worker. The SSI sector can adjust the working days. This kind of flexibility is major demand even of the large industrial sector in the name flexibility in labour market. The following table depicts the working days of the sample SSI workers.

Table 3: Working Days of SSI Workers.

Type	*1990-91*	*95-96*	*00-01*
Skilled	272.35	274.22	270.68
Semi Skilled	259.31	259.87	258.36
Unskilled	253.91	242.21	195.76
Total	**258.31**	**254.55**	**237.52**

Source: As per table 1.

The working days for workers increases with increase in their skill. The employer tries to retain the skilled worker for longer duration for his self interest.

The number of days employed for the workers declined from 258 to 237 during the period under study. The decline in working days is highest for the unskilled workers (254 to 195) followed by semiskilled workers (259 to 258) and for skilled workers it was a decline from 272 to 271 days.

Reforms and Wages

The reduction in demand for labour creates a downward pressure on the wages of the workers. The monetary wage may increase but the price rise may take away the benefits of such wage rise. The net impact on workers real wages will be negative. The trend in case of nominal and real wages for the sample workers is presented in the following table.

Table 4: Nominal and Real Wages.

Type	*1990-91 Wages (in Rs)*	*00-01 Wages (in Rs)*	*% change*
Skilled (Current)	1583	3595	127.1004
(Real)	1583	1455.466	-8.0565
Semi Unskilled (Current)	1086	2658	144.7514
(Real)	1086	1076.113	-0.91037
Unskilled (Current)	686	1742	153.9359
(Real)	686	705.2632	2.808041
Total (Current)	933	2570	175.4555
Real	933	1040.486	11.52045

Source: AS per table 1.

Note: For real wages CPI deflator is used.

In the table no. 4 the impact of reforms o the wages is measured. We get following conclusions from it.

1. In the reform period the nominal wages went up from Rs.933 to Rs.2570 in the decade under study. This means in nominal terms the wages went up by 175.45%. This gives an average growth in wages 17.5%. However the real wages had shown a change of 11.52 resulting in 1.15% growth in real wages.
2. The wages of skilled workers went from Rs.686 to Rs.1742 during reform decade showing an increase of 154% in nominal terms. But the real wages came down by 8%. This shows that the reform process in terms of real wage affected adversely on skilled workers.
3. The wages of semi-skilled workers went from Rs.1086 to Rs.2658 during reform decade showing an increase of 145% in nominal terms. But the real wages came down by 0.98%. This shows that the reform process in terms of real wage affected adversely on semi-skilled workers also. However the magnitude is less compared to skilled workers.
4. The wages of unskilled workers went from Rs.1583 to Rs.3595 during reform decade showing an increase of 127% in nominal terms. The real wages went up by 2.8%. This shows that the reform process in terms of wages affected positively on un- skilled workers.

The economic reform affected the wages of the workers adversely. The adverse impact of reforms shows direct co-relation between the skill and the impact. The unskilled workers were less affected compared to their counterparts. This may be due to very low wages of unskilled wages where there is no scope for further reduction.

Living Standard and Reforms

The standard of living as measured in terms of consumption expenditure helps to understand the adverse impact on workers' family. In the following table the change in consumption expenditure is presented.

The change in the expenditure of the SSI workers in sample shows that the aggregate workers' expenditure (Total) went up from Rs.780 to 1964 showing an increase of 252% in nominal terms and merely 1.94% in real terms. This gives annual increase in consumption expenditure by 25.2% in nominal terms and 0.19% in real terms.

The expenditure of skilled workers shows an increase of 174% over the decade in nominal terms but in real terms it declined by 29%. The reforms have taken some share from the workers' family basket.

Table 5: Consumption Expenditure.

(in Rs)

Type	*1990-91 Expenditure*	*00-01 Expenditure*	*91-01 % Change*
Skilled	1398	2439	174.4635
(Real Expenditure)	1398	987.4494	-29.367
Semi Skilled	901	2127	236.071
(Real Expenditure)	901	861.1336	-4.42468
Unskilled	554	1478	266.787
(Real Expenditure)	554	598.3806	8.010933
Total	780	1964	251.7949
(Real Expenditure)	780	795.1417	1.941244

Source: As per table 1.

In the case of expenditure of semi-skilled workers shows an increase of 236% over the decade in nominal terms but in real terms it declined by 4.42%. The reforms have taken some share from the workers' family basket for semi-skilled workers too.

In the case of expenditure of un-skilled workers shows an increase of 267% over the decade in nominal terms and in real terms by 8%.

Indebtedness of Workers

The fall in employment and reduction in real wages push the workers under the debt. The increase in indebtedness shows the deterioration in the economic condition of the workers. The data in the following table regarding the indebtedness of the sample workers is presented.

Table 6: Indebtedness of Workers.

Type	*1990-91*	*2000-01*	*% Change*
Skilled	Rs. 13362	Rs. 13318	-0.32929
Semi Skilled	Rs. 13500	Rs. 16016	18.63704
Unskilled	Rs. 9460	Rs. 17616	86.21564
Total	**Rs. 11136**	**Rs. 15693**	**40.92134**

Source: As per table 1.

The indebtedness of the workers during the reforms period shows following trends:

1. The overall indebtedness of the workers went up from Rs.11136 to Rs.15693 which shows an increase of 40%.

2. The indebtedness of the skilled workers shows a marginal decline of 0.32%/. However the indebtedness Rs.13300 in absolute terms remains as it was in 1990.
3. For semi-skilled workers the indebtedness went up from Rs.13500 to 16016 which means an increase of 18.63%. in indebtedness.
4. The indebtedness of unskilled workers went up from Rs.11136 to Rs.15693 showing an increase of 40.93%.
5. The indebtedness of the workers had increased over the reform period and the increase shows inverse relation between the skill and indebtedness.

Section IV

The economic reforms were expected to create certain adverse impact on the workers. Hence the concept of safety net and the human face to the reforms were given discussed. The process of reforms affected adversely the workers in the SSI sector for there is no formal mechanism of protection. The summary of the findings of the present study helps to highlight the trend.

1. The demand for labour shifted from unskilled workers to skilled workers during the period under study. The unskilled workers who tried to acquire the skill were succeeded in maintaining their job while other were forced to leave the job.
2. The regularity of job in terms of permanent workers as proportion to total workers shows a positive trend but it is very weak. The temporary workers remain the major section of the SSI workers.(87%)
3. The working days of all the workers were reduced during the period under study. The reduction in working days is higher for the unskilled workers.
4. The economic reforms affected the wages of the workers adversely. The adverse impact of reforms shows direct co-relation between the skill and the impact. The unskilled workers were less affected compared to their counterparts. This may be due to very low wages of unskilled wages where there is no scope for further reduction.
5. The expenditure of the SSI workers shows that the aggregate workers' expenditure (Total) went up from Rs.780 to 1964 showing an increase of 252% in nominal terms and merely 1.94% in real terms. This gives annual increase in consumption expenditure by 25.2% in nominal terms and 0.19% in real terms.

6. The indebtedness of the workers had increased over the reform period and the increase shows inverse relation between the skill and indebtedness.

7. The reform process in nutshell affected the SSI workers in terms of employment and wages which in turn resulted into increase in indebtedness of the workers. The absence of any social security or assistance has pushed the workers in poverty and malnutrition. This calls for effective state intervention in terms of social security net. The reform has generated the demand for skilled workers at the cost of unskilled workers.

15

Changing Social Dimensions and Economic Development of the Selected Countries of the World

Dr. R.S. Gadage*

Introduction

Structural reforms introduced in various countries of the world have already passed the first phase of ten years and entered in the phase of second generation reforms, but the reforms did not involve each level of income group. In 1950's and 1960's emphasis was given to stages of economic growth. The structuralist tends to emphasis external and internal constraints on economic development. Then emphasis was placed on policies needed to reduce poverty unemployment and economic inequalities. The recent approach emphasis combination of economic development of underdevelopment. The growth in GNP or GDP did not correspond the non-economic social indicators like gains in literacy, schooling, health, conditions and other access of social services. Some of the third world countries achieved the economic growth but levels of living remain unchanged. High GNP during 1960-1970 shows no improvement in bottom 40 per cent of population. Simultaneously 2 billion of the world are in the clutches of poverty (Denis Goulet). Even 3 per cent of economic growth can achieve social development, but the experience shows that 5 to 6 per cent of growth failed to achieve the desired objectives as it was proved in trickle down effect.

* Chintamanrao College of Commerce, Sangli–416415
This paper is presented in the ICSSR sponsored National Seminar on Social Dimensions of Economic Reforms held in Department of Economics, Shivaji University, Kolhapur during 29-30 January 2003.

Along with economic sector, social sector, which involves education, health and nutrition is the key component for well being of the society. Earlier A.O. Harshman emphasised unbalancing of the economy with social overhead capital (SOC). A large investment in SOC will encourage private investment later directly productive activities. The UNDP defines HRD approach as a process of enlarging peoples' choices. Again the concept encompasses employment, co-operation, equity in basic capabilities and opportunities, sustainability and the security. People occupy centre stage and measures such as education, health and nutrition are emphasised for their intrinsic value and their role enhancing the basic capabilities of the people. The emergence of concept can also be traced by Amartya Sen who defined standard of living (1985-87) in terms of functioning and capabilities rather than in terms of commodity possessions. Acquisition of education, health, nutrition and other services was also emphasised by T.W. Schultz (1961), Jocob Vinar (1963) and A.K. Sen (1966). In the process of physical development, non physical development plays an important role. Hence, expenditure on social sector enhances the productivity. Economic growth in India and other parts in the world reveals that there is no automatic link between growth and human development. The development requires reduction in unemployment, poverty and participation in growth and long run sustainability. These welfare components can be achieved through public policy by emphasising the social sectors. The state should act as service provider rather than facilitator because social inequalities are not allowing equitable sharing of public goods. Policy initiatives of the state must protect all the groups. The growth of social sector along with economic sector helps to build strong democracy, strong economy, just and humane society. Further social sector has strong backward and forward linkage effects with economic sector. Thus, process should envisage a balanced pattern of growth in both the sectors. Hence all the third world should make mandatory to develop the social sector as a state responsibility.

Investment in Social Sector

As stated earlier, public expenditure on social sectors enhances the socio-economic development. In fact, it depends on annual growth of GNP, GNP PCI, and decision to spend on social sector. The index of development based on good number of indicator provides satisfactory measures of social and personal welfare. Economists have used comprehensive indices of development by assigning weights to various indicators of development, for example, Evertt E. Hagen (1962) eleven indicators, Donald H. Niewiaroski (1965) fourteen indicators, UNIRSD (1970) sixteen indicators, and Irma Andlmen and Enythia Taft and Morris (1967) forty-one indicators. Purposely five countries are selected from high, medium and low human development countries with few social indicators of developments.

Achievements

High and medium human development countries achieved remarkable progress in the non-material development despite type of socio-economic reforms. Table No. 1 indicates that, HDI, GNP annual growth, GNP PCI, PCI rank, and public expenditure on education and health as per cent of GNP and GDP. In high human development countries, GNP annual growth, GNP PCI growth was in the range of 6.90 to 8.70 & 4.4 to 7.30 per cent except of Uruguay and Mexico. But public Expenditure in Uruguay and Mexico on Education was 3.20 and 4.90 as a per cent of GNP and on health 1.90 and 2.80 per cent of GDP respectively. As a result these countries were placed at better HDI rank. Simultaneously these countries maintained GNP PCI ranks except Thailand. Whereas, in low human developed countries GNP annual Growth was in the range of 4.80 to 7.7 per cent in 1998–99. These countries maintained better GNP growth but GNP PCI rank was above 162. The public expenditure on education and health as a per cent of GNP and GDP was in the range of 2 to 3 per cent and 0.6 to 1.8 per cent respectively. High GNP, GNP PCI and public expenditure on education and health results into remarkable progress in literacy, infant mortality rate, and poverty in high human developed countries.

Tables 2 and 3 indicate that, population below poverty line, life expectancy at birth and infant mortality rate. In high and human developed countries as per international norm $1 a day absolute poverty was < 2 per cent. Whereas, in low human developed countries it was around 40 per cent. The life expectancy in high human developed countries was 75 years and in low human developed countries it was 60 years in 2000. The infant mortality was substantially reduced from 88 to 7 in high human developed countries. Whereas, in low human developed countries it was reduced slowly from 168 to 99 per thousands during 1960 to 2000.

Table No. 4 indicates Adult literacy rate and population with access of education, health services, safe water and sanitation. Access of these facilities has significant impact on the socio-economic development of the countries. The literacy rate was more than 95 per cent in high human development countries, but it was below 50 per cent in low human development countries. High human development countries (1990-95) have better access of these facilities for example. Korea Rep., Uruguay, Mexico, Thailand, Malaysia, the range of access of these facilities were, health services 80 to 100, safe water 75 to 93, sanitation 50 to 100 per cent. In medium human development countries like Brazil, Algeria, Tunisia, Srilanka, Morocco, the access range of services were health, 70 to 98 safe water 53 to 99, sanitation, 41 to 96 per

Table 1: I HDI, GNP, GNP, PC Annual Ranks and Public Expenditures on Education, Health, in Selected Countries.

Countries	*HDI*			*GNP*	*Annual growth rate*	*Gnp PCI annual growth*			*GNP rank*	*PCI rank*	*Education as a % of GNP*				*Health as % of GDP*		*SSB Exp.% of GDP*
	1996	*98*	*2*	*80–95*	*98–99*	*65–80*	*80–95*	*98–99*	*98–99*	*98–99*	*80*	*85–87*	*92*	*97*	*90*	*90–98*	*93*
H.H.D.	–	–	–	3.2	–	4.8	1.4	–	–	–	–	–	4.2	–	2	–	–
Korea Rep.	29	30	27	8.7	11	7.3	7.5	10.1	13	51	3.7	3.8	4.2	3.7	2.7	2.5	2.3
Uruguay	32	38	40	– 0.4	– 3.4	2.5	– 0.6	– 4.1	65	63	2.3	3.2	2.8	3.2	2.5	1.9	14.8
Mexico	48	49	54	1.2	4.1	3.6	– 0.9	2.4	12	71	4.7	3.5	4.9	4.9	1.7	2.8	–
Thailand	52	59	70	7.9	4.9	4.4	6.3	4.1	31	102	3.4	3.4	4	4.8	1.1	1.7	0.1
Malaysia	53	60	59	6.9	4.3	4.7	4	1.9	41	82	6	6.9	5.5	4.9	1.3	1.3	2.3
M.H.D.	–	–	–	4.9	2.6	3.8	3.1	2.1	–	–	–	–	3.9	–	2.3	–	–
ex–China	–	–	96	3	7.2	3.2	0.6	6.3	7	140	2.5	2.3	4.7	2.3	2.3	2	–
Brazil	58	62	73	1.4	– 2	6.3	0.4	– 3.2	8	70	3.6	4.7	4.6	5.1	2.8	3.4	–
Algeria	69	82	106	1.8	2.8	4.2	0.9	1.3	52	115	7.8	9.8	8.1	5.1	5.4	3.3	–
Tunisia	78	83	97	3.6	6.2	4.7	1.2	4.9	63	101	5.4	6.2	6.1	7.7	3.3	3.3	4.1
Sri Lanka	89	90	89	4.6	3.8	2.8	3.2	2.7	76	117	2.7	2.7	3.3	3.4	1.8	1.4	2.5
Morocco	123	125	123	2.8	0.6	2.7	0.7	– 1	57	126	6.1	6.2	5.8	5.3	0.9	1.3	1.8
L H.D.	–	–	–	4.4	2.7	1.4	2.4	1.3	–	–	–	–	3.5		1.5	–	–
ex. India	–	–	–	5.3	6.9	1.5	3.2	–	11	162	2.8	3.2	3.1	3.2	1.3	0.6	0.3
Ghana	129	133	129	2.8	4.8	– 0.8	– 0.3	2.1	96	164	3.1	3.4	3.1	4	1.7	1.8	0.1
India	135	139	124	5.3	6.9	1.5	3.2	4.9	11	162	2.8	3.2	3.1	3.2	1.3	0.6	0.3

(Table Contd...)

Table 1: (Contd...)

Countries	*HDI*			*GNP*	*Annual growth rate*	*Gnp PCI annual growth*			*GNP rank*	*PCI rank*	*Education as a % of GNP*			*Health as % of GDP*		*SSB Exp.% of GDP*	
	1996	*98*	*2*	*80–95*	*98–99*	*65–80*	*80–95*	*98–99*	*98–99*	*98–99*	*80*	*85–87*	*92*	*97*	*90*	*90–98*	*93*
Bangladesh	143	147	145	4.5	5	– 0.3	2.2	3.3	50	167	1.5	1.4	2.3	2.2	1.4	1.6	–
Nepal	151	152	142	4.9	4.6		2.2	2.2	109	194	1.8	2.2	2.9	3.2	2.2	1.3	–
Uganda	155	160	150	–	7.7	– 2.2		4.8	99	176	1.2	3.5	2	2.6	1.6	1.8	–
All Developed	–	–	–	4.1	3	2.1	–	–	–	–	–	–	3.9	3.3	2	1.3	–
Least Developed Countries	–	–	–	2.1	4.4	0.4	–0.4	2.5	–	–	–	–	3	4.1	1.8	1.9	–
Ind. Countries	–	–	–	2.2	–	2.2	–	–	–	–	–	–	5.4	5.4	2.4	6.2	–
World	–	–	–	2.6	2.7	2.6	–	1.3	–	–	–	–	5.1	4.8	–	2.5	–

Source: Human Development Reports 1996, 1998, 2001.

Note: H.H.D.: High Human Development M.H.D.: Medium Human Development L.H.D.: Low Human Development S.D. B.: Social Security Benefit Expenditure.

Table 2: Population Below Poverty Line in Selected Countries.

Countries	National Poverty Line							International Poverty lines Population poverty gap below $1 a day%	at $1a day %	National Poverty Line 1987--2000
	Year	Rural	Urban	Year	Rural	Urban	Year			
H.H.D.										–
Korea Rep.							1993	<2	<0.5	
Uruguay							1989	<2	<0.5	–
Mexico	1988	R + U 10.1	–	–	–	–	1995	17.9	6.1	10.1
Thailand	1990	R + U 18.0		1992	15.5	10.2	1998	<2	<0.5	13.1
Malaysia	1973	55.3	48.8	1987	24.7	7.3	–	–	–	15.5
M.H.D.	–	–	–	–	–	–				–
ex–China	1978	33.0	4.4	1998	4.6	<1	1998	18.5	4.2	4.6
Brazil	1990	32.6	13.1	1995	41.5	13.2	1997	5.1	1.3	17.4
Algeria	1988	16.6	7.3	1995	30.3	14.7	1995	<2	<0.5	22.6
Tunisia	1985	29.2	12.0	1990	21.6	8.9	1990	<2	<0.5	14.1
Sri Lanka	1985-86	45.5	26.8	1990-91	38.1	28.4	1995	6.6	1.0	25.0
Morocco	1984-85	32.7	17.3	1998-99	27.2	12.0	1990-91	<2	<0.5	19.0
L.H.D.	–	–	–	–	–	–	–	–	–	–
ex. India	–	–	–	–	–	–	–	–	–	–
Ghana	1987-88	41.9	27.4	1991-92	33.9	26.5	–	–	–	31.4
India	1957-58	52.2	47.8	1997	34.2	27.9	1997	44.2	12.0	35.0
Bangladesh	1991-92	46.0	23.3	1995-96	39.8	14.3	1996	29.1	5.9	35.6
Nepal	1995-96	44.0	23.0	–	–	–	1995	37.7	9.7	42.0
Uganda	1992	59.4	29.4	1997	48.2	16.3	1992	36.7	11.4	55.0

Source: Human Development Reports 1996, 1998, 2001, 2003.

Note: H.H.D.: High Human Development M.H.D.: Medium Human Development L.H.D.: Low Human Development.

Table 3: Life Expectancy at Birth and Infant Mortality Rate per 1000 in Selected Countries.

	Life Expectancy at birth						*Infant mortality rate per 1000*					
Countries	*1960*	*1970-75*	*1980*	*1988*	*1993*	*2000*	*1960*	*1970*	*1980*	*1993*	*1998*	*2000*
H.H.D.	–	–	–	–	73.8	–	88	25	–	28	–	7
Korea Rep.	54	62.6	65	70	71.3	74.9	85	43	34	11	11	5
Uruguay	68	68.7	71	72	72.6	74.4	51	48	40	20	19	14
Mexico	58	62.4	65	69	71.6	72.6	92	79	56	35	35	25
Thailand	52	69.5	63	65	69.2	70.2	103	74	55	36	33	25
Malaysia	53	63.0	64	70	70.9	72.5	73	46	31	13	12	8
M.H.D.	–	–	–	–	67.0	–	143	100	–	48	–	46
ex–China	–	63.2	64	70	68.6	70.5	–	85	56	–	36	32
Brazil	55	59.5	63	65	66.5	67.7	116	95	77	57		32
Algeria	47	54.5	56	64	67.3	69.6	168	143	118	54	40	50
Tunisia	48	55.6	60	66	68.0	70.2	159	135	90	43	32	22
Sri Lanka	62	65.1	66	71	72.0	72.1	71	65	44	17	18	17
Morocco	47	52.9	56	61	63.6	67.6	163	119	107	67	61	41
L.H.D.	–	–	–	–	56.0	–	168	141	–	92		99
ex. India	43	50.3	52	58	60.7	–	–	–	–	–		69
Ghana	40	59.9	49	54	56.2	56.8	132	112	103	80	96	58
India	43	50.3	52	58	60.7	63.3	165	127	123	81	83	69
Bangladesh	37	44.9	46	51	55.9	59.4	156	145	136	106	96	54
Nepal	38	43.3	44	51	53.8	58.6	187	165	150	98	107	72
Uganda	44	46.4	54	48	44.7	44.0	133	110	97	115	170	81
All developed Countries	–	–	–	–	61.5	–	150	108	–	70	–	61
Least developed	–	–	–	–	51.0	–	173	148	–	110	–	98
Ind. Countries	–	–	–	–	74.3	–	–	–	–	–	–	–
World	–	–	–	–	63.0	–	–	96	–	–	75	56

Source: Human Development Reports 1996, 1998, 2001.
Note: H.H.D.: High Human Development M.H.D.: Medium Human Development L.H.D.: Low Human Development

cent. Whereas in low human development countries poor access was found for example. Ghana, India, Bangladesh, Nepal, Uganda the access of health services, safe water and sanitation was in the range of 45 to 85, 34 to 97, 21 to 57 respectively.

Table 4: Percent of Adult Literacy Rate and Percent of Population with Access of Health Services, Safe Water and Sanitation in Selected Countries.

Courntries	*% of adult literacy rate*				*% of population with access of health services, safe water and sanitation*					
	1960	*1977*	*1993*	*2000*	*1990-95*	*1990-95*	*1990-95*	*2000*	*2001*	*1999*
H.H.D.	–	–	–	–	83	84	71	–	—	
Korea Rep.	–	93	4	97.8	100	93	100	95-100	92	63
Uruguay	–	94	7	97.7	82	75	61	50-79	98	95
Mexico	65	81	11	91.4	78	83	50	80-94	86	73
Thailand	68	84	7	95.5	90	86	74	95-100	80	96
Malaysia	53	–	18	87.5	–	78	94	50-79	–	–
M.H.D.	–	–	–	–	89	69	40	–80-94	81	52
ex-China	–	66	25	84.1	–	–	–	–	75	38
Brazil	65	76	16	85.2	–	87	83	0-49	87	77
Algeria	10	35	46	66.7	98	79	77	95-100	94	73
Tunisia	16	62	42	71.0	90	99	96	50-79	–	–
Sri Lanka	75	85	12	91.6	93	53	61	95-100	83	83
Morocco	14	28	66	48.9	70	55	41	50-79	82	75
L.H.D.	–	–	–	–	70	68	32	–	67	50
ex. India	–	–	–	–	–	–	–	–	88	31
Ghana	27	–	40	71.5	60	56	42	0.49	64	63
India	28	36	57	·57.2	85	81	29	0.49	88	31
Bangladesh	22	26	71	41.3	45	97	34	50.79	97	53
Nepal	9	19	78	41.8	–	46	21	0.49	81	27
Uganda	35	48	46	67.1	49	34	57	50.79	50	75
All developed-Countries	–	–	–	73.7	80	70	39	–	78	52
Least developed Countries	–	–	–	52.8	50	52	31	–	63	45
Ind. Countries	–	–	–	–	–	–	–	–	–	–
World	–	–	32	–	–	–	–	–	81	56

Source: Human Development Reports 1996, 1998, 2001.

Note: H.H.D.: High Human Development M.H.D.: Medium Human Development L.H.D.: Low Human Development

Conclusion

The quality and structure of growth needs more attention to human development and long run sustainability. Policy makers should avoid the growth i.e. jobless, voiceless, ruthless and futureless. Higher investment in social sector is essential for achievement of education, health, nutrition, political participation and human security. Human development is much deeper that any other composite index. Faster economic growth has capacity to finance for social sector if the role of public policy plays an important role. A.K. Sen emphasised the Government intervention in social sector is crucial. The government in poor countries should emphasize the social expenditure to meet the societal goals in the areas of education and health irrespective of economic growth.

The social sector development brings the income equality, which creates condition of self-sustaining growth and also helps to reduce poverty, but in 1980s and 1990s LDCs faced the debt crisis and also implementation of structural adjustment programs affected public expenditure retrenchment, which also affected the slow development of social sectors. After 1990, a change in economic policy at global level has led to slow down of social sector development. Further LDCs are also characterised by low PCI GNP and high population growth as well as low gross domestic savings and investment. Therefore LDCs largely depend on foreign aid. Now third world countries are trapped into debt crisis and more than a fifth of their annual budget has spent on debt service in 1990. In order to achieve social sector development transfer to income is needed who bypassed growth with efficient and dedicated administration. Country should also require commitment to fundamental changes in domestic policies and social development priorities.

REFERENCES

1. Human Development Reports 1996, 1998, 2000, 2001.
2. Employment New 6-12 April 2002.

16

WTO and Human Rights–Issues and Remedies

Dr. P. Bhuvaneswari*

Introduction

International Law was solely concerned with States in the classical period which was influenced by the theory of State Sovereignty. The view was based that only States create rules in International Law and as such rules are valid for them alone. Thus, no place was left for the individuals, and, therefore, they had no significance from the International law point of view. Individuals were related to one state through the bond of citizenship or nationality. If an injury was caused to an individual it was the State (to which the individual belonged) alone owed the responsibility under International Law to another State. The individuals concerned not as rights in International law enjoyed rights in questions but as rights derived from national law.[1]

Human rights are no doubt the inherent rights of a man. According to BOSANQUET, "A right is a claim recognised by society and enforced by the State." EARNEST BARKER says "Any particular right which we have, is a capacity of enjoying some particular status or employing some particular power of action, which has secured and guaranteed to me by law" A perusal of the above definitions of rights shows that there are certain inherent characteristics of rights. The demand of an individual becomes a right only after it is accepted by other members of the society and recognised by the State.[2] The conditions of good life and without them the human personality cannot develop. Rights are not absolute and are subject to reasonable

* Lecturer, PSG College of Arts and Science, Coimbatore 641 014.

restrictions in the larger interest of the society. A state does not create rights; it merely recognizes them. A state is known by the rights it enjoys.

The United Nations System divides human rights into two kinds. 1. Civil and Political Rights and 2. Economic, Social and cultural rights. Civil rights or liberties are referred to those rights which are related to the protection of the right to life and personal liberty political rights may be referred to those rights may be referred to those rights which allow a person to participate in the Government of a State. Economic, social and cultural rights are related to the guarantee of minimum necessities of the life to human being right to adequate food, clothing, housing and adequate standard of living and freedom from hunger, right to work, right to social security, right to physical and mental health and right to education are included in this category of rights.

WTO and Human Rights

Globalisation is essentially a process of interaction and negotiation involving multiple powers. This process should not lead to the overpowering primacy of human rights and creation of primacy of the so-called "Law of the market". This holds for developed countries as much as developing countries. During the UN conference on Human Rights held at Vienna in 1993[3], it was clearly stated that no argument, not even that of development, could justify a restriction of rights and freedoms. The so-called imperatives of growth can under no circumstances legitimate the failure of states to comply with their international obligations in the field of human rights. Incidently, all indicators tend to show that economic mechanisms are more efficient when human rights (be it civil and political rights, or economic, social and cultural rights) are respected and protected.

The UN declaration in 1986 states "The human being is at the center of development." It further stated that markets are not the touchstone of human development....... Globalisation should serve individuals and not just profits." Inequalities and situations of chronic underdevelopment, new forms of massive violations of human rights require that the process of liberalisation be controlled and subordinated to rule of law.

The following will clearly indicate inequalities:

- According to World Bank, the average annual individual income worldwide are spread on a scale from 1 to 400, with Ethiopia, Mozambique and Rwanda at the bottom and Switzerland on top: which means that the average daily income of Swiss equals the average annual income of an Ethiopian.

- According to UNDP, the share of the world's poorest 20% went from 2.4% of the world's total income in 1960 to 1.1% in 1994: conversely, the share of the wealthiest 20% went from 69% to 86% over the same period. This means that the inequality is increasing.
- UNCTAD estimates that the least-developed countries will lose between 163 and 265 millions US$ in order to finance their alimentary imports. Free trade has led to progressive dismantlement of the Welfare State, which in turn has entailed the increase of inequalities within developed countries.

Globalisation can hence be said to be unbalanced process: if some countries have benefited from the growth in world trade, some others have become increasingly marginalised. One cannot leave liberalisation in the sole hands of corporate entities-when one considers that the 10 largest transnational companies holds assets worth three times the total GDP of the poorest countries (excluding China and India). The legitimacy of the WTO hinges on its fully integrating the goal of human rights and sustainable development for all. The WTO has concentrated on an extremely narrow mandate of liberalising trade, with no attention given to the broader social, economic and political context. It has not weighed the potential negative impact its policies on human rights. In its present form, the international system of regulation tends to hold growth, with trade as its kernel, as sole criterion for economic development. It is true that trade can help improve the situation of populations in some countries-there is a major risk of seeing human rights neglected and leveled down.

The Universal Declaration of Human Rights (UDHR)

The Universal Declaration of Human Rights (UDHR) laid down the rights to human beings under the UN charter. Right to promote and protect human rights its essential for the prevention of violations of human rights. In order to provide this right to individuals and other groups in the State Assembly[4] on December 9, 1998, on the recommendation of the Economic and Social Council[5] adopted a resolution entitled: "Declaration on the Right and Responsibility of Individuals, Groups and organs of Society to promote and protect universally Recognised Human Right and Fundamental Freedoms.

The last paragraph of its preamble, the UDHR refers to itself as 'a common standard of achievement for all peoples and all nations, to the end that every individual and every organ of society (...) shall strive to secure their universal and effective recognition and observance."[6] This clearly means that human rights promotion is not confined to governments only. This is applicable to multilateral institutions as well as to transnational corporations.

The UDHR prevails over any trade agreement and that it is for every WTO Member State as well as to that institution as such, to observe the fundamental principles of human rights-and even promote their development.

Every country is entitled to take any measures required for the protection of its public order and public morals. Article XX of GATT and Article XIV of GATS allows protection of public morals of public order and of human and vegetal life. Furthermore, both GATT and GATS provide any member may take any action in pursuance of its obligations under the United National Charter for the maintenance of international peace and security.

Agreements under WTO

The agreements that were adopted under WTO undermine are human rights. The rights under threat include the right to sustainable development, the right to health, the right to education, the right to information, the right to culture, labor rights and the right to make use of natural resources.

The General Agreement on Trade in Services (GATS)

The share of services in international trade keeps growing. This has the fundamental principles governing goods trade (most favoured nation clause, national treatment, transparent trade policies). But it does not cover the whole range of services for instance audio-visual services were left out. The health and education (public service) are not of a commercial nature. Privatising public goods entails a number of serious dangers, as private-sector entities are oriented to their own particular interests, and are therefore unable to guarantee the fundamental rights attached to them. Thus, a State where public and private health systems coexist might be forced into complete liberalisation of its market.

The fourth mode of services supply (human flows) remains largely out of bounds, owing to opposition from developed countries. One can only deplore the hypocrisy and inconsistency of these countries, which apply the principles of free trade according to their own limited interests, but fail to push the logic of liberalisation one step further and extend it to free movement of individuals.

The Agreement over Trade-related aspects of International Property Rights (TRIPS)

Intellectual property rights were first raised, as an issue in 1986. The idea was to restrain trade in counterfeit products and for trade liberalisation to go hand in hand with reinforced controls over technology. The TRIPs agreement came into force in 1995 and sets minimum standard on patents, royalties, trade names and trade secrets. Since all these originate in developed countries, which are more stringent than those of developing countries (where agriculture or pharmaceutical products are often left out). As a result, TRIPs rules and regulations pose more dangers to developing countries than to any other, as industrial countries hold 97% of the world's patents, and multinational corporations, just under 90% of the total. This means that large groups will enjoy complete domination in areas involving fundamental rights. Now, the pursuit of short-term profitability poses serious threats to biodiversity, biological safety, health rights and individual fulfillment of vital needs. More specifically, TRIPs entails one particular, direct threat on health rights; as its provisions allow for the patenting not just of manufacturing methods, but also of the products themselves, developing countries may be denied that new technologies which they might have accessed through adjustments and changes in generic drugs at markedly lower costs than original brands.

The Agreement on Technical Barriers to Trade (TBT)

This agreement came into force in 1995 and entails serious dangers for human rights, notably because it may force public authorities to ratchet rights protection down to the lowest existing level. TBT Article 2.2 prevents governments from raising unnecessary barriers to trade. To this end, governments must make sure that technical regulations 'are not more trade-restrictive than necessary to fulfill a legitimate objective."

Any initiative aimed at the protection or the promotion of universally recognised human rights can only be deemed to be a "legitimate objective", rather than a technical barrier to trade. The Freedom is calling on the WTO, its various committees and its dispute settlement body to allow for a broad interpretation of TBT Article 2.2, in order to further genuine observance and implementation of human rights in member countries.

Recommendations

1. In view of its superior standing in the international legal framework, the Universal Declaration of Human Rights (UDHR) prevails over any trade agreement and on every WTO member state, as well as to that institution as such to observe the fundamental principles of human rights. A need to introduce "human rights clause" in the preamble of each of the Marrakech Agreements that would lay down the principle of unconditional observance of the international human rights standards included in the UDHR.
2. In order to subordinate the WTO to the principles set out in the United Nations Charter, the Universal Declaration of Human Rights,

the WTO must be brought into the United Nations system as a specialised agency.

3. Since its ambit extends beyond the strict boundaries of trade issues, the WTO must develop cooperation with other international institutions, with a view to harmonising international rules and regulations.
4. The members should open the fourth mode, in order to include persons in the scope of the free movement granted to goods and services.
5. Within the WTO, of a permanent body must be created. That would report to the General Council and maintain a close working relationship with the ILO. ILO to be granted observer status with the WTO.

Conclusion

Development is not to be measured against only, but there should be full observance of all human rights in an integral part of it. Trade liberalisation and economic growth can in no way to serve to justify human rights violations. It is therefore crucial that the WTO helps create the fair conditions without which international trade is bound to lose all legitimacy, and integrates the frame defined by the UN charter, aiming at the full realisation of indivisible and interdependent human rights for all.

REFERENCES

1. David Vogel, "Social Regulations as Tray Barriers" The Brookings Review, Winter 1998.
2. Griffin, Ricky and Michael Pustay, International Business: A Managerial Perspective, New York: Addison–Wesley Publishing Company, 1996.
3. Jackson, John H. The World Trading System: Law and Policy of International Economic Relation (London: MIT Press, 1997)
4. John Humphery, "No Distant Millennium: The International of Human Rights" (Paris, Unesco, 1989)

FOOT NOTES

1. Oppenheim (1992): 'International Law', Volume. 1 Ninth Edition, p.847.
2. George. H. Sabine (1952): 'A History of Political Theory'. Oxford and JBH Publishing Co., Delhi, pp. 150-51.
3. The conference adopted a two-part Vienna Declaration and a six part 150 paragraph programme of action. The Declaration consisted of 16 preambular paragraphs and 39 operative paragraphs.

4. General Assembly Resolution 53/144, dated December 9, 1998.
5. Economic and Social Council. Resolution 1998/33 of July 30, 1998. Earlier the text of the Draft Declaration was approved by the Commission on Human Rights on April 7, 1998.
6. UDHR Adopted and proclaimed by General assembly Resolution 217 A(111) of 10 December 1948.

17

Employment of Expatriates vis-à-vis Nationals in the Private Sector in GCC Countries

A Case Study

Mokhtar M Metwally*

Introduction

Well-over 90 per cent of the citizens are employed in the Government sector in most GCC countries. Some of these employees have zero or negative marginal productivity (i.e. disguised unemployed). On the other hand, over 95 per cent of the employees in the private sectors of these countries are expatriates, *i.e.* imported labour. This misallocation of manpower is creating serious problems of budgetary deficit and disguised unemployment amongst nationals in the thinly populated rich oil producing countries. The decision makers of the GCC countries ask the question: why does the private sector prefer to employ expatriates rather than nationals. This paper attempts to answer this question by analysing the attitudes of the private sector towards employing nationals in the State of Qatar as a case study.

The labour market in GCC countries has many peculiar characteristics. There is no wage policy of any form and the Law does not impose a minimum wage. In addition, there are virtually no restrictions on importing labour (as

* Professor Mokhtar M. Metwally is QNB Chair of Economics and the Dean of the College of Business and Economics, University of Qatar. He can be contacted at P.O. Box 2713, Doha Qatar. Tel (974) 4852823, Fax (974) 4832923, e-mail: metwally@qu.edu.qa. This study is part of a major research project conducted by the National Research at Center at QU which is financially sponsored by Qatar National Bank.

long as the expatriate has no criminal or political record and passes the set health test). Some states impose quotas on the number of imported employees from various countries to keep a balance in the population structure. Some states also require government departments and firms operating in the mixed sector to employ a minimum proportion of nationals. However, this restriction does not apply to firms operating in the private sector. Moreover, there is a significant difference between the level of wages paid in the Government sector and those paid in the private sector. In addition, there is a huge difference between the wage rate paid to nationals and that paid to expatriates in the same occupation (Metwally, 1997). Furthermore, while tenure, superannuation and other matters related to employment in the Government and mixed sectors are subject to the terms and conditions set by the Civil Service Laws, these laws do not seem to apply to the vast majority of firms operating in the private sector.

The main objective of the paper is to find out why firms operating in the private sector in the State of Qatar prefer to employ expatriates rather than Qatari citizens. The paper is divided into five sections. Section one discusses the main characteristics of the sample. Section two briefly outlines the methodology of the paper. The results of factor and multiple discriminant analyses are given in sections three and four respectively. Finally, section five summarizes the main conclusions of the study.

Main Sample Characteristics

This study is based on a survey conducted during the three months of April-June 2001. Three hundred and eighty five employers of different sizes representing various sectors in the Qatari economy were personally interviewed to give their views on employing Qatari nationals. The sample size was determined using 95 per cent confidence level, 0.05 level of precision and 0.5 population proportion. This sample size reflects the maximum possible variation in the population.

Level of precision and 0.5 population proportion. This sample size reflects the maximum possible variation in the population.

The respondents were selected at random using the table of random numbers and the telephone directory. The respondents were asked to indicate their line of business, size of their firms in terms of capital and number of employees, age of their business, type of ownership, nationality of employees, sex of employees and wage levels of employees of different nationalities. The sample was representative and has properties that conform to the latest Census data (1997).

The respondents were also asked to indicate their agreement or disagreement regarding the following reasons for not employing Qatari nationals:

V1: Nationals ask for much higher wages than expatriates

V2: Nationals like to obtain frequent leaves

V3: Nationals like to occupy leading positions

V4: Nationals like to occupy more than one job

V5: Nationals refuse to work for two shifts

V6: The national employee is not committed to official work timing

V7: The national employee has a relatively low productivity

V8: The national employee is not serious about his/her work

V9: A Qatari employee always seeks excuses to escape duties

V10: There is fear that the national employee may not settle down at work

V11: Most nationals who seek employment lack necessary experience

V12: Most nationals who apply for a particular job lack necessary qualifications

V13: Most nationals who seek employment lack knowledge of English language and computer work

V14: The national may favour his/her relatives when performing his/her duties

V15: The national employee desires to occupy positions that require higher qualifications and richer experience than that he/she possesses

V16: Nationals like to occupy managerial positions

V17: The nationals reject to work in most activities in the private sector

V18: It is difficult to create positions that meet nationals' desires

V19: Nationals ask for fringe benefits that the private sector cannot afford

V20: Nationals seek to obtain early retirement at lucrative terms

V21: National females ask for special arrangements at work (e.g. separation)

V22: It is difficult to rehabilitate and train nationals to perform certain tasks

Table 1 gives the means and standard deviations of the scope for each variable. It is clear that the highest score was given to the variable representing the wage level requested by the nationals (Qatari citizens) compared to that offered to expatriates. Other variables that score relatively high are preferences of nationals to occupy leading and managerial positions, lack of commitment to official work timing, the desire to occupy positions that require high qualifications and experience and refusal to work for two shifts. On the other hand, the mean score of the variables representing the desire to occupy more than one job, favoritism in performing duties and difficulty to rehabilitate and train Qatari citizens to perform certain tasks were not too high.

Table 1: Means and Standard Deviations of Scores.

	Mean	*Std. Deviation*	*Analysis N*
Nationals ask for much higher wages than expatriates	4.6390	.6630	385
Nationals like to obtain frequent leaves	3.7506	1.1204	385
Nationals like to occupy leading positions	4.2123	1.2427	385
Nationals like to occupy more than one job	3.2571	1.3145	385
Nationals refuse to work for two shifts	4.1987	1.2614	385
The national employee is not committed to official work timing	4.2063	1.1696	385
The national employee has a relatively low productivity	3.7896	1.1180	385
The national employee is not serious about his/her work	3.9792	1.1317	385
A national employee always seeks execuses to escape duties	3.4909	1.2228	385
There is fear that the national employees may not settle down at work	3.1169	1.3880	385
Most nationals who seek employment lack necessary experience	3.8649	1.2022	385
Most nationals who apply for the job lack necessary qualifications	3.6675	1.2536	385
Most nationals lack knowledge of English language and computer work	3.7247	1.1646	385
National may favour relatives or friends while performing his/her duties	3.2026	1.2668	385
National desires to occupy positions which require higher qualifications and richer experience than that they posses	4.2226	1.0825	385
Nationals like to occupy managerial positions	4.1099	1.3297	385
The nationals reject to work in most activities in the private sector	3.8442	1.2795	385
It is difficult to create positions that meet nationals' desires	3.8649	1.1075	385
Nationals ask for fringe benefits that the private sector cannot afford	4.0234	1.1143	385
Nationals seek to obtain early retirement at lucrative terms	3.8156	1.1814	385
National females ask for special arrangements at work (e.g. separation)	4.2255	1.4072	385
It is difficult to rehabilitate and train nationals to perform certain tasks	3.4649	1.4214	385

Results of Factor Analysis

The survey contained a large number of variables, most of which are correlated. This section tries to examine the relationships among the interrelated variables and represent them in terms of a few underlying factors. This is done through the use of the technique of "Factor Analysis."

Due to space limitations, it is not possible to report every statistical result of the factor analysis. The Anti-image Correlation Matrix, the Correlation Matrix and the Reproduced Correlation Matrix are available from the Author on request. The coefficients on the diagonals of the Anti-image correlation matrix are greater than 0.5 for each variable. Therefore, none of the 22 variables was eliminated. The correlation matrix shows that well-over 50% of the coefficients are statistically significant at the 5 per cent level of significance and all variables have a large correlation coefficient with more than one of the other variables. The results related to residuals reveal that only 32% of the residuals are greater than 0.5 (in absolute value). All these suggest goodness of fit and adequacy of the factor model.

The main results of factor analysis are given in Table 2. Bartlett's test of sphericity was used to test the null hypothesis that the variables are non-correlated in the population. The test gave a value of 4556.923 which is highly significant favouring a rejection of the null hypothesis [Dillon and Goldstein, 1984]. Also, the Kaiser-Meyer-Olkin [KMO] measure of sampling adequacy was calculated. A value of 0.820 was obtained which indicate that correlations between pairs of variables can be explained by other variables and hence factor analysis is appropriate [Hair, et. al, 1992]. Actually, a KMO value of 0.820 is considered "meritorious".

The Table labelled "Total variance explained" shows the "final statistics" that give relevant information after the desired number of factors have been extracted (Dunteman, 1989). The table gives the commonalties for the variables, along with the variance accounted for by each factor that is retained. It can be seen that the 22 explanatory variables are reduced to only six factors with an eigenvalue greater than one. The six factors account for approximately 68 per cent of the total variance.

The component matrix gives factor loadings. For example the rating for variable V1 (Nationals ask for much higher wages than expatriates) can be expressed as:

$$V1 = .286\ F_1 + .016\ F_2 + .070\ F_3 - .245\ F_4 + .254\ F_5 + .675\ F_6$$

Although the component matrix indicates the relationship between the factors and individual variables, it does not result in factors that can be interpreted. For example, factor 1 is highly correlated with 13 out of the 22 variables. In such a complex matrix, it is difficult to interpret the factors. Therefore, through rotation, the factor matrix is transformed into a simpler one that is easier to interpret.

The rotated factor matrix obtained by the *varimax procedure* suggests that:

1. Factor 1 has high coefficients for the following variables:
   - Nationals like to occupy leading positions
   - Nationals refuse to work for two shifts
   - The national desires to occupy positions which require higher qualifications and richer experience than he/she possesses.
   - Nationals like to occupy managerial positions
   - The nationals reject to work in most activities of the private sector

   Therefore, this factor may be labeled *"work preference."*
2. Factor 2 has high coefficients on the following variables:
   - Nationals like to obtain frequent leaves
   - The national employee is not committed to official work timing
   - The national employee has a relatively low productivity
   - The national employee is not serious about his/her work
   - A national employee always seeks execuses to escape duties

   Therefore, this factor may be labeled *"work commitment"*.
3. Factor 3 is highly correlated with the following variables:
   - Nationals like to occupy more than one job
   - There is fear that the national employee may not settle down at work
   - The national may favour relatives and friends while performing duties
   - It is difficult to rehabilitate and train nationals to perform certain tasks
   - It is difficult to create positions that meet nationals' desires

Hence this variable may be labeled *"job satisfaction."*

4. Factor 4 has high coefficients on the following variables:
   - Most nationals who see employment lack necessary experience.
   - Most nationals who apply for the job lack necessary qualifications
   - Most nationals lack knowledge of English and computer work.

Factor 4 may, therefore, be labeled *"Qualification and experience."*

5. Factor 5 is highly correlated with the following variables:
   - Nationals ask for fringe benefits that the private sector can not afford
   - Nationals seek to obtain early retirement at lucarative terms
   - National females ask for special arrangements at work (e.g. separation)

Therefore, this factor may be labeled *"Fringe benefits."*

6. Factor 6 is highly related to the variables representing the level of wages of National vis-à-vis expatriates. Hence, this factor may be labeled *"wages."*

Thus, using the principal component method and varimax rotation, the 22 explanatory variables for the tendency of the private sector to offer positions to expatriates rather than nationals have been reduced to the following six factors:

F1: Work Preference

F2: Work commitment

F3: Job Satisfaction

F4: Qualifications and experience

F5: Fringe benefits

F6: Wages

Table 2: Statistical Results of Factor Analysis.

KMO and Bartlett's Test

Kaiser-Meyer-Olkin Measure of Sampling Adequacy		.820
Bartlett's Test of Sphericity	Approx. Chi-Square	4556.923
	df	231
	Sig.	.000

Total Variance Explained

Component	*Initial Eigenvalues*			*Extraction Sums of Squared Loadings*			*Rotation Sums of Squared Loadings*		
	Total	*% of Variance*	*Cumulative%*	*Total*	*% of Variance*	*Cumulative %*	*Total*	*% of Variance*	*Cumulative%*
1	6.219	28.268	28.268	6.219	28.268	28.268	4.304	19.562	19.562
2	3.192	14.511	42.779	3.192	14.511	42.779	3.388	15.399	34.961
3	1.759	7.997	50.776	1.759	7.997	50.779	2.227	10.123	45.084
4	1.510	6.865	57.641	1.510	6.865	57.641	2.156	9.798	54.882
5	1.260	5.727	63.368	1.260	5.727	63.368	1.706	7.756	62.639
6	1.018	4.627	67.995	1.018	4.627	67.995	1.178	5.357	67.995
7	.952	4.328	72.323						
8	.798	3.629	75.952						
9	.689	3.134	79.086						
10	.633	2.875	81.961						
11	.582	2.646	84.606						
12	.541	2.459	87.066						
13	.486	2.209	89.275						
14	.430	1.955	91.230						
15	.403	1.832	93.062						
16	.348	1.583	94.645						
17	.331	1.504	96.150						
18	.271	1.232	97.381						
19	.214	.971	98.352						
20	.193	.876	99.228						
21	9.6E-02	.436	99.664						
22	7.4E-02	.336	100.00						

Extraction Method: Principal Component Analysis.

Component Matrix[a]

	Component					
	1	*2*	*3*	*4*	*5*	*6*
Nationals ask for much higher wages than expatriates	.286	.017	.070	–.245	.254	.675
Nationals like to obtain frequent leaves	.565	.318	–.384	–.325	.112	–.298
Nationals like to occupy leading positions	.677	–.593	.036	–.159	–.076	.014
Nationals like to occupy more than one job	.512	.062	–.229	.413	–.323	–.051
Nationals refuse to work for two shifts	.705	–.549	.043	–.148	–.059	.029
The national employee is not committed to official work timing	.601	.306	–.045	–.090	.160	.054
The national employee has a relatively low productivity	.576	.526	–.305	–.336	–.006	–.090
The national employee is not serious about his/her work	.494	.357	–.358	–.103	.006	.334
A national employee always seeks execuses to escape duties	.532	.575	–.163	–.006	.017	.089
There is fear that the national employees may not settle down at work	.474	.242	–.137	–.582	–.206	.042
Most national who seek employment lack necessary experience	.478	.093	.460	–.305	–.301	–.065
Most nationals who apply for the job lack necessary qualifications	.317	.395	.615	–.037	–.340	.061
Most nationals lack knowledge of English language and computer work	.270	.510	.519	.095	–.099	–.080
National may favour relatives or friends while performing duties	.536	–.016	.059	.447	.021	–.218
Nationals desire to occupy positions which require higher qualifications and richer experience than they posses	.620	–.344	.230	–.242	–.017	–.106
Nationals like to occupy managerial positions	.696	–.600	–.042	–.053	.026	–.106
The nationals reject to work in most activities in the private sector	.707	–.602	–.015	.012	–.063	–.004
It is difficult to create positions that meet nationals' desires	.615	.310	–.262	–.073	.021	–.238
Nationals ask for fringe benefits that the private sector can not afford	.459	.091	.309	.165	.473	.068
Nationals seek to obtain early retirement at lucrative terms	.260	.351	.449	.007	.449	–.181
National females ask for special arrangements at work (e.g. separation)	.361	–.229	–.001	.441	.550	–.025
It is difficult to rehabiliate and train nationals to perform certain tasks	.559	.009	.008	.302	–.225	.398

Extraction Method: Principal Component Analysis.
a. 6 components extracted.

Rotated Component Matrix[a]

	Component					
	1	2	3	*4*	5	6
Nationals ask for much higher wages than expatriates	.150	.110	−1.E-01	4.4E-02	.137	.776
Nationals like to obtain frequent leaves	.190	.851	−1.E-02	−2.E-02	5.9E-02	−.108
Nationals like to occupy leading positions	.904	6.8E-02	9.8E-02	6.6E-03	2.3E-02	.101
Nationals like to occupy more than one job	.205	.240	.697	3.1E-02	−5.E-02	-9.E-02
Nationals refuse to work for two shifts	.885	9.8E-02	.117	2.8E-02	5.2E-02	.124
The national employee is not committed to official work timing	.161	.548	.155	.180	.261	.206
The national employee has a relatively low productivity	4.8E-02	.883	6.6E-02	.168	−2.E-02	9.0E-02
The national employee is not serious about his/her work	2.2E-02	.601	.264	−2.E-02	−4.E-02	.434
A national employee always seeks execuses to escape duties	−9.5E-02	.662	.305	.219	.131	.205
There is fear that the national employees may not settle down at work	2.1E-03	.205	.787	8.9E-02	.126	−5.E-03
Most nationals who seek employment lack necessary experience	.376	.182	−3.E-02	.677	−5.E-02	2.8E-02
Most nationals who apply for the job lack necessary qualifications	−1.8E-04	6.0E-02	.155	.848	3.3E-02	9.1E-02
Most nationals lack knowledge of English language and computer work	-.160	.146	.163	.698	.257	-3.E-02
Nationals may favour relatives or friends while performing duties	.276	.129	.517	9.6E-02	.362	−.197
The national desires to occupy positions which require higher qualifications and richer experience than that they posses	.727	.142	−4.E-02	.238	.132	1.8E-02
Nationals like to occupy managerial positions	.893	.106	.151	−.104	.136	−1.E-02
The nationals reject to work in most activities in the private sector	.888	4.4E-02	.248	-6.E-02	8.5E-02	6.1E-02
It is difficult to create positions that meet nationals' desires	.183	.229	.700	7.7E-02	.120	-1.E-01
Nationals ask for fringe benefits that the private sector can not afford	.168	.121	9.5E-02	.174	.671	.196
Nationals seek to obtain early retirement at lucrative terms	-7.5E-02	.196	-.132	.382	.646	-3.E-02
National females ask for special arrangements at work (*e.g.* separation)	.258	-2.E-02	.237	-2.85	.670	3.9E-02
It is difficult to rehabiliate and trainationals to perform certain tasks	.268	8.5E-02	.599	.168	2.1E-02	.383

Extraction Method: Principal Component Analysis.
Rotation Method: Varimax with Kaiser Normalization.
a. Rotation converged in 7 iterations.

Results of Multiple Discriminant Analysis of Factor Scores

The factor scores for the six factors were introduced in multiple discriminant analysis as explanatory variables. The size of employer, measured in terms of capital, represents the dependent variable. Employers were divided into three groups: Group 1 comprises *small* firms whose capital is less than five million Qatari Riyals (US$1.4m). Group 2 refers to *medium-sised* firms whose capital is more than five million Qatari Riyals but less than 20 million Qatari Riyals (US$1.4-5.5 m). Group 3 consists of *large* firms whose capital exceeds 20 million Qatari Riyals (Over US$5.5m).

Since we have three groups and six predictors, we can estimate *two* discriminant functions (Klecka, 1980). Table 3 presents the results of estimating three-group discriminant analysis. The following comments can be made about these results:

1. An examination of group means indicates that factors 3, 4, 5 and 6, which stand for "job satisfaction", "qualifications and experience", "fringe benefits" and "wages" respectively, separate the groups more widely than the other two factors.
2. The pooled within-groups correlation matrix that is computed by averaging the separate covariance matrices for all groups (Lachenbruch, 1975) indicates low correlation coefficients between predictors. Hence there is no serious problem of multi-collinearity.
3. The significance attached to the univariate F ratios indicates that when the predictors are considered individually, all predictors are significant in discriminating between the three groups, with the exception of factor 1 (work preference) and factor 2 (work commitment).
4. The level of significance of Box's M suggests that we should reject the null hypothesis that the covariance matrices are equal (Metwally, 1999).
5. The eigenvalue for function 1 is 2.625. For function 2, it is 1.529. The first function has the largest between-groups variability (as it is usually the case). This function accounts for 63.2% of the variability while function 2 accounts for the remaining 36.8% of the between-groups variability.
6. The Wilks' lambda associated with function 1 is.109. This transforms to a chi-square value of 840.813 which is statistically significant at .000 level. The Wilks' lambda of function 2 after function 1 has been removed is 0.395. This transforms to a chi-square value of 352.035

which is also statistically significant at.000 level, indicating that the function does contribute significantly to group differences (Manly, 1994). These results suggest a simultaneous Wilks' lambda =.043055.

7. Since the value of Chi-square of each function is statistically significant beyond the 5% level, we reject the null hypothesis that the means of both functions are equal. Hence, both functions contribute to group separation.

8. The canonical correlation for function 1 is.851; while for function 2, the correlation is .778. Hence, the proportion of total variability explained by differences between groups is 72.4% for function 1 and 60.5% for function 2.

9. The standardised canonical discriminant function coefficients indicate large positive coefficients for factor 3 (job satisfaction) and a large negative coefficient for factor 2 (qualifications and experience), where as function 2 has a relatively large positive coefficient for factor 6 (wages) and a relatively large negative coefficient for factor 3 (job satisfaction). A similar conclusion is reached by an examination of the structure matrix (Manly, 1994).

10. The unstandardised canonical discriminant function coefficients give the following two discriminant functions:

$$Z_1 = -.393 +.047\ F_1 +.029\ F_2 +.890\ F_3 -.798\ F_4 +.005\ F_5 +.215\ F_6$$

$$Z_2 = .344 +.044\ F_1 +.040\ F_2 + -.528\ F_3 -.304\ F_4 +.030\ F_5 +.719\ F_6$$

11. The canonical discriminant functions evaluated at group means (group centroid) suggest that group 1, *small employers,* has a large positive value on function 2 and also a positive value on function 1. Since the "wage" factor has a large positive sign on function 2 and also a positive sign on function 1, this suggests that small firms who do not employ nationals are concerned mainly about the wage levels these employees would want to obtain. These firms believe that nationals citizens ask for much higher wages than expatriates.

12. Medium-sized employers, on the other hand have a large positive value on function 1 and a large negative value on function 2. Since the "job satisfaction" factor has a large positive coefficient on function 1 and a large negative coefficient on function 2, this suggests that medium-sized employers are not too eager to employ nationals for fear that those employees would not be satisfied with the offered positions and may not stay in employment for long periods.

Table 3: Results of Multiple Discriminant Analysis.

Group Statistics

Size in terms of Capital		*Mean*	*Std. Deviation*	*Valid N (listwise)* Unweighted	*Valid N (listwise)* Weighted
Small Companies	Work Preference	–4.9E-03	.9456478	187	187.000
	Work Commitment	9.97E-03	1.0217139	187	187.000
	Job Satisfaction	8.84E-02	1.0114345	187	187.000
	Qualifications and Experience	–9.6E-02	1.0388398	187	187.000
	Fringe Benefits	.1408497	1.0093258	187	187.000
	Wages	2.2403138	.9514222	187	187.000
Medium-sized companies	Work Preference	8.96E-02	.9670070	117	117.00
	Work Commitment	–2.5E-02	.9046086	117	117.00
	Job Satisfaction	2.2276149	.5617120	117	117.00
	Qualifications and Experience	1.42E-02	.8769956	117	117.00
	Fringe Benefits	–.2027147	.9347663	117	117.00
	Wages	.1850023	1.0265256	117	117.00
Large Companies	Work Preference	–.1228533	1.1558786	81	81.000
	Work Commitment	1.25E-02	1.0886234	81	81.000
	Job Satisfaction	–.6053456	.8654259	81	81.000
	Qualifications and Experience	2.4250720	.4954433	81	81.000
	Fringe Benefits	–3.2E-02	1.0280604	81	81.000
	Wages	–.1566573	1.2474054	81	81.000
Total	Work Preference	–1.0E-03	.9998074	385	385.000
	Work Commitment	1.29E-16	1.0000000	385	385.000
	Job Satisfaction	.5925216	1.4099313	385	385.000
	Qualifications and Experience	.4676849	1.3535201	385	385.000
	Fringe Benefits	–.18E-17	1.0000000	385	385.000
	Wages	1.1114148	1.5173159	385	385.000

Tests of Equality of Group Means.

	Wilks'Lambda	*F*	*df1*	*df2*	*Sig.*
Work Preference	.994	1.084	2	382	.339
Work Commitment	1.000	.051	2	382	.951
Job Satisfaction	.376	317.380	2	382	.000
Qualifications and Experience	.440	243.025	2	382	.000
Fringe Benefits	.978	4.377	2	382	.013
Wages	.470	215.799	2	382	.000

Pooled Within-Groups Matrices

		Work Preference	*Work Committ-ment*	*Job Satisfa-ction*	*Qualification and Experience*	*Fringe Benefits*	*Wages*
Correlation	Work Preference	1.000	.001	.060	.062	.004	–.015
	Work Commitment	.001	1.000	.002	.045	–.002	–.023
	Job Satisfaction	.060	.002	1.000	.123	–.056	–.136
	Qualifications and Experience	.062	.045	.123	1.000	.008	–.068
	Fringe Benefits	.004	–.002	–.056	.008	1.000	.086
	Wages	–.015	–.023	–.136	–.068	.086	1.000

Box's Test of Equality of Covariance Matrices

Log Determinants

Size in terms of Capital	*Rank*	*Log Determinant*
Small Companies	6	–.184
Medium-sized companies	6	–1.977
Large Companies	6	–1.186
Pooled within-groups	6	–.483

The ranks and natural logarithms of determinants printed are those of the group covariance matrices.

Test Results

Box's M		173.883
F	Approx.	4.035
	df1	42
	df2	217886.0
	Sig.	.000

Tests null hypothesis of equal population covariance matrices.

Summary of Canonical Discriminant Functions

Eigenvalues

Function	*Eigenvalue*	*% of Variance*	*Cumulative %*	*Canonical Correlation*
1.	2.625[a]	63.2	63.2	.851
2.	1.529[a]	36.8	100.0	.778

a. First 2 canonical discriminant functions were used in the analysis.

Wilks' Lambda

Test of Function(s)	*Wilks' Lambda*	*Chi-square*	*df*	*Sig.*
1 through 2	.109	840.813	12	.000
2	.395	352.035	5	.000

Standardised Canonical Discriminant Function Coefficients

	Function	
	1	*2*
Work Preference	.047	.044
Work Committment	.029	.040
Job Satisfaction	.771	–.457
Qualifications and Experience	–.718	–.273
Fringe Benefits	.005	.030
Wages	.224	.749

Structure Matrix

	Function	
	1	*2*
Job Satisfaction	.655*	–.592
Qualifications and	–.634*	–.376
ExperienceWork Preference	.046*	–.012
Wages	.167	.831*
Fringe Benefits	–.025	.118*
Work Committment	–.007	.009*

Pooled within-groups correlations between discriminating variables and standardised canonical discriminant functions Variables ordered by absolute size of correlation within function.

* Largest absolute correlation between each variable and any discriminant function.

Canonical Discriminant Function Coefficients

	Function	
	1	*2*
Work Preference	.047	.044
Work Committment	.029	.040
Job Satisfaction	.890	–.528
Qualifications andExperience	–.798	–.304
Fringe Benefits	.005	.030
Wages	.215	.719
(Constant)	–.393	–.344

Unstandardised coefficients.

Functions at Group Centroids

Size in terms of capital	Function 1	Function 2
Small Companies	.245	1.253
Medium-sized companies	1.621	–1.394
Large Companies	–2.907	–8.79

Unstandardised canonical discriminant functions evaluated at group means.

Classification Statistics

Prior Probabilities for Groups

Size in terms of Capital	*Prior*	*Cases Used in Analysis*	
		Unweighted	*Weighted*
Small Companies	.486	187	187.00
Medium-sized Companies	.304	117	117.00
Large Companies	.210	81	81.000
Total	**1.000**	**385**	**385.000**

Classification Results[a]

		Sized in terms of Capital	*Predicted Group Membership*			*Total*
			Small Companies	*Medium-Sized Companies*	*Large Companies*	
Original	Count	Small Companies	178	4	5	187
		Medium-sized companies	4	113	0	117
		Large Companies	2	0	79	81
	%	Small Companies	95.2	2.1	2.7	100.0
		Medium-sized companies	3.4	96.6	.0	100.0
		Large Companies	2.5	.0	97.5	100.0

a. 96.1% of original grouped cases correctly classified.

13. Group 3 which represent large employers have a large negative value on function 1 and also a negative value on function 2. Since the "qualifications and experience" factor carries a large negative sign in both functions, this suggests that large employers who elect to employ expatriates rather than nationals do so because they believe that Qatari citizens do not possess the necessary qualifications and experience for the kind of positions these employees wish to occupy.

14. The classification results based on the analysis sample suggest a hit ratio equal to 96.1%. This suggests that 96.1% of the cases are

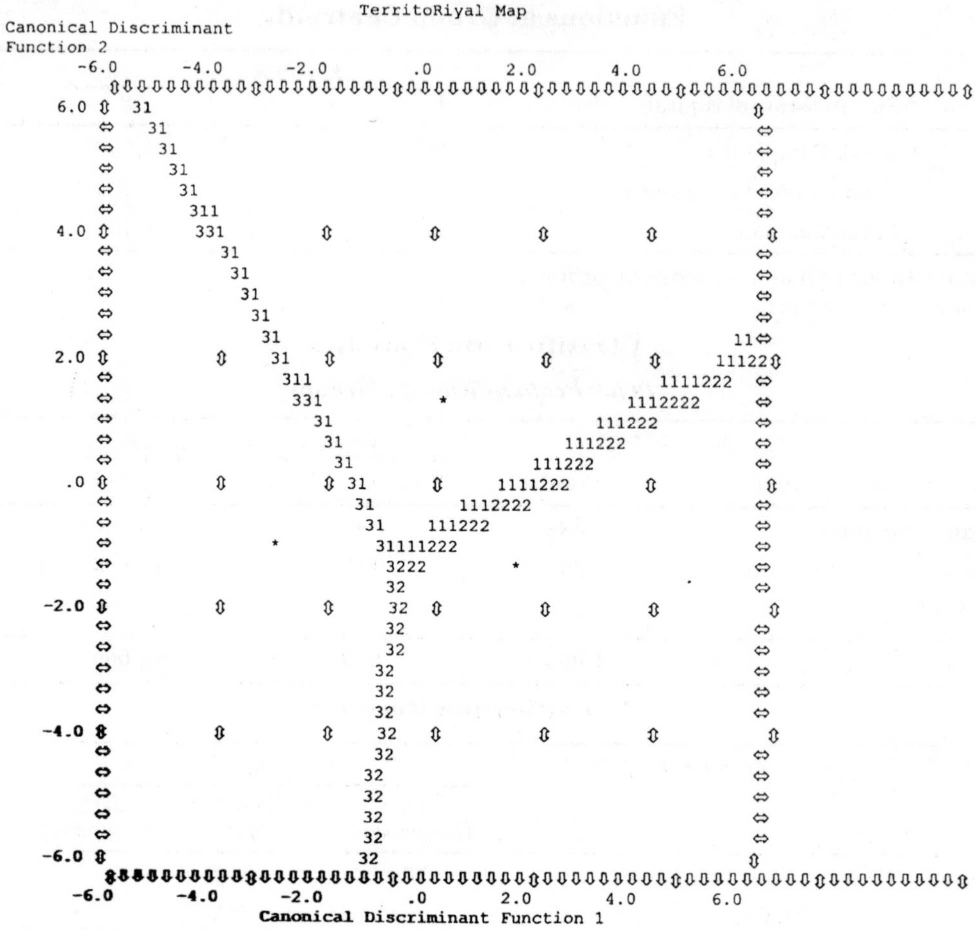

```
                                   TerritoRiyal Map
Canonical Discriminant
Function 2
     -6.0      -4.0      -2.0        .0       2.0       4.0       6.0
      ⇕⇕⇕⇕⇕⇕⇕⇕⇕⇕⇕⇕⇕⇕⇕⇕⇕⇕⇕⇕⇕⇕⇕⇕⇕⇕⇕⇕⇕⇕⇕⇕⇕⇕⇕⇕⇕⇕⇕⇕⇕⇕⇕⇕⇕⇕⇕⇕⇕⇕⇕⇕⇕⇕⇕⇕⇕⇕⇕⇕⇕⇕
  6.0 ⇕ 31                                                            ⇕
      ⇔   31                                                          ⇔
      ⇔    31                                                         ⇔
      ⇔     31                                                        ⇔
      ⇔      31                                                       ⇔
      ⇔       311                                                     ⇔
  4.0 ⇕        331         ⇕         ⇕         ⇕         ⇕            ⇕
      ⇔          31                                                   ⇔
      ⇔           31                                                  ⇔
      ⇔            31                                                 ⇔
      ⇔             31                                                ⇔
      ⇔              31                                             11⇔
  2.0 ⇕          ⇕    31   ⇕         ⇕         ⇕               11122⇕
      ⇔                311                                 1111222 ⇔
      ⇔                 331          *                  1112222    ⇔
      ⇔                   31                         111222        ⇔
      ⇔                    31                     111222           ⇔
      ⇔                     31                 111222              ⇔
   .0 ⇕          ⇕         ⇕ 31      ⇕     1111222           ⇕       ⇕
      ⇔                       31       1112222                     ⇔
      ⇔                        31   111222                         ⇔
      ⇔               *         31111222                           ⇔
      ⇔                          3222          *                   ⇔
      ⇔                          32                                ⇔
 -2.0 ⇕          ⇕         ⇕      32 ⇕         ⇕         ⇕         ⇕
      ⇔                          32                                ⇔
      ⇔                          32                                ⇔
      ⇔                         32                                 ⇔
      ⇔                         32                                 ⇔
      ⇔                         32                                 ⇔
 -4.0 ⇕          ⇕         ⇕     32  ⇕         ⇕         ⇕         ⇕
      ⇔                         32                                 ⇔
      ⇔                        32                                  ⇔
      ⇔                        32                                  ⇔
      ⇔                        32                                  ⇔
      ⇔                        32                                  ⇔
 -6.0 ⇕                        32                                 ⇕
      ⇕⇕⇕⇕⇕⇕⇕⇕⇕⇕⇕⇕⇕⇕⇕⇕⇕⇕⇕⇕⇕⇕⇕⇕⇕⇕⇕⇕⇕⇕⇕⇕⇕⇕⇕⇕⇕⇕⇕⇕⇕⇕⇕⇕⇕⇕⇕⇕⇕⇕⇕⇕⇕⇕⇕⇕⇕⇕⇕⇕⇕⇕
     -6.0      -4.0      -2.0        .0       2.0       4.0       6.0
                     Canonical Discriminant Function 1
```

Symbols used in territoriyal map

Symbol	Group	Label
1	1	Small Companies
2	2	Medium-sized companies
3	3	Large Companies
*		Indicates a group centroid

correctly classified. Since we have three groups of equal size, a chance hit ratio would be 1/3 = 33.3%. The improvement over chance is more than 25% indicating a least satisfactory validity (Malhotra et al, 1996). The *Press's Q* statistic is given by:

$$Press's\ Q = \{385 - (370)\ (3)\}^2/\{385\ (2)\} = 682.6$$

This value exceeds by far the critical value at a significance level of.01 which is 6.63, suggesting that the predictions are significantly better than chance.

15. The territorial map can be used to predict the demand by employers of different sizes for labour services of nationals.

Conclusions

The main conclusions of this paper may be summarised in the following:

1. Bartlett's test of sphericity, Kaiser-Meyer-Olkin [KMO] measure of sampling adequacy and the magnitudes of the residuals suggest goodness of fit of the factor model.
2. Using the principal component method and varimax rotation, it was possible to extract six factors which can explain the tendency of the private sector to offer positions to expatriates rather than nationals. These factors are: the level of wages, fringe benefits, qualifications and experience, work preference, work commitment and job satisfaction.
3. The factor scores were used as predictors in multiple discriminant analysis. Two discriminant functions were obtained. The eigenvalue for both functions were greater than 1. The first function accounts for 63.2% of the variability while the second function accounts for the remaining 36.8% of the between-groups variability. The Wilks' lambda associated with both functions transformed to a chi-square value which is statistically significant at.000 level. This suggests that both functions contribute to group separation.
4. The canonical discriminant functions evaluated at group means (group centroids) suggest the *small firms* who do not employ nationals are concerned mainly about the wage levels these employees would want to obtain. These firms believe that nationals ask for much higher wages than expatriates. Medium-sized employers are not too eager to employ nationals for fear that those employees would not be satisfied with the offered positions and may not stay in employment for long periods. Large employers who elect to employ expatriates rather than nationals do so because they believe that nationals do not possess the necessary qualifications and experience for the kind of positions these employees wish to occupy.

The above results have some serious policy implications. The private sector must play a much stronger role in creating jobs for Citizens. Any economic project that creates jobs only for expatriates, depends on imported equipment, materials and supply does not pay tax and exports most, if not all, of its profits, does not make any contribution to the national economy. Some radical and brave measures must be taken, the sooner the better, to ensure that the private sector carries its responsibilities. Some of these measures are:

(a) No work permit should be granted to any expatriate employee unless the employer can prove that there is *no Qatari citizen of equal qualifications and experience is currently unemployed and searching for the kind of job open to the expatriate.*

(b) No contract for an expatriate employee should be renewed unless the employer can prove that there is no Qatari citizen of equal *qualifications and experience is currently unemployed and searching for the kind of job occupied by the expatriate.*

(c) The enforcement of a *minimum wage,* so the private firms would not rush to employ expatriate cheap labour.

(d) The design of a *wage policy* that ensures minimum differential between the wage rates paid in the Government sector and in the private sector.

(e) The establishment of a *Price-wage Tribunal* whose main function is to ensure that the private sector pays wages to Qatari employees in line with its pricing of goods service. The *policy of charging USA prices and paying Bangladesh wages must be stopped.*

REFERENCES

1. Coakes, S.J. and L.G. Steed (1999), *SPSS: Analysis without Anguish,* Jacaranda Wiley Ltd., Sydney.
2. Dillon, W.R. and M. Goldstein (1984), *Multivariate Analysis: Methods and Applications,* New York, J. Wiley.
3. Dunteman, G.H. (1989), *Principal Component Analysis,* Newburg Park, CA: Saga Publications
4. Fisher, R.A. (1936), The use of Multiple Measurements in Taxonomic Problems" *Annals of Eugenics,* pp. 179-188
5. Hair, J., R.E. Anderson. et. al (1992), *Multivariate Data Analysis with Readings,* 3rd edition, New York, Macmillan Publishing Company
6. Johnson, R.A. and D.W. Wichern (1982), *Applied Multivariate Statistical Analysis.*
7. Klecka, W.R. (1980), *Discriminant Analysis,* Beverly Hills, CA: Sage.
8. Lachenbruch, P.A. (1975), *Discriminant Analysis*, New York, Hafner Press.
9. Maddala, G.S. (1983), *Limited Dependent and Quantitative Variables in Econometrics, Cambridge,* Cambridge University Press.
10. Maddala, G.S. (1992), *Introduction to Econometrics,* 2nd ed., Engelwood Cliffs, Prentice-Hall.

11. Malhotra, N.K., J. Hall, M. Shour and M. Crisp (1996), *Marketing Research: An Applied Orientation,* New York, Prentice-Hall.

12. Manly, B.F.J. (1994), Multivariate *Statistical Methods,* 2nd. Ed., London, Champon & Hall.

13. Metwally, M.M. (1999), *Applied Multivariate Statistical Techniques,* D.E Publishing, Wollongong.

14. Metwally; M.M. (1997),' Causes and Consequences of Wage Differentials in the GCC Countries: A Case Study' *The Middle East Business and Economic Review,* Vol. 9, No.2 PP.22-32

15. Morrison, D.G. (1969), "On the Interpretation of Discriminant Analysis' *Journal of Marketing Research,* Vol. 6, PP. 156-63.

16. Muliak, S.A. (1972). *The Foundation of Factor Analysis,* New York, McGraw-Hill Planning Council, The General Secretariat, State of Qatar,: *Annual Statistical Abstract,* 20th Issue, October 2000.

18

Globalisation of Indian Economy Agenda for the Future

Dr. A. P. Biradar-Patil*

During the last fifty years the performance of Indian economy has been dominated by the regime of multiple controls, regulations and a high degree of state intervention. Industrial economy of the country protected by the state and insulated against the foreign competition was thrown behind the Indian economy. By 1989 the situation of the front of balance of payments and foreign exchange became intolerable. As a result the foreign exchange reserves got depleted to such an extent that we had just enough of them to last for paying a couple of weeks imports. Under such critical situation we were forced to devalue our currency twice, pledge our gold and accept IMF conditionalities for receiving assistance to tide over the balance of payments crisis. Our credibility reached the bottom and no country was ready to advance to India. Such a kind of economic crisis built up in the Indian economy left no choice but to act fast and bring major economic reforms which could assist in revival of our economy. So as to bring the economic crisis under control the then Union Government decided to cut down fiscal deficit and to adopt a structural adjustment policy with liberalisation, privatisation and globalisation agenda in 1991. The two broad objectives of the measures introduced by the Union Government were the reorientation of the economy from centrally directed and highly controlled economy to what is known as a market friendly economy and attaining the macro-economic stabilisation.

* Prof & Head, Dept of Economics, KLE Society's, S.S.M.S College, Athani–591 304. [Research Guide in Economics, Karnatak University, Dharwad]

Globalisation involves the increasing interaction of national economic systems like more integrated financial markets, higher factor mobility and spectacular change in information technology, leading to the spread of knowledge throughout the world. It is quite clear that the process of globalisation does not evolve equally worldwide. The benefits of globalisation are only available to the countries which best managed their economies.

Competition is indeed the crux of globalisation. The higher level of competition, higher the economic growth, the higher the income level, the higher the quality of products and thus the higher the living standards of the people that the globalisation process would bring ultimately. If India is to reap maximum benefits from globalisation we have to complete the unfinished agenda of economic reforms.

Economic Reforms

Our major economic reforms introduced to overcome the critical situation were:

1. Nearly 80% of the Indian Industries were delicensed.
2. The MRTP restrictions relating to assets were removed.
3. Our Foreign Trade was liberalised by reducing tariffs on imports, removing quota system and eliminating export subsidies.
4. Our Rupee was made partially convertible along with inbuilt mechanism to link a portion of imports with actual exports earnings.
5. Foreign Investment was liberalised by simplification of rules and regulations.
6. Private sector was allocated a major role for economic growth, and various procedures were simplified and many of them were eliminated.

New Government rationalised the fiscal system by trying to reduce subsidies, curtail government expenses, rationalize taxes and review incentives. All these measures marked by their boldness did make a positive impact on the Indian economy. Within a short period, deficit has been reduced, foreign exchange reserves have improved, trade balance has been brought under control, government expenses have been restricted and credibility of India has been restored and world is once again towards India with great hope and promise. Indian economy is now more guided by market forces and less by administrative dictates. The policies announced by Union Government not have the desired impact until they are adopted and implemented by the state governments.

Recent economic reforms and initiatives taken by the Union Government have indeed placed a much greater responsibility on the business community of India. The days of protection and shortages have gone, Indian business now has to grow with competition where only the best can survive. Governments have to pay much greater attention on research and development.

Efficiency and competitiveness are the two major hallmarks of globalisation. They have served to drive the terms of trade in favour of the ultimate consumer all across the globe. Singapore, Thailand and Taiwan, which are well accepted as role models of economic progress in East Asia, have all adopted an approach to an economic development, which is similar to our own agricultural growth model.

To be globally competitive a country must be blessed with two favourable factors like an unlimited reservoir of talented and skilled labour and an abundance of capital available for new projects. World Bank in its recent report remarked that, "India has both these factors in abundance."

Sir William Ryrie the Executive Vice-President of International Finance Corporation (IFC) recently said that, "India has some of the most creative entrepreneurs, most dynamic business leaders and the sharpest financial brains in the world." IFC has invested nearly 750 million dollars in the private sector of India during the fiscal year 2000–2001 raising the country to the status of Number One in its world wide portfolio.

It is quite interesting to note that India has become the second largest investor next only to USA which has about 51 million investors and about 7700 domestic companies by the end 2000.

One of the recent issues of the American business magazine "Forbes", mentioned that 'there is twice as much American direct investment now going into China. Unlike China, India operates within the rule of law. When you invest in India, you invest in democracy. India has much larger and more capable infrastructure of local companies which serve as good partners and tough competitors.

The Centre for Monitoring the Indian Economy (CMIE) places the value of total investments on ongoing projects at the end of 2000 at rupees 850,000 crores comprising 4129 projects.

The most unfortunate truth is that, in the last 50 years of freedom India has missed the opportunity to take its proper place both in social and economic spheres. Presently we are in the bottom twenty amongst all the countries in terms of Human Development Index. In the year 2020 we should be amongst the first twenty. This is possible only when we build the necessary consensus for accelerated reforms and implement them more effectively.

Constraints

Some of the major constraints which have held back our socio-economic progress include:

1. Wrong economic philosophy of self-sufficiency.
2. Undue phobia of Foreign Investment
3. Excessive emphasis on Public sector
4. Unwise Agricultural Policy
5. Distrust of Foreign Investment
6. Institution of License Raj.
7. Inadequate Social Investment and
8. Low Ethics in Administration.

Priorities

To overcome all these constraints our immediate priorities should be as under:

1. We must make education as priority of priorities
2. We must privatise the public sector units.
3. We must overcome the shortages of infrastructural facilities
4. We should change our labour - laws
5. We must root-out the age old curse of casteism
6. We should put an end to the problem of corruption
7. We must see that, fruits of liberalisation reach the masses
8. We must stop the wastage of time and energy of the people
9. We should have a down sizing and stable government.
10. We must focus on the use of modern information and technology.
11. We must maintain sustained growth of agricultural sector.
12. We should improve tax administration to raise larger revenue and reduce subsidies.

No doubt, India is blessed with most of the basic potentialities for speedy socio-economic development, a hard working and thrifty population, a long tradition of scholarship, enterprising businessmen, good judicial and civil services and fair endowment of natural fair recourses. We need to assess where we went wrong despite these blessings and to identify the policy measures for liberating India, which has been characterised as a 'caged tiger' by 'Economist' a journal known for its valuable views.

Tasks Ahead

The Rate of growth of Indian economy since 1980, has been hardly around 5% per annum, while China with almost similar endowments and problems like India has been growing at about 9 to 10% per annum.

With discipline, hard work and integrity India can also match the progress made in China and eradicate the poverty and open opportunities for all her people. It is only through higher economic growth that we can reduce poverty and provide sustainable economic security.

For the success of any reform and restructuring programme it is necessary that domestic liberalisation be sequenced before external liberalisation. The experience of successfully liberalising economies like South Korea also suggests that internal economic reforms is crucial to the success of external reforms. That is the lesson to Indian policy makers to learn and act quickly for better and immediate results.

In fact one of the biggest challenges facing the Indian economy today is to step up infrastructure investment and to upgrade the technology for better services. Much more needs to be done for sectoral reforms and rationalisation of user charges and strengthening of institutional, legal and regulatory frame work for ensuring fair competition among private and public operators and protecting consumer interests. A sustainable agricultural production calls for effective planning and environment friendly technologies and policies.

Economic reforms process will remain incomplete without agrarian, social and political reforms. The end product of all economic policies is social well being. What we need is not less government and more market but better government and genuine market. Tomorrow's problem cannot be solved with yesterday's strategies.

No being able to tailor the reforms to suit the specific socio-economic problems has been our major weakness. Further in the process of implementation of reforms a number of distortions have crept in. Correcting such distortions and attending to the neglected segments should therefore be claimed as pre-eminent position on the agenda for our future reforms.

There will not only be challenges but also opportunities. We need to get prepared to overcome the challenges and exploit the opportunities. Let us step into the future with great confidence and commitment.

REFERENCES

1. 'India in the year 2000': J.C. Kapur, New Delhi Publication Division India International Centre, 1975.
2. 'Technology Transfer': The Need for a New Perspective, Viren J. Shah., Bombay 1979.
3. 'India': Vision Reality Gap., Dr. P.M. Bharghava and Chandana Chakrubarti, Yojana Oct 16-31, 1988
4. 'The Changing Nature of Global Security and its Impact on South Asia 'Robert S McNamara., India International Centre, New Delhi 1992.
5. Development and Change (Ed): P. Bardhan M. Datta Chaudhuri and T.N. Krishnan, Oxford University Press, 1993.
6. India's Economy in the 21st Century (Ed) Raj Kapila and Uma Kapila, Academic Foundation New Delhi, 2002.

19

Globalisation, Growth and Poverty In Indian Context

Dr. (Mrs) Kavita Bhatnagar*

Globalisation is the term being used to cover a wide variety of reforms aimed at opening up the economy. This involves freeing trade by reducing/ eliminating quantitative restrictions, de-canalising imports and exports of many commodities, bringing down customs tariffs and removal of various forms of control such as licenses and permits as well as other barriers to investment represented by MRTP and FEMA. A welcome change has taken place in the world scenario during the last decade when then Finance Minister of India Dr. Man Mohan Singh has presented the 1991 Budget of Indian government unveiling the New economic policy. The much debated New Economic Policy was the outcome of acute financial crisis faced by the country in mid 1991 caused primarily by the political uncertainty and aggravated by the impact of Gulf-War. During the period the country was passing through an unprecedented economic crises following strain on balance of payment, galloping inflation, frustrating position of foreign exchange reserves and other Macro economic imbalances. The New Economic Policy was based on a combination of measures aimed at economic stabilisation and structural reforms to overcome the shortcomings of socialistic pattern of economy adopted by India for the last 40 years.

The liberalisation or globalisation process was started when India was faced with the prospect of defaulting on its international commitments; access to external commercial credit market was completely denied; international credit rating had been downgraded; and the international financial

* Sr. Lecturer, Economics. Gokuldas Girls PG College, Moradabad.

community's confidence in India's ability to manage its economy had been seriously eroded. Our growth rate has slumped to 1.4 per cent, industrial production stagnated, inflation raged peaked to 14 per cent, Government fiscal deficit ballooned uncontrollably to 8.4 per cent of GDP, foreign exchange reserves tumbled to merely a month's imports ($1.1 billion) and country was on the verge of a payment default in its international obligations. Trade deficit in 1990-91 soared to Rs. 16934 core and our current account deficit was large as 17369 crore. Our total export value in 1990-91 was able to meet only 48 per cent of our import value. India's share in world export was 2 per cent in 1950, 1 per cent in 1960, 0.66 per cent in 1970 and 0.42 per cent in 1980. It means world expansion in the export sector was larger than the Indian export expansion. In this period our economy was much surrounded with economic crisis. So policy maker had not alternative to correct the economic illness. Our credit was falling fastly in international market, so there was no option to adopt privatisation, liberalisation and globalisation.

In recent years, the Indian Government has been making serious efforts to free the Indian economy from the regulations and restrictions of the past few decades in order to restore freedom of the market and to integrate Indian industry and agriculture with the global economy. India's economic reform programme since the 1990s has involved two basic sets of policy measures. The first set aims to achieve macroeconomic stabilisation by reducing both fiscal (budgetary) and the balance of payments deficits. Reducing fiscal deficits involves a cut in public expenditure, and also an attempt to raise public revenue to bring about a balanced budget over time. Our medium term objective was to progressively reduce the public sector deficit from the high of 12.5% of GDP to about 4 % of GDP in the next 10 years. To reduce the BOP deficits, the economic reform programme in India has heavily relied on currency devaluation to boost exports and reduce imports. So far, measures taken to achieve macroeconomic stabilisation in India have been less than successful.

Economy (growth in per cent)

	1991–92	*1998–99*	*1999–2000*	*2000–01*	*2001–02*	*2002–03 Nine months*
GDP at constant Factor cost	1.3	6.5	6.2	4.3	6.0	4.2
Industrial production	0.6	4.1	6.7	5.0	2.7	5.3
Agricultural production	–2.0	7.6	–0.6	–5.4	5.9	–11.9
Exports (US$)	–1.1	–3.9	10.8	21.0	–1.6	20.4
Imports (US$)	–24.5	–7.1	17.2	1.7	1.7	14.5

Source: Business Standard.

India has experienced one of the most severe droughts in 2002, so the agricultural production has slumped to the negative territory during 2002-2003. Lack of agricultural reforms is also the key factor for negative growth in the agricultural sector. Food grains production which was 168.4 million tones in 1991-92 has increased to 212.0 million tones in 2001-02 subsequently projected to be decreased to 183.2 million tones in 2002-03. Apart from agriculture the recovery appears to be quite broad based. Industrial production which plummeted to 1.6 per cent in 1991-92 has risen to 4.1 per cent in 1998-99, 6.7 per cent in 1999-2000, 5.0 per cent in 2000-01, moderate 2.7 per cent in 2001-02 and 5.3 per cent in 2002-03 (nine months). National savings as a percentage of gross domestic product have been slowly increasing in India: from 16 per cent in 1972 to 21 per cent in 1992, and then to 26 per cent in 1998. Despite such welcome increases, there is still a huge savings gap, both in private and public sectors. Good governance, coupled with a top priority to eliminate corruption and red tape, would not doubt help to generate more domestic savings in India. However, capital shortages are likely to continue in India in the foreseeable future. To overcome such shortages, India will need to create an investment environment, which is both acceptable to foreign investors, and in some broad terms, confirms with the accepted principles of "good governance." In the next decade and beyond India will require an investment and saving rate at a much higher level than ever before, for at least three reasons: First, there is the need for structural adjustments which will call for massive injunctions of new capital in enterprises, particularly high-tech industries. Second, India has to move fast to modernise the entire infra-structure of the economy such as roads and railways, water and electricity supply, and telecommunications to attract new investments from overseas. J.S. Mill, the last great exponent of Classical Economics, forcefully argued the need for heavy government investments in infra-structure projects in a series of articles published in the Morning Chronicle in 1846-1847. Third, a significant level of investment will be required to ensure that the rapidly growing population and the labour force are productively employed, as otherwise a growing level of unemployment would pose a serious threat to political and economic stability.

Another important lesson from the teachings of Classical Economics is the urgent need to tackle the problem of over-population, excessive urbanisation and environmental degradation. It is clear that an economic reform programme that overlooks, or ignores the population and the population-related issues is essentially bankrupt in the Classical context. During 1981 to 2001 the total population have increased from 683 million to 1027 million. This gives an annual compound rate of growth of population

2.05 per cent. Extra mouths to feed will require a high level of investment all around including the provision of infrastructure facilities. When elementary needs of even the current population remain significantly unmet, the task ahead is very large, indeed. The Indian economy is ill placed to support a current population growth of around 2 per cent per annum. The conclusion emerging from the above is that overpopulation coupled with a current annual population growth rate of around 2 per cent in India will put intolerable burden on the future growth capacity of the economy and condemn the poorer sections of the community to economic deprivations over many, certain figures are worthy of consideration in this context. It is estimated that India still has about 36 per cent of the population who live below the poverty line. In absolute numbers this amounts to a staggering figure of over 300 million people who are very poor in India even today. It is true that in the longer term poverty eradication programmes must go hand-in-hand with programmes for economic development and industrialisation. It is also true that since the opening up of the Indian economy in July 1991, the annual growth rate of GDP accelerated to 7 per cent in 1996-97. Since then the GDP growth rate has marginally declined to around 6 per cent. No economic reform programme can therefore fail to ignore the demographic dimensions of India's current economic malaise. Even a superficial observer might argue that the battle against overpopulation in India may have already been lost after he (or she) experiences the level of urban degradation in major metropolitan cities. The NDA government had decided on 15th Feb. 2000 to adopt the National Population Policy with a view to encourage two child norms and at stabilising the population by 2046 AD. This population policy is a step in the right direction and demonstrates growing commitment of the government to population concern.

Liberalisation of the Indian economy and the programme of economic reforms have reduced the capacity of public sector enterprises to carry the large stock of surplus labour. The need for fiscal discipline has also made it necessary to get rid of surplus workers in government offices. At present, the Indian labour market is characterised by dualism. First, there is the huge unorganised sector employing nearly 270-300 million people, and secondly, there is the organised sector, representing less than 10 per cent of the labour market. The agricultural labourers constitute 26.3 per cent of the total work force and more or less in the position of slaves or serfs. They do not receive wages in cash but are generally paid in kind. In fact, the problem of landless or bonded labourers is the most serious problem in the rural sector. The Central and State Governments sought to influence wages in un-organised sectors through the instruments of statutory minimum wages for different industries. But a recent ILO study 17 shows that statutory minimum wages have been largely ineffective in influencing actual wages.

Indeed, in many Indian states, the statutory minimum wages have actually been lower in some cases than the poverty line wage. Indeed the fixation of minimum wages is no guarantee for their payment and this depends mainly on the role of State Government and on the extent of unionisation among the labourers. Another area of labour problem is labour redundancy and to face the problem of labour redundancy in the future, the Government of India established a National Renewal Fund (NRF), which is intended to fund the costs of voluntary early retirement and also to fund area regeneration schemes for areas with high incidence of job losses. National Renewal Fund (NRF) which is meant to finance voluntary retirement schemes, programmes for counseling retraining and redeployment of the workers accepting voluntary retirement and area regeneration schemes for areas with high incidence of job losses. First, statutory minimum wages should set a minimum price of labour in the economy in such a way that a wage worker is able to attain a minimum acceptable standard of living. Second, while labour market dualism exists and will undoubtedly persist for quite a while, state policies must not legitimize and institutionalize this. Third, in the organised sector, ways must be found to link wages with productivity and profitability without rendering labour incomes highly unstable. Finally, collective bargaining must be assigned an important role in the wage determination process." The progress of the NRF scheme has been disappointing so far.

The Indian economy is now facing a paradoxical situation. The rate of growth of agricultural output decelerated during the post liberalisation period as compared to pre-liberalisation period on the one hand and there is mounting stock of food grains on the other. The stock of good grains (mainly wheat and rice) increased from 18.1 million tonnes in 1997-98 to 44.7 million tonnes in 2000-01. Till late eighties, Indian agriculture was relatively closed to global market, as the export market was confined only to some commercial crops like, spices, tea, coffee, etc. and imports were largely restricted. However, with the removal of restrictions and export orientation of the sector many non-traditional commodities like, marine products, oil meals, cashew, tobacco, castor oil, groundnut, sesame, fresh fruits, vegetables, etc., were exported to more than 110 countries. The share of agricultural exports in total GDP which was on the decline in the eighties rose from 1.3 per cent in 1990-91 to 2.0 per cent in 1995-96 but since then it declined to 1.5 per cent in 2000-01. It seems that the degree of openness of the agricultural sector has increased after trade liberalisation but to a lesser extent than the economy as a whole. Agriculture generates about 27 per cent of India's GDP and provides employment to nearly 62 per cent its population. Despite the country's pre-eminent status in the world in terms of cultivable area (in certain food and non-food crops), livestock population, other natural endowments, etc., it lags far behind in productivity as well as income generation. The on-going liberalisation and trade policies in tune with the WTO provisions are focussing attention on this aspect of efficiency in Indian agriculture with comparative advantage as the fundamental watch-word.

Table 1: Pre and Post-liberalisation Growth in Agriculture.

Crops	*1980-81 to 1991-92*	*1992-93 to 1999-00*
Agriculture & Allied GDP (CARG at 1993-94 prices)	3.9	3.6
Agriculture (Crops, Animal Husbandry, Dairying)	4.2	3.7
Forestry	–0.1	0.8
Fishing	5.4	5.5
Crop Agriculture (CARG with base Triennium ending 1981-82)	3.4	2.2
Food grains	2.9	2.0
Cereals	3.1	2.1
Rice	3.7	2.2
Wheat	3.6	3.6
Coarse Cereals	0.0	–1.6
Pulses	1.4	0.8
Non Food grains	4.3	2.4

Source: Economy Survey (2000-01).

Now we have entered into the second generation reforms and it is the time to judge the achievement of objectives of the globalisation. It may be rightly observed that the globalisation has reduced the role of public sector in the economy and the private sector has failed to fill the vaccum created by the public sector investment of social objectives of poverty elimination. Our development strategy in this globalisation period should lead to the following ends:

1. A higher and sustainable growth of GDP.
2. Reducing the population living below poverty line and thus attaining the objective of poverty elevation.
3. Enlargement of employment potential leading to full employment.
4. Better opportunities of the development for the poorer of the society by providing them education, training in skill formation and better health and sanitation facilities.
5. reductions in regional disparities.

Our Former Finance Minister Mr. Yashwant Sinha has stated in his budget speech 2000-01 – "Growth is not just an end in itself. It is critical vehicle for increasing employment and raising the living standard of our people, specially of the poorest. Sustained broad based growth, combined with all our programmes for accelerating rural development, building roads, promoting housing, boosting knowledge based industries and enhancing the quality of the human resources, will impart a strong impetus to employment expansion. There is no better cure for poverty than this in our country."

REFERENCES

1. Hensman, R., 2001, 'World Trade and Workers' Rights: In Search of an Internationalist Position', in Waterman, Peter, and Wills, Jane (eds), *Place, Space and the New Labour Internationalism,* Blackwell Publishers, Oxford.

2. Kumar, Nagesh, 1995, 'Industrialisation, Liberalisation and Two Way Flows of Foreign Direct Investments: Case of India', *Economic and Political Weekly,* Vol. XXX No., 16 December, 3228-37.

3. Mahendra Dev, S., 2000(*a*), 'Economic Reforms, Poverty, Income Distribution and Employment', *Economic and Political Weekly,* Vol. XXXV No. 10, 4 March, 823-35.

4. Petras, James, 1999, 'Globalisation: A Socialists Perspective', *Economic and Political Weekly,* Vol. XXXIV No. 8, 20 February, 459-64.

5. Antony, M.J., 2001 (b), 'Bid to dilute contract labour law fails', *Business Standard,* 21 February.

6. The World Bank, India: Five Years of Stabilisation and Reform and the Challenging Ahead, Washington D.C. 1996, p.xxviii.

20

Trade Liberalisation and Intellectual Property Rights

Some Issues for India

B.K. Mohanty*

Introduction

With passage of time, learning rate increases. The society shifts from equilibrium at a lower level of knowledge to equilibrium at a higher level. At each subsequent state of equilibrium, some new but unique ideas evolve which shift the knowledge horizon further. The advent of new ideas and their application to practice temporarily unsettles the present state of equilibrium and undoubtedly renders the exiting arrangement of objects much complicated but such arrival is inevitable in a market economy. One such new idea in economics in general and economics of international trade in particular has been the idea of 'intellectual property rights' which was never heard in its present description and arrangement before December 20, 1991- the date on which Arthur Dunkel, the then Director General of the General Agreement on Tariffs and Trade (GATT) submitted a comprehensive document to the Uruguay Round of Multilateral Trade Negotiations. In the Uruguay Round, at the insistence of the USA, the issues relating to intellectual property were placed for negotiation among the member nations. Intellectual property rights (IPRs) can be defined as the rights enjoyed by people over the creation of their intellect (mind). These rights confer the creators with exclusive ownership entitlement over their own creations for a certain period of time. The conferment of such rights meets two broad objectives. This promotes

* Reader In Economics. Ravenshaw College, Cuttack-753 003, Orissa.

creative and inventive ideas and at the same time, restrains plagiarism which is believed to be a strong force of psychological deterrent to inventiveness and creativity in a man. Conventionally, such rights are categorised under two, viz., intellectual property (copy rights and related rights, production of phonograms and broadcasting organisations etc.) and industrial property (patents, trade marks, industrial designs etc.). Intellectual property by definition does not include industrial property. But in the Uruguay Round, the developed countries pressed for a comprehensive definition of the term to include industrial property and in fact, it happened so.

The development of the concept of IPRs and its application to multilateral trading system in normally linked with the name of World Trade Organisation (WTO) which came into existence on January 1, 1995 as the first and the foremost world trade regulatory body having enjoyed the status of a permanent organisation with a sound legal basis. The most avowed objective of the WTO is to create an atmosphere within which trade among nations to take place 'as freely as possible'. Moreover, the WTO is to provide a forum to its member countries to negotiate on the matters relating to international trade and commerce. Prior to the formation of WTO, cross-border trade in merchandise was guided by the rules and provisions of the GATT which was formed in 1947 to constitute both as an international agreement and an international organisation. The Bretton Woods Agreement of 1944 gave birth to three global institutions namely, the International Monetary Fund (IMF), the World Bank and the GATT. Being an international organisation, it was to support and implement the provisions covered under the Agreement which are the outcomes of bargaining and deal-making among the contracting parties. Though GATT was initially formed as a formal body to work with the World Bank and the International Monetary Fund (IMF) to meet the noble goal of looking after the post-War reconstruction of the world economy, by the end of 1970s it was perceived that the GATT has failed to deal with the complexities of world trade and equate the problem of trade with a part of the problem of development of underdeveloped countries in general. Moreover, the GATT remained as a 'rich men's club'. All these flaws in the manner of functioning of the GATT and the invasion of recession into the economies of developed countries during 1979, made it imperative to negotiate at a larger scale, Initially, GATT had to look after multilateral trading system involving trade in goods only. Now it was felt to extend the scope of functioning of the GATT, of course under a new description, to cover multilateral trade involving services, technology and investment. With a view to giving an acceptable design to extended system of plurilateral trade, the Uruguay Round of Multilateral Trade Negotiations was launched in

September 1986 which lasted for 8 years only to be concluded in December 1994. On the basis of the resolutions achieved at the Uruguay Round, a new international organisation called WTO was formed on January 1, 1995 with an objective to achieve unification of world trade rules and extending trade liberalisation to services not covered under the scope of operation of the erstwhile GATT and high-tech sectors. Unlike GATT, WTO is to cover three aspects of trade among nations *i.e.*, trade in goods to be regulated under new GATT rule 1994, trade in services to be governed under General Agreement on Trade in Services (GATS) and international flow of intellectual property to be guided by Trade Related Intellectual Property Rights (TRIPS) Agreement. All these three Agreements constitute a single package - WTO's jargon, a 'single undertaking' having accepted to all member nations.

Before the Uruguay Round (1986-1994), the framework of the GATT multilateral trading system, no specific agreement in any form ever achieved on IPRs among the member nations. However, some clauses in the GATT has limited reference to the cross-border movement of intellectual property which might have some bearings on the imports and exports of the concerned countries. For example, in old GATT constitution 1947, specific reference was made to IPRs. It wrote "measures which would otherwise be inconsistent with the General Agreement could be taken (subject to certain conditions) to secure compliance with laws or regulations relating, among other things, to intellectual property rights". Howver, an explicit and extended version of the intellectual property measures was contained in the Agreement reached for the WTO in December 1994.

The United Nations has been having an agency of its own known as the World Intellectual Property Organisation (WIPO) which was established by a convention of July 14, 1967 and came into effect in 1970. The WIPO administers the unions, treaties, resolutions achieved in the area of intellectual property. WIPO's objectives are three fold. First, it promotes intellectual property protection throughout the world through cooperation among the countries and while doing so, depending upon the necessity, in certain circumstances, it may collaborate with international organisations. Second, it also aims at ensuring administrative cooperation among the intellectual property unions. Third, it also undertakes development cooperation for developing countries through advice, training and furnishing of documents. The WIPO and the WTO entered into an Agreement which came into force on January 1, 1996. On the basis of the Agreement, both the organisations are to act in cooperation in three main areas like (1) notification of, access to an translation of national laws and regulations, (2) implementation of procedures for the protection of national emblems and (3) technical cooperation. Thus, WTO in addition to performing its usual functions and discharging its responsibilities towards its member countries is seen to have collaborated with an organ of the UN to promote intellectual property protection among the countries of the world. Though WTO is the successor of the GATT, the success or failure of the trade negotiations on which the WTO was formed, will point to its prospect of continuation as a global body for the promotion of world trade and commerce under free trade regime.

Trade Related Intellectual Property Rights (TRIPS)

Anything material or immaterial which is the creation of human mind or human intellect is called intellectual property. Since these objects are the creations of exceptional and specialised talents owned by the individuals, therefore are akin to private property to which the principle of exclusion applies. These creations are tradable on the international market. But the creators enjoy rights over the sale and purchase of such objects. The rights enjoyed over the commercial use of such creations are called trade related intellectual property rights (TRIPS). The conferment of such rights guarantees the right holders to exclude all illegal and unauthorised uses of such creations. The Agreement on TRIPS is built on the existing international conventions dealing with IPRs and therefore, enjoys legal status. The concept of TRIPS though has its implications for international trade, is associated with the name of WTO as the theory of TRIPS and its application to practice in a sound systematic basis and form was developed for the first time under the framework of the GATT multilateral trade negotiations which led to the formation of WTO. The objectives of TRIPS are explicit. The TRIPS Agreement once fully implemented will undoubtedly strengthen intellectual property protection globally and promote competition among nations.

In the preamble of the TRIPS Agreement, it is explicitly stated that the measures to implement intellectual property rights do not themselves be the sources of deterrence and barriers to genuine trade among nations. As it stands, the member nations are to implement the provisions of the Agreement. Once implemented, it is believed to promote free and fair trade in intellectual property among nations. But the less developed countries like India are apprehensive of its non-discriminatory consequences. The sources of growth of intellectual property are attributed to many of which the principal ones are the height of economic development of a country, its influence in the world market for trade and commerce, its access to scientific research and the possibility and extent of promotion of domestic R&D activity. Since member nations are heterogeneous in terms of providing for the above requirements, giving effect to such Agreement may harm the economic interest of countries having less of every thing or some such things. In common, implementation of the TRIPS Agreement may fail to generate conditions for balanced distribution of gains from free trade so long as countries with unequal bargaining power are the trade partners. Enormous benefits may accrue to research-based multinational corporations having operated from economically and industrially advanced countries. These corporations thus enjoy supremacy in respect of the supply of intellectual property having immediate application to manufacturing. Once they enjoy such monopoly power, will encourage them to charge high cost for technology transfer to less developed countries. Thus TRIPS Agreement by itself may turn as a barrier to free trade not only in intellectual property but also in merchandise and services as the trade in these three (merchandise, services and intellectual property) are interrelated.

Like any other agreements based on international conventions, the TRIPS Agreement also bears some unique features. The Agreement provides freedom to member nations to frame rules on protection of intellectual property. All the member nations are not bound by the Agreement to frame uniform rules. The Agreement provides some minimum standard for the protection of IPRs. The member nations may select to go for a wider coverage and therefore, the TRIPS Agreement is described as a 'minimum standard agreement.' It is not obligatory on the part of the countries to apply the provisions under the TRIPS Agreement at once *i.e.,* on the date of WTO came into being. Countries are allowed some general transition period within which they are to implement the provisions under the Agreement. But the duration of general transition period is not uniform for all member countries. (i) Developed countries are granted a maximum period of one year with effect from January 1, 1995. (ii) Develoing countries are allowed a transition period of five years till January 1, 2000. (iii) Transition economies- the economies of the countries which have voted to shift from centrally-planned or some such regimentation to market are allowed the same time duration of five years to expire on January 1, 2000. (iv) Least-developed countries (those countries having recognised as the least-developed by the United Nations) are granted the longest time duration of eleven years till January 1, 2006 to delay the implementation of the provisions under the Agreement with the allowance for further extension of time. However, the benefit of general transition period applies only to the original members of the WTO. The allowance for such period to countries is based on the fact that each country has to frame certain legislation to conform to TRIPS Agreement. Another essential feature of the Agreement is that the member nations of the WTO are under obligation to comply with the requirements of 'national treatment' and 'more-favoured-nation treatment'. While under the former requirement, the member countries are to treat foreign and domestic individuals and companies equal, under the latter, no discrimination is to be drawn between foreign individuals and companies and own individuals and companies.

Member countries of the WTO are under obligation to comply with the requirements of the TRIPS Agreement. In the event of any measure taken by any member nation detrimental to the economic and trade interest of some other member or members, the latter can choose to return the action of the former by amending its draft domestic legislation or taking some other measures. If a trading partner raises tariff wall or goes to impose some other quantitative restrictions on trade such that the exports of the other partner are adversely affected, the latter can amend its own legislation to retaliate the actions of the former which was framed on the basis of the TRIPS Agreement. But such retaliation is not always possible, sometimes becomes too difficult to pursue. IPRs are the rights granted to private persons for their own creations and these rights are protected under domestic legislation. If an executive decision is taken on any matter relating to trade which adversely affects the trade of the other, the latter cannot seek for a redressal in the courts of law. On the contrary, the violation of any law which has already been framed by appropriate legislation can be pursued in the courts of law. Since IPRs are the outcomes of legislative decisions, its violation by any member by any means even though it is desired on the ground of safeguarding its own interest, can be at once challenged in the courts of law. Therefore, the retaliating power of the TRIPS Agreement is highly susceptible to challenge. Moreover, it is the international politics which raises insurmountable barrier before the member nations to use TRIPS Agreement as an instrument of retaliation.

Another feature of the TRIPS Agreement relates to the procedure of licensing in respect of the use of patents by persons or company other than its inventor. Acquiring license is compulsory to use a patent and it is to be acquired from the right holder who is its original creator. But under certain circumstances, the Agreement allows the government to use a patent without the authorisation of its owner and/or to provide for 'compulsory licensing.' If an individual or a company desires to use the patent whose right rests with its creator, will have to first approach the right holder to issue licence in their favour. In that case, the person or the company must have offered the right holder a decent and adequate remuneration for his/her work and all such things should have been carried out on reasonable commercial terms. In the event of the failure to acquire the license due to the refusal of the original right holder, the government, as the Agreement provides, is free to use the patent without any license from the right holder or it may allow the agent (the person or the company) requesting for license to produce the patented product without the consent of the original patent owner which is referred to as the system of 'compulsory licensing.' However, under the TRIPS Agreement, supplying the domestic market is one of the pre-conditions to seek a license to use a patent.

The scope of protecting IPRs under the TRIPS Agreement is not unlimited. It is restricted to seven only namely patents, copyrights and related rights, trade marks, industrial designs, layout designs of integrated circuits, geographical indications and undisclosed information and trade secrets. *Patents:* Under WTO obligations, inventions in all fields of technology whether 'product' or process' having stood the test of being novel such that these inventions should have industrial applications and can be capable of solving any specific problem shall be patented. The TRIPS Agreement allows the countries to grant patents for such inventions and the patent right rests with the original creator. Patent right is granted by the government to its inventor for a fixed period of time to exclude other persons from imitation, production, using and selling of such patented product or process. May be very novel and unique invention, following are excluded from being patented like (i) diagnostic, therapeutic and surgical methods for treatment of humans and animals, (ii) plants and animals other than micro-organisms and (iii) biological processes for the production of plants and animals. In respect of agriculture and plant varieties, as it happens for India, it is expected to provide a protection either by 'patents' or 'under an effective *sui-generis* system' or 'any combination of the two'. The TRIPS Agreements is silent on the details of an effective *sui-generis* system. The system captures flexibility. It is left to member countries to define an effective *sui-generis* system appropriate to their local needs in the frame work of the Agreement and its coverage. *Copyrights and related rights:* The TRIPS Agreement requires the member countries to comply with the provisions of the Berne Convention in respect of the copyrights and other related rights. Any original work (not necessarily the original idea but the form in which it is expressed) falling within the domain of literature, science and art is to be protected under copyrights act. Such rights include the rights of performers, producers of phonograms and broadcasting organisations. Computer programmes are to be protected as literary works. The assumption of copyrights excludes others to use the form of the work without prior permission of the right holder. The Agreement stipulates that the term of protection for copyrights and right of performers and producers of phonograms should not be less than 50 years and for broadcasting organisations, it must not fall below 20 years. *Trade marks:* WTO obligations require member countries to give protection to both trade marks and service marks. A trade mark is defined as a sign which may consist of 'words, letters, numerals, figurative elements and combination of colours' of such other marks being used to distinguish the product of one firm (may be industrial or commercial enterprise) from that of the other. The TRIPS Agreement provides for conferment of exclusive rights on trade mark owners and also necessary guidelines as to when the trade marks are to be cancelled. It can be cancelled 'only after an un-interrupted period of last three years of non-use.' *Industrial designs:* The TRIPS Agreement necessitates that the member countries are to protect independently created industrial designs that are new and original. Industrial designs include 'shapes, lines, motifs and colours', therefore are treated to be the ornamental features of a product. Member countries however enjoy the option to exclude from protection, the designs dictated by technical and functional considerations. *Layout designs of integrated circuits:* Washington treaty which is otherwise referred to as WIPO covers protection of intellectual property in respect of layout designs of integrated circuits provided these are the original creations. The WTO obligations in this respect require the member nations to comply with the terms and conditions of the said treaty with little more extension in its coverage. The extended version of the obligations requires the member countries to give equal national treatment to foreign right holders and term of protection for 10 years. *Geographical indications:* By geographical indication it is meant the place of origin of the good in question. Such indications are used to tell the consumer that the good originates from a particular place and therefore, possesses certain specific characteristics as distinguished from other goods. Such characteristics are basically qualitative. The obligations under the TRIPS Agreement require each member nation shall have to provide for domestic legislation in order to prevent the misuse of such geographical indications. *Undisclosed information and trade secrets:* The TRIPS Agreement provides for the protection of trade secrets. Trade secrets do have commercial value and the person concerned is the lawful owner of such secrets. The WTO obligations require that legislations be framed by the member countries so as to prevent others to use such trade secrets without proper consent of its owner in violation of honest and genuine commercial practices.

WIPO as a specialist agency of the United nations was administering the international treaties till 1995 relating to intellectual property initiated by the Paris and Berne Conventions. Since the TRIPS Agreement holds the WTO member countries to comply with the substantive obligations of the Paris and Berne Conventions, it is sometimes referred to as a "Berne and Paris-plus" Agreement. While the Paris Convention of 1883 for the first time dealt with the areas relating to industrial property like inventions, trade marks and industrial designs, the Berne Convention of 1886 gave coverage to literary and artistic works. The Paris Convention 1883 has been revised six times till date, the latest being in the year 1967 and a major amendment and a major amendment in 1979. Each revision and amendment allows more monopolistic privilege to patent holders. One of the inventions of the Paris Convention is the national treatment *i.e.*, the same treatment for nationals and foreigners which has been borrowed by treatment *i.e.,* the same treatment for nationals and foreigners which has been borrowed by the TRIPS Agreement. Many a freedom which was available under the Paris Convention has been taken away by the WTO. Accordingly, the WTO has restricted the freedom of the member nations for formulating their own intellectual property laws. Though the TRIPS Agreement has drawn heavily on the Paris Convention, the former is different from both the Paris and Berne Conventions. While the latter two conventions are free-standing and do not constitute any organ of any international treaty or convention or agreement, the TRIPS Agreement is a part of the WTO Agreement. IPRs to a great extent relate to industrial property. Very limited reference has been made to agriculture related intellectual property. Thc UPOV (Union International pour la Protections des Obtentions Vegetables) Conventions of 1961 for the first time on the basis of multilateral treaty emphasised the protection of new plant varieties. But almost a negligible outcome has emerged out of the Convention. This failure is basically attributed to its laws being framed by developed and industrialised countries that are innocent of the existing and potential problems and actual status of farm sector in agrarian economies. The Rio Earth Summit in 1992 and the Fourth WTO Ministerial Conference held at Doha in 2001 achieved something notable in this respect.

In the preamble of the TRIPS Agreement, it has been neatly mentioned that any measure to enforce intellectual property rights do not themselves become 'barriers to legitimate trade' among nations. But a close scrutiny of the provisions under the Agreement, more particularly the provisions relating to 'innovation, transfer and dissemination of technology' points to the existence of certain over-burdening clauses. The enforcement of these clauses may raise barriers in the realisation of trade and economic interest of countries particularly of less developed countries. For less developed countries, trade has been one of the fundamental forces of accelerating the speed of economic development. Having felt the urgency of trade for overall development of less developed countries, the WTO maintains that these countries need to secure a share in the growth of international trade in proportion to their requirements for economic development. As the situation stands, less developed countries lack adequate technology in appropriate quantity. They rely on the technology transfer from the developed block. This will be strongly hindered if the TRIPS Agreement is implemented in its current form. It is because the holders of IPRs having secured a monopoly or near monopoly position may be tempted to charge on exorbitant price for dissemination of such technology. In this case, the TRIPS Agreement by itself will become a cause of discrimination against the poorer partners in trade.

Another limitation in the existing WTO Agreement is found in terms of its failure to recognize the issues and their resolutions which may arise out of trade-development-environment nexus. GATT as such had not any direct reference to the protection of environment which might become inevitable due to liberalised trade regime. WTO, however made reference to the relevance of sustainable or environmental-friendly development while emphasising the expansion of world trade on mutually agreed basis by recognising the importance of "allowing for the optimal use of the world's resources in accordance with the objective of sustainable development, seeking both to protect and preserve the environment and to enhance the means for doing so in a manner consistent with their respective needs and concerns at different levels of economic development." In fact, WTO basically deals with trade-development issues, it does not deal with its extended but more realistic version i.e., trade-development-environment issue. WTO's main concern being the effects of regulations on trade has made the trade-development-environment issue a peripheral one. This has been a strong cause of resentment among green activists and members of the civil society groups to the acceptance of the obligations under WTO Agreement. While emphasising the expansion of world trade, necessary restrictions in proper shape and adequate quantity must be made to ensure environmental protection if such trade endangers 'human, animal, plant life and health' and goes counter to the policies of conserving exhaustible natural resources. Liberalised and free trade regime affects trade and at the same time is likely to affect environment adversely. Domestic manufacturers under a free trade regime may be encouraged to increase their activity by overexploiting natural resources in order to secure a larger share in world trade. It may also tempt the countries having no standardised domestic regulations to contain environmental problems to go for more industries which may be a source of rapid depletion in exhaustible natural resources, thus having adverse implications for environment. Under such a situation, increased exports of the countries may be acquired by overexploiting environmental (common property land, water and forest) resources which threatens the sustainability of development. Any international convention or treaty on trade must not clash with the objectives of such convention or treaty on environment. The former must come with a package of measures to deal with local and global environmental problems, if arise in the event of the implementation of the measures relating to the promotion of world trade. But this has not happened with the WTO. No systematic and clear-cut provisions are there in the WTO Agreement to address environmental problems if arise due to trade-development relationship which is the main focal attention of the Organisation. In this respect, the Mexican tuna-dolphin case and India-Malaysia-Pakistan-Thailand (IMPT) shrimp-turtle case seem grave[1]. The Doha Declaration (2001) having acknowledged the import of such conflicts, clearly iterated that any such areas not explicitly included in the original agenda of the WTO could be interpreted to have been included. The WTO Agreement just says that trade affecting human, animal or plant life or health is to be excluded from the scope of normal GATT discipline and also no patent right can be granted in favour of its inventor if such patent threatens the existence and continuation of human, animal or plant life or causes health hazards and acts as a source of environmental damage. Though these green provisions exist in the original WTO Agreement, no rule has been prescribed for the member countries to deal with such problems which may arise on account of expanded trade among nations. Only iteration of certain problems does not automatically point to their solution. The member countries enjoy freedom to impose restrictions on trade under the WTO obligations if such trade goes contrary to the general principles of preservation of ecology. Accordingly, trade restrictions may serve appropriate policy measures in a regime of liberalised trade. Moreover, better management of environmental resources can be expected from expanded trade. WTO Agreement itself is an international agreement for expanded trade. Trade among nations with varied level of economic development helps the less developed partners to have access to several policy measures adopted by the developed ones to preserve ecology and environment and hence, the latter can acquire knowledge as to how their own such problems can be solved. This happens due to international transmission of ideas which has been a consequence of expanded trade among nations.

Intellectual Property Rights and India

India is a founder member of the WTO and also a signatory in the TRIPS Agreement. Accordingly, India is under obligation to formulate its own laws for strict protection of IPRs. India being a developing country, was allowed a transition period of five years till January 1, 2000 to formulate its own laws in conformity with TRIPS Agreement. But India did not act haste. After careful study of the ground reality and close observations of the public opinions on the issue, it took measures to collaborate with the full implementation of the TRIPS Agreement. Some such new laws so framed to give effect to the implementation of the TRIPS Agreement in India, are seen to have been at par with international practice. These laws include (1) Patents (Amendment) Ordinance, 1994, (2) Copyright Law 1994 which came into force with effect from May, 1995 in conformity with the Berne Convention on Copyrights, (3) Patents (Amendment) Act, 1999, (4) Trade Marks Bill, 1999, (5) Copyright (Amendment) Act, 1999, (6) Geographical Indications of Goods (Registration and Protection) Bill, 1999 which was intended to provide a *sui generis* legislation for the protection of geographical indications, (7) Industrial Designs Bill, 1999 and (8) Patents (Second Amendment) Bill, 1999 approved by the Parliament in 2002 in compliance with the TRIPS Agreement.

India, much earlier than the formation of the WTO, has taken certain measures to strengthen the intellectual property administration system in the country. Such measures consist of (1) setting up of the Office of Patent Information System in 1980 and (2) taking up a project for modernisation of trade marks registry in 1993. The Patent Information System was intended to provide information contained in patent documents to the users consisting of scientists and researchers working at the Indian Institutes of Technology, universities and research institutes/organisations. Trade mark registry is essential to benefit the consumers. Trade marks provide adequate information about the origin of the commodities without which there remains the likelihood of the consumers being deceived. India was not a member of the Paris Convention. But India framed certain laws consistent with the Paris Convention prior to the formation of the WTO relating to intellectual property protection of which Indian Patent Act, 1970 is one. This Act came into force in 1972. All these point to India's sincerity in fulfilling the obligations under the TRIPS Agreement by enacting its own laws. After the constitution of the WTO in 1995, Indian trade marks law has been stretched to include service marks in addition to trade marks for goods. Piracy in computer software had been a common problem in India thwarting the effective implementation of the IPRs clauses. The International Intellectual Property Association (IIPA) estimated a trade loss to US companies in India during 1997 due to piracy in computer programmes for business applications and entertainment software respectively as 76 and 82 per cents of the total loss in these sectors.[2]

The extent of such piracy has been reduced substantially through court orders. And also computer database has been protected in India. In addition to the above measures, few more measures like enforcement of copyright law and reforms in judicial process have also been implemented by the Government of India to strengthen the intellectual property administration in the country. Hence, India has made all possible efforts to strengthen the protection of IPRs.

With the formation of the WTO, a lot of hopes and expectations were projected on its beneficial consequences on world trade and commerce. The World Bank, OECD and GATT Secretariat drew an optimistic note on its likely achievements. It was forecast that the implementation of the Uruguay Round package would add to world income ranging between 213 and 274 billion dollars. The GATT Secretariat went one step ahead by projecting that most of the benefits from meeting the obligations under the WTO framework would go in favour of trade in clothing (60%), agriculture, forestry and fishery products (20%) and processed food and beverages (19%). Since India enjoys export competitiveness in these product groups, it was estimated that its market share in world exports might increase from 0.5 per cent to 1 per cent after the full implementation of the WTO obligations.[3] The transition period granted to India as a matter of policy under the WTO Agreement expired on January 1, 2000. Over two years 2000-01 – 2001-02, the exports of India measured in rupee terms in respect of (1) clothing which includes cotton yarn, fabrics and made-ups and ready made garments and (2) agriculture, forestry and fishery products diminished by 11.07 and 0.09 per cents respectively. But there has been a 12.98 per cent increase in the exports of processed food and beverages of India over the last two years.[4] All this does not support the optimism with which the prediction was made for India.

Some case Studies

While complying with the WTO obligations in respect of intellectual property administration, certain areas of the national economy of India are likely to be affected of which agriculture and pharmaceuticals are the most important ones.

Intellectual Property Rights and Indian Agriculture

Agriculture was kept out of the purview of the original GATT (1947) till 1994. It was felt to bring agriculture within the purview of an international agreement with an objective to make it more competitive and therefore, more productive. In the Final Act of the Uruguay Round, a comprehensive Agreement on Agriculture (AoA) was arrived at in which specific importance was placed on policies relating to market access, export competition and domestic support. Market access policy is to be governed by a 'tariffs only' regime whereby the member countries of the WTO will substitute subsidies by tariffs. Export competition policy needs the countries to compete in the world market to sell their exports. The domestic support policy requires identifying acceptable measures of support to farmers. In the Third WTO Ministerial Conference held at Seattle in 1999, countries like the USA wanted to complete negotiations and extend the work of the Uruguay Round on the Agreement on Agriculture. But the Seattle sitting was a failure which ended in confusion without having reached a Declaration due mostly to the disagreement among the advanced countries on several areas of concern of which TRIPS was one. Till Seattle (Singapore in 1996, Geneva in 1998), India has been emphatic on the negotiation on international protection for two types for intellectual properties namely, (1) indigenous knowledge and genetic resources and (2) geographical indications like Darjeeling tea, Basmati rice, Alphonsa mango. The Fourth WTO Ministerial Conference held at Doha in 2001 achieved something substantial in respect of negotiations in agriculture. At Doha, the countries were unanimous to accept that among all forms of intellectual properties, it is patent which has direct and immediate implications for agriculture in developing countries. In fact, Doha Declaration is a declaration on TRIPS Agreement relating to agriculture and plant variety. The negotiations provided for substantial improvements in market access for developing countries and phasing out of all forms of export subsidies. Such negotiations recognize the development needs of the developing, less developed and underdeveloped countries including food security and rural development and therefore, allowed differential treatment of these country groups. The Doha declaration granted the member nations to complete the modalities for negotiations in agriculture by 31st March, 2003 and the schedule of obligations based on these modalities by September, 2003.

From among the seven categories of IPRs, patents, trade marks, geographical indications and trade secrets are directly applicable to agriculture and plant varieties. Patenting of an agricultural product not only confers the patentee with the right to prevent the third parties from making, using or selling the product, but also encourages further scientific research in the line to develop better varieties. As a part of the conditions of the TRIPS Agreement, the member countries shall provide for the protection of plant varieties either by patents or by an effective *sui generis* system or by a judicious combination of both. On ground of convenience to the growers of plants, India opted to provide protection through an effective *sui generis* system by keeping in view the privileges of both farmers and researchers. While doing so, the government is committed to protect farmers' rights in the Indian plant variety legislation. At Doha, India submitted a proposal containing two main requirements in Agreement on Agriculture. It insisted on taking measures which would safeguard the food and livelihood security of the Indian farmers who basically lead subsistence living. The second proposal was in respect of reducing high tariffs and subsidies prevalent in developed countries so as to maximize India's export opportunities for its farm products.

Inclusion of agriculture sector under the scope of TRIPS Agreement created a lot of confusion and discomfort to the sympathizers of the third world agriculture. To the critics of such an attempt, once agriculture is brought under the TRIPS Agreement, it would be highly disadvantages for the farming communities of the third world countries where agriculture is not only undeveloped but also lacks provisions for scientific research. Once agricultural sector is opened to competition as a part fulfillment of the WTO obligations and patenting is granted, most of the benefits would accrue to the developed countries and multinationals operating from these countries. Among such benefits which are likely to be withdrawn outright from the farmers due to the patenting of seeds, the most important one is the 'farmers' privilege' which includes farmers' own seed supply. Once the seeds are patented, use of uncertified seeds will be treated as an offence and hence, farmers using such seeds will be liable for punishment.[5] This amounts to stealing the right of farmers and imposing on them the compulsory acceptance of a certified brand with uncertified quality. The multinationals, with a view to capturing the largest market share in patented products can invest an unimaginable amount on R&D activities which remains as a dream for less developed countries. In addition to this, it is apprehended that once agriculture is brought under the TRIPS Agreement, the prices of seeds would increase manifold thereby threatening the food security of the country. In India, such apprehension led to protests through demonstrations against the plant variety clauses of the TRIPS Agreement. In order to allay such fear, the Ministry of Commerce, Government of India made a declaration that India did not have to accept the clauses in the Dunkel Draft relating to patenting of plant varieties. It had to devise an effective *sui generis* system which would protect the national interest. It is still doubted whether such a declaration could be able to erase such deep seated fear from the minds of the adversaries of the Dunkel Draft.

Another area of IPRs is geographical indications which find its full application to agriculture. Some agricultural products attract export market on ground of their places of origin. One such example is the Indian grown basmati rice. In 1997, a controversy arose in India in respect of the issuance of patent in the United States to Ricetec, a US company for its claim to have invented novel basmati rice[6]. ".... In September, 1997, Ricetec was granted a patent for allegedly novel basmati lines and grains which were created from the crossing of the basmati germplasm (of Pakistani origin) taken from an *ex situ* gene bank in the US with American long grained variety of rice. Ricetec has claimed that the new varieties have the same or better aroma, grain length and other characteristics than the original basmati variety grown in India and Pakistan and can be grown successfully in specified geographical areas in North America. The Agricultural Export Development Agency (APEDA) of the Ministry of Commerce in the Government of India has been entrusted with the task of representing the rice exporters in any re-examination of the patent in the US Patent and Trademarks Office (USPTO), if it is decided that there are sufficient grounds for the eventual revocation of the patent." Here the question is whether Ricetec can use the title basmati for the product that it has claimed to have invented. This is possible only when basmati is treated as a generic name having referred to a variety of rice and therefore, no protection can be available for it. If basmati is 'placed specific' and it refers only to India or Pakistan, then no patent can be granted to Ricetec and adequate protection has to be granted for such variety. This is again a lesson for India while framing an effective *sui generis* system.

The Agreement on Agriculture (AoA) necessitates the member nations of the WTO to agree with the areas like domestic support and export competition. These two areas are complementary. In order to make own exports competitive in the world market, other things being given, the countries are to make such exportable items price attractive and prices of such items can be kept artificially low if high farm support (subsidy etc.) is granted. The developed countries like the members of the European Union, Japan and Korea etc. provide high farm support. A small farm support will bring to them a disproportionately high return. These countries allow such farm support on economic grounds. They are convinced that demand for their farm products is highly elastic in international market mainly because of the severe competition from other substitutes. If they hold the price lower by bearing a part of the cost of production through subsidy or any variant of farm support, there will immediately be more than proportionate gain from such exercise. But the conditions of third world countries including India are different. Agriculture is traditional and it provides livelihood to a majority of their population. In order these countries to compete in the world market for export of farm products, the current trend must be reversed by increasing the productivity of their farm sector which necessitates increasing R&D expenditure on agriculture and granting and protecting farmers' rights. More particularly, the farm sector is to be left under the nurture of science and technology (S&T).

Intellectual Property Rights and Indian Pharmaceutical Industry

The pharmaceutical industry of India is one of the fastest growing industries. It has earned the reputation of manufacturing high-quality drugs at low cost. Of the total internal demand for medicines, 95 per cent is met from indigenous production. The remaining 5 per cent consisting mainly of life-saving medicines is met out of imports. Prior to January 1, 1995, Indian patent laws did not allow product patent on pharmaceuticals. But process patenting was available. The Pharmaceutical Research and Manufacturers' Association (PhRMA) of India was emphatic on India adopting a patent law which should provide immediate product patent protection to pharmaceuticals. From this date, product patenting has been incorporated. The provision of such product patent is expected to have two-fold consequences. Firstly, it may affect the pharmaceutical units differently. Such affects could be skewed in favour of large units and multi-national corporations and in against of small units dealing with the production of pharmaceuticals. Secondly, the drugs prices in India may increase manifold. It is apprehended that such price rise may range between 5 to 10 times of the price prevailing in the post-patent period and hence, it would cause loss of consumer surplus. But such argument has been countered by the Indian Export Register (A Brief Guide to the WTO for Small Businesses, 2000). It holds that in the list of essential drugs prepared by the WHO, hardly 10 per cent of these drugs are under the patent regime and hence, such expectation regarding soaring of drugs prices is hardly with any sound base.

Adoption of IPRs and patenting of products in pharmaceutical industry of India will create new challenge for that sector by exposing the sector to competition both from within and outside. Once competition becomes optimum, it will encourage the scientists to work for the creation of something very novel in the line and at the same time, the industry itself will rise to face the challenge which has been emphasised by one of the most reputed pharmaceutical industries functioning from India. The Chief Managing Director of Ranbaxy Laboratories Ltd. says "... by agreeing to comply with the TRIPS Agreement, we have set the clock in motion. We now need to take measures to ensure that we are prepared to meet this challenge... from being technology driven, the industry need to be innovation led. There is a lot to be gained from the synergies that remain untapped between government laboratories, industry and academic. Even though we have lost precious time (in debating when to allow product patent), it is still (perhaps) not too late in leveraging the situation to our benefit"[7]. In spite of all such efforts created from within, if the implementation of TRIPS Agreement will impose any cost on the pharmaceutical sector of India, it can be mitigated by the system of compulsory licensing and devising an effective policy of competition.

In the Fourth WTO Ministerial Conference held at Doha, India along with some other like minded countries from the developing world demanded flexibility in the interpretation of the Agreement on TRIPS. Such flexibility was sought in respect of access to essential medicines and life saving drugs at affordable prices and formulating their own public health policies by keeping in view their own requirements. It ultimately brought success to their claim. At the conclusion, the Doha Declaration affirmed that the TRIPS Agreement can be interpreted and implemented by the member countries in a manner appropriate to their requirements to protect public health and allow access to medicines for all. Thus it was a victory of the third world member countries of the WTO. The Indian Patent Act provides for 14 years terms for all patents and 7 years in the case of pharmaceuticals. New patent law for pharmaceuticals in the framework of TRIPS Agreement will be implemented in India effective from January 1, 2005.

Conclusion

Liberalised trade regime has the twin objectives of achieving export oriented growth and increasing gains from trade. Pre-conditions for export oriented growth are not only to make exports of the residents cheap in international market but also an assurance of quality. This happens only when the industries supplying exports extend their own R&D activities in conformity with an international standard. These industries will be encouraged to do so if their own creations are protected against plagiarism through legislation. This exhibits the presence of a linkage between export oriented growth and intellectual property protection. It is thus believed that the Indian objective of export led growth will be realised for its being a signatory in the TRIPS Agreement. The policy of trade liberalisation in India has proved conducive to the promotion of patents. The Government of India introduced economic reform measures in the mid-1990s. The number of applications for patent licensing in India has increased from 3552 in 1990-91 to 8562 in 1996-97. This stands a testimony to the positive response of Indians to the acceptance of TRIPS Agreement in general and granting of patent rights in particular.

Intellectual property rights create a new protection regime and cause technology upgradation and development. But Indian acceptance of the international agreement on TRIPS must not compromise with its own economic interest, more particularly in agriculture. In any international forum whenever any matter relating to intellectual property protection in agriculture has ever been placed for negotiation, the member countries are seen to have divided in their deliberations and opinions. In some cases, the matter has ended with confusion and conflict. Intellectual property protection, more particularly patenting in agriculture was one of the items on the agenda for negotiation in the Seattle and Doha Conferences of the Ministers of the WTO member countries. While Seattle Conference was concluded with no declaration, at Doha, finally it came with Declaration for agriculture favouring the opinions of the representatives of the agrarian countries.

The success from India's acceptance of TRIPS Agreement depends on its readiness and capability to provide for the basic requirements. Intellectual property protection can be successful if the countries can provide for the requirements like taking certain legislative measures, constituting administrative machinery and evolving one judicial mechanism to deal with those conflicts which may arise while administering the intellectual property protection. It is a fact that all developing countries cannot provide for these basic requirements at once on ground of their paucity of resources for the purpose. But India's sincerity in this respect is never doubted.

NOTES

1. **Case-I:** Mexican 'Tuna-dolphin' Case:

   In 1988, the USA amended its Marine Mammal Protection Act. The objective of such amendment was to restrict the imports of fish caught with technologies that do not meet the protection standard set by the USA. From such legislation, Mexican export to America was adversely affected. In 1991, it approached the GATT panel to rule on the issue. Mexico put its argument for lifting such restriction for five heads that (1) it was a form of quantitative restriction on imports which violates Article XI, (2) it was a discrimination against a particular geographical region inconsistent with Article XIII, (3) it was against the 'national treatment' clause, (4) the term 'exhaustible' in the Amendment did not apply to renewable resources and (5) Article XX was inoperative as measures taken outside the geographical territory of the nation (by the USA) did not apply to the country taking the measure (the USA). The panel ruled in favour of Mexico under the following arguments. (1) The USA was not competent under the existing GATT obligations to impose any restriction on imports from Mexico on the ground that Mexican way of producing tuna did not satisfy the US specification. However, it could do so on the ground of the quality and/or contents of the tuna product likely to be exported to the USA. (2) In the framework of the GATT's rule, no country could impose any restriction on trade with a view to enforcing its own domestic law. (3) This was not the only measure available to the USA to pursue against the import of Mexican tuna product. Thus, the USA lost the case.

   Case-II: The 'Shrimp-turtle' Case:

   It is a dispute between the US on the one hand and India, Malaysia, Pakistan and Thailand on the other which dates back to 1996. Under the authority of the Endangered Species Act, the US imposed embargoes on the imports of shrimp and shrimp products from these countries that did not certify that the shrimp were caught by employing catching technologies that made use of 'turtle excluding devices' (TED) in areas with high presence of sea turtles. The US rationalised the imposition of such embargo on the ground that it was aimed at protecting sea turtles which are declared as endangered species and that sea turtles are highly migratory and therefore, a globally shared resource whose conservation is a global responsibility. India, Malaysia, Pakistan and Thailand requested the dispute settlement panel of the WTO to rule on the imposition of the embargo by the USA as such imposition violates the principle of 'most favoured nation' treatment. The panel ruled that the US action could not be upheld as it amounted to a violation of the GATT principle of 'general elimination of quantitative restriction.' The panel further ruled that though the protection of sea turtle was a serious issue, the unilateral measure taken by the US was a bare threat to the multilateral trading system as comprehended under GATT framework. Hence the US action was invalidated under the chapeau of Article XX which relates to environment-trade issues. The panel's ruling was followed by a US appeal. The appellate body of the WTO did not reverse the ruling of the panel. It took a decision which provided a greater responsibility to the USA for negotiating with the member nations of the WTO on the protection of the endangered species like sea turtle. In the decision of the appellate body, the US embargo imposition was legitimate having environmental objective. Further the body held that sea turtles are 'exhaustible resources' which are highly migratory and therefore could occur in waters over which the US exercises jurisdiction. The body asked the US to negotiate with concerned governments on the protection of sea turtles and provision of technical training to them in the use of TED within a reasonable period of time.

2. Source: Policy Statements on 'Intellectual Property Rights in India', Embassy of India, Washington, DC, 2002.
3. Source: Economic Survey, Government of India, Ministry of Finance, 1994-95.
4. Source: Economic Survey, Government of India, Ministry of Finance, 2002-03.
5. In a system of farming where patenting of seeds is not made, farmers are granted privilege to use their own seeds raised by themselves. In the event of the issuance of patents for seeds, the rights of farmers in general and that of farmers of less developed countries in particular will be seriously undermined. This is evident from a dispute which arose in Bavaria. In Bavaria, commercial (patented) seeds are available. A farmer in the village of Oberding having not satisfied with the quality of such seeds developed his own ecological variety of wheat seeds. Few other farmers from the neighbouring villages procured the wheat seeds from him. This went to the ears of the Government of Upper Bavaria. Since the farmer used and traded in uncertified seeds, was fined by the Government of Upper Bavaria (Shiva Vandana, 1997).
6. This and the following evidence is based on 'Watal Jayashree (1988): Intellectual Property Rights in Indian Agriculture, Working Paper No. 44, Indian Council for Research on International Economic Relations, New Delhi".
7. Source: The Economic Times, December 29, 1998.

REFERENCES

1. Alagh, Y. K. (2001): Globalisation Debate, The Indian Economic conference 84th Volume pp. 1-9.
2. Chadha, G.K. (2000): Indian Economy under the WTO Regime: Happenings, Non-happenings and Missing Links, The Indian Economic Conference 83rd Volume, pp. 13-35.
3. Chandiramani No. (2002): Legal Factors in TRIPS, Economic and Political Weekly, Vol. 37, No. 3, pp. 200-203.
4. Chimni, B.S. (2002): WTO and Environment: Legitimisation of Unilateral Trade Sanctions, Vol. 37, No. 2, pp. 133-139.
5. Desai, Ashok V. (1988): India and the Uruguay Round, Economic and Political Weekly (Special Number), Vol. 23, Nos. 45-47, pp. 2371-2384.
6. Dhar, B. (1995): An Anatomy of the Emerging Trading System, the Indian Economic Conference 78th Volume, pp. 301-308.
7. Rao, C.H. Hanumanth (2001): WTO and Viability of Indian Agriculture, Economic and Political Weekly, Vol. 36, No. 36, pp. 3453-3457.
8. Ruta, Giovanni (2002): Economic and Institutional Aspects of the Trade and Environment Debate, Environmental Economics and Development Policy-V, World Bank Institute.
9. Shiva Vandana (1997): Bio-diversity, Totalitarianism, IPRs and Seed Monopolies, Economic and Political Weekly, Vol. 32, No. 41, pp. 2582-2585.
10. Srivastava, Jayati and Rajeev Ahuja (2002): Shrimp-Turtle Decision in WTO: Economic and Systematic Implication for Developing Countries, Economic and Political Weekly, Vol. 37, No. 33, pp. 3445-3455.
11. Subramanian, Arvind (1999): Indian as User and Creator of Intellectual Property: The Challenges Post-Seattle, Paper Presented at the Workshop on 'South Asia and The WTO', New Delhi, December 20-21.
12. Watal Jayashree (1998): Intellectual Property Rights in Indian Agriculture, Working Paper No. 44, Indian Council for Research on International Economic Relations, New Delhi, July.

21

Growth, Poverty and Economic Reforms in India

A Macro View

Talwar Sabanna*

Introduction

Reduction of poverty issue is so central to development and policy that it warrants further examination. The basic question is the following: Does the pursuit of economic growth along GDP maximising lines tend to improve, worsen or have no necessary effect on the distribution of income and the extent of poverty in developing countries? Unfortunately, economists do not at present possess any definitive knowledge of the specific factors that affect changes in the distribution of income over time for individual countries. Professor Kuznets has suggested that in the early stages of economic growth, the distribution of income will tend to worsen while later stages it will improve.

It was found through the empirical study in various developing countries that the principal impact of economic development on income distribution has been, on average, to decrease both the absolute and the relative incomes of the poor. There was no evidence of any automatic "trickle-down" of the benefits of economic growth to the very poor.

The necessity of reorienting development priorities away from exclusive pre-occupation with maximising rates of GDP growth and toward broader social objectives such as the eradication of poverty and the reduction of

* Faculty, Department of Economics, Karnatak University, K.R.C. P.G. Centre, Belgaum.

excessive income disparities is now widely recognised in the developing economies.

In the Indian context, alleviation of poverty coupled with employment have remained the central challenge of development right since the beginning of plan periods, for the society as a whole, employment, equity and growth are the three pillars to support its survival-employment to provide means of livelihood to its members, equity to provide social justice and cohesion, and growth to translate an outward shift in the frontiers of knowledge for the benefit of mankind (Mathur, 1998).

No doubt, in recent years, a number of studies are available on various aspects of poverty (such as Tendulkar and Jain, 1995; Hashim, 1999; Gupta, 1999; Sundaram, 2001; Vaidyanathan, 2001; Angus and Jean, 2002; Rao C.H.H., 2003 etc). An additional leap has been attempted in this paper to examine some dynamic aspects of poverty and its implications on Indian economy (especially during the post-reforms regime).

Growth and Poverty Issues in India

Currently, there is an interesting debate in India on the impact of growth and economic reform on poverty alleviation. The data and analysis, whether in terms of direct poverty ratios or indirectly looking at unemployment and wages are reported to suggest that in the 1990s, especially in the years after the onset of reform in mid 1991, rural poverty reduction has been arrested, while urban recorded a decline. It is noteworthy that the increased GDP growth and moderate inflationary pressures have helped to alleviate poverty. Thus, growth helps to reduce poverty due to three central reasons:

1. It creates jobs that 'pull up' the poor into gainful employment by providing more economic opportunity;
2. It provides the revenues with which we can build more schools and provide more health facilities for the poor; and
3. It creates the incentives that enable the poor to access these facilities and also for the advancement of progressive social agendas generally.

It is a fact that few serious economists thought of growth as an instrument for reducing poverty. The focus on poverty was always there, at least in India. True, we could redistribute incomes, assuming that was politically possible, but we had to think of sustainable attack on poverty, not a one shot-effect.

There was a mega-debate that growth with Green Revolution would harm the poor introducing a new divide between rich and poor, the former using and the latter unable or unwilling to use the new seeds; many feared and some hoped that the Green Revolution would then usher in the Red Revolution! This did not transpire; the Green Revolution increased the demand for labour and worked benignly with regard to workers wages (Jagadish Bhagawati, 2001).

In linking poverty reduction with reform and growth in India in the 'nineties', the first question that crisis is with regard to the counter factual, viz. if there were no reform, would the reduction in poverty ratios have continued. Then again, we might ask: has GDP growth once achieved, managed to improve poverty levels in India? In the 1980s, as Table 1 shows, we changed to a higher GDP growth rate of 5.7 per cent annually; but most analysts agree that it was based on unsustainable borrowing and spending policies. In fact, these policies, produced the 1990-91 crisis. After 1991, we have had similar GDP growth rates, i.e. 5.8 per cent annually, and these are more sustainable and do reflect the ongoing reforms. Further, it could be argued that, in view of the international and domestic uncertainties, particularly in the recent years, the vulnerability of the economy and also of the poor would have been severe in the absence of reform.

Table 1: Annual Growth Rate of GDP at Constant Prices. (1993-94)

Pre-Reform Period		*Post-Reform Period*	
Years	*Per cent Per Annum*	*Years*	*Per cent Per Annum*
1981-82	6.0	1991-92	1.3
1982-83	3.1	1992-93	5.1
1983-84	7.7	1993-94	5.9
1984-85	4.3	1994-95	7.3
1985-86	4.5	1995-96	7.3
1986-87	4.3	1996-97	7.8
1987-88	3.8	1997-98	4.8
1988-89	10.5	1998-99	6.6
1989-90	6.7	1999-00	6.4
1990-91	5.6	2000-01	5.2
Average (1981-91)	5.7	Average (1991-01)	5.8

Source: Hand Book of Statistics on Indian Economy, RBI, 2001.

Poverty - at the National Level

A 'poor' is defined as one who cannot afford to spend a stipulated minimum real expenditure per capita. Poverty in today's official definition depends on the level of per capita consumption. Further the level of per capita consumption depends on; (i) productivity and earnings per employed labour in a household; (ii) number of people employed in a household; (iii) household size; and (iv) the saving propensity of a household.

Before going into the explanations of poverty trends, we briefly mention here the determinants of poverty in both rural and urban areas. There are essentially three factors; agricultural growth, food prices and anti-programmes which influence rural poverty. Agricultural growth is very important for rural areas for not only increasing production but also for income generation to the labourers in the form of employment and wages and its linkages with non-agriculture. Its indirect impact to prices is also quite high. The changes in food prices affect the real incomes of the poor as foodgrains are the basic need that has a large share of consumption in the budgets of the rural poor. Equally important is of public action in influencing changes in rural poverty. Because, the expenditure on anti-poverty programmes and public management of food economy have significant influence on rural poverty.

In case of urban areas, the per capita non-agricultural income and food prices play an important role in influencing poverty. The agricultural performance has an indirect impact on urban poverty through food prices and also via migration. Urban poverty is concentrated in the informal sector and growth in the organised sector may not percolate to the unorganised sector.

Now, we present, in Table 2, the estimates of the proportion of population in households below the poverty line by rural-urban location, at the All-India level, from 1983 to 2000.

Table 2: Poverty Ratio at the National Level.

(Per cent)

Year	*Rural*	*Urban*	*Combined*
1983	45.1	40.0	43.9
1987-88	39.1	38.2	38.9
1989-90	33.7	36.0	34.3
1990-91	35.0	35.3	35.1
1992	41.7	37.8	40.7
1993-94	37.3	32.4	35.2
1994-95	38.0	34.2	36.9
1995-96	38.1	33.9	37.2
1999-2000	27.1	23.6	26.1

Source: Household Consumption Survey, NSSO, Government of India (Various Rounds).

At the All-India level, there is a definite and unambiguous decline in the proportion of population that lie below the poverty line. Table 2 shows that there has been a remarkable fall of rural poverty in India from 45.1 per cent in 1983 to 37.3 per cent in 1993-94 and further to 27.1 per cent in 1999-2000, and this is indeed a significant achievement. On the other hand, the urban poverty has also declined from 40.8 per cent in 1983 to 32.4 per cent in 1993-94 to 23.6 per cent in 1999-2000. Thus, the incidence of poverty expressed as a percentage of people living below the poverty line has witnessed a steady decline from 43.9 per cent in 1983 to 35.2 per cent in 1993-94 and to 26.1 per cent in 1999-2000.

The performance of economy during the post-reforms period is urban biased and have bypassed the rural sectors where majority of the poor are concentrated, leading to a divergent growth between rural and urban India. Economic reforms have neglected rural investment and the food security, employment generation, resulting in a slow agricultural growth, reduced employment opportunities in rural areas. All these are likely to be associated with increasing poverty in rural areas than urban India, especially during 90s.

Poverty at the State Level

In India the issue of growth versus poverty has been debated quite extensively. It has been argued by some analysis that because of institutional rigidities, rapid growth does not percolate down and therefore fails to make any dent on poverty. In fact, some scholars have even suggested that growth has led to immeseration in some states like Punjab and Haryana, the view that cannot be substantiated from the data.

Higher economic growth is important for several reasons. More resources will be available for further investments and social development. It will also create better opportunities for the population if the growth is labour intensive.

Table 3 gives data regarding the growth rates of gross state domestic product and per capita income at state level during 1980-81 to 1990-91 and 1993 to 2000-01 along with their ranks. It is clear from the table that Karnataka (7.92 per cent), West Bengal (6.88 per cent), Rajasthan (6.26 per cent) and Tamil Nadu (6.04 per cent) are the states which have a highest level of growth rates of Gross State Domestic Product during the 1993 to 2000-01. On the extreme, the States which have had low growth rate of gross state domestic product are Assam (2.59 per cent), Orissa (3.22 per cent), Madhya Pradesh (4.33 per cent) and Bihar (4.50 per cent) in the same period.

The table further shows that States with highest growth showed in case of per capita income are Karnataka (6.41 per cent), West Bengal (5.32 per

Table 3: Growth Rates (GR) of GSDP and Per Capita GSDP (Percentage) and Ranks for Major States.

State	*GR in GSDP (Per cent)*		*GR in Per Capita GSDP (Per cent)*		*Rank for GR in GSDP (Per cent)*		*Rank for GR in Per Capita SDP*	
	1980-81 to 1990-91	*1993-94 to 2000-01*	*1980-81 to 1990-91*	*1993-94 to 2000-01*	*1980-81 to 1990-91*	*1993-94 to 2000-01*	*1980-81 to 1990-91*	*1993-94 to 2000-01*
Andhra Pradesh	5.50	5.31	3.33	4.04	4	8	5	8
Assam	3.51	2.59	1.37	0.98	14	15	15	15
Bihar	4.55	4.50	2.4	2.81	11	12	10	12
Gujarat	4.96	5.98	3.00	4.39	8	5	8	4
Haryana	6.23	5.57	3.81	3.68	2	7	2	9
Karnataka	5.16	7.92	3.20	6.41	7	1	7	1
Kerala	3.51	5.17	2.13	4.05	14	10	13	7
Madhya Pradesh	4.46	4.33	2.10	2.36	12	13	14	13
Maharashtra	5.85	5.75	3.56	4.30	3	6	4	5
Orissa	4.20	3.22	2.39	2.00	13	14	12	14
Punjab	5.18	4.96	3.30	3.01	6	11	6	11
Rajasthan	6.39	6.26	3.84	4.22	1	3	1	6
Tamil Nadu	5.24	6.04	3.80	4.99	5	4	3	3
Uttar Pradesh	4.83	5.26	5.24	3.10	9	9	9	10
West Bengal	4.60	6.88	2.41	5.32	10	2	11	2
All India	**5.37**	**6.13**	**3.24**	**4.38**	-	-	-	-

Source: Adapted from Economic and Political Weekly, Vol. XXXVIII, Nos. 12 & 13, March 22-28 and April 4, 2003, p. 1145.

cent), Tamil Nadu (4.99 per cent) and Gujarat (4.39 per cent) between 1993 to 2000-01. On the other hand, the states like Assam (0.98 per cent), Orissa (2.0 per cent), Madhya Pradesh (2.36 per cent) and Bihar (2.81 per cent) have recorded slow growth in the same period.

This shows the few states during the post reforms period have done well and others continued the same backwardness and slow growth in respect of Gross State Domestic Product and Per Capita Income.

Tables 4 and 5 shows the estimates of poverty prevalence ratios for 15 major states during the 1983, 1993-94 and 1999-2000. These estimates are presented separately for the rural and urban populations in each state. The main exception is Assam, where poverty has stagnated in both rural and urban areas. In Orissa, there has been very little poverty decline in the second sub-period i.e. between 1993-94 and 1999-2000, with the result that Orissa (48.01 per cent) now has the highest level of rural poverty among all Indian States according to 1999-2000 year data.

Table 4: Rural Poverty Ratio at the State Level.

(In Per cent)

State	*1983*	*1993-94*	*1999-2000*	*Rank*		
	I	*II*	*III*	*I*	*II*	*II*
Andhara Pradesh	30.32	15.92	11.05	13	14	12
Assam	42.44	45.01	40.04	8	3	3
Bihar	62.48	58.21	44.30	1	1	2
Gujarat	44.43	22.18	13.17	7	13	11
Haryana	20.14	28.02	8.27	14	10	14
Karnataka	47.88	29.88	17.38	6	9	9
Kerala	39.07	25.76	9.38	11	12	13
Madhya Pradesh	41.71	40.64	37.06	9	6	4
Maharashtra	50.71	37.93	23.72	5	7	7
Orissa	57.74	49.72	48.01	4	2	1
Punjab	14.72	11.95	6.35	15	15	15
Rajasthan	32.37	26.46	13.74	12	11	10
Tamil Nadu	54.06	32.48	20.55	3	8	8
Uttar Pradesh	40.85	42.28	31.22	10	4	6
West Bengal	59.34	40.80	31.85	2	5	5
All India	**45.07**	**37.28**	**27.09**	–	–	–

Source: Economic Survey, Ministry of Finance, Government of India, New Delhi, 2002-03.

Table 5: Urban Poverty Ratio at State Level.

(In Per cent)

State	*1983*	*1993-94*	*1999-2000*	*Rank*		
	I	*II*	*III*	*I*	*II*	*II*
Andhra Pradesh	30.81	38.33	26.63	12	5	6
Assam	11.39	7.73	7.47	15	15	14
Bihar	49.28	34.50	32.91	1	8	3
Gujarat	40.05	27.89	15.59	7	10	11
Haryana	26.93	16.38	9.99	13	13	13
Karnataka	49.20	40.14	25.25	2	3	7
Kerala	37.76	24.55	20.27	10	11	9
Madhya Pradesh	42.06	48.38	38.44	5	1	2
Maharashtra	38.82	35.15	26.81	8	7	5
Orissa	37.29	41.64	42.83	11	2	1
Punjab	13.76	11.35	5.75	14	14	15
Rajasthan	37.90	30.49	19.85	9	9	10
Tamil Nadu	46.80	39.77	22.11	3	4	8
Uttar Pradesh	44.19	35.39	30.89	4	6	4
West Bengal	40.82	22.41	14.86	6	12	12
All India	**40.03**	**32.36**	**23.62**	–	–	–

Source: Economic Survey, Ministry of Finance, Government of India, New Delhi, 2002-03.

Further table 6 gives details on the proportion of total population below the poverty line. It is interesting to note that in 1983, Bihar (60.76 per cent) and Orissa (55.16 per cent) had the highest incidence of poverty closely followed by the West Bengal (54.37 per cent), Tamil Nadu (51.63 per cent) and Maharashtra (46.45 per cent). Whereas the developed States such as Punjab (19.35 per cent) and Haryana (21.69 per cent) had the lowest proportion of population below poverty line. By 1993-94, the incidence of poverty seems to have decreased in all the States except Bihar (54.96 per cent), Orissa (48.56 per cent) and Madhya Pradesh (42.52 per cent). Whereas, in 1999-2000 one can find a steep decline in poverty in almost all the States. However, in 1999-2000, States like Orissa (47.15 per cent), Bihar (42.60 per cent) and Madhya Pradesh (37.43 per cent) had taken the highest position. On the other extreme, the Punjab (6.16 per cent) followed by the Haryana (8.74 per cent) and Kerala (12.72 per cent) were having the lowest proportion of poor persons.

Table 6: Total Poverty Ratio at the State Level.

(In Per cent)

State	*1983*	*1993-94*	*1999-2000*	*Rank*		
	I	*II*	*III*	*I*	*II*	*II*
Andhra Pradesh	30.44	22.19	15.77	13	14	10
Assam	41.58	40.86	36.09	9	4	4
Bihar	60.76	54.96	42.60	1	1	2
Gujarat	43.04	24.21	14.07	7	13	12
Haryana	21.69	25.05	8.74	14	12	14
Karnataka	45.11	33.16	20.04	6	9	9
Kerala	38.82	25.43	12.72	11	11	13
Madhya Pradesh	41.78	42.52	37.43	8	3	3
Maharashtra	46.45	36.86	25.02	5	6	7
Orissa	55.16	48.56	47.15	2	2	1
Punjab	19.35	11.77	6.16	15	15	15
Rajasthan	33.58	27.41	15.28	12	10	11
Tamil Nadu	51.63	35.03	21.12	4	8	8
Uttar Pradesh	41.48	40.85	31.15	10	5	5
West Bengal	54.37	35.66	27.02	3	7	6
All India	**43.90**	**35.97**	**26.10**	–	–	–

Source: Economic Survey, Ministry of Finance, Government of India, New Delhi, 2002-03.

Thus, from tables, it may appear that the 'Pace' of poverty decline in the nineties has been fairly rapid, but this is not uniformly present across all the major states, while in a majority of the 15 states analysed poverty ratios have indeed declined between 1993-94 and 1999-2000, in both the rural and urban areas.

Per Annum Poverty Reduction at the State Level

Inequality refers to the relative standard of living across the whole society. It is always assumed that a high level of inequality contributes to a high level of poverty in different ways. At the maximum inequality level, one person has everything and the other has nothing. Clearly, in such a situation, levels of poverty of the deprived will be very high (Rakhee Byhattacharya). One can see from the table 7 the annual percentage decline in rural, urban and total poverty. The results shows that the rural rates of decline were slightly higher than the urban rates. Further, the total poverty declined at the National level was 0.79 per cent per annum between 1983 and 1993-94, which was 1.65 per cent per annum during 1993-94 to 1999-2000.

Table 7: Per Annum Poverty Reduction at the State Level.

(In Per cent)

States	*Rural*		*Urban*		*Total*	
	1983 to 1993-94	*1993-94 to 1999-2000*	*1983 to 1993-94*	*1993-94 to 1999-2000*	*1983 to 1993-94*	*1993-94 to 1999-2000*
Andhra Pradesh	1.44	0.81	–0.75	1.95	0.83	1.07
Assam	– 0.26	0.83	0.37	0.04	0.07	0.80
Bihar	0.43	2.28	1.48	0.27	0.58	2.06
Gujarat	2.23	1.50	1.22	2.05	1.58	1.69
Haryana	–0.79	3.29	1.06	1.07	0.34	2.72
Karnataka	1.80	2.08	0.91	2.48	1.20	2.19
Kerala	1.33	2.73	1.32	0.71	1.34	2.12
Madhya Pradesh	0.11	0.60	–0.63	1.66	0.07	0.85
Maharashtra	1.28	2.37	0.37	1.39	0.96	1.97
Orissa	0.80	0.29	–0.44	–0.20	0.66	0.24
Punjab	0.28	0.93	0.24	0.93	0.76	0.94
Rajasthan	0.59	2.12	0.74	1.77	0.62	2.02
Tamil Nadu	2.16	1.99	0.70	2.94	1.66	2.32
Uttar Pradesh	–0.14	1.84	0.89	0.75	0.06	1.62
West Bengal	1.85	1.49	1.84	1.26	1.87	1.44
All India	**0.78**	**1.70**	**0.77**	**1.46**	**0.79**	**1.65**

Source: Results are based on tables 4, 5 and 6.

Of India's 15 largest states, Bihar, Haryana, Karnataka, Kerala, Rajasthan and Tamil Nadu accounted for the highest decline of poverty per annum between 1993-94 and 1999-2000 (more than two per cent per annum). Table 7 presents that the total poverty rate in Bihar has decreased by 2.06 per cent points per year during the 1993-94 to 1999-2000. The discrepancies are less but still significant for Haryana i.e. 2.72 percentage point per year reduction in total poverty during the 1993-94 to 1999-2000, in contrast to a 0.34 percentage point reduction in 1983 to 1993-94. Tamil Nadu is another State that accounts for a significant decline of poverty in India (2.32 per cent per annum) during 1993-94 to 1999-2000. In contrast, the rates of total poverty reduction agree quite closely for some states—Karnataka (2.19 per cent), Kerala (2.12 per cent), Rajasthan (2.32 per cent), Maharashtra (1.97

per cent) and Gujarat (1.69 per cent) during the post-reforms period (i.e. from 1993-94 to 1999-2000).

The above analysis shows that there have been large changes towards equality observed in most parts of rural India and to a degree in urban India. This overwhelming evidence suggests that inequality has worsened in India over the last two decades, is somewhat erroneous.

Employment and Poverty

There is an ongoing debate among several development economists about the relationship between a country's economic growth and its rate of employment, poverty level and income distribution. Many of them believe that growth and poverty reduction are directly correlated. Regarding the relationship between growth and employment generation, there are questions raised on whether growth necessarily creates corresponding employment. In this part of our paper, we have discussed about the employment growth, worker-population ratios and poverty at the national level.

Growth of Labour Force and Employment

An important objective of development planning in India has been to provide for increasing employment opportunities not only to meet the backlog of the unemployed but also the new additions to the labour force. The increasing diversification of the economy together with acceleration in economic growth has resulted in structural changes in the nature of the job market.

As noted in Table 8, the various rounds of surveys conducted by the National Sample Survey Organisation (NSSO) reveal-that the average annual growth rate of overall employment was 1.54 per cent per annum in the period 1983 to 1987-88, which increased to 2.45 per cent per annum over 1987-88 to

Table 8: Rate of Growth of Population, Labour Force and Employment

(Per cent per annum)

Period	*Rate of Growth of Population*	*Rate of Growth of Labour Force (UPSS)**	*Rate of Growth of Employment (UPSS)**
1983 to 1987-88	2.14	1.74	1.54
1987-88 to 1993-94	2.10	2.29	2.45
1993-94 to 1999-2000	1.93	1.03	0.98

* Usual principal and subsidiary status.

Source: Economic Survey, 2001-2002, Ministry of Finance, Government of India, New Delhi, 2002.

1993-94. As per the 55th round of the Survey on Employment conducted by the NSSO, overall employment grew by about 1 per cent per annum during 1993-94 to 1999-2000. The labour force participation rate declined in 1999-2000 as compared with 1993-94, and which is reflected in a sharp deceleration in the growth of the labour force from 2.29 per cent per annum in 1987-88 to 1993-94, to 1.03 per cent per annum in the period 1993-94 to 1999-2000. Thus, the deceleration in employment is also associated with a sharp decline in the growth of the labour force.

Worker-Population Ratios (WPRs)

Table 9 presents the age-specific, usual status worker-population ratios (WPRs) by rural-urban location and by gender from 1987-88 to 1999-2000. From table it is seen that:

1. In the case of both rural males and rural females, in all the younger age-groups, up to and including the 25-29 age-group, there is a broad downward drift in age-specific work-participation rates. The same holds true for urban males and urban females as well but only up to the 20-24 age-group. In the 40-44 and the 45-49 age-groups the rise in WPRs between 1987-88 and 1993-94 serves to exaggerate the subsequent decline in 1999-2000.
2. In all the three population segments a decline over time in the worker population ratios in the open-ended age-group '60 and above' is to be expected with the rising share of the older population. This is confirmed for both urban males and urban females. In the case of both rural males and rural females there was an unusual increase in WPRs in the 60+ age-group between 1987-88 and 1993-94 which tends to exaggerate the decline in WPRs in this age-group between 1993-94 and 1999-2000.
3. In respect of rural women in the 50-54 age-group were an exception to the general pattern that the decline (between 1993-94 and 1999-2000) in WPRs in the 25 and above age-groups were due entirely to declines in WPRs on the subsidiary status.

Overall, while the decline in WPRs in the younger age-group between 1993-94 and 1999-2000 in all the three population segments is a beneficial rise in student-population ratios over this period, the decline between 1993-94 and 1999-2000 in the WPRs in the 25 and above age-group for both rural and urban women largely, reflects a decline in participation rates on the subsidiary status. Whereas, for men in both rural and the urban areas, variations in WPRs in the prime age-group between 30 and 49 are fairly small (Sundaram, 2001).

Table 9: Age-Specific Usual Status (PS + SS) Worker Population Ratios by Rural-Urban Residence and Gender in India

Age Group (years)	*Males* 1987-88	1993-94	1999-2000	*Females* 1987-88	1993-94	1999-2000
I. Rural						
10-14	190	138	91	182	141	96
20-24	872	859	844	465	456	409
25-29	959	957	950	523	525	491
30-34	982	983	979	577	585	555
35-39	986	989	984	596	608	579
40-44	979	987	983	610	606	586
50-54	959	970	953	523	542	515
60+	668	699	639	218	241	218
All	539	553	–	323	328	–
II. Urban						
10-14	85	66	49	65	45	36
20-24	674	674	658	185	180	155
25-29	914	904	883	223	224	194
30-34	969	964	960	272	301	235
35-39	981	983	975	309	301	285
40-44	983	981	974	308	320	283
50-54	938	942	935	268	286	262
60+	480	442	402	123	113	94
All	506	521	–	152	155	–

Source: 1. Sarvekshana, September 1990 and July-September 1996.
2. NSSO 55th Round July 1999-June 2000, December 2000.

The percentage of people below the poverty line significantly fell from 44.5 per cent of population in 1983 to 35.1 per cent in 1990-91 and to 26.1 per cent in 1999-2000. A majority of Indians live in the rural area and it is precisely in the rural area that poverty is worsening. Reduction in urban poverty has almost all along seen showing a downward trend. As against this, the employment growth went down to 0.98 per cent during 1990s from 1.54 per cent in the 1980s. The case for a direct 'employment generation policy' gains more strength if we see the future projection of population, labour force and availability of employment opportunities. Thus, if we look at the employment growth and the employment elasticity to GDP growth that have been witnessed over the last two decades, the picture is very alarming. And, the problems of poverty and unemployment in the years to come, place a big challenge before our society. Because, the dualism in the labour market is getting further sharpened. A market for educated, trained and skilled job aspirants, typically characterised by new and upcoming production/marketing/ management standards, significantly higher levels of productivity, wage rates and earnings, is steadily expanding simultaneously with sluggishness or a steady decline in the job market for their less educated, semi-or-unskilled and untrained brethren. Employment prospects are thus brighter for the more qualified while a squeesing scenerio sets in for the untrained and the uneducated job-seekers; differences in employment and wage-period jobs, and still more significantly, job espirants, especially females, suffer far more severe setbacks, primarily because of their own educational and skill deficiencies.

Poverty Reduction in the Pre and Post-Reform Period

This part of our paper analyses the development of policies on poverty reduction in India. This is essential for understanding more clearly the scope of using such strategies in the frame of a shift in emphasis to market forces under liberalisation.

Poverty Reduction in the Pre-Reform Period

The key policies which have had an impact on curbing poverty historically include the following:

Growth-based Strategies

The role of poverty programmes have to be placed in the backdrop of India's market economy, with the state playing a significant role in planning. In the post-independence phase particularly in the mid of 1980s and early 1990s, an emphasis on market forces under neo-liberalism has prevailed. The Indian experience shows that a combination of inadequate growth and failure of growth to 'trickle-down' has resulted in inability to meet the basic needs of the poor, coupled with widening of disparities over the years. "Trickle-down" of growth may demand fairly high rates of growth over a long period. Some economists have attributed to inadequacy of growth and the failure of Indian planning to make a significant dent in poverty. During 1980's we saw an overall growth rate trend of 3-4 per cent per annum against high rates of population growth. This was considered to be the explanation for low living standards and persistence of poverty.

Institutional Measures and Decentralisation

Institutional measures have centred on creating a basis for changing the asset distribution to establish more equal socio-economic structure. This can enable a more equal sharing of the economic structure and gains from growth.

In this context, land redistribution has been a major feature of public policy. Land reform has been seen as a major force in integrating programmes for growth and poverty alleviation, to form a comprehensive strategy for the development of the rural economy.

Poverty Reduction in the Post-Reform Period

In India, the process of adjustment and reform was initiated from the second half of 1991. However, it is widely accepted that the impact of stabilisation and adjustment on the poor is adverse, for the following reasons:

Firstly, a compression of government spending, restrictions on the import of essential raw materials and capital goods slows the rate of growth of the economy and thereby corresponding result in a lower rate of employment growth.

Secondly, a reduction in the government expenditure, necessitated by the objective of reducing the fiscal deficit, would inevitably affect spending on social sectors such as education, health and welfare, and programmes of poverty alleviation.

Thirdly, the lower government expenditure there may be a compulsion to reduce subsidies. A fall in food subsidies should have a direct bearing on the real incomes of the poor, as prices of foodgrains supplied through the public distribution system would rise. Again, a reduction in fertilizer subsidy would imply a rise in the cost of inputs to farmers producing cereals resulting in a higher cost of output.

Fourthly, the distribution of land holdings, productivity of land, quality of labour force and opportunities outside the agriculture sector etc are more instrinsically responsible for the archaic structure of rural economy. Agricultural labourers still constitute a historically deprived social group in the country—they are the poorest of the poor. All these factors have their malevolent consequences on productivity. The labour productivity in Indian agriculture is only about one third that outside it and the wages/earnings are also lower when compared to those prevalent in the other sectors. Thus, rural poverty in the country is more due to human failure rather than natural factors.

Lastly, there has been a decline in central plan assistance to the states as a proportion of total public sector outlay. The shortfall in some plans is a cause for concern, particularly because, in such sectors as agriculture, irrigation, education and health, expenditure is incurred largely out of state plan funds. Thus, the state plan outlays have fallen far short of targets, particularly in the poorer states and that these have led to considerable shortfalls in agriculture, irrigation and social sector outlays. Investments in these sectors are critical for upliftment of the poor from existing levels of poverty and ignorance.

Policy Measures and Conclusion

Our discussion above leads us to suggest the following policy measures:

- There is a need for improving education, training and for creating opportunities for the rural poor so that they too could enter in the higher productivities areas including non-agricultural activities. In case of urban poor, it seems that they have over this period been comparatively more successful in sharing the benefits of faster productivity occupations. Further, for this group, the poverty alleviation policy should be concentrated on improving the productivity of urban industries and services; especially in the large informal sectors that provide subsidiary occupation.
- Development under market-led growth benefits those who are qualified enough and socially well placed to take advantage of the opportunities of capital intensive and labour displacing global technologies. The Government and the community as a whole is to ensure that in the long-run, all sections of the society will be able to achieve those levels of skill that can avail of the opportunities to enter the mainstream job market.
- Help the 'left-out' groups, during the reforms period, like marginal farmers, unskilled labour and people in the backward areas, so that they can maintain a reasonably good standard of living and making the reform processes socially acceptable. For this, appropriate social, demographic and economic policies will have to be developed to bring this under-privileged section with improved skill, to enter the mainstream market activities.
- What would be the role of local bodies, which are being revamped in many states, and of Non-Governmental Organisations, in both growth oriented and poverty alleviation programmes? It is appropriate to consider them as good vehicles for such centrally designed programmes and encouraged to take interest in multi-dimensional approach to poverty alleviation and empowerment of the poor.

The conclusion of this paper is that jobless growth during reforms period is not tenable if poverty has to be ameliorated. Thus, the permanent solution to the problem is to bring the rural and the urban poor in the high growth productivity activities by proper training skill formation and accessibility to basic infrastructures. Domestic Research and Development (R&D) for developing appropriate technology has to be encouraged. A continuous training process of labour force on jobs should be there because of the appropriate faster changes in technology and management style in the present globalised world.

REFERENCES

1. Bhagwati Jagdish, (2001) *"Growth, Poverty and Reforms"*, Economic and Political Weekly, Vol. XXVI, No. 10, March 10-16, p. 843-846.
2. Bhalla Surjit S., (2003) *"Recounting the Poor, Poverty in India, 1983-99"*, Economic and Political Weekly, Vol. XXXVIII, No. 4, January 25-31, p. 338-349.
3. Bhattacharya Rakhee, (2002) *"Rural Poverty in India: A Review"*, Indian Journal of Regional Science, Vol. XXXIV, No. 2, p. 10-22.
4. Deation Angus and Dreze Jean, (2002) *"Poverty and Inequality in India: A Re-examination"*. Economic and Political Weekly, Vol. XXXVII, No. 36, September 7-13, p. 3729-3748.
5. Dev Mahendra S. and Ravi C. (2003) *"Macro-economic Scene: Performance and Policies"*, Economic and Political Weekly, Vol. XXXVIII, No. 12 and 13, March 22-28 to April 4, p. 1143-1157.
6. Government of India, (2002-03) *"Economic Survey, 2001-02"*, Ministry of Finance, Economic Division, New Delhi.
7. Gupta S.P., (1999) *"Trickle Down Theory Revisited; The Role of Employment and Poverty"*, V.B. Singh Memorial Lecture, 41st Annual Conference, Indian Society of Labour Economics, Mumbai.
8. Hashim S.R., (1999) *"Employment and unemployment in a Society in Transition"*, Presidential Address, 41st Annual Conference, Indian Society of Labour Economics, Mumbai.
9. Kuznets Simon, (1971) *"Economic Growth of Nations: Total Output and Production Structure"*, Harward University Press, Cambridge.
10. Mathur A., (1998) *"Employment, Equity, Growth"*, Presidential Address Delivered at the 39th Annual Conference of the Indian Society of Labour Economics, Thiruvanathapuram, January.
11. National Sample Survey Organisation, (2000) *Employment and Unemployment in India,* 1999-2000, Key Results of NSS 55th Round.
12. National Sample Survey Organisation, (1996) Sarvekshana, Vol. 20, No. 1, 68th Issue, July-September.
13. Parikh S. Kirit, (1997) *"India Development Report-1997"*, Oxford University Press, Mumbai.

14. Rao Hanumantha C.H. and Dev Mahendra S. (2003) *"Economic Reforms and Challenges Ahead"*, Economic and Political Weekly, Vol. XXXVIII, No. 12 and 13, March 22-28 to April 4, p. 1130-1141.

15. Reserve Bank of India, (2001) *Hand Book of Statistics on Indian Economy.*

16. Sen Amartya, (1981) *"Poverty and Famines"*, Oxford University Press, Delhi.

17. Sundaram K., (2001) *"Employment and Poverty in 1990s"*, Economic and Political Weekly, Vol-XXXVI, No. 32, August 11-17, p. 3039-3049.

18. Tendulkar S.D. and Jain L.R., (1995) *"Economic Reforms and Poverty"*, Economic and Political Weekly, Vol. 30, No. 23, June 10, pp. 1373-83.

19. Vaidyanathan A., (2001) *"Poverty and Development Policy"*, Economic and Political Weekly, Vol. XXXVII, No. 21, May 26 to June 1, p. 1807-1822.

22

Output, Exchange Rate, Inflation, and Monetary Dynamics in Transitional Southeast European Economies
Evidence Through a Panel Country Set

Nicholas Apergis*
Dimitrios Kyrkilis**

Introduction

Many macroeconomists have attempted to describe empirically the sources of fluctuations in output and inflation in many countries. These studies focuses on the question whether stabilisation programmes can be successful, especially in developing or transitional economies that seriously suffer from high inflation rates. So far in the relevant literature three main sources have been identifies as those that determine the course of output and inflation, namely, monetary, fiscal, and balance of payments policies. The first two sources are closely linked, especially in the case where fiscal deficits are highly monetised.

There exists a substantial body of literature focusing, mainly, on developing economies. Ndung'u (1993) investigated the dynamic interaction of certain macroeconomic variables, e.g. money supply, prices, the exchange

Acknowledgments: The authors wish to express their gratitude to Professor Pedroni (University of Indiana) for providing the software that estimates the cointegration results.
* Nicholas Apergis, Department of International European Economics and Political Studies, University of Macedonia, Thessaloniki, Greece.
** Dimitrios Kyrkilis, Department of Balkan, Slavic and Oriental Studies, University of Macedonia, Thessaloniki, Greece.

rate, real output, and the interest rate, in order to explain inflation behaviours in Kenya, while Rodriguez and Diaz (1995), Rogers and Wang (1995), and Hoffmaister and Vegh (1996) used practically the same macroeconomic variables in order to investigate the determinants of output growth for the economies of Peru, Mexico, and Uruguay, respectively. Montiel (1989), Dornbusch, Sturzenbegger, and Wolf (1990), Kamin (1996), and Odedokun (1996) employed Vector Autoregressive (VAR) models to study the sources of hyperinflation in selected high inflation Latin American and African countries. All of the above studies indicated that exchange rate changes were the main factor in determining the future course of output and inflation.

The purpose of this study is to investigate, by applying the novel methodology of panel data, the main sources of output growth and inflation in four transitional Southeast European countries, namely, Bulgaria, Romania, Croatia, and Slovenia. Although it was initially intended to include more transitional Southeast European economies in the sample, the unavailability of statistical data prevented the authors from doing so. There are strong reasons to believe that there is significant heterogeneity in cross-country dynamics, and that no panel-data estimations mislead inferences due to the neglect of such heterogeneity. This study is expected to contribute to the literature in the following respects. Applying developed panel techniques would allow both the presence of heterogeneity in the estimated parameters and dynamics across countries to be explicitly considered. This would generate more credible results given that panel data estimation enables a researcher to capture certain interesting time-series relations that cross-sectional analysis alone cannot. In this paper a multi-country panel data set is used in order to exploit both time-series and cross-sectional information. More specifically, panel unit root and cointegration tests allow for both parameter and dynamic heterogeneity across the chosen country groups, which have been proven to generate more powerful results (Harris and Tzavalis, 1999). Moreover, a panel data set from four different Southeast European countries is employed from 1990 to 2002. Finally, the paper contributes to the literature by investigating for the first time the dynamics among certain macroeconomic variables for those Southeast European countries in a panel data set.

Transition in the four countries under investigation was initially marked by a decline of real GDP, which was accompanied primarily by high inflation, external imbalances and public deficits (Table 1), reflecting a series of problems including poor initial conditions combined with ethnic conflicts, politically instability, uneven implementation of reform programs, inconsistent macroeconomic stabilisation policies, unbalanced industrial structures, lack of tradition in institutional development, and inadequate infrastructure. All

Table 1: Selected Macroeconomic Variables.

Countries	*Years*												
	1990	*1991*	*1992*	*1993*	*1994*	*1995*	*1996*	*1997*	*1998*	*1999*	*2000*	*2001*	*2002**
Bulgaria													
Real GDP Growth %	–9.1	–11.7	–7.3	–1.5	1.8	2.9	–9.4	–5.6	4.0	2.3	5.4	4.0	4.2
Inflation, CPI annual %	26.3	333.5	82.0	73.0	96.3	62.0	123.0	1.082.0	22.2	0.7	9.9	7.4	5.8
Current Account Balance. % of GDP	–8.2	–1.0	–4.2	–10.1	–0.3	–0.2	0.2	4.1	–0.5	–5.3	–5.6	–6.5	–4.2
General Government Balance, % of GDP	–8.1	–4.5	–2.9	–8.7	–3.9	–5.7	–10.3	–2.0	0.9	–0.9	–1.0	–0.9	–0.8
Croatia													
Real GDP Growth %	–7.1	–21.1	–11.7	–0.8	5.9	6.8	6.0	6.5	2.5	–0.9	2.9	3.8	3.5
Inflation, CPI annual %	609.5	123.0	665.5	1.517.5	97.6	2.0	3.5	3.6	5.7	4.2	6.2	4.9	2.3
Current Account Balance. % of GDP	n.a.	–3.4	3.2	5.7	5.9	–7.7	–5.5	–11.6	–7.1	–7.0	–2.3	–3.3	–3.5
General Government Balance, % of GDP	n.a.	n.a.	–3.9	–0.8	1.2	–1.4	–1.0	–1.9	–1.0	–6.5	–7.1	–5.8	–4.6
Romania													
Real GDP Growth %	–5.6	–12.9	–8.8	1.5	3.9	7.1	3.9	–6.1	–5.4	–3.2	1.8	5.3	3.5
Inflation, CPI annual%	5.1	170.2	210.4	256.1	136.7	32.3	38.8	154.8	59.1	45.8	45.7	34.5	22.5
Current Account Balance. % of GDP	–9.6	–3.5	–8.0	–4.5	–1.4	–5.0	–7.3	–6.2	–7.0	–3.7	–3.7	–6.1	–5.0
General Government Balance, % of GDP	n.a.	n.a.	–3.9	–0.8	1.2	–1.4	–1.0	–1.9	–1.0	–6.5	–7.1	–5.8	–4.6
Slovenia													
Real GDP Growth %	–4.7	–8.9	–5.5	2.8	5.3	4.1	3.5	4.6	3.8	5.2	4.6	3.0	2.7
Inflation. CPI annual %	549.7	117.7	207.3	32.9	21.0	13.5	9.9	8.4	7.9	6.1	8.9	8.4	7.4
Current Account Balance. % of GDP	3.0	1.0	7.4	1.5	4.0	–0.5	0.2	0.1	–0.8	–3.9	–3.4	–0.4	1.2
General Government Balance, % of GDP	n.a.	2.6	0.3	0.6	–0.2	–0.3	–0.2	–1.7	–1.4	–0.9	–1.3	–1.2	–2.9
	n.a.	n.a.	–4.6	–0.4	–2.2	–2.5	–3.9	–4.6	–5.0	–3.5	–3.7	–3.5	–3.0

Notes: *Estimations
Source: European Bank of Reconstruction and Development. Transition Reports. various years.

countries adopted a strategy of macroeconomic stabilisation as a means among others, for creating favourable conditions for sustained economic development. However, the specific policy mix and its effectiveness differ between countries. Even, the same country in some cases shifted from one type of stabilisation policy to another during the 1990's. Initially, all four countries implemented a monetary targeting stabilisation policy accompanied by a flexible exchange rate regime. This policy had some effectiveness in reducing inflation with the exception of Slovenia. The limitation of this policy effectiveness in reducing inflation with the exception of Slovenia. The limitation of this policy effectiveness was due to the lack of independence and accountability of monetary authorities, the mismanagement of macroeconomic policies meaning basically the absence of strict ex ante stabilisation rules, in conjunction with a high policy content of discretionary measures in conformity with policy and social pressures. Public deficits were often financed through quasi-fiscal operations aiming at subsidising various economic sectors.

Bulgaria changed its stabilisation policy to a currency board regime implementing a fixed exchange rate against the DM in the beginning and the euro after the introduction of the latter. Money supply growth became subordinate to the target of maintaining the exchange rate parity. Croatia adopted also an exchange rate targeting policy but within a specified zone allowing for some fluctuation in order to adjust the balance of payments. Exchange rate targeting in both countries resulting in improved macroeconomic stabilisation performance with most pronounced effects the disinflation of the economy and the fiscal discipline. Inflation (CPI annual average) in Bulgaria went down from 123.0% in 1996, the year before the currency board regime was established, to 5.8% in 2002. The balance of general government reduced its deficit from –10.3% of GDP to a –0.8% of GDP in the same period, while the current account balance continued to record deficits. The current accounts recorded an estimated deficit of –4.2% of GDP in 2002 compared to –6.5% in 2001 and –0.5% in 1998. GDP recorded positive growth rates, and in 2001 it had recovered 80.0% of its pre-transition (1989) level. Croatia managed to decelerate inflation from 97.6% in 1994, when the exchange rate targeting policy was introduced to 2.3% in 2002 while both the general government balance and the current accounts recorded deficits as percentage of GDP. The latter achieved positive growth rates; with the exception of 1999 and in 2001 it stood at 85.0% of its 1989 level.

By contrast, Romania maintained monetary targeting throughout the whole period achieving some, albeit poor, results. Inflation is still at two-digit level. The CPI increased by 22.5% year-on-year in 2002 compared with an average annual rate of 41.0% in the period between 1998 and 2002. The general government balance recorded a deficit of –3.4% of GDP in average for the 1999-2002 period compared with –4.0% in the period between 1995 and 1998. Meanwhile, the current accounts balance maintained a sizeable deficit, standing at an estimated –4.1% of GDP in 2002. Throughout the 1990's the external deficit the ratio of which GDP recorded a 6.8% average for the 1996-1998 period declining after to –3.7% for each one of the following two years and jumped back to –6.1% in 2001 constrained the economic policy calling for restrictive measures that hindered domestic demand, hence economic growth. The latter after a period of positive trend, between 1993 and 1996, reversed to negative rates before recovering again in the last three years.

Slovenia adopted a managed flexible exchange rate regime along restrictive monetary and fiscal policies, achieving sustained economic growth since 1993. Although monetary targeting managed to reduce inflation to single digit levels, CPI is maintained at the upper band of the single digits range, mainly due to wage pressure and vulnerable oil price shocks. Part of the inflation can be attributed to the Balassa-Samuelson effect. The managed floating exchange rate regime allows for nominal devaluation of the currency for accommodating balance of payment problems but it feeds into inflation. Current accounts have been either balanced or positive as percentage of GDP for the most part of the 1990's but their balance has been negative since 1998. The general government budget runs modest deficits, but it is estimated to have increased to just below –3.0% of GDP in 2002.

All four countries maintained high interest rates either for realising net capital inflows in order to sustain the exchange rate target, in the countries pursuing an exchange rate targeting stabilisation policy; or to combat inflation in the remaining countries. In all cases high interest rates reflect limited competition in the banking sector, low domestic savings, and high-risk profiles of businesses.

The remaining text of this paper is organised as follows. Section 2 describes the methodology employed. Section 3 presents the empirical analysis and discusses the empirical results. Finally, section 4 concludes the paper.

Methodology

For the empirical purposes of this paper the methodology of a structural VAR model supplied by Blanchard and Watson (1986) and Bernanke (1986) is employed. According to this methodology, certain restrictions are imposed on a contemporaneous VAR setting. Our VAR system involves five variables, namely, the exchange rate, the interest rate, income, prices, and money supply. The restrictions are imposed on the contemporaneous residuals out of that VAR model:

$$\varepsilon^{e} = v^{e}$$
$$\varepsilon^{INT} = v^{INT}$$
$$\varepsilon^{y} = a_1\,\varepsilon I^{NT} + a_2\,\varepsilon^{p} + v^{y}$$
$$\varepsilon^{p} = a_3\,\varepsilon^{e} + a_4\,\varepsilon^{y} + a_5\,\varepsilon^{m} + v^{p}$$
$$\varepsilon^{m} = a_6\,\varepsilon^{e} + a_7\,\varepsilon^{y} + a_8\,\varepsilon^{p} + v^{m}$$

where as are parameters to be estimated. The first equation shows that shocks in the nominal exchange rate are due only to own shocks. In other words, no other macroeconomic variable plays any role in determining the course of the exchange rate policy in our country sample. This is an indication that the exchange rate system of the four countries under study was administratively managed (adjustable peg). In such a system the exchange rate does not reflect the dictate of the market fundamentals.

The second equation in the system also shows that interest rate shocks respond only to their own shocks. This is an indication that over the majority of the period under study interest rates were administratively fixed. Some countries, i.e. Bulgaria and Slovenia, experienced a modest deregulation in their monetary system. However, with the presence of high inflation it was difficult for those systems to allow interest rates to reflect market forces.

The third equation displays that output shocks reflect the impact of interest rate and inflation shocks (plus, of course, their own shocks). At the same time, the fourth equation shows that inflation shocks are monitored by shocks originated in the goods and money market, i.e. output and money supply shocks. Moreover, they are also affected by exchange rate and own shocks.

Finally, the fifth equation of the system exhibits that monetary shocks, i.e. money supply shocks, respond to shocks in the exchange rate, output, prices, and own. The own shocks reflect shocks through the monetary policy rule followed by the central banks of the countries under investigation.

Overall, the structure of the contemporaneous model implies that monetary factors seem to dominate the course of the system. Actually, that was the case for the countries under study. Although, fiscal policies have been also used to drive the system to its equilibrium, deficits were always monetised. Moreover, Blanchard and Quah (1989) argued that the impact of fiscal variables on output in the long run is negligible.

The Data

To explore output, inflation and exchange rate dynamics in transitional economies the used data come from certain sources. The time period under examination is from 1990 to 2002 for the following countries: Bulgaria, Romania, Croatia, and Slovenia. Annual data on the following variables were obtained: Nominal exchange rates (E) are proxied by the units of the national currency with respect to one dollar, nominal interest rates (INT) proxied by lending yields, real output (Y) measured by GDP, prices (P) measured by the consumer price index, and money supply (M) proxied by M2. For the empirical purposes of this study real GDP was used. Real GDP was obtained by dividing nominal GDP by the price level. Data for Bulgaria come from the Monthly Bulletin of the Bulgarian National Bank, data for Croatia come from the Croatian Statistical Service, data for Romania come from the Monthly Bulletin of the National Commission for Statistics, and data for Slovenia come from the Statistical Yearbook of the Bank of Slovenia. For the empirical purposes of the paper all nominal exchange rates were transformed into an index in such a manner as an increase in the exchange rate index to represent a depreciation of the domestic currency. Throughout the paper, small letters indicate variables in logs. Finally, the RATS, Version 4.2, software assisted the empirical analysis.

Empirical Analysis

Dynamic Heterogeneity

The dynamic heterogeneity, i.e. variation of the intercept over countries and time, across a cross-section of the relevant variables can be assessed in a number of ways. In the first step, an ADF(n) equation for each relationship in the panel is estimated; then, the hypothesis of whether regression parameters are equal across these equations. Next, a similar test of parameter equality is performed by estimating a n-order autoregressive model for each relationship under study. Standard Chow-type F tests under the null of parameter equality across all relationships are also performed. If the results reject the null, this indicates heterogeneity in cross-sectional parameters. Finally, homogeneity error variance across groups is also examined as another measure of dynamic heterogeneity. White's tests for group-wise heteroscedasticity are employed to serve this objective. The results are reported in Table 2 for the relationship between exchange rates, interest rates, output, prices, and money supply. The results indicate that the relationship under investigation is characterised by heterogeneity of dynamics and error variance across groups.

Panel Integration Analysis

The null hypothesis of non-stationarity versus the alternative that the variable is stationary is tested using the group mean panel unit root test (or

Table 2. Tests of Dynamic Heterogeneity Across Groups.

	ADF(3)	*AR(4)*	*WHITE'S TEST*
e-INT-y-p-m	25.71*	19.84*	43.91*

Notes: The ADF(3) column reports the parameter equality test (F test) across all relationships in the panel. The AR(4) column reports the F test of parameter equality conducted in a fourth-order autoregressive model of the relationships under study. Finally, the White's test reports White's test of equality of variances across the investigated relationships in the panel. The White's test was computed by regressing the squared residual of the ADF(3) regression on the original regressor(s) and its (their) square(s). The test statistic is (NT) × R^2, which x^2 distributed with the number of regressors in the second regression as the degrees of freedom.

* Significant at 1%.

't-bar' test) of Im, *et al.* (1995). This test is based on the Augmented Dickey-Fuller (ADF) statistic for each country (Dickey and Fuller, 1981) and allows each member of the cross section to have a different autoregressive root and different autocorrelation structures under the alternative hypothesis. The results are reported without and with a trend and are presented in Table 3. The hypothesis that variables *e*, INT, *y*, *p*, and *m* (in levels) contain a unit root cannot be rejected at the 1% significant level. When first differences are used, unit root nonstationarity is rejected at the 1% significant level, suggesting that the variables under study are I(1) variables. These results

Table 3: Panel Unit Root Tests.

Variables	*Without Trend*	*With Trend*
e	–1.11(2)	–1.28(2)
Δe	–4.77(1)*	–5.49(1)*
INT	–1.02(2)	–1.38(2)
ΔINT	–5.73(1)*	–5.82(1)*
y	–1.23(3)	–1.53(3)
Δy	–4.56(2)*	–4.97(1)*
p	–1.34(2)	–1.25(2)
Δy	–4.91(1)*	–5.09(1)*
m	–1.19(3)	–1.47(2)
Δm	–4.77(1)*	–4.93(1)*

Notes: Figures in brackets denote the number of lags in the augmented term that ensures white-noise residuals. The optimal lag length was determined through the Akaike information Criterion (AIC) and the Schwarz-Bayes Information Criterion (SBIC).

* Significant at 1%.

open the possibility of cointegration among those variables commensurate on the testable hypothesis.

Panel Cointegration Analysis

Once the order of stationarity has been established, we can more to a panel cointegration approach, developed by Pedroni (1997, 1999). The panel cointegration technique makes use of a residual-based ADF test. The specific cointegrating relationships estimated are:

$$y_{it} = \beta_{1i}\, e_{it} + \beta_{2i}\, \mathrm{INT}_{it} + \beta_{3i}\, p_{it} + \beta_{4i}\, m_{it} + \varepsilon_{it}$$

where i runs from 1 to N countries (here N = 4) and t runs from 1 to T observations (here T = 13). The term ε_{it} estimates the deviation from the modelled long-run relationship. If the series are cointegrated, this term will be a stationary variable. In other words, stationarity can be achieved by establishing whether ρ_i in:

$$\varepsilon_{it} = \rho_i\, \varepsilon_{i\,(t-1)} + \xi_{it}$$

is unity. The null hypothesis, associated with Pedroni's test procedure is that $\rho_{is} = 1$. In other words, the null hypothesis associated with Pedroni's test procedure is equivalent to testing the null of nonstationarity (no cointegration) for all i. Pedroni (1997, 1999) developed four panel cointegration statistics and three group mean panel cointegration statistics. The Pedroni cointegration results are reported in Table 4. The results accept the null hypothesis of no cointegration, confirming that the panel is non-stationary. In other words, the results indicate that the variables do not share a long-run cointegrating relationship. We do not find support for the presence of a long-run relationship between the variables under investigation by accounting for dynamic heterogeneity.

Table 4: Panel Cointegration Tests.

Panel v-stat	–0.45128
Panel rho-stat	–0.11119
Panel pp-stat	–0.96796
Panel adf-stat	–0.48263
Group rho-stat	–0.87809
Group pp-stat	–0.24881
Group adf-stat	–0.54245

Estimates of the Structural Model

This section estimates the contemporaneous relationships from the structural VAR model. The results are presented below:

$$\varepsilon^{e} = \upsilon^{e}$$

$$\varepsilon^{INT} = \upsilon^{INT}$$

$$\varepsilon^{y} = -\underset{(0.012)^{*}}{0.505}\,\varepsilon^{INT} - \underset{(0.075)^{*}}{0.604}\,\varepsilon^{p} + \upsilon^{y}$$

$$\varepsilon^{p} = \underset{(0.123)^{*}}{0.484}\,\varepsilon^{e} + \underset{(0.384)}{0.436}\,\varepsilon^{y} + \underset{(0.279)}{0.392}\,\varepsilon^{m} + \upsilon^{p}$$

$$\varepsilon^{m} = \underset{(0.147)^{*}}{0.524}\,\varepsilon^{e} + \underset{(0.158)^{*}}{0.578}\,\varepsilon^{y} - \underset{(0.161)}{0.102}\,\varepsilon^{p} + \upsilon^{m}$$

where ε represent the residuals from the unrestricted VAR model and υ represent the own exogenous shocks. Figures in parentheses indicate standard errors while an asterisk indicates significance at the 5 per cent level. Commenting on the estimations of the structural model we can say the following: First, in the equation of output shocks, those shocks are negatively related to lending rate shocks as well as to price shocks. The presence of a negative relationship between lending rate shocks and output shocks is not in agreement with the McKinnon-haw hypothesis of financial deregulation. This hypothesis postulates that higher interest rates lead to an enhanced saving behaviour as well as to increased financial intermediation. Both of those positive responses increase the efficiency of the economy leading to higher economic growth. The empirical findings rather suggest that higher lending rates have an impact on the working capital due to the negative effects on output (Van Wijnbergen, 1986). Moreover, the presence of the negative effect of price shocks on output shocks could be explained through the impact of demand shocks. In particular, unexpected prices increases lead to lower demand which, in turn, lowers output growth.

The equation of inflation depicts that output shocks, exchange rate shocks, and money supply shocks generate positive inflation shocks. More precisely, the positive association between output and price shocks agrees with the empirical findings by Turner (1993) and Kamin and Klau (1998), while that between price and money shocks agrees with the results offered by Barungi (1997) and Kaminsky (1997).

Finally, the equation of money supply shows that there exists a positive relationship between monetary and output shocks, indicating that the monetary authorities follow an accommodating monetary policy when the output rises. The same explanation holds for the positive relationship between monetary and exchange rate shocks. The monetary authorities increase the money supply whenever the domestic currency depreciates against the U.S.

dollar. Finally, the negative association between monetary and price shocks could be explained through the fact that the monetary authorities tend to mop-up liquidity from the economy whenever inflation is becoming to much trouble.

Variance Decompositions

The variance decomposition technique describes the fraction of the *k*-step ahead squared prediction error of one variable attributed to the innovation-variance of another. The results are reported in Table 5. In all five panels, the empirical analysis shows that 'own' shocks explain a substantial part of the forecast error variance of the variable under study. Moreover, the results in Panel 1 indicate that price shocks play the dominant factor in explaining the forecast error variance of the exchange rate. Panel 2 results reveal that over both short- and long-run horizons, money supply shocks as well as nominal exchange rate shocks account for half of the forecast error variance of the interest rate. The remaining is explained through the own interest rate shocks. In Panel 3 the empirical findings show that price shocks, money shocks, exchange rate shocks and interest rate shocks account for the forecast error variance of income. Next, Panel 4 results show that income as well as exchange rate shocks account for the forecast error variance of inflation. Finally, the results in Panel 5 indicate that income shocks account for half of the forecast error variance of money supply.

Impulse Responses

Figures 1 through 5 show the responses of the variables under investigation to a one-time shock in each of the variables entering the system, i.e. the exchange rate, the interest rate, income, inflation, and money supply, respectively. All variables entering the system are expressed in first differences. In such a manner, a one-time shock to the first difference in a variable indicates a permanent shock to the level of that variable.

Commenting selectively on impulse responses, Figure 1 depicts that a depreciation of the domestic currency in all countries in the panel set has an expansionary effect on output. The results are similar to those reached by Edwards (1989), Reinhart and Reinhart (1991), Kamin and Klau (1998), and Kamin and Rogers (1997) for developing countries. Moreover, inflation responded positively to exchange rate shocks (depreciation), as in Dordunoo and Njinkeu (1997) for certain African countries. Finally, those exchange rate shocks also tend to lead to positive money supply responses. From Figure 3 it can be deduced that positive output shocks (a stronger economy) tend to appreciate the domestic currency. Those findings are in agreement with those

Table 5: Variance Decompositions.

Panel 1. One Standard Deviation Shock in the Exchange Rate.

Forecasting	*Forecast Error Variance due to*				
Horizon / Years	*e*	*INT*	*y*	*p*	*m*
1	100.00	0.00	0.00	0.00	0.00
4	48.19	0.76	0.06	50.97	0.01
8	48.25	0.65	0.06	51.02	0.02
10	48.26	0.65	0.05	51.02	0.02

Panel 2. One Standard Deviation Shock in the Interest Rate.

Forecasting	*Forecast Error Variance due to*				
Horizon / Years	*e*	*INT*	*y*	*p*	*m*
1	0.00	100.00	0.00	0.00	0.00
4	25.00	49.84	0.00	0.01	25.13
8	25.10	49.78	0.00	0.01	25.07
10	25.08	49.78	0.00	0.01	25.10

Panel 3. One Standard Deviation Shock in Income.

Forecasting	*Forecast Error Variance due to*				
Horizon / Years	*e*	*INT*	*y*	*p*	*m*
1	19.00	20.34	30.62	20.00	10.00
4	20.50	29.36	30.09	10.00	10.00
8	20.50	29.36	30.09	10.04	9.96
10	20.50	29.36	30.09	10.00	10.00

Panel 4. One Standard Deviation Shock in Inflation.

Forecasting	*Forecast Error Variance due to*				
Horizon / Years	*e*	*INT*	*y*	*p*	*m*
1	20.00	0.00	50.64	29.36	0.00
4	20.01	0.00	50.63	29.37	0.00
8	20.02	0.00	50.62	29.36	0.01
10	20.02	0.00	50.62	29.36	0.01

Panel 5. One Standard Deviation Shock in the Money Supply.

Forecasting	*Forecast Error Variance due to*				
Horizon / Years	*e*	*INT*	*y*	*p*	*m*
1	0.02	0.09	50.57	0.02	49.29
4	0.02	0.08	50.57	0.02	49.30
8	0.02	0.08	50.57	0.02	49.30
10	0.01	0.07	50.58	0.02	49.31

Notes: Figures came from rounding-off.

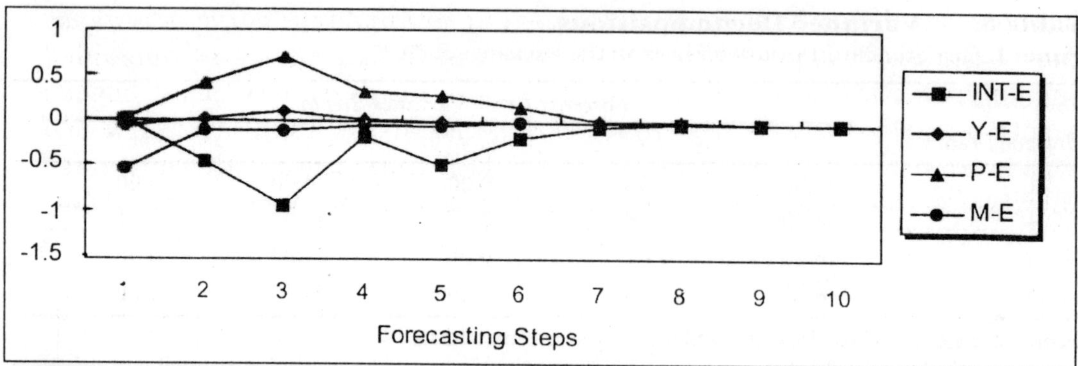

Fig. 1: Responses to One S.D. Innovations of the Exchange Rate.

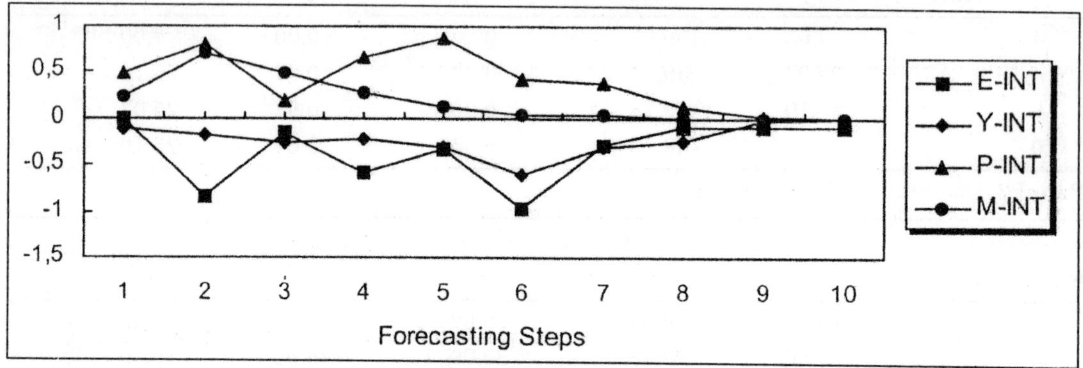

Fig. 2: Responses to One S.D. Innovations of the Interest Rate.

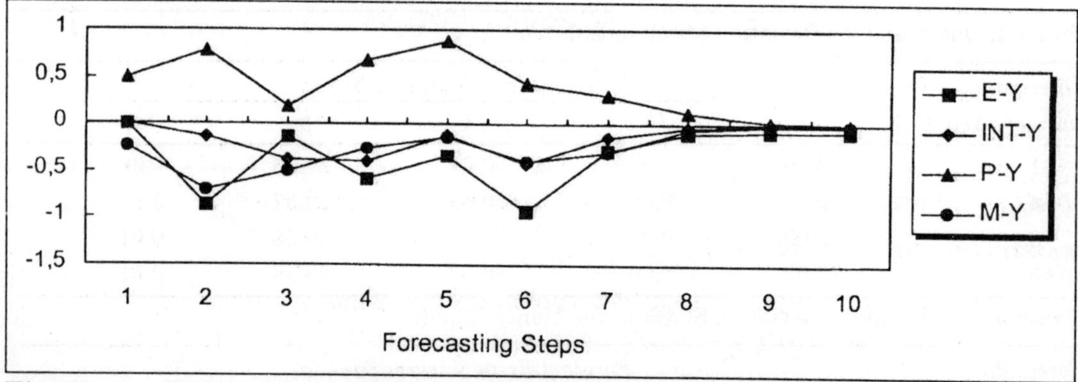

Fig. 3: Responses to One S.D. Innovations of Income.

offered by Ndung (1997). In addition, positive output shocks are accompanied by negative responses of money supply, an indication that monetary authorities implement a restrictive monetary policy when the economy expands in order to avoid inflationary pressures. Finally, positive supply (output) shocks are accompanied by positive inflationary responses, an indication that the economy is characterised by Phillips-type curve behaviour. Figure 4 depicts that price shocks (increases in finflation) are accompanied by an appreciation of the domestic currency. Furthermore, price shocks generate positive money supply responses, since higher inflation drains the economy from the necessary liquidity needed, thus, urging the monetary authorities to implement accommodating monetary policy to avoid recession.

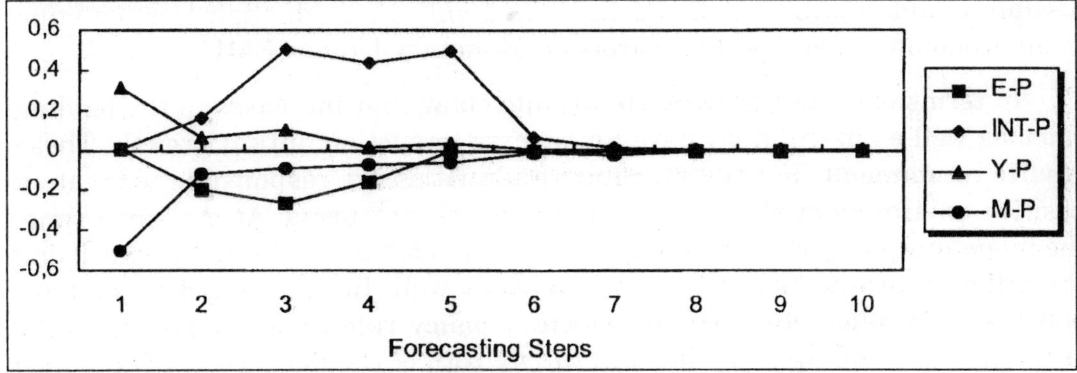

Fig. 4: Responses to One S.D. Innovations of Inflation.

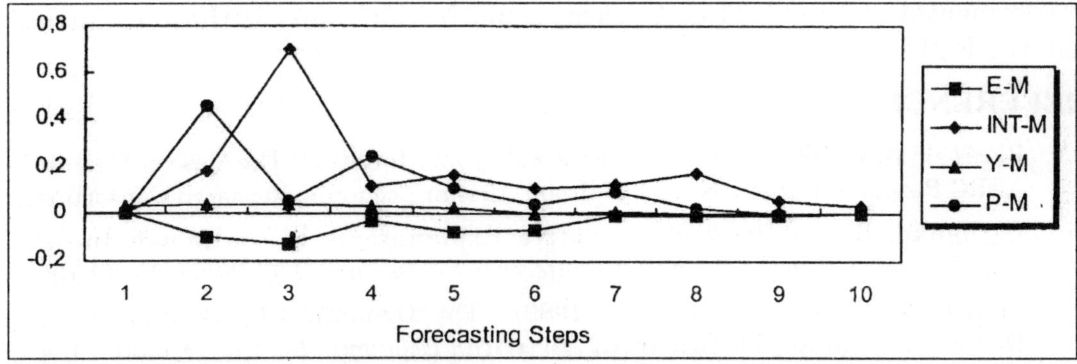

Fig. 5: Responses to One S.D. Innovations of Money Supply.

Conclusions and Policy Implications

This paper investigates dynamic relationships among output, inflation, exchange rates and monetary dynamics. Using a panel data set from four different Southeast European transition economies, namely, Bulgaria, Romania, Croatia, and Slovenia, from 1990 to 2002, first it applies panel cointegration methodology. After finding no statistical evidence for a relationship among those variables, the paper moves into a variance decompositions and impulse responses analysis in the short-run.

The analysis through the impulse responses show that exchange rate depreciations exert an expansionary effect on output. That is an indication that the adoption of a flexible exchange rate system seems to be extremely desirable. However, the results also suggest that changes in exchange rates are followed by increases in prices and money supply. This last evidence indicates that these countries need more than a flexible exchange rate system. They need more discipline and credibility in the manner the economic authorities pursue their economic policy. If the latter fact is valid, then this discipline and credibility should be gained only through their participation in an economic union, i.e. the European Monetary Union (EMU).

In terms of output growth, the results show that increases in the lending rates as well as in inflation have an adverse impact on output growth. These results recommend that the monetary authorities are responsible to create a positive environment that will promote growth prospects. At the same time, the monetary policy should be implemented in such a way for not jeopardising the inflation prospects of those economies as well. In other words, monetary policy should follow an optimal monetary policy rule i.e. through the strike of the optimal lending rate, that will satisfy both of the main goals of economic policy, i.e. high growth and stable inflation. Needless to say, the latter could be achieved only by separating the central bank in these countries from the governmental embrace. This, in turn, could be done only if these countries join the E.M.U.

REFERENCES

1. Barungi, M.B. (1997). "Exchange Rate Policy and Inflation: The Case of Uganda". AERC Research Papers, No. 59, Nairobi: African Economic Research Consortium.
2. Bernanke, B. S. (1986). "Alternative Explanations of the Money-Income Correlation". *Carnegie-Rochester Conference Series on Public Policy* 25, 49-100.
3. Blanchard, O. J. and Quah, D. (1989). "The Dynamic Effects of Aggregate Demand and Supply Disturbances". *American Economic Review* 79, 1146-1164.
4. Blanchard, O. J. and Watson, M. (1986). "Are Business All Alike? " In *The American Business Cycle: Continuity and Change*, edited by R. J. Gordon. Chicago, III: University of Chicago Press.
5. Dickey, David A. and Fuller, Wayne A. (1981). "Likelihood Ratio Statistics for Autoregressive Time Series With a Unit Root". *Econometrica* 49, 1057-1072.
6. Dordunoo, C. K. and Njinkeu, D. (1997). "Foreign Exchange Rate Region and Macroeconomic Performance in Sub-Saharan Africa". *Journal of African Economies*, Supplementary to Vol. 6, 121-149.
7. Dornbusch, R., Sturzenbegger, F. and Wolf, H. (1990). "Extreme Inflation: Dynamics and Stabilisation". *Brooking Papers on Economic Activity*, 1-64.
8. Edwards, S. (1989). *Real Exchange Rates, Devaluation and Adjustment: Exchange Rate Policy in Developing Countries.* Cambridge, Mass.: MIT Press.

9. Engle, Rober F. (1978). "Testing Price Equations for Stability Across Spectral Frequency Bands". *Economertica* 46, 869-881.

10. Harris, R. D. F. and Tzavalis, E. (1999). "Inference for Unit Roots in Dynamic Panels where the Time Dimension is Fixed". *Journal of Econometrics* 91, 201-226.

11. Hoffmaister, A. W. and Vegh, C. A. (1996). "Disinflation and the Recession-Now-versus-Recession-Later Hypothesis: Evidence from Uruguay". *IMF Staff Papers* 43, 355-394.

12. Im, Kyung S., Pesaran, M. Hashem, and Shin Yonacheol. (1995). "Testing for Unit Roots in Heterogeneous Panels". Working Paper 9526. Department of Applied Economics, Cambridge University.

13. Kamin, S. (1996). "Exchange Rates and Inflation in Exchange-Rate Based Stabilisation: An Empirical Examination". International Finance Discussion Paper, No. 554. Washington, D.C.: Federal Reserve Board.

14. Kamin, S. and Klau, M. (1998). "Some Multi-Country Evidence on the Effects of Real Exchange Rates on Output". International Finance Discussion Paper, No. 611. Washington, D.C.: Federal Reserve Board.

15. Kamin, S. and Rogers, J. H. (1997), "Output and the Real Exchange Rate in Developing Countries: An Application to Mexico". International Finance Discussion Paper, No. 580. Washington, D.C.: Federal Reserve Board.

16. Kaminsky, G. L. (1997). "Dual Exchange Rates: The Mexican Experience, 1982-1987". In *Parallel exchange Rates in Developing Countries*. Edited by M. A. Kiguel, J. S. Lizondo and S. A. O'Connell. Basingstoke: Macmillan.

17. Montiel, P. (1989). "Empirical Analysis of High-Inflation Episodes in Argentina, Brazil and Israel". *IMF Staff Papers* 36, 527-549.

18. Ndung'u, N. (1997). *Price and Exchange Rate Dynamics in Kenya: An Empirical Investigation (1970-1993)*. AERC Research Paper No. 58. Nairobi: African Economic Research Consortium.

19. Ndung'u, N. (1993). "Dynamics of the Inflationary Process in Kenya". Goteborg, Sweden: University of Goteborg.

20. Odedokun, M. O. (1996). "Dynamics of Inflation in Sub-Saharan Africa: The Role of Foreign Inflation: Official and Parallel Market Exchange Rates and Monetary Growth". Dundee, Scotland: University of Dundee.

21. Pedroni, Peter. (1995). Panel Cointegration: Asymptotic and Finite Sample Properties of Pooled Time Series Tests With an Application to the PPP Hypothesis, Indiana University, Working Paper in Economics. No. 95-013.

22. Pedroni, Peter. (1997). Panel Cointegration: Asymptotic and Finite Sample Properties of Pooled Time Series Tests With an Application to the PPP Hypothesis, New Results. Mimeo, Indiana University.

23. Reinhard, C. M. and Reinhart, V. R. (1991). "Output Fluctuations and Monetary Shocks: Evidence from Colombia". *IMF Staff papers* 38, 251-266.

24. Rodriguez, G. H. and Diaz, G. G. (1995). "Fluctuations Macroeconomics en la Economia Peruana". Working Paper. Lima: Banco Central de Reserva del Peru.

25. Rogers, J. H. and Wang, P. (1995). "Output, Inflation and Stabilisation in a Small Open Economy: Evidence from Mexico". *Journal of Development Economics* 46, 271-293.

26. Turner, P. M. (1993). "A Structural Vector Autoregression Model of the UK Business Cycle". *Scottish Journal of Political Economy* 40, 143-164.

27. Van Wijnbergen, S. (1986). "Exchange Rate Management and Stabilisation Policies in Developing Countries". *Journal of Development Economics* 23, 227-247.

23

Grobalisation and Sectoral Change

Prof. Doddanagouda Patil*

Globalisation is defined as the free movement of goods, services, people and information across national boundaries. It creates and in turn is driven by an integrated global economy, which influences both economic as well as social relations within and across the countries. The opening up of an economy increases the competition internally as well as externally, leads to structural changes in the economy. Globalisation affects developed and developing countries differently.

After over a decade of implementing economic reforms, an assessment of the globalisation process is a very relevant and useful exercise not only for Indian economy but also for states economy which have and/or are going to initiate the process of reforms. In order to make an assessment of the impact of globalisation on sectoral development in India and Karnataka state, we must consider the initial conditions prior to globalisation.

This paper addresses some of these issues of economic development.

The specific objectives of the paper are as follows:

1. Study the trends of growth of GDP, GSDP and its main sector during Pre-Reforms and Post-Reforms period.
2. Compare the sectoral growth and its fluctuations in 1980-91 and 1992-93 to 2000-01.

* Faculty, Deptt. of Economics, Karnatak University, KRC PG Centre, Belgaum.

3. Study the shift in the sectorial composition of GDP during the period under study.
4. Study the occupational structure during the 1990-91 and 1999-2000.

Hence, in this paper I attempt to discuss about globalisation and sectoral change during the period of pre-reforms and post-reforms. This paper is organised in three sections. In the section I, I will discuss Review of literature, in Section II about globalisation and sectoral change in India and in Section III globalisation and sectoral changes in Karnataka state. For this we have considered the following three sectors of the economy.

1. Agriculture and allied: Forestry, fishing and mining.
2. Industry: Manufacturing, construction, electricity, gas and water supply.
3. Service: Trade, transport, communication, banking, insurance real estate business services, public administration, defence and other services.

I. Review of Literature

In this section, I undertake a brief review of the available literature to understand the problem more precisely.

Starper (1959) studied the sectoral analysis of GNP of East Germany by dividing the economy into agriculture, industry, construction, transport and communication. The gross national products attributable to transport and communication has increased almost parallel to that of industrial sector. Apparently, as compared to 1936, the output of industry and transport sector of East Germany have increased in 1956; that of agriculture declined and other sectors have more or less remain unchanged.

Swamy (1972) analysed the rate of growth of national income and share of different sectors to national income for China and India for the period 1952-1970. The rate of growth of national income in China declined from 4.8 per cent in 1952-57 to 1.4 per cent in 1957-65 and was 1.7 per cent during 1960-70. In India, the rate of growth of national income increased from 3.1 per cent during 1952-59 to 4.0 per cent during 1957-65 and declined to 2.3 per cent during 1960-70.

The share of agriculture to total production in India and China has declined over time. In China, the decline was from 45.3 per cent to 43.8 per cent while in India it was from 48.8 per cent to 42.4 per cent. The share of mining sectors rose sharply in China from 10.1 per cent to 33.3 per cent in

1970 but hardly changed in India. The service sector showed a different trend, it declined from 38.6 per cent to 22.9 per cent in China and increased from 34.6 per cent to 40.6 per cent in India.

Malenbaum (1982) compared the growth of India and China for the period 1950-80 GNP recorded a growth rate of 3.6 per cent India and 6.7 per cent in China. Sectoral composition of China has changed dramatically over time. The contribution of agriculture declined from 51 per cent in 1950 to 19 per cent in 1980. The importance of services sector has reduced through nominal (from 34 per cent to 26 per cent). A noteworthy shift has been recorded in the industrial activity, its share having increased to 55 per cent in 1980 from 15 per cent in 1952. On the other hand, sectoral composition of India showed much less dramatic changes. The contribution of agriculture declined from 62 per cent in 1950-51 to 42 per cent in 1980-81; that of industrial sectoral elevated to 24 per cent from 14 per cent while service sector contribution increased to 34 per cent from 24 per cent.

Rao (1979) analysed national income data to bring out the important structural changes having taken place in the Indian economy during the period 1950-51 to 1976-77. These changes are in the direction of modernisation and an increasing role for secondary and tertiary sectors. Nevertheless, the Indian economy continues to be dominated by the primary sector and by unorganised enterprises.

Dadibhavi (1986) analysed the annual compound growth rate of different sectors for India and Karnataka state for the period 1960-70. The rate of growth of primary sector was 2.26 per cent for India and 3.83 for Karnataka state. The secondary sector has recorded a growth rate of 5.17 per cent in India and 5.74 per cent in Karnataka state. The rate of growth of tertiary sector was 5.12 per cent for India and 4.14 per cent for Karnataka state.

All these studies and surveys indicate the increase in share of tertiary and secondary sectors and decrease in share of primary sector in GDP.

II. Behaviour of Growth Rates in India

Higher economic growth is important for several reasons. More resources will be available for further investments and social development. It will also create better opportunities for the population in the growth is labour-intensive. In this section, we examine the trends in economic growth, sectoral composition of GDP and structural changes in occupation in Indian economy during the period of 1980s and 1990s. The data on GDP is obtained from Central Statistical Organisation, New Delhi.

Sectoral Growth Rates

Table 1 examines the growth of gross product under different sectors and sub-sectors at constant prices. First to begin with, let us evaluate the changing growth profile of the Indian economy on a trend basis during the pre-reforms and the post-reforms period. It is evident that services sector has emerged as the dominant growth driver of the economy. If annual GDP growth has moved up from 5.4 per cent in the pre-reforms period to 6.4 per cent in the post-reforms period, it is the entirely due to the services sector growth surging from 6.4 per cent to 8.2 per cent during these two separate phase. In contrast, the industrial sector has remained struck at around 6.5 per cent annual growth. It is however, noted that in primary sector, the trend growth rate decelerated during post-reforms as compared to the pre-reforms.

Table 1: Sectoral Real Growth Rates in GDP.
(at factor cost)

(In percentage)

	Item	*1980-81 to* 1991-92	*1992-93 to* 2000-01
1	Agriculture and allied	3.9	3.3
2	Industry of which	6.3	6.5
	Manufacturing	6.1	7.4
3	Services of which	6.4	8.2
	Trade, hotels, transport and communications	5.5	8.3
	Financial, real estate and business services	9.4	8.8
	Community, Social and Personal services	5.6	7.4
4	Total GDP	5.4	6.4

Source: Obtained from Indian Industry in Post-Liberalisation Era, Forum of Free Enterprise, Mumbai, 20 July 2001.

National Income of the country has been increased considerably during the globalisation period. Due to changes in the sectoral share in National income, the structural transformation has taken place in recent years. The structural changes in national Income occurred due to an increase in the share of services sector and decrease in the share of primary and secondary sector.

The strong winds of globalisation have made the Indian corporate sector feel shy of manufacturing sector and they are now attracted more towards service sector.

Sectoral Composition of GDP

Economic development is the result of co-ordinated efforts of Agriculture and allied Industry and service sectors. The relative importance of each sector depends on the stage of economic development. The sectoral composition of GDP in India is presented in Table 2 at current prices. The structure of the economy is rapidly shifting to service sector economy with rapid rise in the share of service sector in GDP from 43.69 per cent in 1990-91 to 52.3 per cent in 1999-2000. The share of agriculture sector decreased from 30.93 per cent to 25.54 per cent. Even the share of Industry sector has fallen from 25.38 per cent to 22.1 per cent during this period, which is highly disturbing. Rate of industrial growth has slowed down. The share of services sector in GDP is quite higher as compared with the primary sector and the secondary sector. It shows the growing importance of services sector in our domestic economy. This is a sign of diversification of our eccnomy during the 1990s.

Table 2: Percentage Share of GDP by Industry of Origin.

	Sector	*1990-91*	*1999-2000*
1	Agriculture and allied sector	30.93	25.5
2	Industry sector	25.38	22.1
3	Services sector	43.69	52.3
	Total	**100**	**100**

Source: C.S.O. National Accounts Statistics (1991-92 and 2000-01).

Structural Changes in Occupation

The changing occupational pattern is interesting to note. Table 3 presents the distribution of work force by origin of industry based on the 1990-91 census and 2000 NSSO data. The occupational structure in the country has also been changed during globalisation period. Workforce in agriculture sector declined from 67.4 per cent in 1990-91 to 59.8 per cent in 1999-2000. The performance of industry sector in workforce has been improved from 20.5 in 1990-91 to 22.7 per cent in 1999-2000. The services sector in workforce has

Table 3: Labour force in Three Broad Industrial Sectors.

(In Percentage)

	Sector	*1990-91*	*1999-2000*
1	Agriculture and allied sector	67.4	59.8
2	Industry sector	12.1	17.5
3	Services sector	20.5	22.7
	Total	**100**	**100**

Source: (i) Census of India 1991, Series I, Final Population Tables Paper II of 1992, Statement VI, P. 18.

(ii) NSSO 2000, NSS Survey, 55th Round.

been increased to 22.7 per cent in 1999-2000 to 20.5 in 1990-91. The share of services sector in workforce is quite higher as compared with the agriculture sector and industry sector. It shows the shift of employment to services sector.

III. Growth Behaviour of Sectoral and District Incomes in Karnataka

The study of growth of different sectors in the district may indicate the trend differences in their economic inequalities. And the inter-sectoral income growth differences can also explain the changing importance of different sectors in the district economics. In this section, we examine the trends in economic growth of Karnataka. The annual average growth rates of sectoral and district income in Karnataka are worked out for the periods 1980-81 to 1990-91 and 1993-94 to 1998-99 at constant prices. The data on NSDP is obtained from Directorate of Economics and Statistics, Bangalore.

The calculated growth rates of Net District Domestic Product by broad sectors for the periods 1980-81 to 1990-91 and 1993-94 to 1998-99 are given in Table 4.

It is evident from the data provided in the table, that there are significant variations in the growth of every sector and there are also differences in inter-sectoral growth rates. When one looks at the individual annual average growth rates of Net District Domestic Product, Bangalore and Kodagu districts turned out to be the fastest and the slowest growing districts, respectively, in Karnataka between 1980-81 to 1990-91. The overall growth rates of Bangalore, Belgaum, Bijapur, Dakshina Kannada and Kolar are found to be faster than state's overall growth rate of 6.38% between 1980-81 to 1990-91. In eight districts, namely, Bangalore, Belgaum, Bellary, Bidar, Bijapur, Hassan, Kolar and Shimoga, the agriculture and allied sectors grew faster than the state level. Such a trend, perhaps may indicate the importance of primary sector in the development of these districts. In all the districts, except Bangalore, Belgaum, Gulbarga, Mysore and Uttara Kannada, the industrial sector growth rate is less than the state level. And service sector growth rates were found to be higher than state growth rate for Bangalore, Belgaum, Bijapur, Dakshina Kannada, Gulbarga and Mysore during the eighties.

Between 1993-94 to 1998-99, Bangalore and Shimoga districts emerged the fastest and the slowest growing districts respectively. The overall growth rates of Bangalore, Bellary, Chitradurga and Dakshina Kannada is higher than state level between 1993-94 to 1998-99. The annual average growth rate of agriculture and allied sector in Bangalore, Belgaum, Bijapur, Chitradurga, Dharwad, Kolar, Mysore and Tumkur is higher than state rate. It is in Bellary and Dakshina Kannada, industry and service sector grew faster than state rate during 1993-94 to 1998-99.

Table 4: District wise Sectoral Net District Income Annual Average Growth Rates in 1980s and 1990s

(In Percentage)

	District	*1980-81 to 1990-91 (Pre-reforms)				**1993-94 to 1998-99 (Post-reforms)			
		Agriculture and allied	*Industry*	*Services*	*Net District Income*	*Agriculture and allied*	*Industry*	*Services*	*Net District Income*
1 2	Bangalore Bangalore Rural }	2.99	12.05	11.19	10.64	7.32	8.48	18.15	12.90
3	Belgaum	3.69	12.32	13.02	7.86	4.94	3.36	9.09	5.91
4	Bellary	2.98	6.12	10.11	5.61	3.46	30.88	15.11	11.82
5	Bidar	3.28	4.10	9.78	5.17	2.56	6.06	8.36	8.25
6	Bijapur	10.19	6.34	12.04	10.07	3.58	8.93	12.00	7.23
7	Chikmagalur	1.88	5.13	9.67	4.01	–3.53	2.93	3.16	–0.83
8	Chitradurga	1.34	3.61	8.30	3.68	12.38	8.01	13.79	12.09
9	Dakshina Kannada	2.37	7.56	10.94	6.56	2.86	39.02	18.25	18.96
10	Dharwad	–0.47	8.97	9.95	4.89	4.51	4.86	9.81	6.67
11	Gulbarga	0.08	15.74	10.88	6.02	0.92	3.24	10.63	4.88
12	Hassan	2.65	3.23	7.77	4.06	0.77	3.51	7.62	3.47
13	Kodagu	1.07	1.65	7.49	2.59	0.30	8.86	8.93	3.30
14	Kolar	7.44	7.52	9.35	8.18	5.63	7.54	7.89	6.68
15	Mandya	1.69	5.00	8.05	3.59	3.17	0.75	8.12	4.35
16	Mysore	0.55	10.05	10.52	5.36	5.67	3.01	12.18	7.30
17	Raichur	1.74	1.22	10.06	3.83	2.25	13.17	10.03	6.49
18	Shimoga	3.51	0.59	6.74	3.85	–3.18	0.91	5.88	0.51
19	Tumkur	2.26	8.42	10.14	5.58	5.80	11.95	9.02	7.95
20	Uttara Kannada	–0.50	9.98	6.49	3.53	1.41	10.76	10.32	7.04
	State	2.37	9.13	10.21	6.38	3.51	9.66	12.65	8.45

Source: Directorate of Economics and Statistics (1991-92 and 2001). State Domestic Product Karnataka, Bangalore.

Note: * Old series with 1980-81 base.

** New series of NSDP with 1993-94 base.

A comparative study of growth rates given in Table 4, indicates that the agriculture and allied sector's growth is accelerated in the eighties and nineties in as many as 12 districts, namely, Bangalore, Belgaum, Bellary, Chitradurga, Dakshina Kannada, Dharwad, Gulbarga, Mandya, Mysore, Raichur, Tumkur and Uttara Kannada of Karnataka. And in as many as seven districts, viz., Bangalore, Belgaum, Chikmagalur, Dharwad, Gulbarga, Mandya and Mysore, growth rates of industrial sector are decelerated during 1990s. However, in the eight districts, that is Bangalore, Bellary, Chitradurga, Dakshina Kannada, Kodagu, Mandya, Mysore and Uttara Kannada, there is a remarkable increase in the growth of service sector in the nineties over that of the eighties. The growth rates of district domestic product for the two periods indicate that the overall growth rates of six districts, i.e., Belgaum, Bijapur, Chikmagalur, Gulbarga, Hassan and Shimoga, are decelerated during the nineties.

Table 4 examines the ranking of district wise sectoral growth rates of Net District Income. Relative rank of eight districts, viz. Bangalore, Belgaum, Bijapur, Chimagalur, Gulbarga, Hassan, Kolar and Shimoga deteriorated over the years in growth rate of Net District Income. And ranks of Bangalore, Chitradurga, Mysore and Uttara Kannada improved in terms of growth rates of agriculture and services sector. However, Bangalore, Belgaum, Chikmagalur, Dharwad, Gulbarga, Kolar, Mandya and Mysore lost their earlier position in 1990s.

Sectoral Composition of District Product

The sectoral composition of NSDP in Karnataka is presented in Table 5 at current prices. The maximum contribution of the agriculture and allied sector (67.3%) and the least contribution of the Industry (4.5%), the service (28.2%) sectors, to the total income is found in Kodagu for the period of 1990-91. On other hand, the least contribution of the agriculture and allied (2.6%) and the maximum contribution of the Industry (45.9%), the service (51.5%) sectors to the total income is observed in Bangalore. However, the contribution of agriculture, except three district, viz Bangalore, Dakshina Kannada and Dharwad is above and contribution of industry, except five district namely, Bangalore, Dakshina Kannada, Dharwad, Gulbarga and Mysore is below the state's share. And the share of service sector to the total income is above the state's share of 38.8% in Bangalore, Dakshina Kannada, Dharwad and Uttrara Kannada districts.

In the period 1998-99, the highest (61.6%) and the lowest (5.8%) contribution of agriculture and industry sectors, respectively, to the District Income is found in Kodagu, whereas the least contribution of the agriculture

Table 5: Ranking of District Wise Sectoral Growth of Net District Income.

	District	1980-81 to 1990-91 (Pre-reforms)				1993-94 to 1998-99 (Post-reforms)			
		Agriculture and allied	*Industry*	*Services*	*Net District Income*	*Agriculture and allied*	*Industry*	*Services*	*Net District Income*
1	Bangalore }	6	3	3	1	2	8	2	2
2	Bangalore Rural }								
3	Belgaum	3	2	1	4	6	14	11	13
4	Bellary	7	11	8	7	9	2	3	4
5	Bidar	5	14	11	10	12	11	14	5
6	Bijapur	1	10	2	2	8	6	6	8
7	Chikmagalur	11	12	12	13	19	17	19	19
8	Chitradurga	14	15	14	16	1	9	4	3
9	Dakshina Kannada	9	8	4	5	11	1	1	1
10	Dharwad	18	6	10	11	7	12	10	11
11	Gulbarga	17	1	5	6	15	15	7	14
12	Hassan	8	16	16	12	16	13	17	16
13	Kodagu	15	17	17	19	17	7	13	17
14	Kolar	2	9	13	3	5	10	16	10
15	Mandya	13	13	15	17	10	19	15	15
16	Mysore	16	4	6	9	4	16	5	7
17	Raichur	12	18	9	15	13	3	9	12
18	Shimoga	4	19	18	14	18	18	18	18
19	Tumkur	10	7	7	8	3	4	12	6
20	Uttara Kannada	19	5	19	18	14	5	8	9

Source: Computed from Table 4.

(3.6%) and the maximum contribution of industry (37.9%), service (58.5%) sectors is observed in Bangalore. Share of agriculture, except three districts, viz. Bangalore, Dakshina Kannada and Uttar kannada is above and share of industry except, four districts of Bangalore, Bellary, Dakshina Kannada and Uttara Kannada is below the state's share. And the share of service sector to the total income is above the state's share of 44.0% in Bangalore, Bidar and Dharwad district.

Table 6, indicates that share of agriculture and allied sector increased during the 1990-91 to 1998-99 in the seven districts, namely, Bangalore, Bangalore rural, Belgaum, Chitradurga, Dharwad and Gulbarga. And share

Table 6: Industrial Composition of District Income at Current Prices.

(In Percentage)

District	*1990-91*			*1998-99*		
	Agriculture Allied	*Industry*	*Services*	*Agriculture and Allied*	*Industry*	*Services*
1 Bangalore	2.6	45.9	51.5	3.6	37.9	58.5
2 Bangalore Rural	37.1	24.8	38.1	40.0	23.0	37.0
3 Belgaum	40.9	24.0	35.1	43.2	20.1	36.7
4 Bellary	46.4	16.3	37.3	35.9	24.2	39.9
5 Bidar	48.1	15.1	36.8	39.5	14.8	45.7
6 Bijapur	50.3	16.7	33.0	42.5	17.4	40.1
7 Chikmagalur	59.0	7.5	33.5	55.2	7.4	37.4
8 Chitradurga	46.0	19.0	35.0	48.9	14.9	36.2
9 Dakshina Kannada	31.2	29.5	39.3	19.2	37.7	43.1
10 Dharwad	31.9	25.3	42.8	36.0	19.1	44.9
11 Gulbarga	37.3	28.2	34.5	37.4	19.2	43.4
12 Hassan	56.8	10.8	32.4	47.4	12.1	40.5
13 Kodagu	67.3	4.5	28.2	61.6	5.8	32.6
14 Kolar	49.4	13.8	36.8	49.2	12.7	38.1
15 Mandya	54.3	14.4	31.3	46.5	14.9	38.6
16 Mysore	37.8	25.2	37.0	34.7	21.9	43.4
17 Raichur	53.5	11.3	35.2	43.7	14.8	41.5
18 Shimoga	48.5	18.1	33.4	41.0	17.5	41.5
19 Tumkur	45.4	19.3	35.3	45.4	18.7	35.9
20 Uttara Kannada	37.8	22.1	40.1	32.0	24.3	43.7
State	36.4	24.8	38.8	32.2	23.8	44.0

Source: Directorate of Economics and Statics (1991-92 and 2001), State Domestic Product Karnataka, Bangalore.

of industry sector declined in 11 districts viz. Bangalore, Bangalore rural, Belgaum, Bidar, Chitradurga, Dharwad, Gulbarga, Kolar, Mysore, Shimoga and Tumkur. However, except Bangalore rural remarkably increase in the share of service sector to the District income in all districts of the Karnataka. It shows the growing importance of service sector in state domestic economy. Thus, the service sector has, in fact gained the expanse of both and over performed since 1991.

IV. Conclusion

Our study shows that the policy of decontrol put the Indian economy and Karnataka on a economy higher growth trajectory in the eighties. Economic reform during the nineties helped the state and nation to maintain this high growth trajectory, despite with the marginal increase in agricultural growth in the state and deceleration in agricultural growth at the national level. This is largely due to the increase in the share of non-agricultural earnings. It also indicates a strong structural shift in favour of the service sector of the economy. The distortion in development process is not because the industrial sector has lagged behind but because the service sector has grown at a higher rate pulling down the shares of others. This means that industry has to grow faster, otherwise it will drag down the growth process in the economy. Improvement in the growth of income in the non-agricultural sector has been able to control the wise fluctuations in the overall growth rate of the GDP, but this has increased the variations in the growth of non-agricultural sectors. It is thus, seems that market-oriented economic policies have thrown up more uncertainties for the growth processes.

REFERENCES

1. Ganesh Kawadia (2002): Trends and Direction of India's Growth Process (1980-81 to 1999-2000), Man and Development March, pp. 29-36.
2. Sukumar Mukhopadhyay (2002): Globalisation and Indian Services Sector, Economic and Political Weekly, October 2, pp. 4097-4098.
3. Dr. M. D. Mohite and A. D. Sharma (1990): Wage Share Aspect in National Income, Structural Changes and Issues of Indian Economy, Himalaya Publishing House, March, pp. 27-32, Bombay.
4. G. S. Kainth and R. S. Bawa (1985): Economic Development and Structural Changes, Inter-India Publications, New Delhi.
5. Dr. O.P. Mahajan (1982): Economic Planning and Regional Development in India, ESS Publications, New Delhi.
6. R. V. Dadibhavi (1986): Income, Productivity and Industrial Structure, Chugh Publications, Allahabad.

7. Starper, W.F. (1959): The National Product of East Germany, Kyklos, Vol. 12, 1959.

8. Swamy S. (1972): Economic Growth in China and India: 1952-70, Economic Development and Cultural Change, Vol. 21, No. 4, Part II.

9. Rao V.K.R.V. (1979): Changing Structure of Indian Economy: As Seen Through National Accounts Data, Economic and Political Weekly, Vol. 14, No. 50, December.

10. Government of India: National Accounts Statistics (1991 and 2000): Central Statistical Organisation, Ministry of Planning.

11. Government of Karnataka: State Domestic Product (1991 and 2001): Directorate of Economics and Statistics.

12. Govt. of India (2001): Indian Economic Survey, 2000-2001.

13. Malenbaum, Wilfred: Modern Economic Growth in India and China: The Comparison Revisited, 1950-80, Economic Development and Cultural Changes, Vol. 31, No. 1, October 1982.

14. R.S. Bawa (2001): Challenges and Opportunities of Globalisation Implications for India, presidential address, in 84th Annual Conference IEA held at Vellore (T.N.)

15. S.S. Bhandare (2001): Indian Industry in Post-Liberalisation Era, Forum of Free Enterprise, Mumbai.

24

Globalisation and Foreign Direct Investment with Reference to Indian Economy[1]

*Ms. Sandeepa Malhotra**

Globalisation refers to the process of increasing economic integration and growing economic interdependence in the movement of goods and services, technology transfer, flow of capital, people and information amongst different nations in the world economy. It is beneficial because all countries have not been endowed by nature with the same productive facilities because of differences in geographical and climatic conditions. It creates more opportunities in term of large market for trade, large private capital inflows, and improved access to technology. The wave of globalisation in recent years has been expected to open a new vista in the field of productivity, efficiency, consciousness, quality, management and competitiveness.

In the pre-independence era, Indian economy was considered to be colonial economy which was characterised by mass poverty, unemployment, high degree of dependence on agriculture, lack of industrial base, inequality, more inflatory pressure, low level of productivity etc. During the post independence era, the economy may be described as one making an effort to attain self-sufficiency in food, fighting against poverty, unemployment and technological backwardness etc. Till 1991 the Indian economy, designed largely on a socialistic pattern, was characterised by a highly regulated

1 I am grateful to my guide Dr. P.L. Sablok, Prof. and Head, S.O.S. in Economics, Jiwaji University, Gwalior for his guidance and co-operation.

* Visiting Faculty, School of Studies in Economics, Jiwaji University, Gwalior-474011, India

business environment, a pervasive license system and high tariff barriers. Sweeping reforms since introduced by successive governments have radically changed the course of the economy. Today the Indian economy is far more simple, liberal, transparent and geared towards promoting private investments, both domestic and foreign. External trade has been liberalised, tariffs steadily lowered and import controls progressively reduced, while the few that remain are proposed to be freed within a fixed time frame. Globalisation besides encouraging competitive strength of the Indian economy should also reduce poverty to minimum. Opening up the gates of Indian economy has facilitated the flow of foreign investment into the country that will help the country to meet the internal shortage in internal finance. It also helps India to tide over the problem of BOP.

The Industrial Policy 1991, is based on the view that while freeing Indian Industry from official controls, opportunities for promoting foreign investments in India should also be fully exploited. It is felt that foreign investment would bring advantages of technology transfer, marketing expertise, introduction of modern managerial techniques and new possibilities for promotion of exports.

India is the fifth largest economy and has the second largest among emerging economies, based on purchasing power parity. India also ranks as the 11th largest economy in terms of industrial output and has the 3rd largest pool of scientific and technical manpower. The introduction of cable television has brought TV shows and news from around the world into the living rooms of Indian households. The Hong Kong based Star TV, BBC, CNBC and CNN broadcast news bulletins around the clock. Other popular channels like Zee, Sony, Sahara provide awareness and information about product and services to the common men. Brand-name awareness has permeated even among the cities and villages poorest population. In any village you go, you may not get drinking water, but you may get Coke or Pepsi. Children can readily identify Barbie and Mickey Mouse. This results in the development of large and rapidly growing consumer's market of approximately 300 million people for branded consumer products. Several multinationals have established their presence in the Indian market either through wholly owned subsidiaries or through joint ventures. Some of them are Suzuki, Ford, Coke, Avon, Pepsi, Revlon, Colgate etc. India opened its borders to the world, paving the way for foreign investment and imports from cars to computers. This also results in openings of movie theaters, bowling alleys, restaurants and malls. MNC's were energetic about business prospects in India, mainly on account of the huge market and the availability of skilled and cheap labour. Initially, most multinationals view India as a platform for exports and then capture the domestic market.

In the past, a more pronounced multinational presence was seen in non-core sectors, such as consumer goods, intermediates and services. Primarily because the core sectors were reserved for the public sector. Currently foreign investment is being encouraged in the core sectors, such as basic infrastructure. Investments are needed over coming years, till 2005-06, for the development of national and state highways estimated to total US$ 34 billion of which private sector investment required is US $ 8.3 billion. Opportunities exist in four-lane highway construction of over 35,000 km. Other related enroute activities like restaurants, motels, parking areas, real estate development etc. are needed. Consequently, a large number of foreign investors have entered various sectors of the Indian market. These include Fortune 500 companies as well as small and medium enterprises from all over the world. The success stories of these companies have encouraged others to follow suit. The opening up of capital intensive infrastructure industries such as power, telecom, oil and natural gas, roads and highways, and ports offer vast opportunities to foreign investors.

The Government has announced guidelines for private/foreign participation that permit formation of joint ventures between major ports and foreign ports, between major ports and minor ports and between major ports and companies. The measures are aimed at attracting new technology, fostering strategic alliances with minor ports to create an optimal port infrastructure and enhancing private sector confidence in the funding of ports. Gujarat Pipavav Port Limited was the first port to be established in the joint sector. The Port of Singapore Authority holds 26% equity in the project. The Commonwealth Development Corporation has offered to acquire equity worth Rs. 600 million. Land has been offered on lease to Indian Oil Corporation and Bharat Petroleum Corporation Limited to set up terminals and pipelines at the port site. The Kakinada port project has been awarded to a consortium of three companies led by International Seaports Ltd. (ISPL) of Singapore.

India possesses a rich wealth of mineral resources and a flourishing mining industry producing 84 minerals out of which 4 are fuel minerals, 11 metallic, 49 non-metallic and 20 minor minerals. Being aware of the vast potential of this sector, the Indian Government, has been consistently and in a pragmatic manner opening up the previously controlled regime to usher private investment, technology and managerial expertise. The opening up of the Indian mining sector has, therefore, generated considerable global interest. The Indian mining sector was opened up to Foreign Direct Investment in

1993 after the announcement of the New Mineral Policy which was further reviewed by the Department of Mines on 11th February 2000 for further liberalisation. For all minerals other than diamonds & precious stones, foreign equity holding upto 100% will be allowed on the automatic route, for both exploration and mining. In case of diamonds & precious stones, foreign equity upto 74% will be allowed. Some of the Joint Venture is between Hindustan Zinc Ltd. and BHP Minerals International, Australia; Indian Aluminum Ltd. and Alcan Ltd. Canada.

Tourism has been declared a high priority industry. No approval is required for foreign equity upto 51 per cent for developing restaurants, beach resorts and other tourism complexes that provide accommodation and catering to tourists. This draws attention of NRI, foreign institutions to invest money in above area. Growing popularity of Continental, Thai, Mexican, Chinese and American fast food also facilitates the flow of foreign investment in India. Some of the large multinational fast food chains present in the country are Wimpy, McDonald's, Domino's Pizza, Pizza Hut.

A number of facilities are available to NRIs, persons of Indian origin for investing in India. Some of these include maintenance of bank accounts, investment in securities, shares and deposits of Indian firms and companies. NRIs are permitted to make direct investments in firms/companies in India and in government securities, national savings certificates and units of the Unit Trust of India. Sale proceeds on these instruments can be repatriated provided they were bought out of funds remitted from abroad or from the investor's repatriable accounts in India.

The slow pace of reforms has made India somewhat unattractive as a destination for foreign direct investment (FDI). India has slipped to number 11 in consultancy firm AT Kearney's FDI Confidence Index for January 2000 from number 6 in June 1999. India ranks below China, Brazil and Mexico but above Thailand, Argentina, Hungary and Malaysia from the emerging markets. It is also above France, Canada and Japan. FDI inflows into India have always around US$2-3 billion against China's US$30-40 billion.

India has vast market potential, which lures foreign companies. But its demanding consumers can be difficult to read, and local rivals can be surprisingly tough. Political squabbles, bureaucratic delays, infrastructure headaches, and unprofessional business practices create one obstacle after another. Foreign companies are often viewed with suspiciousness. The factors detracting inflows are an obstructionist bureaucracy; slower reforms; poor infrastructure and cultural barriers.

The critics argue how country be self-reliant when the doors are discriminatory open to foreign capital and technology. By patenting products, process technology will not be shared but rented. Foreign company will reap the advantage of foreign exchange through equity participation rather than selling once for all. It is in this context that one must understand the need for emphasising Swadeṣhi against the powerful MNC's. Today's India remembers all too well what life was like before liberalisation. The most popular car was the Ambassador, a wide, heavy vehicle designed for India's rugged roads. Conglomerates headed by families like Tata and Birla made everything from shoes to trucks.

Present age is the age of borderless world, a world where physical distances matter little. The need of time is not to reverse the process of globalisation and foreign direct investment but to take bold steps to solve the problem created by the process of globalisation. There is only one way forward i.e. more integration, more interactions, more interrelations and more co-ordination and co-operation between domestic and foreign investments. Therefore, a well thought strategy and cautious approach should be adopted, so that Indian and foreign companies contribute to the economy simultaneously.

REFERENCES

1. Ahluwalia, Montek S. (1994): Structural Adjustment and Reform in Developing Countries, International Monetary and Financial Issues for the 1990s Vol. IV, Special Issue: Proceedings of a Conference Sponsored by the G-24 on the occasion of the 50th Anniversary of Bretton Woods (NY:UNCTAD).
2. Ashok Upadhyay: The History of Globalising, Business India, 2002.
3. Ashok Upadhyay: Why are we poor when we are so Rich, Business India, Dec. 2001.
4. Asian Development Bank, (2000): Asian Development Outlook, Oxford University Press, NY.
5. Bery, Suman K. (1992): India; Reform of the Financial Sector, Mimeeo, Reserve Bank of India, Bombay.
6. Bhattacharyya, B. (1994): Foreign Direct Investment in India, Foreign Trade Review, Jan-March.
7. Chakarvarty, Vikram (1996): Getting the best out of Foreign Capital Inflows, The Economic Times, Feb. 24.
8. Diwan R. (1995): Foreign Capital: Economic Reforms or Swadeshi, The Statesman Nov. 4.
9. Economic Policy and Performance (2001): B. L. Mathur.

25

Targeting the Poor and Social Development under New Paradigm of Microcredit Programme

An Approach Through SHGs in West Bengal

Debnarayan Sarker*

Microcredit Programmes in the world, especially in the third world countries, have emerged as an important institutional devices for providing small credit to the rural poor in order to alleviate poverty. These programmes, first developed and initiated in Bangladesh in the late seventies and replicated in many other developing countries including the Southeast Asian and some African countries, have now been recognised as a useful instrument for poverty alleviation. Under this programme, collateral free loans are provided to the rural poor who have limited access to the formal financial institutions mainly due to lack of assets to offer as collateral. The prime objective of these microcredit programmes is to ease such constraints in the credit market and thereby create self employment and increase the productivity and earning of the rural poor. This paper examines empirical evidence of SHG-led microcredit programmes in West Bengal in respect of targeting the poor, increase in income and some social change for better quality of life.

The paper in divided into four sections. In section I, we bring out the context in which the new paradigm of microcredit programme has emerged in the literature. In section II, we make a short review of this microcredit programme. In section-III, we present the data set and empirical evidence of

* Professor, Centre for Economic Studies, Presidency College, Kolkata.

our study. Conclusions and implications in the light of our empirical finings are made in section IV.

Introduction

There are two schools of thought on rural credit policy in developing countries (Egaitsa, 1988). One is the conventional supply-side approach that tries to inject subsidised credit from the outside in order to get rid of informal lenders, who enjoy usurious practices, and modernize the credit market. The other approach advocated mainly by researchers at Ohio state University emphasizes the importance of saving mobilisation and the viability of rural credit markets. More importantly, the old paradigm of microcredit programme in India, the conventional supply-side approach, failed in terms of both efficiency and equity. Under this programme, subsidised credit was monopolised by wealthier farmers though the programme was intended basically for the poor. The programme terminated with high default rate mainly because of 'intentional' non-repayment by the beneficiaries. Thus the old paradigm' of microcredit programme in India failed mainly for two reasons—non-viability of these programmes to the target group and poor recovery performance[1].

But the new paradigm of microcredit programme in India which emphasises qualitative as well as quantitative outreach of the poor and self-sustainability of the micro-finance institutions tied with their programmes[2], advocates the principle of 'Ohio schools of thought' - saving mobilisation and the viability of rural credit market. Under this programme, many non-Govt. organisations enter into the rural credit scene by way of organising the poor into informal groups for self-help through mutual aid along with the practice of their regular saving programmes. The initiative to organise Self-Help Groups was taken by the NGO in the early part of 1980s. Almost at the same time (1982-83), the group approach was initiated by the Government under a programme called Development of Women and Children in Rural Areas (DWCRA) in order to use the collective strength of groups of poor women's to break social barriers that have denied their income-generating and self fulfilling opportunities. With a view to evolving supplementary credit strategies for reaching unserved rural poor, NABARD introduced the pilot project in 1992-93 for linking SHGs with credit Institutions. With IRDP being subsumed in SGSY effective from 01.04.99, formation of Self-help Groups has become the principal mode of poverty alleviation through self-help and development of micro-enterprise. In addition to the practice of self-mobilised savings and the regular credit needs for self-employment opportunities of the group members. SHGs have developed as a decentralised channel of group members to make collective decision making, to solve conflicts through collective leadership, to meet the emergent needs on mutual help-basis, to participate in the welfare programmes, to build up awareness and capacity through group action and the organise themselves for gaining access to social opportunities. Thus microcredit programmes also provide positive externalities to those SHG member households which are not the direct borrowers of microcredit but enjoy the access to social opportunities through building up awareness and capacity by the collective efforts.

Review

The result of the performance of new microfinance programmes of the world are reasonably supportive as an efficient means of reducing poverty, but not of extreme poverty (Hulme and Mosley, 1996; Mosley and Hulme, 1998; Hulme, 2000, Navajas et al., 2000; Fujita; 2000; Meyer et al., 2000). But some studies argue that microfinance has very beneficial economic and social impacts. (Hossain, 1988; Remenyi, 1991; Otero and Rhyne, 1994; Holcombe, 1995; Schuler et al, 1997; Khandkar, 1998; BIDS, 1990), although some writers caution against such optimism and point to the negative impacts that microfinance can have (Adms and von Pischke, 1992, Montgomery, 1996; Rongaly, 1996; Wood and sharrif, 1997). The study of Paul Mosley (2001) reveals that the Bolivian achievement in microfinance has been impressive and Bangladesh and Indonesia are the only other countries in the world which can reasonably claim to have reached a similar level of creativity, but not always vulnerability and not extreme poverty. Navajas et al. (2000), in their studies on five microfinance organisation in Bolivia, observe that most of the poor households reached by the microfinance organisations were near the poverty line—they were the richest of the poor. Group leaders had more depth of outreach than the individual leaders. The urban poorest were more likely to be among the poorest. Although the average cost of reducing poverty through microfinance was cheaper than any of the anti-poverty modalities with the exception of rural health expenditure, the issue of appropriate insurance has not been resolved for poverty alleviation. It is observed that microfinance clients, urban and rural, are highly vulnerable and open to risks of decapitalisation and major reason for this is their lack of access to viable insurance managements. For eight years Bancosol used a forced saving arrangement in which 20 per cent of the interest charge was used as a group insurance premium to protect the repayment of loans, but this arrangement was done away with in 1994, so that the impact of negative shock on borrowers income is now thrown on to coping mechanism such as reciprocal lending solidarity group. In rural areas, where poverty is the worst, the insurance issue is particularly urgent because of the instability of income and high associated level of risk.

In comparison with other anti-poverty measures, microfinance appears to be successful and cheaper at reducing the poverty of those close to poverty line but inefficient by comparison with labour market and infrastructural means in reducing poverty (Paul Mosley, 2001). A variety of lending models have achieved the reduction of income and asset poverty, but have little impact on extreme poverty. The vulnerability of microfinance clients on the liability side has often been increased by borrowing and the coping strategies which those clients use have often been especially risky in the case of poorest clients. As a consequence, a number of gaps still remain in the structure of microfinance. The tentative inference we draw in that Bolivian MFOs are relatively effective at reaching the poor, not the poorest. For a total survey of nearly 2000 non-poor, poor and extremely poor over six years, Paul Mosley (2001) finds a single case where a MFO had managed to reduce extreme poverty and that was in an indirect manner (ibid, P. 129).

It has been argued that since the debt absorbtion capacity of the very poor is low, most of them are unable to borrow sufficient amounts to raise them above the established poverty line (Copestake, 1995). Moreover a system based on the quick-repayment of very small loans does not allow for funds to go into income-bearing activities that have a gestation period of any significance. Only project with very quick rates of return and high rates of return relative to the tiny investment can meet existing repayment schedules and this is not usually possible for the poorest of the poor. Some evidences also suggest that poverty alleviation by microcredit programmes (such as by the Grameen Bank) is attained through the generation of self-employment opportunities by the poor, not by the poorest of the poor, is not correct or is at least misleading (Fujita, 2000; Rutherford, 1998, Ito, 1999). The evidence supports that loans are, for the poor (not the poorest) with regular income, functioning as advances for savings. The point is that the regular repayment (for example, weekly repayment) is afforded by saving from already established regular income sources and not by labour income (and/or) profit from micro-enterprises financed by microcredit programme (Fujita 2000; p. 370). Moreover, there is the fore evidence that in order to maintain regular repayment schedule the borrowers of microcredit have to enter a loan recycling process which intensifies their debt liabilities or debt cycles' with various lenders (Rahman, 1999). Thus a more important aspect of microcredit programme through SHGs is to see how far such programmes have been in buildings/upgrading the asset-base (including technology, skill, information etc.) of poor micro-entrepreneurs not merely as saving-lending-repayment microcredit programmes.

The Data Set and Results

This paper is based on published data (Secondary source) of State Institute of Panchayet and Rural Development (SIPRD), Kalyani, West Bengal, which conducted a field survey in July 1999 on 50 SHGs randomly selected from total women SHGs promoted by different agencies in West Bengal (SIPRD, 2000 and 2001). The sample SHGs were almost in rural areas.

In order to study the different aspects of empirical findings tabular analysis, proportion, averages etc. have been used. Moreover, a simple mathematical model on positive externalities and the related figures have been presented based on the empirical findings of this study.

As regards some usual characteristics, this survey shows that all the 366 members under 50 SHGs are women and 94 per cent of them are within the age group 18-45. 30 per cent of the members belong to scheduled caste and 16 per cent to scheduled tribe. 83 per cent of them are married and 81 per cent are having family of not more than 6 members.

Targeting the Poor

Microfinance organisations (MFOs) in most of the developing countries have not explored how their targeting criteria relate to the comprehensive national poverty measures. The targeting criteria used by some MFOs, such as housing indices, involve variables that can not be as easily related to national poverty assessments as is land ownership in rural Bangaladesh (Meyer et al. 2000; P. 177). Some of the most important MFOs in Bangladesh have developed techniques to target the poor. Both the Grameen Bank (GB) and the Bangladesh Rural Advancement Committee (BRAC) use simple criteria to target clients for their credit programmes. The GB requires that its members have less than 50 decimals (0.5 acres) of land. BRAC requires that households have less than 50 decimals of land and have at least one family member engaged in manual labour as their main occupation. Analysis have revealed that mis-targeting (providing services to households that do not qualify) by the GB has reached 20-30 per cent in recent years (Matin, 1998), while estimates reach 15 to 20 per cent for BRAC (Zaman 1998). Research in Bangladesh sheds some light on the relationship between land ownership and rural poverty. A study of 62 village survey in Bangladesh during 1989-90 appears that land ownership is correlated with rural poverty because nearly 72 per cent of the extremely rural poor and 60 per cent of the extreme and moderately poor had no land or less than. 0.5 acres (Hossain 1995). Wodon (1997) explored alternative indicators of poverty as measured by the 1991-92 Household Expenditure Survey. He found that education was always a better targeting indicator than land ownership in urban areas, while in most cases land ownership was better than education in rural area. Housing variables also worked fairly in both rural and urban areas.

Our study relating to the size of land holding (Table-1) indicates that only 4.37 per cent of the members' families have land of more than one acre. 34.70 per cent of SHG households possess upto 1 acre of land. Although the break-up of data relating to SHG households less than 50 decimals (0.5 acres) of land are not explicitly stated, about 61 per cent of SHG households, (223 out of 366 cases) possess no land. As to the housing condition, the survey indicates that about 76 per cent of the SHG households live in kucha house (Table 2). Concerning to the educational characteristics of SHG members, Table-3 shows that only 10 per cent members are illieterate. This seems to be in conformity with Wodon's (1997), observation who found that education was not a better indicator than land in rural areas. These finding thus suggest that most of the people (about 61 per cent) of target group have come up under the SHG programme. Hence the question arises of whether all the members who have come under SHG Programme are the beneficiaries of microcredit. Saving-Credit status of SHG member seems to be important for explaining this issue.

Table 1: Distribution of SHG Member Households by Size-Class of Land-Holding.

Size of Land-holding (in acre)	*No. of Members*	*Percentage of Total*
Upto I	127	34.70
Above I	16	4.37
Landless	223	60.93

Table 2: Distribution of Households of SHG Members by Nature of Dwelling House.

Nature of Dwelling House	*No. of Households*	*Percentage of Total*
Kutcha	277	75.68
Pucca	55	15.03
Semi-Pucca	33	9.02
Rental	01	0.27

Quantum of savings depends upon the duration of membership. About 95 per cent of SHG members (346 out of 366 cases) are in the group for more

Table 3: Distribution of SHG Members by Educational Status.

Educational Status	*No. of Members*	*Percentage of Total*
Illiterate	27	10.11
Literate	147	40.16
Primary	75	20.49
Secondary	95	25.96
Collegiate	12	3.28

than one year upto 3 years. Membership upto 6 months and from 6 months upto 1 year are in the possession of 4.10 per cent (15 cases) and 1.10 per cent (4 cases) of total members respectively. The study also reveals that 40.7 per cent of SHG members (149 out of 366 cases) have saved more than Rs. 500 in the group (Table 4). As the duration of SHG membership is of short period, majority of SHG members are expected to have saving size upto Rs. 500 in the group. It is also observed that cent per cent of members are saving regularly and such savings are mobilised mostly from income of self (Table 5). Turning to the distribution of SHG members by the size of microcredit, the data show that 44 per cent of saving linked SHGs are not linked with microcredit under the microcredit programme (Table 6). As to the size of credit facility, majority of the borrowers of microcredit receive credit above the range Rs. 1000. However in comparison with the distribution of SHG member by size of saving (Table 4), it is usually said that if all of the SHG members under the size of saving above Rs. 500 are provided credit, total quantum of credit will be usually greater than their savings. But as the data do not specify the distribution of the recipient of credit as per their

Table 4: Distribution of SHG Members by Size of Saving.

Size of Saving (Rs.)	*No. of Members*	*Percentage of Total*
Upto 200	127	34.70
201 - 500	90	24.59
Above 500	149	40.71

Table 5: Distribution of SHG Members by Source of Saving.

Source of Saving	*No. of Members*	*Percentage of Total*
Family Income	109	29.78
Own Income	202	55.12
Cut in Family Expenditure	55	15.03

Table 6: Distribution of SHG Members by Size of Credit Facility from the Micro-Credit Institution.

Size of Credit Facility (Rs.)	*No. of Members*	*Percentage of Total*
Upto 500	54	26.34
501 – 1000	33	16.10
Above 1000	118	57.56

saving range, nor do it specify according to the distribution of land-holding, it may not be possible to identify the beneficiaries of microcredit neither by the size of saving nor by the land status. With these findings, it can not, however, be said that all beneficiaries of microcredit belong to target group judged by the criteria of land status and housing variable and educational characteristics, although about 44 per cent of the saving-linked SHGs are not beneficiaries of microcredit. This may not indicate high performance of the involvement of target group under this microcredit programme. It needs mentioning that in an empirical study Sarkar (2001) observes that majority of the saving linked SHG are out of credit linkage with SHG-Non-NGO models of microfinancing in West Bengal, whereas about 90 per cent saving-linked SHGs were credit linked under SHG-NGO models of microfinancing in West Bengal[3]. It is however expected that saving linked SHGs have higher access to credit for SHG-NGO microfinancing models in West Bengal.

Increase in Income

Any study about earning and assets is beset with several difficulties, such as under reporting, recall bias and inaccurate evaluation of earnings in kind. In the absence of properly maintained accounts in the case of small household enterprises, commonly observed in rural areas, the problem of income measurement is likely to be more acute. The methodology of calculating income changes requires accurate estimates of base year as well as final year incomes (Swaminathan, 1990). A reliable method can be to calculate income mobility of households given that one has income data collected during the two corresponding years. The studies conducted by Hossain (1988), Hulme and Mosley (1996), Todd (1996), Khandkar and Choudhury, (1996) on the beneficiaries of Gramen Bank (GB) show a positive change in income of the beneficiaries using a recall method and, therefore, their results are likely to suffer from memory bias Any change in asset position is also Calculated either by the recall method or by the calculation of asset changes of base year as well as final year estimates. Changes in working capital by the SHG member from base year to final year have been used for the calculation of asset position of SHG households (Hossain 1988). This survey does not mention the methodology of the calculation either of increase in earnings or of increase in asset position of SHG households which are the beneficiaries under microcredit programme.

Relating to the distribution of monthly income of SHG members before their involvement in the microcredit programme, the study reveals that the majority of SHG members (62.30 per cent) had monthly income upto Rs. 1000 and 30.05 per cent of members had monthly income above Rs. 2000 on an average (Table 7). As mentioned earliers although all the member are saving linked under SHG programme, 44 per cent of them are not linked with microcredit (Table 6). But this study represents increase in money income of those members who are dependent on loan only from microcredit. 63.41 per cent (130 out of 205) of microcredit beneficiaries, who had neither access to bank credit nor receive loan from informal credit tied with high rate of interest, are entirely depended on microcredit loan. Table 8, reveals that majority of SHG households entirely on microcredit had an average increase in monthly income upto Rs. 200 for their participation in the microcredit programme. But as the data of SHG members who had an increase in income for their only dependence on microcredit, were not categorised according to their initial income range when they received microcredit for the first time, the degree of the change in income for those beneficiaries according to the

Table 7: Distribution of SHG Members by Monthly Income before their Participation in Micro Credit Programme.

Income Range (Rs.)	*No. of* Members	*Percentage of* Total
Upto 500	54	14.75
501 – 1000	174	47.55
1001 – 2000	28	7.65
Above 2000	110	30.05

Table 8: Distribution of SHG Members by Increase in Monthly Income through use to micro-credit.

Increase in Monthly Income (Rs.)	*No. of Members*	*Percentage of Total*
Upto 200	91	70.00
201 – 500	31	23.85
501 – 1000	06	4.61
Above 1000	02	1.54

respective range of income can not be clearly represented. But it may suggest that microcredit plays a positive role for the increase in income of its beneficiaries, who relied on loan only from microcredit source. Studies on Grameen Bank have in generals shown a positive change in the income of the beneficiaries [Hossain 1988, Hulme and Mosley 1996, Todd 1996, Khandkar and Choudhury 1996]. However, all these studies use recall method and therefore their results are likely to suffer from recall bias. Kurian (1987), reporting results from a countryside survey of IRDP beneficiaries, found that about 84 per cent of the households enjoyed a positive increment in income after a period of two years. Within these, about 38 per cent of households enjoyed an increase in income of about 50 per cent. In another review of IRDP, Guha (1986: p. 32) reached the conclusion that IRDP failed to generate income to the expected level (Chavan and Ramkumar, 2002, p. 958). Our study suggests an increase in income in 100 per cases, who relied only on loan from micro credit programme, although the magnitude of the change in income is small for the use of small size of credit.

As to the distribution of the sectorial use of microcredit, it is observed that agriculture, animal husbandry, household industry and services are the combined sectors where microcredit beneficiaries find their major use (Table 9) Contrary to the popular belief that microcredit is mostly used for consumption expenditure, this study reveals that the recipient of microcredit uses their credit mostly for production purposes (about 71 per cent cases of total) suggesting that microcredit loan is income-generating for its beneficiaries.

Table 9: Distribution of Beneficiaries by Sectorial use of Micro-credit.

Source	*No. of Member*	*Percentage of Total*
Agriculture	47	26.86
Animal Husbadry	27	15.43
Household Industry	46	26.29
Services	04	2.28
Consumption	51	29.14

Data relating to the 'distribution of microcredit beneficiaries by repayment period', Table 10 shows that in major cases (109 out of 205) the period of repayment is 6 months and above. In about 46.83 per cent cases the repayment period for full repayment of each loan is upto 6 months. The repayment of all microcredit is usually fix at weekly basis, although the data do not specify whether the repayment period is made on specific term (first/ 2nd/3rd.......) or on all terms of microcredit. The available information suggest that about 87 per cent of members who received microcredit, have repaid

Table 10: Distribution of Beneficiaries by Repayment Period.

Repayment Period	*No. of Members*	*Percentage of Total*
Upto 6 months	96	46.83
6 Months upto 1 Year	42	20.49
Above 1 Year	67	32.68

their loans in time. Except the groups promoted by the rural financial institutions which were changing administered rate of interest, micro-credit attracts rate of interest higher than the bank rate but lower than the market rate. Peer pressure and need for more credit seem to be the motivating factor for timely repayment. (Table 11). It is usually expected that as the burden of weekly repayment is of small amount, it helped the beneficiaries of microcredit for timely repayment. It is relevant to mention that Bank Rakyat Indonesia's (BRI's), Unit Desa, Bangladesh Grameen Bank (GB), Baneosol of Bolivia have maintained high repayment rates and lent at commercial rate of interest (Kaladhar, 1997, p. 2688), But for state-led programme like Rural Regional Banks' (RRBs) loan of India, which are charging administered rate of interest, the average default rate was 47.5 per cent during 1983-91 and the six months arrears rate RRBs in 1992 was the highest among the 13 institutions that mosley and Hulme (1998) examined across different countries.

Table 11: Distribution of Beneficiaries of Micro-credit by Factors for Timely Repayment of Loan.

Factor	*No. of Beneficiaries*	*Percentage of Total*
Peer Pressure	44	24.72
Self-respect	8	4.49
More Credit Need	126	70.79

A record of near 100 per cent repayment is a major success of NGO-led microcredit programme (Hossain, 1988, Mosley and Humes 1998, Chavan and Ramkumer, 2002). But high repayment rate of NGO-led microcredit programme is directly related to high transaction cost and high rate of interest (Rahman, 1999 and Bhat and Tang, 1998, cited in Chavan and Ramkumar 2002, and Ramchandran and Swaminathan 2002). This is because NGOs heavily invest on supervision, monitoring and inforcing loan repayment. As the Grameen Bank, for instance, expanded its activities, administrative costs rose from 8.6 per cent of liabilities in 1988 to 18.1 per cent of liabilities in 1992 (Hossain, 1988). This study also suggests that despite the charging of high rate of interest on microcredit and its high recovery rate compared with State-led programme, the microcredit is found to be income-generating in all cases of its beneficiaries, who receive loans only from microcredit programme, though income generation is small for the use of small size of credit. This study, however does not bring to the fore evidence of income-generation for those beneficiaries who receive loan not only from microcredit source but also from other sources. Not unexpectedly, the beneficiaries of credit from various sources may enter into a loan recycling process in order to maintain their regular repayment schedule leading to the creation of "debt cycle" for those beneficiaries with various sources of credit.

Social Issues

Turning to the social aspects, though about 56 per cent of SHG members are the direct borrowers of microcredit, the microcredit programme is also found to have positive impact on the quality of life to an SHG members households, irrespective of direct beneficiaries of microcredit. Table 12 shows positive social changes like enrolment of children in school, immunisation of children, use of safe drinking water, organised resistance to social injustice, problem' solving (without external intervention), participation in social action are visible among almost all members irrespective of direct beneficiaries of microcredit. Thus the microcredit programmes through SHGs confirms some positive extenalities for those SHG member households which are not direct beneficiaries of microcredit for their participation in the group activities.

Table 12: Distribution of SHG Member Households as Beneficiaries of Social Aspects.

Indicators	*Number of Housechild*	*Percentage of Total*
Enrolment of Children in School	317	86.61
Immunisation of Children	346	94.53
Use of Safe Drinking Water	366	100.00
Problem Solving (Without external intervention)	365	99.73
Participation in Social Action	366	100.00
Organised Resistance to Social Injustice	346	94.53

In theoretical forms, this problem, thus relates to positive externalities in which there is no property right and no market or price for these social services. The SHGs; the recipient households of microcredit, are the suppliers of social services. The consumer, the SHG member households', which are the non-recipients of microcredit, are the potential buyers (along with the borrower member households of microcredit). Since the commodity (x) is good, we can anticipate that consumer will buy this good only if they are given subsidy to buy it.

Suppose there are two firms. Firm I, for examples SHG member households which are the borrowers of microcredit, operates in a perfectly competitive market[4] and produces an output x (for example good qualities of social services) which imposes a subsidy S(x) on firm 2 (e.g. the SHG member households which are not the beneficiaries of microcredit). The profits of the two firms are:

$\pi_1 = Px - c(x)\ \pi_2 = S(x)$ [p = Price per unit, C = cost]

We assume $\frac{dc}{dx} > 0$ and $\frac{ds}{dx} < 0$, Also C" $(x) > 0$ and S"$(x) < 0$, Private profitability consideration will lead firm to produce x such that $p = c'(x)$; but there will be an underallocation of resources. From the social point of view, the external benefits should be taken into account. Then the socially optimal level of output will be obtained by maximising $\pi = Px - c(x) + S(x)$.

The first order condition is:

$$P + S'(x) = C'(x)$$

The second order condition for the optimal solution is that the slope of MC will be greater than the slope of social marginal benefit.

In the following figure the demand and supply curve for a competitive industry intersect initially (i.e., when the external benefits are not taken into account) at point E, which, therefore, is the point of equilibrium. The

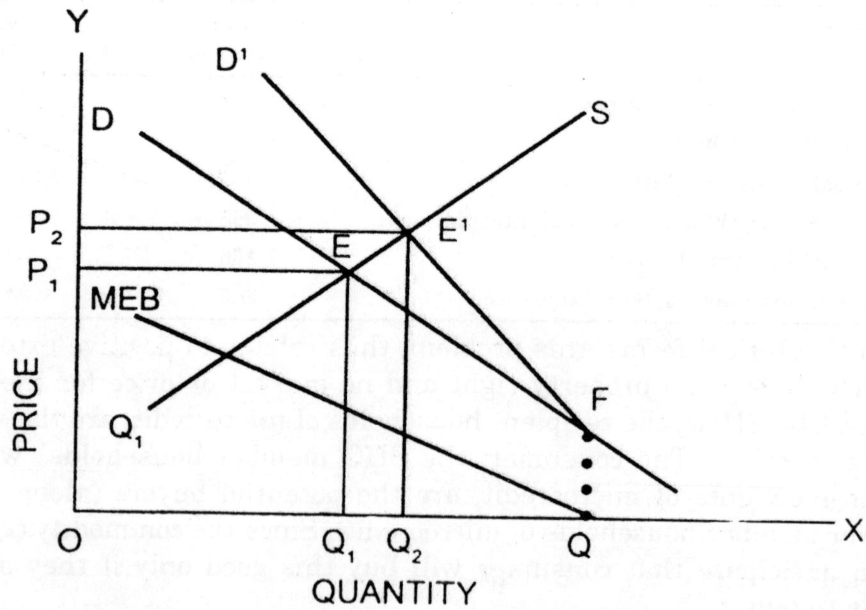

equilibrium price OP_1 and equilibrium output is OQ_1. Let us now consider external benefits. In the figure, the Marginal External Benefit, (MEB) curve shows the external benefit per unit of consumption. This curve is taken as downward sloping because as the consumption of the good increases, additional consumption yields lower and lower marginal benefits to other people. Social marginal benefits are indicated by vertically summing up the demand curve D and the marginal external benefit curve MEB. The social marginal benefit curve is D′E′F. As can be seen from the figure. MEB becomes zero at OQ, level of output and hence the D′E′F curve and D curve coincide after that point. The point of intersection of the new demand curve D′E′F with the supply curve S gives the optimal or efficient level of output OQ_2. This is the efficient level of output as it takes into account the benefits accruing not only to direct consumers who are the borrowers of microcredit but to other members of SHGs also. Thus in the case of positive externalities initial equilibrium guided by profit motive leads to a sub-optimal output (OQ_1) of the good conferring positive externalities as compared with efficient level OQ_2. Thus when individual (member's of SHGs who are the direct borrowers of microcredit) decide privately, individual do not take into account of the benefit of others. There will be sub-optimal output, which is lower than efficient level of output. Hence the relevant issue is to what extent SHG member households, which are not the direct beneficiaries of microcredit, can enjoy the external benefit. More importantly, whilst everyone within the group can enjoy the benefit equally, the access to basic social services and social mobilisation among the SHG member households depends upon the development of awareness, consciousness, capacity and self-confidence of the individual household for their participation in the group activities in these microcredit programmes.

Conclusions

The simple criteria used to identify the target group of the SHG member households based on land status, housing variables and educational characteristics suggests that majority of SHG member households under this study belong to target group, although the extent of poverty among the target group remains unexplored. Despite the inclusion of a little more than 50 per cent of SHG members (about 56 per cent) as the beneficiaries of microcredit, it can not be said that all the beneficiaries of microcredit belong to target group judged by the targeting indicators. The study also suggests that the microcredit programme through SHGs charges high rate of interest from its beneficiaries and the repayment rate is high compared with State-led microcredit programmes. But the microcredit programme is found to be income-generating in all cases of its beneficiaries, who receive loan only from microcredit sources, although income-generation is small for the use of small size of credit. No evidence of income-generation is found among the beneficiaries, who receive credit from various sources along with microcredit. It may lead to 'debt cycle' for those beneficiaries with different lenders for maintaining their regular repayment schedule. Moreover, this programme has positive impact on social development for all the SHG member households, irrespective of direct beneficiaries of microcredit, leading to the better quality of life for all. This programme confirms some positive externalities for those SHG member households, which are not direct beneficiaries of microcredit, for their participation in the group activities.

Thus the impact of microcredit programme through SHGs has been effective is making some positive social change to all member households, irrespective of direct borrowers of microcredit. In convention with this, to make the microcredit programme more effective in economic front, it needs to make higher coverage of the target group as the direct beneficiaries of microcredit under this programme and large-scale funds are to be spent for target group through microcredit programmes.

NOTES

1. For extensive discussion on this point see, Rangarajan, 1996; p. 68; Ramchandran and Swaminathan, 2002, p. 238; Kaladhar, 1997, p. 2687-8; Meyer et al., 2000, p. 173.
2. The new paradigm emphasises financial intermediation with self-sustainability of institutions and qualitative/quantitative outreach of the poor (Robinson, 1995): See, Kaladhar, 1997, p. 2688 for a discussion on this point.
3. Bradly there are mainly two different models - SHG-NGO and SHG-non-NGO - Which have emerged under the SHG linkage approach operating micro-credit programmes in West Bengal. Each of this two different models are future classified into there linkage approaches, see, Sarker (2001) for the details.
4. Though the cost of credit per unit is observed to differ between NGO-led microcredit programmes and State-led microcredit Programmes, the cost of credit is almost same within NGO-led programmes or within State-led Programmes in West Bengal, amount SHG members receive microcredit from these two sources (Draft Report, SIPRD, 2000).

REFERENCES

1. Adams, D., and Von Pischke, J.D. (1992): Microenterprise Credit Programs: Deja ve. *World Development*, 20.
2. Bhat, N. and Tans, Shui-Yan (1998) "The Problems of Transaction Costs in Group Band Micro-landing: A Institutional Perspective", *World Development*, 26(4) April.

3. BIDS (1990): Bangladesh Institute of Development Studies. *Evaluation of Poverty Alleviation Programs in Bangladesh.* (Mimeo) BIBDS, Dhaka.

4. Chavan P. and Ramakumar, R. (2002): "Microcredit and Rural Poverty: An Analysis of Empirical Evidence", *Economic and Political Weekly*, March, 9.

5. Copestake, J. (1995): *IRDP Revised* (Mimco).

6. De, S and Sarker, D. (2002): "Increasing Women's Participation and Self Employment Generation in Household Industries: An Approach Through SHGs in West Bengal, *22nd Conference Volume, Bangiya "Ardhanite Parishad.*

7. Egaistu, F. (1988): 'Rural Financial Market: Two school of thought In Farm Finance and Agricultural Development of Asian Productivity organisations. Tokyo Asian Productivity Orgazation.

8. Fujita, K. (2000): "Credit Flowing From The Poor to the Rich: The Financial Market and The Role of the Grameen Bank in Rural Bangladesh". *The Developing Economics*, XXXVIII-3 (Sept).

9. Guha, S. (1986): "Rural Poverty Alleviation in India: Poverty, Performance and Possibilities, Paper Presented at the Franco-India Colloquium on technological choices for Rural Development, Montpellier, France 18-20 March: reproduced in S. Subrmanian (ed) Indian Development Experience: *Selected Writings of S. Guhan*, Oxford University Press, New Delhi, 2001.

10. Holcombe, S (1995): Managing to empower: *The Grameen Bank's experience of Poverty Alleviation*, London: Zed press.

11. Hossain, M (1988): *Credit for Alleviation of Rural Poverty. The Gramen Bank in Bangladesh,* Washington, D.C.; IFPRI.

12. Hossain, M. (1995): "Socio-economic Characteristics of the poor", in Hossain Zillur Rahman and Mahabub Hossain, eds., *Rethinking Rural Poverty: Bangladesh* as a case study. Bangladesh: University Press Limited.

13. Hulme, D and Mosley, p (1996b): *Finance Against Poverty*, Vol. 1, Routledge Publication, London.

14. Hulme, D. and Mosley P. (1996): *Finance Against Poverty*, Vol. 1 & 2, Routledge Publication London.

15. Hulme, Devid (2000): Impact Assessment Methodologies for Microfinance: Theory, Exprience and Better practice, *World Development* Vol. 28, No. 1.

16. Ito, S. (1999): "The Grameen Bank: Rhetoric and Reality". *Ph. D. diss, University of Sussex.*

17. Khandker, S.R. and Chowdhury, O.H. (1996): "Targeted Credit Programmes and Rural Poverty in Bangladesh," in *Proceedings of the Workshop, Credit Programmes for the poor: Household and Intrahousehold Impact and Programme Sustainability*, held in March 19-21, 1995 Edited by Latif M.A., Khandkar, S.R. and Khan, Z.H. Dhaka.

18. Khandhar. S.R. (1998): *Fighting Poverty with Microcredit: Experience in Bangladesh* Weshington, D.C.: Oxford University Press for World Bank.

19. Khandker, S.R. (2000): Savint, Informal Borrowing and Microfinance. *The Bangladesh Development Studies*, Vol. XXVI, July-Sept.

20. Kurian, N.J. (1987): "IRDP: How Relevant is it? " *Economic and Political weekly*, 22(52).

21. Latif, A.M. (2001): "Microcredit and Savings of Rural Households in Bangladesh" *The Bangladesh Development Studies*, Vol. 27, March.

22. Matin, I. (1998): "Mis targeting by the Grameen Bank: A possible explanation" *IDS Bulletin*, Vol. 29, No. 4.

23. Meyer, R.L. Nagarajan, G. and Dunn, E.G. (2000): Measuring Depth of Outreach: Tools for Microfinance. *The Bangladesh Development Studies*. Vol. XXV, June-Sept.

24. Montgomery, R. (1996): "Disciplinign or protecting the Poor? Avoiding the Social costs of peer pressure in Microcredit Schemes", *Journal of International Development*, 8(2).

25. Mosley, P. (1996a): India: Regional Rural Banks' in Hulme, D. and Mosley, P (1996b).

26. Mosley, P. (2001): "Microfinance and Poverty in Bolivia", *Journal of Development Studies*, Vol. 37, No. 4.

27. Mosley, P and Hulme, D (1998): Microenterprise Finance: In there a conflict between growth and poverty Alleviation. *World Development*, Vol. 26, No. 5.

28. Nair, T.S. (1998): Meting the Credit Needs of the Microenterprise Sector: Issues in Focus. *The Indian Journal of Labour Economics*, Vol. 41, No. 3.

29. Navajas, E., Richard, L.M., Claudio, G. and Jorje R. (2000): Microcredit and the Poorest of the Poor: Theory and Evidence from Bolivia, *World Development* Vol. 28, No. 2.

30. Otero, M. and Rhyne, E. (1994): *The New World Micro Enterprise Finance*, IT London. Pitt. M.M. (2000): The Effect of Non-agricultural Self-employment credit on Contractual Relations and Employment in Agriculture. The case of Microcredit Programmes in Bangladesh. *The Bangladesh Studies*, Vol. XXVI, June-Sept.

31. Pitt. M. & Khandker, S. (1995) "Household and Interhousehold Impacts of the Grameen Bank and Similar Targeted Credit Programs in Bangladesh. "Paper presented at Workshop on "Credit Programs for the Poor: Household and Intrahousehold Impacts an Program sustainability." Dhaka: *World Bank and Bangladesh Institute of Development Studies.*

32. Rahman, A. (1999): "Microcredit Initiatives for Equitable and sustainable Development: Who Pays? " *World Development,* 27(1) (January) pp: 67-82.

33. Ramachandran, V.K. and Swaminathan, M. (2002): "Rural Banking and Landler Labour Households: Institutional Reform and Rural Credit Markets in India" *Journal of Agrarian Change*, Vol. 2, No. 4 (October).

34. Remenyi, J. (1991): *Where credit is due.* London IT Publication.

35. Rogaly, B (1996): Microfinance Evangelism, Destitute Women and Hard Selling of a New Anti-poverty Formula. *Development in Practice* 6(2).

36. Rangarajan, C. (1996): "Rural India, the Role of Credit" *Reserve Bank of India Bulletin*, May, Bombay, Reserve Bank of India.

37. Rutherford, S. (1998): "The savings of the Poor, Improving Financial Services in Bangladesh", *Journal of International Development* 10, No. 1.

38. SIPRD (2000; 2001) 'Study of Rural Credit in West Bengal, *Draft Report*. Edited by Manab Sen.

39. Sarker, D. (2001): "A study of SHG-NGO and SHG-non-NGO models of Rural Microfinancing in West Bengal, Indian *Journal of Agricultural Economics*, July-Sept.

40. Schuler, S.R., Hashemi, S.M. and Riley, A.P. (1997): The influence of women's changing roles and status of Bangladesh's fertility Transmission: Evidence from a study of credit programms and Contraceptive use, *World Development*, 25(4).

41. Swaminathan, M. (1990): "Village Level Implementation of IRDP: Comparison of West Bengal and Tamil Nadu" *Economic and Political Weekly*, 35(13), March 31.

42. Todd, H. (1996),: *'Women at the Centre: Grameen Bank Borrowers after One Dcade. Dhaka:* University Press.

43. Wodon, Q.T. (1997): "Targeting the poor Using ROC Curves", *World Development,* Vol. 25, No. 12.

44. Wood, G. and Sharrif. S. (1997): *Credit: where credit is due*, Dhaka and London VPL and Zed Press.

45. Zaman, H. (1998): "Can Mis-targeting be Justified' *IDS Bulletin*, Vol. 29, No. 4.

26

Impact of Globalisation on Export-Import of Agro-Products

*Prof. Sathya Prema**

Trends in Export-Import of Agro Products

With a new Economic Policy of 1991, both internal and external trade policies were liberalised, various policy reforms viz., withdrawal of quantitative restrictions, tariff rate quotas, export subsidies etc., were introduced to create competitive environment for Indian agriculture. As a result of liberalisation policy import of agricultural products especially in the case of edible oil, cereals increased considerably. Import of bulk consumption goods (Agro-products) increased from Rs. 5513 Crore in 1997-98 to Rs. 10619 Crore in 1998-99.

Similarly India's export of Agricultural and allied products increased from Rs. 24626 Crore in the same period i.e. 1997-98 – 1998-99. Even though World trade declined from 12.2% to 10.9% during the period between 1990-97, India's export has increased from 19.5% to 21.3%.

Another notable trend with regard to India's export of Agro-Products is that, export of spices—tea, coffee, tobacco, cashew nut, fruits and vegetables increased considerably during the period between 1993-1998.

Therefore, it is clear that there is more scope for boosting export of commercial crops because these commercial crops-tea, coffee, fruit, herbs, tobacco, spices, vegetables have comparative advantage.

* Chairperson, Department of Studies in Economics, Karnataka State Open University, Manasagangotri, Mysore.

Problems and Suggestions

There is a strong argument against Globalisation on two grounds:

- Due to low quality and High price, Inadequate supply it is impossible to face foreign competition.
- Eliminating subsidies and quota restrictions, Incorporation of Intellectual Property rights affect agricultural sector.

The quality of the product can be improved with the help of modernisation and technological upgradation. No doubt this reduces the cost and thereby the price. Proper steps should be taken to provide good quality of infrastructure facilities like cold storage, power etc., More and more dry land should be used for growing fruits, flowers and plantations-to increase the export surplus.

Government should, announce a phased programme of withdrawing subsidies. In Globalisation game, since the stipulated process of tariffication is gradual, India has been given ample time for adjustment.

Thus by following these measures, it is possible to overcome the constraints and reap the benefits from Globalisation.

Introduction

The main objective of this paper is to analyze the impact of globalisation on export-import of Agro-Products in India. Globalisation, which aims to integrate nations within the framework of WTO, is nothing but modern version based on comparative cost advantage. The aim is to have export led pattern of growth to replace import substitution trade policies. With the high degree of openness, it minimizes numerous rigidities and distortions in the product commodity market and helps to exploit the comparative advantages. Global competition and imports keeps price at lower level, as a result of which inflation is less likely to derail economic development. Global competition spurs innovations with new ideas from foreign countries. India has number of favourable factors like low cost of labour, large pool of scientific and technical power, broad resource and agricultural base, favourable weather conditions, expanding market, recent liberalisation policy—which encourage globalisation. With all these conducive factors India can face the challenge and can participate successfully in globalisation.

In recent years, world has undergone a significant structural changes. The process and product diversification, growing importance of capital movements, technology transfers—all these not only influenced the world trade but also created potentials of limitless opportunities. Besides developing countries like India felt in different degrees the impact of changes viz., change in exchange rate, changes in terms of trade. Therefore they could never stay outside the arena of global economy. Thus under changing scenario and far reaching changes in economic policies led to considerable changes in our Foreign trade—The process of globalisation initiated in 1991.

Globalisation and Agricultural Trade

Globalisation offers our country a good opportunity to push up our trade in Agro Products. If various provisions of the Agreement on Agriculture (AOA) viz. Reduction of tariffs, Elimination of non trade barriers, Reduction of export subsidies are properly implemented, our agricultural exports will gain competitive advantage. The conditions spelled out for liberal and free trade in WTO charter already existed in India, even before signing the WTO. The government of India has been announcing liberal policies to pave the way for free flow of goods, capital and technology. As a result of this, structure of Indian Agricultural Trade is undergoing significant changes. With the new economic policy of 1991 both internal and external trade policies were liberalised.

Trends in Import-Export Sector

Trends in Import

As a result of liberalisation policy import worth of cereals and edible oil increased from Rs. 1240 Crore in 1992-93 to Rs. 1383 Crore in 1998-99. Import of bulk consumption increased from Rs. 5513 Crore in 1997-98 to Rs. 10619 Crore in 1998-99. The Tables 1 and 2 indicate an increase in the import of principal commodities during 1991-92 to 1997-98.

Table 1. Trends in Imports.

(Rs. in Crore)

Agricultural Products	*91-92*	*92-93*	*93-94*	*94-95*	*95-96*	*96-97*	*97-98*
Cereals and Cereal Preparations	173	966	290	92	80	487	1083
Cereal-Wheat	–	710	126	–	10	404	971
Cereal-Rice	11	73	55	9	–	–	–
Pulses	255	334	567	593	686	890	1195
Cashewnuts raw	267	376	483	691	760	688	744
Sugar	1	–	1	2283	216	3	470
Vegetable Oil fixed (edible)	248	167	167	624	2262	2929	2765

From Table-1 it is clear that except rice there is an increase in the import of other agricultural products, especially in the case of cashewnuts and edible oil, rise in the imports is continuous and rapid.

Table-2 reveals the rapid growth in edible oil and other principal products during the two-year period i.e. 1997-98—1998-99.

Thus, as a result of liberalisation, import of agricultural products, especially in case of edible oil increased rapidly.

Table 2.

(Rs. in Crore)

Principal Commodities	*1997-98*	*1998-99*
Cereal and preparation	1083	1210
Edible Oil	2765	7589
Sugar	470	1111

Source: [X].

QRs

In accordance with the rules of globalisation game, the removal of quantitative restrictions on imports, except for balance of repayment reasons is presently being negotiated. Under the WTO agreement, India has begun the process of phased dismantling of QRs since the later half of 90's.

As per the phase out plan with respect to balance of payment related to QRs on imports (1429 items, announced on March 21st 2000) QRs on 714 items were removed on March 31st 2000 and QRs on the remaining 715 items were removed on March 31st 2001. These included 147 items of agricultural products.

A study by Gulati and Sharma states that "with no QRs and zero import-export duties would lead to an increase in agricultural trade balance by 25% - 40%". In the case of Wheat, Non Basmathi rice, coarse cereals, Sugar and Diary Products, Government should take measures to discourage imports through tariffs. On the other hand, removal of QRs on Basmathi rice, cotton, tobacco, tea would not affect domestic products because they are capable of remaining export competitive. Similarly removal of QRs on onions, potatoes, mangoes, grapes, bananas and floriculture does not hamper production and income from these crops because these crops enjoy strong advantage for exports.

Trends in Export Sector

The trade policy reforms have provided already a good opportunity to our exporters to export agricultural products to overseas markets. To increase the export of agricultural products, Exim policy envisages the setting up of "Agricultural Export Zones" which are supposed to be the Regional Rural Motors of Indian Export Economy. Agricultural and allied sectors export increased from 13.02 thousand Crore in 1993-94 to 23.69 thousand Crore in 1997-98.

Table 3 reveals that the export of rice, coffee, tea is growing during the period 1997-98 and 1998-99. Even though World trade declined 12.2% to 10.9% during the period between 1990-1997, India's export has increased from 19.5% to 21.3%. The Export performance across the commodity group was rather asymmetric. During 1997-98, export of primary products declined by 7% in comparison with 10.3% in 1996-97. Their share in total export dropped by 2% points to 22.2% but the intake of Indian tea, coffee, non-manufactured tobacco and cashewnut increased considerably during 1997-98. Besides, export of spices, fruit, vegetable and other agricultural products increased considerably. India is the largest exporter of spices viz., Pepper, Chili, Turmeric, etc. During 1999-2000, Spices contributed 6.93% in total value of agricultural exports. Table 4 reveals an upward trend in some of the other principal commercial crops during the period between 1993-94 – 1997-98.

Table 3. Export Performance.

(Rs. in Crore)

Agricultural Agro Products	*91-92*	*92-93*	*93-94*	*94-95*	*95-96*	*96-97*	*97-98*	*98-99*	*1999-(p)*
Rice	NA	NA	NA	NA	NA	NA	3371	6281	3105
Tea	1212	977	1059	975	1171	1037	1876	2265	1766
Coffee	332	376	546	1053	1503	1467	1708	1728	1364
Cashew Nuts	676	749	1048	1247	1237	1288	1391 (p)	NA	NA
Sugar & Molasses	157	354	178	62	506	1078	248	NA	NA
Tobacco	377	474	461	255	447	757	1059 (p)	NA	NA

(p) = Provisional, **Source:** [X, XI, XII]*.

The export trend (Table 4) clearly indicate there is more scope for boosting export of commercial crops. Since cultivation of commercial crops is profit-oriented and also export-oriented there is a rapid rate of transformation from subsistence farming to commercial farming.

Besides, immense Agro-climatic diversity is highly favourable to the cultivation of variety of plantation and horticulture and other types of commercial crops. The data reveals that per cent share of agricultural goods in total export has increase from 14.7% in 1992-93 to 17.7% in 1996-97.

Table 4. Export Performance.

(US $ Million)

Agricultural Products	*1993-94*	*1994-95*	*1995-96*	*1996-97*	*1997-98*
Spices	181.4	195.0	237.2	338.6	378.8
Fruits & Vegetables	132.1	139.1	157.7	163.0	152.2
Processes fruit and juices	90.6	115.0	265.4	307.1	173.3
Marine Products	813.6	1126.4	1010.9	1128.9	1160.4

Source: [X].

Table 5 shows the details of increase in export of agricultural commodities during different periods. This indicates that there is scope of boosting export of agricultural products.

Table 5. Total Exports – Agricultural Exports - Comparison.

(Rs. in Crore)

Year	*Country's Exports - Total*	*Agricultural Exports*	*Per cent share*
1992-93	53,688	7,884	14.7
1993-94	69,751	10,811	15.5
1994-95	82,674	11,051	13.4
1995-96	1,06,353	17,496	16.5
1996-97*	1,18,817	21,021	17.7

Source: Southern Economist, July 15, 1998.

With this background it is possible to increase the export of both food and commercial crops if the government takes proper and suitable measure to increase the quantity and improve the quality of agricultural products.

At present India's export in World trade in Agro-Products is only 0.6%. The aim of export strategy of our government is to push this up to 1%.

Constraints

There is a strong argument against globalisation on two grounds:

- Due to low quality, high price and inadequate supply it is impossible to face foreign competition.
- Eliminating subsidies and quota restrictions, incorporation of intellectual property rights affect agricultural sector.

But even before signing the AOA, the conditions of agricultural sector regarding quality and efficiency were not favourable. Besides, since the stipulated process of tariffication is gradual it gives ample scope for adjustment (1). Of course it is true that in 1998 export of basmathi rice, Non Basmathi rice, tea and other cash crops declined. This decline was mainly due to stiff competition.

Another major disturbing feature of agricultural policy is the growing amount of input subsidies.

These subsidies were justified only on the ground those agricultural producers as much as the consumers of agricultural products are poor. It is also justifiable in introduction of new input or transferring income to poor consumers. Close scrutiny at the functioning of subsidy regime in agriculture reveals that none of the arguments apply in this situation.

Another constraint is that, increasing use of subsidised input is not contributing to the productivity at margin, but still the farmers have become addicted to subsidy (1). These subsidies are losing their relevance and becoming fiscal burden. Another difficulty is that if heavy protection is suddenly and expectedly removed it results in losses but in globalisation game the developing countries like India have been given ample time for adjustment.

Besides the farmers are asking for higher procurement prices on the plea of rise in the cost of production due to lack of infrastructure, delay in supplying credit and other inputs. Regarding agricultural trade policies, the major issue is our stance on Food self-sufficiency. The wide spread move towards globalisation, Import Liberalisation and secular decline in the food prices—all these increase the pressure to wean away from the stance on food self-sufficiency. In addition to this Import Liberalisation has paved the way for inflow of food crops along with other non-essential goods, ex. China supplying good quality rice at Rs. 6 per Kg. No doubt this would create negative impact on agricultural sector.

In the case of export sector major constraints are low quality, high price and adequate supply.

Suggestions

It is true of course, the restrictive economic policies of the past, poor-infrastructure, poor quality, lack of experience affected the competitiveness of our exporters. Inspite of these constraints, India has number of favourable factors like low cost of labour, large pool of scientific and technical power, broad resource, and agricultural base, recent liberalisation policy. These factors encourage our traders to face foreign competition.

Constraints in the export sector can be overcome by increasing the export surplus especially in the case of commercial crops, which have comparative advantage and fulfill important criteria namely adequate surplus and growing International demand. State governments could identify agricultural export zones for export of specific products from a geographically contiguous area. State governments should evolve a comprehensive package of services to be provided by state government agencies, state agricultural universities and all the institutions of the union government.

To solve the problem of subsidy the government should announce a phased program of progressively withdrawing subsidies and the same amount thus saved should be used for strengthening rural infrastructure, research and technological development purposes.

Regarding minimum price support policy it could continue till we are able to have comprehensive coverage through crop insurance and more crops are brought under forward marketing. To face the stiff competition government should take measures like doing away with asymmetric information among concerned agents. Many exporters are unaware of the quality requirements of their exports. Therefore research and innovation are crucial and both public and private sectors should play a major role in the national research system. The Government should take measures to improve the quality of the product with the help of modernisation which reduces the cost and thereby the price. In this regards we should follow China which started its economic reforms in 1978 with the launch of full modernisation which mainly involved technological upgradation. Today China is able to complete with developed countries.

Measures should be taken to provide good quality of infrastructure facilities like cold storage, power, irrigation etc., Besides proper steps should be taken to increase the export surplus especially in the case of commercial crops which have comparative advantage. This implies transformation from food crops to cash crops, which are export oriented. More and more dry land should be used for growing vegetables, flowers, and plantation crops for which there is more foreign demand. Thus by following these measures it is possible to overcome the constraints and reap the benefits from globalisation.

REFERENCES

1. V.S. Vyas: *Agriculture: The Second Round of Economic Reforms*. The Indian Economic Journal Volume 48, January-March, 2000-2001, m p. 24.

2. Michael Mussa: *Macro-Economic Policy and Trade Liberalisation*. The World Bank, Research Observer Vol. 2, 1, January 1987, p. 61.

3. S. Jayaram: *Changing Dimensions of Foreign Investment in a Developing Country*. The Indian Economic Association Conference, Vol. p. 61.

4. Y.V. Krishna Rao: *Agrarian Scenario*. Nava Karnataka Publications, Bangalore - 1999.

5. Arjun Sengupta: *Financial Management on Globalisation*. Economic and Political Weekly, Jan. 15th, 2000.

6. V. Vaidyanathan: *Research for Agriculture - some current issues*. Economic and Political Weekly - August 12, 2000.

7. Nilanjan Bank: *An Analysis of India's Exports during the 1990's*. Economic and Political Weekly November 3, 2000.

8. S. Kannaiyan, C. Ramaswamy, K.N. Selvaraj and N. Ajjan: *Issues and Challenges in Agriculture Lessons from Freer Trade.* National Seminar on WTO and Allied Issues—Indian Institute of Foreign Trade, New Delhi, 3rd Feb. 2002.

9. Prof. Sathyaprema: *Globalisation and Trade in Agro-Products*. National Seminar on WTO & Allied Issues, Indian Institute of Foreign Trade, New Delhi 2-3 Feb. 2002.

10. *Report on Currency and Finance*, 1997-98, p. 253 & 254.

11. *RBI Report* p. 234 & 235 – 1999-2000.

12. *RBI Report* p. 934 & 942 – 2001.

27

Development Experience of Southeast Asian Countries and a Lesson for India

*Radhika Lobo**
*Vinayak Deshpande***

An array of academicians and development planners, apart from national, regional and international development agencies have been attracted to the development experience of Southeast Asian countries. The three Southeast Asian economies of Indonesia, Malaysia and Thailand adopted open economic policies, liberalising both the real and financial sector. Following such a strategy they were able to secure a high degree of exposure to trade and capital flows leading to growth beginning in the mid 1980s and continuing in to the mid 1990s, as in new well-documented in economic history. This was an euphoric decade during which the gross domestic product grew at a fast pace, exports surged, inflation was maintained at moderate/low rates, foreign investment inflows boomed and, in general, the economies were very buoyant.

By 1995 the first signs of trouble could be seen on the export horizon. There was a decline in the growth rate of exports. Suspicions were aired that there had been over-investment in the non-tradable property and financial sector. This led to the creation of a 'bubble economy.' Another area of concern was related to the change in the pattern of capital inflows. The FDI inflows were being replaced by short term banking inflows. Such vulnerability ultimately snowballed into a full-fledged financial crisis.

* Flat No. 41, Bldg. No. 45-A, Brindawan Colony, Thane.
** *Faculty Member, Deptt. of Economics, Nagpur University, Nagpur.*

From being 'miracle economies' in the early nineties they turned into 'debacle economies' by the end of the decade. While they rode the boom their economies were lauded and accolades were showered on them by none less than the international financial community. But once a crisis emerged they were criticised and their policy framework considered avoidable like the plague. The international financial institutions that praised their policies and had recommended the same to the rest of the developing world were also attacked and accused of making false claims.

The development experience of the Southeast Asian economies has been eventful and offers a panorama of lessons for developing countries like India.

This paper has broadly been divided into the following sections:

Section I: Reasons for Adopting Open Economic Policies in Southeast Asia.

Section II: Features of Southeast Asian Development Experience (pre crisis period)

Section III: Financial Crisis

Section IV: Implications for India

Reasons for Adopting Open Economics Policies

According to Tariq Banuri[1] openness is a description of the economy indicating, its degree of integration with global economy forces. It can be divided into 2 categories:

1. *Trade Openness*, which refers to the exposure of the goods market to the international economy and is measured by the ratio of exports to GDP.
2. *Financial Openness*, which indicates the exposure of the domestic financial system to world capital markets and is measured by the volume, nature and regulation of international capital flows, including the size of the foreign debt, or the existence of capital controls.

It would be pertinent to enquire into the reasons as to why these countries adopted open economic policies and were on the way to globalisation well before the other developing countries like India. Certain historical events and the international institutions including World Bank, International Monetary Fund influenced the course of economic policies in Southeast Asia and the same are discussed below.

The *US influence* in the post World War II period has had a major bearing on policy making in Southeast Asia. In Southeast Asia economic and security reasons led the US to create global economic and strategic environments, which were favourable to the success of open development policies.[2] The decision-makers in East Asia were taken in by the economic ideas of liberalism propagated by the US. The US provided access to its markets, provided capital, technology and managerial skills to support the ideas that these countries were advocating.[3] This dispelled skepticism that remained in the minds of those adopting open policies but they were reassured about the likely benefits in post execution policy period.

The most dominant and long lasting influence on the economic choices of Southeast Asia has been the creation of global economic institutions like IMF (1944), IBRD (1945) and GATT (1947). It is the US leadership that provided the impetus for creating these institutions. Of these, the first two are financial institutions and have a greater bearing on the economic policies due to the financial power they wield. As a matter of fact, since the early 1980s the development dialogues the world over have chiefly been dominated by the policy and research agenda of the World Bank and International Monetary Fund. These institutions made out autarky to be a less viable proposition and instead promoted/advocated a system of international trade with minimum barriers.

The introduction of the Structural Adjustment Lending (SAL) enshrining the neo-classical paradigm as the official and authoritative doctrine of the international development community has exerted strong influence in thinking and practice of economic policies adopted by these countries.[4] Indonesia and Thailand received assistance from the World Bank/ International Monetary Fund in the early 1980s. Consequently, the development strategy adopted by the Southeast Asian countries is essentially the policy package and institutional reforms prescribed and endorsed by the International Monetary Fund/World Bank.

The First Oil Shock of 1973 also had a great bearing on the policy making in Southeast Asia. The OPEC countries announced an embargo on supply of crude oil to countries supporting Israel. Subsequently, this led to an increase in the prices by about 125 per cent. As such in the early 1970s there was a general rise in prices and the rise in oil prices only propelled it further. The end result was a slow down in the pace of development of the ASEAN3.

In the case of Indonesia (a part of the OPEC group) the effect of increase in oil prices was positive, though the gain was not too significant. (In comparison to Saudi Arabia and Iran that produced 8.4 m and 6.1 m barrels per day respectively, Indonesia produced only 1.4 m.) But Thailand being a net importer (upto 90% of its energy needs), about 1/7th of its merchandise exports were used to pay for energy imports. Moreover, due to the first oil crisis international investors shied away from Malaysia and Thailand. While the flow of FDI had doubled in the early 1970s, it stagnated between 1973-79.

To make up for these losses, loans were availed of. Loans had now become easily available from the international banks that were flush with petro dollars coming from OPEC countries. Such flows (loans) clubbed with remittances from nationals working in the OPEC countries helped overcome the problem to a large extent.

The high indebtedness was sustainable as the money was being used for investment rather than consumption. However, such loans definitely had a bearing on the policy measures implemented in these economies in later years.

After the First Oil Shock the prices stabilised and with the high investment financed from international borrowing, there was a spur in growth. Most countries had not adjusted to the shock but had learned to live with a current account deficit. But the *Second Oil Shock occurred* and oil prices increased from $12 in 1979 a barrel to $32 in 1981. The Second Oil Shock increased the cost of imports, reduced economic growth rates, and slowed the expansion of world trade especially between 1980 and 1982. By 1983 current account deficits in the ASEAN3 were as follows: 7.5% of GDP in Indonesia, 11.5% of GDP in Malaysia and 7.% of GDP in Thailand.

A loss of confidence of international banks and private lenders in the developing countries brought about a *reduction in their foreign lending.* At this time, bilateral and multilateral sources like IMF and the WB became an important source of aid. With the loan commitment made by IMF/WB, investor confidence returned in developing economies in general; and Southeast Asia in particular.

Thus to *sum up,* the First and Second Oil Shocks (which made the Southeast Asian economics vulnerable) and the indebtedness to international banks left the Southeast Asian economies with little choice but to borrowings from international financial institutions like the IMF and the WB. *The situation put pressure on the policy makers to adopt a new line of thinking and make efforts to correct the BOP situation.* In other words, these countries were left with a Hobson's choice-either liberalize, privatize or globalize and hope to achieve high growth or else continue on the path of low growth. The choice was obvious.

The rest of the developing world kept away from open policies initially but most of them succumbed to the lure of these policies by the end of 1980s/ early 1990s.

Features of South Asian Development Experience

This Section examines features observed in the development experience in the ASEAN3 since the mid-1980s to the mid 1990s (now referred to as the pre-crisis period).

Pre-crisis period (1986-95)

There is considerable similarity in form and timing throughout the region. Hence, it is possible to generalize and collectivise. The features listed below (1-6) influenced the development of the ASEAN3 and the econometric evidence presented in *Tables 5 to 10* show to what extent they were beneficial for growth or otherwise.

Macroeconomic Stability

Macroeconomic stability is generally considered a key factor stimulating economic growth. There are various ways in which macroeconomic stability can be attained: maintaining a low rate of inflation, low budgetary deficit, exchange rate stability etc. Here only the low budgetary deficit aspect is considered as the variable for achieving macroeconomic stability. In Indonesia and Thailand, at the behest of the IMF/WB, sharp cuts were made in government's expenditure. On the revenue front, efforts were made to increase receipts. In the case of Malaysia it was able to finance its budgetary deficits without much difficulty. Financial savings levels here were quite high and much of these savings went into the domestic financial system[5] (as opposed to real assets or capital flight as in the case of Latin America). The government's provident fund mobilised domestic savings in large measures to finance the budget in a non-inflationary manner. Secondly, since the growth rate of GDP was quite high in Malaysia, much of the monetary financing could be absorbed without resulting in inflation.

Trade Openness

The Southeast Asian economies made a decisive switch towards outward oriented strategies by actively encouraging exports, reducing import tariffs and removing quantitative restrictions.

In *Indonesia and Thailand,* the structural reforms undertaken to push exports and create openness included: devaluation, rationalisation of trade and tariff laws and less restriction on foreign investment. Local content regulation was done away with. Export taxes were reduced. In general, the economies shifted explicitly towards export promotion.

The decline in the world demand for *Malaysian* exports in 1980-82, necessitated adjustments in its trade policy in 1985-86. The reforms included reducing the restrictions on foreign ownership and liberalising the same by tying them to exports and employment requirements. Tariffs were revised to support a shift from import substitution to export oriented investment. Exchange control measures like repatriation of export proceeds in any foreign currency were also introduced. Tax incentives for export were increased and imports were liberalised.

The outcome of such open policies towards trade was an *increase in exports.* It may be judged by observing Table 1. The average annual growth rate of exports was 23.08 during 1986-95 for Thailand. For Malaysia the same was 16.78%. Only for Indonesia it has been relatively lower at 9.3%.

Table 1: Growth Rate of Exports.

Country	*Average annual growth rate of per capital GDP (1986-95)*	*Average annual growth rate of Exports (1986-95)*
Indonesia	5.3	9.3
Malaysia	5.1	16.78
Thailand	7.7	23.08

Source: IMF Data.

The ***extent of openness*** of the policies and their results can also be observed from the exports of goods and services as a per cent of GDP. For Malaysia exports of goods and services as a per cent of GDP steadily increased from 55.0% in 1985 to 95.4% in 1995. For Thailand too there was a rise from 22.8% to 42.2% between 1985-95. Finally, for Indonesia, it had increased marginally from 21.9% to 26.2% for the same period.

Financial openness through creation of a favourable environment for foreign direct investment (FDI)

Over time these countries dismantled barriers to capital inflows and outflows.[6] Foreign capital was welcomed in the ASEAN3 whatever form it took-short term and long term borrowing, or FDI or portfolio investment. Of these, FDI played a very important role in the economic development of these countries. FDI is said to be the most stable of capital flows since others tend to reverse during times of political and economic difficulty.

Policies to attract FDI in *Indonesia* were initiated by setting up of the investment co-ordinating board BKPM. Others included the simplification of the application procedures for foreign investment, all new investment projects were granted a one-year tax exemption on imported equipment and raw material, visa requirements on businessmen from 29 countries were lifted, foreign companies were granted the same privileges enjoyed by local companies, foreign investors were granted access to the stock exchange and so on. In *Malaysia* foreign ownership restrictions were liberalised by tying them to exports and employment requirements. Here FDI helped build the electronics and semiconductors sector and expand the existing textiles and apparel industry. In *Thailand,* foreign investment was strongly encouraged with major concessions allowing ownership of land, repatriation of capital, waiving of duties on imported capital goods and tax holidays. To generate interest amongst foreign investors for portfolio investment in Thailand, Thai Fund was established in New York and London in 1986. Relaxation was also introduced for forex controls to permit free inflows and outflows of funds by the Bank of Thailand in 1989 resulted in a large influx of foreign investment.

A simplified *gauge of the degree of financial openness* is the *FDI/GDP* percentage. An increase in this would indicate that the policies have been fairly open and that they have been effective in increasing GDP growth as is evident from Table 2. The advantage of taking this indicator is that it removes the effect of market size inflation and currency movements.

Resource Mobilisation

The financial sector acts as an intermediary between savers and investors in mobilising funds both domestic and foreign that determines the level of investment and thus economic growth. In general there is said to exist a strong positive correlation between various measures of financial system sophistication and the of level of economic development as measure by the real GNP.[7]

All the three countries adopted a wide-ranging programme of financial deregulation and liberalisation. The financial sector was open to private sector participation for establishment of new banks and financial companies. Interest rates were deregulated, lifting of ceilings on sectoral credit and abolishing of subsidised liquidity credit. Withholding tax on deposit interest rates was introduced to level the playing field vis-à-vis stock market dividends. Measures to promote investment include establishment of bond markets, equity markets and the creation of a wide range of financial institution. *The financial sector liberalisation helped to increase savings and investment.*

Industrial Policy (IP)

The industrial policy regimes followed a distinct pattern. Initially they promoted import substitute industries, later they were export oriented

Table 2: Net FDI Inflows as a % of GDP. (1970-97)

Country	*1970*	*1971*	*1972*	*1973*	*1974*	*1975*	*1976*	*1977*	*1978*	*1979*	*1980*	*1981*	*1982*	*1983*
Indonesia	0.80	1.40	1.80	0.10	–0.20	1.50	0.70	0.50	0.40	0.30	0.20	0.10	0.20	0.40
Malaysia	2.20	2.20	2.10	2.10	6.20	3.80	3.60	3.20	3.20	2.80	3.80	5.30	5.60	4.40
Thailand	0.60	0.50	0.80	0.70	1.30	0.20	0.40	0.50	0.30	0.20	0.60	0.80	0.50	0.80

Table 2: (Contd...)

Country	*1984*	*1985*	*1986*	*1987*	*1988*	*1989*	*1990*	*1991*	*1992*	*1993*	*1994*	*1995*	*1996*	*1997*
Indonesia	0.30	0.40	0.30	0.40	0.70	0.80	1.00	1.20	1.30	1.30	1.20	2.30	2.70	2.10
Malaysia	2.30	2.20	1.80	1.50	2.20	4.70	5.80	8.30	9.00	7.80	5.80	4.80	5.20	5.30
Thailand	0.90	0.40	0.60	0.60	1.70	2.50	2.90	2.10	1.90	1.00	0.60	1.20	1.30	

Source: *OECD Proceedings, "FDI & Recovery in Asia," OECD, France, 1999.*

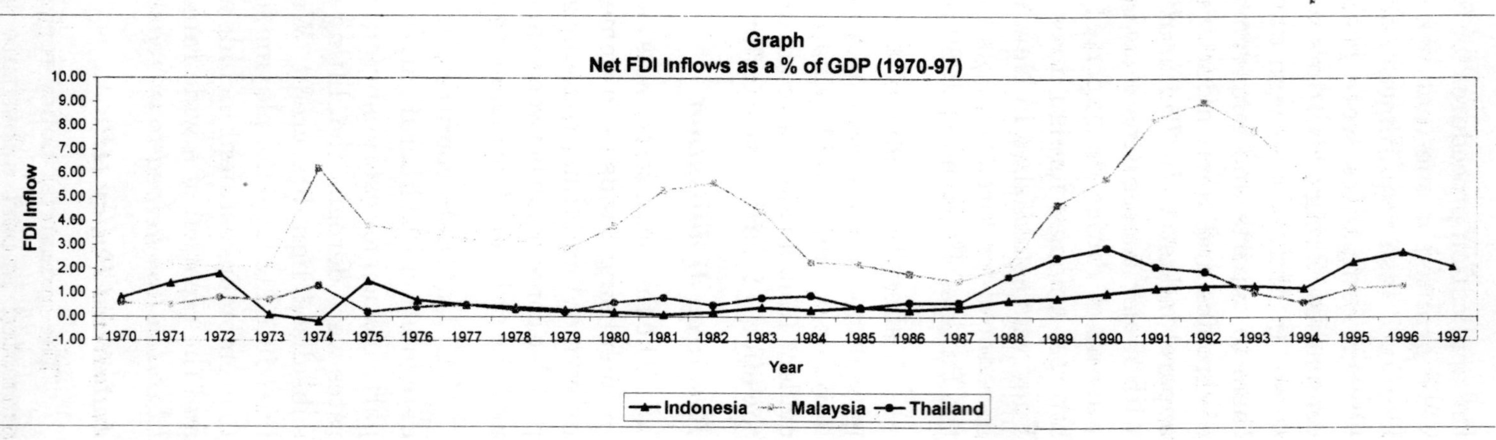

policies. Booms favoured greater state intervention while foreign exchange constraints led to more liberal policy stance.[8] The Southeast Asian industrial policy emphasised on development of export industries. The selection of industries was guided by the principle of comparative advantage determined by existing and evolving factor endowments. Hence, initially production in resource-based industries dominated. This gradually shifted to labour intensive and finally to skill based industries. The policy was open to utilisation of foreign human resources. It heavily relied on industrial linkage with the East Asian subregion as a whole and emphasised a great deal on FDI and capital markets.

Efficacy of the IP can be assessed through the favourable effect that the industrial policy had on the *manufacturing value added.* (MA). Table 3 indicates that over the time period (1986-95), MVA as a percentage of GDP in Indonesia has increased from 6.6 to 10.6. The change has been more dramatic in Malaysia where the increase in from 4.6% in 1986 to 13.1% in 1985. Similarly, in Thailand it increased from 7.9% in 1986 to 11.9% in 1995.

Table 3: Annual Increase in Value Added in Industry as a % of GDP (1986-95).

Country	*1986*	*1987*	*1988*	*1989*	*1990*	*1991*	*1992*	*1993*	*1994*	*1995*
Indonesia	6.6	5.2	5.2	8.2	11.5	11.7	8.2	9.8	11.2	10.6
Malaysia	4.6	6.7	12.7	11.0	13.2	11.2	8.9	10.1	12.4	13.1
Thailand	7.9	12.8	17.4	16.2	16.1	12.1	9.9	10.6	9.9	11.9

Source: Industrial Trade Statistics Year Book 1996, UN, New York, 1997.

An observation to be made here is that in all three economies the MVA as a per cent of GDP increased between 1986-90/91, after which it dropped marginally until 1992 and after that it started rising again. Such a wavelike pattern is seen because initially all the economies had resource based on labour intensive manufacturing. Gradually they started shifting to skill based manufacturing. During this transition period there was a drop in the value added, but it rose again once the structural adjustments were made. The value addition to industry has been one of the most important factors contributing to the growth in GDP. The next section providing quantitative evidence will prove the same.

Labour Inputs

According to growth accounting concepts of development economics, a country's economic growth can be divided into three contributory parts: growth of *labour input, growth of capital input and growth of total factor productivity*

(TFP)[9]. The fact that capital inputs like increased domestic and foreign investment have resulted in a high GDP growth is already established above. This leads to the next question that whether growth in the Southeast Asian economies has been propelled by technological innovation/TFP or by increased labour inputs.

TFP is the residual element after eliminating the contribution of labour and capital to growth. Notable economist Paul Krugman has equated the mechanism of East Asian growth (this included Southeast Asia), to that of the former Soviet Union that relied on massive capital inputs. Krugman is of the opinion that it is not TFP but increased labour and capital inputs that has propelled growth in Southeast Asia.

The question whether *labour inputs* have or not helped growth can easily confirmed seeing the growth of labour employed in manufacture. There has been a definite increase in the number of labour employed in manufacture as is evident from Table 4.

Table 4: Annual Labour Force Employed in Manufacturing Sector in Thousands.

Country	*1986*	*1987*	*1988*	*1989*	*1990*	*1991*	*1992*	*1993*	*1994*	*1995*	*1996*
Indonesia	5606	5818	5997	7335	7693	7946	8255	8784	10841	10127	10773
Malaysia	861	929	961	1171	1333	1470	1639	1742	1892	2052	2178
Thailand	2069	2438	2461	2770	3133	3465	3600	3961	3851	4377	4334

Source: *International Trade Statistics Year Book 1996, UN, New York, 1997.*

Econometric Model-GDPs responsiveness to its Determinants

This sub-section deals with responsiveness of the Gross Domestic Product to its various determinants.* The response of the GDP (the dependent variable) to the factors (independent variables) affecting it studies with the help of the technique of regression. The regression analysis is carried out for all countries selected for this study. An attempt has been made to establish the interrelationship between the growth rate of GDP and different macroeconomic variables for the decade 1986-95 for Indonesia, Malaysia and Thailand.

Dependent Variable: GDP growth rate (Y)

Independent Variables:	**Proxy Variables**
1. Macroeconomic Stability (Ms)	Budget deficit/surplus

* Based on a similar model constructed by Bende-Nabende, Anthony for the ASEAN5 in Bende-Nabende, Anthony (1999), 'FDI, Regionalism, Government Policy and Endogenous Growth', England, Ashgate Publishing House.

2. Outward Orientation in Trade (Ot) — Exports of Goods and Services
3. Outward Orientation in Investment (FDI) — Foreign Direct Investment
4. Savings (S) — Gross Domestic Saving
5. Industrial Policy (Ip) — Manufacturing Value added
6. Labour inputs (L) — Employment in manufacturing

Thus,

Y = f {Ms, Ot, FDI, S, Ip, L}

In equation form

$$\mathbf{Y} = \propto_0 + \propto_1 \mathbf{Ms} + \propto_2 \mathbf{Ot} + \propto_3 \mathbf{FDI} + \propto_4 \mathbf{S} + \propto_5 \mathbf{Ip} + \propto_6 \mathrm{L}$$

The following results were obtained from the time series data collected for the selected countries for the time period 1986-97.

Correlation Coefficients

The correlation matrix for all the three countries is presented in Table 5, 6 and 7 for Indonesia, Malaysia and Thailand respectively. As expected, the value of correlation between the variables was quite high. Notwithstanding this general observation, a few exceptions are observed. For

Table 5: Correlation Matrix - Indonesia.

		GDP	*BD*	*EX*	*FDI*	*GDS*	*MVA*	*EMP*
GDP	Pearson Correlation	1.000	0.583	0.998**	0.27	0.999*	1.000*	0.978**
	Sig. (2-tailed)	-	0.077	0.000	0.43	0.000	0.000	0.000
	N	10	10	10	1	10	10	10
BD	Pearson Correlation	0.583	1.000	0.581	0.59	0.609	0.591	0.653*
	Sig. (2-tailed)	0.077	-	0.078	0.07	0.061	0.072	0.041
	N	10	10	10	1	10	10	10
EX	Pearson Correlation	0.998*	0.581	1.000	0.26	0.997**	0.997*	0.971**
	Sig. (2-tailed)	0.000	0.078	-	0.46	0.000	0.000	0.000
	N	10	10	10	1	10	10	10
FDI	Pearson Correlation	0.279	0.590	0.264	1.00	0.305	0.296	0.372
	Sig. (2-tailed)	0.435	0.073	0.461	-	0.392	0.407	0.290
	N	10	10	10	1	10	10	10
GDS	Pearson Correlation	0.999**	0.609	0.997**	0.30	1.000	0.999*	0.979**
	Sig. (2-tailed)	0.000	0.061	0.000	0.39	-	0.000	0.000
	N	10	10	10	1	10	10	10
MVA	Pearson Correlation	1.000**	0.591	0.997**	0.29	0.999**	1.000	0.982**
	Sig. (2-tailed)	0.000	0.072	0.000	0.40	0.000	-	0.000
	N	10	10	10	1	10	10	10
EMP	Pearson Correlation	0.978**	0.653	0.971**	0.37	0.979**	0.982*	1.000
	Sig. (2-tailed)	0.000	0.041	0.000	0.29	0.000	0.000	-
	N	10	10	10	1	10	10	10

** Correlation is significant at the 0.01 level (2-tailed).

* Correlation is significant at the 0.05 level (2-tailed).

Table 6: Correlation Matrix - Malaysia

		GDP	BD	EX	FDI	GDS	MVA	EMP
GDP	Pearson Correlation	1.000	0.930**	0.996**	0.908**	0.995**	0.999**	0.989**
	Sig. (2-tailed)	-	0.000	0.000	0.000	0.000	0.000	0.000
	N	10	10	10	10	10	10	10
BD	Pearson Correlation	0.930**	1.000	0.924**	0.892**	0.931**	0.925**	0.922**
	Sig. (2-tailed)	0.000	-	0.000	0.003	0.000	0.000	0.000
	N	10	10	10	10	10	10	10
EX	Pearson Correlation	0.996**	0.924**	1.000	0.893**	0.994**	0.998**	0.974**
	Sig. (2-tailed)	0.000	0.000	-	0.000	0.000	0.000	0.000
	N	10	10	10	10	10	10	10
FDI	Pearson Correlation	0.908**	0.829	0.893**	1.000	0.918**	0.906**	0.901**
	Sig. (2-tailed)	0.000	0.003	0.000	-	0.000	0.000	0.000
	N	10	10	10	10	10	10	10
GDS	Pearson Correlation	0.995**	0.931**	0.994**	0.918**	1.000	0.996*	0.971**
	Sig. (2-tailed)	0.000	0.000	0.000	0.000	-	0.000	0.000
	N	10	10	10	10	10	10	10
MVA	Pearson Correlation	0.999**	0.925**	0.998**	0.906**	0.996**	1.000	0.983**
	Sig. (2-tailed)	0.000	0.000	0.000	0.000	0.000	-	0.000
	N	10	10	10	10	10	10	10
EMP	Pearson Correlation	0.989**	0.922**	0.974**	0.901**	0.971**	0.983**	1.000
	Sig. (2-tailed)	0.000	0.000	0.000	0.000	0.000	0.000	-
	N	10	10	10	10	10	10	10

** *Corelation is significant at the 0.01 level. (2-tailed)*

instance, in the case on Indonesia the correlation between the budget deficit and other macro variables is the range of 0.581 to 0.653.

Regression Coefficient

The enter method was used to obtain regression coefficients. The regression coefficients in the case of *Indonesia* are shown in Table 8. The same indicates that the *regression coefficients* for Manufacturing Value Added (MVA) in industry works out to 0.841 and is higher than the corresponding regression co-efficient for other variables. In other words, MVA is the most significant variable affecting GDP. The *elasticity* of GDP with respect to MVA works out to 0.1639. Thus, a 1% increase in average MVA raised the GDP by 0.1639. The higher value of R^2 of the multiple regression indicates that the six independent variables considered together explain 99% of the total variation in the GDP.

Table 7: Correlation Matrix - Thailand.

		GDP	*BD*	*EX*	*FDI*	*GDS*	*MVA*	*EMP*
GDP	Pearson Correlation	1.000	0.847**	0.998**	0.924**	0.992**	.999**	0.958**
	Sig. (2-tailed)	-	0.002	0.000	0.000	0.000	0.000	0.000
	N	10	10	10	10	10	10	10
BD	Pearson Correlation	0.847**	1.000	0.814**	0.857**	0.788**	0.863**	0.784**
	Sig. (2-tailed)	0.002	-	0.004	0.002	0.007	0.001	0.007
	N	10	10	10	10	10	10	10
EX	Pearson Correlation	0.998*	0.814**	1.000	0.997**	0.997**	0.995*	0.957**
	Sig. (2-tailed)	0.000	0.004	-	0.000	0.000	0.000	0.000
	N	10	10	10	10	10	10	10
FDI	Pearson Correlation	0.924**	0.857**	0.917**	1.000	0.899**	0.928**	0.789**
	Sig. (2-tailed)	0.000	0.002	0.000	-	0.000	0.000	0.000
	N	10	10	10	10	10	10	10
GDS	Pearson Correlation	0.992**	0.788**	0.997**	0.899**	1.000	0.988**	0.964**
	Sig. (2-tailed)	0.000	0.007	0.000	0.000	-	-	0.000
	N	10	10	10	10	10	10	10
MVA	Pearson Correlation	0.999**	0.863**	0.995**	0.928**	0.988**	1.000**	0.954**
	Sig. (2-tailed)	0.000	0.001	0.000	0.000	0.000	0.000	0.000
	N	10	10	10	10	10	10	10
EMP	Pearson Correlation	0.958**	00.784**	0.957**	0.789**	0.964**	0.954**	1.000
	Sig. (2-tailed)	0.000	0.007	0.000	0.007	0.000	0.000	-
	N	10	10	10	10	10	10	10

** Corelation is significant at the 0.01 level. (2-tailed)

For *Malaysia,* too similar result are obtained and the same is presented in Table 9. The most significant variable affecting GDP is MVA. The *beta coefficient* is 1.003. Here the *elasticity* of GDP with respect of MVA is 0.247. Thus, a 1% rise in average MVA raised the GDP by 0.247.

The results are consistent even in the case of *Thailand* (Table 10). Her too MVA is the most significant factor affecting GDP. The *regression coefficient* for the same is 0.912. The *elasticity* of GDP with respect to MVA is 0.2491. In other words, a 1% rise in average value addition to industry increases the GDP by 0.2491. R^2 shows that all the six variables taken together account for 99% of the total variation in GDP.

The values of elasticity indicate that change in GDP cannot occur independently with one single variable. The effect on GDP becomes significant when all the variables act together.

Table 8: Regression Results for Indonesia.

Independent Variables Entered	*Method*
Budget Deficit/Surplus	Enter
Exports of Goods and Services	
Foreign Direct Investment	
Gross Domestic Savings	
Manufacturing Value Added	
Employment in Manufacturing	
Dependent Variable: GDP	

Model Summary

R	*R Square*	*Adjusted R Square*	*Std Error of the Estimate*
1*	1	0.999	2963.3476

* Independent Variables

ANOVA

	Sum of Squares	*df*	*Mean Square*	*F*	*Sig*
Regression	1.21E + 11	6	2.01E + 1	2287.264	0
Residual	26344287.1	3	8781429.04		
Total	**1.21E+11**	**9**			

Coefficients

		Beta Coefficient	*t*	*Significance*
Constant	2029.318		0.09	0.934
Budget Deficit/Surplus		–0.057	–1.101	0.351
Exports of Goods and Services		0.068	0.222	0.839
Foreign DirectInvestment		0.07	1.229	0.307
Gross Domestic Savings		–0.025	–0.151	0.89
Manufacturing Value Added		0.841	3.145	0.051
Employment in Manufacturing		0.104	1.335	0.274

Therefore, the result of the regression analysis confirm that the independent variables Ms, Ot, FDI, S, Ip, and L have a positive effect on GDP. In other words, GDP responds positively to a low budget deficit, higher growth of exports, larger inflow of FDI, higher savings, increased value addition to industry and increased labour inputs.

Table 9: Regression Results for Malaysia

Independent Variables Entered	*Method*
Budget Deficit/Surplus	Enter
Exports of Goods and Services	
Foreign Direct Investment	
Gross Domestic Savings	
Manufacturing Value Added	
Employment in Manufacturing	
Dependent Variable: GDP	

Model Summary

R	*R Square*	*Adjusted R Square*	*Std Error of the Estimate*
			the Estimate
1*	1	1	371.7852

* Independent Variables

ANOVA

	Sum of Squares	*df*	*Mean Square*	*F*	*Sig*
Regression	2.15E + 10	6	3.58E + 09	25921.769	0
Residual	414672.639	3	138224.213		
Total	**2.15E+10**	**9**			

Coefficients

		Beta Coefficient	*t*	*Significance*
Constant	26198.481		7.38	0.005
Budget Deficit/Surplus		0.021	2.429	0.093
Exports of Goods and Services		–0.172	–2.515	0.087
Foreign Direct Investment		–0.005	–0.617	0.581
Gross Domestic Savings		0.007	0.123	0.91
Manufacturing Value Added		1.003	7.999	0.004
Employment in Manufacturing		0.148	5.017	0.015

Financial Crises

The preceding section has emphasised the remarkable success of the Southeast Asian economies of Indonesia, Malaysia and Thailand in the decade from the mid 1980s to the mid 1990s. The image of success, measured by indicators such as GNP, manufacturing capacity and export performance had

Table 10: Regression Results for Thailand.

Independent Variables Entered	*Method*
Budget Deficit/Surplus	Enter
Exports of Goods and Services	
Foreign Direct Investment	
Gross Domestic Savings	
Manufacturing Value Added	
Employment in Manufacturing	
Dependent Variable: GDP	

Model Summary

R	*R Square*	*Adjusted R Square*	*Std Error of the Estimate*
			the Estimate
1*	1	0.999	35858.7993

* Independent Variable

ANOVA

	Sum of Squares	*df*	*Mean Square*	*F*	*Sig*
Regression	9.35E + 12	6	1.56E + 15	1211.998	0
Residual	3.86E + 09	3	1.29E+ 09		
Total	**9.36E+12**	**9**			

Coefficients

		Beta Coefficient	*t*	*Significance*
Constant	338025.25		1.682	0.191
Budget Deficit/Surplus		0.001	0.047	0.966
Exports of Goods and Services		0.217	1.125	0.342
Foreign Direct Investment		–0.007	–0.456	0.68
Gross Domestic Savings		–0.096	–0.188	0.863
Manufacturing Value Added		0.912	1.675	0.192
Employment in Manufacturing		–0.031	–0.305	0.781

gained wide publicity worldwide and the decade 1986-95 was termed as the boom period. However, since 1995, there was a slow down in the economy. First signs of the end of the miracle could be seen by 1896 when growth rate of GDP and exports started to decline. In retrospect, these two indicators *viz.* decline in the GDP growth rate and the export growth rate could be termed as the early signs of vulnerability of these economies, ending in a financial crash.

A study conducted by the IMF staff published in *World Economic Outlook May 1998, IMF, Washington, December, 1998* has assessed the vulnerability of six Asian economies (Indonesia, Korea, Malaysia, Philippines, Singapore and Thailand) to crisis, in the pre crisis period. An *index of macroeconomic vulnerability* was constructed. The index was constructed using, *the appreciation of the real exchange rate, the growth of domestic credit and the growth of unbacked domestic banking sector liabilities* (the ratio os M2 to international reserves). The index showed that beginning in early 1997, *vulnerability increased* in almost all of the East Asian economies especially Thailand and Malaysia and to a lesser extent in Indonesia. There was a sustained build-up in macroeconomic imbalances (current account deficit) lead to a pressure on the forex market leading to a currency crisis.

Grancarlo Corsettim, Poaolo Pesenti and Nuriel Roubini[10] conducted another study. Here a *crisis index* that was a weighted average of the percentage rate of exchange rate depreciation relative to the US dollar and the percentage rate of change in foreign reserves between the end of December 1996 and *end of December 1997* was constructed. A speculative attack against a currency is signaled by a sharp depreciation of the exchange rate or a contraction in forex reserves to help prevent the same. Quite obviously the results showed the crisis index to be *–38.3 for Indonesia, -38.8 for Malaysia* and *–47.8 for Thailand.* This study has hypothesised that both financial and real sector imbalances have caused the crisis and these countries displayed vulnerability in the pre-crisis period. Due to weakness in the banking system the Non-performing loans were high and there was a lending boom directed towards non-tradable sector. Also a sizable current account deficit and a significant real appreciation of the currency was a worrisome signal. In general, the results suggested that structural imbalances (current account deficit, currency appreciation, non-performing loans and a lending boom) created a vulnerable situation and made a speculative attack possible. The results of this study are presented in Table 11.

The very factors, which brought about a boom, now became a bane for the ASEAN3. The rising inflows (shift from FDI to Short-Term), increasing investment (unfortunately in unproductive areas) and the policy choices (as directed by the IMF-WB) helped to maintain high rate of growth initially. However, these factors among others themselves were responsible for causing a crisis.

Table 11: Crisis and Economic Indicators, December 1996-December 1997.

Country	*Crisis Index (IND)*	*Real Appreciation (RER)*	*Current Account (CA)*	*Lending Boom (LB)*	*Non-Performing Loans*	*Reserves adequacy (M2/RES)*	*Reserves adequacy (M1/RES)*	*Reserves adequacy (STD/RES)*
Argentina	4.9	38.6	–1.9	16.5	9.4	351.0	108.2	147.8
Brazil	–0.5	75.8	–2.0	–26.3	5.8	345.9	66.8	78.3
Chile	–1.4	37.5	–1.7	24.1	1.0	188.2	41.9	53.3
China	7.6	4.9	0.8	6.9	14.0	828.9	334.0	26.7
Colombia	–9.1	26.6	–5	35.0	4.6	209.4	104.3	73.9
Crech Rep.	–19.5	50.7	–4.4	22.7	12.0	356.9	139.5	42.9
Hong Kong	5.7	31.8	–1.6	25.5	3.4	411.9	34.2	20.0
Hungry	–1.6	–38.8	–6.5	–56.5	3.2	167.1	83.3	52.3
India	5.7	–29.1	–1.2	–2.3	17.3	860.0	296.5	37.2
Indonesia	–38.3	17.5	–2.9	9.6	12.9	614.8	114.3	188.9
Jordan	9.8	6.1	–4.5	1.4	6.0	437.8	141.4	33.9
Korea	–38.6	11.1	–2.5	11.2	8.4	665.4	147.6	217.0
Malaysia	–38.8	19.9	–6.4	31.1	9.9	364.8	115.6	45.3
Mexico	10.9	8.9	–2.7	–10.9	12.5	444.8	129.3	142.9
Pakistan	11.4	–2.0	–5.3	–3.7	17.5	3369.9	1822.8	399.0
Peru	0.7	–20.4	–6.2	177.2	5.1	123.6	32.4	61.6
Philippines	–29.8	38.9	–4.6	150.8	14.0	465.6	91.8	849.3
Poland	3.5	30.0	0.9	38.5	6.0	262.3	95.9	14.2
Singapore	–15.7	4.7	16.5	16.7	4.0	103.5	25.0	20.0
Sri Lanka	–1	17.7	–5.7	28.4	5.0	236.4	72.9	26.8
Taiwan	11.4	–7.0	2.9	43.4	3.9	575.1	141.0	22.8
Thailand	–47.8	20.0	–7.2	58.0	13.3	380.5	43.3	121.5
Turkey	4.3	–16.1	–0.1	43.2	0.8	302.6	48.9	76.0
Venezuela	4.9	2.2	6.8	–51.5	3.8	102.4	58.5	28.2

Causes of the Crisis

Financial Sector Liberalisation

The ASEAN 3 had embarked upon ambitious policies of financial deregulation in the late 1980s and the process was intensified during the 1990s. The extensive liberalisation of the financial sector was consistent with the policy goal of providing a large supply of low cost funds to national financial institutions and the domestic corporate sector to encourage exports and assist growth. Such policies of financial liberalisation brought in many benefits but they also increased risk.

The policies of financial liberalisation were coupled with the policy of high interest rates and this led to problems. High interest rates were maintained to limit aggregate dividend and keep inflation low (Tight monetary policy suggested by IMF-WB). But these high interest rates made it cheaper to borrow foreign loans at a cheaper cost and lend them in the form of foreign currency to local borrowers. The spread in local deposit rates and the Libor rate was high in Thailand and Indonesia. (Information relating to this is presented in Table 12) This spread provided an opportunity for local agents to borrow abroad and lend locally. This way they made a clean profit by relending the dollars to local customers at lower rates than those of domestic currency loans, because the interest rates on the dollar loans were 4-6% lower than the domestic currency loans[11]. The central banks tried to slow down the overheated economy by further raising interest rates. But this caused foreign borrowing to increase more rapidly. These were mainly short-term loans and most were not hedged against currency fluctuations. Quite obviously a situation like this makes the economy vulnerable to a speculative attack. *Hence it was the very same measures of financial liberalisation, which, helped the economy during the boom period, caused a doom too.*

Table 12: Incentive for Foreign Borrowing. (1992-96)

Country	*Spread of International Rate and Labour*	*Aug Annual Appreciation*	*Exchange Rate Volalibity**
Indonesia	11.5	–3.8	0.7
Malaysia	1.6	1.2	2.6
Thailand	4	–0.3	1.2

* S.D. on Basis of % Deviation of Regression on a Time Trend.
Source: World Bank, Global Economic Prospects 1998-99, Page: 68.

The crisis countries had long pursued conservative macro economic policies as suggested by the IMF-WB. When the capital inflows increased on account of financial liberalisation (another suggestion of IMF-WB), the countries faced new challenges of tougher decisions often outside the purview of macro economic policy. The crisis countries unfortunately tried to use monetary policy to sterilize inflows. But attempt to tighten credit only encouraged the same, especially under relatively fixed exchange rates. The exchange rate policy was designed in the first place to encourage exports (IMF-WB directed) so that cross border traders and, investors and borrowers can carry on their activities smoothly. These policy choices helped growth for a while, but gradually as inflows increased, it encouraged unhedged positions.

Changing Pattern of Inflows

The composition of the inflows started to vary over a period of time. Initially, (mid 1980s) the major part of the inflows constituted FDI. This was quite in tune with the policy reforms undertaken by the ASEAN3. They had made the investment climate conducive to FDI inflows especially to promote the export sector.

FDI flows were being replaced by portfolio investment and short-term banking flows in the early 1990s. Having liberalised FDI flows in the 1980s, in the early 1990s, the ASEAN3 started concentrating on liberalisation of financial capital flows. In fact the reduction in FDI flows prompted these economies to diversify their sources of foreign capital inflows. Hence, they adopted liberal equity market policies, allowing free entry and exit without much restrictions on repatriation of income and capital. They also shifted to a more flexible policy with respect to foreign banks entry into the domestic market. Such a commitment to capital inflows liberalisation and financial market opening, particularly in banking enabled large entry of portfolio investment and short-term capital.

Table 13 gives a clear picture of capital inflows in terms of percentage of GDP and their changing pattern. It can be seen that the proportion of portfolio investment began to increase in relative terms vis-à-vis FDI over the years. The ratio of portfolio to FDI inflows for Thailand was very low upto 1992 but it increased suddenly in 1993 to 3.01 from 0.43 of the previous year. In subsequent years it remained more than 1.5 through 1994-96. The proportion of inflows in the category others that included short terms inflows to the banking sector remained very high in the total inflows. It varied between 0.53 to 0.74 during 1989-96. Thus about two thirds of the private capital flowed into banking sector and other related activities.

Portfolio to FDI inflow ratio became very high after 1993 in Indonesia. The proportion of others in the total was also high. Only Malaysia stands out as a distinct case as there was a net outflow of portfolio investment from Malaysia, barring a few years. Therefore, disproportionate portfolio investment has not really contributed to the crisis in Malaysia as in Indonesia and Thailand.

During the boom period since the currencies were relatively stable there was no inherent danger for the investors. But since 1995-96 there was a gradual decline in the level of forex reserves relative to stock of portfolio and short term funds. This situation made portfolio and short term funds volatile.

Table 13: Capital Inflows in the SE Asian Countries. (1989-96)

Country	*1989*	*1990*	*1991*	*1992*	*1993*	*1994*	*1995*	*1996*
Thailand								
FDI	2.46	2.82	2.02	1.91	1.46	0.95	1.25	1.28
Portfolio*	2.06	–0.04	–0.08	9.83	4.4	1.73	2.46	1.97
Others**	5.12	8.07	9.67	5.85	5.44	6.86	11.7	6.52
Total	9.64	10.85	11.61	8.59	11.3	9.54	15.41	9.77
Portfolio/FDI	0.83	–0.014	–0.039	0.43	3.01	1.82	1.97	1.54
Others/Total	0.53	0.74	0.83	0.68	0.48	0.72	0.76	0.67
Indonesia								
FDI	0.96	1.51	1.86	1.94	1.76	1.77	3.28	3.25
Portfolio*	–0.24	–0.13	–0.02	–0.1	1.59	3.26	3.09	4.5
Others**	3.24	4.83	5.3	4.84	1.91	–1.29	1.92	1.94
Total	3.96	6.21	7.14	6.68	5.26	3.74	8.29	9.69
Portfolio/FDI	–0.25	–0.08	0.01	–0.05	0.9	1.84	0.94	1.24
Others/Total	0.82	0.78	0.74	0.72	0.36	–0.34	0.23	0.25
Malaysia								
FDI	4.4	5.44	8.23	9.16	8.19	5.84	4.8	3.8
Portfolio*	–0.28	–0.6	0.35	–1.98	–1.16	–2.22	–0.51	–0.63
Others**	–0.68	–0.21	1.02	5.63	12.17	–2.59	3.78	4.87
Total	3.44	4.63	9.6	12.31	19.2	1.03	8.07	8.07
Portfolio/FDI	–0.06	–0.11	0.04	–0.21	–0.14	–0.38	–0.1	–
Others/Total	–0.19	–0.04	0.1	0.45	0.63	–2.51	0.47	–

A mention may also be made of the role of credit flows in meeting the liquidity needs of the private sector, which is apparent from the rising leverage ratio of the corporate sector. The pace of financial innovation created a situation where finance became dissociated from real spheres of activities and got diverted to high profit high risk speculative activity. Table 14 shows that the mean value of foreign debt to equity ratio of corporate ranged between 1.88 and 2.36 in the ASEAN3 economies in 1996. Moreover, short-term debt to total debt was in the range of 0.54 to 0.64 (mean value) for 1996. Such highly leveraged corporate structure left the economies in a very weak position and added to the financial crisis.

Financial Sector Weakness and Imbalances

There is no doubt that the weaknesses in the financial sector were an important factor contributing to vulnerability in the Southeast Asian economies. Insufficient capital adequacy ratios, inadequate legal lending limits on single borrowers or groups of related borrowers, inadequate asset classification system and poor provisioning for possible losses, poor disclosure and transparency of bank operation and the lack of provision for an exit policy for troubled institutions all contributed to financial fragility.

Table 14: Selected Indicators of Corporate Finance. (1996)

Country	*Debt to Equity Ratio*		*Ratio of Short Term Debt to Total Debt*	
	Mean	*Median*	*Mean*	*Median*
Indonesia	1.88	1.83	0.54	0.57
Malaysia	1.18	0.90	0.64	0.70
Thailand	2.36	1.85	0.63	0.67

Source: *Bank for International Settlement. (1997)*

Apart from poor supervision and regulatory controls, there was also the problem of connected lending[12]. This implies lending to bank directors, managers and their related businesses. Again, due to crony capitalism, there was the danger of concentration of credit risk and lack of prudent credit decisions. Finally, there was excessive ownership of and/or government involvement in banks. Banks often became the quasi-fiscal agents of governments, providing an oblique mechanism for channeling government assistance (off budget) to ailing industries[13].

The imbalances created were as follows:

- The foreign liabilities of the banks in relation to their assets increased tremendously. The foreign liabilities of commercial banks in the crisis hit countries (including Philippines and Korea) increased by about 12% per year while foreign assets increased by 7% per year. By contrast in the unaffected Asian countries, banking sectors foreign liability and assets increased at the same rate and the net foreign debt position remained virtually unchanged.[14]
- Much of the collateral that the banking sector accepted for loans were real estate and equities, assets whose prices contained a large bubble element.
- The maturity structure was mismatched as banks borrowed for short-term a period and lent for long-term period.
- A currency mismatch also emerged as banks borrowed in foreign currency and lent in domestic.

To sum up, premature financial deregulation and capital account convertibility greatly facilitated external borrowing in the form of bank loans with increasingly short maturity structure. This situation coupled with inadequate financial supervision and poor risk assessment, allowed domestic banks to lend indiscriminately. The end result was that the financial institutions found themselves with various imbalances making the economy vulnerable.

External Sector Developments

(Current account deficit, rising real exchange rates and export slow down)

The ASEAN3 did not display vulnerability in the fiscal deficit, but since 1990s a growing current account deficit was evident, especially in Malaysia and Thailand. The current account deficit to GDP averaged 6.4% in both Malaysia and Thailand during 1991-95 and 2.3% in Indonesia. In 1996 it was about 8% in Thailand, 5% in Malaysia and 3.3% in Indonesia. (Table 5) Such deficits were not viewed with skepticism in the early 1990s as the foreign borrowings were mainly used for an increase in investment rather than consumption. In other words the economies were building the capacity to service those debts.[15] Also since the exports were growing there would be adequate foreign exchange earnings for the repayment of the debts. But, in the couple of years prior to the crisis, the situation started to alter. The large current account deficit could not be sustained as the *quality of investment* had started to deteriorate. Also, the *real effective exchange rate (REER) was rising*. Relatively speaking Malaysia was the only one of the ASEAN3 economies that had a genuine basket system. The other two had a defacto peg to the US$. The weight of the US$ in the basket peg in the case of Thailand was 80%. Therefore, when the US$ appreciated against the Yen in the mid nineties, the currencies of the ASEAN3 recorded an appreciation in REERs. By itself such appreciation in the REER would not create much problems. However, when real appreciation occurs along with large current account imbalances, it becomes a source of increased vulnerability.

The third reasons for the widening of the current account deficit was the *export deceleration*. Table 15 shows that growth of total exports declined from 12.1%, 20.3% and 19.6% during 1990-95 to 9.7, 5.8 and –1.3% for Indonesia, Malaysia and Thailand respectively. The export deceleration in turn took place due to the following reasons:

(i) defacto peg with the US$, (ii) the depreciation of the Japanese yen (iii) the decline in growth rate of the ASEAN4 economies (iv) the worldwide computer related recession in 1996, (v) the emergence of China as a competition for goods exported from the ASEAN3 economies and (vi) rapid growth in wages during the early 1990s.

Table 15: Data on Macroeconomic Fundamentals, East Asian Countries, 1994-98.

	Indonesia					*Malaysia*					*Thailand*				
	1994	*1995*	*1996*	*1997*	*1998*	*1994*	*1995*[1]	*1996*	*1997*	*1998*	*1994*	*1995*	*1996*	*1997*	*1998*
Real GDP Growth (in%)	7.5	8.2	8.	5.0	–17.0	9.2	9.5	8.6	7.8	2.5	8.9	8.	5.5	–0.4	–3.
CPI Inflation Rate	8.5	9.4	7.	6.6	39.1	3.7	3.4	3.5	2.7	5.1	5.1	5.	5.9	5.6	10.1
Money Supply Growth	20.0	27.2	27.2	23.2	17.7	14.7	24.0	20.9	22.6	16.1	12.9	17.0	12.6	16.5	15.4
Saving/GDP	29.2	29.0	28.8	27.3	29.2	32.7	33.5	36.7	37.0	36	34.9	34.3	33.1	31.8	32.6
Fiscal Balance/GDP	0.0	0.8	1.	2.0	3.	2.5	3.8	4.2	1.6	3.2	2.0	2.	1.6	–0.4	3.
Current Acct. Balance/GDP	–1.7	–3.3	–3.	–2.6	1.	–7.8	–10.0	–4.9	–4.8	–0.5	–5.6	–7.	–7.9	–2.2	3.
Growth of Exports in US$	8.8	13.4	9.	7.3	–2.	24.7	25.8	6.0	0.8	–12.9	19.8	26.2	–0.8	4.4	3.
External Debt/GDP	61.0	61.5	56.7	58.8	49.2	40.4	39.3	40.1	40.2	40.3	45.8	49.7	49.3	49.7	47.5
Short-term/External Debt	61.8	61.9	61.7	58.7	5.	48.8	47.2	50.3	56.3	48.4	71	69.4	65.2	63.7	53.6
Official Reserves (US$ billion)	12.1	13.7	18.3	16.6	15.5	25.4	23.8	27.0	21.7	20.4	29.3	36.0	37.7	26.2	28.6
in months of imports	4.5	4.0	5.	4.8	7.	5.1	3.7	4.1	3.3	3.7	6.5	6.	6.2	5.0	7.

Various Sources

Thus, large current account deficits, deteriorating quality of investment, appreciation in real exchange rate and a slow down in export rate all taken together contributed to the vulnerability of the ASEAN3 economies.

The sharp *slow down in exports giving rise to* a rapid deterioration in the current account and *liberalisation of the capital account* not accompanied by prudent regulations in the related sector that were the villains of the piece.

Currently these economies have bounced back (although not to the pre crises level as far as all the economic indictors are concerned) and are continuing on the much trodden path of liberalisation but of course with caution and prudence.

Implications for India

The development experience of Southeast Asia has certain lessons to offer that India and other developing nations cannot afford to ignore or overlook. The South Asian countries looked upon the Southeast Asian economic performance with envy till 1997 and had been prompted to emulate the same. However, in the post 1997 period the South Asian policy makers are relieved that their economies escaped the contagion and experienced no major turbulence. Notwithstanding the above, India and other such economies need to prepare themselves for the future and gear up to new challenges that liberalisation and globalisation have thrown up.

Why India escaped the crisis?

India has experienced 4 instances of crises between the mid 1960s and early 1990s (1965-1967, 1975-1976 and 1979-1981 and in 1991). All of them were balance of payment crisis (BOP) accompanied by inflation[16]. All these BOP crisis resulted mainly on account of the inward looking policy followed by India. This policy not only discouraged non-essential imports but it also ensured that exports could not grow.[17] Thus India was beset with problems of low external reserves on the one hand and restricted capacity to finance any unexpected increase in imports or their prices on the other hand.

However, since 1991 with the change in the policy stance and the satisfactory growth rates that India had achieved when compared to its previous standards it was less susceptible to a BOP crisis. The outward oriented policy reforms had to some extent cushioned the impact of external shocks. The question that remains to be answered is that although India was, by 1997 less vulnerable to a BOP crisis, was it also less vulnerable to a currency crisis? By virtue of the nature of the policies followed prior to 1991, India never experienced a currency crisis. But in the post 1991 period has India's vulnerability increased? These questions can be answered after examining for India the macroeconomic parameters that contributed to the crisis in Southeast Asia. The major contributors to the crisis in Southeast Asia were the high current account deficit, a pegged exchange rate arrangement, increasing inflow of portfolio investment vis-à-vis FDI, high short-term debt, financial sector weakness and decline in exports.

In India the *current account deficit* was less than about 2 per cent of GDP over the period 1991-1998. As compared to the 8 per cent in Indonesia and 10 per cent in Malaysia, during 1995 and about 5 per cent during 1990-1996 in Thailand, India's current account deficit is very modest. So at least as far as current account deficit is concerned, it was maintained within safe levels and kept India away from the crisis. However, it may be mentioned here that the ratio of current account deficit to GDP was low in India due to industrial recession, which had caused a slow down in non-oil imports. Moreover, in India consumer goods still constitute a part of the negative list.

Another important factor that insulated India from a currency crisis in 1997 was that the goal of *capital account convertibility* (CAC) had not yet been achieved. Due to restrictions in the capital account large-scale capital transfers in short periods cannot take place in India. In recent times the path towards achieving CAC is being traversed but complete convertibility is yet to be achieved.

The foreign exchange market operated only on the basis of the current account transactions with a number of small players and a few big players. The latter included the State Bank of India, which is 55 per cent owned by the Government of India. With hardly any players and foreign exchange dealers not being allowed to speculate even for a microsecond, the central bank was in complete control. Thus India was unlikely to be affected by the currency crisis in Southeast Asia. Hence the kind of currency switching that took place in Southeast Asia, with domestic residents dumping their own currency in a wild scramble for foreign currencies, was far less likely[18].

The insulation provided by the absence of full capital account convertibility is not always an insurance against a currency crisis. This is because capital controls are never completely effective and currency black markets always run parallel to controls. Moreover, the maturity profile of foreign debt is an important factor adding to vulnerability. If there is an excessive portfolio dependence on short-term debt or if portfolio investment is increasing, they can contribute to vulnerability.

Portfolio to FDI ratio was rather high at 6.25 in 1993-1994. But since then it has decreased and stood at 0.57 for 1997-1998. It may be mentioned here that this ratio was very high in Indonesia and Thailand. Since in the pre-crisis period this ratio was low in India it therefore helped India escape the crisis. India needs to be watchful of this indicator and has therefore to be careful that portfolio inflows do not increase excessively in proportion to FDI as the portfolio investments are volatile and can be reversed.

Another factor that can cause volatility is the *quantity of short-term debt.* For India this ratio was less than 25 per cent from 1993-1994 onwards and was well within safe limits through 1991-1998. Hence, due to the low short-term debt to FER ratio, India did not run the risk, of being destabilised by a speculative attack on the currency.

However, complacency in the above matter is definitely not right if one looks a little more deeply rather than just superficially. This is because in India, the large component of the foreign exchange reserves is the NRI deposits that constitute a volatile source.

As far as the *financial sector* is concerned there is a lot of improvement as a result of the reforms since 1991. According to the Reserve Bank of India there has been a reduction in gross non-performing assets (NPAs) as a proportion of advances to about 18 per cent in 1996-1997. As is now well recognised rapid growth of credit to the private sector tends to lower the quality of bank loan portfolios, as more credit goes to poor quality projects and creditors, and actual NPAs may increase without being immediately brought to light. But the growth of bank credit to the private sector did not increase; in fact, it fell in 1996-1997 to 8.9 per cent from 17.7 per cent in the previous year.

The external liabilities of banks were to 2.8 per cent of GDP in 1996-1997 and for non-bank private sector it was higher at 8.5 per cent of GDP. The bank borrowings abroad though low, constituted US$ 10.1 billion *i.e.* 37.2 per cent of foreign exchange reserves as of June 1998.

As far as the share of goods *exports* in the total GDP of India is concerned, it has been very modest as India has never really been an export-oriented economy. This ratio was about 6.7 per cent in 1991-1992 and peaked to 8-9 per cent in 1995-1996 and declined marginally to 8.3 per cent in 1998-1999. It is worth noting that growth rate of exports has declined from about 20 per cent to about 2 per cent between 1995-1996 and 1998-1999. Thus, although, as mentioned above India is not following an export-led growth like Southeast Asia, yet a continued decline in export does not portend well for the economy as a whole.[19]

Lessons from the Southeast Asian Crisis

India can draw many inferences from the Asian crisis. The big lesson of the East Asian crisis and its aftermath for India and South Asia is the importance of following a path of fundamental and sustained reform, while paying due attention to their proper sequencing and timing[20]. Indian policy makers have to be continuously alert and appropriate adjustment has to be made at the right time. Any delay can prove costly. Deregulation need not be equated to a *laissez faire* system. Along with openness and liberalisation of the economy there must exist a *supervisory and regulatory role for the Government.*

Symptoms of financial ailments do exist in India and hence India must exercise caution. Financial and real sector liberalisation must be preceded by and continuously supported by a *sound financial structure* a sound financial system and sound banking practices are *sine qua non.* In fact, the Asian financial crisis has sent this message worldwide and now a country's ability to attract investment from abroad depends on whether the banking standards practiced match up to international standards. At the micro level the banks and other financial institutions must be prudent in their lending activities and be able to assess the risk factor objectively. The RBI has indicated from time to time that it will not allow too much short-term cross border transactions.

The next lesson to be remembered by India is to keep the *current account deficit under control.* In fact a large current account deficit often encourages large borrowing especially for a short-term period. Moreover in India's case particularly since the exports cannot sustain a large deficit, the same must be constantly monitored. It must not be overlooked that a deceleration in exports among others was primary cause of the crisis. Also the quantity of India's foreign exchange has to be adequate to support the current account deficit.

The most important inference that India must draw from the Southeast Asian development experience is relating to the *timing* of capital account convertibility (CAC). India is certainly likely to heed the message from the East Asian crisis: caution is needed in moving to capital account convertibility[21] In the post crisis period it has been decided to postpone the CAC to a later time as against by the year 2000 as had been suggested by the Tarapore Committee Report. However this does not mean that India must never adopt a free capital account. The integration of the foreign exchange market and the money market require more sustainable foreign exchange reserves backed by a high growth rate of exports, and a strong financial sector. A premature freeing of the capital account can result in speculative and destablising capital inflows. Hence till

India's position is more secure it would do good to postpone the CAC, else it will have to pay with a currency crisis. However the sole objective of policy making cannot be avoiding of a crisis. As mentioned earlier it should just be sequenced properly to avoid costly turbulence.

Finally when India does adopt CAC, it must also simultaneously *adopt a prudent exchange rate policy.* A pegged exchange rate and a free capital account are incompatible. Thus it is better to have a free-floating exchange rate policy, whenever CAC is adopted. This can bring down the chances of a currency crisis risk. A negative side effect of flexible exchange rates is that the appreciation of the currency, resulting from capital inflows, has an adverse effect on the competitiveness of the country's exports. This was perhaps a key reason why the countries in east and Southeast Asia opted for fixed exchange rates. To the extent that exports affect growth, under flexible rates, the countries would have had to sacrifice real income. Flexible exchange rates also do not rule out banking crisis that result from capital mobility. This is especially true when banking sector is itself vulnerable as in India.

Unlike the goods markets, the liberalisation of financial markets is a complex affair. Before we embark upon full currency convertibility, it is advisable to at least get our banking sector on its feet. Otherwise, we risk currency and banking crisis and with them the risk of administering a serious setback to the more urgent reforms.

REFERENCES

1. Banuri, Tariq (1991), *'Economic Liberalisation: No Panacea',* New York, Oxford University Press, p 10.
2. Bowie, Alasdain and Danny Unger (1997), *'The Politics of Open economies: Indonesia, Malaysia, the Philippines, and Thailand,'* London, Cambridge University Press, p 27.
3. Ibid.
4. Yangihara, Toru (1997), *'East Asian Development Experience: Economic System Approach and Application'*, Tokyo, Institute of Development Economics.
5. World Bank (1993), *'The East Asian Miracle',* Washington, Oxford University Press, p 109.
6. Asian Development Bank (1999), *'Asian Development Outlook 1999',* New York, Oxford University Press.
7. Asian Development Bank (1992), *'Asian Development Outlook 1992',* Manila, Oxford University Press.
8. Rowen, Henry (1998), *'Behind East Asian Growth: The Political Foundations of Prosperity',* New York, Routledge, p 97.

9. Masuyama, Seiichi (1997), *'The Evolving Nature of Industrial Policy in East Asia. Liberalising, Upgrading and Integration,'* in Seiichi Masuyama et al (eds) 'industrial Policies in East Asia' Singapore, ISEAS, p 3.

10. Corsetti, Giancarlo et al (2000), *'The Asian Financial Crisis, Causes Contagion and Consequences',* Yale University, p 127-141 *Contagion and Consequences',* Yale University, p 127-141.

11. Doner, Richard et al (1999), *'Thailand: From Economic Miracle to Economic Crisis',* in Karl Jackson (ed), 'Asian Contagion. The Causes and Consequences of a Financial Crisis', Singapore, Institute of Southeast Asian Studies.

12. Goldstein, Morris (1998), *'The Asian Financial Crisis. Causes, Cures and Systematic Implications',* Washington DC, Institute for International Economics, p 37.

13. Ibid.

14. Asian Development Bank (1998), *'Asian Development Outlook 1998',* New York, Oxford University Press.

15. Goldstein, Morris (1998), *'The Asian Financial Crisis. Causes, Cures and Systematic Implications',* Washington DC, Institute for International Economics, p 37.

16. Ibid, p 134.

17. Jayasuria, Sisira (1998), 'India', in Ross Mclead et al (eds), 'East Asia in Crisis', London/New York, Routledge, p 133.

18. Yadav, Surendra and P.K. Jain (2000), 'Economic Crisis in Southeast Asia', Delhi, Hindustan Publishing Corporation, p 86.

19. Jayasuria, Sisira (1998), 'India', in Ross Mclead et al (eds), 'East Asia in Crisis', London/New York, Routledge, p 133.

20. Speech by Joseph Stiglitz in New Delhi on 19 May 1998, Business Line, 20 May 1998.

28

Globalisation and its Implications for Indian Agriculture

Dr. D. Rudrappan*

Introduction

Professor Gunnar Myrdal, a Noble Laureate has strongly emphasised the imperative need for agricultural progress, as the basis of long term economic development. The vast majority of poor people in India are located in rural areas and are engaged primarily in subsistence agriculture for their survival, even today. The core problems of widespread poverty, growing inequality, rapid population growth and rising unemployment, find their origin in the stagnation and often retrogression of economic life in rural areas. Millions of people have been bypassed by whatever economic "progress" that has been attained in India before and after Independence. If "development" is to take place and becomes self-sustaining really and substantially encompassing especially the poor, it will have to start in the rural areas in general, and the agricultural sector in particular.

In India, terms of trade always worked against agriculture as a result of high protection policy to industry, and also due to an over-valued exchange rate. The underlying assumption perhaps was that a rapidly growing manufacturing sector and the urban areas would siphon off excess labour from agriculture in due course. This would allow the agricultural sector too to modernize itself with a more favourable land-man ratio, and raise productivity in agriculture. But history has proved it otherwise. The share of

* Reader, Department of P.G. and Research Studies in Economics, *Presidency College, Chennai–600 005.*

agriculture in national GDP slid from 56% to 25%, in the year 2000 (India 2001). It's share in the working population fell only marginally from 71% to 64%. As a consequence, intersectoral inequalities in income and assets have increased, creating a chasm between rural-urban India. Rural India appears to have lagged much behind even with occasional injections of technological breakthroughs like green revolution and subsidies.

The political economy of food compelled our policy makers to periodically look back to agriculture, whenever the spectre of hunger loomed large. Therefore, new agricultural strategy was sought to be implemented with the import of 18,000 tonnes of HYV wheat seeds, besides constitution of Food Corporation of India in mid 1960's for food grains distribution and Agricultural Prices Commission for recommending minimum support prices. With these dramatic changes, a negative price policy era (1951-65), turned into one of a positive price policy era, along with the advent of Green Revolution (Krishna, 1980)

Genesis of Globalisation and Paradigm shift in Indian Agriculture

A study on the periodisation of globalisation has stated that the Capitalist economic foundation (had been) laid in as early as 16th century (Wallerstein, 1990). However, the forces of globalisation have emerged strongly and pervaded in all the countries from the early 1990s (Sengupta, 2001). Apart from liberalisation and privatisation, globalisation is one of the components of New Economic Policy initiated by the Government of India, in 1991. Among them, globalisation extended its area of influence vastly encompassing all the sphere of the economy. Globalisation is increasingly viewed as the only explanatory background for the analysis of almost all the current social and economic issues. In simple terms it refers to the opening up of the economy and free movement of all financial resources reducing all kinds of tariff and non-tariff barriers and quantitative restrictions gradually. It is expected that this will result in higher level of economic activity and with higher rates of employment and higher volume of trade with higher availability of goods.

Globalisation measures especially the trade policy reforms, perhaps for the first time, aimed at correcting 'anti-agriculture' bias in trade policies. Protection to industry should be brought to the same level as that of agriculture, to provide momentum for the development of agriculture. Indian agriculture needs a 'level playing field' with domestic industry. This would be a precondition, not necessarily a sufficient one, for a new paradigm of growth, where agriculture triggers growth impulses in other sectors, through its backward and forward linkages. This would lead to distribution of growth among villages where the soul of India resides.

Before 1991, India's decision makers took the economy on a state controlled development path with launching of the Second Five Year Plan in 1956. The subsequent decades were marked by crises of low rate of economic development. The paradigm shift in India's economic policy took place in 1991 when the Government of India made a decisive shift to a more open and liberal economy, integrating Indian economy with the World economy, albeit gradually.

The process of opening up and economy involves replacing quantitative controls on imports and exports by 'tariffication', and then lowering the tariffs; removing biases in incentive structures to produce for exports or the home market, by allowing the exchange rate to be determined by market conditions; and removing restrictions on the flow of foreign capital in various sectors.

Opening up Trade

The rupee was devalued by 22 per cent in July 1991 to facilitate the expansion of foreign trade. Further, in February 1992, the Liberalised Exchange Rate Management System (LERMS) was introduced, resulting in partial convertibility of the rupee, allowing 60 per cent of the foreign exchange earnings to be converted at the market-determined exchange rate. Invisibles were added to this list in August 1994, thus completing full convertibility of the rupee on current account.

The signing of GATT on 15 April 1994 at Marrakesh, implied that physical controls on exports and imports of agricultural commodities would have to be replaced while tariffs have to be bound, and then gradually reduced-faster by the developed countries than by the developing countries like India. It also implied that the export subsidies on agricultural commodities have to be reduced and also the domestic support as measured by Aggregate Measure of Support (AMS). The import weighted average level of tariffs was to be brought down from 89% in 1989-90 to 45% by 1995-96 and to 25% in 1990-91 (GOI, 1991). However, Indian tariffs are high when compared to other developing countries such as Mexico and Indonesia where less than 10% tariff prevailed (Ahluwalia, 1996). Nevertheless, compared to its own past, the progress in tariff reductions in India has been reasonably impressive, except in consumer goods.

Out of 5021 tariff lines, by December 1995, over 3000 tariff lines covering raw materials, intermediate and capital goods, were freed from import licensing requirements (Economic Survey, 1995-96). This is a major initiative towards Globalisation of the economy. The inflow of foreign capital has been liberalised. Automatic approval for FDI (equity participation) upto 74 per cent has been entrusted to the Reserve Bank of India in capital goods, consumer goods and financial sectors.

Opening up Agriculture

India also became a signatory to the Uruguay Round trade negotiations, including agriculture. Consequently, the Tax Reforms Committee (Government of India, 1993) had recommended that agriculture commodities should basically attract three rates of import duties. First, essential agricultural commodities like wheat and rice should be imported at zero per cent duty; secondly, commodities like oilseeds and pulses should attract 10 per cent duty; and thirdly, non-essential agricultural goods like almond and cashewnuts should be imported at 50 per cent import duty. All this transformation in import duties should be achieved by 1996-97 or latest by 1997-98. However, the performance of trade policy so far in agriculture is not satisfactory. Thus, overall it appears that India has taken rapid strides towards globalising the economy since the 1991 reforms but the larger part of this remained restricted to the industrial sector. Agriculture experienced lot of hiccups in trade liberalisation.

Implications of Globalisation

Theoretically, the process of economic reforms in the Indian Economy would involve reduction of import duties on the highly protected manufacturing sector, and freeing agricultural exports, which are somewhat unprotected. This should inevitably lead to the terms of trade moving in favour of agriculture, and improvements in the relative environment for agriculture. Other things remaining constant, it should invite higher private investments, spurring growth in agriculture. Enhanced agricultural incomes should then generate enough demand for industrial products through its backward and forward linkages. It would also stimulate and sustain off-farm activities in the rural areas.

The manufacturing sector was protected by about 46 per cent while agriculture was being disprotected by about 20 per cent leading to a large implicit 'discrimination against agriculture. The aggregate measure of support (AMS) for Indian agriculture worked out at (–) 22 per cent for the triennium ending (TE) 1998-99, (–) 21 per cent for the TE 1992-93 and (–) 17.6 per cent for the TE 1994-95 (Gulati, 1996).

The results are on expected lines; liberalisation triggers growth in agriculture, the impact is more from industrial liberalisation than from agricultural liberalisation *per se*. However, the poor are in the short run adversely affected by the liberalisation of agriculture, necessitating at 'safety net.' The Economic Survey, 2002-03, observes that the robust agricultural performance in the last four years is not just the result of normal monsoons, but also due to improved incentives for the agricultural sector as a whole. Comprehensive reforms of tariff rates, trade policy, and the exchange rate system have greatly reduced the earlier bias in favour of manufacturing industries arising from high levels of protection and has improved the relative profitability of agriculture.

Problems and Prospects

The first set consists of bottlenecks in the supply side factors: irrigation, credit, research and development, institutional factors governing patterns of landholdings, and so on. The second set of threats consists of issues relating to food-security.

So far as supply side bottlenecks are concerned, the most critical seems to be irrigation. It is well known that public investment in irrigation fell drastically during 1980s and early 1990s. This trend needs to be reversed, preferably by cutting down on input subsidies, which lately have exceeded even the plan expenditure on agriculture (IMF, 2000). Allocation of greater resources to irrigation alone may not solve the problem. Research in that area reveals that the irrigation sector is in acute need for institutional and price reforms, enabling the farmers to participate in the management of these irrigation projects. In this, the distribution of water and the maintenance is being handed over to farmers, who also collect charges for sharing water amongst themselves.

Criticisms: The following are the remarks voiced by the anti-globalisation blocs in India.

1. Developed countries had muscled through their agenda irrespective of National Parliaments and that global capital would have a free run. India was forced to capitulate to the pressure of WTO and Parliament was being suffocated at the behest of corporate sectors.
2. Opening up of agriculture would lead to diversification of cropping patterns away from cereals and thereby pose a threat to food security at the national level. Food prices will increase with the opening up of exports of agriculture, and the poor would suffer, atleast in the short run.
3. The commitment on the removal of input subsidy may lead to deceleration of crop output leading to untold miseries among the resource poor farmers specifically in developing countries.

4. Fears have been articulated that new risk dimensions for the environment and for human health could occur due to the direct manipulation of transgenic crops. This may result in loss of bio-diversity through vertical and horizontal transfer. Another risk of insect-resistant crops is the pest population could develop resistance to the toxins produced by the terminator seeds and further that these crops could have detrimental effects on beneficial insects and other non-target organisms. Possible health risk of transgenic crops for human consumption include the occurrence of undesirable toxic by-products and unknown allergic reactions due to new proteins entering the food chain.

5. Trans National Corporations may dominate the seed market and this will have its baneful effects on the peasants of poor countries.

6. Protection of plant breeders rights under globalisation will have its adverse effect on farmers traditional rights to develop and sell seeds.

Critics Answered

1. The linking of domestic reform agenda to trade negotiations by WTO regime should be welcomed since this will ensure commitment, transparency and responsibility among our politicians and bureaucrats. Among some groups, it is said that it is not in our interest in combined social issues with trade. Being a democratic country with an active judiciary, social welfare and reform, India is far more progressive than other Asian countries including China. Infact by virtue of our legislation, we end up with higher effective labour cost in organised manufacturing. Thus, agreeing to a social cost may not necessarily hurt us as much as our potential competitors.

2. Indian Government complain about the unfairness of allowing subsidies given by developed countries to their farmers while prohibiting ours. The fact is our subsidies are poorly designed and distort the operation of the market forces. Minimum support price distort the economics of surplus and deficit states in the case of food and non-food production and thus, has created huge stocks of foodgrains along with deprivation. Poor management of Targeted Public Distribution System could be cited as a reason for the prevailing persistent deprivation in some parts of the country. Subsidy scheme could be redesigned as income support programmes and they would be less distortionary and more equitable. By this way, India can escape subsidy removal restriction also, besides

improving conditions for balanced production and increased availability of food.

3. Developments in the international trade arena are unlikely to offer any succour to India agriculture unless it devises a strategy to reduce the present high cost structure with the assistance of cost-reducing technologies for increasing farm efficiency.

4. Participatory Management practices such as Water User's Associations and Self-Help Groups should be promoted to increase and manage farm infrastructure and other farm service for enhancing farm productivity.

5. Field testing and application of transgenic crops did not reveal any undesired impacts. Further, insecticidal genes have been identified for being used to broaden the spectrum of protection. To avoid health risks, comprehensive laboratory and feeding tests are necessary before a new modified crop is approved from commercialisation. Transgenic field trials are being conducted at Indian Agricultural Research Institute, New Delhi for brinjal, tomato and mustard. Transgenic crops are tolerant crops into which a gene from the soil bacterium *Bacillus thuringenesis* (Bt) has been inserted to make them resistant to certain tracts. In the early 2002, Genetic Engineering Approval Committee (GEAC) as well as Government of India have permitted cultivation of genetically engineered bollworm resistant Bt. cotton hybrid varieties of U.S.A.'s Mahyco-Monsonto Corporation in India. Already 44 million hectares were commercially grown with transgenic crops at the global level in year, 2000.

The targeted group may be given a higher subsidy per unit of grain. To plug the leakages, the fair-price shops may be brought under the supervision of local bodies such as the panchayats. This, would make the food subsidies more effective in providing a safety net to the poor. The other option is to strengthen major efforts in the countryside to community assets, housing for the poor and Primary Health Centres. But again, unless this is accompanied by institutional reforms where local people have a say in decision-making and supervision of these works, mere allocation of greater resources would not be very productive.

Impact of Globalisation

1. While reviewing the trade policy and practices of India on June 19 and 20, 2002, WTO Secretariat highlighted the progress made by the Indian economy by pointing out that the economy has grown

rapidly over the past decade, with real GDP growth averaging 6 per cost annually (Economic Survey, 2002-03).

2. However, WTO Secretariat voiced concern over subsides for agricultural products and inputs, which have contributed to large grain-stocks and export restrictions on agricultural goods. As a corrective measure, WTO emphasised further liberalisation of Indian agricultural sector (by the way of) and reduction of subsidy; both consumer subsidy and producer subsidy, while India reiterated its support for WTO and the Doha work programme, it was added that if further progress was to be made, the onus remained on the developed countries in reducing the agricultural subsidy and to keep the promises made in Doha. The need for accelerating the reforms further was, however emphasised given the ambitious Tenth Plan growth targets to be achieved.
3. The latest RBI currency and Finance report, published in April 2003 pointed out that the aggregate activity has not only decelerated but is also far below its potential growth as a result of poor performance of agriculture and allied sections. The report further states that the primary sectors long run trend rate of growth since Indian Independence has been 3 per cent, and the post-reform period marks the first period when it has actually fallen well below that. Indeed, this low rate of growth reflects the stagnation or even decline of agriculture in the more recent period. The report added that globalisation of trade liberalisation has kept the crop prices down in India even when there is a fall in the domestic output (Chandrasekar, 2003).
4. Gross capital formation in Indian agriculture 1993-94 prices has decelerated from 1.6 per cent GDP in 1993-94 to 1.3 per cent in 2001-02 causing concern among planners and policy makers. This decline was attributed mainly to near stagnation early nineties. Further, this has led to inadequate provision of infrastructure in agriculture.

For instance, as against the targeted growth of irrigation potential at 3.4 m.ha in Ninth Plan, annual average irrigation potential has been created at the rate of 1.80 m.ha on account of declining investment in agriculture (Economic Survey, 2002-03).

Reforms in Agriculture Marketing

Liberalisation of world trade in agriculture has provided new opportunity to the farm sector to access markets for agricultural commodities world-wide.

However, to make this happen, reforms have to be brought about in agriculture sector to remove all barriers, whether legal or policy induced, which introduce inefficiencies and monopoly rents or policy induced, which introduce inefficiencies and monopoly rents in the functioning of agricultural markets. At present, though agricultural production is largely free from controls, the same is not true of marketing of agricultural commodities. Under the Agricultural Produce Marketing Control Act (APMC Act), State Governments alone are empowered to initiate the process of setting up of markets for agri products within a defined area. As a result, private and co-operative sectors cannot take initiative in setting up markets equipped with modern facilities.

High investments together with entrepreneurial skills required for creation and managing the market infrastructures have to come from private sector. In order to encourage private sector participation and investments required for development of alternative marketing infrastructure and supporting services, provisions of the State Agricultural Produce Marketing Regulation Act would need modification to create a lawful role for the private sector in market development and to establish integrate facility for marketing of agricultural produce. At a National Conference on Agricultural Marketing Reforms organised by the Ministry of Agriculture on 27th September 2002 in New Delhi, all the State Governments were requested to implement reform measures such as provision of direct marketing, development of agricultural markets in private and cooperative sectors, stepping up of pledge financing, expansion of futures trading to cover all agricultural commodities, introduction of negotiable warehousing receipt system and use of information technology to provide market led extension services to farmers. Curtailment of excessive bureaucratisation of markets is necessary for healthy growth of such markets. It is suggested that the Governments role should be that of a facilitator rather than that of exercising control over the management of markets.

An essential task prior to any analysis of the costs and benefits of Globalisation is to determine exactly the extent of international integration of an economy. In the case of India, there has been a significant advancement in the country's external economic integration compared with its own past record as has been pointed out by the World Bank Database in the year 1999.

Four elements are considered in determining the country's openness to the world economy and to find out the impact of the changed openness of the Indian economy of India's economy.

1. Foreign trade in goods and services: The proportion of the country's Gross Domestic Product (GDP) involved in the international trade of goods and services has gone up from 17.70% to 24.78% in 1998.

2. Tariff levels: The related element of the level of tariff determines the degree of protection accorded to local production against imports from the world economy. Import duties as percentage of imports has decelerated from 45.88% in 1991 to 25% in 2002-03.
3. Transnationalisation of production: Total foreign investment comprising of Foreign Direct Investment (FDI) and Portfolio Foreign Investment (PFI) has enhanced from $74 million in 1991 to $5693.10 in 1998 accounting for 0.03% of GDP and 0.85% GDP respectively.
4. State controls in capital movement: Due to globalisation measure, restrictions were loosened first in respect of trade, current account payments and foreign direct investment followed by liberalisation of portfolio foreign investment.

It is evident that there has been a significant increase in India's external economic integration, compared with its past record. But this advancement has been modest and gradual. Despite these measures of globalisation, an IMF analysis maintains that many restrictions on capital flows remain and that India's system remains relatively restrictive.

Conclusion

Thus, in conclusion, the globalisation process in the economy offers an opportunity to correct the 'anti-agriculture' bias in Indian trade policies that have been in existence since 1950s. With this, the hidden 'implicit taxation' on agriculture sector would get an opportunity to respond favourably to these signals. India, which has significant technical skills in the field of agriculture, must develop self-reliance in technology. Moreover, there is no need for the country to function as the purveyors of Multi-National Corporation technologies with their patent rights. Agriculture can move on to a higher growth trajectory, if supply side bottlenecks are freed, and a protective cover is accorded to the poor, at least for some time. If this happens, agriculture can propel growth in other sectors too on a sustainable basis, while promoting intersectoral and interpersonal equity and linkages.

Unless supply side bottlenecks are removed and Public Distribution System in restructured, reforms can prove to be a threat and stall the process of globalisation in other sectors as well. Needless to say, given the plethora of issues, the country has to take concerted steps to further the country's economic interests and to improve its performance both internally and externally. Hence, our domestic policy framework must move in synchronisation with the structure of global trade rules. Doing this requires building a more realistic domestic consensus on trade and globalisation than has been done so far.

REFERENCES

1. Ahluwalia, Isher Judge *et al.*, (1996) "India Opening up to Trade and Investment" in Policy Reform in India (Ed) Charles Oman, *Development Centre Seminars, OECD, Paris.*

2. Chandrasekar, C.P. and Jayati Ghosh. (2003) "Economic Reforms, The RBI's Assessment," *The Hindu Business Line,* dt. 08.04.2003.

3. *Economic Survey* (1995-96), Ministry of Finance, Government of India, New Delhi.

4. Government of India (1992-93) *Tax Reform Committee Final Report, Ministry* of Finance, New Delhi.

5. Gulati, Ashok and Garry Pursell (1996) *Trade Policies, Incentives and Resource allocation in Indian Agriculture* mimeo, The World Bank, Washington, D.C.

6. IMF, (2000) "Capital controls: Country Experiences with their use and Liberalisation," *IMF Report Washington,* DC.

7. India (2000) *Agriculture* Government of India, New Delhi.

8. Krishna, Raj and Ray Chandhuri, (1980) "Some Aspects of wheat and rice price policy in India," *World Bank Staff Working Paper* No. 381, April, Washington, D.C.

9. Sengupta, Chandan (2001) "Conceptualising Globalisation: Issues and Implications," *Economic and Political Weakly,* vol. XXXVI, No. 33, August 18.

10. Wallerstein, Immanuel (1990) "Societal Development or Development of the World System" in *Globalisation knowledge and Society: Readings from International Sociology,* (Eds) Martin Albrow and Elizabeth King, Sage Publications, London.

29

Economic Reforms and Poverty in India

Ravi M. Tirlapur*

Introduction

India began economic reforms on a massive scale in the year 1991, though its origin can be traced to mid 1980s. We are now into the second decade of the LPG era. The immediate reason for the launching of the policies of economic liberalisation was the balance of payments crisis faced by India in 1991. However the real reason behind the reforms was the deep dissatisfaction with earlier regime, where India was caught in the low level equilibrium trap with the so called 'Hindu Growth Rate' of about 3.5 per cent per annum for more than three and half decades of planning. For the country like India- with subcontinental size and the second most populous country - this level of growth was grossly insufficient to make any serious dent on the levels of poverty, inequality and unemployment.

With the objective of accelerating the pace of economic growth India was initiated into the reform mode and resultant higher growth was expected to make inroads into the domain of the poor population. The impact of reforms of 1990s on GDP growth has been satisfactory both by the international and by our own historical standards. In fact India turned to be one of the fastest growing economies in the world during the period. Since India happens to be the home for the largest number of poor in the world, the impact of GDP growth on poverty reduction was much awaited by both the domestic and international observers, policy makers and the academics. "What happens to

* Faculty, Department of Economics, Bangalore University, *Bangalore.*

India is quantitatively important to the world's overall progress in fighting absolute poverty" (Datt and Ravallion, 2002). For the international institutions (like IMF and World Bank) the gains, if any, in terms of poverty reduction could be used for pushing forward with Globalisation and liberalisation policies elsewhere in the world more rigorously. Domestically the poverty reduction could be posed as the vindication of the break in the policy paradigm and as a proof of efficacy and desirability of reform process initiated in early 1990s.

Hence poverty, one of the hotly debated issues in India is in news again, even after the five decades of planning and economic development. The debate on poverty - its measurement, monitoring and evaluation continues unabated even in the 1990s. In this background the present paper seeks to examine the impact of economic reforms on poverty reduction in India, especially in the light of the latest 55th Round NSSO Survey (1999-2002) released in 2001-02.

Measurement of Poverty in India

The idea of eradication and issues related to poverty is not new to India. Dadabhai Naoroji's book 'Poverty and Unbritish Rule' dates back to pre-independence period. The Indian National Congress which spearheaded the struggle for Indian freedom also widely deliberated on this issue and the ways and means of reducing it. After independence it has been one of the main planks of the Five Year Plans. The estimates of poverty are available in India since 1958. It was the late 1960s which witnessed spurt of interest among economists in the study of poverty both at the conceptual and empirical levels (Vaidyanathan, 2001). Dandekar and Rath (1974) in their 'Poverty in India' advocated that poverty be defined on the basis of minimum income required for nutritional diet and other essentials. They provided their own estimates of poverty and strategies to meet the challenge. The studies by many other individual researchers – Minhas, Vaidyanathan, Bardhan, Ahluwalia etc. also provide estimates of poverty in India.

Planning Commission has since adopted the definition provided by the 'Task Force on Projections on Minimum Needs and Effective Consumption Demands.' According to the Task force report the poverty line is defined as mid point of monthly per capital expenditure class having a daily calorie intake of 2400 per person in rural areas and 2100 in urban areas. Accordingly the cut of points were estimated at Rs. 76/- and Rs. 88/- per capita per month for rural and urban areas respectively, at 1979-80 prices (GOI, Planning Commission, VI Plan). The data on the estimates of Consumer Expenditure is obtained from the 'Household Consumer Expenditure Surveys' conducted by National Sample Survey Organisation (NSSO). The poverty line arrived at in 1979-80 is updated using price deflator (to adjust for the price changes) for the later years. Following Lakdawala Committee (GOI, 1993) recommendations the earlier practice of using single national level poverty line and single deflator for state level estimates was given up. Now separate state level price indices are used to make adjustment for the differences with respect to base year price levels.

NSSO carries out small scale sample surveys every year and large scale quinquennial sample surveys periodically. Poverty estimates are based on the latter. The large scale sample surveys of household income and consumption, education and health are also conducted by NCAER. However NCAER surveys are less detailed as compared to NSSO. For long there has been divergence between NSS and NAS (National Accounts Statistics) estimates and this divergence seems to be growing over the years. Compared to the NAS data, the NSS data persistently underestimated consumption and thereby and overestimated poverty. Therefore it has been suggested by experts that NSS estimates be revised upwards as a reconciliation for the divergence. The current debate however, is with respect to the controversy over the new methodology in the design of the questionnaire and the resultant underestimation poverty in the 1999-2002, 55th NSS round.

Growth Performance in 1990s

Many experts have hailed India's growth performance in 1990s. After a slow start (1991-92 and 1992-93), growth later picked up well. The initial sluggishness was obvious due to stabilisation policies. That followed the Balance of Payments crisis. However many argue that the i nproved growth performance in the later years is still below India's potential. On top of it, this growth could not be sustained after 1996-97, but still remained high by international and by India's own historical standards.

Table 1: Annual Growth rates of GDP in 1990s at factor cost. (1993-94 prices)

Year	*GDP Growth Rate (%)*
1990–91	5.6
1991–92	1.3
1992–93	5.1
1993–94	5.9
1994–95	7.3
1995–96	7.3
1996–97	7.8
1997–98	4.8
1998–99	6.5
1999–00	6.1

Source: Economic Survey 2001-02, GOI.

This high growth in 1990s is quite encouraging compared to GDP growth of about 3.5% in 1960s and 1970s. The decade of 1980s also recorded higher growth which however became unsustainable for the reasons well known in Indian Economic Literature. The 1990s growth thus marks a structural break, when India conclusively come out the clutches of low level equilibrium trap. Much of the growth in 1990s is attributed to economic reforms-policies of economic liberalisation and globalisation.

But the moot question is, did this growth get translated into poverty reduction? The estimates by Ravallion and Dutt (1996) show that for the pre-1991 period (i.e. from 1958-1991) elasticity of incidence poverty with respect to NDP per capita was minus 0.75 and with respect to private consumption per capita it was minus 0.9. This suggests that in the past, growth in India has been poverty reducing. Are there reasons to believe that this happened in 1990s too? Has 1990s left the poor behind, as is argued? Or as it is believed, has poverty fallen more rapidly in 1990s compared to the previous period?

Evidence of Poverty in 1990s

Evidence on poverty reduction 1990s prior to the NSS 55th round has been contentious. Bhalla (2000) argued that poverty in 1990s has fallen more rapidly compared to the earlier period. But Dutt (1999) and Jha (2000) argued, poverty reduction in 1990s was lower compared to 1980s. After the release of NSS 55th round data (1999-00) in 2001, this issue has become even more contentious. Let us however first look at the official explanation based on the latest round. Table 2 shows the official estimates of poverty in India in the recent years.

Table 2: Estimate of Poverty in India.

Year	*All India No (Million)*	*Poverty Ratio (%)*	*Rural Number (Million)*	*Poverty Ratio (%)*	*Urban Number (Million)*	*Poverty Ratio (%)*
1973-74	321	54.9	261	56.4	60	49.0
1977-78	329	51.3	264	53.1	65	45.2
1983	323	44.5	252	45.7	71	40.8
1987-88	307	38.9	232	39.1	75	38.2
1993-94	320	36.0	244	37.3	76	32.4
1999-2000	260	26.1	193	27.1	67	23.6

Sources: Economic Survey of India, 2001-02, GOI.

According to the latest NSSO round, poverty in India has declined significantly both in absolute and percentage terms. In absolute terms, after remaining at about 320 million for a considerable period of time the number of poor under poverty line has in 1999-2000 has fallen to 260 million. In percentage terms too, poverty has witnessed steady decline from 55% in 1973-74 to 36% in 1993-94 and 26% in 1999-2000. This is hailed as significant achievement of the liberalisation process.

As always there are opinions to the contrary, disputing the official claims. The opposition to the latest estimates is mainly to the change in the design of the questionnaire used by NSSO, thus casting doubts on the comparability of the data. The change in design has been in placing the multiple recall period (7 days, 30 days, 365 days) in addition to the 30 days recall period on the same schedule. The more worrying aspect has been putting 7 days and 30 days recall for food for the same set of households with the columns appearing side by side on the same page of the questionnaire. This, as is widely agreed, promotes convergence thereby leading to over estimation of consumption and hence underestimation of poverty (Datt and Ravallion, 2002). This therefore, it is opined renders the latest official estimates non-comparable with their own earlier estimates. Number of efforts have been made by private researchers to restore the inter temporal comparability by making appropriate adjustment to the official estimates.

Angus Deaton (January 2003) adjusts the official estimates to ensure comparability. Accordingly the overall proverty ratio works out to be 29% for all India and 30.2% and 24.7% for rural and urban area respectively. This constitutes the decline of 1.2 percentage points per annum between 1993-94 and 1999-00. This decline is considerable, though lower than the official estimates. According to the adjustments by Sundaram and Tendulkar (2003) the poverty ratio all India is at 28%, marking 8% decline compared with the earlier round. This again corroborates the official evidence that poverty declined in 1990s. Estimates by the same authors shows a faster decline in latter half of the 1990s as compared the previous half.

Table 3: Estimates of Poverty in India in 1999-2000.

	All India	*Rural*	*Urban*
Official Estimates	26.1	27.1	23.6
Angus Deaton	28.8	30.2	24.7
Sundaram & Tendulkar	28.0	–	–
Datta & Ravallion	34	–	–
Surjit Bhalla	15	–	–

Source: Compiled by the Author.

The adjustments by Datt and Ravallion (2002, 2003) show far greater divergence between their official estimates. The poverty ratio in this study stands at 34% for all India in 1999-00 and the overall reduction in 1990s is lower (albeit slightly) compared to 1980s. This they attribute to slower progress in poverty reduction in the states which account for India's large number of poor. Surjit Bhalla's (2003) estimates would make the mandarins in the Finance Ministry happier. His estimates based on the data from NAS and NCAER show poverty ratio in India to be at 15% in 1999-00, nearly half the official estimates of 26%.

Poverty at Desegregate Level

Poverty at the aggregate level conceals more than it reveals. For more meaningful analysis and effective policy prescription, a close look at state level poverty data is essential. As Table 4 indicates there is great divergence with respect to poverty performance among states. This arises from the divergence in growth performance too (growth of GDP and GDP as per capita) across the states during 1990s.

Kerala shows the highest reduction in poverty from 26% to 13% between 1993-94 and 1999-00. Where as for the BIMARU states the reduction is not as significant. Therefore for poverty reduction at all India level the reduction in the states where it matters most is essential. Thus it is noted that "if not for the (sectoral and) geographic pattern of growth, India's macroeconomic growth in 1990s would have delivered the rate of poverty reduction roughly double the historical trend (Datt and Ravallion, 2002).

Conclusion

Despite the controversy over the designing of the questionnaire in the 55th round NSSO Survey (1999-00), there is widespread evidence that the economic reforms of 1990s have not left the poor behind (though much more is desired), thus proving the sceptics wrong. However the evidence in India and elsewhere (China, South East Asia) suggests that growth is necessary, but not a sufficient condition for poverty reduction. The role of faster economic growth in poverty reduction cannot be discounted. But growth needs to be complemented with social development viz. improvements in literacy, skills, health status, life expectancy etc., so that the growth and development process becomes shared one and the benefits percolate down to the poor. This is essential to make the poor the co-passengers in the journey of higher economic growth.

At the same time, the regional divergence in the growth performance and the disparities in poverty reduction also need serious consideration and

Table 4: Poverty Ratio at the State Level.

Sl. No.	*State*	*Combined*		
		1973-74	*1993-94*	*1999-2000*
1.	Andhra Pradesh	48.86	22.19	15.77
2.	Arunachal Pradesh	51.93	39.35	33.47
3.	Assam	51.21	40.86	36.09
4.	Bihar	61.91	54.96	42.60
5.	Goa	44.26	14.92	4.40
6.	Gujarat	48.15	24.21	14.07
7.	Haryana	35.36	25.05	8.74
8.	Himachal Pradesh	26.39	28.44	7.63
9.	Jammu and Kashmir	40.83	25.17	3.48
10.	Karnataka	54.47	33.16	20.04
11.	Kerala	59.79	25.43	12.72
12.	Madhya Pradesh	61.78	42.52	37.43
13.	Maharashtra	53.24	36.86	25.02
14.	Manipur	49.96	33.78	28.54
15.	Meghalaya	50.20	37.92	33.87
16.	Mizoram	50.32	25.66	19.47
17.	Nagaland	50.81	37.92	32.67
18.	Orissa	66.18	48.56	47.15
19.	Punjab	28.15	11.77	6.16
20.	Rajasthan	46.14	27.41	15.28
21.	Sikkim	50.86	41.43	36.55
22.	Tamil Nadu	54.94	35.03	21.12
23.	Tripura	51.00	39.01	34.44
24.	Uttar Pradesh	57.07	40.85	31.15
25.	West Bengal	63.43	35.66	27.02
26.	A & N Island	55.56	34.47	20.99
27.	Chandigarh	27.96	11.35	5.75
28.	Dadra & Nagar Haveli	46.55	50.84	17.14
29.	Daman & Diu	NA	15.80	4.44
30.	Delhi	49.61	14.69	8.23
31.	Lakshadweep	59.68	25.04	15.60
32.	Pondicherry	53.82	37.40	21.67
	All India	**54.88**	**35.97**	**26.10**

Source: Economic Survey, GOI, 2001-02.

action. Otherwise, however high may be the income growth, if it does not carry the backward states along the overall poverty figure would continue to look as grave as ever, both in absolute and relative terms.

REFERENCES

1. Bhagwati Jagdish (2001), "Growth Poverty and Reforms," Economic and Political Weekly, May 15, 2001.
2. Balla Surjit (2003), "Recounting the Poor: Poverty in India, 1983-99," Economic and Political Weekly, Jan 25, 2003.
3. Datt Gaurav and Ravallion Martin (2002), "Is India's Economic Growth Leaving the Poor Behind? ", World Bank, Policy Research Working Paper No. 2846, May, 2002.
4. Deaton Angus (2003), "Adjusted Indian Poverty Estimates for 1999-00, Economic and Political Weekly Jan 25, 2003.
5. Dollar David and Kraay Aart (2001), "Trade, Growth and Poverty", World Bank Policy Research Working Paper No. 2615, June 2001.
6. Economic Survey, Government of India, Various Issues.
7. Jha Raghavendra (2000), "Growth, Inequality and Poverty in India: Spatial and Temporal Characteristics," Economic and Political Weekly, March 2000.
8. Krishna Swamy K.S. (2001), "Growth, Poverty and Reforms," Economic and Political Weekly, April 21-27, 2001.
9. Nayya Dhiraj (2000), "Role of Good Governance and Constitutional Reform," Economic and Political Weekly, Oct. 14, 2000.
10. Vaidyanathan A (2001), "Poverty and Development Policy," Economic and Political Weekly, May 26, 2001.

30

Changing Pattern of Employment in the Primary Sector in Goa

Silvia Maria de Mendonca Noronha*

Introduction

The Primary Sector refers to agriculture proper and other allied activities like mining, quarrying, livestock, forestry, hunting, plantations, etc. This sector plays a pivotal role in an economy, especially in the early stages of development. Once this sector develops it paves the way for other sectors to emerge and grow.

Objectives of the Study

This paper seeks to analyse:

1. The trends in the employment pattern in the primary sector as a whole and the sex distribution.
2. The intra-sectoral distribution of the total workforce in the primary sector and the sex distribution and finally.
3. To draw appropriate conclusions from the above findings.

To facilitate discussion, the paper has been divided into 3 sections. Section I deals with the trends in the total workforce (TWF) in the primary sector together with the sex distribution. Section II relates to the intra-sectoral distribution of the TWF and its sex distribution and Section III concentrates on the policy implications.

* Reader & Head, Department of Economics, *Goa University, Goa-403 206.*

Workforce Trends

In this section we consider the total workforce in the primary sector as a whole, as well as in the main sub-sectors *i.e.* in Agriculture Proper (AP) and in other than Agriculture Proper (OTAP). Agriculture Proper consists of workers employed as agricultural labourers and cultivators and other than agriculture proper consists of workers engaged in mining, quarrying, livestock, fishing, forestry, plantations, orchard, etc.

Table 1 shows the total workforce employed in the primary sector and its main sub-sectors from 1961-1991.

Table 1: Workforce Trends in the Primary Sector and It's Main Sub-Sectors.

Year	*TWF in AP*	*TWF in OTAP*	*TWF in the Primary Sector*
1961	142,096 (82.6)	29,997 (17.4)	172,093 (100)
1971	98,815 (78.7)	26,733 (21.3)	125,548 (100)
1981 Main	88, 932 (72.6)	33,568 (27.4)	122,500 (100)
Marginal	35,511 (94.6)	2,027 (5.4)	37,538 (100)
Total	**124,443** **(77.8)**	**35,595** **(22.2)**	**1,60,038** **(100)**
1991 Main	91,812 (74)	32,049 (26)	123,861 (100)
Marginal	21,599 (93.5)	1,500 (6.5)	23,099 (100)
Total	**113,411** **(77)**	**33,549** **(23)**	**1,46,960** **(100)**

Source: Census of India, Goa, Daman and Diu, Economics Tables, 1961, 1971, 1981, 1991.

Note: AP - Agriculture Proper
OTAP - Other than Agriculture Proper.

From the above table we observe the following:

1. The absolute workforce as well as the percentage in Agriculture Proper has been declining from 1961-1991.
2. In percentage terms the fall has been 3.9% points from 1961-1971 to 6.1 points from 1971-1981 (Main workers) and from 1981 to 1991 (TW) it has been 0.6% points. The fall was greater from 1971-1981.

3. In Other than Agriculture Proper (OTAP) the absolute workforce shows a fall from 1961-1971, but a rise from 1971-1981 (Main). From 1981-1991 (TW) there is a fall in absolute terms.

4. In its percentage to the total work force in the primary sector, OTAP shows a rise of 3.9% points from 1961-1971 and 6.1% points from 1971-1981. From 1981-1991 (TW), there was a marginal rise to 0.6 points. In percentage terms, OTAP has shown a rise from 1961-1991, though the rise from 1981-1991 is negligible.

Thus, from the above, we note that the total workforce in AP has been declining, both in absolute, as well as in percentage terms, from 1961-1991, whereas, in the case of OTAP, in absolute terms, it shows a fall from 1961-1971 and 1981-1991 but, a rise from 1971-1981. In percentage terms, the total workforce in OTAP to the total workforce in the primary sector, has been growing from 1961-1991, though rather slowly from 1981-1991.

We conclude from the above observations, that in Goa, Agriculture Proper still continues to employ the bulk of the labour force *i.e.* 77.2% in 1991, but, the employment in this sub-sector is declining, unlike that in OTAP which shows a growing trend. So we conclude that, within the Primary Sector, the people are increasingly being employed in OTAP as compared to AP.

Table 2 shows the sex distribution of the Total workforce in the Primary Sector as well as the sub-sectors.

From the table we observe the following:

1. The male workforce in the primary sector, shows a fall in absolute terms from 1961-1991, but a rise in its percentage to the total workforce in the primary sector.

2. In percentage terms, it increased by 15.3% points from 1961-1971 and negligibly by 0.2% points from 1961-1971 (Main). From 1981-1991 (TW) the increase was 1.3% points.

3. The female workforce in the primary sector also shows a fall in absolute terms from 1961-1991, as well as in percentage terms.

4. In percentage terms it fell by 15.3% points from 1961-1971 and by 0.2% points in 1971-1981 (Main) and from 1981-1991 (TW) it fell by 1.3% points.

Thus from the above observations, we conclude that the female workforce in the primary sector, has been declining both in absolute as well as percentage terms from 1961-1981, whereas, the male workforce has been

Table 2: Sex Distribution of the Workforce Trends in the Primary Sector and its Main Sub-Sectors.

Year	*Total Workforce in the Primary Sector*			*Total Workforce in AP*			*Total Workforce in OTAP*		
	M	*F*	*Total*	*M*	*F*	*Total*	*M*	*F*	*Total*
1961	88,546 (51.5)	835,547 (48.5)	172,093 (100)	66,394 (46.7)	755,702 (53.3)	142,096 (100)	22,152 (73.8)	7,845 (26.2)	29,997 (100)
1971	83,856 (66.8)	41,692 (33.2)	125,548 (100)	61,975 (62.7)	36,840 (37.3)	98,815 (100)	21,881 (81.9)	4,852 (18.1)	26,733 (100)
1981 Main	82,230 (67)	40,270 (33)	122,500 (100)	53,775 (60)	35,157 (40)	88,932 (100)	28,455 (84.8)	5,113 (15.2)	33,568 (100)
Marginal	8,976 (24)	28,562 (76)	37,538 (100)	7,959 (22.4)	27,552 (77.6)	35,511 (100)	1,017 (50.2)	1,010 (49.8)	2,027 (100)
Total	**91,206 (57)**	**68,832 (43)**	**160,038 (100)**	**61,734 (49.6)**	**62,709 (50.4)**	**1,24,443 (100)**	**29,472 (82.8)**	**6,123 (17.2)**	**35,595 (100)**
1991 Main	81,008 (65.4)	42,853 (34.6)	123,861 (100)	54,370 (59.2)	37,442 (40.8)	91,812 (100)	26,638 (83)	5,411 (17)	32,049 (100)
Marginal	4,734 (20.5)	18,365 (79.5)	23,099 (100)	4,179 (19.3)	17,420 (80.7)	21,599 (100)	555 (37)	945 (63)	1,500 (100)
Total	**85,742 (58.3)**	**61,218 (41.7)**	**1,46,960 (100)**	**58,549 (51.6)**	**54,862 (48.4)**	**1,13,411 (100)**	**27,193 (81)**	**6,356 (19)**	**33,549 (100)**

Source: Census of India, Goa Daman and Diu, Economic Table, 1961, 1971, 1981, 1991.

Note: AP - Agriculture Proper
OTAP - Other Than Agriculture Proper

declining in absolute terms, but shows a rise in its percentage terms. So we conclude that, more males are increasingly finding employment in the primary sector compared to females.

5. In Agriculture Proper, we note that the male workforce shows a declining trend in absolute terms from 1961-1991, and, a rising trend in percentage terms. From 1961-1971, there was a rise of 16% points in the male workforce in Agriculture Proper. From 1971-1981 (Main) there was a fall of 2.7% points. From 1981-1991 (TW) there was a rise of 2% points.

6. With regard to female workers, we note a fall in absolute terms from 1961-1991, as well as in percentage terms, except from the decade 1971-1981, where there is a rise in percentage terms. We also note that there are more female marginal workers in Agriculture Proper than males.

Thus, we conclude that, more males are finding employment in Agriculture Proper than females from 1961-1991 and there are a higher percentage of females engaged as marginal workers in Agriculture Proper.

7. In Other Than Agriculture Proper, we also note a fall in absolute terms in the male workforce, with the exception of the decade 1971-1981 and a rise in percentage terms. In the case of the female workforce, there is a fall in absolute terms from 1961-1971, but, a rise from 1971-1981 and 1981-1991. In percentage terms, there is a fall from 1961-1971 of 8.1% points and 2.9% points from 1971-1981 (Main). However, there was a rise of 1.8% points from 1981-1991 (TW).

We conclude from the above that, through the female workforce showed a fall in percentage terms in Other Than Agriculture Proper from 1961-1981, unlike the male workforce, which showed a rise, it has shown a rise from 1981-1991, both in percentage, as well as, in absolute terms in Other Than Agriculture Proper unlike the male workforce, which showed a fall both in absolute and percentage terms from 1981-1991 (TW). This shows that, within the primary sector, there is a rising percentage as well as absolute numbers of the female workforce in Other Than Agriculture Proper, as compared to the male workforce.

Summary of Conclusions in Section I.

1. In Goa, Agriculture Proper (AP), still continues to employ the bulk of the labour force in the primary sector but, at a declining rate.
2. Other Than Agriculture Proper (OTAP) shows a growing trend in employment, leading us to conclude that, within the Primary Sector, the workforce is increasingly being employed in OTAP as compared to AP.
3. More males are increasingly finding employment in the primary sector compared to females.
4. Within the Primary Sector, more males as well as females are employed in AP from 1961-1991, but from 1981-1991 (TW) an increasing percentage of females are employed in OTAP than males.

Intra-Sectoral Distribution of the Workforce and its Sex Distribution

In this section we will consider the distribution of the total workforce in the various sub-sectors in the primary sector. We consider here figures from 1971-1991 as separate figures for mining and quarrying, livestock, fishery etc. are not available in 1961.

Table 3: Intra-Sectoral Distribution of the Workforce in the Primary Sector in Goa.

Year	*TWF in Agriculture Proper (AP)*		*TWF in Other Than Agriculture Proper (OATP)*		*TWF in the primary sector*
	As agricultural Labourers	*As Cultivators*	*In Mining & Quarrying*	*In Forestry, Fishery, Livestock, Plantation, Orchards & Allied Activities*	
1961	37,957 (22.1)	104,139 (60.5)	–	–	172,093 (100)
1971	38,296 (30.5)	60,519 (48.2)	16,237 (12.9)	10,496 (8.4)	125,548 (100)
1981 Main	30,556 (25)	58,376 (47.6)	18.985 (15.4)	14,583 (12)	122,500 (100)
Marginal	16,039 (42.7)	19,472 (51.9)	405 (1.1)	1,623 (4.3)	37,538 (100)
Total	46,595 (29)	77,848 (48.6)	19,390 (12.1)	16,206 (10.1)	160,038 (100)
1991 Main	35,284 (28.5)	56,528 (45.6)	16,432 (13.3)	15,617 (12.6)	123,861 (100)
Marginal	9,491 (41.1)	12,108 (52.4)	250 (1.1)	1,250 (5.4)	23,099 (100)
Total	**44,775 (30.4)**	**68,636 (46.7)**	**16,682 (11.4)**	**16,867 (11.5)**	**1,46,960 (100**

Source: Census of India, Goa, Daman and Diu, Economic Tables, 1961, 1971, 1981 and 1991.

1. From 1971-1991, we note from the table that, a large percentage of the workforce in the primary sector has been employed as cultivators, though this percentage has shown a declining trend from 1971-1991. It has declined by 0.6% points from 1971-1981 (Main) and by 1.9% points from 1981-1991 (TW). In absolute terms, there has been a fall from 1971-1981(Main) and from 1981-1991 (TW).

2. The next sub-sector to employ a large percentage of the workforce in the primary sector is agricultural labourers. In this sub-sector, there was a fall of 5.5% points from 1971-1981 (Main) and a rise of 1.3% points from 1981-1991 (Main). In absolute terms, this sub-sector has shown a rise from 1971-1981 (Main) and a fall from 1981-1991 (TW).

3. The sub-sector of mining and quarrying showed a rise of 2.5% points from 1971-1981 (Main) and a fall of 0.7% points from 1981-1991 (TW). In absolute terms, this sub-sector has shown a rise from 1971-1981 (Main) and a fall from 1981-1991 (TW).

4. The sub-sector of forestry, fishery, livestock, plantations etc., showed a rise of 3.6% points from 1971-1981 (Main) and a rise of 1.4% points from 1981-1991 (TW). In absolute terms, this sub-sector has shown a rise from 1971-1981 (Main) as well as from 1981-1991 (TW), The only sub-sector to show a rise both in absolute as well as the percentage terms from 1971-1991.

From the above observations, we conclude that, within the primary sector, an increasing percentage of workers are finding employment in forestry, fishery, livestock, plantations, etc. The mining and quarrying sub-sector which other wise was the dominant sector with regard to employment in OTAP, has shown a declining trend in employment from 1961-1991 (TW). Angle P (2001) has observed that, the contribution of the mining industry to the State GDP, in relative terms, has been declining over the years. This could have a relation to the declining employment trend in this sector.

Table 4: Sex Distribution of the Infra-Sectoral Distribution of the Workforce in Goa.

Year	*TWF Engaged As Agricultural Labourers*		*TWF Engaged As Cultivators*		*TWF in mining & Quarrying*		*TWF in Forestry, Fishery, Livestock, Hunting, Plantation, Orchards & Allied Activities*		*TWF in the Primary Sector*
	M	*F*	*M*	*F*	*M*	*F*	*M*	*F*	*Total*
1971	20,076 (16)	18,220 (14.5)	41,899 (33.4)	18,620 (14.8)	12,634 (10.1)	3,603 (3)	9,247 (7.4)	1,249 (1)	125,548 (100)
1981 Main	16,454 (13.4)	14,102 (11.5)	37,321 (30.5)	21,055 (17.2)	16,036 (13.1)	2,949 (2.4)	12,419 (10)	2,164 (1.8)	122,500 (100)
Marginal	3,723 (10)	12,316 (32.8)	4,236 (11.3)	15,236 (40.6)	256 (0.7)	149 (0.4)	760 (2)	863 (2.3)	37,538 (100)
Total	20,177 (12.6)	26,418 (16.5)	41,557 (26)	36,291 (22.7)	16,292 (10.2)	3,098 (2)	13,179 (8.2)	3,027 (2)	160,038 (100)
1991 Main	19,169 (15.5)	16,115 (13)	35,201 (28.4)	21,327 (17.2)	13,184 (10.6)	3,248 (2.6)	13,454 (11)	2,163 (1.7)	123,861 (100)
Marginal	2,043 (9)	7,448 (32.2)	2,136 (9.2)	9,972 (43.2)	137 (0.6)	113 (0.5)	418 (2)	832 (3.6)	23,099 (100)
Total	**21,212 (14.4)**	**23,563 (16.1)**	**37,337 (25.4)**	**31,299 (21.3)**	**13,321 (9.1)**	**3,361 (2.3)**	**13,872 (9.4)**	**2,995 (2)**	**1,46,960 (100)**

Source: Census of India, Goa, Daman and Diu, Economic Tables, 1971, 1981, 1991.

The following observations can be drawn from Table No. 4.

1. The total male workforce in the primary sector working as agricultural labourers shows a fall from 1971-1981 (Main) in both absolute and percentage terms.

However, from 1981-1991 (TW) there is a rise in both absolute and percentage terms, in the total male workforce employed as agricultural labourers in the primary sector, From 1971-1981 (Main), there was a fall of 2.6% points. From 1981-1991 (TW) there was a 1.8% point rise.

2. As regards the female workforce engaged as agricultural labourers there was also a fall in absolute as well as in terms of percentage from 1971-1981 (Main). The percentage fall was 3% points for this decade. From 1981-1991 (TW), we note once again a fall in absolute as well as percentage terms. The percentage fall was negligible *i.e.* 0.3% points from 1981-1991 (TW).

We conclude from the above, that the percentage of the male workforce employed as agricultural labourers in the primary sector, shows a positive trend compared to that of the female from 1981-1991 (TW) though there was a fall from 1971-1991 (Main).

3. The total male workforce working a cultivators in the primary sector, shows a decline both in absolute as well as percentage terms, from 1971-1981 (Main). It declined by 2.9% points from 1971-1981 (Main). From 1981-1991 (TW), we also note a fall in both absolute as well as in terms of percentage. The fall in percentage terms was marginal i.e. 0.6% points from 1981-1991 (TW).

We conclude that a lower percentage of males are employed as cultivators in the primary sector.

4. With regard to the female workforce employed as cultivators in the primary sector, we note that there was a rise both in absolute and percentage terms from 1971-1981 (Main). The rise was 2.4% points from 1971-1981. From 1981-1991 (TW), we note a fall in both absolute as well as percentage terms in the total female workforce employed as cultivators in the primary sector. The fall was 1.4% point from 1981-1991 (TW).

Thus, we conclude that the percentage of females employed as cultivators have also declined in the primary sector. However, we note that, from 1971-1991 (Main), there has been a fall in the percentage of the male workforce engaged as both, agricultural labourers as well as cultivators, but a rise in the percentage of the female workforce in the case of cultivators.

5. The total male workforce employed in the sub-sector of mining and quarrying rose both in absolute as well as percentage terms from

1971-1981 (Main). In percentage terms, the rise was by 3% points for this period. However, from 1981-1991 (TW), there was a fall both in absolute as well as percentage terms. The fall in percentage terms was by 1.1% point.

6. With regard to the female workforce employed in mining and quarrying in the primary sector, we note a fall both in absolute and percentage terms from 1971-1981 (Main). In percentage terms, the fall was by 0.6% points. From 1981-1991, we note a rise in the absolute number as well as percentage of the female workforce in mining and quarrying, although, the rise was marginal. In percentage terms, it was 0.3% point. From the above, we conclude that, although, the absolute number and percentage of males employed in mining and quarrying, continues to be higher than that of the females, their absolute number and percentage is decreasing from 1981-1991 (TW).

7. In the sub-sector of forestry, fishery, livestock, hunting, plantations, orchards and allied activities, we note that, the total male workforce in the primary sector employed here, rose both in absolute as well as percentage terms from 1971-1991. From 1971-1981 (Main) the rise was by 2.6% points and from 1981-1991 (TW), it was by 1.2% point. This is the only sub-sector in the primary sector, that shows a rise in both absolute and percentage terms in the male workforce from 1971-1991.

We conclude from the above, that in OTAP, this sector is emerging as the main employer for males overtaking mining and quarrying.

8. With regard to the female workforce in this sub-sector, we note a rise in absolute as well as percentage terms from 1971-1981 (Main). The percentage rise was 0.8% point. However, from 1981-1991 (TW), we note a marginal fall in absolute terms and the percentage remained the same *i.e.* 2%.

We conclude from the above, that the highest percentage of males in the primary sector are employed as cultivators, followed by agricultural labourers, forestry, fishery, livestock etc. and then in mining and quarrying. The highest percentage of females are found engaged as cultivators, followed by agricultural labourers, mining and quarrying and then forestry, fishery, livestock etc.

The percentage of the male workforce in the primary sector in forestry, fishery, livestock etc. shows a rise from 1971-1981 (Main), whereas in the case of females the rise in the case of cultivators, and forestry, livestock, fishery, etc. from 1971-1991 (Main).

Policy Implications

We have noted in this paper that, although, agriculture proper in the primary sector, still employs a large percentage of the workforce as per the 1991 census data, the percentage of employment here is decreasing and more people are finding employment in 'Other Than Agriculture Proper' (OTAP). Normally, this would be welcomed, but, in the case of Goa, this shift of the workforce is not because agriculture has developed and therefore, requires relatively less workers but, because it was found to be a low remuneration employment.

Agriculture is a much neglected sector in Goa. Angle P. (2001) states that, "although statistically over 60% of Goa's working population was engaged in agricultural pursuits, this sector contributed hardly 16 per cent of the state's income in 1960. Even four decades later, the position in this regard is no different then what it was in pre-liberation days and the contribution of agriculture to Goa's Net Domestic Product is around 15 per cent, whereas at the national level, it contributes around 30 per cent of the national product." This is indicative of the fact that, the Government of Goa has to take strong measures to encourage agricultural development in Goa.

The Tenancy Act of 1964 has been largely responsible for this scenario. The aims of the Act were noble *i.e.* to provide security to the tenants and thus induce them to increase production, by making them the owners of the land they cultivate. But this goal has not been met as, many tenants did not cultivate that land except a small area that would produce for their home consumption. The lands have many a times been kept fallow and subsequently sold for non-agricultural purposes at a high market price. This legislation also resulted in small size of operational holdings as, the land was divided among the tenants. Infact, the Agricultural Census of 1990-1991 shows that 81% of holdings are under 1.0 hectare. As long as this prevails, agriculture in Goa will suffer. So an effort has to be made to consolidate these holdings in the form of co-operatives and make production more economically viable. This can be a step the Government of Goa can take to increase agricultural productivity in the state and make agriculture a more lucrative avenue of employment.

It is no doubt a healthy trend that employment in OTAP has increased from 1961-1991, but the percentage of the total workforce in the primary sector employed here is still very low *i.e.* 22.8% in 1991. In OTAP, Mining and Quarrying and Forestry, Fishery, Livestock etc. are the two sectors considered. From 1961-1981 a higher percentage of the workforce was engaged in Mining and Quarrying in OTAP but in 1991, this percentage declined compared to Forestry, Fishery etc. and this is not surprising. Minerals are a non-replenishable resource and as mining has gone on for the last so many years the possibility is always there of a depletion in this resource. So, we cannot always rely on this sub-sector for employment. Besides, mining poses an environmental risk, as it is ecologically unfriendly. Very often, large excavations of the over-burden and rejects are dumped on surrounding land, resulting in adverse on forestry and agriculture. Forestry, fishery, livestock, plantation and other allied activities should be developed, so that people can increasingly find employment in this sub-sector.

The fishery sector can be developed to provide more employment opportunities. Goa, with a coastline of 105 kms., inland waterways and a good number of tanks, is capable of producing quantities of fish, that can satisfy the requirements of the locals as well as areas across the borders. Data shows that, export of marine products from Goa has shown a decline over the period 1994-1999. The quantity has decreased from 17,153 tons in 1994 to 9,054 tons in 1992. This has to be looked into and measures have to be taken to reverse the trend.

Sugarcane, rubber and oil palm are the chief commercial crops of Goa. Their production should be increased by suitable incentives. This can be another source of revenue for the government and employment for the people.

Forests in Goa suffered losses due to the cultivation by cumerins[1] which was carried out by burning the trees and using the ash to turn the land fertile and also by mining activity. Forests can be a source of revenue, besides its importance in maintaining the ecological balance of the place can by no means be undermined.

Conclusions

We therefore conclude that, in Goa, there is a shift in the employment pattern in the primary sector from 1961-1991. We find that an increasing number of people in the Primary Sector, are finding employment in OTAP as compared to Agriculture Proper. In OTAP, the sub-sector of Forestry, Fishery, Plantations, Livestock etc. is providing more employment compared to Mining and Quarrying.

With regard to the sex distribution, we find that more males are employed in both Agriculture Proper as well as in OTAP from 1961-1991. Within OTAP, males as well as females are increasingly finding employment in Forestry, Fishery, Livestock, Plantations etc. from 1971-1991 (Main).

NOTES

1. System of burning the wood

REFERENCES

1. Angle P., (2001), Goa: An Economic Update, The Goa Hindu Association, Kala Vibhag, Mumbai.
2. Almeida J.C. (1967), Aspects of the Agricultural Activity in Goa, Daman and Diu, Govt. Printing Press, Panaji, Goa.
3. Director of Census Operations, Census of India, 1961, 1971, 1981, Goa, Daman and Diu, Economic Tables.
4. Director of Census Operations, Census of India, 1991, Goa, Economic Tables.

31

Poverty Alleviation Programmes and Wasteland Development in India with Special Reference to Karnataka

Dr. C.K. Renukarya*
Dr. B. Gopal Singh**

Absolute poverty is a curse on society where as relative poverty is a soothing concept. There is a controversy in India in the 1990's, over using national accounts statistics (NAS) estimate of private final consumption expenditure (PFCE) in place of NSS based estimate for calculating the proportion of the population below poverty line or head count ratio. The greater availability of NSS data sets has prompted a flurry of studies of poverty in India. The statistics of poverty are not as A.K. Sen once remarked an issue for 'Unleashing one's personal morals' (1981: 17) yet they seem to become a stone on which many people are happy to grind their axes.' The problem is that all sources of statistics have their strength and weaknesses.

The following table shows the population below the poverty line in few part of the world.

The data up to 1993-94 is based on Dr. Lakdawala group, Planning commission, for 1996-97 and 2001-02 are based on planning commission projections, for 1993-94 state wise data on population below poverty line indicates that Bihar (55%) & Orissa (48.6%) had highest percentage, where as Punjab (11.8%) & Delhi (14.7%) had lowest percentage of population below

*Prof. of Economics, PG Studies, *Manasagangothri, Mysore.*
***Prof. of Economics, G.F.G.C. Sira.*

1996-2000 Population Below Poverty Line in a Few Parts of the World.

Region	*1990 (Millions)*	*2000 (Millions)*
South Asia	526	511
East Asia	169	73
Sub-Sahara Africa	216	304
East & North Africa Region	73	89
Latin America & Carribean	108	126
Total	**1092**	**1103**

Source: Technical report, Second Ed. F.A.O. *Conf.* 1996.

The Following Table Shows the Population Below Poverty Line in India.

	2001-02	*1996-97*	*1993-94*	*1987-88*	*1973-74*
No. of Poor (Mn.)					
Rural	137.5	210.0	244.0	231.9	261.3
Urban	44.5	63.0	76.3	75.2	60.0
Total	**182.0**	**273.0**	**320.3**	**307.0**	**321.3**
Poverty Ratio (%)					
Rural	18.6	30.5	37.3	39.1	56.4
Urban	16.6	25.6	32.4	38.2	49.2
Total	**35.2**	**56.1**	**69.7**	**77.3**	**105.6**

poverty line. In case of Karnataka it was 33.2% which is little below the National average of 36%. The percentage of families below poverty line in Karnataka was 56.69% as per BPL survey conducted during the 8th plan period. At that point of time families with an income of less than Rs. 1100/ annum were classified as families below the poverty line.

In this paper an attempt is made to examine the poverty alleviation programmes mainly the wasteland development and poverty alleviation with special reference to Karnataka.

There are many poverty alleviation programmes in Karnataka which have attempted to generate income and employment. Some of them are CDP, (Community Development programme) IRDP, (Integrated Rural Development Programme) NREP, (National Rural Employment Programme) RLEGP, (Rural Landless Employment Guarantee Programme) TRYSEM (Training Rural Youth for Self Employment) EGS, (Employment Guarantee Scheme) RWCD, (Rural Women & Children Development) Development of SC/ST's, SEU (Self

Employment for educated un-employed) SFDA, (Small Farmers Development Agency) (Now renamed as District Rural Development Agency) MFAL, (Marginal Farmers and Agricultural Labourers Development Agency) JRY, (Jawahar Rozgar Yojana) PMRY, (Prime Minister's Rozgar Yojana) NRY, (Nehru Rozgar Yojana) SJSRY, (Swarna Jayanthi Shahari Rozgar Yojana) SGSY, (Swarna Jayanthi Grama Swarozgar Yojana) DDP, (Desert Development Programme) MNP, (Minimum Needs Programme) 20 points Programme, Vishwa Plan, Ashraya plan, RWP, (Rural Work Programme) IDLAD, (Integrated Dryland Agriculture Development) ADS, (Area Development Scheme) CPRE, (Crash Programme for Rural Employment) OFDD, (Operation Flood Dairy Development) HADP, (Hill Area Development Programme) Anthodaya, CAPART and finally the new avenue wasteland development in which this paper probes in to.

Wasteland Development Programmes in India and Karnataka have to some extent generated income and employment for not only rural poor but also for the urban poor.

The three important aims of Wasteland Development Programmes are Food, Fuel, and Fodder, in turn it will generate income and employment.

The total geographical area of India is about 329 million hectares, poverty women drudgery, environment and ecology are all inextricably linked with the conditions of productivity of wasteland. According to Agarwal "Wastelands are those lands which are producing much less than their potential", they are not utilised to their full potential and their productivity could be increased by making reasonable efforts and investment. Different types of wastelands are gullies, upland, waterlogged, salt affected, shifting cultivation, degraded forest land, pastures, striplands, sands, mining spoils, barren rocky, snowcovered area, fallow lands, wind erosion etc., The estimates of wasteland in India differs to a great extent, Ministry of Agriculture and Co-operation, New Delhi estimated it as high as 175 million hectares (53.2%) where as National Commission on Agriculture and Irrigation, Govt., of India has estimated it as 45 M.H. (13.7%). National Wasteland Development Board put it as 123 M.H. (37.5%), NRSA has estimated it as 53.3 M.H. (16.2%). We should note that 'No land is wasteland'. The sustainable development needs ecological balance and increase in net sown area and reclamation of wastelands.

In case of Karnataka the total geographical area is 1,91,77000 Hectares, the wasteland details are as follows:

Category	*Hectares*
Salt affected land	32400
Gullied and ravinous land	78900
Upland with or without scrub	1182400
Jhum or forest blanks	79900
Sandy area	1300
Barren/Rocky/Stony waste/Sheet rock	268000
Total	**1642900**

But the reported wasteland is only 1,38,300 Hectares.

During 80's the annual growth rate of Karnataka was 5.1% as against 5.4% in the country. Under wage employment programme in Karnataka 48% of the 9th plan allocation amounting to Rs. 152 Crores (at 1996-97 prices) has been spent during the first three years of 9th plan. 3586 village tanks, 616 field channels, 6272 water harvesting structures under minor irrigation, 9944 road works, 10068 culverts, 4637 soil conservation works, 10643 school buildings, 6230 panchayat ghars/mahila mandals/anganawadi were executed and 75 lakh trees were planted in the first two years of 9th plan generating employment to the extent of 15 crore mandays (in 3 years) for tackling poverty directly. Under IRDP 1.5 lakh families provided with income generating assets through subsidy and institutional credit. 25826 youths were trained under TRYSEM, 4177 groups were assisted under DWCRA to take up income generating activities. 23758 artisans were provided with improved tool kits, 6.4 lakh beneficiaries were covered under rural group life insurance scheme.

SGSY aims at assisting poor families above the poverty line and it has been targeted to cover 30% of the poor in each block in the next five years, it ensures that beneficiary families are assured monthly income of atleast Rs. 2,000.

As per the economic survey 1994-95 of Govt. of Karnataka there has been marginal improvement in employment during 1994-95. Integrated rural

Dryland Development (Area covered)

(Lakh Hectares)

Year	*Within the water shed*	*Outside the water shed*	*Total*
1992-93	1.770	0.140	1.910
1993-94	2.710	0.100	2.810
1994-95	2.410	0.120	2.530

Source: Director of Agriculture (Soil conservation) GOK.

development programme was the most important institutional credit linked programme for poverty alleviation. Karnataka is predominantly a dry farming state, hence importance is given to wasteland development. The following table indicates the achievements in dryland development and soil conservation in Karnataka.

The area covered under soil conservation is as follows

(Lakh Hectares)

Year	*During the Year*	*Cumulative*
1991-92	0.48	36.47
1994-95	1.92	41.26
1997-98	1.30	45.13
1998-99	1.42	46.55
1999-2000 (A)	1.14	47.69

Source: Director of Agriculture, (Soil conservation) GOK.

Command Area Development Programme in Karnataka has also provided income and employment, Command Area Development Programme for Karnataka for the Year 1997-98 to 1999-2000 is given below:

(000 Hectares)

	Item of work	*1994-95*	*1997-98*	*1998-99*	*1999-2000 (A)*
1.	Construction of field Irrigation channels	48.03	11.03	10.53	11.94
2.	Land levelling	39.12	18.82	17.63	19.10
3.	Construction of field drains	15.38	0.25	3.05	5.94
4.	Warabandhi	39.23	16.23	8.23	12.10

Source: Irrigation Department GOK.

Social forestry in Karnataka has contributed much towards the wasteland development in turn generated income and employment in rural areas. The following table indicates the revenue realised and expenditure on forestry...

(Rs. Crores)

Year	*Revenue*	*Expenditure*
1992-93	68.35	111.90
1994-95	86.72	94.73
1997-98	112.740	205.870
1998-99	106.170	283.050
1999-2000 (A)	100.00	295.00

Source: Forest Department, GOK.

Social Forestry is assumed to be a source of poverty alleviation programme and the wastelands are used for social forestry purposes. The additional area brought under forestry in Karnataka is as follows:

(In Hectares)

	1997-98	*1998-99*	*1999-2000*
Eucalyptus plantations	1090	1252	1300
Teak Plantations	1986	2170	2200
Miscellaneous plantations	40929	86158	86025
Canal & Avenue plantations (Km's)	2521	3441	2400

Source: Forest Department GOK.

Farm forestry is said to be more useful in Karnataka in wasteland development and in poverty alleviation. Irrigation works have also provided a source of income and contribute towards development of wastelands.

Most of the externally aided projects under wasteland development have assured income in Karnataka. Karnataka state has good potential for wasteland development which is clear from the following table.

Arable land in Karnataka, India & world

(1000 Hectares)

Sl. No.	*Item*	*World*	*India*	*Karnataka*
1.	Total Geographical Area	1,33,92,798	3,28,727	19050
2.	Arable Land`	13,71,618	1,64,850	11972
3.	Percentage of Arable land to Geographical Area	10	50	63

Source: Fertilizer Statistics: 1984-85.

Basically there are two types of wastelands in Karnataka such as culturable and un-culturable wastelands.

Comprehensive land use management project is in vogue in Karnataka. Karnataka has many successful watershed development programmes such as Kabbalanala, Kalyana kere-Mavathur kere, Chitravathi, Bindehalli-Lokapavani, Hirehalla & Devihalla & Mittemari project etc.

Employment generation is possible through ravine reclamation, sodic-land reclamation, afforestation, people's participation is very much required in these programmes.

A survey has been conducted by the authors in three districts of Karnataka state viz. Hassan, Mandya & Tumkur Districts, the results are as follows.

The reasons for leaving the land fallow are many viz. laziness, failure of rains, labour problems, lack of water facilities. Many farmers accept that afforestation has succeeded in greening wastelands, soil and water conservation measures by government have not helped them, they believe that construction of check dams, gully-plugging, cross cultivation, farm forestry, use of cowdung as manure, contour bunds, planting of Khus grass, soil testing will go a long way in wasteland development.

In India various models have been built such as using Remote Sensing Technology for identification of wastelands, wasteland mapping, participatory approach *i.e.* Ralegon Siddi model, model of water resource management, technology for Arid regions and sodic wasteland management, Agro-forestry model with integration of domesticated birds, growing of medicinal plants, wasteland development by women's groups such as 'SARTHI', Mittemari project in Karnataka, watershed approach, use of Bio-fertilizer, ravinous land management of Chambal valley, Bhoomisena project, community land watershed management of Shivalik hills etc.,

Watershed is no doubt best method for wasteland development but it does not mean that only Agricultural lands which are waste has to be developed, it involves that wastelands lying in canal beds, both sides of Roads & Railways, rocky lands, backyards of residential houses have to be developed. We have to keep in mind as said earlier 'No land is wasteland.' These programmes invariably reduce the poverty level of the masses.

In May 1985 National land use Board was reconstituted at the centre as the National land use and wasteland development council. Two Boards were setup to function under the council such as (*i*) National Land use and Conservation Board (*ii*) The National Wasteland Development Board. The council is the highest policy planning and co-ordinating agency for all issues concerning the proper management of country's land resources.

Various technologies have to be developed which should be ecologically effective, economically desirable and socially acceptable. The technology for the development of wastelands may differ according to the type of wastelands and degree of limiting factors.

There are certain research gaps in wasteland development which has to be filled up by appropriate research. Research on silvipasture methods, suitable tree species, planting geometry, spacing etc., and suitable shade tolerant grasses to maximise production is necessary.

Detailed statistics/data has to be prepared on the different category of wastelands, there is an urgent need for microlevel planning. Usufruct benefits should be assured. There is a need for perspective plan for next 10 to 15 years for wasteland development. There should be a co-ordinating authority to co-ordinate the activities of all the departments in wasteland development. Wasteland maps should be prepared at taluk level, conversion of agricultural lands for Non-agricultural purposes should be halted. Farmers should be encouraged to form their Co-operative society to develop their wastelands and make further arrangements for processing and marketing. Soft loans should be provided, NGO's should also be involved, proper land use policy needed in Karnataka. Tribals/Poor/SC/ST's rights of common lands should be protected. Government Departments/KSRTC/Railway etc., should cover their un-utilised land with greencover.

Fly-ash can be used for salt-affected lands, Carribean stylo legume can be grown in wastelands, edible cactus can also be grown in wastelands, JoJoba is a new desert gold which can be grown in wastelands. National symposium should be conducted on the proper use of wastelands, desilting of canals has to made, further settlements of Industry, roads should be only on wastelands. Awareness should be created among people regarding wasteland development. Natural resource management committees should be started in all the villages, there must be proper grasing policy. The dried stem of cotton, Jowar, Wheat, Pulses, Coconut and Betelnut leaves should be converted in to briquettes as alternate fuel.

It is earnestly hoped that the above suggestions are implemented the wasteland development takes place quickly in the state along with its concomitment purposes of employment generation and poverty alleviation.

REFERENCES

1. *Abhalakshmi Singh (1985)*: 'The Problems of wastelands in India' B.R. Publishers, New Delhi.
2. *Adisheshaiah Malcom (Ed.) 1989*: 'Economics of Wasteland Development' Lancer, New Delhi.
3. *Bali. B.S. (1972)*: 'Ravine Reclamation Needs for India' New Delhi.
4. *Government of India (1961)*: 'Report on the Location & Utilisation of Waste Land Development' part X, U.P. New-Delhi.
5. *Government of India (1986)*: 'Guidelines for Microlevel Planning' NWDB, New Delhi.
6. *Government of Indià (1988)*: *'National Land Use Policy Outline-Action Points'* National Land use and Conservation Board, New Delhi.
7. *Government of Karnataka*: *'Statistical Outline of Karnataka'* Director of Economics & Statistics, 1989-90, 1996-97, Bangalore.

8. *Government of Karnataka*: *'Karnataka at a Glance'* 1995-96, 1999-2000, Director of Economics and Statistics, Bangalore.
9. *Government of Karnataka: 'Approach Plan for Wasteland Development in Karnataka'* Forest department, Aranya Bhavan, Bangalore.
10. *Madhava Gadgil & N.H. Ravindranath*: *'Draft Guideline for Microlevel Planning for Integrated Development of Wastelands*, IISc Bangalore.
11. *Rohit Shukla:* 'Focus on Wasteland Development' Economic Times, April 3, 1995.
12. *Statistical Outline of India*: 1990-2000, TATA Services Ltd., Department of Economics and Statistics, Mumbai.
13. *Seminar Proceedings:* 'Seminar on Opportunities and Problems of Wasteland Development', "Wasteland News", Vol. I, No. 2, November 1985, Jan. 1986.

32

Human Development

An Alternative Paradigm to Combat Poverty

Dr. (Mrs.) B Shyamala*

The first Prime Minister Pandit Jawaharlal Nehru in his speech in the Constituent Assembly at the midnight of the day of independence said "the service of India means the service of the millions who suffer. It means the ending of poverty, ignorance, diseases and inequality of opportunity". Ironically even after fifty years of independence the distributive justice and economic equality have remained a distance dream. Though the concept of poverty, measurement of poverty and magnitude of poverty are outside the purview of this paper it is better to discuss the same briefly.

The estimates of poverty in India is clearly given in the Table 1.

Table 1: Population Below Poverty Line (%).

Areas	*1977-78*	*1983-84*	*1987-88*	*1990-91*	*1992-93*	*1994-95*
Rural	51.2	40.4	33.3	19.7	22.9	19.3
Urban	38.2	28.1	20.1	10.8	13.0	9.5
Combined	48.3	37.4	29.9	17.4	20.3	16.6

Source: Govt. of India, Planning Commission, VII Five Year Plan.

The Planning Commission has attributed its achievement of bringing down the over all poverty ratio from 48.3 in 1977-78 to 16.6 in 1994-95 mainly

* M.A. Ph.D., Reader and Head of the Dept. Post Graduate Department of Economics, Fatima College (Autonomous), Mary Land. Madurai-625 018, Tamil Nadu.

due to the higher rate of growth, increased agricultural production and a sustained effort in providing employment. However some economists have raised serious doubts about the claims of the Planning Commission. Mihas, Jain and Tendulkar have estimated the overall poverty ratio as 48.1 in 1983-84 and 45.9 in 1987-88. Whatever be the discrepancy in the estimates of poverty ratio, a large gap exists between haves and have nots in the rural areas are still drawers of water and hewears of wood and a majority of them are living under abject poverty. Recently the World Bank Report says that three out of four Indians and 77% of the Indians are poor. Inspite of the persistent was against poverty for fifty long years the poor remain poorer. If we probe into this matter, seriously we may be able to find a solid reason. All the anti poverty programmes in India are lacking the human touch. i.e. human resources are totally neglected. Hence the development of human resources is the only way to combat poverty in India.

The intention of this paper is to draw attention of the planners and policy makers towards the urgency of the situation and to study seriously the possible strategies for escaping from poverty which is multidimensional in character. Development of human resources which is one such dimensions of poverty reduction is emphasised in this paper. In other words this paper has tried to establish a synergistic relationship between development of social sector and poverty reduction. The paper is organised in such a manner that the first part concentrates on concept of poverty, treatment of poverty during five year plans and evaluation of Anti poverty programmes. The second part deals with the need for attention towards Human Development, human poverty index in India, Govt.'s role in addressing human development in India and finally the policy issues are suggested. The sources of data are mostly from Human Development Reports and Reports of Planning Commission.

Treatment of Poverty During Five Year Plans

Though the First Five Year Plan (1951-56) noted the social and economic inequalities, the real planning starts only with the Second Five Year Plan (1956-61). In tune with Bombay Plan and Mahalanobis model a strategy of industrialisation was set out with a combined emphasis on reduction in social and economic inequalities. The Third Five Year Plan (1961-66) was committed to a socialist pattern of society. The Fourth Plan (1969-74) talked of improvement in the conditions of the Common man and the weaker sections, through a recognition of small farmers and landless labourers. Despite of all the attached sentiments for the weaker sections the number of the poor continued to swell in the country. The Parliamentary election of 1971 brought into sharp focus on the problem of poverty through a powerful slogan Garibi

Hatao (Remove Poverty). A clear cut diagnosis of poverty was made during the Fifth Five Year Plan (1974-79). This Plan identified that unemployment, under-employment and low resource base of multitudes in agriculture are the causes of poverty. The so called 20 point programme was launched. The Sixth Plan (1980-85) defined poverty in terms of calorie consumption and also defined poverty line on the basis of recommended nutritional requirements of 2400 calorie per person per day for rural areas and 2100 calorie for the urban areas. The Seventh Plan (1985-90) started reviewing the impact of Anti poverty programmes. It was suggested that the process of economic growth and anti poverty programmes have made a significant dent in the problem of poverty. This is clearly given in the Table 2.

Table 2: Impact of Poverty During Sixth and Seventh Five Year Plans.

Year	*No. of poor (million)*		
	Rural	*Urban*	*Total*
1977-78	253 (51.2)	54 (38.2)	307 (48.3)
1984-85	222 (39.9)	51 (27.7)	273 (36.9)
1989-90	169 (28.2)	42 (19.3)	211 (25.8)

Source: Planning Commission, Seventh Five Year Plan. Vol. 1, p. 23.
Figures in parenthesis indicate percentage.

The Eighth Five Year Plan (1992-97) pursued employment oriented strategy through special employment programmes such as IRDP, JRY and NRY. But these programmes met the short term objective of providing temporary work to the unemployed. This would be better achieved by a greater integration of the existing special employment programmes with other sectoral programmes. The Ninth Plan (1997-2002) relies essentially on the trickle down effects of economic growth for poverty alleviation. It nevertheless recognises the role of anti poverty programmes. This plan has tried to alleviate poverty through PDS. According to the Ninth Plan projections, the planners are too optimistic and hope to practically eliminate poverty by the year 2012 A.D. This would require a transfer of consumption expenditure from the top 10 per cent to the bottom 10 per cent of the population. Though the Ninth Plan has desired to have such transfer but has not suggested the mechanism for such transfers.

Evaluation of Poverty Alleviation Programme

A careful examination of the poverty alleviation programmes reveals that the planners have made the assumption that the poor constitute a homogeneous category. The planners made no attempt to segment the group in terms of common characters an their requirements. Moreover the attempts of poverty alleviation in our country has been a general guided by the dominant view that poverty could best be addressed by raising the economic standards of the poor through the 'tickle down effect' of economic growth at macro level. They continued their poverty alleviation efforts with emphasis on GNP growth. But the situation remained unchanged and the number of poor kept on mounting. Many reasons can be attributed for this state on affairs.

1. The concept and measurement of poverty have arrived at controversial conclusions. The systematic study of concept, measurement and estimate of poverty has been tried since 1960. In fact estimation depends on techniques of measurement and conceptualisation of poverty. The methodologies of poverty measurement have been changed over years.

2. Surveying the development scenario obtained in the villages, it is felt that the whole effort become state sponsored and people's participation remained just a slogan. It is surprising that in our anxiety to reduce the level of rural poverty. We become unconcerned with providing the basic minimum services to the people.

3. The income and expenditure generation of poverty alleviation programme do not recognise the importance of increased flow of social inputs through family welfare, nutrition, social security and minimum needs programme in alleviating condition of poverty on a long term basis.

4. These programmes have done little for disabled, sick, socially handicapped individuals who can not participate in formal economic activities. The strategy for poverty alleviation has also foiled to do justice to women in intra-family distributions.

5. The Government has failed to make necessary changes in anti-poor laws and policies.

6. Poverty alleviation programmes often ignore the consequences of the earning activities of the poor in terms of occupational health hazards and adverse ecological consequences.

7. In the exploitation of Government schemes, the non-poor are also included in the poor class. Thus the per capita income and income norms fail to identity the proportion of people living below the poverty line. So techniques like inequality of income, calorie intake and consumption expenditure have been earmarked for the purpose.

8. Anti poverty programmes such as IRDP and NREP are basically employment oriented or security based, they are essentially adhoc and not well designed or planned. IRDP is a bureaucratic programme in which innumerable steps involved and lacks sincerity at all operational levels. Though IRDP is the Kingpin of anti-poverty programmes it is neither integrated nor related to rural development.
9. The National policy measures so far implemented in the area of poverty reduction are not based on pragmatism or practical experience. Most of the policies are influenced by the political manifestoes of the various political parties at the State and the Centre. As a result the development programmes lack practical approach, inappropriate policies and selling of unrealistic goals and targets.
10. Many studies have highlighted the shade of administration in the failure of anti poverty programmes. Some of the important factors are: poor and defective planning, poor management, supervision, guidance, control, follow up, lack of qualified or trained staff, frequent transfers of officials and vacancy of key posts.
11. Slow process of technology, non-recognition of appropriate technology, and indigenous technology, high cost of technology and non availability of appropriate technology in right place and in right time, have contributed towards the not-so satisfactory performance of anti poverty programmes in India.
12. Negative characters that affect the success of rural development programmes are caste, authoritation background and traditional joint family system have seriously affected the country's anti poverty programmes.
13. Anti poverty programmes are highly politicised, intervention of political interests, political intervention in selection and identification of beneficiaries, prevalence of high degree of corruption, and political pressures on various agencies.
14. Leakage in anti-poverty programmes obstructs the success of these programmes. It is to be admitted that out of every Rs. 100 earmarked for welfare, only about Rs. 15 reached the poor. The rest of the money is spent on meeting official expenses, bribing middlemen and perpetuating social exploitation.
15. A major limitation of existing poverty alleviation strategy is that it has no programmes for these households who neither have assets

nor skill can not benefit from wage-employment programmes. For such a category separate policy measures such as social security schemes would be required.

16. Other problems that have blocked the success of anti poverty programmes are population explosion, neglect of adult education, neglect of role of women in anti poverty programmes, neglect of village industries, cottage industries SSI and neglect of ecological aspects due to excessive dependence on land.

The above discussion gives the impression that there are many loopholes in the concept, execution and performance of anti poverty programmes. It can be generalised that these programmes lack an element of human development. It other words these programmes ever improved neither wealth nor health of the poor. Therefore there is a dire need for an alternative development paradigm giving due stress on human resource utilisation and development. In this paradigm the primary goal of planning and development should be employment generation rather than economic growth Mr. Deva Gowda our former Prime Minister said, "Development should not be analysed in terms of growth rates alone. It should be analysed and understood in terms of the people. Human development and formation of human capabilities and enriching the quality of life of our people is an important and integrated aspect of our reform process". Amaryya Sen also emphasised the need for integration of social sector development.

For most governments a standard recipe to alleviate poverty is to announce a number of anti poverty schemes. Whether the poor really get the benefit of these schemes is of secondary importance. In this context it is right to point out that these schemes have lost focus. We shall have fewer more focused anti poverty schemes which lie in the development of human resources. In other words there is a crucial role to be played by public investment particularly in social sectors like education, health, housing and family welfare.

Human Resource Development

The concept of HRD has been gaining prominence and is in focus in the development debate of the last two decades. Human resources as the active factor of production are considered to be the centre of all development process of the economy. HRD in India is officially identified with social development encompassing quality of life issues. Human development is defined as the process of enlarging peoples' choices as well as raising the level of well being achieved. The most critical choices are to lead a long and healthy life, to be educated and to enjoy a decent standard of living. Human Development is necessary on account of the following reasons.

1. Human development is a means to higher productivity. A well nourished healthy, educated skilled, alert labour force is the most important productive asset.
2. Human development is the end while economic growth is only a means to this end.
3. It helps in lowering the family size by slowing human reproduction.
4. Human development is good for physical environment. Deforestation, desertification and soil erosion decline when poverty declines.
5. Reduced poverty contributed to a healthy civil society, increased democracy and greater social stability.
6. Human development can help in reducing civil disturbances in a society and in increasing political stability.

Against this backdrop, it is appropriate to mention that the Human Development Report for 1996 has estimated that 61.5 per cent of India's population do not have access to basic capabilities. In other words Human Development Report focuses on the deprivation in the four elements of human life—longevity, knowledge, a decent standard of living and health of children.

1. The first deprivation relates to survival—the vulnerability to death at a relatively early age and it is represented in the human poverty index by the percentage of people expected to die before age 40.
2. The second relates to knowledge—being excluded from the world of reading and communication and is measured by the percentage of adults who are illiterate.
3. The third relates to a decent standard of living, which is represented by these variables—the percentage of people without access to safe drinking water, health services and sanitation.
4. The fourth relates to underweight children under age five.

The human poverty index is constructed by taking a simple average of the four variables—Human Poverty in India is presented in Table 3.

This table reflects country's unsatisfactory performance in alleviating human poverty. Since human poverty is as high as 35.9 per cent the human poverty is widespread.

Table 3: Human Poverty in India.

	Deprivation	*Value*
1.	Survival deprivation	16.1
2.	Deprivation in education and knowledge	46.5
3.	Deprivation in economic provisioning:	
	Population without access to safe drinking water.	
	Population without access to health services.	
	Population without access to sanitation.	38.3
4.	Deprivation in the health of the children	53.0
	Human Poverty Index Value	35.9

Source: UNDP. Human Development Report 1999. Table 4 pp. 146-47.

At this juncture, it is appropriate to discuss the Government's role and its contribution in addressing the human development in India. Of late the human deprivations are categorised in a single sector called social sector. Seven basic services are identified for primary attention. They are life expectancy, safe drinking water, availability of primary health services, universalisation of primary education, provision of public housing assistance and Nutritional support to children. The Table 4 furnishes the clear picture of social sector in India. It is observed from the table that after 1996 all the variables started declining.

Table 4: Indicators of Human Development.

Indicators	*1960*	*1990*	*1996*	*1998*
Life Expectancy	44	59	62	58
Under Five mortality (per 1000 live berth)	282	142	72	77
Population with access to safe water (%)	31	75	78	80
Daily calorie supply (% of requirements)	89	94	90	88
Adult Literacy Rate (%)	34	48	52	52
Real GDP per capita	530	910	721	701
Birth Rate	42	30	27	26
Death Rate	23	10	9	9

Source: UNDP, World Development Report. New York, Oxford University Press.

Now we turn to the discussion that how far our five year plans had given attention to the social sector. The Table V givès the overall picture of the role of the Government in the performance of the social sector in India. It is observed from the Table 5 almost all the variables in the social sector have received priority in a decreasing trend. As the total outlay increased the allotment of funds to these variables has been decreased inspite of a rapid increase in the size of Indian population. The allotment of funds never coped up with increased population in India.

(Rs. in crore)

Five year Plan	*Health*	*Educa- tion*	*Nutri- tion*	*Housing*	*Family* Welfare	*Social* Welfare	*Backward* Class	*Total outlay* of the *Plan*
I	137 (6.99)	85 (4.34)	—	1150 (0.57)	1 (0.05)	4 (0.20)	32 (1.63)	1960
II	269 (5.85)	95 (1.63)	—	1300 (0.28)	5 (0.11)	19 (0.41)	90 (1.96)	4600
III	315 (3.67)	178 (2.07)	—	1550 (0.18)	27 (0.31)	31 (0.36)	114 (1.32)	8600
IV	434 (2.75)	235 (1.49)	—	2800 (0.18)	315 (2.0)	93 (0.9)	142 (0.90)	15780
V	681 (1.73)	480 (1.04)	116 (0.29)	4230 (0.11)	497 (1.26)	86 (0.22)	517 (1.31)	39430
VI	1330 (1.22)	900 (0.82)	175 (0.16)	(2.6)	765 (0.70)	131 (0.12)	895 (0.82)	109290
VII	3687 (1.69)	7686 (3.51)	2210 (1.00)	2723 (1.24)	3121 (1.43)	252 (0.11)	1070 (0.49)	218730
VIII	3553 (3.89)	8553 (3.89)	4175 (0.96)	3663 (1.22)	4516 (1.50)	434 (0.09)	1875 (0.54)	434100

Source: Reports of Planning Commission.
Figures in parenthesis indicate percentage.

Current Scenario of Social Sector in India

Health

The investment on health has shown considerable increase over the plan periods. However there has not been any increase in the proportion of the plan outlay allocated to health sector. Hence the health sector is considered as low priority area. There seems to be hardly any distinction in planning for health. Consequently the network of health services happens to be top heavy, over centralised, heavily curative in its approach, urban and elite oriented. These shortcomings can not be cured by small tinkerings here and there. This calls for integrated plans for health and development including family welfare.

Housing

The available housing stock in urban and rural India suggests that between 1951-91 general population has increased about 235 per cent however, the increase in the number of households is about 206 per cent. This indicates that the Government, inspite of its several housing programmes was not able to achieve the demands created by the population explosion and for that matter the Government is not able to meet such huge demands.

Education

The current scenario of primary education clearly reveals that universalisation of primary education by 2005 A.D. is a very complex process and needs considerable and tremendous effort to achieve the desired goal. Unless we give right to education to every citizen we can not accelerate the rate of literacy. Our planners should therefore make vigorous efforts to spread education in rural areas so that the present inequalitarian character of education in the society is changed. The non-formal sector of education needs to be given due priority in the present situation of vast illiteracy.

Safe drinking water

India receives 1194 mm rainfall which is 394 mm. more than the world average of 800 mm. Inspite of this India is faced with a twin problem of non-availability of water because large amount of rain water is allowed to run into the sea and not collected for proper utilisation and also evaporation and concentration of physio-chemical salts in water sheds. Hence there are 27 per cent of villages and 21 per cent of centres where safe drinking water is available. In 1,62,000 villages no potable water is available. In fact 60 per cent villages which have no safe water while liquor shops are there in 90 per cent villages. Against this background the need for formulating a National Water Policy gains more urgency especially in the case of drinking water.

Family Welfare

Population explosion is another great failure in India. If we add more than one Australia every year to our population where do we get food, clothing and housing. Metropolitan slums are developing like cancerous growth eating into the country. There is widespread desertification and deforestation. So how are we going to deal with this problem? It is much better to have a suitable National Population Policy with more emphasis on empowerment of women. Moreover the politicians never diverted their attention towards the reduction of the number of population instead they are particular over the number of voters.

Policy Options

1. Grain Bank is a system suggested to eradicate poverty through which the have nots may not face the hardships for food during the lean

period. This calls for vigorous efforts on the part of the Government to extend the scheme to cover all over the rural areas.

2. Tracing the trend of poverty and extent of inequality neither economic growth nor anti-poverty schemes alone can improve the living conditions of the poor. There is a need for alternative strategy which depends on competent and in corrupt administration. Inspite of liberalisation the government has to play an effective role in managing basic services to the people.

3. For rural India time is running out and it must adopt strategies and methods to transform the socio economic life of the people in which participation by all is both the mean and end itself.

4. The total reorientation of the existing system calls for integrated plans for health and development including family welfare, programmes of nutrition, improvement of the environment and expansion of immunisation coverage.

5. The National Housing Policy calls for a progressive shift from a subsidy based housing to cost-sharing and from target orientation to demand driven approach.

6. Working with the private sector for poverty alleviation is called for.

7. The declining trend in the allocation of funds to agricultural sector shows a declining trend in employment in rural areas. Hence growth of agriculture and allied sectors is a key concern in the alternative development paradigm.

8. There is an urgent need to restructure the curriculum in the present educational system to meet the market demand in the contemporary job market. This calls for an integration of educational institutions and industries so that educational institutions can provide manpower that is best suited to the industries in the country.

REFERENCES

1. Chandhuri, Pramit, 1978, "The Indian Economy—Poverty and Development" Vikas Publishing House, New Delhi.

2. Dev and Ranade, 1997, "Poverty and Public Policy: A mixed Record" Indian Development Report 1997.

3. Gadage, R.S., 1997, "Standard of Living Measurement of Poverty in India". Facts for you, Aug. 1997.

4. Government of India Planning Commission (1999), Ninth Five Year Plan, 1997-2002.

5. Hanumantha Rao, C.H., 1992, "Integrating Poverty Alleviation Programmes with Development Strategies—Indian Experience" Economic and Political Weekly, Nov. 28, 1992.

6. Joshi, Navin, 1996, "Creating New Ambience for rural Social Needs", Kurukshetra, Oct-Nov. 1996.

7. Minhas, B.S. et. al., (1991), "Declining Incidence of Poverty in 1980's—Evidence versus Arte facts Economic and Political Weekly, July 6-13, 1991.

8. Misra, S.K., and Puri V.K., 2000, "Indian Economy" Himalaya Publishing House, 18th Revised and Enlarged Millennium Edition.

9. Oommen, M.A., 1997, "Fifty Years of Planning for the poor: A looking back", Kurukshetra, Aug. 1997.

10. Sen, Abhijit, 1996, "Economic Reforms, Employment and Poverty Trends and Options". Economic and Political weekly, Special Number. Sept. 1996.

11. Streeten, Paul, 1996, "Foreward to Mahhub ul Haq. Reflections on Human Development Oxford University Press.

33

SHG Bank Linkage
A New Paradigm for Combating Poverty

Dr. (Mrs.) Laxmi R. Kulshresthra*
Dr. (Mrs.) Archana Gupta**

Some of the research studies conducted by NABARD during the early eighties showed that despite having an extremely wide network of rural bank branches which implemented specific poverty alleviation programmes that sought creation of self-employment opportunities through bank credit for almost two decades, a very large number of the poorest of the poor continued to remain outside the fold of formal banking system. These studies gave signals that the existing banking policies, systems and procedures and deposit and loan products were perhaps not most suited to meet the immediate needs of the very poor. What they really needed was a better access to these services and products rather than cheap subsidised credit.

Against this background, a need was felt for alternative policies, systems and procedures, savings and loan products, other complementary services and new delivery mechanisms which would fulfill the requirements of the poorest, especially of the women members of such households. The emphasis therefore was on improving the access of the poor to micro Finance (mF) that had led it to develop the Self Help Group (SHG)—Bank linkage model as the core strategy that could be used by the banking system in India for increasing

* Head, Deptt. of Economics & Mgmt), Faculty of Social Sciences, Dayalbagh Educational Institute, (Deemed University), Agra.
** Deptt. of Economics & Mgmt, Faculty of Social Sciences, Dayalbagh Educational Institute, (Deemed University), Agra.

their outreach to the poorest of the poor who were hitherto getting by-passed by them.

Starting with NABARD led limited scale Pilot Project (with the support of the Central Bank of the country, i.e., Reserve Bank of India) in 1992 that aimed at promoting and financing 500 SHGs across the entire country, the SGH-bank linkage strategy has come a long way.

The pilot phase was followed by setting up of a Working Group on NGOs and SHGs by the Reserve Bank of India in 1984, which came out with wide ranging recommendations on internationalisation of the SHG concept as a potential intervention tool in the area of banking with the poor. The Reserve Bank of India was quick to accept most of the major recommendations and advised the banks to consider mainstreaming lendings to the SHGs as part of their rural credit operations.

What is SHG

A Self-Help Group (SHG) is a small economically homogeneous and affinity group of rural poor generally not exceeding 20 members voluntarily coming together.

- To save small amounts regularly.
- To mutually agree to contribute to a common fund
- To meet their emergency needs
- To have collective decision making
- To solve conflicts through collective leadership and mutual discussion.
- To provide collateral free loans with terms decided by the group at market driven rate. (Chart. 1.)

Self-help groups and Bank Linkages

SHGs are mostly informal groups of people where members pool their savings and re-lend in the group on rotational basis, depending upon consumption, production or investment needs. SHGs have a common perception of need and improvise in collective decisions and actions. Many such groups are formed around specific production activities to promote savings among members and use the pooled common resources to meet emergent credit needs of members. Where funds generation is low in the initial phases due to low savings capacities, these are supplemented by external resources by NGOs.

What is a Self help Groups

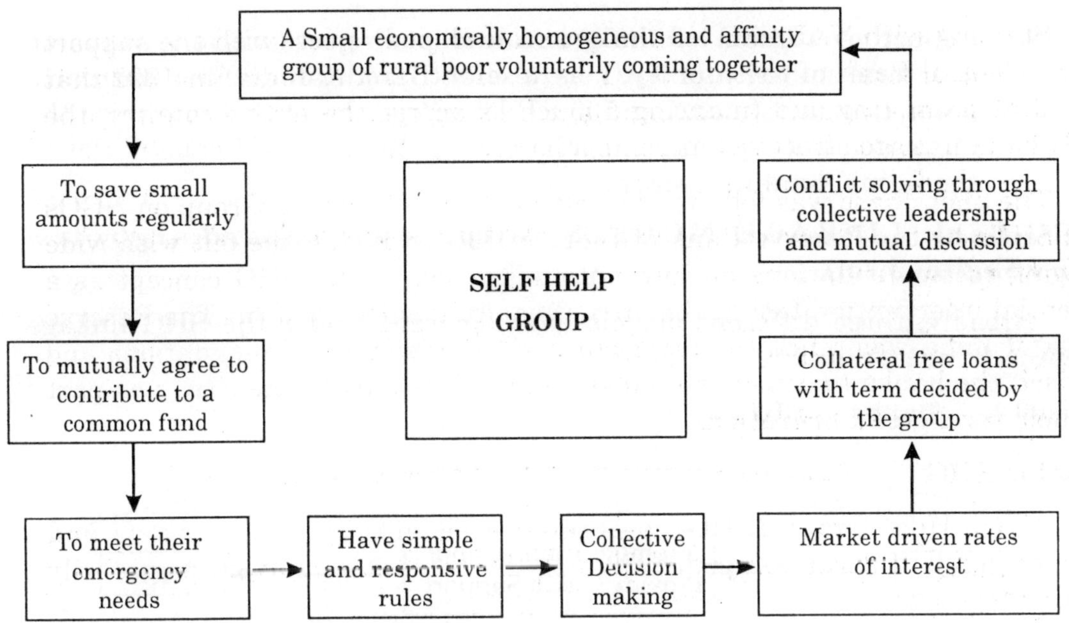

Source: http://www.nabard.org/shg1slide.htm.

It is a small bank of poor people, which is formed by the people, for the people themselves, also formulate rules and regulations; no registration is needed SHGs are authentic and recognised by the RBI; Commercial Banks and other financial institutions. Group is a self-made group, so it thinks for all over development. The conceptual thinking behind the SHG philosophy and the Bank Linkage could be summarised as under:

1. The poor can transit from dependency to self-reliance much faster through social mobilisation and awareness creation than through economic interventions.
2. Women form the basis of social mobilisation and therefore aiming for women's empowerment is the most cost-effective strategy available, even for economic development.
3. Self help supplemented with mutual help can be a powerful vehicle for the poor's efforts in socio-economic upward migration.
4. Participative financial services management is more efficient and responsive. Small affinity groups of poor with initial outside support can effectively manage and supervise micro credit among its members.

5. Poor can save and are bankable. They need not only credit support but also savings and other services.
6. Collective wisdom of the group and peer pressure is a valuable collateral substitute. SHG as a client, facilitates wider outreach, lower transaction cost and much lower risk costs and minimize the mismatch between the expectations of the poor and capabilities of the formal banking system.

SHG-Bank LINKAGE MODELS (http://www.nabard.org/roles/micdShgline.htm)

Broadly, three different models have emerged under the SHG linkage approach in the country.

Model 1: Banks as SHPIs.

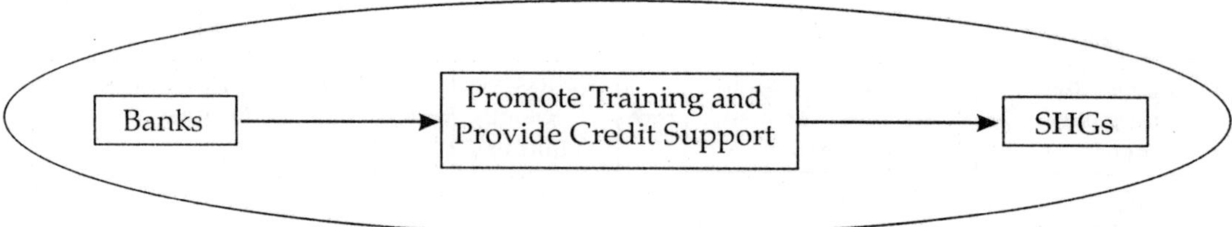

In this model, the bank itself acts as a Self Help Group Promoting Institutions (SHPI). It takes initiatives in forming the groups, nurtures them over a period of time and then provides credit to them after satisfying itself about their maturity to absorb credit.

Model II: NGOs as SHPIs.

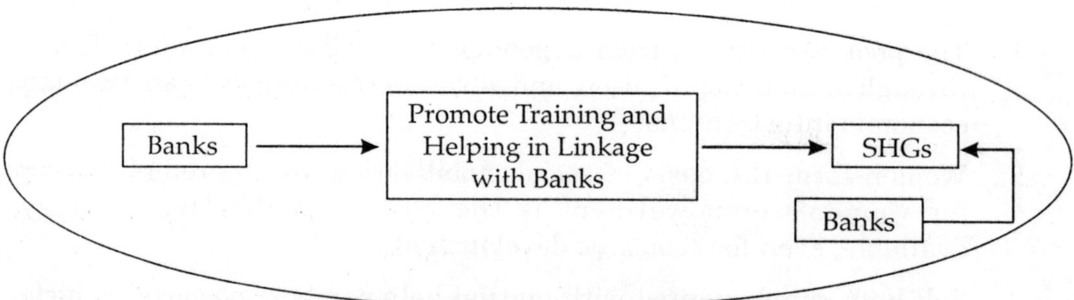

In this model, groups are formed by NGOs (in most of the cases) or by government agencies. The groups are nurtured and trained by these agencies. The bank then provides credit directly to the SHGs after observing their operations and maturity to absorb credit. While the bank provides loans to the groups directly, the facilitating agencies continue their interactions with the SHGs. Most linkage experiences begin with this model with NGOs playing a major role. This model has also been popular and more acceptable to banks, as some of the difficult functions of social dynamics are externalised.

Model III: NGOs as Financial Intermediary.

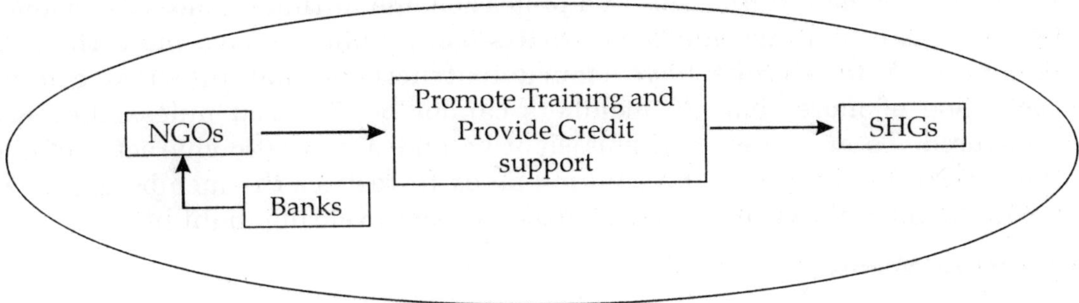

Due to various reasons, banks in some areas are not in a position to even finance SHGs promoted and nurtured by other agencies. In such cases, the NGOs act as both facilitators and micro-finance intermediaries. First, they promote the groups, nuture and train them and then approach banks for bulk loans for on-lending to the SHGs.

The Model-wise linkage of SHGs (as on March 2000 is below)

Model-wise Linkage of SHGs as on March 2000.

(Rs. Million)

Model	*SHG No.*
I	13,51
II	65,636
III	15,448
Total	**94,645**

Source: SDC, NABARD Collaboration in Micro Finance Innovations in India.

Structure of SHGs

Membership of the group

Self-Help Group is small group of poor villagers who are homogeneous in nature, economically and socially. It constitutes of only male or female or combination of both. It should not consist of more than twenty or less than ten members in the group.

Among the group members one management committee is formed which constitutes of president, secretary and treasurer, each pausing some peculiar responsibilities to carry out the functioning of the group smoothly. These management members are elected by the 'say' of every member.

Group Size

SHGs are formed on the basis of the homogeneous character of group members-economic status, sex, and profession and at times, place of residence or even caste. A large number of SHGs were found to have more than 20 members. A few banks have issued instructions that informal groups consisting of more than 20 members cannot be financed unless they are registered. To encourage the participative and democratic character of the groups. NGOs are now-a-days taking steps to restrict the membership size below 20. (http://www.nabard.org/roles/micd/threeyearhighlight.htm)

Security Norms

The RBI has relaxed security norms for lending to SHGs and accordingly group savings are the only security, which can be offered by the SHG. It is thus, envisaged that the credit worthiness of an SHG need not be judged on the basis of the security it can offer. On the contrary, the cohesiveness, vibrancy, group discipline, level of awareness, collective decision-making, etc. should be assessed and given more importance than any tangible security.

Credit Utilisation

A group member must utilize the loan to make products, which he or she can sell; otherwise he or she will be worse off as a result of having borrowed funds at high cost.

Repayment Period

According to RBI/NABARD guidelines on SHGs, banks are required to sanction a term loan for lending to SHGs or NGOs repayable over a period of 3 to 10 years. Flexibility has been provided in collection of interest by the bank (at shorter intervals with quarterly of half-yearly) and in fixation of appropriate installments of the capital depending on the rolling over of funds. Similarly the bank negotiates about appropriate repayment period with SHG and SHG decides on the repayment schedule for its members generally in weekly instalments.

Rate of Interest

RBI directives govern the rate of interest. The rate of interest structure under SHGs is such that it provides some margin to the bank as well as to the NGO when the credit linkage is established through an NGO. However, any change in the rate of interest changed to the ultimate beneficiary or any change subsequent to the linkage disturbs the entire structure and margin available.

Documentation

The banks are allowed to decide the same in consultation with their legal departments. It was however observed that the documents collected by the banks varied from 4 to 11.

The loan being a group loan, some banks were found to have insisted on the signature of all the members of the group instead of their authorised representatives. At times, banks also ask for the photographs of all the SHG members.

Indicative Criteria for selection of SHGs for the Linkage with banks

NABARD has set out simple and specific guidelines for the selection of members, so that the functioning of the group goes on smoothly.

(These criteria are only indicative and are not exhaustive. They may also require to be modified according to the local situations).

- The group should have been in active existence for at least a period of six months.
- The group should have successfully undertaken savings and credit operation from its own resources.
- Democratic working of the group wherein all members feel that they have a say should be evident.
- The group should maintain proper accounts/records.
- The banker should ensure that the group has not come into existence only for the sake of participation in the project and availing benefits (credit) there under. There should be a genuine need to help each other and work together among the members.
- The SHG members should preferably have homogeneous background and interest.
- The interest of the NGO or the Self-Help Promoting Institution (SHPI) concerned, if any, in the group is evident and the agency is helping the SHG by way of training and other support for skill up gradation and proper functioning.

Highlights as on 31 March 2001

With over 4.5 million poor households accessing banking services including micro-credit through their 263 thousand Self-Help Groups (SHGs), the SHG bank linkage programme is now perhaps the largest micro Finance programme of the world in terms of its outreach. The year 2000-2001 witnessed a two-fold jump in the outreach of the SHG-bank linkage programme. both in physical and financial terms. Today, over 750 NGOs and 14,000 branches of 318 banks are associated with the programme. (http://www.nabard.org/roles/micd/threeyearhighlight.htm).

The Hon'ble Union Finance Minister in his Budget Speech for the year 2000-2001, announced the creation of a micro Finance Development Fund in NABARD with a start up contribution of Rs. 1,000 million contributed by RBI, NABARD and selected commercial banks. The fund will be used for capacity building of various mF stakesholders including members of SHGs. The cumulative progress and the Regional Spread of SHG linked as on 31st March 2001 is given table 1 and 2 respectively.

- 149,050 new SHGs were provided credit by the banks under the SHG-Bank linkage programme.
- Rs. 2,878.90 million were disbursed by banks as loans to SHGs which included 21630 earlier financed SHGs who received repeat finance. Against this, the banks claimed Rs. 2,506 million as refinance from NABARD.
- Cumulatively, 263,825 SHGs are now credit linked with different banks.
- Cumulative bank loan disbursed to SHGs stood at Rs. 4808.70 million.
- Cumulative refinance availed of by banks from NABARD for financing SHGs stood at Rs. 4,007 million.
- 4.5 million poor households have gained access to the formal banking system through the SGH bank linkage programme.
- More than 85 per cent SHGs have exclusively women members.
- On-time Repayment of bank loan was above 95 per cent from SHG members.
- The significant success of the programme was due to the active involvement of over 750 NGOs over 14,000 branches of 318 banks.
- Policy support from Govt. of India, RBI and State Governments.
- Development policy initiatives and capacity building of its partner agencies by NABARD.
- SHG-bank linkage programme covered 382 districts in 27 States and Union Territories.

Table 1: SHG Bank Linkage Programme Highlights. (March 1997-2000)

Sl. No.	*SHG-Bank Linkage Programme Highlights* *Items*	*March 1997*	*March 1998*	*March 1999*	*March 2000*	*March 2001*
		March 1997-2000 Rs. in Million As at				
1.	No. of SHGs linked during the year.	3841	5719	18678	81780	149050
2.	No. of SHGs inked (cumulative).	8598	14317	32995	114775	263825
3.	% of women group	76	78	84	85	85
4.	No. of participating banks	120	150	202	266	318
	I Commercial Banks	29	31	38	40	41
	II RRBs	79	102	129	165	166
	III Co-op. Banks	12	17	35	61	111
5.	No. of States/UTs	20	21	24	24	27
6.	No. of districts covered		221	280	362	382
7.	No. of NGOs	220	291	550	718	750
8.	Bank Loan (cumulative Rs. million)	118.36	237.6	570.7	1929.82	4808.7
9.	Refinance	106.5	213.8	520.6	1501.26	4007.2
	(cumulative US$)	2.48	4.97	12.11	34.91	87.11
10.	No. of families assisted	146000	243000	560000	1900000	4485000
11.	Average Loan/SHG (Rs.)	13766	16596	17297	16814	1828
	US$	320.14	385.95	402.26	391.02	39.74
12.	Average Loan/Family (Rs.)	810	978	1019	1016	1072
	US$	18.84	22.74	23.70	23.63	23.30
13.	Model-wise linkage (cumulative)					
	I Directly to SHGs without intervention/facilitation of any NGO	13%	18%	17%	14%	14%
	II Directly to SHGs with facilitation by NGOs and other formal agencies	45%	46%	56%	70%	70%
	III Through NGO as facilitator and financing agency	42%	36%	27%	16%	16%

Source: Micro Credit Innovations Department (MCID), NABARD India.

- NABARD has provided, upto 31 March 2001, Revolving Fund Assistance (RFA) of Rs. 122 million to 22 NGOs, SHG Federations and credit unions for on-lending to SHGs and to build their financial intermediation capacities.

Table 2: Regional Spread of SHGS Linked as on 31st March 2001.

(Rs. in Millions)

S. No.	*Region / State*	*No. of SHGs Credit linked*	*No. of SHGs refinance linked*	*Bank Loan*	*Bank Loan*	*Refinance*	*Refinance*
A	**Northern Region**			Million Rupees	Million US$	Million Rupees	Million US$
1.	Himachal Pradesh	2545	1568	31.90	0.68	25.56	0.56
2.	Rajasthan	5616	3749	111.74	2.43	72.66	1.58
3.	Haryana	537	455	15.57	0.34	12.57	0.27
4.	Punjab	203	192	1.82	0.04	1.52	0.03
5.	Jammu & Kashmir	9012	6055	163.72	3.56	114.41	2.49
	Total (A)	**9012**	**6055**	**163.72**	**3.56**	**114.41**	**2.49**
B	**North Eastern Region**						
6.	Assam	276	216	3.99	0.09	2.32	0.05
7.	Meghalaya	160	118	4.06	0.09	2.12	0.05
8.	Tripura	5	5	0.32	0.01	0.05	0.00
9.	Sikkim	5	5	0.11	0.00	0.11	0.00
10.	Manipur	31	5	0.51	0.10	0.10	0.00
	Total (B)	**477**	**349**	**8.98**	**.20**	**4.70**	**0.10**
C	**Eastern Region**						
11.	Orissa	8888	7889	80.76	1.76	74.44	1.62
12.	Bihar	4592	3199	50.06	1.09	35.81	0.78
13.	West Bengal	8739	8600	58.43	1.27	54.31	1.18
14.	UT of A & N Islands	33	33	0.90	0.02	0.79	0.02
	Total (C)	**2252**	**19721**	**190.15**	**4.13**	**165.3**	**53.59**
D	**Central Region**						
15	Madhya Pradesh	5699	5440	101.26	2.20	76.86	1.67
16	Uttar Pradesh	23152	16013	155.92	3.39	97.21	2.11
	Total (D)	**28851**	**21453**	**257.18**	**5.59**	**174.07**	**3.78**
E	**Western Region**						
17	Gujarat	4929	4218	63.91	1.39	56.90	1.24
18	Maharashtra	10468	10468	179.71	3.91	135.91	2.95
19	Goa	146	46	2.76	0.06	2.72	0.06
	Total (E)	**15543**	**14732**	**246.38**	**5.36**	**195.53**	**4.25**
F	**Southern Region**						
20	Andhra Pradesh	126362	101275	2541.65	55.25	2152.99	46.80
21	Karnataka	18619	14386	367.65	7.99	309.86	6.74
22.	Kerala	9625	6652	191.72	4.17	95.47	2.08
23.	Tamil Nadu	32766	28272	827.62	17.99	781.14	16.98
24.	UT of Pondicherry	318	318	13.74	0.30	13.74	0.30
	Total (F)	**187690**	**150903**	**3942.38**	**85.70**	**3353.20**	**72.90**
	Grand Total	**263825**	**213213**	**4808.79**	**104.54**	**4007.26**	**87.11**

Source: Micro Credit Innovations Department (MCID), NABARD India.

- Over 16,000 bank officials including faculty members of training establishments of banks were trained by NABARD in micro Finance (mF) during 2000-2001.
- Cumulatively, 27,000 bank offices and 300 faculty members of training colleges of banks have been trained by NABARD.
- About 4,000 participants from lesser experienced NGOs in mF were trained during the year in 192 programmes by NABARD in association with experienced NGOs.

Caution

If proper care is not taken self-help group's promotion efforts may also fail to produce desired results. Basically there are two potential sources of weakness, SHGs over time may suffer from factionalism and internal rivalries, from domination by a self-interested, sometimes corrupt leadership or management, from lack of solidarity among members, from shortsighted, inefficient management, etc. Therefore, facilitating institutions have to be careful about these issues and educate the people so as to prevent any such situations.

The other inherent danger comes from the facilitating institutions. They have to clearly orient their staff and operate, with the understanding that self-help promotion is drastically different from the need to guard themselves against the temptation to get involved in western style aid-oriented development work. This is very important to bear in mind because self-help promotion means evolving a people's movement which may not have the kind of short-term visibility which is so characteristic of today's development agencies. Though overtime results will certainly become visible. Thus how to strike a balance between short-term results and building people's movement for self-reliance, is the point to ponder over for development agencies. It is expected to be one of the major programmes of poverty alleviation in India with full participation from the formal banking system and without any interference from the government. However, considering the magnitude of poverty, the outreach of the programme needs to be significantly enhanced.

Summing Up

It is an established fact today that national economic growth alone cannot prevent the growth of mass poverty. Over the years, one-sided emphasis on economic achievements by national policy-makers has set in motion a process of alarming socio-economic polarisation and the deepening of social cleavages in both rural and urban areas. Past technocratic approaches to poverty eradication have failed to produce desired results. Since the poor have become too numerous to be healed from outside, self-help promotion' has emerged as a new paradigm for combating poverty. This, however, requires a different orientation and approach. But how can we afford to overlook, it should be a matter of concern for all those social-consciousness driven people who want to banish poverty from this world.

BIBLIOGRAPHY

1. Desai Murti, 1998, "Policy Approaches to Women and Poverty Eradication'; The Indian Journal of Social Work, Vol. 54, Issue 4, October 1998.
2. Jindal Krishan Basu Kishanjit, 2000, "Micro Finance Emerging Challenges." Bankers Institute of Rural Development, Lucknow.
3. Kaladhar, K., 1997, 'Micro Finance Design Structure and Governance'. Economic and Political Weekly, 32 (42) October 18.
4. NABARD, SHG Bank Linkage Programme, Status as on 31 March 1998. Micro Credit Innovations Department, Nabard, Mumbai.
5. Nabard, 2000; "A. Pamphlet on Self Help Group Programme," Mumbai.
6. Nabard, 1999; "Banking with the Poors, Financing Self Help Groups,' Hyderabad.
7. Naidu G. Venkta, Narasaini M. Laxmi; 'Role of Banking in Rural Development'. Discovery Publishing House, New Delhi.
8. Nair Tara, S. (1998); "Meeting the Micro Credit Needs of the Poor; Issues in Focus', The Indian Journal of Labour Economics, July-September.
9. Nair Tara S. (2001); Institutionalising Micro Finance in India as Overview of Strategic Issues, Economic and Political weekly vol. xxxvi 4a Jan-Feb. 2001.
11. Rashtriya Mahila Kosh (1998); 'A Report on Self Help Group', R.C. Group, New Delhi.
12. Sundaram Stya (1999); 'India 50 years of Independences 1947-97 Rural Development'; B.R. Publishing Corporation.

WEBSITES

1. http://www.nabard.org/roles/micd shglink, bank.htm
2. http://www.nabard.org/shg1chart.htm
3. http://www.nabard.org/vanl.htm
4. http://www.nabard.org/shg2 chart.htm
5. http://nabard.org/shg1/slide.htm
6. http://www.nabard.org/roles/micd/three yearhighlights.htm
7. http//www.nabard.org/roles/micd/introduction.htm
8. http://www.nabard.org/rols/micd/statewise.htm

34

Globalisation and Consumer Behaviour

A Case Study of Indian Automobile Industry

Manjappa, D.H.*

Vinay, M.R.**

Introduction

The 20th century could be described as the Age of Automobiles. As a revolutionary product for travel and transportation, it transformed society and grew into a giant industry that pulled up the economy and led to technological innovations. As a mass production and multidivisional form of a corporate organisation, it has provided representative business models of the modern industries.

The automobile industry worldwide is technology intensive both as regards its process and products. It is also characterised by considerable economies of scale and high degree of specialisation in component manufactures. Largely for these reasons, the world industry has increasingly become internationalised, with component production for individual models located in many countries and with assembly concentrated in large domestic markets or in countries that are a base of regional exports. Automobile industries have been transformed by trade and investment liberalisation

* Professor of Economic

** Research Scholar in Economics

Department of Studies in Economics and Co-operation, University of Mysore, Manasagangothri, Mysore, Karnataka, India-570 006.

This paper was presented in the International Conference of III Asia-Pacific International Association of Canadian, Studies, Mysore.

policies and global expansion of the auto industry in the past decade in developing countries.

The automobile industry, in India, has been subjected to substantial policy changes over the last decades. The policy changes were in two doses and took the form of partial deregulation introduced in 1980's and globalisation measures launched since 1991. As a result of these measures the industry has been dispensed with the bulk of controls and regulations and has been assigned a central role to market forces. The Government of India has provided a suitable economic and business environment conducive to the success of the established and prospective foreign partnership ventures. As a result of this many joint ventures have been set up in India with foreign collaboration, both technical and financial with leading global manufactures. In the dynamics of transition of the Indian economy, the automobile industry is emerging as a leading industry, with increased production and capacity creation and with substantial growth in exports (Surekha Sunil Lomaye 2000). Far-reaching economic reforms have moved India into the front ranks of rapidly growing Asia-Pacific Region in the automobile industry.

It is found that a growing body of literature on Indian Automobile Industry has focused on supply side variables.[1] But the growth of the automobile industry is closely related to the market dynamics, specifically the demand side factors can be contributed to the changes in the perception of consumer to buy products. The aspect of such an importance, specifically changes in the consumer behaviour in the context of globalisation has become the focal point of considerable interest in investigation. In this context, the paper attempts to analyze the changes in both supply and demand side factors determining the behaviour of automobile consumers, under different policy regimes taking the case of car industry.

The paper is organised as follows. The paper begins with the examination of the Indian automobile policies and their importance in determining the growth, development, performance and structure of the auto industry, under regulated and liberal economic policy regimes (section 2 and 3). Section 4 deals demand side variables of economic reforms, which influences the consumer behaviours. The impact of globalisation and macro economic reforms that led to changes in the consumer behaviour has been analyzed in the Section 5. The last section deals with the conclusions.

Growth and Structural Changes of auto-industry under different Policy Regimes

Laissez-faire economy has now become a relic of history. In post-Independence India-in the 50s'-the Nationalist (Autarkic) impulses came to the fore; planning and government intervention became the bases of Industrial Policy. For the 30 years, the automobile industry received the highest level of protection. Starting from Complete Knock Down (CKD) to Semi-Knock Down (SKD), the 'licensed' auto producers were encouraged-through disincentive and directive-to indigenous their production. On the one hand, manufacturers, and vendors, reached over 90% of local content, in the licensing regime. There were controls on price and a large excess demand continued to rule the market with ages-old technologies.

Even though the automobile sector was liberalised prior to 1991 in India. It was in 1990s, under pressure of balance of payments, the Indian government further opened the many domestic sector to all foreign investment. Under this policy international players entered the Indian auto world. This 'globalisation' phase brought dramatic changes in the choices and competitive structure in the Indian auto market.

The Indian automobile industry is now almost sixty years old. Its growth has changed with the changes in the automobile policies of GOI. Its growth can broadly be viewed in terms of three phases: (1) Autarkic (2) Mass-Car and (3) Globalisation phases.

Autarkic Phase

Automobile industry has been operating under the conditions of what is often termed as a 'protected market'. It was protected both from internal and external competition for a fairly long period. Investment behaviour of firms was characterised by the lack of competitive forces that could operate in the product market with the existence of excess demand conditions for a long period of time. The constraints were significant because of numerous entry barriers erected by the government through industrial-licensing, import restrictions and other instruments. Entry barriers were operating not only with regard to new entrants but also in the case of existing firms, because of restrictions on diversification, expansion of capacity, foreign technology collaborations, and imports of capital stock & components. The impact of these restrictions was especially significant in this industry, since most of the firms began their production process with technology imports.

The restrictive set of policies was chiefly aimed at building an indigenous auto industry. However the restrictions on foreign collaborations led to limitations on imports of technology through technical agreements. These policies of GOI did not allow foreign players to set shop in the country. In the absence of adequate technology and purchasing power, the industry resulted in the slow growth even after a long time since independence. The domestic firms, which were able to capture the licenses were able to block the entry & enjoyed the monopoly. Incumbents in domestic industries thus worked without much concern for potential competition, which allowed firms to sell products of sub-standard quality at high prices.

Mass Car Phase

The Industrial Licensing Policies were dismantled in 1980s in some of the sectors including auto industry by allowing the entry of TNC's. The policies aimed at deregulation and technological upgraded of Indian industries, India has adopted this policy in view of the recognition that TNCs would provide a sort of dynamism in development process of developing economy.

The GOI announced its famous broad banding policy in 1985, by giving new licenses to broad groups of automotive products like cars. Though a liberal move, the licensing system was still very much intact. Protection policies continued through the 1980's, though little bit of protection was reduced as a result of broader policies for trade & investment liberalisation.

Globalisation Phase

The New Industrial Policy (NIP) of 1991 swept away most of the hurdles relating to expansion and foreign investment. New firms were allowed to enter all the segments. The government has permitted a tie-up arrangements with foreign firms in the form of technical & financial collaborations with the result of that almost all firms have imported technology through collaborations with emphasis on fuel efficiency, pollution & safety standards. Also the lifting of quantitative restrictions on imports by the recent policy is added up the flurry of foreign cars into the country. The decontrol, delicensicing and deregulation of the auto industry have changed the growth of the Indian Auto world. They opened the gates to a virtual flood of international auto-makers into the country with improved technology.

Structure of the Car Industry

Globalisation has largely determined the political actions and economic initiatives of government at the end of this century. The force of its impact has modified the economics and social structures of nations involved in it. Alongwith the entry of multinational auto companies, the profile of domestic companies too witnessed a structural change. In the US car market of over 10 million a year, there are just six players that dominate, Europe has eight, Japan has six, where as, the Indian car market after globalisation has at least a dozen or more contenders.

But before 1983 the passenger car sector of the Indian automobile industry consists of only three firms with limited capacity. Those were

Premier Automobiles Ltd. Hindustan Motors Ltd. Standard Motor Production. The GOI entered the car business with a 74% stake in Maruthi Udyog. Ltd. (MUL), the joint ventures with Suzuki Motors Ltd. of Japan during mass car production stage.

After 1991 Telco has diversified the passenger car segment. Subsequently, other world-class assemblers entered the Indian passenger car industry. Firms like Daewoo, Ford, General Motros, Honda Siel Cars India, Hyundai Motors, Mercedes-Benz India, Telco, and Toyota Kirloskar Motors & Fiat entered in to the market. Most of these MNC's have entered as joint ventures with Indian firms, and also are fighting the battle for supremacy in different categories of vehicles.

Supply Side of Passenger Cars

The demand for cars in past was supply driven whereas supply did not match demand. This led to high premium and long waiting periods for the cars. During the globalisation period due to change in government policies coupled with aggressive capacity creation, introduction and upgradation of new models by existing and new car companies in the nineties led to increase in supply of cars with different models.

The table-1 indicates the supply trends of passenger cars in India.

Table 1: Supply of Passenger Cars.

(in thousand)

Year	*Supply of Cars*
1981	42,475
1991	181,420
1994	207,658
1995	264,468
1996	348,146
1997	407,539
1998	401,002
1999	390,355
2000	577,243

Source: AAMA.

Impact of Macro-Economic Reforms on Demand side

India has adopted LPG policy since 1991. This policy has changed the economic environment not only on supply side but also on demand side of the economy. In the previous section, we examined the changes that took place in supply side of the car industry due to global perception. On the other hand, there are considerable changes even in the demand side variables or factors in the economy which have been analyzed below.

Income

GDP has grown at modest rate of a 3.8% per annum in the last fifty years of the economic planning. Over the last decade GDP has grown at an annual average rate of 6.0%. Most of the income growth has swelled size of the middle class located at the higher end of the consumer durable market. (Natarajan 1998).[3] Murali Patibandla (2002) argues that the rapid growth of income in emerging countries which expands the consumer markets for more income elastic products, coupled with the fact local incumbents are stuck with large sunk costs in their existing product lines, leads to natural strategy of product quality choice for TNCs. Thus, TNCs enjoy higher income elasticity for their differentiated products, than local firms given the typical nature of incumbents' technology and the income growth process.

Ten Years back, the country embarked on a policy of economic liberalisation. Since then it has been seen that households have moved up the income ladder with the number of households in the lower income groups actually declining. According to NCAER from FY 93 to FY96. The proportion of lower income household has declined rapidly than in the pre-reform period. In absolute term, 10mm, household graduated outside the lower income group. At the same time the proportion of households in the high-income group went up. Alongwith, the purchasing power of rural people is also increased. Table 2 compares the distribution of households in various income groups in the pre-reform and post-reform periods:

Table 2: Distribution of Households in Different Income Groups in the Pre-Reform and Post Reform Periods.

(In percentage)

Annual Income (Rs)	*Income*	*FY 90*			*FY96*		
FY96	*Group*	*Urban*	*Rural*	*Total*	*Urban*	*Rural*	*Total*
Less than 25,000	Lower	37.1	67.3	58.8	27.9	57.2	48.9
25,001-50,000	Lower Middle	34.8	26.9	26.9	34.9	29.0	30.7
50,001-77,000	Middle	17.9	10.1	10.1	20.3	8.6	11.9
77,001-106,000	Upper Middle	6.5	1.2	2.7	9.6	3.1	5.0
More than 106,000	High	3.8	0.5	1.4	7.3	2.0	3.5

Source: NCAER.

Disposable income, household and corporate savings have improved over the years.

Financial Sector Reforms

Commercial Bank's lending approach has changed in 1990's. The personal banking emerged as retail banking in financial sector. Bank finances are available with flexible terms and low interest rates. The stiff competition in banking sector has lead to more friendly to customers as compared to pre-reforms period. In addition to banking sector, the non-financial intermediaries have been expanded in post reform period.

The market interest rate has been declining in post-reform period. In view of this trend the consumer's surplus as well as purchasing power of the people has increased.

Economic Reforms and Fiscal Policy

Government also no longer views passenger cars as a luxury product. This is reflected in the continuous reduction of excise and custom duties for passenger cars, particularly on the economy models.

The perception of a car as a luxury good lead to heavy excise duty on cars. The excise duty doubles from 25% in FY 1987 to 56% in FY 1991. But with the onset of liberalisation process in the early nineties, the government has continually rationalised the excise duty regime. Presently, there is a duty of 40% on motor vehicles, designed for transport of more than six persons, but not more than the twelve persons, the duty is 32%. Over and above the excise duty, cess by the government, states are now charging a uniform sales tax of 12%.

Excise Duty Variations under the Different Policy Regime.

Years	*1984-85*	*1987-88*	*1990-91*	*1991-92*	*1996-97*
Excise duty	15%	25%	42%	56%	40%

The depreciation norms have changed for different types of machineries. With this the companies are benefited from tax shelter provided by depreciation of 25%. In the 80's, import duties varied between 150 to 200% based on the engine capacity of a car. The import duty on cars and components has come down in the last few years with general reduction in import tariffs. In the FY' 1998 budget, the import duty on cars has also been further brought from 50% to 40% ad-valorem. The import duty on catalytic converters and parts thereof has been reduced from 25% to 5%. The duty on CNG kits and parts thereof has been reduced from 10% to 5%.

Exogenous Factors

Exogenous factors like exchange rates, demand condition in international market, export-import policy, quantitative and qualitative trade barriers, etc.

also have changed. The exchange rate of rupee against the U.S. dollar continued to be broadly market determined.

Impact of Globalisation and Economic Reforms on Consumer Behaviour—An Assessment

Globalisation has opened up the floodgates of global competitive forces for the Indian economy. At the same time the macro-economic policy reforms have also impact substantially on different sectors of the economy. The market oriented growth model that is pursued now is changing the economic environment and market structure of Indian industries.

Consumer preference has been changing at a faster pace alongwith the global changes. The decontrol, de licensing and deregulation of the auto industry have changed the both demand and supply structure of the automobile industry. Alongwith globalisation the other economic reforms in the economy have led consumers to have more choice, freedom and good knowledge to reveal his preference. Several factors from both demand and supply side have been contributed for this revolutionary change in the preference of automobile consumers. These factors have been examined below.

Car-Ownership Pattern in India

Car ownership pattern has been changing at a faster phase along with the changes in the economic and social environment, in India. Car penetration rate was very high due to low number of car owners, led by low level of income, savings and lack of financial facilities, in the pre-reform period. Even though the cars usage is still very low (3 per thousand, as compared to 559. in US and 326 in Japan), the Indian car-buyer's attitude has been changed, in the wake of globalisation and other economic reforms (Ivan Antonio Pinheiro and Arun D Sinher 1999). Car penetration rate has been decreased with the significant increase in the number of car owners led by reforms in both the demand and supply side variables. Gradually, at the same time passenger car have become necessity to have a personal vehicles, as a result of inefficient or deficient public transportation. The following table 3 shows decreasing tendency of the car penetration rate in India.

Competition

The decontrol, delicensing and deregulation of the auto industry have changed the growth of the Indian Auto World. They opened the gates to a virtual flood of international auto-makers into the country with improved technology. These trends have encouraged many multinational automakers from Japan, U.S.A. and Europe to enter the Indian market mainly through

Table 3: Four Wheeler Penetration Rates in India.

Year	*Automobile Ownership*	*Population (mn)*	*Penetration (People / vehicle)*
1980-81	46	679	14760
1985-86	103	755	7330
1990-91	181	839	4635
1995-96	5846	919	157
1999-00	6388	1001	156

Source: Society of Indian Automobile Industry.

joint ventures with Indian firms. Almost all the global players in the automobile industry have set up/are in the process of setting up their facilities in India.

The flood of new entrants into the car industry as a result of liberalisation has led to the complete transformation of this segment. This has resulted in the market being witnessing not only more choice of models with increased production capacities, but also more competition. The car segment is flooded with new models from new and existing players, a visible shift from a constrained supply situation of only three players to the players of twelve. As many as 30 models have entered the car market in these days.

With the release of new models in the higher end of the economy segment, the demand for and supply of second hand economy car is expected to increase substantially, which will be costing just about two times price of premium range two wheelers. This could affect the demand for first hand/ new cars even though there is an increased demand for the same.

Introduction of new models, product differentiation, advertisement and supply of second hand cars, have led to unhealthy competition and thus to price war among the firms.

As Morris (1994) argued that shift in the higher growth & profit frontier usually takes place with a change in the economic environment in which the firms operate, mainly due to technological changes. Therefore the changes in the extent and direction of technology efforts of firms have changed both the demand and supply structure of automobile industry.[2] During the post 1985 period, firms in this industry concentrated primarily on creating capacity and obtaining a large market share, with the intense competition that has come to characterize the industry. Since the 1991 policy regimes, firms would have attempted to shift to a higher growth profit frontier in view of created more demand.

Changes in the Market Share

Consumer in the earlier decades had no such type of choice, freedom and even knowledge to reveal his preference. The demand for cars in the past was *supply driven*, as supply did not match the demand. There were only few car companies, producing limited products and with limited models. This part, consumer had to bind his preference for few products and models or brands. They were compelled to buy the poor quality vehicles at the demanded prices. The Indian corporations, which were able to capture the licenses, were able to block entry and enjoyed monopoly rent. Incumbents in the domestic market thus worked without much concern for potential competition, which allowed firms to sell products of substandard quality at high prices. At that time firms in the automobile industry in India had also been experiencing excess demand condition for a long time. This excess demand was largely due to strict capacity licensing followed by government. This led to high premium and long waiting periods for the cars. Besides a rigid form of price control on vehicles was imposed in 1953 as a sequel to the protection granted to the industry at that time. This continues till 1975.

The flood of new entrants into the car industry as result of globalisation has led to complete transformation of the industry. The car segment is flooded with new models from new and existing players a visible shift from a constrained supply situation to a surplus. At that same time, with the onset of liberalisation and globalisation, cars are gradually declassified as luxury items. Now they have become as essential commodities. Demand for passenger cars has shot up rapidly, since 1994. This is due to reforms influenced on both the demand and supply sides. The following Table 4 presents the changing tendency of market share of car companies.

Household Sector Income and Demand for Cars

As pointed out in the demand side analysis that the people have shifted from lower income group to middle income group. On the other hand there is a decline in the interest rate in the economy. As a result the purchasing power of the people has increased during the post reform period. This has created more permanent income to middle class families. But the household sector savings and private corporate sector savings have not influenced to the greater extent in creating demand for cars. This indicates that savings have not influenced on creating demand for cars. The Regression result is insignificant as given below. Similarly there is no relationship between the growth rate of household sector savings as well as private corporate sectors' savings to demand for cars. This is given in the table 5.

Table 4: Market Share of the Firms in the Car Sector

Company	*Man Products*	*1981*	*1983*	*1985*	*1986*	*1988*	*1990*	*1992/93*	*1994/95*	*2000*
S Motor	—	0.01	0.00	0.01	1.15	0.15	0.00	—	—	—
H Motor	Ambassador Contessa	41.95	40.15	19.11	16.25	14.15	12.43	13.4	10.7	3.9
Maruthi	Maruthi 1000. Esteem. Omni	0.00	0.00	40.08	44.82	51.62	53.50	74.8%	73%	52.4%
Mahindra	Commander, Bolero, Marshal	22.15	25.64	16.93	18.47	14.99	13.92	—	—	—
Premier	Premier Padmini NE 118	35.89	34.21	23.88	19.31	19.1	20.15	9.4	11	—
Telco	Tata Sierra, Tata Estate							2.4	4.9	9.9%
Hyundai	Santro, Accent									14.4%
Daewoo	Ciero, Nexia,									11.5%
Motors	Matiz									
Indauto	—									2.1
Honda SIEL	City									1.7
Others										4.1%
Total		**100.00**	**100.00**	**100.00**	**100.00**	**100.00**	**100.00**	**100.00**	**100.00**	**100.00**

Source: SIAM: Society of Indian Automobile Manufactures.

AIAM: Associative of Indian Automobile Manufactures.

ACMR: Automotive Component Manufactures Association of India.

Car Demand (D) = 0.11HSS + 0.20 PSS
See (0.40) (0.17)
$R^2 = 0.93$ DW = 2.2
Where HSS-Household Sector Savings
PSS-Private Corporate Sector Savings

Table 5: Savings and Car Production.

Year	*Gross Domestic Savings**		*Car Demand Number*	*% Growth in Production*
	House Hold Sector	*Private Corporate Sector*		
1979-80	13.8	2.0	42475	—
1980-81	13.8	1.6	46942	10.5
1983-84	12.8	1.5	99304	111.5
1985-86	14.3	2.0	103000	3.72
1988-89	16.8	2.0	222587	116.10
1989-90	17.9	2.4	224000	0.63
1990-91	19.3	2.7	181420	-19.0
1991-92	17.0	3.1	164600	-9.27
1992-93	17.5	2.7	160600	-2.4
1993-94	18.4	3.5	209203	30.26
1994-95	19.7	3.5	264822	26.58
1995-96	18.2	4.9	345486	30.45
1996-97	7.0	4.5	410992	19.0
1997-98	7.6	4.2	417736	2.0
1998-99	18.9	3.7	409624	-2.0
1999-00	20.3	3.7	638815	55.8

* As percentage of GDP at Current market prices.
Source: Economic Survey 2001-02 at 1993-94 prices
Society of Indian Automobile Industry.

Car Finance

Car finance also plays a vital role in augmenting the demand. At present, more than two-thirds of cars are sold through this route. Most of the auto manufacturers have set up car financing companies and some of them in collaboration with global car finance players. Major Indian public sector banks have also started financing to cars in a big way, making the car finance market more attractive to the borrowers. This has resulted due to reduction in the interest rates. At the same time, car-financing companies have shifted their focus from metro to small towns and villages, where there is a sizable pent-up demand. Thus, with increasing car finance facilities, the purchase decision of Indian car buyers are executed earlier, which helps to boost the car demand in the country. The premium segment cars are mainly targeted at businessmen and are usually bought through consumer finance.

According to Premier's Doshi, half of car purchases in India now are financed up from virtually zero in 1990. This has been a crucial catalyst for new-car demand in India. It is also the key to create a mass car market.

Banking institution is major sources of finance for car. Their lending to car is included in the personal loan.[3] An attempt is made to measure the relationship between personal loan and car demand by using OLS. The result is quite significant at 1% level. The regression result is as follows.

Car Demand (CD) = –173.5 + 0.30 Personal Loan

See (0.06)

R^2 = 0.73 R-Bar Squares = 0.70 DW = 1.45

Other Factors

Further there are 21 million two wheelers population in India, the owners of which predominantly belong to middle income group. A major portion of them is in the way to graduate themselves into car owners, as a result of increase in income, financial facilities etc. Availability of safety and distance in working place to home, good infrastructure facilities, good roads, urbanisation etc., are also responsible for creating demand for cars.

At the same time advertisement and demonstration effects (Duessenbery) have become the important aspects of non-price rivalry among firms. Consumers are easily evolving for these effects without much constrains. But the flood of variations in existing and new models provides wide range of choice for the customer. Also, these models will be able to carve a niche themselves in the crowded market.

State-Wise Sales of Passengers Cars

State-wise analysis revealed that states where the NSDP increased during the globalisation period the car demand has increased. In other words states responded positively to globalisation created increase in demand for car. This has been given in the appendix-I.

The car sale has increased in the states, which have responded to globalisation and macro economic reforms. At the same time, in the states, which have failed to attract foreign investment, the sale of car is at lower level.

Car Classification and Market Share

The Indian car industries can be classified based on the price of the car, into the small car or the economy segment and luxury car segment. The models in the car market can be sited to different segments as given in table 7.

Table 7: Classification of Car according to Price.

Category	*Models*
Economy segment (upto 4 lakhs)	Maruthi Omni, Maruthi 800, Padmini Premier 118NE, Ambassador Nova, Fiat UNO, Zen, Hyundai Santo, Daewoo Matiz, Tata Indica, Maruthi 1000, Contessa.
Luxury car segment (above Rs. 4 lakhs)	Peugeot Zoa, Tata estate, Tata Sierra, Maruthi Esteem, Ceilo Executive, Honda City, Mitsubishi Lancer, Ford Ikon, Opel Astra, Fiat Sienna, Opel Corsa, Daewoo Nexia, Hyundai Accent Mercedes Benz & other imported models.

Source: SIAM.

As a result of globalisation of auto industry and macro reforms which are favourable to middle and lower level of income group in India, the demand for car has increased substantially in post reform period. The distribution of cars sales in FY 2000 in terms of the above mentioned segments is as given in the chart below:

Classification of Cars and Changes in the Market Share.

(in per cent)

Segment	*Price range (Rs. '000)*	*Approximate market share of the segment (in 2000)*		
		1980	*1990*	*2000*
Economy	250-500	15.9	63.5	90.9
Premium	500 & above	84.1	36.5	10.1

The table shows that the demand for economy car segment has been increased due to increase in the purchasing power of lower and middle-income group with increase in household income, saving and financial facilities. However, in the last two years, sales in the mid-sized car segment has also picked up due to the wider choice set available and a study rise in household income and savings.

Conclusion

- The growth of the passenger car industry in related to the market dynamics as the economic reforms and globalisation have paved the way for increased activities in this vital industry. Earlier the restrictive policies of the GOI did not allow foreign players to set up their shop in India. But with the opening up of the economy several global automobile companies have set up their plants and started production. The study revealed that the government policy has played the key role in changing the structure and performance of car industry.

- The structure of the auto industry has been changing at a faster pace along with the changes in the industry. Globalisation factors like foreign collaborations, technology acquisition, foreign direct investment, factor substitution, competition, different models suitable to different type of customers, decrease in price, advertisement have led to change the supply side of the industry which resulting an unprecedented boom in the demand for all types of vehicles. At the same time liberalisation and economic reforms have led to change the demand side factors, like increasing Gross Domestic Product, cost effective car financing schemes, household savings, depreciation norms deficient and inefficient public transport facilities, resulting in accelerating the demand. The overall results of the study revealed that change in supply side factors not alone is adequate for creating the demand. The changes in other factors related to demand as explained in the study are essential for creating the demand for the products. The initial changes in demand side factors have effected the changes in the supply side factors, particularly in car industry during the globalisation period.
- The reorganisation of the Indian consumer preference reflects not only global forces but also rather the interplay of changing institutional factors influencing the demand structure in the economy. The globalisation policy along with the domestic reforms must favourable to consumers is essential for changes in industrial environment as revealed by the study.

NOTES

1. The following studies [Annavajhula J.C. Bose (1990), Krishnan Vishwanathan (1996), Narayanan, K. (1997), Chugen, P.K. (1997), Chugan, P.K. (1998), Kesripradeep Kumar (1998), Agarwal R.N. (1998), John Humphery (1999), Surekha Sunil Limaye (2000), Wibbenlink, R.P. and Heng M.S.H. (2000), Kamal Saggi (2000), Hrishikesh Panda (2000), Julius Spatiz and Peter Nunnen Kamp (2002), Agarwal, Aradhna (2002), Murali Patibandla (2002)] have concerned only with the supply side variables.
2. Studies [Ansal 1990, Rao 1993, Basant 1997 & Narayanan 1998] have pointed out that economic policy force have their impact on the extent and direction of technology efforts of firms.

3. Personal Loans includes all types of loan availed by the people for purchasing consumer durable goods. This includes car loan.

REFERENCES

1. Agarwal R.N. 1988, *"Indian Automobile Industry', Problems and Prospects'.* The Indian Economic Journal, No. 2, Vol. 36, Oct-Dec. 1988 pp. 50-61.
2. Amsden, A.H. and J. Kang, *'Learning to be Lean in an Emerging Economy: The Case of South Korea',* IMVP Sponsors Meeting, Toronto, 1995.
3. Ansal, Hacer K., 1990, *'Technical Change & Industrial Policy: The case of Trunch'.*
4. Avinandan, M. and Trilochan S, 1996, *'The Automotive Industry in Emerging Economics: A Comparison of Korea, Brazil, China and India',* IIM, Ahmedabad 380.
5. Basant, Rakesh, 2000, *'Corporate Response to Economic Reforms',* Economic & Political Weekly, Vol. 35, No. 10, PD 813-22.
6. Chugan P.K. (1998), *'Factors Affecting the Inter-firm Variations in Export Performance: A case of Indian Autoparts Industry.* Indian Journal of Economics No. 312 Vol. Lxxxx, July 98.
7. D-Costa,-Anthony, 1995, *'The Restructuring of the Indian Automobile Industry; Indian State and Japanese Capital',* World-Development; 23(3), March 1995, pp. 485-502.
8. Donnefield, S and S. Weber, 1992, *'Vertical Product Differentiation with Entry';* International Journal of Industrial Organisation 10(3) 449-472.
9. Garry Pursell, 2002, *'Australia's Experience with Local Content Programs in the Auto Industry: Lessons for India and Other Developing Countries',* Consultant, Development Research Group (Trade), World Bank, Washington, DC USA.
10. John Humphrey, 1999, *'Globalisation and Supply Chain Networks: The Auto Industry in Brazil and India'.*
11. Kumar Nagas, 1987, *'Multinational Enterprises and Export Promotion: The case of Indian',* Discussion Paper, New Delhi.

    Manufacturing in Turkey', *World Development',* Vol. 18, No. 11, pp. 1513-28.
12. Marris, Robin, 1964, *'The Economic Theory of Managerial Capitalism, Glances,'* (Free Press, New York).
13. Murali Patibandla, 2002, *'Product Differentiation and Market Demand for TNC's in an Emerging Economy: The case of India Durable Consumer Goods Industries.* The Indian Journal of labour Economic, Vol. 44, No. 2, April-June, 2001, pp. 205 to 221.
14. Narayanan, K., 1998, *"Technology Acquition, De-regulation & competitiveness: A study of Indian Automobile Industry',* Research Policy, Vol. 27, No. 2, PD, 217-230.

15. Narayanan, K, 2001, *"Evolution of Automobile Industry in India through Changing Policy Regimes'* in Carello, Torge, Yanniak Lung and Robvan Tuder [Eds.]

16. Natarajan, 1998, *"India Market Demographic Report',* National Council for Applied Economic Research, New Delhi.

17. Pankaj Chandra, P.R. Shukla, 1994, *'Manufacturing Excellence and Global Competitiveness', Challenges & Opportunity for Indian Industries'.* Economic & Political Weekly Feb. 26, 1994.

18. Surekha Sunil Limaye, 2000, *"An Introduction to the Indian Automobile Industry"* suite 101.com.

19. Takahiro F. and Akira T, 2001, *"Automobile: Strategy Based Lean Production System"* University of Tokyo & Hitotsubashi University.

20. Vishwanthan Krishan, 2001, *"Indian Automotive Industry: Opportunities & Challenges Posed by Recent Development".*

21. Wadhva, D. Charan (1977), *'Multinational Enterprises in India and their Export performance. The Case of Hindusthan Lever Ltd.'* Global Giants, pp. 50-63.

22. Williamson, Oliver E. 1985, *"The Economic Institutions of Capitalism',* (The Free Press, New York).

35

Revitalising Micro-Income Generating Activities Through SHGs and Micro-Credit For Rural Women

*Dr. Falendra K. Sudan**

Introduction

Globalisation and economic liberalisation with the doctrine of free markets have opened up tremendous opportunities for development and growth and consequent modifications in livelihood strategies. However, these economic changes are making the marginalised and poor sections of society more vulnerable without adequate safety net. The profit of the huge commercial conglomerates: multinational corporations and transnational corporations (MNCs and TNCs) concentrate on cost cutting through technological improvements and ignore the needs of the poor people. The developed countries and institutions like the International Monetary Fund (IMF) and the World Bank are increasingly dictating economic and social policies under the policy of structural adjustment and economic liberalisation. In the present situation, the economic transformation is being hammered through at the cost of social development. Economic development without social development can only increase tensions and friction within any society. In developing countries, where only a handful of the population is rich, ignoring the poorer sections of the population is a sure recipe for disaster. In India, if civilised society is to be maintained, all development efforts have to be people-oriented. After many year of centralised planing, it is clear that the government cannot ensure employment to all. The industrial and

* Reader, P.G. Deptt. of Economic University of Jammu, Jammu (J. & K.), 180 006.

agricultural sector is unable to absorb the growing labor force. Not only this, the spread and strengthening of neo-liberal economic agenda across the developing world, and its emphasis on marketisation and structure adjustment, women participation in development programmes have assumed significance. There is inadequate understanding of the ways in which liberalisation affects women's participation in markets, in terms of both productive and reproductive activities. However, the women are entering the hitherto reserved arenas of economic endeavours in a big way.

Besides, the growing population pressure as well as extreme poverty in the Third World has brought about a situation wherein the means available with the poor are not sufficient for them to live a normal human life. Despite considerable efforts in the last five decades to overcome widespread poverty and economic stagnation, a majority of the population still has little access to the market economy to support their private initiative. It is now increasingly believed that the government aid and assistance creates dependency and disincentives. Besides, corruption and nepotism has made matters much worse in developing countries [UNDP (2000)]. In India, even the 'targeted schemes' like Integrated Rural Development Programme (IRDP) and Development of Women and Children in Rural Areas (DWCRA) fails to benefit the rural women in desired manner. Keeping in view the widespread rural poverty, there is need not only to ameliorate the economic condition of the marginalised and disadvantaged social groups, but also to transform their social structures. In the context of rural women, their economic condition becomes more vulnerable due to unequal distribution of resources. Poverty and deprivation increase gender inequality, which favours a policy for empowerment of women through increasing their greater access to credit through Self-Help Groups (SHGs) so that these marginalised sections of rural society would be able to acquire the capability and assets that can help facilitate in realising strategic gender needs. Thus, the SHGs can be built on the social capital of the local community especially women, to carry out savings and credit activities to initiate micro-income-generating activities (MIGAs) to eke out a sustainable livelihood [Moser (1989) and Hydan (2000)].

During the recent past, the new types of institutions have been promoted to meet the credit needs of those groups who have hitherto been excluded from formal credit markets [Prakash (2002]. SHGs are mostly informal groups whose members have a common perception and impulse towards collective action. These groups promote savings among their members and use the pooled resources to meet the emergent needs of their members, including the consumption needs. Sometimes, the generated internal savings are supplemented by external resources loaned/donated by the Non-Governmental

Organisations (NGOs) who promote them. SHGs are thus able to provide banking services to their members, which may not be sophisticated but are cost-effective, simple, flexible, accessible to their members and above all without any defaults in repayments of loans. The linking of SHGs to banks helps in overcoming the problem of high transaction costs to banks in providing credit to the poor, by transferring some banking responsibilities, such as loan appraisal, follow-up, recovery, etc., to the poor themselves [Satish(2001)]. Several studies reveal that the most of the groups formed and financed were of poor women. This feature was more conspicuous in the resource-poor regions, predominated by poor people. The demand for credit for credit from these groups was frequent and for small amounts, at unpredictable times and more often for consumption purposes [Puhazhendi (1995)]. These studies also indicated a reduction in transaction costs for both banks and SHG members and almost 100 per cent recovery of loans [Srinivasan and Rao (1996)].

In rural context, the SHGs have facilitated the poor, especially the women to overcome the existing constraints grappling the formal credit institutions. These groups provide considerable social protection and income opportunities to their members. These emerging rural institutions have sought to explore new ways and alternatives, based on value system that introduces new type of relationships and takes into account the social and economic aspects of collective living and livelihood improvement. Besides, these groups also help facilitate the poor women to overcome the difficulty of providing collateral to raise the finance to initiate MIGAs and due to better performance, the SHGs have acquired a prominent status with a view to maximize social and financial returns. The promotion of MIGAs for the poor rural women is perceived as a powerful medium to ameliorate several socio-economic problems such as reduction in poverty, provision of goods and services appropriate to the local needs, redistribution of both income and opportunities in the community in general. Th redistribution of wealth and opportunity lead to decentralisation of economic power within the community [Bhat (1999)]. Keeping above in view, in the present paper an attempt has been made to examine the issues related to revitalising the Micro-Income-Generating Activities (MIGAs) through Self-Help Groups (SHGs) by utilising micro-credit for rural poor women in the context of the Integrated Watershed Development Project (IWDP), Hills-II, Jammu and Kashmir.

SHGs and MIGAs

In developing countries with vast sections of rural population caught up in the web of poverty, the challenge is to generate employment and income opportunities for the marginalised groups, but in the sustainable manner. MIGAs whether in the informal organised sectors provides opportunities for or gainful employment, while preserving the social structure. MIGAs can play an important role in improving the quality of life and poverty alleviation. Ensuring their success is cost-effective and enables the vulnerable groups, such as woman and disadvantaged communities, to smoothen the seasonal fluctuations in household income. It has emerged as a real boon for the poor and helped in generating additional income for families. Tailoring, embroidery work, pickle making, fruit canning, bookbinding, incense stick making etc. provide ample prospects for illiterate and poor rural women to make a livelihood. Further, it is ideal for many poor women who prefer part-time employment. Most women confirming to the conventional and traditional roles accept domestic responsibilities as mothers and wives MIGAs facilities women to have flexible working hours. Besides, it trains them to acquire entrepreneurial ability and at the same time obtained economic independence. In most economically depressed poor sections, men desert the families shirking their responsibilities as principal earners. In such cases, it becomes the women's lot to provide for family and children. These female-headed households are the poorest of the poor, because women have less access then men to training, credit, property, resources and income generation. Development of MIGA can help to create immediate employment opportunities involving a number of women at low investment level. Besides, it provides for full utilisation of capital and also reduces the wastage of human resources particularly women [Sundari and Geetha (2000)].

There are three types of situation in which the poor members of SHG may take up MIGAs: (1) they may take up individual activities like farming, animal husbandry, artisans work, wage labour and petty trade; (ii) they may also come together to own common inventories by sharing capital and operating costs, however, their principal economic activity is individual-based; and (iii) they may take up collective activities such as social forestry, which are run by the group with responsibilities divided between the members. The area of concern for MIGAs is: (a) identification of demand-led potential; (b) timely supply/availability of raw materials; (c) technology/skill upgradation; (d) access to market information; (e) availability of proper supportive infrastructure; and (f) other backward and forward linkages. Another area of concern is the non-availability of adequate and timely credit. Bank needs to develop new financial products and adopt innovative approaches to meet the growing financial requirement of micro-enterprises. Micro-credit in rural areas is meaningful only if poor are empowered with crucial skill to run MIGAs successfully. The long-term entrepreneurial education, access to cheap loans and the formation of SHGs will enable to poor to fight poverty with dignity and build up various skills.

Prior to 1990s, there were hardly any credit schemes designed for rural women. They have limited access to resources or employment opportunities that would make them financially independent. They live in conditions that do not permit them to meet their minimum consumption needs. They do not control even the money earned by them from hard physical labour. Institutional credit is difficult to access as women rarely have any property rights to mortgage or collateral to offer, as they have to depend on rural money-lenders for their production-cum-consumption needs. This entraps them into a vicious cycle of perpetual poverty and indebtedness. Some banks notably State Bank of India (SBI) have formulated specific schemes for rural women entrepreneurs and specific training courses for developing their skills. However, their credit needs were not attended to in desirable manner. Given the situation, the micro-credit approach has been considered appropriate through which their potential or small savings should be utilised and their investment and production-cum-consumption needs should be met. The micro-credit to the SHGs to operationalised MIGAs is rarely misused. In fact, the income from the MIGAs is generally used for the betterment of the families, especially children. It reduces the transaction and monitoring costs and enhances the repayment capacity. Women are able to manage their credit operations very practically and are able to face the future with greater degree of confidence.

Micro-Credit for MIGAs

The concept of micro-credit to finance MIGAs in rural areas has developed considerably during the recent past. It is working neither on donation nor on subsidy. It is basically rotational investment done to motivate poor to empower themselves and apply the existing theory of 'save for the future and use those resources during the time of need'. Theoretically, micro-credit means making provisions for smaller working capital loans to poor to take up MIGAs like daily farming, poultry rearing, weaving, handloom, handicrafts, etc. [Naithani (2001)]. According to *Grameen* Bank, micro-credit symbolizes small loans extended to the poor for undertaking MIGAs that would generate income and enable them to provide for themselves and their families. The targeted groups include women micro-entrepreneurs to which credit up to Rs. 25,000 is provided without any collateral [RBI (1999)]. Under micro-credit scheme, the non-poor is discouraged from borrowing [Hulme and Mosley (1996)], through group formation [Yunus (1999)]. The formation of micro-credit groups ensures the solidarity among like-minded people living in similar socio-economic milieu. The loans are given for pre-identified local raw materials and skill based MGAs that cannot go wrong in terms of repayment of the loan or it turning into a bad investment [Hulme and Mosley (1996)]. The administrative and monitoring costs are minimised as the loan usage and enforcement is taken care of individually as well through the group [Hussain (1998)].

The popularisation of micro-credit has given an opportunity to put gender back in focus in the issue related to development planning. The empirical studies on the relationship between micro-credit and women welfare have shown mixed results. Pitt and Khandker (1996) projected that credit programmes like the *Grameen* Bank are an affective means to empower women by increasing their contribution to household consumption expenditure, their hours devoted to production for the market and the value to their assets. Rahman (1999), however, brought the rather uncanny face of *Grameen* programme. The insistence on increase disbursement of loans and high recovery rates force the bank workers and borrowing peers to inflict excessive pressure on women clients and escalation of domestic violence. Goetz and Sen Gupta (1996) argued that overemphasis on enhancing women productively in home-based work by disbursing credit is bound to subvert the basic feminist concern for redistribution of gendered domestic responsibilities and thus undermine women's control over resources generated through loans and investment. Pearson (2000) emphasised that micro-credit programmes focuses on resources and policies targeted at women and not in terms of improving gender position on transforming gender relations, but in terms of the ways in which credit might successfully allow donors to provide appropriate resources to the poor household.

Government Programmes for Micro-Credit

The fulfillment of the objective of rural development is very much connected to the availability of bank credit to the marginalised and disadvantaged groups in rural areas Traditionally, rural women have tended to borrow from the informal sector only. With structural changes transforming the rural areas, institutional credit for women has assumed critical importance. Often, it is the legal provisions and the loan policies and procedures that make credit inaccessible to rural women and keep them out of the mainstream of the development process. IRDP launched for poverty alleviation in India was a target-oriented programme with a focus on identifying the poorest of the poor and helping them to acquire productive assets through bank loan and subsidy from government. The underlying assumption was that lack of productive assets was responsible for the poor being unable to better their lot. IRDP, however, was not successful as was visualised. Several drawbacks were seen in the implementation of the programme [Rath (1985)]. In 1982-83, DWCRA was launched as a sub-scheme of IRDP. This was an attempt to involve women more intensively in economic activities (NABARD, 1999). The focus of DWCRA was on economic activities for rural women to be taken up in-groups. DWCRA was successful to some extent in Andhra Pradesh [Dev (1999)]. However, on the whole, DWCRA too met with limited success and was failed to take off. Despite these schemes and several others [Training of Rural Youth for self-employment (TRYSEM), supply of Improved Toolkits to Rural Artisans (SITRA), the credit and poverty problem in rural areas continues [Madheswaran and Dharmadhikary (2001)].

The rural poor are still dependent on informal sources of credit despite an impressive expansion of bank branch network. Although this dependence has come down from 83.7 per cent of the rural population in 1961 to 36 per cent in 1991, the problem still persists. Given the levels of rural poverty, unemployment and underemployment, "the self-employment programmes assume significance for, they alone can provide income to the rural poor on a sustainable basis" (Government of India, 1999, p. 10). Against this background, the schemes of micro-credit through SHGs were designed NABARD (1999) advocated 'SHG-Bank Linkage' model as a core strategy for provisioning micro-credit to operationalised MIGAs to alleviate rural poverty and livelihood enhancement. The SHG-Bank Linkage approach stresses the importance of links between commercial banks, NGOs and SHGs as a mechanism for channelising credit to the poor on a sustainable basis. In this model, rural women are expected to form groups and borrow from the banks as a group. The default of the bank loan by any one member is the responsibility of all the members. The loan can also be used for consumption purposes. Besides, to begin with, the group has to save certain amount of money to be eligible for bank credit, which help inculcate the habits of savings. Unlike, DWCRA, the funds under micro-credit programme keeps revolving, which can be used by the women to take up MIGA at their own pace and have better chance of success.

Government programmes like Rural Labour Employment Guarantee programme (RLEGP), Self-Employment for Educated Unemployed Youth (SEEUY), etc. have also not been very useful to the rural poor women. A large number of rural poor women are not prepared by way of skills, attitudes and enterprise to manage income generating activities involving relatively large financial outlays. This explains the relatively low level of loan amounts disbursed per beneficiary under the IRDP programme. The average credit disbursed per assisted family averaged Rs. 2,566; Rs. 2,289; and Rs. 2,880 in the primary, secondary and territory sectors, respectively as against the maximum limit ranging from Rs. 3,000 to Rs. 9,000. Institutional agencies are also finding it difficult to meet the credit requirements of the poor sections in view of accounts scattered over a wide area, stringent asset classification and income recognition norms, lack of proper assessment of credit needs, mounting over dues, staff problems, lack of consumption loans, etc. The general impression is that government is obsessed with targets. The bankers are worried about the recovery and none is bothered about the development of rural poor women [Kulshrestha (2000)].

Some of the development programmes, which are operational in Jammu and Kashmir are (i) *Swaranjayanti Gram Swarozgar Yojana* (SGSY) through District Rural Development Agency (DRDA); (ii) Schemes for Economic Empowerment of Females under Women Development Corporation (WDC); (iii) Schemes of Department of Animal Husbandry for Dairy Farming; and (iv) NABARD and other Banks. SGSY has been launched in April 1999 and is operational in the project area. The objective of SGSY is to bring every assisted family above the poverty line within a period of 3 years through the provision of micro-enterprise. This is a holistic programme covering all aspects of self-employment such as the organisation of poor into SHGs' training, credit, technology, infrastructure and marketing SGSY lays stress on cluster approach, so that *Swarozgaries* can draw sustainable incomes from their investments. The choice of activity is based on the local sources, the aptitude as well as the skills of the people. It is also necessary that the products have ready market. SGSY supplements the traditional knowledge of the poor households and facilities the identification of suitable activities. As regards non-form activities, under SGSY care have been taken to identify only those activities that result in the production of goods and services that have a ready market. Infrastructure already available in the district in terms of production, service, training facilities as well as market are being utilised and that choice of activity does not require a new effort in all direction-production as well as marketing. SGSY focused on group approach and involves organisation of the poor into SHGs; and their capacity building. Group activities are being given preference and progressively, majority of the funding will be for SHGs.

SGSY is a credit-cum-subsidy programme. There are two ways in which a SHG can receive this assistance: (i) Loan-cum-subsidy of SGSY to individuals in a group, provided the prospective *Swarozaries* in the group are capable of and willing to take up income generating activities and (ii) Loan-cum-subsidy to the group where all members in the group want to take up a group activity. Subsidy under SGSY is uniform at 30 per cent of the activity, subject to a maximum of Rs. 7500. In respect of SC/STs, however, subsidy is 50 per cent and Rs. 10000 respectively. For the groups of *Swarozgaries,* the subsidy is 50 per cent of the cost of the scheme to a ceiling of 1.25 lac. SGSY particularly focussed on the vulnerable groups among the rural poor. Accordingly, the SC/STs accounts for at least 50 per cent of the *Swarozgaries,* women for 40 per cent and the disabled for 30 per cent. SGSY is being implemented by the DRDAs at district level and BDOs at block level. The size of the loan for micro enterprise depends on the nature of the activity. Nominal interest is being charged as per the guidelines issued by Reserve Bank of India/National Bank for Agriculture and Rural Development from time to time. The sanctioning procedure is easy and the banks take no more than 15 days to sanction the loan. The repayment system is also easy. SGSY proposes a number of measures for upgrading the capacity of *Swarozgaries* both in individual as well as group oriented activities. In case, the *Swarozgaries* possesses the required skills, they may be put through a basic orientation programme after the loan is sanctioned and before it is disbursed. The *Swarozgaries* who needed additional skill development/upgradation of skills, appropriate training may be identified and suitable training programmes organised. In case of targeted people in project area, they also possess some skills, which needs upgradation and some women needs appropriate training. SGSY recognizes that for any successful enterprise, appropriate technology and marketing is of paramount importance, for which the services of KVIC, KVKs, ITIs, etc. are being utilised.

J&K State WDC undertakes a number of schemes for economic empowerment of females. The objectives are to assist women in starting income generation units by providing financial assistance, grant-in-aid, subsidy, margin money, etc.; and conduct training programmes to promote talent amongst females. The poor women of the project area are eligible for financial assistance (loan/grant-in-aid) under different schemes being implemented by WDC for setting up of viable MIGAs. The prescribed income ceiling determining eligibility for availing credit/loan varies from scheme to scheme. However, the ultimate/end beneficiaries should be variably belonging to weaker sections/ living below poverty line. Under the scheme of setting up of Training-cum-Production Centre, registered societies/NGOs are given 100 per cent finance by Government of India to impact skill upgradation training in traditional and non-traditional sectors and later on converting training centres into production centres, providing employment to females. Likewise, under the socio-economic scheme of setting up of Production Centre, Central Welfare Board through its socio-economic programme being implemented through registered societies/NGOs endeavours to provide them opportunity for "Work and Wage". These activities provide the women an opportunity to engage themselves in full time and/or part time work to earn either a full or a wage to supplement the meager income of the families of the middle income and lower income groups. It also helps these women to earn a wage while working at homes, as far as possible, so as not to cause dislocation to domestic life.

Another scheme called Support to Trainee and Employment Programme (STEP) envisages imparting training and providing employment. Under this scheme, vocational training is being imparted to females. The Department of Women and Child Development, Ministry of Human resource Development, Government of India provides 90 per cent of the project cost and the remaining 10 per cent of the cost is provided by J&K State Women Development Corporation. The scheme of direct financing under *Rashtriya Mahila Kosh* envisages meeting small credit needs of females with a view to enabling them, to start some income generating activity. Short term and mid-term assistance is provided to the women belonging to the families living below poverty line at nominal rate of interest. The loan range is from Rs. 4000-6000 for each beneficiary, through NGOs. Though individual ventures are financed, yet major thrust is on group activities. *Rashtriya Mahila Kosh* provides incentives to NGOs/Societies who help in formation of SHG and promote group activity. The system of post-dated cheques secures the repayment of the loan advanced under direct financing scheme through WDC from the beneficiaries. WDC organizes training in identified trades for women entrepreneurs through the training institutions run by government/NGOs/Societies in tailoring and cutting, fashion designing, shawl and blanket, ceramic works, vegetable and fruit processing, spinning and weaving, etc. The Corporation also provides market tie-up to women artisans by organising craft *bazar* / exhibitions and deputing female artisans to exhibition/gram Melas organised by other departments within and outside the state.

Besides above, line departments also provide assistance to the targeted groups. For the activities like bee-keeping and mushroom cultivation, 50 per cent subsidy is available through department of agriculture to SC/STs families. The department of agriculture provides training in this regard. The department of animal husbandry provides training in dairy technology and poultry rearing; and provides subsidy on the purchase of *Jersy* cows. The department of sericulture also provides subsidy on raw silkworm, mulberry saplings and purchase of dry cocoons at district level. There is no provision of direct financial assistance for processing of dry cocoon by the women themselves, however, if cooperatives are formed, financial assistance is available. The directorate of handloom imparts training to the potential and existing weavers to improve their skills and designs. Under the Share Capital Loan Assistance Scheme, the directorate provides working capital loan to the weavers of primary cooperative societies. The financial assistance is available in the shape of 50 per cent subsidy and 50 per cent loan at about 9 per cent interest rate. However, in most cases, financial assistance is available to cooperatives only. NABARD/other banks provides financial assistance to SHGs for taking up MIGAs, provided they are six months old and the SHGs are potent of becoming self-sustaining over the period. The major problem with most schemes for poverty alleviation and channelising credit to the rural areas seems to be that they are not based on unrealistic assumptions and analysis of the rural credit markets. In most of the cases, the beneficiaries' perceived the loan as grant and they do not feel the responsibility of repaying it. Bankers and development agencies too concentrated on disbursing the loan. They did not have the time or the mechanism for monitoring the repayment. This led to poor loan recovery and resulted in the scheme becoming non-viable [Rath (1985) and Rao et al. (1990)]. In contrast, the repayment of loans in micro-credit schemes using SHG is reported to be satisfactory from almost all places, which may be due to better information and peer monitoring [Hoff and Stiglir (1990)].

With increasing criticism of the State-led formal credit system and its utilisation for poverty alleration [Shetty (1997) and RBI (1991)], in recent years, India has moved towards a new mechanisms of lending such as micro-credit. Micro-credit has been claimed to be a solution to most of the problems that originated out of the state's efforts to alleviate poverty using the instrument of credit [Yunus (1999)]. The implementation of any formal lending programme directed towards the poor is often beset by three important difficulties: problem of exact targeting, screening problem of distinguishing the good from bad borrowers, and poor monitoring to ensure productive usage of loans [Hulme and Mosley (1996) and Cornia and Steward (1993)]. In order to create an environment that enables the micro-credit providers to evolve into institutions capable of achieving wider outreach and critical mass in operations, the Reserve Bank of India (RBI) had set up a micro-credit special cell to examine the policy issues on regular basis. Recently, the RBI has permitted banks to adopt any model to cater to the needs of micro-financial services. Similarly, the RBI has given total freedom [Capoor (2001)] in regard to designing of appropriate loan and savings products and related terms and conditions including the loan amount, unit cost, unit size, maturity period, grace period, margin, etc., with an intention to provide maximum flexibility. The banks have also been permitted to provide credit for consumption purposes [Todd (2000)]. Indian banking policy has attempted to involve the public banking network in the provision of micro-credit to the poor through credit groups. Public banks adopt the approach of group lending to the credit groups. Such a policy has three variants that differ in the mode of linkage between the banks and borrowers. These variants are: (*i*) Public banks to take initiatives in forming the groups, nurtures them over a period of time and then provides credit to them after satisfying itself about their maturity to absorb credit (ii) Public banks and borrowers (credit groups) are linked through facilitating agencies, which are either NGOs working locally or government agencies. (iii) The functions of forming groups, nurturing them and providing credit to them are performed by NGOs, while banks confine themselves to provide credit to NGOs. This is practiced in regions where the banks are not in a position to even finance credit groups promoted and nurtured by other agencies. However, the utilisation of the public banking network for the supply of micro-credit does not necessarily mean the continuation of public regulation or accountability in its operations. It has been pointed out that it is "desirable and appropriate to support evolution of a self-regulatory mechanism for micro-finance institutions such as NGOs, which would prescribe codes of conduct and ground rules" [RBI (2001)]. Hence, the degree of accountability of NGO-led micro-credit institutions in India still remains unclear.

MIGAs under IWDP (Hills-II), J&K

Integrated Watershed Development Project (IWDP), Hills-II, Jammu and Kashmir has been launched in the State of Jammu and Kashmir for a period of 5 years viz. September 1999-March 2005. The "bottom-up" approach is an integral part of the project design and involves all stockholders during project planning and implementation. The need for designing and operationalising the MIGAs for the targeted groups has been emphasised in the Project Appraisal Document (PAD) and funds have been earmarked for this purpose [World Bank (1999)]. One of the objectives of IWDP (Hills-II) is to diversify the rural livelihood conditions of the people inhibiting the watersheds lying in the *Shivaliks* through active community participation at each stage and in all project interventions. An important component of the project is institutional strengthening. The objective of the institutional strengthening is to (a) support beneficiary capacity building in planning, implementing project activities; (b) strengthen implementing agencies capacity of reaching the communities through training, field exposure and better incentives, (c) support the effort to increase awareness of sustainability measures and project development objectives; and (d) support the project to implement policy and institutional reforms essential for sustainability of the project activities and building partnerships with other local level institutions. The main sub-components of the institutional strengthening component includes. (a) improve community capacity building; (b) strengthen policy reforms, studies and human resource development; (c) improve women's capacity to manage development by promoting income generating activities; (d) improve knowledge management, monitoring and evaluation; and support and strengthen project management [World Bank (1998)].

During the implementation of the phase-I of the project, women participation was reportedly scanty and was constrained by low literacy, inadequate decision-making, token representation in watershed institutions, lack of technical skill and training, economic dependence, gender bias and above all absence of all women groups [Sadhu and Sudan, (1999)]. To overcome the above constraints and better participation of women, the project in its II-phase has started formation of all women SHGs. Most of the project interventions are land-based and the women are not the sole owners of the land, so they are deprived of the benefits of most of the interventions directly. Women constitute about half of the population in the project area and their involvement is ensured to enhance the sustainability of the project interventions. Likewise, other disadvantaged groups viz. landless, Scheduled Castes/Scheduled Tribes and nomadic and semi-nomadic pastoral communities inhibiting the sub-watershed are also roped in to take up suitable MIGAs to raise their livelihoods and make the project interventions sustainable. Women of these disadvantaged groups, though insignificant in number, are encouraged to participate in MIGAs and training programmes in large scale. The demand driven MIGAs are being implemented for tribal (nomadic and semi-nomadic pastoral communities) and decided through a participatory approach. The project is promoting MIGAs on group basis, but in the case of nomadic and semi-nomadic pastoral communities, those types of activities are being implemented, wherein more benefits accrue to individuals [Sudan (2002)].

Table 1: Proportion of Targeted Groups to be involved in Broad Group of Activities (in percentage).

Targeted Groups	*Off-Land IGAs*	*Land-Based IGAs*	*Training-based IGAs*
Women	28	34	34
Landless	34	Nil	22
SCs	12	22	14
STs	8	18	12
Sedentary Gujjars	0	12	12
Nomadic and Semi-nomadic	8	14	8

Source: IWDP, Hill-II, J.&K. (2001).

The targeted population possesses traditional skills, which could be utilised properly by upgrading the skills through training as well as extending/ providing, other support services like credit and marketing. By doing so, not only the targeted groups could be able to utilize their spare/free time productively, but also poverty alleviation will be the outcome due to increased socio-economic status [Sadhu and Sudan (2000)]. On the basis of PRA exercises carried out by Participatory Social Development functionaries and technical staff of the project, the proportion of different targeted groups to be benefited from various off-land, land-based, and training-based MIGAs are given in table 1. A mere perusal of the data reveals that women is the most dominant social group targeted for implementation of MIGAs under IWDP (Hills-II) followed by landless and other disadvantaged groups such as SCs, STs, sedentary *gujjars* and nomadic and semi-nomadic transhumance communities.

Principles of MIGA Strategy

One of the major reasons for deterioration in the ecological balance in the *Shivaliks* has been the excessive pressure of population on land. With the increase in population, marginal lands were brought under cultivation and pastures and forests encroached upon. Deforestation, soil erosion and decline in the productivity of village common lands have also adversely affected women more, as their main household duties usually consist of collecting fuel, fodder and water, all of which had become scarcer. The young girls are mostly engaged in the tasks of collecting firewood and fodder, fetching water, washing utensils, tending animals, looking after young siblings besides attending other domestic chores, which have affected their scooling after primary or middle standard and drop-out rates are quite high in case of girls. All this will likely to worsen the future poverty status of the population inhibiting the project area, if corrective and timely measures are not initiated. Therefore, unless alternative sources of income are provided to the population inhibiting the project area, any attempt to promote optimum use of land and water cannot succeed, in spite of the improved dryland agricultural practices [Sudan (2002)].

In order to operationalize the approach, SHGs have been created. The project place special emphasis on the building the capacity of SHGs to take up MIGAs on sustainable basis for which PRA exercises have been conducted to reflect their priorities. The project focuses on the most degraded watersheds in the *Shivaliks* and, thus, the proportion of the poor inhibiting the project area is quite high. The project aim to ensure that benefit streams must reach the more marginalised and vulnerable section of the rural community, which includes those who subsist on the most marginal of resources as well as women, whose role in overall livelihood strategies have often been ignored in the past. The participatory development functionaries of the project are taking steps to incorporate the interests of these marginalised and vulnerable sections of the rural community in operationalisation of MIGAs. The continuous dialogue are being initiated with their representatives and SHGs. Special attention has been given to incorporate the interests of the transhumance community in the MIGAs. In order to ensure that women participates in project activities, women-specific MIGAs are identified, for which special attention are being given to their skill development programmes, awareness campaigns, development of close links with other gender related poverty alleviation and social programmes, and opportunities for income generation.

To operationalize the identified MIGAs, skill development of the targeted groups in various aspects of micro-enterprises is not over-emphasised. Women, landless and other disadvantaged sections of the rural community have traditionally been at the fag end of development conduit and hence to bring them in the mainstream of the society, capacity building process needs to be strengthened. Through initiation of MIGAs, it is hoped that pressure on environmental resources will be curtailed and the project will be able to realize the goal of watershed development and protection along with poverty alleviation. Most of the identified MIGAs are based on traditional skills and local resources, which have ready-made local markets. A large proportion of the rural poor women is engaged in household activities and available to take up MIGAs on sustainable basis, if opportunities are made available. The existing MIGAs and skill possession by the women needs to be strengthened. The targeted group needs training in various issues of MIGAs, which includes technical, financial and marketing aspects [Sadhu and Sudan (2000)]. The SHGs created in the project area by the participatory development functionaries are implementing most of the identified MIGAs. SHGs capacity is being strengthened through continuous training in various aspects of MIGAs including technical, financial, marketing and record keeping. The overall objective of initiation and operationalisation of MIGAs is to strengthen the processes of social and economic development of women and other targeted groups and create an environment for social change to improve their quality of life. The selected MIGAs are being operationalised through adopting "bottom up approach" evolving and strengthening participatory process.

The matrix of MIGA action plan is shown in box 1, which contains various stages of MIGA, the key issues, responsibilities of stakeholders, and the role of the project. The main stages of the MIGA are selection of MIGA, selection

Box 1: Matrix of MIGA Action Plan.

Stages of IGA	*Key Issues*	*Responsibility*	*Role of project*
• Selection of MIGA	• Skill possession • Raw-material availability • Local demand • Profit expected	SHGs	• Role of facilitators • Disseminate information • Market related issues • Training
• Selection of Beneficiary Group/ Individual	• Group motivation • Skill possession • Available free time	SHGs	• Role of facilitators in formation of SHGs • Capacity building for institutionaldevelopment
• Financial Support	• Total financial requirement • SHG contribution • Existing development schemes • Gestation period	• Participatory development functionaries of the project to motivate SHGs to procure loans/funds for equipment and loan for raw materials • Project to bear the cost of training, etc.	• Financial assistance of Rs. 15,000 to each SHG for equipment • Interest free loan of Rs. 20,000 for raw materials to each SHG • Training assistance of Rs. 30,000 to each SHG, equipment on rotational basis • Engagement of local trainer.
• Marketing	• Local demand • Consumer linkages • Sales price • Transportation • Storage	• Project functionaries to arrange finance and training • SHGs to assess training needs	• Role of facilitator in forging marketing linkages • Ensure sustainability of MIGA after project
• Training	• MIGA based skills • Skill in marketing • Management skills • Bookkeeping and account maintenance • Follow up training	• Project functionaries	• Training needs assessment • Identification of trainers • Organisation of training • Forging training linkages • Trainer exchange facilitation • Organisation of exposure visits etc.
• Documentation and Publicity	• Disseminating success stories • Preparation of training manuals • Organisation of • Organisation of exhibitions/fairs • Publicity • Disseminating through workshops	• Project functionaries	• Meet the cost of dissemination • Cost of preparation of • Cost of preparation of training manuals • Training related expenses • Organisation of exhibitions/fairs • Establishment of linkages, etc.

Source: Sudan (2002).

of beneficiary group/individual, financial support, marketing, training, documentation and publicity. The key issues in MIGA are selection of MIGA, selection of beneficiary group/individual, financial support, marketing, training, documentation and publicity. The key issues in MIGA selection are skill possession, raw material availability, local demand and level of profit expected. In the selection of MIGA, the main responsibility lies with SHGs, which are facilitated by social development facilitators through information dissemination on market-related issues and training. The next stage of MIGA is selection of beneficiary group/individual beneficiaries in which the key issues are motivation of the group, skill possession and availability of free spare time to take up the enterprise. The SHGs have the responsibility in beneficiaries' group/individual beneficiaries' identification and the project facilitators have to facilitate the SHGs formation and their capacity building for institutional development. The financial support to SHGs is a very crucial stage in taking up the MIGA and its sustainability. Only those types of MIGAs are to be selected which have lesser financial requirements. A higher proportion of the finances are to be met from the contribution of the SHGs, and the gap is to be met from existing development schemes for which suitable linkages needs to be forged with government and non-government development agencies. As the SHGs have meager finances of their own, the participatory social development functionaries of the project must motivate them to procure loans/funds for equipment and raw materials. The project intends to give a financial assistance of Rs. 15,000 for equipment, interest free loan of Rs. 20,000 for raw materials and training assistance of Rs. 30,000 to each SHG, besides equipment of rotational basis.

Other important stages of MIGA are marketing, training, documentation and publicity. The key issues for marketing is that the products must have local demand for which suitable consumer linkages are to be forged. The sale price, transportation and storage facilities also assume importance. The project functionaries are required to arrange the finances and training in marketing aspects of the identified MIGAs, which could be based on training needs assessment carried out by the SHGs. The project facilitators have to facilitate the SHGs in identifying the marketing outlets and in making suitable linkages with them, which could ensure the sustainability of the MIGAs after the project. The stage of training is very vital and is linked with each and every aspect of the MIGAs such as technical skill formation and development, marketing skill, managerial skills, bookkeeping and accounts maintenance skills, etc. The project functionaries have a major role to play in areas such as training needs assessment, identification of trainers, organisation of training, forging training linkages, organisation of exposure of visits, etc. Last but not the least, documentation and publicity is an important stage in sustainability of MIGAs and help in disseminating success stories, preparing training manuals, publicity etc. the project has a major role in this regard and has to met the cost of dissemination, training expenses, exposure visits, linkage formation etc.

The key objectives and performance indicators of MIGAs are shown in box 2. The main objectives of MIGAs are institutional strengthening, support to MIGAs, capacity building of SHGs, capacity building of participating agencies, mobilisation of funds, and business management and technical support services. The outcomes of the objective of institutional strengthening are to be judged by SHG sustainability, financial sustainability and training effectiveness. The mobilisation of investment funds and training in business management and technical aspects to SHGs are significant objectives of MIGAs, where the outcomes are assessed by credit mobilisation ratio, number of SHGs receiving loans for MIGAs, proportion of the loan used, increase in income levels of the beneficiaries, etc. The outcomes of the capacity building of the SHGs are measured by extent of mutual support, achievement of self-reliance and self confidence, cost-effectiveness of financial and technical services and overall improvement in socio-economic status of the beneficiaries. Likewise, the outcomes of the capacity building of the participating agencies are measured by improved orientation and attitude, greater awareness of priorities and needs, and improved level of services for the targeted groups. The greater mobilisation of investment funds for MIGA are assessed by inculcation of saving habits, development of credit management skills, building a pool of creditworthy clients, more access to credit, and reduction in risks and transaction costs of the banks. Finally, the performance of business management and technical support services are measured by increased level of income of the targeted groups, improved management and technical skills of the beneficiaries, and establishment of suitable linkages with concerned stakeholders.

Implementation Process

The first step in operationalisation of MIGAs through SHG is their formation. In the selected villages, the poor women from marginalised, vulnerable and disadvantaged groups have been identified through PRA techniques. The services of reputed local NGOs were hired to facilitate the formation and operationalisation of sustainable SHGs. The greater emphasis has been laid on sustainability of groups, as wherein the poor had formed groups with the sole objective of receiving government grants or bank loans, the chances of survival and sustenance of such groups were bleak as they

Box 2: Key Objectives of MIGAs and Performance Indicators.

Objectives	*Outcomes*

• Institutional Strengthening
• Establishment of SHGs
• Sensitisation and capacity building
	• SHG Sustainability
	• Drop out rates
	• Accumulation of savings
	• Average loan size
	• Financial Sustainability
	• Repayment rates.
	• Portfolio at risk rate
	• Transaction costs
	• Training Effectiveness
	  • Proportion maintaining systematic records
	  • Number of groups formed by mature SHGs

• Support to MIGAs • Mobilisation of investment funds • Training in business management and technical aspects to SHGs	• Credit mobilisation ratio • Number of SHGs receiving loans for MIGA • Source of loan • Proportion of loans used for MGA vs. consumption • Increase in income from MiGA
• Capacity Building of SHGs	• Income and resource control within household • Mutual support to manage their own affairs • Increased self-reliance and self-confidence • Cost-effectiveness of financial & technical services • Improved socio-economic status
• Capacity Building of Participating Agencies	• Improved orientation and attitude • More awareness of priorities and needs • Improved level of services
• Mobilisation of Investment Funds	• Inculcation of savings habits • Development of credit management skills • Building a pool of creditworthy clients • Access to credit • Reduction in risks and transaction costs of the banks
• Business Management and Technical Support Services	• Increased level of income of targeted groups • Improved management and technical skills • Establishment of suitable linkages

Source: Sudan (2002).

generally disintegrated once their limited purpose of availing grant/credit was served [Fernandez (1995)]. The groups formed with the genuine purpose of self-help in the wake of felt needs had much better chances of success [Gain and Satish (1995)]. The social development functionaries mainly the female coordinator, facilitators, and motivators are drawn from the local population. These field functionaries of the project were given intensive training on various aspects of group formation and operationalisation of MIGAs, before entrusting with the tasks.

The PRAs reveals that social development functionaries have adopted a systematic approach by taking necessary sequential steps in SHG formation. The first step was the initial interaction to appraise the women stakeholders of the objectives of the project and group formation. This was done in their own settings to extract their preferences and perceptions. Later, other field functionaries including local leaders were also requested to participate in the PRAs and informed about the advantages of group formation. Subsequently, female facilitators and motivators have made follow-up visits. The suspicion, fear and anxiety of members about the group were discussed and dealt with. Gradually, the women themselves have decided the composition of their respective groups. The PRA approach has been adopted in each and every steps of operationalisation of identified MIGAs. In order to improve community capacity building, steps are being initiated to mobilize the community through participatory approach. To ensure community ownership in project activities, the project is providing extensive training to beneficiaries on technical, financial and social aspects of watershed management. The project interventions are likely to improve availability of fuel wood, drinking water and fodder, thus reducing drudgery and increasing time available for women to be engaged in skill development programmes, technical know-how and opportunities for income generation. The social assessment and participatory planning exercises carried out by the participatory development functionaries have identified needs and constraints faced by the women in the project area, and integrated into the plan for operationalisation of MIGAs. Special attention is being given to gender training, awareness campaigns and development of close links with other gender related poverty alleviation and social programmes. To ensure that women fully participate and benefit from project activities, the participatory development functionaries along with members of SHGs have been encouraged to find specific ways to incorporate the interests of women in the Village Development Plans (VDPs).

The participatory development staffs have also initiated the participatory process to motivate the various stakeholders regarding the objectives of the project, rationale for initiating MIGAs and other vital issues related to the project, which includes:

1. Discussion with the community leaders and village level stakeholders.
2. Identification of their problems.
3. Raising the level of awareness regarding project objectives.
4. Building the confidence of the village level stakeholders.

5. Collection of data and information about community and resource availability.
6. Undertaking of participatory planning and exploring the views of different group of stakeholders and integrating them with participatory planning process, and
7. Formation of SHGs and their operationalisation viz. creation of thrift habits, opening of accounts in bank, creation of users group, etc.

To begin with, the participatory development functionaries and hired consultants have undertaken the PRA exercises. They carried the baseline survey of the potential, socio-economic milieu, existing traditional institutions, their strengths and weaknesses, etc. The participatory development functionaries have organised awareness and motivational camps in the project area to propagate the policies and programmes among the stakeholders like the women, landless, disadvantaged sections of the population, NGOs, *Panchayats, Mahila Mandals,* functionaries of NABARD, DRDA, BDO and reputed local persons. On average, 2-3 camps have been organised in each micro-watershed to motivate and create awareness regarding MIGAs and other activities to be carried out under the watershed development and protection. The project field staffs in respective sub-watersheds have played a vital role in organising these camps, A view separate camps have also been organised for the women especially from the disadvantaged sections of population including tribal nomadic and semi-nomadic pastoral communities. This section of watershed community is traditional, introvert and shy in nature, without experience of handling money and material, and dependent on male folk for even minor decision-making. The local ethics like *purdah* system are also not conducive to encourage them to come in forefront to take up MIGAs on sustainable basis. In the second year of the project, a few SHGs have been formed to inculcate the saving habits among the members and to initiate the training programme and MIGAs on experimental basis. The beneficiaries have been trained and started taking up MIGAs on sustainable basis, which have resulted into their increased income and improved livelihoods.

The project is being paying special emphasis on developing rural poor women's leadership, conflict-resolution abilities, and capacity to identify the full economic, social and political contexts of the disadvantages they suffer, and would eventually plan joint action to address these problems. The project is being providing a supportive role in responding to their requests to help them and would provide training in the necessary interpersonal or leadership spheres. Through PRA exercises, the participatory development functionaries

Box 3: Implementation Process of MIGAs under IWDP (Hills-II), J.&K.

Activity and Participants	*Process*
• Activity: Participatory process • Participants: Community and social development functionaries of the project	• Discussion with village level stakeholders • Interaction with village community and PRA process • Identification of their problems • Identification of MIGAs based on different parameters • Raising the awareness of different stakeholders • Building the confidence of community.
• Activity: Formation of SHGs • Participants: Community and social development functionaries of the project and SHGs	• Operationalisation of SHGs • Creation of thrift habits • Opening of saving accounts • Creation of inter-loaning scheme
• Activity: Training • Participants: Local crafts-person/ development agencies/project staff/NGOs	• Provision of training and skill up-gradation • Training in financial and marketing issues
• Activity: Linkages with other development agencies • Participants: Govt./Non-govt. agencies/project staff/NGOs	• Initiation of MIGAs • Training • Linkages for marketing and micro credit Finance
• Activity: Monitoring and evaluation • Participants: SHGs/NGOs/project staff/govt./non-govt. development functionaries	• Evolving participatory monitoring and evaluation

Source: Sudan (2002).

have identified the existing moderately homogeneous groups, which may undertake MIGAs. The consultations were held with the various interest groups at micro-watershed level. The participatory development functionaries have motivated the poor women folk especially from the disadvantaged and tribal communities to organize themselves in small homogenous SHGs. SHGs are being provided elaborate training in technical, financial, and marketing aspects of the MIGAs and in record keeping. Clear roles, functions and accountability modes have been jointly worked out for the different members of SHG. A mere perusal of the data in table 2 makes it evident that the performance of the SHGs has been comparatively better in Akhnoor and Ramnagar sub-watershed than other two sub-watersheds. The members of the SHGs contribute a small sum ranging between Rs. 20-50 on monthly basis, for the purposes of inter-loaning among themselves. Most of the SHGs have already opened their accounts in the banks and some of them have started inter-loaning. However, the performance of the SHGs in opening bank accounts as well as operationalising inter-loaning scheme is reportedly very poor across the project area. It is ironical to note that none of the SHG has initiated the process of inter-loaning in sub-watersheds of Rambiyara and Rajwar. SHGs have been considered as an appropriate entry point for initiating the MIGAs. The project would help the SHGs to take advantage of the NABARD's loans to undertake MIGAs. The SHGs would be financially integrated with mainstream rural credit, and are envisaged to become self-sustaining, so that at the end of the project they will continue to function.

Table 2: SHGs' Profile in Project Area. (No. and Rs.)

Sub-watershed	*SHGs*	*Members*	*SHG Linked with Banks*	*Av. Monthly Saving*	*Training Centers*	*Inter-loaning Scheme*
Akhnoor	45	911	39	500	33	4
Ramnagar	30	589	28	700	35	3
Rambiyara	8	154	8	550	8	–
Rajwar	4	79	4	1200	8	–

Source: IWDP, Hills-II, J.&K. (2001).

The PRA exercises also reveals that non-poor had dominated the SHG functioning, and the visibly poorest were generally not members of any SHG. In some villages, the poor women were even not aware of the project and its activities. Whereas in some other villages, those who knew about the project and group formation were diffident in joining a group because they were not comfortable about the rigid discipline insisted by the SHGs and also they were not confident about their capacity to save regularly. Thus, most of the poor women were left out of the process as well as invariably the poorest of the poor were diffident and unwilling to join the group. The project functionaries have reported that "trickle down effect" would take place and due to "demonstration effect" the poorest were bound to come forward to form group in near future. However, there is no denying the fact that the provision of micro-credit through SHGs for operationalisation of MIGAs has brought about modest changes in rural livelihood amelioration. The concerted efforts of the project field functionaries and poor women stakeholders have resulted in successful initiation and implementation of subsidiary occupations such as dairy, poultry rearing, mushroom cultivation, handloom, etc. and diversification of agricultural activities. As a result, the levels of living had modestly improved, and noticeable social changes can be seen in the project area. The women, the hitherto neglected social groups have created their own space in the family and village society, and can be seen in participating in family decision-making and watershed development and management.

To ensure that the process of institutional strengthening is self-sustaining, the participatory development functionaries should facilitate in building SHGs, which must have the capacity to further their development on an ongoing basis. The targeted groups "owned" SHGs are crucial to the empowerment process as they provide mutual support for members and confidence to strive collectively for social and economic development and critically analyze their situations and devise strategies to overcome their difficulties. In the interests of sustainability and repeatability, emphasis should be placed on the capacity of mature SHGs to support the formation of additional groups. The formation of association of mature SHGs should also be encouraged, both as a means of providing ongoing support to existing groups and to further the expansion of the SHG movement.

Table 3: IGAs' Profile of Project Area (No.).

Activity	*1999-2000*	*2000-2001*	*2001-2000*
Poly-Green House	30	89	50
Mushroom Development	18	80	1087
Apiculture	4	18	16
Dairy Units	46	122	95
Poultry Units	45	512	80
Sheep Units	23	72	15

Source: IWDP, Hills-II, J&K (2001).

Sadhu and Sudan (2000) have identified the viable MIGAs based on the factors like: Skill possession, raw material availability, less training inputs required, better marketing potential, better financial viability, profit margin expected and existence of linkages with government/non-government agencies. The sedentary Gujjars and nomadic and semi-nomadic pastoral communities are roped in for off-land MIGAs like dairy and poultry; land-based MIGAs like sericulture and sheep rearing; and training-based MIGAs like tailoring and spinning and weaving. However, the MIGAs and training are area specific as well as group specific and are determined by participatory process. The MIGAs identifid are given as under: dairy farming, poultry rearing, sheep rearing, sericulture, mushroom cultivation, *dhingri* cultivation, canning and fruit preservation, budding and grafting, vegetable growing, rope making, basket making, artificial flower making, spinning and weaving, carpet weaving, *fulkari* work, sisal fibre handicrafts, knitting and weaving, and tailoring. Out of the identified MIGAs, the activities such as poly-green house, mushroom development, apiculture, dairy, poultry, and sheep rearing have been operationalised by the project through SHGs for which micro-credit schemes operational in the project area have been utilised (See table 3). All these MIGAs have shown increasing performance over the period except sheep rearing. It has been proposed that other identified MIGAs will be initiated in due course by utilising the available micro-credit schemes in the project area.

MIGAs and Micro-Credit

With the existing system, availability of credit resources is restricted to the few who are able to have resources to credit under various government sponsored programme like IRDP, Prime Minister Rozgar Yojana (PMRY), Jawahar Razgar Yojana (JRY), etc. The majority of the rural poor is unable to avail the benefits of these credit programmes due to the past indebtedness, lack of specific knowledge about these schemes, inability to interact with bank and government official, etc. Beside, the banks do not provide credit to meet the real urgent needs of the poor. Their income level thus, stays at such a low level that very little can ever be saved and invested to let their economic base expand. The poor are one of the more productive segments of the population. However, their labour does not yield adequate returns because the financial resources are inaccessible to them. The ideal way out would be a credit programme for the poor, so that their genuine credit needs are met. The credit programme should be integrated with training, marketing, transportation facilities, technology, etc. While designing an appropriate programme, sound financial principles, as also clear social objective must be kept in mind. A key factor is their participation in programmes for poverty alleviation especially those in rural development sphere. The success is possible, if the poor participate in the process of their poverty alleviation.

Suitable micro-credit linkages are planned to be forge with the existing development programmes and schemes of the WDC and government agencies for poverty alleviation. The Ministry of Rural Development implement poverty alleviation schemes by DRDA through BDOs of the respective blocks in the project area. The outside sources of micro-credit have to be tapped, as the poor women, landless, disadvantaged and tribal nomadic and semi-nomadic pastoral communities are not having finances at their own. Even if they save some meager sum, they never risk these in MIGAs, as they have numerous social obligations to meet. The initiation of MIGAs requires investment in equipment, raw materials etc. for which funds must be made available with the SHGs. The following sources of micro-credit should be tapped to sustain the MIGAs.

1. SHGs should utilize the funds available with them to take up a viable IGA, which is to be decided by the members.

2. The project should also provide the funds to SHGs at a rate of interest, lower than bank rates.

3. The members of SHGs should also utilize the loans from the nationalised banks for taking up of MIGAs.

4. The SHGs should also raise loans from NABARD/other banks, provided they are six months old.

5. The existing government schemes for income generation and poverty alleviation should be utilised for implementing MIGAs. SGSY provides finance for micro enterprises for SC/ST, disabled and IRDP beneficiaries. Suitable linkages should be forged with the government functionaries like the Project Officers, DRDA and BDOs in respective sub-watersheds. Through these agencies, the targeted groups should be able to utilize the funds from on-going developmental activities to take up viable MIGAs on sustainable basis.

6. Various line departments also providee subsidies to beneficiaries to take up micro enterprises related to dairy, mushroom cultivation, etc. which could be utilised, for which the IWDP project functionaries should forge suitable linkages.

7. Women (from weaker sections/living below poverty line) are eligible for financial assistance (loan/grant-in-aid) under different schemes being implemented by J&K WDC for setting up of income generating units. The project functionaries should initiate the process of establishing linkages with WDC to facilitate the targeted groups to take loans/grants-in-aids for taking up of MIGAs.

The provision of financial assistance by the agencies mentioned above except NABARD/other banks will not cover the targeted groups as a whole. Even NABARD/other banks extend loans to self-sustainable SHGs, whereas the targeted groups are potent stakeholders in the project and their socio-economic upliftment is the prime responsibility of the project. Due to many bottlenecks in the procedures and conditions of getting loans from NABARD/ banks, the past experience in getting financial assistance/loan from these sources have not been encouraging. The project should share the major responsibilities in facilitating the procurement of financial assistance/loan from the agencies mentioned above. SHGs crated under the project have not created large savings due to poverty. The level of capacity building in terms of participatory development and institutional strengthening is also not vibrant. The technical, managerial, financial and marketing related aspects of MIGAs are also inadequate among the members of SHGs created so far in the project area. Keeping above constraints in view, the targeted groups should be assisted in various aspects of sustainable MIGAs like capacity building, institutional strengthening, mobilisation of investment funds from ongoing schemes, technical support services to SHG members both for on-farm and off-farm activities, and training services on business management and marketing.

Conclusions and Suggestions

The advocates of micro-credit programmes view poverty as a cash-flow problem and seek its solution through credit and MIGAs. Poverty, particularly that of rural women cannot be defined only in terms of cash-flow, since it has strong linkages with inequitable distribution of resources, unequal power relations, illiteracy, lower wages, cuts in developmental spending and anti-poor macroeconomics policies that disproportionaly affect poor rural women. It also needs to be emphasised that micro-credit is not a substitute for social sector spending and anti-poverty programmes. In the rural context, women's control over and ownership of land can play an important role not only in economic betterment, but also in terms of social and economic empowerment, as land is a symbol of political power and social status. Furthermore, micro-credit programmes have to be visualised in the context of the new global economic order as liberalisation, privatisation and globalisation policies have led to job losses in the formal sector, decline in social sector spending and growing unemployment. In this scenario, the last option left for poor rural women is self-employment, which micro-credit aims to promote. But poor rural women are placed at a disadvantageous position in the market. How can the products of poor women complete with those of big business and MNCs and TNCs, which not only have strong financial backing, but also send millions on advertising, brand selling and marketing. Until and unless poor women are provided access to market information, technology, management and marketing skills, their economic ventures will remain uncompetitive. Since the efficacy of micro-credit programmes is not independent of other development interventions, it could at best be one of the component of a wider developmental agenda. In order to intensify the social movements in developing and strengthening SHGs and MIGAs, the following steps could be very useful.

Formation of SHGs

With the assistance of the village leaders and existing social groups, more sustainable and robust SHGs should be formed. The following suggestions should be taken into consideration in forming SHGs.

1. Only the targeted people should be the members of a SHG. It should be homogenous in terms of members' income, sex and social status, place of residence and like-mindedness.

2. Gender bias may be avoided while forming the SHG. All women SHG should be promoted.
3. One person per households should be the member of SHG.
4. The size of the group should be manageable and restricted to below 25 members.
5. The Executive Committee (EC) should be ready to assists SHG members in identifying and MIGAs and identifying different avenues for marketing the products and procuring raw material through group ventures.
6. Regular fortnightly meeting with compulsory attendance should be held.
7. SHG should open a saving account in the bank as decided by the group with at least three signatories-president, secretary and accountant.
8. All transaction needs to be approved in the group meeting through a resolution.
9. The amount spent toward administrative costs and bank charges should be met out of the savings and accordingly, recorded in the account registrar.

Implementation of MIGAs

With regards to MIGAs, the following suggestions should be given due consideration:

1. Member intending to undertake MIGAs may do so through the SHG.
2. Identification of activities and market feasibility should be made in consultation with group members.
3. Assets required for any MIGA should be purchased through the SHG.
4. SHG should assess the feasibility of the activity before approaching for credit assistance.

Micro-Credit

There is need for reorientation as regards micro-credit needs of rural women using new production, distribution channels and promotional services, based on the perceived needs:

1. The need for credit is in frequent but small doses, innovative savings-linked cash credits, may be answer, as these will provide safety, liquidity and lower transaction costs.

2. The credit programmes should be based on savings, and credit alone should not be made the basis for SHG formation.

3. These savings can also be used for emergent family needs such as consumption and medical needs and for social/religious needs.

4. A composite loan system (including term and working capital requirements) can be devised for women entrepreneurs running MIGAs, so as to ensure timely credit both for assets and working capital.

5. Insurance needs also have to be met and rural credit agencies could provide for integration of income with credit after discussion with insurance companies. Insurance should be required for the life of women borrowers, for the asset purchased with the loan and for loan repayment in the events of borrower's death.

6. Finally, training in cash and funds management, marketing and packaging, and credit management has to be provided to women micro-entrepreneurs.

Although the project is being implemented by the government agency, the project ultimately has to withdraw from the villages. To ensure sustainability, village level organisations should be scaled up. They should be so strengthened that withdrawals become smooth. Before withdrawal, the policy of clustering of SHGs should be encouraged to enhance the mutual support between the SHGs, facilitate formal links with *panchayati raj* institutions, and engender confidence among villagers in seeking outside inputs, after project withdrawals, through line agencies or reputed local NGOs. As with SHGs, the emphasis of the clusters should be production-oriented. It is expected that SHGs would contribute to a cluster revolving fund, which would support wider entrepreneurial initiatives. These large bodies should have greater capability and bargaining power in seeking market outlets, sources of training and support from other agencies. Similarly, they should have the resources to employ villagers as para-professionals to improve the production-base, support income generation activities and seek market outlets for cluster produce. Consequently, cluster office-bearers will need training in management, accounting and marketing skills. In nutshell, the pre-requisites for successful implementation of MIGAs should include extensive capacity building and institutional strengthening of the SHGs in all aspects of MIGAs; extensive re-orientation training programmes in participatory methods, for the line agency staff, and introduction of strong institutional mechanisms to ensure an integrated approach.

REFERENCES

1. Bhat, G., 1999, "Rural Entrepreneurship and NGOs, *Kurukshetra,* November, Capoor, J. (2001), Development Issues in Micro Credit, *Reserve Bank of India Bulletin,* Vol. 55, No. 3, March.
2. Cornia, G.A. and F. Stewert, 1993, Two Errors of Targeting, Economic Policy Series, UNCIEP International Child Development Centre, Italy.
3. Dev, S. Mahendra, 1999, Stated Interventions and Women's Employment, in T.S. Papola and Alakh N. Sharma (Eds.), *Gender and Employment in India,* Vikas Publishing House Pvt. Ltd., New Delhi, pp. 373-411.
4. Fernandez, A.P., 1995, The MYRADA Experience-Alternate Management Systems for Savings and Credit of the Rural Poor, The Mysore Resettlement and Development Agency, Bangalore.
5. Gain, T.S. Raji and P. Satish, 1995, A Micro Study on Group Dynamics and Group Functioning, Working Paper No. 6, Bankers Institute of Rural Development, Lucknow.
6. Goetz, A.M. and R.N. Gupta, 1996, Who Takes Credit? Gender, Power and Control over Loan use in Rural Credit Programmes in Bangladesh, *World Development,* Vol. 24, No. 1.
7. Government of India, 1999, *Swarnjayanti Gram Swarozgar Yojana: Guidelines,* Ministry of Rural Development, New Delhi, p. 9.
8. Hoff, K. and J.E. Stiglitz, 1990, Introduction: Imperfect Information and Rural Credit Markets-Puzzles and Policy Perspectives, *The World Bank Economic Review,* Vol. 4, No. 3, September.
9. Hussain, M., 1988, Credit for Alleviation of Rural Poverty: The Grameen Bank in Bangladesh, Research Report No. 4, International Food Policy Research Institute, Washington.
10. Hulme, D. and Paul M. (1996), *Finance Against Poverty,* Volume 1, Routledge Publication, London.
11. Hydan, G. (2000, Governance for Sustainable Livelihood, www: http/ www.undp.org.
12. IWDP, Hills-II (2001), *Status Report for Suprvision Mission of World Bank,* Integrated Watershed Development Project, Hills-II, Jammu and Kashmir.
13. Kulshreshtha, C.R., 2000, Micro-Finance: The New Development Paradigm for Poor Rural Women, *Kurukshetra,* November.
14. Madheswaran, S. and A. Dharmadhikary, 2001, Empowering Rural Women through Self-Help Groups: Lessons from Maharashtra Rural Credit Project, *Indian Journal of Agricultural Economics,* Vol. 56, No. 3, July-September, pp. 427-443.
15. Moser, C.O.N. (1989), Gender Planning in the Third World: Meeting Practical and Strategic Gender Needs, *World Development,* Vol. 17, No.

16. NABARD, 1999, *Report of the Task Force on Supportive Policy and Regulatory Framework for Micro Finance,* Mumbai.

17. Naithani, P., 2001, Micro-Financing the Self-Employment Activities, *Kurukshetra,* July.

18. Pearson, R., 2000, Rethinking Gender Matters in Development, in Tim Allen and Alan Thomas (eds.), *Poverty and Development into the 21st Century,* Oxford University Press.

19. Pitt, M.M. and S.R. Khandker, 1996, Household and Intrahousehold Impact of the Grameen Bank and Similar Targeted Credit Programmes in Bangladesh, *World Bank Discussion Paper,* No. 320, The World Bank, Washington, DC.

20. Prakash, A., 2002, Micro-Credit Groups-How Empowering? The Economic and Social Context, *The Indian Journal of Labour Economics,* Vol. 45, No. 4.

21. Puhazhendhi, V., 1995, Transaction Costs of Lending to the Poor-Non-Governmental Organisations and Self-Help Groups of the Poor as Intermediaries for Banks in India, The Foundation for Development Corporation, Brisbane, Australia.

22. Rahman, A., 1999, Micro-Credit Initiatives for Equitable and Sustainable Development: Who Pays? *World Development,* Vol. 27, No. 1.

23. Rao, D.K.: V.A. Despande and A. Dharmadhikary, 1990, *Development of Women and Children in Rural Areas (DWRCA), Velhe District Pune,* An Action Research project sponsored by UNICEF India, National Institute of Bank Management, Pune.

24. Rath, N., 1985, Garibi Hatao: Can IRDP Do it? *Economic and Political Weekly,* Vol. 20, No. 6, February 9, pp. 238-246.

25. RBI, 1991, *"Report of the Committee on the Financial System,"* (Narasimham Committee), Reserve Bank of India, Mumbai.

26. RBI, 1999, "Report on Micro-Credit, Micro Credit Special Cell, Central Office, Mumbai.

27. RBI, 2001, "Development Issues in Micro-Credit, speech by Jagdish Capoor, RBI Bulletin, March, pp. 305-309.

28. Sadhu, A.N. and F.K. Sudan, 1999, *Retrospective Study, IWDP (Hills-I), Jammu and Kashmir,* Integrated Watershed Development Project, Hills-II, Jammu and Kashmir.

29. Sadhu, A.N. and F.K. Sudan, 2000, "Study of Viable Income Generating Activities for Rural Women, Landless and Disadvantaged Groups, Integrated Watershed Development Project, Hills-II, Jammu and Kashmir.

30. Sudan, F.K., 2002, *Action-Cum-Implementation Plan,* Income Generating Activities Under IWDP (Hills-II), Jammu and Kashmir, Integrated Watershed Development Project, Hills-II, J.&K.

31. Satish, P., 2001, "Some Issues in the Formation of Self-Help Groups," *Indian Journal of Agricultural Economics,* Vol. 56, No. 3, July-September, pp. 410-418.

32. Shetty, S.L., 1997, "Financial Sector Reforms in India: An Evaluation, *Prajnan,* 25 (3-4), pp. 253-287.
33. Srinivasan, G. and D.S.K. Rao, 1996, Financing of Self Help Groups by Banks: Some Issue, Working Paper No. 8, Banking Institute of Rural Development, Lucknow.
34. Sundari, S. and N. Geetha, 2002, Poverty, Credit and Micro Enterprises: A Gender Study, *Kurukshetra,* November.
35. Todd, H., 2000, mainstreaming of Micro Credit in India, Cashpor, Inc., June, Seremban, Malaysia.
36. UNDP, 2000, *World Development Report,* Oxford University Press, New York.
37. World Bank, 1998, *Project Concept Document: Integrated Watershed Development (Hills-II) Project,* Rural Development Sector Unit, South Asia Region, New Delhi.
38. World Bank, 1999, *Project Appraisal Document: Integrated Watershed Development (Hills-II) Project,* Rural Development Sector Unit, South Asia Region, New Delhi.
39. Yunus, Muhammad, 1999, "Banker to the Poor-Micro-Lending and the Battle against World Poverty", Pacific Affairs, New York.

36

Indian Small Scale Industries and Globalisation

*Dr. G.L. Bhong**

Introduction

Small Scale Industries (SSI hereafter) represent a key segment of an Indian economy. The Small-Scale industrial sector which plays a pivotal role in the Indian economy in terms of employment and growth has recorded a high rate of growth since independence in spite of stiff competition from the large sector and without much support from the Government. The Government of India followed a policy of protection, subsidies and reservation for the development of SSI over last fifty years.

The role of SSI has been emphasised from time to time, keeping in view the overall planned objectives of economic growth continued with social justice. It play's a vital role in the growth of the country. It contributes almost 40% of Gross Industrial value in Indian economy. It has created large number of employment opportunities for Indian populace next to agriculture and it generated 18.56 million employment by 2001-2002. It has been observed that a million of Rupees of Investments in Fixed Assets in small scale sector produces 4.62 million worth of goods or services with a approximate value addition of 10% points.

The SSI sector has grown rapidly over the years. The number of SSI units has increased from an estimated 0.87 million units in 1980-81 to over 3 million in the year 2002.

* Reader & Head, Department of Economics, Abasaheb Garware College, Karve Road, Pune 411 004, Maharashtra State, India.

Present Position of Small Scale Industries in India

The number of small scale units has been increasing in the comprehensive manner in recent years, more particularly after the introduction of economic reforms from 1991. The following table shows the present position of SSI units in India.

Table 1: Overall Performance of SSI Sector.

Year	*No. of Units (in lakh)*	*Output at Current Prices Rs. Crores*	*Employment Lakh nos.*	*Export at Current Prices Rs. Crores*
1991-92	20.82 (6.9)	1,78,699 (15.0)	129.80 (3.6)	13,883 (43.7)
1992-93	22.46 (7.9)	2,09,300 (17.1)	134.06 (3.3)	17,785 (28.1)
1993-94	23.81 (6.0)	2,41,648 (15.5)	139.38 (4.0)	25,307 (42.3)
1994-95	25.71 (8.0)	2,93,990 (21.7)	146.56 (5.2)	29,068 (14.9)
1995-96	27.24 (6.0)	3,56,213 (21.2)	156.61 (4.1)	36,470 (25.5)
1996-97	28.57 (4.9)	4,12,636 (15.8)	160.00 (4.8)	39,249 (7.6)
1997-98	30.14 (5.5)	4,65,171 (12.7)	167.20 (4.5)	43,946 (12.0)
1998-99	31.21 (3.6)	5,27,515 (13.4)	171.58 (2.6)	48.979 (11.5)
1999-2000	32.25 (3.3)	5,78,470 (9.7)	178.50 (4.0)	53,975 (10.2)

Note: Figures in the brackets give the increase over previous year.
Source: Economic Survey, Government of India, 2000-2001.

The above table reveals that the total number of SSI units of India has increased from 20.82 lakhs in 1991-92 to 32.25 lakhs in 1999-2000 which shows a 3.3 per cent increase in 1998-99 over the previous year figure or 31.21 lakhs.

The value of production of SSI units of the country has increased from Rs. 1,78,699 crores in 1991-92 to Rs. 4,12,636 crores in 1996-97 and then to Rs. 5,78,470 crores in 1999-2000 showing a growth rate of 9.7 per cent over the previous year. Total number of persons employed in these SSI units has also increased from 129.80 lakhs in 1991-92 to 160.00 lakhs in 1996-97 and then to 178.50 lakhs in 1999-2000 showing an increase of 4.0 per cent over the previous year.

SSI sector produces 35% of total exports of Indian economy in recent times. Total value of exports of SSI units has increased from Rs. 13,883 crores in 1991-92 to 39,249 crores in 1996-97 and to Rs. 53,975 crores in 1999-2000 showing an increase of 10.2 per cent over the previous year.

SSI sector is maintaining an important position in the industrial map of the country. The SSI sector being a labour intensive project, can employ on an average 18 to 19 persons with an investment of Rs. 1 lakh. Moreover, the SSI sector is also maintaining a good number of export oriented units (EOUs) producing goods for meeting demands coming from international market. But in the era of globalisation SSI units are facing some serious problems. In the context of globalisation, it is imperative to solve these problems, so as to utilize the opportunities created by globalisation.

Globalisation

In modern times globalisation gathered momentum with the birth of General Agreement on Tariffs and Trade (GATT) in 1947 signed by 23 nations. GATT was a set of rules and multilateral agreements having the main objective of expanding production and international trade. This provisional arrangement continued till 1995. On January 1, 1995, World Trade Organisation (WTO)—a permanent institution to monitor the global trade and decide the other related things-came into existence. India is one of the founder members of the WTO. The WTO commitments are full and permanent. Its rules are applicable to trade in merchandise, trade in service and trade in related aspects of intellectual property.

The term 'Globalisation' is defined by the International Monetary Fund (IMF) as, "the growing economic dependence of countries worldwide through increasing volume and variety of cross-border transactions in goods and services and of international capital flows and through more rapid and widespread diffusion of technology." Globalisation is a trend towards a more integrated, borderless global economic system. It implies globalisation of marketing, production, investment and technology.

Globalisation and India

In India the real thrust of globalisation was provided in 1991. The huge fiscal deficit, debt crisis, falling foreign exchange reserves and conditions imposed by IMF and the IBRD (World Bank) led to the announcement of the New Economic Policy by the Government of India in July 1991 based on liberalisation, privatisation and globalisation. Since then the Government has taken various measures to further the globalisation process. Those affecting the SSI include import liberalisation, reducing the tariff rates and lifting the quantitative restrictions on imports etc. India has signed a number of agreements which will affect the fortunes of SSI. For example General Agreement on Tariffs and Trade (GATT) requires India to remove all quantitative restrictions (QRs) by 2003. Article XVII of GATT provides for imposition of QRs on imports for balance of payments reasons. India's plan of phasing out QRs was challenged by USA in WTO. India lost this case, which implies that it has to phase out all QRs even before 2003. The Government has already initiated the process of removal of QRs. On April 1, 2001 QRs on 715 items were lifted. The list includes items like processed foods, two wheelers, electric appliances, consumer products, liquor, garments, toys and 650 add highly—visible others. Most of the items were reserved for SSI sector Mr. Jayant Ajinkya of SSI Projects Division comments on this action of the government in these words, "The WTO is not providing a level playing field. Beset by increasing deregulation, imminent dismantling of protective trade barriers, under WTO regime and dumping of cheap products from China and Taiwan, India's SSI is fearing for its very survival."

Investment limit of Small Scale Industries

The definition of the SSIs and ancillary units has undergone both qualitative and quantitative changes, from 1955 to 1999-2000.

Table 2: SSI-Investment in Plant and Machinery.

(Rs. in lakhs)

Year	*S.S. Unit*	*Ancillary Unit*	*Tiny Unit*
1966	7.50	10.00	—
1975	10.00	15.00	—
1980	20.00	25.00	2.00
1985	35.00	45.00	2.00
1991	60.00	75.00	5.00
1997	300.00	300.00	25.00
1999	100.00	100.00	25.00
2000	100.00	100.00	25.00

Source: Economic Times June' 2000.

The enhancement of investment limit in plant and machinery for SSI to Rs. 3 crores in December 1997 due to higher costs of plant and machinery was a step towards technological upgradation. With lowering of customs tariffs and reservation of items for SSI, it was more logical for government to increase the investment limit to enable SS sector to face competition from imports more effectively by modernisation and quality improvements in their products. However, this limit of 3 crores was too high for manufacturers operating in residential areas who came nowhere near this limit. As a result government reduced investment limit in this sector in 1999 bringing it down to one crore rupees.

Policy of Reservation

Prior to 1997, the total number of items reserved exclusively for SS production was 843 Post WTO, the items reserved for SS Production came down to 822. The Abid Hussain Committee had forcefully argued in favour of scrapping it in 1997. The government reservation policy to encourage and protect SSI has failed to benefit the small enterprises.

Through over 800 items are reserved for SSI production, 80% of units are engaged in manufacturing of only items 39. In addition, it is surprising to note that about six units manufacture 529 items and only one unit produces 90 items. The second census of SSI reveals a drastic figure of 233 items not being produced at all by small scale industries in India. If fact, reservation of 14 items viz. Garments, rubber soles, plastic toys, footwear etc., in June 2001, constitute a major share in exports of India. In all the policy of reservation of certain items has little relevance today with most of reserved items placed on open general license.

Impact of Globalisation on SSI in India

In the context of globalisation of Indian Economy, there is a need for transparency of operations and accountability on the part of Indian industries involve a great amount of economic and social interest. The object of globalisation in the economy is to make Indian industry efficient and competitive at international level along with the development of Indian multinationals. The impact of globalisation on SSIs in India could be analysed as under:

Many of the SSI units have closed their activities because they are of ancillary nature. Some large industrial units are taken over by the MNCs. The tendency of merger, amalgamation and absorption has been increased from 1991.

A more passing danger awaits small scale industries. While all along India has been protecting SSI units from competitions from larger units through reservation, concessions under the WTO agreement would mean that the markets in India are open globally for more than half of (480 out of 812) all the product lines of SSIs. We have thus reserved most of our products of small scale units for global manufacturers.

In view of the change in the policy of large and medium size wrists regarding make or buy decision, the dependence of these units on SSI units has diminished, because of their own production.

The Voluntary Retirement Scheme and Compulsory Retirement Scheme with a gold plated name such as Golden Shake-Hand; Exit Policy etc. are launched by Large, Medium and also Small Scale Units.

After 1997, there is a major depression in all the industries sector including small scale industries. The demand from customers to consumable goods and from industries to industrial goods reduced enormously.

There is a great fear amongst the small scale industrialists in India that the globalisation of the economy will make way for multinationals rich in technology and financial resources and world create an atmosphere of unhealthy competition. Such type of unhealthy competition has already started.

Some of the SSI units have tried to compete in the global market but have failed because the cost of their product is more than the price of the same foreign products.

Due to steep competition in global market, closing down of the activities by majority of SSI units, implementation of VRS and CRS as well as Hire and Fire Policies the social atmosphere get polluted to some extent. Because the voluntarily or compulsorily retired persons because the burden to their families and the society.

The confidence in the minds of Entrepreneurs is declining day by day. They are not supposing the globalisation as an opportunity but according them it is a great constraint.

Suggestions

There is no alternative for accepting the situation created by globalisation for SSIs in India. The competitive situation, decrease in tariff, quality products with lesser price, customer orientation etc. are main features of this global environment. The closed and protected market has now ended. The internal competitions have almost ended. The SSIs in India have to compete with foreign and international organisation.

The SSI units have to increase their strength that those units are not only to keep their existence but have to develop themselves to the extent possible.

The due importance must be given to the 'Cost Management' The 'Cost. Volume Profit Analysis, is necessary for SSI units, to minimize the cost and to avoid unnecessary expenditure.

The tendency among the large company to out source their requirement will provide new opportunities to small and ancillary units in India. But they will have to upgrade their technologies and improve the quality of the products. Quality consciousness is quite necessary now a days.

There are certain products such as handicrafts, hand-knitted carpets, high value handloom saris. Custom-made garments and leather products that cannot be produced in standardised large scale processes. These labour intensive areas requiring traditional skills continue to remain the preserve of the small scale sector.

Entrepreneurial firms can globalise their business by using any one or a port-folio of the following strategies:

1. By exporting the products to the foreign markets directly under their own brand names.
2. Exporting the products to some foreign firms/departmental stores/ chain stores which may distribute them in the local market under their own brand-names.
3. By establishing a partnership or granting franchise for production/ sell of Indian products in foreign market.
4. By promoting locally owned subsidiary companies in the foreign countries.
5. By setting up joint venture companies with foreign forms in Indian or abroad.
6. Acquisition of foreign companies to get an easy access to the foreign market.

The process of globalisation should be gradual and be linked with the objectives of the industry of the country. It should be helpful in solving the constraints in marketing of products of small business entrepreneurs in the changing global bushiness environment.

There is a need for forgoing linkages between the small entrepreneurial sector and large sector so that the transition of small into big becomes easy and even automatic. The medium and large scale units have to adopt the policy of "Live and Let Lie" in result of SSIs.

Problems of small scale entrepreneurs in marketing the products, are multi-dimensional and these can be solved by the co-ordinated efforts of entrepreneurs and functioning of promotional agencies and government assistance without red-tape or bureaucratic delays.

Simplification of the procedure and liberalised financing by the banks to this sector at concessional rate of interest shall help the small scale industry in modernisation and competition. Non-co-operation of the financial institution is presently making this sector sick which is adding to the problems of unemployment creating a social stigma as well. The banks and financial institutions should provide funds to SSIs for fixed and working capital in time.

Multinationals and industries in the organised sector have an edge in marketing their products advertising and using the electronic media, whereas the small scale industry finds it difficult to expose its technology and product at national and international levels. It is, therefore, requested that 'Marketing Development Fund' of at least Rs. 500 crores may be created immediately for assisting the units in different constitutions, industrial association and organizers of exhibitions for publicity of product to enable participation in domestic and international exhibitions to give them exposure to technology and products manufactured by this sector. Experts Committee for SSI set up by the Government has also supported it. Creation of marketing estates, information and trade centers. Holding of seminars and support by the electronic media will go a long way helping the marketing of the goods manufactured by this sector.

The role of effective communication and the right information are important tools for development. There is an urgent need for speedier dissipation of information on the latest market trends and polices being followed by the government and the developments in other countries on industrialisations. Laghu Udyog Bharati has set up its own website and it is connected with the world network. It has inaugurated by Shri Yashwant Sinha, Hon. Union Minister of Finance, on 16th August 1999. It is for the first time that any organisation of SSI has developed webside. The SSI units can get facilities of visual search information about new products of various countries, on line order facility, bullion and share market updates, currency counters, listing of financial institutions and banks, member's list and other allied information on industry.

While deserving the products from SSI, the Abid Hussain Committee had recommended that the Government should provide annual resources of the order of Rs. 500 crores over next five years thereby totaling Rs. 2500 crores. The committee had also recommended that Government and industry representative should setup a joint mechanism where by they could help the SSI units whose products have been deserved for a smooth transaction. This provision should be made at the earliest.

The credit should be given to SSI with 'Prime Interest Rate' The interest rates. The Prime rate of interest in western countries mean the interest rate charged by the bank for their best commercial customers.

Tiny sector will definitely be a boon of self employment oriented youth, lacking in resources and experience. The personnel in the tiny sector is always changing. Because the employees leave the tiny unit for want of new advanced job, so these units become only the training centers. The laws relating Minimum Wages Act and other law, will have to be reviewed and changed to the tune that tiny units can survive themselves. A separate set of package of incentive should be given to the tiny sector.

In respect of SSI, in India globalisation should be accepted and implementation for the shake of increasing their competitive strength and long term survival. The globalisation should not be accepted for the sake of globalisation only. Otherwise the situation in the SSI sector is that, "Operation is successful, but the patient is dead." Market oriented globalisation is necessary.

Our business should accept the foreign technology, foreign capital, foreign management but we should not accept the ownership of foreigners. The ownership must vests with Indian organisation. Otherwise FDI (Foreign Direct Investment) will become "Future Death Investment." Foreign investor do not want to invest in building, machinery, etc. but they want to invest in purchasing market.

Our Central Government, State Governments, Large Business Houses and Financial Organsiations must have to increase confidence in the minds of entrepreneurs and should support them in all respects e.g. offering package of incentive, advances and loans at the lowest possible interest rate, providing information of international market etc.

Quality is a subjective analysis. The prices of product should be appropriate with the quality. So SSIs should obtained ISO certificate. Demonstration of the product in the international exhibitions is necessary.

All the SSIs organisations should join their hands with national level SSIs organisation. The national level SSIs organisation should have to form an Agency. Which can maintain liaison between SSI units and Government.

The Agency can advise the Government to frame appropriate policy for SSIs in India.

In the context of globalisation the SSI units in India must have to accept all the challenges. If the SSIs have to survive and play a useful and productive role in the economy it is time we make SSIs in India have the potential to play a major role in alleviating poverty can not be under estimated. If the SSIs are brought back on the road of progress and are allowed to exploit vast potential, the poverty of Idia's teeming millions could be turned into prosperity. We firmly believe that the SSI sector of India will also lead the other nations and show the path of prosperity to the world in the next millennium, being the main source of economy and employment generation.

Government Policy and Measures

Government of India has not stopped itself from protecting SS sector. In its constant efforts to enable the SSUs to continue to develop. Commercial banks in India have sanctioned so far as whooping amount of more than Rs. 20000 crores to SS sector. Besides Plan resources, quite a large investment has taken place on private account financed partly by financial institution and partly from promoters' own financial and non-financial resources.

With the policy of globalisation and opening of economy, government has adopted a number of safety measures for smooth functioning of SS sector, an important pillar of Indian economy. As per budget 2001-2002, 4 UNIDO projects have been started under Cluster Development Programme. Schemes like National Equity Fund Scheme and Technology Development and Modernisation Fund are of a great help for developing SS sector. Moreover, to upgrade technology and enhance quality consciousness among small-scale entrepreneurs, government has started new branches for SSI to obtain ISO certification. Various incentives for exports like free trade zones, software technology parks, duty drawback schemes, etc. play a great role in increasing exports from small scale sector.

REFERENCES

1. Desai Vacant, 2001, "Small Scale Industries Management", Vol. 2, No. 2, "Economic Political Weekly", February, 2002.
2. Report of the Study Group on Development of SSI", 2001, "Planning Commission." "Economic Survey of India", 2002.
3. Neg Biswaji, 2000, "WTO Regime and its Implication for Indian Small and Medium Enterprises Sector', Sedme, Vol. 27, No. 03.
4. Busines Today, 2002: "Life after QRS", Vol. 27, No. 03.

5. P. Subba Rao, 2001, Ibid.
6. Gharpure, Y.H., 2002, "Globalisation" Sampada.
7. Rao N. Janardan, 2002, "Chinese Competitiveness. The arch of the dragon".
8. Dutta, Ruddar and K.P.M. Sundaram, 2002.
9. "Indian Economy", New Delhi, S. Chand and Co. Ltd., Vol. 46.
10. Desai S.S.M. & Bhalerao, Nirmal, 2002, "Industrial Economy of India", Mumbai, Himalaya Publishing House.
11. Batra, G.S. & Dangwal, R.C., 2002, "Entrepreneurship and Small Scale Enterprises", New Delhi, Kanishka Publishers and Distributors.
12. Minakshi Sundaram, N. 2002, "Financial Management in Small Scale Enterprises", New Delhi, Kanishka Publishers and Distributors.

37

Empowerment of Weaker Sections
Problems and Prospects

Dr. D. Rudrappan*

Introduction

Even after 55 years of freedom, India still has millions of poverty—stricken people, caught up in the vicious circle of economic and social deprivation. There is a tale of tears and trauma, taking place as a result of mass illiteracy and poverty. Vicissitudes of poverty and vagaries of fortune are the order of the day for these miserable ones, who constitute one-third of Indian population. Weaker sections in India are a miserable lot. Only a few are well in control of their destinies now, on account of their educational empowerment. Others eke out their livelihood somehow believing that their fate is already sealed and that there is nothing they could do to change their destiny.

The challenge for the Government both at the Centre and at States today is to bridge the vast gap between its performance and its promise. On the one hand, India remains as the poorest, the most illiterate and the most malnourished country. On the other, it has all the potential to become the most dynamic power of Asia in the twenty first century, if only there is massive investment in human development, particularly in those relating to depressed classes.

Social security, possible abroad because of limited population, is an impossible alternative as of now in India. Therefore, the need of the hour is

* M.A., M. Phil., Ph.D., Reader, Dept. of Post-Graduate and Research Studies in Economics, Presidency College, Chennai-600 005.

to empower weaker sections so that they can make an informed choice in economic, political, social and cultural activities. Improvement of livelihood, effective implementation of land reform measures in rural areas, Government accountability in protecting the poor, capacity building and effective advocacy constitute an overarching part of empowerment strategy. Moreover, it is equally important to endow the weaker sections, by means of education and awareness, the power to possess the will, the will to withstand social, economic and emotional pressure and to assert their rights.

As the people belonging to the depressed classes suffer from certain disabilities, the Constitution of India has made certain provisions of protective discrimination for their welfare and upliftment. Based on the policy of protective discrimination, the Government has laid down reservation arrangement for the people belonging to the category of Scheduled Castes, Scheduled Tribes and after 1990 for Other Backward Classes.

First, there has been reservation of seats for these groups in the Parliament and State legislatures. Second, there has been reservation of jobs for them in Government and Quasi-Government services except in defense and highly meritorious services. Third, seats have been reserved for them in the educational institutions of higher learning such as colleges and universities, for their social and educational advancement. Hence, a certain percentage of quota is fixed, keeping in mind the population size of the SCs/STs.

Reservation for B.C., S.C. & S.T.

As far as the affirmative action for Backward Classes are concerned, the Central Government has taken the following stand in the year 1994, after the recommendations of the Mandal Commission. Admitting the *"creamy layer"* concept, the Centre has divided the whole Backward Classes into Backward Classes and Other Backward Classes. It is for the Other Backward Classes among Backward Classes whose annual income does not exceed Rs. 1 lakh that the Government provided protective discrimination at 27%. Thus, on the whole, the overall quota of reservation does not exceed 50%. For SCs, it is 15% and for STs 7.5% and for other OBCs 27%; all totalling up to 49.5%. However, the reservation quota of 15% for SC's and 7.5% for the tribals seem to be a little lower, as their population accounts for 16.5% and 8.01% respectively, as per the census of 1991 (Virginius Xaxa, 2001).

The process of filing up the above quota as fixed by the Government is a problem even today and even this meagre quota in certain categories could not be filled up. And the reasons put forward range from apathy and indifference on the part of the Government to the non-availability of suitable candidates especially for the top-ranking posts from the weaker sections, on account of their social, economic and educational backwardness.

Need for Caste-Based Empowerment

In a democratic setup every individual and community has a legitimate right and aspiration to participate in the governance of the country. However, poverty and illiteracy are the greatest impediments to such a goal. Poverty is a direct consequence of two crippling caste based handicaps such as socio-economic and educational backwardness. Hence, for the removal of poverty, caste based empowerment in the form of target-group strategies is necessary.

Strategies for Amelioration of Poverty

The World Development Report 2000-01, with its focal theme on attacking poverty, recognises three major strategies for reducing poverty. They are, *promoting opportunity, facilitating empowerment* and *enhancing security* for poor people. Therefore, the poor people are those who experience multiple deprivations in nutritious food, shelter, education and health facilities which Amartya Sen would call as *entitlements*. Thus, poverty is seen as deprivations in opportunities that can result in lesser accumulation of human capabilities, which are essential for leading a decent life. Education is considered as an integral important opportunity for the development of human capital or human capabilities, the deprivation of which by itself represents poverty of education which becomes in turn an integral part of the human poverty (Tilak, 2000).

'Human history' as H.G. Wells remarked a few decades ago, 'becomes more and more a race between education and catastrophe'. Further, several studies including one by Tilak in 1999, have analysed the relation between educational attainment and poverty level in different states of India. A strong inverse relationship has been noticed between poverty and education. Educational attainment has been observed in terms of major educational indices such as illiteracy, enrollment, dropout, mean years of schooling and attendance. Taking the example of Tamil Nadu in this case, the Noon-Meal Scheme adopted since the reign of Kamaraj, had resulted in increased enrollment, retention and educational attainment.

The Ministry of Social Justice and Empowerment, Government of India undertakes programmes aimed at ensuring social justice to and empowerment of, the disadvantaged and marginalised sections of society such as Scheduled Castes, Scheduled Tribes and Backward Classes. For the Tenth Five Plan, an allocation of Rs. 8,530 crore has been made available. The focus would be on equitable distribution and growth with social justice, through a three-pronged strategy i.e., social empowerment through removing all this persisting inequalities, disparities and other problems besides providing easy access to basic minimum services; economic empowerment through promotion of employment—cum—income generation activities and social justice through eliminating all types of discrimination with the strength of legislative support, affirmative action, awareness generation and requisite change in the mind-set of people (Economic Survey, 2002-03).

Some may argue that removal of poverty could be undertaken through various welfare measures under Five Year Plans such as land reforms, enlargement of rural credit facilities, supply of subsidised seeds, implements and fertilizer, starting of rural, tiny and small scale industries. These have mostly been skimmed off in the end by the neo-capitalists and industrialists making them richer and leaving the poor to become poorer. Hence, this kind of economic remedy cannot solve the social and educational backwardness, unless some special treatment is devised and implemented. The policy of reservation in one of the available means to uplift the downtrodden and backward people.

An argument advanced against reservation is that it will impair the quality and efficiency of government services. At present, almost all of the top echelons of government services are manned predominantly by open competition candidates and their poor performance in recent years is a glaring instance for public criticism. But on the other hand, people belonging to the weaker sections will have the great advantage of possessing first hand knowledge of the sufferings and problems of the backward sections of society, for whom they are called upon to serve.

As regards the displeasure which may be caused to upper castes by the application of reservation policy, they should bear in mind that they have been enjoying the benefits of Government services for many years, while their fellow countrymen belonging to weaker sections have been made to starve and stand at the gates of Government offices. Therefore, natural justice demands that those who have been enjoying government patronage in full be made to wait, and *the excluded people* should be cared first. Until such time when all communities are made equals, in all walks of life, the reservation policy is indispensable to provide equal chances for all.

Further, Government services in India has always been looked upon as a symbol of prestige and power. By increasing the representation of weaker sections in Government service, an immediate feeling of participation the governance of the country is given to them. Moreover, the psychological spin off of this phenomenon is tremendous in that, that the entire community of the weaker section candidate feels socially elevated. Even when there are no tangible benefits to the community, it acts as a moral booster.

Universal Primary Education

Accordingly to provide opportunities for the livelihood of weaker sections, a firm basis for equitable growth was laid by massive investment in basic education for all, combined with great emphasis on technical education. Education strategy pursued in India towards three broad parameters i.e. universal access, universal retention and universal achievement stemmed from the Directive Principles of the Indian Constitution and 83rd Constitutional Amendment and they were instrumental not only in accelerating economic growth but also in distributing resources more equitably coupled with empowerment of people.

The Directive Principles of State Policy in Article 45 of the Indian Constitution elaborated the goal of universal primary education and directed the state that it shall endeavor to provide, within a period of 10 years from the commencement of the Constitution, *free and compulsory education* for all children until they complete the age of 14 years. Yet, about five and a half decades later, the goal of universal basic education remains elusive and unfulfilled. Realising the importance of primary education, the constitutional 93rd Amendment seeks to provide Education. For All (EFA) by making free and compulsory elementary education for all children as a fundamental right in the age group of 6-14 years. In order to fulfill this Constitutional obligation, *Sarva Shiksha Abhiyan* has been launched through a community owned approach and ensuring quality elementary education in a mission mode by the year 2010.

As against the goal of 6% of GDP laid down by the Kothari Education Commission, the total expenditure on education in India is 3.99% of GDP in 2001-02 (Economic Survey, 2002-03). Within the education sector, elementary education has been given the highest priority in terms of sub-sectoral allocations and a number of schemes launched by he Central Government to meet the needs of the educationally disadvantaged viz., Operation Blackboard, District Primary Education Programme, Education Guarantee Scheme and Alternative and Innovative Education, Teacher Education, National Programme of Nutritional Education, National Programme of Nutritional Support to Primary Education in 1995 and Pradhan Mantri Gramodaya Yojana in 2000-01 (elementary education component). Besides, another programme known as *National Literacy Mission* (NLM) has also started *Total Literacy Campaign* to achieve full literacy i.e., a sustainable threshold level of 75 per cent literacy by 2005.

The imperative need to provide education, the single most decisive factor of human resources development, has been succinctly underscored in the Article 21 of the Universal Declaration of Human Rights, 1948, by the U.N.O. The article reads "Everyone has a right to education". What is critical for human progress is education and opportunity. Poverty hinders both the access to education and opportunity. Especially poverty of income is often the result, poverty of opportunity is often the cause, for low attainment of education. Poverty of opportunity is a multi-dimensional phenomenon, embracing lack of education and health, lack of economic assets, social exclusion, and political marginalisation.

Paradigm Shift in Development

The real answer lies in changing the very model of development from the traditional economic growth pattern to human development, where human capabilities are built up and human opportunities enlarged and wherein people become the real agents and beneficiaries of economic growth, rather than remain an abstract residual of inhuman development processes. Such human development model rely on certain core strategies for the elimination of poverty—in particular educational empowerment, land reforms, credit to the poor, equitable growth, women's empowerment and good governance for all, particularly the depressed classes.

Education as An Engine of Growth

Education is a critical component for economic and social development. As education is the prime requirement for the education empowerment, it is crucial for building human capabilities and for opening up of opportunities among depressed classes. It is the true essence and indicator of human development also. Without education, development can be neither broad-based nor sustained. In terms of human development objectives, education is an end in itself, not just a means to an end. Education is a basic human right. It is also the key which opens many economic, social and political doors for people. It increases access to income-earning capabilities and employment opportunities.

The importance of education for development not a new discovery. It was fully recognised by classical economists such as Adam Smith, Alfred Marshall, and has been reconfirmed by more recent writers such as Schultz and Sen. The political leaders of India have not been far behind in extolling the virtues of providing education to the masses. However, around 424 million people are steeped in ignorance in India in the year 1997 and it has the largest illiterate population in the world exceeding the North American Continent and Japan (Mahlub-hul Haq, 1998).

Development of Human Capital

Human capital is defined as the stock of useful productive, valuable, and relevant knowledge acquired and built up in the process of education and training. Education provides the basis for building human capital which is a vital ingredient in building a nation. Of course, as will be argued later, education must be relevant to the needs of modern societies and to the demands of global markets, and it must be available to the members of society.

Human capital formation hypothesis suggests that investment in education is conceptually identical to an investment in physical capital. Rates of return studies convincingly show that social returns to investment in education are among the highest in a society. Primary education has the highest social rate of return, followed by secondary education. As national income increases, the returns to all levels of education decline, but primary education still has the highest return.

Along side improvements in children's nutrition are essential to ensure that educational performance is not hampered by poor health. In short, it is necessary for making the input of education a part of the wider human development strategy and a driving force behind all economic development. From the theoretical and empirical studies which link education and economic growth, it is very clear that no educated society remains underdeveloped far long, while no illiterate society can achieve sustained rate of economic expansion.

As the labour force becomes more and more educated, income is redistributed from the top 20 per cent to the lower 80 per cent of the population. Education is also a basic component of social cohesion and national identity. The foundation for a conscious and active citizenship are often laid in school. As such education plays a key role in the democratisation process. Literacy leads directly to an improvement in the depth and quality of public opinion as well as more active participation of the poor in the democratic process. Economic miracles are based on education miracles. Once educational base expands, it is also the best safety net to cushion any economic or political shocks.

Merits of Empowerment

The economic and social costs of such neglect of education in India are simply enormous. Whenever and wherever basic education has spread, the social and economic benefits were quite dramatic and visible. In urban India when mothers were illiterates, the child mortality rate was as high as 82 per thousand, but it dropped sharply to 34 per thousand when mothers became literates. A one-year increase in the average number of years of primary schooling of the work force would raise output by 23 per cent in India. Population stabilisation is possible only with improvement in literacy rates in India. Further, population stabilisation is crucial for the achievement of the goal of sustainable development and an equitable distribution of resources and opportunities. Improved access to primary and secondary education, extension of basic amenities, the empowerment of women, awareness generation and a better standard of living would and ultimately contribute towards inculcation of the required consciousness regarding the desirability of a small family size.

Education leads to many social benefits including improvements in the standard of hygiene, reduction in infant and child mortality rates, increase in labour productivity, rise in civic consciousness, greater political empowerment and democratisation, and an improved sense of national unity. Mark Blaug has pointed out some widely held shibboleths about the role of education. He has outlined that education is a necessary complement to sanitation and nutrition programmes and these work directly to eliminate the consequences of poverty. Further in his view 'education acts to reduce the birth rate, directly via the education of women and indirectly via an increase in the period for which children are dependent on their parents' (Mark Blaug, 1974).

Educational Challenges Ahead

In education, the elementary sector is besieged by numerous systematic problems such as inadequate school infrastructure, presence of single—teacher schools, high teacher absenteeism (specially in rural areas), large scale teacher vacancies and inadequate equipment. This brings into focus the role of decentralisation and people's participation in the provision of basic services. It is essential that control over schools and teachers be transferred to local bodies, having a direct interest in teacher performance. The key need in India is not just to bring all children to school but to improve the ability of these schools to teach children effectively. This is a challenge that India is yet to meet. Several straight-forward actions have been suggested that would go a long way towards improving school quality and enhancing learning achievement.

India's educational challenge consists of the following major tasks:

1. enrolling all children primary schools compulsorily through the incentive mechanism of free meals, clothing, books, notebooks and introduction of Community Monitoring Mechanism.

2. improving the quality and relevance of education through pre-service and in-service education for teachers.
3. providing more and better qualified teachers and creating a performance based career structure for teachers.

Prevalence of Child Labour

Despite the strenuous efforts of the government, the goal of universal primary education has not been achieved so far, resulting in large scale prevalence of child labour. Although, child labour has been abolished by law long back, the system continuous to prevail invariably in all parts of India due to the legal loopholes. The abominable act of employing children stems from a number of socio-economic factors, associated with poverty and ignorance.

Enrolement of children belonging to weaker sections remains far below their number and the sops offered by the government in the form of clothing, books, notebooks and free lunches have not allured them, because there is a lingering doubt on their very survival in the world, in the face of poverty and squalor. Consequently, the agenda remains unfinished inspite of the implementation of a number of programmes such as Total Literacy Mission Programme, Shiksha Karmi Project and Mass Literacy Programmes, besides a new policy approach for the achievement of Universal Primary Education (UPE) outlined in the National Policy on Education, 1986. However, even now in our country, about 35 million children in the 6-10 age group do not attend primary schools and the drop outs of primary school children account for 37%. As the goal of Education for All (EFA) has not been met, Adult Education Programmes were started. Adult Literacy Schemes signify in a way, the past failures to meet the Education for all challenge (An Economic Appraisal, 1997-98). However, the relentless fight on illiteracy should be continued with emphasis on the strict enforcement of law on compulsory primary education.

Present Position of Reservation in Higher Education

One of the major prerequisites for filling up positions meant for the Scheduled Castes and Scheduled Tribes in Government/Quasi-Government services is the attainment of the minimum educational qualification specified for jobs or positions. Hence, reservation has also been provided for in the educational institutions especially in higher education. Now, the scenario with respect of enrolment of the SCs and STs in institutions of higher learning such as colleges and university departments is almost similar to the situation in the sphere of services.

Table 1: Faculty Wise Percentage Position of SC/ST Enrolment (1992-93) in Colleges and Universities.

Faculty	*SC*	*ST*	*SC and ST*
Arts	8.0	3.9	11.9
Science	5.8	2.1	7.9
Engg/Tech	8.1	2.1	10.2
Medicine	11.9	4.4	16.3
Agriculture	10.7	5.4	16.1
Law	11.7	2.7	14.4

Source: UGC, 'Representation of Scheduled Castes and Scheduled Tribes in Enrolment, Teaching and Non-Teaching Staff in University Teaching Departments/University College', p. 5.

Though reservations have been provided for the Scheduled Castes and Scheduled Tribes, the filling up of these seats especially in service and higher education is not routine and mechanical. Rather, it is dependent upon their performances in test, examinations and interviews, besides of course, the prerequisites of appropriate educational attainments. This partly explains as to why the state has not been able to fill up these posts and seats for both the Scheduled Tribes and Scheduled Castes. However, Special Training Programmes are being conducted by the Centre and States to reduce the handicaps faced by these candidates in this regard.

Reservation in Political Field

As pointed out earlier, the provision of reservations for the weaker sections has been analysed in the educational field so far. With reference to reservation in politics, the share of the Scheduled Castes and Scheduled Tribes in the Parliament was 79 (14.5 per cent) and 41 (7.5 per cent) respectively in 1999. The corresponding figure for the legislative assemblies was 562 (13.8 per cent) for the Scheduled Castes and 539 (13.2 per cent) for the Scheduled Tribes [Planning Commission 2000]. The higher share of the Scheduled Tribes in the State Assemblies is due to the creation of tribal states, mainly in the north-eastern region. Now, reservation for weaker sections have also been ensured at the grassroots democracy level i.e., Village Panchayats.

Reservation in Government Services

Education without adequate, remunerative and productive jobs rarely leads to sustainable economic growth. As on January 1, 1995 the share of the Scheduled Tribes in respect of A, B, C, and D group of services has been that of 2.89, 2.68, 5.69 and 6.48 per cent respectively as against 10.15, 12.67,

16.15 and 21.26 respectively in the case of the scheduled caste. The following table highlights greater shortfall of SCs and STs at the higher groups of services such as A and B grades.

Table 2: Share of SCs and STs at various levels of the Government Services in 1995.

Group	*Percentage of SC*	*Percentage of ST*
'A'	10.15	2.89
'B'	12.67	2.68
'C'	16.15	5.69
'D'	21.26	6.48
Total	**17.43**	**5.78**

Source: Report of the National Commission for Scheduled Caste and Scheduled Tribe, Vol. 1, 1996-97 and 1997-98.

In contrast, the scheduled castes fall short of the stipulated quota only in respect of group A and B services and that too, if one may add, not substantially. In respcct of C and D, their share exceeds the required quota of 15.5 per cent of reservation.

Conclusion

Poverty and oppression have multiple causes and, therefore multiple issues have to be addressed to overcome them. India, being an agrarian economy, people could also be empowered through the distribution of quality land under land reforms; livelihood could be improved through satisfactory tenancy rights, reasonable minimum wage and alternative employment possibilities. Besides organising the people for achieving social justice, Government accountability is required for protecting the poor (John, 2001).

So far, it has been observed that the laws enacted for the educational and employment empowerment of weaker sections have not yielded the desired results on account of the socio-politico, economic and administrative bottlenecks. Moreover, loopholes in the existing laws aimed at the empowerment of weaker sections have to be plugged and the law should be implemented with determination and political will, so that everybody is benefited. Along with this, the country needs committed leaders. Thus, only a committed bureaucracy and political system could implement the reservation laws with full spirit, resulting in the creation of opportunities for sustained livelihoods, community participation in nation-building activities, economic, social and political upliftment of weaker sections, sustained and equitable economic growth leading to all-round development.

The more we delay the empowerment of the weaker sections, the larger looms the peril of successively growing weaker generations who may be not fully brought into the tough task of development for the general good of all society—a prospect the nation can ill-afford to harbour.

REFERENCES

1. *Economic Survey*, (2002-03), Ministry of Finance, Government of India, New Delhi, p. 222 to 245.
2. John, Sommer, G. (2001), *Empowering the Oppressed: Grassroots Advocacy Movements in India,* Sage Publications, India Pvt. Ltd., New Delhi, p. 101.
3. Loh. J. (1995) "Education and Economic Growth in India: an Aggregate Production Function Approach", NCERT, *School Effectiveness and Learning Achievement at Primary Stage: International Perspective,* New Delhi.
4. Mahlub hul Haq and Khadija Haq (1988), *Human development in South Asia,* Oxford Univesity Press, Karachi, p. 48.
5. Mark Blaug (1974), *Education and the Employment Problem in Developing Countries,* The Macmillan Company of India Limited, New Delhi, p. 85.
6. Director of Evaluation and Applied Research (1997-98), *Tamil Nadu—An Economic Appraisal,* Government of Tamil Nadu, Chennai-108, p. 144.
7. Tilak, J.B.G. (1999), "Investment inhuman Capital in India: An Inter-State Analysis of Stock and Flow of Human Capital", *Journal of India School of Political Economy,* 11(1), January—March, p. 48.
8. Tilak, J.B.G. (2000), "Education Poverty in India" *NIEPA Occasional Paper 29, International Symposium on Development Policies for the New Millennium,* Mumbai, July 12-14.
9. Virginius Xaxa (2001), "Protective Discrimination: Why Scheduled Tribes Lag behind Scheduled Castes", *Economic and Political Weekly,* Vol. XXXVI, No. 29, July 21, p. 2773.
10. *World Development Report (2000-01),* Oxford University Press Inc., New York.

38

Prospects and the Challenging Issues of Globalisation

Prof. N. Narayana*

The mid 1980s and the first half of the 1990s thus became a period when many developing countries, with the initiation from the institutions such as the World Bank and International Monetary Fund, unilaterally opened up their markets to imports from developed and other developing countries. Having reassessed the value to themselves of foreign investment, they moved away from relative isolationism to greater integration into the world economy. In broad economic terms, the initial results have indicated in the form of markedly higher growth rates in developing countries that opened their markets particularly in Asia. Some of the countries of Latin America have managed to avoid financial catastrophes. New structures of production have developed with greater international linkages, more rapid technical change, and a shift of the economic weight in the world from Europe and North America to the Pacific. The trade liberalisation elements of these changes were confirmed in the Uruguay Round and the creation of the World Trade Organisation.

All these factors, combined with increase in speed and scope of communications, have contributed to the process that is called 'Globalisation'. Depending on the angle from which one approaches it, Globalisation is seen either as a blessing or a curse. Some welcome it as a path to new patterns of growth and development; others use it as a synonym for unwelcome, over-rapid change and loss of control of the economic and social environment. However, ever-closer linkages and the extension of competition into more

* Department of Economics, University of Botswana, Private Bag–0022, Gaborone, Botswana.

areas than before characterize globalisation. This means, for instance, that for emerging markets, international dependence is replaced by competition, which offers them enormous opportunities.

An attempt is made in this chapter to analyse how the process of globalisation has contributed to improve the economic prospects of the nations that have adopted market system. The challenging issues of globalisation such as sustainable development, socio-cultural adversities are also highlighted to understand the implications.

Some of the definitions of globalisation that are offered are presented here:

- "The growing economic interdependence of countries worldwide though the increasing volume and variety of cross-border transactions in goods and services and of international capital flows through the more rapid and widespread diffusion of technology" (IMF, 1997)
- "The widening of the spectrum of goods and services entering international trade as a consequence of trade liberalisation, increased freedom of establishment and technical innovations allowing long-distance delivery of services" (Ronald W. Jones and Henry. K. Kierzkowski, 1997).
- "A process whereby producers and investors increasingly behave as if the world economy consisted of a single market and production area with regional or national sub sectors, rather than of a set of national economies linked by trade and investment flows" (UNCTAD, 1996).
- "The absorption of all countries and systems into one" (Rob van Drimmelen, 1998).

The Main Features of the Globalisation Process

- There has been an immense increase in the volume of goods and services traded internationally, associated with the steady and continuing process of trade liberalisation; during the period from 1985 to 2000, the volume of world merchandise exports consistently grew more rapidly than world output, with average annual rates of 6 per cent and 2.5 per cent respectively from 1990 to 2000. Consequently, trade has been greatly influencing on the economies of most countries (World Bank, 2001).
- An equally important shift in the country and product structure of international trade between 1985 and 2000 indicates that the

developing countries raised their share of trade from 23 to 29 per cent, increased their share of trade among themselves from 31 to 37 per cent, and increased the share of manufactures in their exports from 47 per cent to a staggering 83 per cent (World Bank, 2001).

- An even larger increase has been noticed in the volume, speed and complexity of financial and direct investment flows and a multiplication of financial markets. Again with greater integration of developing countries, private capital inflows to developing countries rose from an average of one-half of one per cent of their GDP in the period from 1983 to 1989, to between 2 and 4 per cent from 1990 to 2000, with the share of bank lending falling and that of direct investment rising (World Bank, 2001).
- Continuing economic growth is achieved in some developing countries at a speed never seen before in the post-second world war period. In some cases this was helped by well-directed state intervention, and in other cases by the withdrawal of the state from economic intervention.
- Concomitant changes in patterns of production of goods and services have taken place. This is seen partly in an increasing shift away from manufacturing to services in Western economies, while manufacturing rises in developing countries, and partly in the fragmentation of production processes previously undertaken in one place.

Some of the elements that have contributed to the globalisation process are:

- Trade liberalisation, first in goods then in services took place and there is clear evidence that nations taking an active part in the process of liberalisation have advanced more rapidly than those that have not.
- Freer movement of capital than of labour and freer movement of skilled labour than of unskilled labour, including the development of new skills in an educated workforce in the fields of computer programming, engineering, finance. This trend that cuts across boundaries between "developed" and "developing" countries has been noticed.
- Transfer and adaptation of technologies (new agricultural methods under the Green Revolution and its successors; the application of computer technology to a whole variety of processes).

- More rapid, widespread and affordable communications (travel, telecomm, Internet).

Based on the above analysis, it is now possible to say that economic globalisation is a process, which combines several elements. In the first place, it is the contemporary expression of a strong historical trend that created the world economic system through the internationalisation of some markets and the transnationalisation of economic enterprises. Second, the globalisation of markets has been accelerated in recent decades by technological developments, especially in the realm of computer science and communications. Third, a global market, more integrated than ever before, has been shaped for raw materials, manufactured goods, financial and derivative products. As a result, prevailing global trends are expressions of the different ways the market functions. They are based on the accumulation of instruments, especially at the technological level, which have enabled the creation and development of complex economic devices.

Many world leaders have unambiguously endorsed globalisation, arguing that it is the key to global prosperity. Behind this promise of an improvement of economic life lies an implicit hope that the process would increase the productivity of ordinary working people by ensuring relative prosperity for the large majority of citizens and also substantially improving the current global distribution of income and wealth. In the process of globalisation, hundreds of millions of new jobs are being created, though in new sectors and areas, since industries change under competitive pressure. In addition, the end of the USSR and changes in Eastern Europe have led many to argue that there is no alternative to the market system (Michael Schluter and David Lee, 1993).

It is evident that a number of independent but inter-related activities such as finance, communications, trade, power, and technology have been globalised. Furthermore there is a globalisation of problems in health and the natural environment, exemplified by the HIV/AIDS pandemic and the spread of plant and animal life forms to regions of the world where they upset an historic ecological balance. Cultural exchanges, which enable peoples to share their values and traditions but also create new tensions, are also described in terms of globalisation (Steward M. Hoover, 1995).

Of course, there are many who accept the prevailing economic system on the basis of empirical considerations while others reject this single frame of reference. There are indeed some positive outcomes of the prevailing process. The technological changes, which make possible the integration of markets, have also contributed to a greater extent.

The Role of Technology

Globalisation has been made possible by changes in technology. It is now easier, quicker and cheaper to communicate with others and transport goods over long distances than it used to be. What was visualised, two centuries ago, by Adam Smith about the critical role that transportation plays in increasing national prosperity has proved correct (Adam Smith, 1776). The key to economic growth, he observed, is "the division of labour", the specialisation of workers that enables a rural family specialising in farming to produce more per year than a family that must also make its own clothes and soap and other non-farm necessities as well. As transportation improves, more specialisation can occur because the same producer can serve a larger market. Economists today tend to look at international transport of goods in the same way. Larger physical markets through globalisation allow for even greater efficiencies and thus increased prosperity.

One need not be a Marxist to recognize the truth underlying Karl Marx's materialist interpretation of history. For our purposes, we can think of this insight as having two parts. The first is that when technological change occurs, it has far-reaching influence on humans and their social institutions. The second is that technological change itself appears as an independent force in our common life because it seems to be inevitable. It is extremely rare that an improvement in a production process, once discovered, is not implemented. While Marx extended the impact of such changes in the forces of production into the realm of ideas to an extent many find historically inaccurate, those two initial insights are quite relevant to the debate over globalisation.

The far-reaching influence of technological change on humans and their social institutions would seem undeniable. While we today would probably think immediately of the tremendous impact of the invention of the computer in this connection, revolutionary change produced by technological developments is not a new phenomenon. The fact is that each of these technological changes whose implementation and widespread use seemed virtually inevitable in the process of globalisation.

Costs of Globalisation

Like any transformation, the process of globalisation has not been achieved without costs, and fears about its effects are understandable.

- In many developed economies, unemployment has increased and real wages have fallen, even though the worst fears of "de-industrialisation" stemming from the combination of trade, capital movements and technology have not been realised. Some countries and communities have managed to surmount the changes more or less successfully.

- Development has also been uneven in the "developing" world. Although statistics show a general increase in economic welfare, relative income distribution has worsened in many cases.
- In all economies the balance between skilled/educated and unskilled/uneducated people has increasingly tilted in favour of the more educated and hence more flexible. This leaves less skilled or less educated people and populations more vulnerable and marginalised (Nicanor Perlas, 1996).
- There is a general impression that the autonomy of governments in policy-making has declined. "The market" is seen as too powerful and potentially destabilising and there is a feeling that "business has become the most powerful force shaping the world" (Jeffrey Garten, 1997). At the same time, however, markets are what we all rely on.

Political developments, sometimes linked to systemic economic change, have been equally dramatic:

- The major painful and destabilising political transformations in Russia and Eastern Europe have not yet been consolidated.
- Equally strong economic reforms have taken place in China, leading to double-digit economic growth but within a very controlled political system.
- In the former GATT and now in the WTO, this change in international relationships has been visible both in the much greater integration and influence of the nations of the South in the work of the organisation, and in changing alliances among nations in trade negotiations. Fundamental new alliances are also being forged in Latin America, Asia, Africa and Europe. In Latin America, the drive for regional cooperation is strengthening. In the Asia-Pacific region, ASEAN (which has expanded to ten members) and the APEC group, which takes in the whole of the Pacific basin, are becoming important cross-cultural groupings. The expansion of the influence of the European Union to Central and Eastern Europe and the Baltic states is filling the vacuum left by the downfall of the Soviet system. The political transformation in South Africa has raised hopes that it may be a positive and dynamic economic and political force in southern Africa if not the whole of the continent (Ian Morrison and Greg Schmidt, 1994).

These changes are part of the new framework for the interaction between economics and politics. They are the most fundamental factors. We must recognize that rapid change often means severe adjustment and disruption. Therefore, we should encourage and promote policies that do not deny change, but seek to minimize or compensate for its disruptive effects, while looking out for new opportunities to bring about positive change.

It needs to be noted that the markets, if undistorted, generally do operate efficiently and to the benefit of consumers. Most efforts to protect special interest groups have not worked and may in the long run do more harm than good to the people they seek to protect. Effective competition is essential to the good functioning of markets, and those monopolies, which necessarily distort, should be discouraged. It is evident that the privatisation of some important companies on a monopoly basis has not benefited consumers, while the privatisation of organisations like telecommunications on a competitive basis has done so. While trade liberalisation is in broad terms desirable, it is not a sufficient condition for economic growth and, in turn, that economic growth is not a sufficient condition for social development or improved income distribution.

We must recognize that there is need for active policies by governments to ensure both that markets function and that exploitation is minimised and the pain of adjustment alleviated. But we cannot deny that change is part of our lives. We must also recognize that relatively few governments meet the criterion of being "of the people, by the people, for the people".

Before we address the issues of globalisation adequately, it is necessary to analyse the impact of globalisation on economic prospects of the economies.

Globalisation - Impact on the Economies

The process that has grown into globalisation has benefited humankind in many ways. Taken together with education and other elements of social and economic development, trade and economic liberalisation have lifted many people out of the subsistence economy into participation in economic development, even at a time when the population of the world is still growing very fast. For example, Kenya has had thirty years of over 3 per cent population growth; yet there is evidence that the country can still feed itself and that there is a growing African middle class. The academic discussions of 30 years ago about whether India could feed its rapidly increasing population have also been belied by events: the growth rate of India's population has declined and access to food has improved.

Globalisation brought enormous gains in prosperity worldwide. In many richer economies, structural adjustment triggered by globalisation has added to an already high rate of unemployment. At the same time, however, overall gains in well being are unprecedented in history. Within the last ten years, according to UN Development Programme statistics, 500 to 600 million people have been newly established above the poverty line. According to UNDP forecasts, the group of people living on revenues above the poverty line is expected to increase further by 1.5 to 2 billion in the 30 years to come. It is true that 600 to 700 million people may remain below the poverty line in the next 30 years, because the market mechanism will not be able to solve all problems by then. But the impact of globalisation is clearly working in the right direction (UNDP, 2002).

Along with higher incomes for billions of people, more and better jobs and a rapidly increasing middle class in emerging economies, a wider choice of goods and services is being produced more efficiently. It is consumers all over the world who must be seen as the main winners in this process - and not the firms (due to increased competition). The outlook, based on World Bank data, suggests that, according to the regional pattern of future gains from Globalisation, even Africa will gain from Globalisation over the next 15 years.

Projected annual growth in per capita Gross Domestic Product 1994-2010.

Two World Bank Scenarios

Countries	*"Divergent" scenario Percentage of growth per annum*	*"Globalisation" scenario Percentage of growth per annum*	*Difference between the two scenarios Additional wealth accumulated*
OECD countries	1.6	2.3	+12 percent
East Asia	3.0	4.4	+24 percent
China	2.3	3.9	+28 percent
South Asia	2.4	4.0	+28 percent
Latin America	1.4	3.3	+35 percent
North Africa/Middle East	1.4	3.4	+37 percent
Sub-Saharan Africa	-0.3	1.7	+37 percent

Source: IBRD World Development Report 1995.

There are a number of parallel developments - partly distinct from globalisation, partly overlapping with it, partly stimulated by it, and partly accelerating it - that may be mentioned. One is the expansion of technology in general, and in particular information technology. There is also the process of de-industrialisation and the growth of the service sector. The global knowledge base has increased, with a doubling of the scientific literature every

10 to 15 years. One aspect of the slow-down in population growth is the increase in learning, made possible in part because parents have more time and resources to invest in their children. It is learning which makes knowledge out of the mass of information. In many countries of the developing world there is autonomous opening, deregulation, modernisation and globalisation of rules and institutions relevant to business. Company behaviour is also changing, seen for example in the outsourcing to India of software development.

Of course, there has been a slow-down in economic growth in industrialised countries. But any conclusion drawn from these statistics should take into account the error in inflation measures, improvements in health care (which does not just involve higher prices of the health-care system) and the impact of the ageing of the population.

The correction of wage compression should also be noted. Low wages act as a starting point for people joining the labour market in the United States; and 95 per cent of those identified as belonging to the lowest quintile of income distribution in 1975 are no longer in that group. In Europe, the phenomenon of high minimum wages acts as a means to keep newcomers out of the job market. In industrialised countries today, income differentiation runs along the lines of education and skills, and no longer according to entitlements, or because someone comes from a middle-class family.

Issues of Globalisation

The concern of people in developing countries has rightfully been aroused by the fact that many people, especially among the world's poor, have been left worse off than before by this process. This has led many people to condemn globalisation as a fundamentally misdirected process. Globalisation has not only left many people worse off, but has also left many people better off - including many of the world's poor. When poor people are made better off, they obviously become less poor and perhaps no longer poor at all. Thus the fact that globalisation has helped them seems to lose its moral importance in the eyes of many, since the poorest apparently are not being helped (Daniel Rush Finn, 1996). Far greater care must be taken by all our nations for the damage done to people's lives by economic change, but the benefits of that change must enter our moral assessment as well.

The second problem is that many of the effects attributed to globalisation are in fact effects of other processes that would have occurred within individual nations even without increased global connectedness. Even within a single nation, the ordinary developments of economic life regularly leave some people better off and others worse off. Thus responsibly attributing economic problems to globalisation requires more than a simple assertion. Quite rightful moral indignation at the plight of poor people today does not justify, however vociferous the indignation, every conceivable causal connection that might come to mind.

Going further, some critics of globalisation point out the large profits that many multinational corporations make through international trade. Many therefore attribute the basic causal force behind globalisation to these corporations. From there it is often argued that if globalisation has detrimental effects, then it would be a simple moral choice to oppose the interests of these multinationals in an effort to reduce international trade and its detrimental effects. However, the relation between causal analysis and moral assessment is rarely so simple.

Although multinational corporations play an important role in the process of globalisation, it is far more accurate to begin our causal analysis with a view of the role of technology in the developments, which are shaping the world today.

We tend to attribute much of what is happening globally today to three revolutions which have shaped modern life; the *economic* revolution that started with the mercantile capitalism of the 12th century, the *industrial* revolution of the 18th century, the *political* revolutions which gave rise to the ideologies of the 19th and 20th centuries. Of these three revolutions, technology and the market have sidelined the significance of the political one. Interlocking economic interests and the traffic of information via cyberspace increasingly render the nation-state borderless. The market and technology have replaced ideology as a primary force in organising societies. There is a decided shift towards reliance on market forces in resolving what used to be political questions, and a certain sense of inevitability over the globalisation process as technology extends its reach.

With the collapse of socialism, societies have increasingly become market-led. By this is meant not only that countries and their internal policies are being organised around the demands of a globalising economy, but also that people's lives today are much more determined by economics than previously. The ways in which the market is shaping social organisation can be seen in the following global trends:

- **Emergence of middle class:** One of the promises of globalisation is the tremendous redistribution of economic power at the world level. By the end of the year 2000, it was said that East Asia would have arrived at full economic parity with Europe and North America. A world middle class has emerged, made up mostly of the professional elites of Asia, Latin America and Eastern Europe. This change in the global balance of power, together with the addition of 2.5 billion people into the world market as previously closed economies have opened up, means that intense competition is now focused on capturing this emergent middle class, whose consumption patterns are now similar to the middle classes of industrial economies. The uneven spread of growth within societies increases discontent and marginalisation, especially among the urban poor who witness the life-styles of the affluent and erupt into frustration and violence.

- **Marginalisation of the producers of real goods:** Because of the speed with which capital moves across borders and the power of transnational corporations to outsource labour and other services from anywhere in the world, trade will increasingly be in money and ideas rather than actual goods. It is predicted that over the next decade, financial transactions and trade in product patents will grow two to three times faster than the movement of goods. Already, about US$1.5 trillion is circulating in the global market. Those in information industries who control software, their price and value bears little relationship to actual costs or the direct labour that went into its production. This means that those with real goods to sell will have a far less significant impact on world trade than those with access to mobile capital and technological innovations. The Indian economy is a good example of the kind of vulnerability induced by globalisation.
- **Insecurity of the work force:** The emergence of "virtual corporations" - firms with a fairly small core of competencies but linked to a network of organisational alliances and external experts—is giving rise to a highly individualised work force, operating in isolation. More and more highly skilled professionals depend on short-term contracts, with no job security and none of the usual benefits. In order to compete in the global economy, large transnationals downsize, de-linking corporate profit from employee welfare and security. This growing sense of insecurity in the workplace means that corporate loyalties—a factor, which in the past propelled economies, like that of Japan to perform at a very high rate of productivity—have become fragile.
- **Increased inequality in access to growth:** The head-on mega-competition that is part and parcel of globalisation leads to winner-

take-all situations. The biggest losers are the poor, whose levels of education and skills leave them far behind than those who are knowledge- and communication-oriented. Moreover, their plight is now left to market forces, as seen in the massive funds being poured into micro-credit as a way of training the poor to adapt and survive in the market. The demonstrated unsustainability of welfare systems in the North has made emergent economies unwilling to bail out those at the edges of life. A kind of social disorder is setting in, judging those who fail to adapt themselves to the market as unfit and leaving them behind.

With the ascendancy of the market and the market is the determining factor; the result is marginalisation of human values. The market is not competent to address problems of poverty and equity. We cannot leave the plight of the poor to the operations of blind market forces.

Sustainability and Globalisation

There are several areas in which elements of the process of globalisation affect the requirements of sustainability. Without claiming to provide an exhaustive list, we may mention the following:

1. **Unlimited growth, reasonable human satisfaction and unfair distribution of resources**: Because the world has limited resources, the prevailing economic trend that aims at permanent economic growth - which characterizes the process of globalisation - threatens the sustainability of life and future generations. Furthermore, the product of economic growth is unevenly shared, and the gap between the well off and the poor is widening. Those who aim at sustainability affirm that the rich minority of the world, which profits from the process of globalisation, is wasting a great volume of earth's resources and living far above the level of human need. The debate between those who want more economic growth and those who advocate an "economy of enough" is becoming sharper.

2. **Technology and sustaining humanity**: Technology, which can contribute much to the improvement of life, especially when its innovations take account of the vital needs of human beings and the natural and social environment, is also used to destroy jobs and weaken human communities. This particularly applies to the tensions generated by the exploitation of resources of the South by economic powers who have the knowledge and control of these technologies. Furthermore, a technology that may promote life for some can at the same time be negative for many others. For example, without

any consultation with the wider public, powerful economic agents make critical decisions about genetic manipulations that may threaten human life.

3. **Communications and sustaining humanity**: Although developments in modern technologies of information broaden people's possibilities for communicating and inter-relating, there is a very strong trend towards the concentration of global information on trade in the hands of a few powerful commercial actors (Melba Padilla Maggay, 1998).
4. **Increased human relationships and transactions**: The technological developments on which the process of economic globalisation is based enable quicker contact among people than ever before. The acceleration of trade requires financial transactions and information about markets, which contribute greatly to economic growth. Computer programmes are designed to react almost instantaneously to fluctuations in the market. Trade can also facilitate easier contact among people. But this new phenomenon inherent to the process of globalisation also creates a level of stress and anxiety, which is difficult to manage; and some are asking whether this situation is human or sustainable.
5. **The influence of production trends and finance**: The necessary inter-relation of places of production in today's world helps to make visible the basic solidarity of human beings. One of the disturbing realities of our time, however, is the dominating power of financial capital. The specific interests of global finance seem to impose their power on nearly every aspect of human life. Although the majority of investments in many financial markets may come from pension funds for employees, civil servants, and the like, their managers often behave aggressively; and in the final analysis those most affected are the impoverished, who find little space in which to exercise human freedom or to seek alternatives to sustain their lives.
6. **Trade and foreign direct investment**: Increased international trade and direct foreign investment hold out the hope that the people of the developing world may participate in the prosperity enjoyed by others. After generations of almost exclusively providing primary products to the industrialised world, the building of factories in developing countries to process those products for export and to manufacture a large variety of goods for both export and domestic consumption has enabled some people to move out of poverty. Others

however have become poorer and experience a growing feeling of insecurity; and the fact is that most developing countries are not enjoying these potential benefits of trade and direct foreign investment. Moreover, the terms of trade regularly worsen for most underprivileged people while they improve for some of the wealthy. This significantly reduces any advantages of trade for those most in need while increasing the advantage of those who already have greater advantage. Transnational corporations press governments - especially in the developing world - for concessions on taxes, labour regulations and environmental standards by threatening to move elsewhere if they are not granted. Social justice is thus undermined, and governments are deprived of the revenue to maintain necessary public services. Similarly, international competition leads firms to press governments to delay implementing stricter controls to combat climate change and local pollution. Both physical and social sustainability are thus threatened.

7. **Economic Globalisation and social exclusion**: As a result of market integration millions of jobs are lost at the level of production. More and more people are affected by chronic unemployment, lack the necessary means for a decent life and confront the painful realisation that their socio-economic rights. The mergers and take-overs, which are a chief index of globalisation, are often followed by an announcement that jobs are being cut. At the level of international trade, certain regions of the world, such as Africa and Latin America, have a smaller share today than twenty years ago. This greatly affects the life of many people, whose only chance for survival is the informal sector, where their social rights are not respected.

8. **Mobility and increasing migration**: Mobility has always been a driving force of trade. The present level of world trade would not be possible without the development of more and faster transportation of both persons and goods. Further expanding world trade favours the further increase of mobility. From the point of view of sustainability, this has to be avoided. Those concerned with the environmental crisis believe that new approaches to mobility and transport must be found. A further element of mobility is reflected in the increasing numbers of uprooted people. The phenomenon of economic refugees has reached intensity unforeseen as recently as ten years ago. When the conditions to survive decently are lacking in their native places, people decide to migrate - from rural areas to the cities, from small towns to the big urban centres, from poor

countries to wealthier ones. However, prevailing economic trends are unable to create the conditions necessary to enable societies to face this situation adequately. Indeed, the integration of markets is managed a way that works against this. Current demographic trends, especially in the South, tend to aggravate the situation.

9. **Intercultural tensions**: When economic globalisation is affirmed as the only route to a better human future, those cultures, which experience its impact as a threat or even an attack, will inevitably clash with prevailing trends. Cultural fragmentation is almost inescapable. People's lives are affected adversely. They cannot reject integration into international markets and the accompanying imperatives to be more efficient and competitive. At the same time, they sense that their traditions, values and identities, which often include a respectful and caring attitude to the natural environment, are in danger. These tensions are sometimes unfortunately manifested in violent terms (Danial Katz, 1947).

10. **The role of the state**: A key structural consequence of globalisation has been a weakening of political control over economic life. The contemporary reduction of national political power and sovereignty has not been compensated for by the creation of a transnational political authority, which could appropriately and democratically define the limits within which market activity must occur. International economic institutions, especially financial exchanges, strive to limit the control of national authorities. In this context, the regulatory role of the state in the economic realm must be underlined. If the state should not be an economic actor among others, competing with them, it ought nevertheless to set the framework and to be responsible for the economic process at the national level, including its economic exchanges with other nations. The wealthiest groups of the world would press for quick international agreements that so evidently serve their own interests at the cost of labour standards and environmental policies. It is the responsibility of the state to guarantee that the common national interest is respected and to do so it must fulfill its regulatory role.

Global Trends and Community Life

However, globalisation also threatens community life. Given its dependence on the world of human constructions and the extraordinary nature of most of the elements, which make it possible, globalisation accentuates the instrumental intention of economic activities. It reinforces a "culture of enterprise" which reduces most created beings to things and means (Marshall Mcluham, 1964). Human beings, who can understand themselves by taking account of their living relationships with their environment, are now being detached. The breaking of communion between nature and human beings tempts persons to ignore not only their links with their environment but also their own limits. The particularly devastating effects of the prevailing trends of the globalising economy on the community life of indigenous peoples must be particularly emphasised. Exploitation of natural resources and lack of care for land often threaten the very being of these communities.

But those who want to manage the processes and integration of markets favour globalisation. They look on its development optimistically, encouraged by the unprecedented growth in world trade. They believe that the integration of markets will bring along with it the integration of cultures and peoples. However, many others are fearful and anxious about the high price they must pay to adjust themselves to globalisation. Those who are excluded from the process of globalisation experience bear the price by way of pains and sufferings. They feel that they are not recognised but are considered as objects, as masses, but not as human beings with rights and responsibilities. As part of the mass of excluded people - whether they live in industrialised, developing or less developed nations - they sense that they are discarded, as if they do not count at all. They do not have the chance to live well, but only to survive. This situation leads to social and political problems.

Amidst this paradoxical coexistence of the integration of markets and the exclusion of people are some communities in which men and women associate to affirm life. Not surprisingly, many of the individuals who participate in groups defending human rights are also involved in the ecological movement and in other movements acting for social renewal. The common thread is their affirmation of life—an expression of their awareness that we share a common existence in a world where injustice prevails and life is in danger. These communities question whether sustainability is possible to achieve within the context of ongoing globalisation. But the sustainable society cannot emerge in the framework of prevailing trends of growing world trade and human mobility. However, some communities are ready to resist the threats globalisation poses to human beings and to sustain and affirm a kind of life, which is common to all and can be shared with future generations.

Conclusion

Globalisation has impacted the nations in a variety of ways. A positive effect of globalisation has been witnessed by many nations as it allowed them to achieve higher levels of economic growth and development. With higher levels of trade, world output has increased. This is true especially for rapidly developing countries of Asia through out 1990s. However, nations that had been struggling with achieving sustainable growth and standards of living have been further negatively affected by globalisation. With the countries such as Africa opening up their markets, they have been inundated with imports, but at the same time enabled to sell their exports. This equates to the lower levels of growth for these countries and lower standards of living.

Whether globalisation helps or hurts the poor is one of the most contentious economic issues of modern times. Part of the reason for continued disagreement lies in the very notion of globalisation, which has many dimensions- some economic, some political, some technological, and some cultural- and as such may mean different things to different people. There are those who argue that globalisation is contributing to increasing economic disparities in the world by allowing some countries and some segments of the population to become ever richer while marginalising the poorer countries and poorer population groups. They tend to blame globalisation itself for deepening poverty in parts of the world. Others contend that if some countries and some population groups have failed to benefit from globalisation, fault lies in globalisation itself but in fact that they have not actually embraced globalisation ad fully as the rest of the world.

However the issues of globalisation discussed above indicate that the developing countries cannot bear the costs of globalisation in the short run although the benefits of it will be derived in the long run. Globalisation will help the poor by promoting labour-intensity in labour-abundant developing countries. The inference that can be drawn from this argument is that if the poor are not actually gaining, it must be because globalisation has not gone far enough.

REFERENCES

1. Adam Smith, 1776, 'An Inquiry into the Nature and Causes of Wealth of Nations', London, W. Strahan & T. Cadell, 1776; repr., ed. Edwin Cannan, New York, Modern Library, 1937, p.17.
2. Daniel Rush Finn, 1996, 'Just Trading: On the Ethics and Economics of International Trade', Nashville, Abington.
3. Daniel Katz, 1947, "Psychological Barriers to Communication," *Annals of the American Academy of Political and Social Science*, Vol- 29 (12).
4. IMF, 1997, "Globalisation: Opportunities and Challenges", in *World Economic Outlook*.

5. Ian Morrison and Greg Schmidt, 1994, 'Future Tense: The Business Realities of the Next Ten Years', New York, William Morrow.

6. Jeffrey Garten, 1997, *The Financial Times*, 21 May 1997.

7. Marshall McLuhan, 1964, 'Understanding Media', New York, McGraw-Hill.

8. Melba Padilla Maggay, 1998, 'Cultural Issues of Globalistion', Institute for Studies in Asian Church and Culture, Quezon, Philippines.

9. Michael Schluter and David Lee, 1993, 'The Globalisation Factor', London, Hodder & Stoughton.

10. Nicanor Perlas, 1996, "The Perils of Globalisation", Center for Alternative Development Initiatives, Singapore.

11. Ronald W. Jones and Henry. K. Kierzkowski, 1997, "Globalisation and the Consequences of International Fragmentation", unpublished paper, Geneva, Graduate Institute of International Studies.

12. Steward M. Hoover, 1995, "Mass Media and Religious Pluralism", in Philip Lee, ed., *The Democratisation of Communication*, Cardiff, University of Wales Press.

13. UNCTAD, 1996, 'Globalisation and Liberalisation', New York and Geneva.

14. UNDP, 2002, 'Human Development Report- 2001', Oxford, Oxford University Press.

15. World Bank, 2001, 'Emerging Development Through Globalisation, Washington, D.C.

16. World Bank, 2002, 'Globalisation, Growth and Poverty: Building and Inclusive World Economy', Washington, D.C.

17. WCC, 1998, 'Faith in a Global Economy: A Primer for Christians', Geneva.

39

Neo-Globalisation: *A Discursive Debate*

Dr. P. Jegadish Gandhi*

Introduction

Globalisation is as old as the Roman Empire. When the suzerain empire wanted to subdue all nations and bring under the empire, that was globalisation. When Lenin wanted his socialist society to be replicated in all societies, that was globalisation. At the beginning of the 21st century, "Globalisation"—a term first used in 1985 by Theodore Levitt—has become a household name in all corners of the world. It connotes pervasiveness, inclusiveness and sweepingness with epidemic and pandemic implications in international trade and financial relations. It is a new avatar of the 18th century imperialist, colonisation and exploitation and the 20th century neo-liberal economic fundamentalism. In its global scope and sophisticated operations, it is referred to as the new face of liberal capitalism. The culture of consumerism is intimately linked with the growing strength and the global spread of the market-driven society. Part I deals with the historical compulsions and theoretical dimensions of economic globalisation Part II focuses on the threats and possibilities of the globalised environment. Part III analyses the great globalisation debate with new alternatives. Part IV sheds light on people movements against the forces of globalisation with special reference to the recent Indian developments. Part V visualizes a scenario of humanised "another world" of globalisation in the remaining decades of 21st century.

* Honorary Director, Vellore Institute of Development Studies, Vellore.

Part I

Global Economy

Even though the two terms “world economy” “and global economy” are often used as synonyms, there are certain distinct differentials in their strategic dialects. While the “world economy” has been used traditionally to describe some aggregate behaviour on a world-wide scale, the term “global economy” might be used rather to imply a kind of organic entity of world-wide processes. Therefore, globalisation denotes not just a mere aggregate, but an economic organism, having some laws of behaviour. The “double” part of globalisation signifies that it widens the frontier of economic activities across political boundaries of nation-states and helps the process of increasing economic integration and growing economic interdependence between countries in the world economy.

Apostles of Globalisation

The severe global recession of the 1970s, the worst world-wide Debt Crisis of international financial markets in the early 1980s and the consequent reverse flow of resources from the developing countries to the developed countries, the break up of the USSR in the early 1990s and the uni-polar supremacy of USA had facilitated the economic globalisation a vendable possibility. It is now fast becoming an obsessive global reality. There have been frequent references in public and academic discussions to a set of ideas known as the Washington Consensus. This Consensus is supposed to have been arrived at among the big official development lenders of the developed countries under the leadership of the World Bank.

The ten components of the Washington Consensus are: Fiscal discipline; Redirection of Public expenditure toward education, health, and infrastructure investment; Tax reform-broadening the tax base and cutting marginal tax rates; interest rates that are market-determined and positive in real terms; Competitive exchange rates; Trade liberalisation-replacement of quantitative restrictions with low and uniform tariffs; Openness to foreign direct investment and Privatisation of State enterprises. Deregulation—abolishment of regulations that impede entry or restrict competition, except those justified on safety, environmental and consumer protection grounds and prudential oversight of financial institutions; and Legal security for property rights. The Consensus does not seem to have taken into account the social contract basis of the emergence of the social contract basis of the emergence of the state, in which some components of social justice are necessarily embedded in the contract.

The apostles of World Trade Organisation (WTO) and International Monetary Fund (IMF) and World Bank (WB) are now spreading the gospel of liberalisation, privatisation and globalisation for the universal pseudo economic salvation. The emergence of the WTO as the overarching authority to oversee the free flow of global trade has forced countries to choose between WTO membership which would allow them a chance of find their place in an uncertain global economic order dominated by large multinational corporations or face the inevitable isolation of hermit nations. This message is accepted as a fact of modern life and as a prerequisite to development by most governments in the developing world including India. What makes the WTO so powerful is that it has both the legislative and judicial authority to challenge laws, policies and programmes of countries that do not conform to WTO rules, and strike them down if any are seen to be too 'trade restrict'. A country is obligated to harmonise its laws or face the prospect of perpetual trade sanctions or fines (Maude Barlow). This coercive market evangelism converted the mind-sets of policy pundits in developing countries to concertise and global growth to small regions within the global economy, such as the economies of the Far East in the Asia-Pacific region especially Japan and the economies of South-East Asia region.

Modalities

The main aspect of globalisation is unfettered competition in the "contestability of markets". Business has been increasingly transcending the national borders so much so that for dynamic companies and corporations, it is a world without borders. They strive to enhance their competitiveness by tapping the scope of globalisation in souring, manufacturing and marketing. This business dynamic leads to be development of a network of transitional enterprises dominating international trade, finance, transfer of technology and the global monetary system. Foreign investments take shape of transplants i.e., transplanting production facilities in the foreign markets instead of exporting products manufactured in the home country. A large amount of foreign investment in most countries is associated with joint venturing with local entrepreneurs growing Mergers and Acquisitions, emerging regional grouping/integration and trade pacts and sweeping cross border strategic alliances.

Dynamics

The Washington-based IMF and WB, the Geneva-based WTO and the Rome-based FAO are networking vigorously to speed up dynamics of global economy. Primarily, globalisation has two components—trade and capital flows. Spurred by rapid improvements in information technology, globalisation has caused the transformation not only of economic systems, but also of political, social and cultural institutions. More and more international movements, actions and initiatives on democracy, human rights, environmental concerns and social development issues are considered to be part of globalisation.

Today, intensified integration of the global economy has shown new features like penetrating global brand products into the smallest villages and the largest cities, crafting global environmental concerns and human rights into manufacturing products, multiplying multilateral trade agreements, increasing pace of privatisation and liberalisation, the domineering role of WTO, formalising new regional and global groupings and increasing use of satellite media networks.

Multi-National Companies (MNCs) have, today, become a force in global economic transactions., They number about 63,000 patent firms and around 690,000 affiliates. They span virtually all countries and economic activities. The world's largest MNCs, based almost exclusively in developed countries, are the main drivers of global manufacturing activities. They hold about $2 trillion in foreign assets, employ over six million people and their foreign sales are over $2 trillion. The familiar face of globalisation is Foreign Direct Investment (FDI), and in particular, inter-regional cross—border mergers, Global FDI flows constitute 14 per cent of capital formation around the world, compared with 2 per cent 20 years ago. The number of parent MNCs has increased from 7,000 at the end of 1960 to 40,000 at the end of 1990. One-tenth of global GDP is accounted for by MNC industries. Global FDI flows stood at $865 billion to reach to $1 trillion in 2000.

Part II

Threats and Possibilities

To allow the market mechanism to be sole director of the fate of human being and their natural environment would result in their natural environment would result in the demolition of society. Globalisation is radically changing the face of human societies, shattering cultures and social systems. It has brought instant prosperity to a thin layer of society, but has consigned the rest of marginality. A vast majority number of the world's population has been excluded from the benefits of globalisation. This includes workers laid off due to massive job cuts and the closure of factories, farmers dislocated by widespread land conversion schemes, indigenous peoples driven out of their ancestral lands, migrant workers forced to leave their jobs, and independent local entrepreneurs forced out of business. Women, youth and children are the worst victims of globalisation.

The most visible economic threats of globalisation are manifested in financial volatility and economic turmoil, job and income insecurity, increased levels of poverty. Non-economic threats are: impact on social institutions and culture, health insecurity, environmental insecurity, and inequitable access and exclusion. There is not gainsaying the fact that there are certain possibilities and opportunities inherent in global economic dynamics that can enrich life in this world. These include: spectacular breakthroughs in science and technology, empowered voices of NGOs, people's movements, minority groups, marginalised people and small business, and exciting possibilities of knowledge-based growth.

Overall, globalisation perceives the economy and politics i.e., market and state, as autonomous units and the nation-state as a minimalist entry particularly in its social intervention in favour of the poor. This process not only reinforces and reconstitutes the older forms of exploitative structure in newer forms, but also alters their subjugation from more direct, easily identifiable and confrontable forces to indirect, often invisible and always remote centers of domination. Under the globalisation dispensation, the world is thus reduced to the status of economic territories to be exploited by transnational capital. This process has significantly changed the balance of power between TNCs and governments. Overall, *globalisation begets globalisation.*

Part III

The Great Globalisation Debate

Boomerang Effects

Globalisation plainly is fraught with hitherto undreamt of consequences that will further polarize the rich from the poor within countries and between countries. It will undermine the less powerful in terms of loss of sovereignty, widen and concentrate arenas of marginalisation, increase poverty, catapult unemployment to unmanageable and dangerous levels, degrade the environment, destroy religions and cultures and expand violence and repression, and give a new impetus to the growth of the military-industrial complex of western nations. Understansing globalisation in the contemporary world and explaining the imminent dangers is the responsibility cast on all those concerned individuals and organisations that can perceive the core of this phenomenon. The fact is that globalisation is not only a complex process but is, more importantly, a paradigm and master plan for development with the developed or industrialised countries and their Transnational Corporations (TNCs) at its helm, leading to the exclusion, of people particularly, those who are economically, socially, and politically marginalised. It is spreading its tentacles reapidly, and seemingly successfully, without any under written guarantee from probable disaster with boomerang effects on the creator-countries.

Throughout the world dominated by the "free" market, this very day, there are over one billion people living in degrading poverty and about 40 million people, mostly children, stamped for slow death on account of hunger and/or related diseases during the course of a year. Even in the world's richest country, the United States of America, which controls 25% of global wealth, nearly 30 million people are condemned to undergo the pangs of hunger, four times as many children as that of any other developed country face poverty and, ironically this Mecca of the "free" market system also imprisons a larger percentage of its population than any other developed country in the world. It is well understood that the global market place of today rests on relationships of dependency that permit dominant countries to dictate the rules of economic engagement of the international "community". It is also well documented that this dependency has sustained poverty in South Asia and elsewhere in the world.

Exclusion of Marginal Economy

The globalised economy model has shown that only the modern sector of the developing economies stands to benefit at all from the opportunities that will be opened by the system. The vast majority of society: the ones who work in the marginal economy will remain excluded for a long time (Rand of S. David). Do we opt out of the globalisation process based on multilateral relationship or do we voice our concern by maintaining partly revalrous and partly cooperative relations with the rest of the world? Facts and logic seem to support the second alternative (S. Ambirajan). For an effective alternative programme for developing countries there should be three minimum conditions. They are: (1) an end to economic dualism (small modern sector vs. large traditional sector, (2) resistance to the logic of comparative advantage and an affirmative role of the state in economic planning and (3) increasing structural reform of domestic economy with the widest participation of the organised sectors (Roberto Unger). For nations to be able to do that, however, Walden Bellor believes that some difficult decisions have to be made by governments. The new economic agenda may include: Developing countries must learn to finance their growth primarily from local savings and domestic investments. In this regard, they will have to tax their elites, production will have to be reoriented to serve the domestic market in order to avoid the dangers of heavy dependence on the export market. The domestic market will have to be enlarged primarily through a comprehensive programme of assets and income reform.

Thrust of Modernity

Globalisation is the highest form of modernity in human history and is an interlocking phenomenon of a dynamic nature. The power of capital is such today that a financially-led globalised capitalism is structurally evolving with the tremendous support of advances in tendentious information technology. In the era of globalisation the most powerful non-state actors are the transnational corporations. The increasing marginalisation of the state as an economic actor leads to a contrary role for the state. The concomitment consequences are: a major shift in the paradigm of state intervention, a fundamental change in its welfare commitment, a substantial reduction in sovereignty, the addition of supra-territorial constituents, reduction of social security provisions and weaker realisation of democracy through the state. After 9/11, globalisation and militarisation is the legitimisation of super-power terrorisation. The dilemma of our time, in the words of Ninan Koshy, is that "Globalisation promotes inequality, unrest, conflict, economic inequality is greening: more conflicts and civil wars are emerging. It is important to see a connection between these two situations." We are only victims and witnesses. Today, civil society is considered to be the main locus of resistance against the state and the main moral reserve of the social order, but whether civil society is capable of coping with the demands that result from the processes of structural adjustment and the downsizing of the state is a moot question.

Globalisation from Below

In his incisive presentation, *The Limits of Capitalism: An Approach to Globalisation without Neo-liberalism,* Wim Dierckxsens of Costa Rica had demonstrated that there are alternatives to neoliberal globalisation. Growing concern about an impending worldwide recession is leading to greater acceptance of debate on alternatives especially following the financial crises in Asia, Russia and Brazil. Such a scenario gives rise to the historic possibility of constructing globalisation without neoliberalisation. Neoliberal theory is dominant and has claimed to be to the unique successful paradigm. In the face of this triumphant position, it has been difficult to construct other paradigms of economic theory without accentuating the cracks in the neoliberal model.

In this context, progressive sectors are faced with the truly historic challenge of helping construct a new society on a global scale that is guided by the Common Good. Such efforts can be characterised as globalisation from below. On the other hand, these sectors are poorly prepared to deal with globalisation that is based on the Common Good for citizens throughout the world. Globalisation based on a worldwide Common Good begins by focusing on the reproduction of human life and of nature, in other words, the citizenry as a whole. This reproduction is not subordinated to the logic of the efficiency of the parts. In the last instance, efficiency of the parts leads to inefficiency on the level of the whole by exclusion or waste of resources on a global level of the whole means working with all human and natural resources, with no wastefulness or exclusion in the system and without needing to achieve maximum efficiency of the parts.

Until recently globalisation and elimination of the state's role were generally thought to be inevitable, even among those on the left. After October 1997, the Asian crisis and opposition to the Multilateral Agreement on Investment (MAI) project represent a shift in the state's role in deregulation. After MAI had been postponed for a year, transnational corporations suffered a serious setback to the hands of OECD member nation-states seeking to defend themselves from an imminent loss of self-determination. This shift eventually marked the beginning of a new era of regulation.

We are at a historical juncture where the cracks in neoliberalism are beginning to show and the still somewhat timid worldwide citizens' organisations are beginning to question that model and suggest citizen-based alternatives. Given impending economic regulations, the question becomes whether political action can still take the form of economic intervention based on a conciliation of citizens; and private interest while respecting efficiency as the last word, in true Keynesian style. Private interests would be allowed to operate but not at the expense of the common good to the citizenry. The vitality of the whole would replace efficiency as the ultimate criterion.

The new economic regulations must be totality-centred rather than focusing on the private parties with conflicting interests. This in turn transforms the economic rationality. It is no longer sufficient that a visible hand guide the invisible one, while still leaving free market forces the last word. Interventions is needed on behalf of the Common Good, along with elimination of preferences given to competitive advantage in the free market. Consequently, inefficiency and protectionism must be re-evaluated when they are used to further the Common Good. We have a historic opportunity to formulate a real MAI based on the rights of citizens in investment recipient countries and the obligations of investors. It would include unconditional respect for existing or future social and environmental norms. I would also require that a given percentage of the aggregate value be created locally a portion of the products be sold on site, and a share of the profits be reinvested. The real problem with neoliberalism lies not in the economy itself but in the exercise of political control over it. Likewise, inverting the global economic rationality is a political, not economic, issue. This same economic globalisation also provides the possibility and even the historical need to subordinate micro-level efficiency to macro-level vitality. By reclaiming the Common Good it becomes possible to transcend the nationalism of the past and, for the first time in history, to function on behalf of humanity as a whole.

"Managed" Globalisation

It has been easy for the international political and economic elites to dismiss public criticism of the impact of globalisation on the developing countries. Governments which murmur in protest do not know what is good for them. Political groups which resist the advance of globalisation are protecting entrenched domestic lobbies. Economists who have offered critiques are clinging to the past. And the street protestors at the late 1990s economic summits are only the rabble. They are all tilting at windmills. A highly respected mainstream economist who was a one-time chairman of the U.S. President's Council of Economic Advisers, a chief economist of the World Bank and a winner of the Nobel Prize, Joseph E Stiglitz, in his latest treatise, *Globalisation and its Discontents* has argued that for globalisation to work effectively it should be a "managed" process in which democratic governments exercise more power than the IMF or global capital markets. He suggests an agenda for reform of the international institutions, where again the focus is on forcing the IMF to change. There is the outline of an agenda for governments of developing countries as well; the focus there is for governments to "assume responsibility for their well-being themselves". Restoration of a measure of autonomy to democratic governments is a must for globalisation with "a more human face".

Part IV

Peoples' Movements—World Social Forum

The World Social Forum (WSF) was conceived as an international forum against neo-liberal policies and capitalist-led globalisation build around the slogan: "Another World Is Possible". It seeks to provide space for discussion alternatives, for exchanging experiences and for strengthening alliances between social movements, unions of the working people and NGOs. The World Social Forum is not an organisation, not a united front platform, but "... an open meeting place for reflective thinking, democratic debate of ideas, formulation of proposals, free exchange of experiences and inter-linking for effective action, by groups and movements of civil society that are opposed to neo-liberalism and to domination of the world by capital and any form of imperialism, and are committed to building a society centred on the human person". The first WSF was held in January 2001, in the city of Porto Alegre, Brazil. The second WSF held in Jan./Feb. 2002. The International Committee of the World Social Forum and Brazil Organising Committee has decided that from the year 2002 onwards, the annual global WSF meeting will be accompanied by regional, continental, and/or thematic Forums across the globe. While the main WSF event was held in 2003 January in Porto Alegre, there is a proposal that the 2004 event shall be held outside Brazil, most probably in India. Use the WSF not only to discuss individual issues and to expose ourselves individually and organisationally to other ways of thinking, but also to find ways of building bridges: between old movements and new, between old politics and new, between different streams of civil and political movement; and between movements and other streams of civil action and concern, including business, the creative world including the media, and the world of faith. The experience of this past year has made clear that, at the minimum it is going to a long hard march to another world. *We need first to move from our singular obsession with economic or capitalist globalisation to looking at and relating to the host of other everyday globalisations that are taking place through the actions of peoples all over the world—and that are equally changing the world.*

Indian Setting-Asian Social Forum

In line with the WSF International Committee's call, the WSF in India organised the Asia Social Forum (ASF) in the city of Hyderabad in India from January 2-7, 2003. In the World Social Forum process, the ASF 2003 is the first Asia level event to be convened with the understanding that the Asia Social Event would be repeated over a period in all the sub-regions of Asia. The ASF provided a forum for an open dialogue among the movements opposed to capitalist-led globalisation. The only criteria is that the participants are opposed to imperialist globalisation as well as religious sectarian violence, and have a commitment to democratic values, plurality and peace. The Asia Social Forum was conducted around the identified six thematic areas: Peace and Security. Debt, Development, Trade, Finance and Investment, Nation State, Democracy and Exclusions, Social Infrastructure, Planning and Co-operation, Ecology, Culture and Knowledge and Alternatives and Peoples Movements.

The six-day Asian Social Forum summit heralded it was time to 'rewrite history' but it should be done by the toiling masses and not by the international and national political rulers, racist, casteist and religious communal chieftains and global corporate regimes and business houses. The summit began with a question "is another world possible?" In all 14,426 delegates, including 780 foreigners, 840 organsiations, 160 seminars and 164 workshops deliberated on the question. The insight into the struggles that people so far only heard or read about strengthened with first-hand accounts of exploitation. Definition and negation of identities by the post-colonial State, environmental concerns, impact of globalisation on marginalised communities and Dalits, population politics and conflicts in West and Central Asia were hotly debated. As the economic issues came to the fore, it became clear that a vast majority was suffering in silence and the responsibility of the knowledgeable ones was even greater. A common theme in every forum was the predicament of women and children.

The ills of imperialist globalisation discussed threw greater focus on the need for forming a *global citizenship.* The summit gave names and faces to the cold statistics and 'collateral damage' of marketed and capital-centric globalisation. The meet asserted the right of the deprived and showed, how despite all the hardships, the victims of the new order are still celebrating life. *It said that a people-centric paradigm would make it possible to live life as a celebration in contrast to a life where consolidation of capital and profits robbed life of contentment and dignity.*

Part V

Towards Humanised Globalisation?

It is now almost conventional wisdom for political leaders and heads of Government and state to express disquiet about some aspect or the other globalisation. In the UN Millennium Summit the top political leaders, discussed how to share the benefits of globalisation among all the world's people and how to control its negative effects. The then U.S. President, Mr. Bill Clinton, had cynically questioned the fallout of globalisation on labour and the environment, the French President, Mr. Jacques Chirac, has raised issues of the threat to national culture and the heads of multilatereal financial institutions such as the World Bank, the International Monetary Fund and even the World Trade Organisation have been warning their audiences about the need to make global economic integration a more equitable phenomenon. The Indian Prime Minister, Mr. Atal Behari Vajpayee maintained that "globalisation is yet to demonstrate that it is of the people, for the people and by the people".

How to humanize globalisation or to win over large masses of people in the developing countries who are seething with rage over the actual or perceived destablisation of their fragile economic security cause by the hectic process of liberalisation? First, stronger policies to protect and promote human development—literacy, education, training, preventive health, gender justice and so forth; second, more international cooperation in human development areas; and third, a participative process of development integrating governments, NGOs and business entities (S. Swaminathan) what is, therefore, needed is a social policy that will, in today's context, reorient the economy and polity to protect and promote the common good with an accent on the basic needs of the majority people. It will be an antidote against the marginalisation syndrome of the market fundamentalism. To quote A.P.J. Abdul Kalam, the President of India: "While aggregated indicators are important, it does not make sense to achieve a developed' status without a major and continuing upliftment of all Indians who exist today and of the many more millions who would be added in the year to come. They should all have a secure and enjoyable" 'present' and also be in a position to look forward to as better 'future'. Such a developed India is what we are looking for".

REFERENCES

1. Abdul Kalam, A.P.J., and Y.S. Rajan, *"India 2002, A Vision for the New Millennium,* Viking, New Delhi, 1998.
2. Ambirajan, S., "Living with Globalisation", *The Hindu,* April 17, 2000.
3. Brahmananda, P.R., "Washington Consensus", *The Hindu—Business Line,* October 21, 28 & Nov. 4, 2000.
4. Jai Sen, "The Long March to Another World", *The Hindu,* January 29-30, 2003.
5. Jegadish Gandhi, P., *"Economic Reforms in India: Mid-way Reflections,* Interest Publications, New Delhi, 1994.
6. Jegadish Gandhi, P., "Globalisation and debt Crisis", *Southern Economist,* June 15, 1999.
7. Jegadish Gandhi, P., "Social Sector and Economic Reforms", *Southern Economist,* May 1, 2000.
8. Jegadish Gandhi, P., "The New Emerging Situation in Asia: A Periscopic View," ACISCA Directors' Meeting, Bangkok, Oct. 15-19, 2000.
9. Jegadish Gandhi, P., "Presidential Address: "Humanising Development: The 21st Century Perspectives, "21st Annual Conference of the Association of Economists of Tamil Nadu & Pondichery, January 20, 2001.
10. Jegadish Gandhi, P., "Dynamics of Global Economy: Its Diagnosis and Prognosis", *Southern Economist,* May 1, 2001 & *Theology for our Times,* ECC, Bangalore, July 2001.
11. Jegadish Gandhi, P., (Ed.), *Globalised Indian Economy: Contemporary Issues & Perspectives,* Deep & Deep Publications, New Delhi, 2003.
12. Jegadish Gandhi, P. & George Cheriyan (Eds.), *"Globalisation: A Challenge to the Church,* ACISCA-NCCI-URM, Chennai, 1998.

13. Joseph E. Stiglitz; Globalisation and Its Discontents, W.W. Norton, 2002.
14. Julio X Labayan, "Human Integrity and Life," A Report on "Understanding Globalisation, Fundamentalism and Global Ecumenism" and Humanity's Response, St. Scholastica's Centre of Spirituality, Philippines, May-June, 20002.
15. Leonora Margolis Briones, "Life in Asia in the Age of Globalisation; Economic Threats and Possibilities," *CTC Bulletin,* Christian Conference of Asia, Vol. XVI, No. 1, Nov. 1999.
16. Maude Barlow, "Global Rules could Paralyse Us", *National Post,* Toronto, Aug.' 99.
17. Mervyn D. de Silva, *"Development—The Other side,* Logos, Vol. 39, No. 1., September 2000, Centre for Society and Religion, Sri Lanka.
18. Mike Moore, *"A World without Walls. Freedom, Development, Free Trade and Global Governance,* Cambridge University Press, 2003.
19. Ninan Koshy (Ed.), *"Globalisation: The Imperial Thrust on Modernity.,* Vikas Adhyaya Kendra, Mumbay, 2003.
20. Rondolf S. David, "Asian Societies in the Age of Globalisation," Faith and Life in contemporary Asian Realities, *Christian Conference of Asia,* Hong Kong, September 1999.'
21. Robert Mangaberia Unger, *Democracy Realised,* 1998.
22. Walden Bello, et. al, *"A Siamese Tragedy,* Zed Books, 1998.
23. Wim Dierckxsens, *"The Limits to Capitalism—An Approach to Globalisations without Neo liberalism,* English Edition, Zed Books, London, 2000.

40

Globalisation and Poverty
Experience of Developing Countries

Paramjit Nanda*
P.S. Raikhy*

Poverty amidst plenty is the world's greatest challenge. During fifties and sixties, to solve the problem of poverty, stress was laid on large investments in physical capital and infrastructure; during seventies, emphasis shifted towards improvements in health and education, and during eighties, there was shift in emphasis towards an improvement in economic management and market forces. During nineties, a two-part strategy was evolved, which included promoting labour-intensive growth through economic openness and investment in infrastructure (World Bank, 1990). The developing countries, with around 3 billion people, undertook series of reforms and made liberalisation efforts after mid-1980s, representing an effective shift in development strategy from an inward-oriented/import substituting strategy to an outward-oriented/export promoting framework, reinforced by increasing flows of foreign direct investment.

In view of the above, the focus of the present paper is to study the impact of globalisation on poverty in developing countries. Poverty in the paper has been defined in terms of percentage of people living below U.S. $ one per day (P) and in terms of share of total income (consumption) held by bottom 20 per cent population (Y). Five indicators of globalisation, viz. (i) exports to GDP (X-GDP) ratio, (ii) imports to GDP (M-GDP) ratio, (iii) (X+M)-GDP i.e.

* Reader & Professor, Punjab School of Economics, Guru Nanak Dev University, Amritsar.

(T-GDP) ratio, (iv) foreign investment to GDP (FI-GDP) ratio and (v) foreign investment to exports (FI-X) ratio have been considered. Foreign investments been defined to include foreign direct investment and portfolio investment. Data for all these variables were available only for 39 countries (having population below poverty line) during late-eighties and for 67 countries during late-nineties from various issues of World Development Reports and World Development Indicators, published by World Bank.

In order to study the nature and extent of association among the variables, coefficients of correlations were worked out. To identify determinants of poverty, simple regression analysis and step-down multiple linear regression analysis were carried out in following way:

Y or P= f(X/GDP, M/GDP, T/GDP, FI/GDP, FI/X).
Y = income share of bottom 20% population
P = Percentage of population living on less than US$ one per day.

Accordingly, paper has been divided into two sections. Section I studies extent of globalisation and incidence of poverty of developing nations during late-eighties and late-nineties, while Section II examines the effect of globalisation on poverty and brings out policy implications.

Globalisation has different facets. It is associated not only with an increasing cross-border movement of goods, services, capital, technology information and people, but also with organisation of economic activities which straddles national boundaries (Shigeru, 1996). It is used in positive sense to describe a process of increasing integration into the world economy and in normative sense to prescribe a strategy of development based on a rapid integration with the world economy (Nayyar, 1996).

Recent wave of globalisation (after 1980s) is not entirely a new phenomenon. It also started around 1870s and continued until the onset of First World War (1870-1914). New wave of globalisation is different from first wave of globalisation (1870-1914) in the sense that first wave was characterised by an integration of markets through an exchange of goods and movement of capital and labour across national boundaries. There was simple vertical division of labour between countries. But the new wave of globalisation is marked by increasing flow of foreign direct investment, intra-firm trade among MNCs, portfolio investment, mergers and acquisitions, internalisation of money market with instant computer-based satellite communications—increase in electronics commerce and growth of consumerism. Thus game is same but players of the game are new and rules of game are different (free flow of goods and services).

The extent of globalisation at a product level means higher growth in world trade as compared to world output. Table 1 shows extent of globalisation during first wave and new wave of globalisation.

Table 1: Growth in World GDP and Merchandise Exports in Real Terms (percent)

Period	*Real GDP*	*Export Volume*	*Export Growth / GDP Growth Rate*
1870-1913	2.5	3.9	1.6
1973-1990	2.7	4.0	1.5
1990-1996	2.5	5.9	2.1

Source: WTO (World Trade Organisation), 1998, p. 34.

Thus extent of globalisation has been more in nineties as compared to eighties or earlier periods as depicted in Table 1.

Table 2, showing extent of globalisation of 39 developing nations, reveals that during late-eighties, X-GDP ratio ranged between 3.96 per cent (for Guatemala) to 66.84 per cent (for Malaysia). In case of 22 nations (56 per cent), X-GDP ratio ranged between 3.96-20 per cent, in 14 nations (36 per cent), the ratio was in-between 20-40 per cent and for only 3 nations (8 per cent), the ratio ranged between 40-60 per cent, M-GDP ratio ranged between 4.95 per cent (for Guatemala) to 121.89 per cent (for Lesotho). In case of 34 countries (88 per cent), the ratio ranged between 4.95-40 per cent, in 3 nations (7 per cent), the ratio was in-between 40-60 per cent and in 2 nations (5 per cent) (Lesotho and Malaysia), the ratio was above 60 per cent. Trade-GDP ratio ranged between 8.91 per cent (for Guatemala) to 134 per cent (for Lesotho). In case of 21 countries (54 per cent), ratio was between 8.91-40 per cent, in 14 countries (36 per cent), it ranged between 40-80 per cent, for 2 countries (5 per cent), it was 80-120 per cent and for the remaining 2 (5 per cent), it was above 120 per cent, FI-GDP ratio ranged between zero per cent (for nations) to 6.01 per cent (for Chile). Thirty six nations (92 per cent) were having FI-GDP ratio ranging between 0-4 per cent, only 3 nations (Botswana, Chile and Malaysia) were having FI-GDP ratio of 5.56 per cent, 6.01 per cent and 4.97 per cent respectively. FI-X ratio ranged between zero per cent to 23.52 per cent (for Guatemala). In case of 23 nations (59 per cent), the ratio ranged between 0-5 per cent, in 6 countries (15 per cent), each it ranged between 5-10 per cent and 10-15 per cent, for 2 (5 per cent), it was between 15-20 per cent and for another 2 nations (5 per cent), it was above 20 per cent. Regarding incidence of poverty in terms of share of bottom 20 per cent population in income, the table shows that share of bottom 20 per cent

Table 2: Measures of Globalisation and incidence of Poverty in Late Eighties.

Countries	*X/GDP*	*M/GDP*	*T/GDP*	*FI/GDP*	*FI/X*	*Y*	*P*
Algeria	14.78	14.31	29.09	.02	.16	6.90	1.6
Bangladesh	6.44	17.41	23.85	.01	.01	9.50	
Bolivia	20.69	16.05	36.74	.24	1.19	5.60	
Brazil	10.77	5.72	16.49	.39	3.68	2.10	28.70
Botswana	56.39	56.31	112.70	5.56	9.85	2.50	33.3
China	17.01	14.61	31.62	.95	5.61	6.40	
Chile	32.43	25.76	58.19	6.01	18.54	3.70	
Colombia	13.66	11.55	25.21	.51	3.80	4.00	
Costa Rica	26.09	33.39	59.48	1.93	7.41	4.00	18.9
Cote'd Ivoire	30.83	20.15	50.98	.67	2.20	6.80	17.7
Dominican Rep.	13.69	33.69	47.38	1.65	12.07	4.20	19.9
Ghana	19.39	17.87	37.26	.28	1.47	7.10	
Guatemala	3.96	4.95	8.91	.93	23.52	2.10	39.8
Honduras	25.46	23.14	48.60	1.18	4.63	2.70	
Hungary	33.05	30.34	63.39	.01	.01	10.90	
India	7.05	9.30	16.35	.10	1.12	8.80	
Indonesia	23.80	20.35	44.15	1.30	5.49	8.70	
Jamaica	33.92	42.44	76.36	3.47	10.24	6.00	4.7
Korea	35.40	30.24	65.64	.42	1.18	7.40	
Lesotho	12.70	121.89	134.59	1.54	12.12	2.80	48.8
Mauritania	48.11	39.22	87.33	.22	.46	3.60	31.4
Malaysia	66.84	60.20	127.04	4.97	7.43	4.60	5.6
Morocco	18.19	32.78	50.97	0.01	0.92	9.80	
Nepal	6.88	19.61	26.49	.01	.01	9.10	
Pakistan	10.59	16.85	27.44	.47	4.43	7.80	53.1
Panama	6.52	21.18	27.70	.81	12.45	2.00	
Peru	10.88	11.16	22.04	.09	.86	4.90	25.6
Philippines	18.04	20.80	38.84	2.38	13.23	6.50	
Poland	19.26	14.76	34.02	.01	.01	9.20	27.5
Rwanda	4.38	13.74	18.12	.87	20.00	9.70	6.8
Sierra Leone	15.39	21.23	36.62	2.47	16.05	1.10	35.7
Sri Lanka	27.36	37.08	64.44	.59	2.41	8.90	57.0

(Table Contd...)

Table 2: (Contd...)

Countries	*X/GDP*	*M/GDP*	*T/GDP*	*FI/GDP*	*FI/X*	*Y*	*P*
Thailand	27.27	30.84	58.11	2.74	10.07	6.10	4.0
Turkmenistan	16.23	22.05	38.28	1.00	6.18	4.00	
Tunisia	31.57	49.37	80.94	.68	2.17	5.90	
Uganda	5.35	16.24	21.59	.01	.01	8.50	3.9
Uruguay	22.30	16.77	39.07	.01	.01	5.40	69.3
Venezuela	35.67	13.18	48.85	.93	2.61	3.60	
Yugoslavia	18.59	20.62	39.21	.09	.50	5.30	

Note: The ratios pertain to particular years for different countries during late-eighties.

Source: World Development Report and World Development Indicators, The World Bank, (Various Issues).

population has varied between less than 2 per cent (for Sierra Leone) to 10.9 per cent (for Hungary). During late eighties, in 2 countries only (5 per cent) share of bottom 20 per cent population was less than 2 per cent, 11 countries (28 per cent) had the share in the range of 2-4 per cent, 16 countries (41 per cent) had it in the range of 4 to 8 per cent and 10 countries (25 per cent) had the share ranging between 8 to 12 per cent. Defining poverty in terms of percentage of population living below US $ one per day, Table 2 clearly indicates that incidence of poverty was maximum in Uganda (69.3 per cent), followed by Sierra Leone (57 per cent), Nepal (53.1 per cent) and Lesotho (48.8 per cent). Incidence of poverty ranged between 1.6 per cent (for Algeria) to 69.3 per cent (for Uganda). Of 20 countries considered, 9 countries (45 per cent) had incidence of poverty ranging between 1.6 to 20 per cent, 7 countries (35 per cent) had 20 to 40 per cent poor population and 4 countries (20 per cent) were worst affected by poverty with percentage of poor people in population being even greater than 40 per cent.

Table 3, showing trends in globalisation measures and incidence of poverty of 67 nations during late nineties, reflects the fact that X-GDP ratio ranged between 6.06 per cent (for Georgia) to 79.10 per cent (for Malaysia). Twenty three nations (34 per cent) had the ratio ranging between 6.06 per cent-20 per cent, in 33 nations (49 per cent), the ratio ranged between 20-40 per cent, for 9 nations (13 per cent) it was in-between 40-60 per cent and for 2 (3 per cent), the ratio ranged between 60-80 per cent. M-GDP ratio ranged from 7.93 per cent (for Brazil) to 81.72 per cent (St. Lucia). Fifteen countries (22 per cent) had the ratio ranging from 0-20 per cent, in 26 countries (38 countries), the ratio was in-between 0-40 per cent, for 18 countries (26 per

Table 3: Measures of Globalisation and Income Share of Bottom 20% Population.

(Late Nineties)

Countries	*X/GDP*	*M/GDP*	*T/GDP*	*FI/GDP*	*FI/X*	*Y*
Algeria	20.74	23.09	43.83	0.01	0.06	7.00
Armenia	19.94	59.28	79.22	1.74	8.72	5.50
Azerbaijan	17.61	27.48	45.09	9.49	53.92	6.90
Bangladesh	12.04	16.07	28.11	.45	3.75	8.70
Belarus	37.61	31.58	69.19	.90	2.84	11.40
Bolivia	14.57	23.39	37.96	9.16	62.90	1.90
Brazil	6.40	7.93	14.33	2.86	44.75	2.60
Bulgaria	41.96	37.84	79.80	6.29	15.00	10.12
Cambodia	20.40	36.53	56.93	6.70	32.85	6.90
China	19.14	14.07	33.21	5.08	26.57	5.90
Chile	20.16	22.63	42.79	6.37	31.62	3.40
Colombia	12.88	16.27	29.15	3.99	30.99	3.00
Costa Rica	31.97	42.94	74.91	4.74	14.85	4.50
Cote d'Ivoire	39.12	27.88	67.00	2.13	5.45	7.10
Croatia	21.21	40.34	61.55	5.22	24.64	8.80
Czech Rep.	39.87	50.48	90.35	2.91	7.30	10.30
Dominican Rep.	31.42	47.92	79.34	4.88	15.53	5.10
Ecuador	24.00	23.37	47.37	2.62	10.93	5.40
El Salvador	12.00	26.29	38.29	2.36	19.67	3.70
Estonia	51.71	73.14	124.85	12.18	23.56	7.00
Ethiopia	8.00	19.54	27.54	.26	3.30	7.10
Egypt. Arab Rep.	7.26	24.79	32.05	1.18	16.30	9.80
Georgia	6.06	20.52	26.58	.92	15.32	6.10
Ghana	24.17	31.27	55.44	.95	3.97	5.90
Guatemala	15.03	22.47	37.50	3.55	23.63	3.80
Honduras	23.00	54.22	77.22	2.71	27.16	1.60
Hungary	43.40	48.32	91.72	4.80	11.60	10.00
India	9.08	10.13	19.21	1.91	21.11	8.10
Indonesia	53.50	33.92	87.42	.11	.21	8.00
Jamaica	30.43	65.88	96.31	4.15	13.65	7.00
Jordan	20.71	55.42	76.13	6.14	29.66	7.60
Kazakhstan	30.00	20.52	50.52	6.60	22.00	6.70
Kyrgyz Rep.	31.24	40.19	71.43	4.70	15.24	6.30
Lao PDR	10.95	23.33	34.28	5.19	47.39	7.60
Latvia	31.44	49.11	80.55	5.64	17.95	7.60

(Table Contd...)

Table 3: (Contd...)

(Late Nineties)

Countries	*X/GDP*	*M/GDP*	*T/GDP*	*FI/GDP*	*FI/X*	*Y*
Lithuania	43.14	58.61	101.75	2.22	5.16	7.80
Madagascar	7.83	16.16	23.99	.39	5.03	5.40
Mauritania	37.83	65.54	103.37	.65	1.73	6.40
Malaysia	79.10	80.88	159.98	4.70	5.96	4.40
Mexico	28.44	29.16	57.60	3.91	13.76	4.00
Moldova	46.74	62.18	108.92	4.05	8.68	5.60
Mongolia	37.63	25.90	63.53	1.13	3.02	7.30
Mexico	20.09	26.62	46.71	.52	2.60	6.50
Mozambique	9.88	46.53	56.41	2.32	23.52	6.50
Nepal	8.03	14.90	22.93	.42	5.30	7.60
Nicaragua	28.85	68.96	97.81	9.16	31.77	2.30
Niger	21.10	16.61	37.71	.37	3.11	2.60
Nigeria	40.21	16.89	57.10	3.87	9.62	4.40
Pakistan	13.99	18.13	32.12	1.56	11.21	9.50
Papua New Guinea	49.45	36.13	85.58	5.76	11.66	4.50
Panama	7.81	36.26	44.07	15.78	201.08	3.60
Paraguay	44.42	45.75	90.17	3.97	8.94	1.90
Peru	8.57	13.04	21.61	9.79	114.14	13.20
Philippines	30.41	46.95	77.36	1.57	5.18	5.40
Poland	20.47	28.57	49.04	4.62	22.58	7.80
Russian Fed.	27.04	20.95	47.99	1.10	4.09	4.40
Senegal	6.99	14.46	21.45	.65	9.41	6.40
Lanka	29.41	40.15	69.56	.90	3.08	8.00
St. Lucia	68.72	81.72	150.44	3.24	4.71	5.20
Thailand	47.38	32.80	80.18	8.67	18.30	6.40
Turkmenistan	41.31	81.91	123.22	5.49	13.29	6.10
Uganda	9.29	11.86	21.15	1.97	21.30	7.10
Ukraine	31.41	37.33	68.74	1.70	5.48	8.80
Venezuela	33.62	13.23	46.85	5.82	17.33	4.10
Vietnam	44.51	52.68	97.19	6.14	13.80	8.00
Yemen, Rep.	34.76	50.97	85.73	5.07	14.59	7.40
Zambia	30.90	49.49	80.39	5.90	19.11	3.30

Note: The ratios pertain to particular years for different countries during late-nineties.

Source: *World Development Report and World Development Indicators,* The World Bank (Various Issues).

cent), the ratio ranged between 40-60 per cent and for 9 nations (13 per cent), the ratio ranged between 60-80 per cent. Trade-GDP ratio ranged between 13.98 per cent (for Brazil) to 159.98 per cent (for Malaysia). Nineteen countries (28 per cent) had the ratio ranging between 0-40 per cent, 30 nations (45 per cent) had the ratio ranging between 40-80 per cent, 14 nations (21 per cent), had the ratio in-between 80-120 per cent and four nations namely Estonia, Malaysia, St. Lucia and Turkmenistan were having the ratio above 120 per cent. FI-GDP ratio was lowest (i.e., 0.01 per cent) for Algeria and highest for Panama (15.78 per cent) following by Estonia (12.18 per cent). In 37 countries (55 per cent) the ratio was between.01-4 per cent, in 23 countries (34 per cent), it ranged between 4-8 per cent, for 4 countries (6 per cent) it was between 8-12 per cent and for three nations namely Estonia, Nicaragua and Panama, the ratio was above 12 per cent. FI-X ratio was lowest for Algeria (0.06 per cent) and was highest for Panama (201.08 per cent). FI-X ratio ranged between 0.06 per cent-20 per cent for 46 countries (69 per cent), between 20-40 per cent for 15 countries (22 per cent); between 40-60 per cent for 3 nations (4 per cent), for Bolivia (78.98 per cent) and above 80 per cent for Panama and Peru. Share of bottom 20 per cent population in income varied between 1.9 per cent (for Bolivia) to 11.4 per cent (for Belgium). During this time period, in three countries (5 per cent), share of bottom 20 per cent population was less than 2 per cent, 10 countries (15 per cent) had the share in the range of 2-4 per cent, 44 countries (65 per cent) had it in the range of 4-8 per cent and 10 countries (14 per cent) had the share ranging between 8 to 12 per cent. Incidence of poverty was maximum in Nigeria (70.2 per cent), followed by Jamaica (68.7 per cent) and Niger (61.4 per cent) and lowest was in Ukraine (2.9 per cent). Of 43 countries considered, 25 countries (58 per cent) had incidence of poverty ranging between 2.9 to 20 per cent, 13 countries (30 per cent) had 20 to 40 per cent poor people, 2 countries (4 per cent) had 40 to 60 per cent poor people and 3 nations (6 per cent) were worst affected by poverty with more than 60 per cent population below poverty line.

As compared to eighties, there has been an increasing trend in X-GDP ratio, M-GDP ratio, Trade-GDP ratio, FI-GDP ratio and in FI-X ratio in late nineties, indicating the spread of globalisation. Regarding incidence of poverty in term of share of bottom 20 per cent population in income, there is marginal decrease. Incidence of poverty, defined in terms of people living below US$ one per day, has declined rapidly during this period.

Globalisation is considered an effective tool of poverty reduction through increase in the manufactured exports (which are labour-intensive) increase in exports of textiles and clothing (due to abolition of MFA) and increase in exports of primary commodities (World Bank, 1990).

Table 4: Measures of Globalisation and Incidence of Poverty.

Countries	*X/GDP*	*M/GDP*	*T/GDP*	*FI/GDP*	*FI/X*	*P*
Armenia	19.94	59.28	79.22	1.74	8.72	7.80
Bangladesh	10.36	21.67	32.03	.16	1.60	29.10
Bolivia	12.85	20.48	33.33	10.15	78.98	14.40
Brazil	6.57	7.41	13.98	4.17	63.46	11.60
Cameroon	19.00	13.01	32.01	.37	1.90	33.40
Chad	19.93	20.91	40.84	.94	4.91	18.50
China	19.72	16.75	36.47	4.29	21.77	18.80
Colombia	11.04	13.61	24.65	2.77	25.12	19.70
Costa Rica	52.93	55.26	108.19	5.84	11.05	12.60
Cote d'Ivoire	39.12	27.88	67.00	2.13	5.45	12.30
Dominican Rep.	29.50	47.83	77.33	.73	2.49	3.20
Ecuador	24.00	23.37	47.37	2.62	10.93	20.20
Egypt. Arab Rep.	7.26	24.79	32.05	1.18	16.30	3.10
El Salvador	20.64	31.32	51.96	9.30	45.04	25.30
Estonia	46.09	63.36	109.45	.00	.00	4.90
Ethiopia	8.00	19.54	27.54	.26	3.30	31.30
Ghana	23.41	45.08	68.49	1.05	4.50	44.80
Guatemala	15.03	22.47	37.50	3.55	23.63	10.00
Honduras	37.55	43.56	81.11	1.84	4.90	24.30
Indonesia	34.14	16.84	50.98	1.06	3.11	12.90
Jamaica	30.43	65.88	96.31	4.15	13.65	3.20
Lanka	29.41	40.15	69.56	.90	3.08	6.60
Lao PDR	10.95	23.33	34.28	5.19	47.39	26.30
Madagascar	14.35	18.48	32.83	.45	3.15	49.10
Mauritania	37.83	65.54	103.37	.65	1.73	28.60
Mexico	29.84	31.86	61.70	3.06	10.25	15.90
Moldova	46.74	62.18	108.92	4.05	8.68	11.30
Mongolia	37.63	25.90	63.53	1.13	3.02	13.90
Mozambique	13.18	45.68	58.86	3.73	32.30	37.90
Nepal	8.22	32.46	40.68	.18	2.29	37.70
Niger	21.10	16.61	37.71	.37	3.11	61.40
Nigeria	40.21	16.89	57.10	3.87	9.62	70.20
Pakistan	14.28	18.21	32.49	2.50	17.50	31.00
Panama	7.81	36.25	44.06	15.78	202.01	14.00

(Table Contd...)

Table 4: (Contd...)

Countries	*X/GDP*	*M/GDP*	*T/GDP*	*FI/GDP*	*FI/X*	*P*
Paraguay	44.42	45.75	90.17	3.97	8.94	19.50
Peru	8.57	13.04	21.61	9.79	114.14	15.50
Russian Fed.	27.04	20.95	47.99	1.10	4.09	7.10
Senegal	6.99	14.46	21.45	.65	9.41	26.30
Turkmenistan	41.31	81.91	123.22	5.49	13.29	12.10
Ukraine	29.95	30.64	60.59	1.28	4.28	2.90
Venezuela	18.48	15.59	34.07	4.79	21.38	23.00
Yemen, Rep.	34.76	50.97	85.73	5.07	14.59	15.70
Zambia	30.90	49.49	80.39	5.90	19.11	63.70

Note: The ratios pertain to particular years for different countries during late-nineties.

Source: *World Development Report and World Development Indicators,* The World Bank (Various Issues).

The association of poverty with different measures of globalisation and inter-correlation amongst measures have been given in correlation matrix in Table 5. The table shows that poverty as measured by income share of bottom 20% and population living below poverty line is negatively associated with measures of globalisation in eighties as well as in nineties.

Income share of bottom 20% population is significantly and negatively related with FI-GDP ratio and FI-X ratio, while incidence of poverty is significantly but negatively related with X-GDP ratio in eighties. The relation between two measures of proverty with different indicators of globalisation has become weak in nineties as compared to in eighties. Different measures of globalisation were also having significant inter-correlation among themselves. X/GDP is significantly related with T/GDP and with FI/GDP, M/GDP with T/GDP, T/GDP with FI/GDP, and FI/GDP with FI/X in eighties. In nineties, X/GDP is significantly associated with FI/GDP and with T/GDP, M/GDP with T/GDP, and FI/GDP with FI/X.

The simple/multiple linear regression results given in Tables 6 and 7 show that during eighties as well as during nineties, globalisation affected poverty at non-significant rates, indicating that globalisation has neither aggravated poverty nor has been successful in eliminating poverty at significant rates, which further indicates that poverty may have been reduced due to some endogenous factors (national and local level).

Table 5: Correlation Matrix Between Different Indicators of Globalisation and Incidence of Poverty.

Variable	*Late Eighties*					*Late Nineties*				
↓ →	*X/GDP*	*M/GDP*	*T/GDP*	*FI/GDP*	*FI/X*	*X/GDP*	*M/GDP*	*T/GDP*	*FI/GDP*	*FI/x*
X/GDP	1					1				
M/GDP	0.42 (0.41)	1				0.67 (0.62)	1			
T/GDP	0.77 (0.76)	0.89 (0.90)	1			0.89 (0.86)	0.93 (0.93)	1		
FI/GDP	0.57 (0.66)	0.39 (0.42)	0.56 (0.61)	1		0.13 (-0.11)	0.24 (0.05)	.20 (-.01)	1	
FI/X	-0.08 (-0.24)	0.15 (0.02)	0.06 (-0.09)	0.59 (0.36)	1	-0.34 (-0.40)	-0.12 (-0.15)	-.24 (-.28)	.72 (.86)	1
Y	-0.16	-0.19	-0.21	-0.41	-0.45	-0.001	-0.050	-.030	-.127	-0.80
P	-0.43	-0.01	-0.22	-0.12	0.24	-0.12	-0.22	-.20	-.08	-.11

Note:

1. Figures in parentheses indicate correlation coefficients when poverty is defined in terms of US$ one per day.
2. Due to differences in number of countries and survey year, correlation coefficients among independent variables are different; Number of countries while considering income share is 39 in eighties and 67 in nineties; While considering population living below US$ one day, number of countries is 20 in eighties and 43 in nineties.

When increasing degree of globalisation has not been successful in reducing poverty in developing countries, solution has to be searched through other measures under the policies of liberalisation, privatisation and globalisation. There is a need for establishing institutions and organsiations for successful development, not only at the national level but at the international level as well (Bawa, R.S., 2001-2002). The developed countries, besides financing different projects for alleviating poverty in the developing countries, should open up their markets to at least selected imports from developing countries, which benefit the poor in these countries. It has been estimated that OECD tariff and subsidies caused annual losses in welfare of almost $20b in developing countries equivalent to abut 40% of aid in 1998 (World Bank, 2001-02). Apart from lowering trade barriers and opening markets, global actions in form of (i) promoting global financial stability (ii) bridging the digital and knowledge divides, thereby bringing technology and information to people (iii) providing financial and non-financial resources for international public goods, especially for medical and agricultural research (iv) increasing aid and providing debt relief to help poor countries and (v) giving a voice to poor countries in global forums are required (World Bank, 2001-02).

Table 6: Effect of Globalisation on Poverty/Income Share (Late Eighties) Results from Simple/Multiple Linear Regression Analysis.

Constant	*X/GDP*	*M/GDP*	*T/GDP*	*FI/GDP*	*FI/X*	r^2/R^2	*F*
With Dependent Variable as Share of Bottom 20% Population in Income							
6.5277	-0.0311					0.0279	1.064
(8.384)	(1.032)						
6.5095		-0.0249				0.0373	1.4339
(9.429)		(1.197)					
6.7819			-0.0193			-0.0462	1.7959
(8.379)			(1.340)				
6.6720				-0.7030		0.1684	7.4949
(13.603)				(2.738)			
6.9340					-0.1884	0.2039	9.4794
(13.395)					(3.079)		
7.7636	-0.0241		-0.0053	-0.836	-0.1794	0.2488	2.8155
(7.345)	(0.437)		(0.24)	(0.166)	(1.778)		
With Dependent Variable as Population living below $ one per day							
37.7294	-0.4886					0.1932	4.3125
(5.623)	(2.077)						
27.0964		-0.0133				0.0003	0.057
(3.717)		(0.076)					
33.1023			-0.1171			0.0491	0.9298
(4.132)			(0.964)				
28.8289				-1.484		0.0147	0.2686
(4.692)				(0.518)			
21.2821					0.6925	0.0624	1.1991
(3.227)					(1.095)		
36.6045	0.8257	1.7362	-1.6254	3.8215	-0.1261	0.2664	1.0067
(2.964)	(0.002)	(0.004)	(0.004)	(0.682)	(0.131)		

Source: Calculated from the data given in Table 2.

Apart from global measures, actions at national as well as local levels are required as poverty is complex problem involving various economic, social and cultural factors. There is need for broader, and more comprehensive policy measures to fight with poverty because world population is expected to grow by $2 billion in next 25 years and 97 per cent of this increase will be in developing world, which may aggravate poverty.

Economic growth and equalities (across gender, ethnic, social and racial) are necessary to provide more opportunities to poor people. Special measures should be taken for encouraging small enterprises. Private investment should be complemented by public investment in infrastructure and in upgradation

Table 7: Effect of Globalisation on Poverty/Income Share (Late Nineties) Results from Simple/Multiple Linear Regression Analysis.

Constant	X/GDP	M/GDP	T/GDP	FI/GDP	FI/X	r^2/R^2	F
With Dependent Variable as Share of Bottom 20% Population in Income							
6.278	-0.001					0.000	0.001
(10.551)	(0.009)						
6.499		-0.0062				0.0024	0.1654
(10.341)		(0.407)					
6.4201			-0.0023			0.0009	0.0620
(9.757)			(0.249)				
6.652				-0.0969		0.0616	1.0675
(14.194)				(1.033)			
6.4078					-0.0067	0.0064	0.4202
(17.869)					(0.648)		
6.5909	0.0603	0.0413	-0.0482	-0.1289	0.0051	0.0192	0.2384
(8.476)	(0.008)	(0.006)	(0.007)	(0.744)	(0.262)		
With Dependent Variable as Population living below $ one per day							
26.059	-0.1626					0.0166	0.6947
(4.870)	(0.833)						
28.6363		-0.1978				0.0490	2.1138
(5.597)		(1.454)					
28.829			-0.1173			0.0411	1.7579
(5.117)			(1.326)				
23.556				-0.4475		0.0078	0.3261
(6.614)				(0.571)			
23.238					-0.0532	0.0138	0.5761
(7.979)					(0.759)		
33.0440	-1.8032	-1.7733	1.5775	1.9885	-0.2567	0.1033	0.8529
(4.861)	(0.005)	(0.005)	(0.004)	(1.066)	(1.413)		

Source: Calculated from the data given in Tables 3 & 4.

of skills. Participation of poor people should be strengthened in local decision making by promoting inclusive decentralisation and community development. Poor people should have complete security from various shocks in the form of ill health, crop failures and draughts etc.

Developing countries should themselves try to achieve international development goals set by international community by 2015 at national level. These goals include (i) reduction in incidence of poverty by half, (ii) universal primary education (iii) elimination of gender disparities in education(iv) reduction in infant and child mortality by two-third (v) reduction of maternal mortality by three-fourth (vi) universal access to reproductive health services and (vii) to achieve sustainable development by 2005 (World Bank, 2001-02).

Developing countries will have to pull-up their own boost straps to alleviate poverty and have respectable position at international fora by improving the level of governance, which is the key factor for the purpose.

REFERENCES

1. Bawa, R.S., 'Challenges and Opportunities of Globalisation-Implications for India', *Indian Economic Journal,* Vol. 49, No. 3, Jan.-March, 2001-02.
2. Nayyar Deepak, 'Globalisation: The Past in Our Present, *The Indian Economic Journal,* Vol. 43, Jan.-March, 1996, pp. 1-19.
3. Shigeru Otsubo, *Globalisation, A New Role for Developing Countries in a Integrating World,* World Bank, Policy Research Working Papers, 1628, 1996.
4. World Bank, *Globalisation, Growth and Poverty,* World Bank Policy Research Report, 2002.
5. World Bank, *World Development Indicators* (Various Issues).
6. World Bank, *World Development Report* (Various Issues).

41

Poverty Reforms and Reaction Impact in Indian Contexts

S. Chinnammi*

In nineties, policy reforms involved market friendly policies. IMF's loan conditionality and World Bank's structural adjustment lending let to the adoption of the policies of liberalisation in deregulation, privatisation, other macro economic reforms and stabilisation programmes but their policies concluded in emphasis on infrastructure, human development, poverty alleviation, employment generation, protection of environment, financial regulation and quality of governance (Bawa, 2000).

The emphasis of development theory shifted from GDP to many other important tasks, in this; reduction of poverty is the most important problematic issues in our country. Knowledge of economic development has been realised that people are not poor but because of poor policies they are poor (Meier 2000). The rich and upper middle classes are benefited by the new economic reforms because all the entire consumer and luxury goods are at their doorsteps. But the condition of the poor and the marginalised has further worsened.

Economic efficiency is hardly a desirable end in itself; it has relevance only in relation to the ultimate social end, which must encompass elements of economic justice (Tisdell, 1999). IMF, World Bank and WTO have to play the role of international public sector for equitable distribution of the benefits of globalisation. All economic ills like poverty, unemployment, and child labour have also to be globally owned. Emerging poverty, and increasing

* Lecturer, Deptt. of Economics, University of Madras, P.G. Extension Centre, Vellore-632 004.

unemployment and inequalities have created doubts whether the process has been instrumental in globalising poverty. Gap between the earnings of the skilled and unskilled workers has widened. Small-scale industries are facing closure, thereby intensifying the problem of unemployment.

The 'attitude of co-operation and conflict', as in case of oligopolistic markets, will go side by side and there is need for new type of capitalism called 'Alliance Capitalism', where success depends upon harmonious interaction between economic agents and governments (Dunning, 1998). 'Beggar by neighbor' approach has to be abandoned. There is need to change the situation from 'winners and loser's to 'win-win' situation.

Since the implementation of the new economic reforms, 6-7% more of our people have joined the ranks of people described as those below poverty level (BPL). Planning Commission report says that in 1993-94, 35.97% (320.97 million) (Table 1) and that in 1996-97, 36.17% (360.17 million) people have been living below the poverty level. The Human Development Report 1997 says that 44% of the Indian population, which constitute about one third of the world's poor, live in absolute poverty. (Mahbub-ul-Haq 1997) Poverty ratios from the 53rd round of the National Sample Survey (NSS) for 1997, and the 54th round conducted in India during January-June 1998 (NSSO 1997 & 1998). These shows no change in the urban poverty ratio (Head count (HC) Index), if economic growth is maintained, urban poverty will be virtually eliminated in the next decade. But critics say that is impossible without radical social reforms.

A rise in the rural and all India poverty ratios since economic reforms were undertaken in 1991 (EPW 2001). One reason could be that the poor spend more than they earn. In other words, they have negative saving and borrow for consumption. We can assume that their income is less than their expenditure. These households are not likely to have any savings and their entire income would be spent on consumption and also, poverty is actually worsening, while millions work as bonded labour slaves. But India has to do to overcome poverty is keep up the pace of economic growth. Economic growth alone will be enough to significantly reduce the numbers of the poor in the social sector. The households in the lower income level, will drop in number. In fact there are indications from urban areas that it is going to be virtually non-existent by 2006-07. In rural areas also it's going to be very small, may be around 15-16 per cent.[1] It could eventually mean good news even for the people who are marginalised at the very bottom of India's extremely stratified caste system, the Dalits or Untouchables.

Table 1: BPL Population in Indian States in 1993-94.

Sl. No.	States	Rural		Urban		Combined		Total Population (Million)
		No. of Persons (in lakhs)	% of total BPL Population	No. of Persons (in lakhs)	% to total BPL Population	No. of Persons (in lakhs)	% to total BPL Population	
1.	Andhra Pradesh	79.49	51.63	74.47	48.37	153.96	22.19	693.90
2.	Arunachal Pradesh	3.62	97.05	0.11	2.95	3.73	39.35	9.48
3.	Assam	94.33	97.89	2.03	2.11	96.36	40.86	235.83
4.	Bihar	450.86	91.38	42.49	8.62	493.35	54.96	897.65
5.	Goa	0.38	19.89	1.53	80.11	1.91	14.92	12.80
6.	Gujarat	62.16	59.09	43.02	40.91	105.18	24.21	434.49
7.	Haryana	36.56	83.31	7.31	16.69	43.87	25.05	175.17
8.	Himachal Pradesh	15.40	73.61	1.86	26.39	17.26	25.17	83.11
9.	Karnataka	95.99	61.35	60.46	38.65	156.45	33.16	471.83
10.	Kerala	55.95	73.22	20.46	26.78	76.41	25.43	300.47
11.	Madhya Pradesh	216.19	72.42	82.33	27.58	298.52	42.52	702.07
12.	Maharashtra	193.33	63.36	111.90	36.66	305.23	36.86	828.05
13.	Manipur	6.33	93.08	0.47	6.92	6.80	33.78	20.13
14.	Meghalaya	7.09	96.07	0.29	3.93	7.38	37.92	19.46
15.	Mizorum	1.64	84.53	0.30	15.47	1.94	25.66	7.64
16.	Nagaland	4.85	96.03	0.20	3.97	5.05	37.92	13.31
17.	Orissa	140.90	87.73	19.70	12.27	160.60	48.56	330.72
18.	Punjab	17.76	70.72	7.35	29.28	25.11	11.77	213.33

(Table Contd...)

Table 1: (Contd...)

Sl. No.	States	*Rural*		*Urban*		*Combined*		
		No. of Persons (in lakhs)	*% of total BPL Population*	*No. of Persons (in lakhs)*	*% to total BPL Population*	*No. of Persons (in lakhs)*	*% to total BPL Population*	*Total Population (Million)*
19.	Rajasthan	94.68	73.68	33.82	26.20	128.50	27.41	468.80
20.	Sikkim	1.81	98.36	0.03	1.64	1.84	41.43	4.44
21.	Tamil Nadu	121.70	60.21	80.40	39.79	202.10	35.03	576.93
22.	Tripura	11.41	96.77	0.38	3.23	11.79	39.01	30.22
23.	Uttar Pradesh	496.17	82.08	108.28	17.92	604.45	40.85	1497.70
24.	West Bengal	209.90	82.45	44.66	17.55	254.56	35.66	713.85
25.	Andman & Nicobar	0.73	68.86	0.33	31.14	1.06	34.47	3.07
26.	Chandigarh	0.07	8.75	0.73	91.25	0.80	11.35	7.04
27.	D. & N. Haveli	0.72	93.50	0.06	6.50	0.78	50.84	1.51
28.	Daman &Diu	0.03	16.67	0.15	83.33	0.18	15.80	1.14
29.	Delhi	0.19	1.22	15.32	98.78	15.51	14.69	105.58
30.	Lakshadweep	0.06	42.85	0.08	57.15	0.14	25.04	0.56
31.	Pondichery	0.93	28.09	2.38	71.91	3.31	37.40	8.85
	All India	**2421.23**	**76.17**	**762.90**	**23.83**	**3184.13**	**35.97**	**8869.13**

Source: Compiled from focus on the poor Government of India, 1997.

Table 2: Percentage Population Below income (MISH) Poverty Line and Official Expenditure Poverty Line, All-India

Year	*MISH*			*Planning Commission*		
	Urban	*Rural*	*All-India*	*Urban*	*Rural*	*All-India*
1987-88	38.20	39.09	38.86	38.86	39.09	38.85
1989-90	35.14	36.89	36.41			
1993-94	24.37	30.86	29.15	32.36	37.27	35.97
1994-95	21.82	27.26	25.80			
1995-96	17.98	24.74	22.90			
1996-97	15.21	20.23	18.86			
1997-98	12.63	17.96	16.52	34.00	38.50	37.20

Source: EPW March 24, 2001.

Table 2 shows during the decade of 1987-1997, the Head Count (HC) ratios based on market information survey of households (MISH) data show a marked decline while the official estimates based on NSS show an initial decline up to 1993-94 and a rise thereafter. Even the decline between 1987-88 and 1993-94 is more moderate. The estimates for the states also show a consistent decline in both rural and urban areas for all the states. The Mumbai Social Sector Reforms Conference also addressed the issue of tacking increasing regional disparities in human development in the country. The findings of the State Human Development Reports inspired by UNDP, and supported by the Planning Commision, indicate that the dimensions of poverty and human deprivation vary dramatically across regions, districts and social categories and conditions[2].

The higher growth has brought down poverty reduction in some states, but the poorer states, in particular need to undertake reforms that would lead to faster growth and poverty reduction. Sharp disparities remain between development-oriented states and laggards. Poverty in rural Bihar, for instance, was almost twice as widespread (a 58 per cent rate of incidence) in 1993-94 as in rural Kerala. Even within a single state, the variance can be striking, for example, between rural poverty incidence in southern (68.8) and northern (45.5) Orissa[3].

Table 4 shows poverty in India remains predominatly rural. Three out of every four poor persons live in rural areas. Changes in urban and rural poverty followed a similar path over most of the last twenty-five years. The large poor states in the north and east, containing 40 per cent of India's population, have lagged in reducing poverty since the late 1970s[4].

Table 3: Percentage of Population Below Poverty Line by States (1987-88 to 1997-98).

State	Year	*MISH*			*Planning Commission*		
		Urban	*Rural*	*Total*	*Urban*	*Rural*	*Total*
Andhra Pradesh	1987-88	40.11	20.92	25.86	40.11	20.92	25.86
	1989-90	36.58	17.42	22.35			
	1993-94	29.67	15.92	19.84	38.33	15.92	22.19
	1997-98	15.01	7.06	9.43			
Assam	1987-88	9.94	39.35	36.21	9.94	39.35	36.21
	1989-90	8.45	33.08	29.88			
	1993-94	5.18	29.50	26.76	7.73	45.01	40.86
	1997-98	1.71	18.73	16.64			
Bihar	1987-88	48.73	52.63	52.13	48.73	52.63	52.13
	1989-90	41.98	50.85	49.61			
	1993-94	35.67	46.65	45.21	34.50	58.21	54.96
	1997-98	24.88	29.79	29.11			
Gujarat	1987-88	37.28	28.67	31.54	37.28	28.67	31.54
	1989-90	27.27	24.07	25.17			
	1993-94	22.79	21.63	22.05	27.89	22.18	24.21
	1997-98	7.65	11.73	10.22			
Haryana	1987-88	17.98	16.22	16.64	17.98	16.22	16.64
	1989-90	13.52	14.95	14.56			
	1993-94	9.09	11.15	10.62	16.38	28.02	25.05
	1997-98	4.58	5.32	5.12			
Himachal Pradesh	1987-88	8.29	18.28	15.45	8.29	18.28	15.45
	1989-90	6.28	17.89	16.78			
	1993-94	4.18	12.17	11.56	9.18	30.34	28.44
	1997-98	1.69	3.94	3.72			
Karnataka	1987-88	48.42	32.82	37.53	48.42	32.82	37.53
	1989-90	42.84	29.01	34.35			
	1993-94	32.51	24.68	27.13	40.14	29.88	33.16
	1997-98	15.45	13.63	14.23			
Kerala	1987-88	40.33	29.10	31.79	40.33	29.10	31.79
	1989-90	34.64	23.81	26.16			
	1993-94	17.65	15.53	16.09	24.55	25.76	25.43
	1997-98	5.45	9.53	8.38			

(Table Contd...)

Table 3: (Contd...)

State	*Year*	*MISH* *Urban*	*MISH* *Rural*	*MISH* *Total*	*Planning Commission* *Urban*	*Planning Commission* *Rural*	*Planning Commission* *Total*
Maharashtra	1987-88	39.78	40.78	40.41	39.78	40.78	40.41
	1989-90	33.19	37.39	35.72			
	1993-94	23.15	34.37	30.02	35.15	37.93	36.86
	1997-98	12.59	16.29	14.84			
Madhya Pradesh	1987-88	47.09	41.92	43.07	47.09	41.92	43.07
	1989-90	37.02	41.29	40.23			
	1993-94	29.80	40.26	37.96	48.38	40.64	42.52
	1997-98	15.49	21.21	19.90			
Orissa	1987-88	41.63	57.04	55.53	41.63	57.04	55.53
	1989-90	40.37	48.17	47.00			
	1993-94	32.46	43.40	41.92	41.64	49.72	48.56
	1997-98	20.20	29.74	28.33			
Punjab	1987-88	14.67	12.60	13.20	14.67	12.60	13.20
	1989-90	9.21	19.69	16.11			
	1993-94	7.67	8.90	8.51	11.35	11.95	11.77
	1997-98	2.12	3.54	3.07			
Rajasthan	1987-88	41.92	33.21	35.15	41.92	33.21	35.15
	1989-90	26.99	30.19	29.41			
	1993-94	24.61	20.57	21.52	30.49	26.45	27.41
	1997-98	17.41	14.96	15.56			
Tamil Nadu	1987-88	38.04	45.60	43.98	38.04	45.60	43.98
	1989-90	33.43	35.67	34.72			
	1993-94	21.66	26.30	24.63	39.77	32.48	35.03
	1997-98	8.00	13.54	11.54			
Uttar Pradesh	1987-88	42.90	41.10	41.46	42.90	41.10	41.46
	1989-90	31.47	37.07	35.87			
	1993-94	25.09	33.20	31.54	35.89	42.28	40.85
	1997-98	15.65	19.34	18.58			
West Bengal	1987-88	35.08	48.30	44.72	35.08	48.30	44.72
	1989-90	28.07	37.14	34.27			
	1993-94	18.86	35.33	30.48	22.41	40.80	35.66
	1997-98	8.25	23.00	18.67			

Source: EPW, March 24, 2001.

Table 4: Estimated Market size of Consumer Durables.

(Rs. in Billion)

Year	*MISH**	*NAS*	*NSS*
1987-88	53	70	54
1993-94	132	158	85
1997-98	268	320	202

*Only 20 selected durables.

A number of factors that may explain the lack of progress in reducing rural poverty. First, the slowdown may reflect inconsistencies in national statistics, underscoring the need to improve their quality in order to provide a firmer basis for policy-making.

The slowdown may also be explained by the higher average inflation in the 1990s compared to the 1980s, especially the more rapid increase in food prices. There are also concerns that the pattern of agricultural growth could be producing less of a rise in labour demand and fall in poverty than in the past.

A wide disparity in poverty across Indian states and their uneven progress in poverty reduction is a key feature of the evolution of poverty in India. In most cases, better-off states remained relatively affluent and reduced poverty, while poorer states remained poor and made less progress in poverty reduction. Growth in the urbanised part of the economy was less significant in reduction poverty across states, reflecting the capital intensive, import-substituting nature of India's industrial development, its requirements for skilled rather than unskilled labour, and labour market regulations that limited the growth of formal sector employment. These factors limited the impact of urban growth on labour demand and kept the proportion of urban population relatively small, so that its proportionate impact was low. While some states were able to take advantage of the stabilisation and reforms to speed up growth and poverty reduction, others increasingly lagged, due to poor governance, insufficient infrastructure, low levels of human development, lack of fiscal adjustment, and compression of development spending.

India's pervasive poverty, is predominantly rural, and is mirrored in health, education, and nutrition indicators that remain too low* even accounting for India's low per capita income.

Economic development is concerned with improved standard of living of human beings and neglect of people at the bottom of the ladder would indicate a failed economy (Sen 1984). However, markets by their very nature are discriminating towards the poor and there is need for enhancing opportunities for the poor in the markets.

A variety of consumer goods, both durable and expendable, entered in the Indian market soon after liberalisation. There was a consumer boom and the country witnessed impressive growth in the consumption of goods and services. Estimates of consumption of these durables based on NSS and MISH along with the sales of these durables as available from various newspaper reports and business magazines are presented in Table 4. Not that everyone in India is poor, by any means, as is clear from the money being spent in luxury jewellry shops. Middle class Indians also enjoy the latest consumer electronics in their homes and employ domestic servants on a scale unimaginable to most of their European or American counterparts.

Globalisation impact will be viewed as positive in the sphere of living standard, job opportunities, high consumption pattern, brotherhood at global level, etc. On the other hand, the impact is likely to be negative so far as commercialisation and advertising blind aping, demonstration effects, malpractices, children's educational goals, household and rural industries, the feeling of swadeshi, five star culture, liberal education, Indian literary heritage, food habits etc. are concerned. The consumption pattern of the bottom 17% corresponding to the population below poverty line is given in Table 5 and 6.

The total market size of the 20 expandable products in MISH was Rs. 800 million in 1997-98. Of this about 7 per cent is consumed by the households classified as poor. Practically every one of them use toilet soap. Nearly 90% use washing cake and cooking oil. Footwear of one kind or other was bought by almost all. Vast majority also bought tea and hair oil. Only nail polish, lipstick and health beverages were bought by less than 5 per cent of these households.

Every tenth households bought shampoo and face cream. Nearly a fourth bought body talcum powder. About 15% per cent bought packaged biscuits. (*Deepak Lal, Rakesh Mohan, Natarajan, 2000-01*). These are all the implication of globalisation and people are educated through hi-tech media.

These households own a variety of consumer durables also. About three fourth of the households owned a wristwatch. Bicycle and radios were owned by 40% and 30% of the households. Black and white television and tape recorders were owned by 10% and 16% respectively. Two per cent had a mechanised two-wheeler. Nearly a tenth had a sewing machine. (*Deepak Lal, Rakesh Mohan, Natarajan, 2000-01*).

Table 5: Consumption of Expendable Goods for Population Below Poverty. Line as Estimated from MISH, 1997-98

(Per cent users)

Product	*Urban*	*Rural*	*Total*
Toilet soap	95.3	95.1	95.1
Washing cake	88.8	87.3	87.6
Washing powder	67.7	49.4	53.3
Tooth paste	46.5	21.1	26.6
Tooth powder	62.2	40.8	45.4
Body Talcum Powder	39.8	20.9	24.9
Shampoo	18.9	4.7	7.8
Hair Oil	78.5	69.8	71.7
Face cream	16.4	83.	10.1
Nail polish	8.7	3.5	4.6
Lip stick	8.9	1.0	2.7
Edible oil	90.4	93.5	92.8
Packaged biscuits	27.3	15.5	18.0
Tea	86.6	78.2	80.0
Health beverages	4.5	0.9	1.7
Electric bulbs	56.2	29.4	35.1
Electric tubes	21.7	3.1	7.1
Sports shoes	20.1	13.4	14.8
Footwear-leather	44.3	26.2	30.1
Footwear-others	52.0	50.9	51.2
Cigarettes	18.9	13.0	14.3

Source: EPW 2001.

Also these are the households of whom more than 85% claim, according to NSS, to be getting two time meals a day throughout the year. The bottom 18% of households in India display such a consumption pattern in provides further evidence that the estimate of 37% being below the poverty line in India 1997-98. Lack of education and health are among the main poverty-related problems named by the poor themselves. Strengthening education and health contributes towards the goal of human well-being and also enhances poor people's capacity for self-help and opportunities for economic activity. The provision of basic social services (basic education, basic health, food and safe water), in particular, and relevant sector reforms are therefore important elements of poverty reduction. The success of education and public health in

Table 6: Ownership of Durables by Population Below Povery Line.
As Estimated from MISH, 1997-98

(Per '000 hhs)

Durables	*Urban*	*Rural*	*Total*
Transistor-Ratio	423	309	319
Cassette Recorders	202	150	155
Pressure Cooker/Pan	260	76	92
Bicycle	419	410	411
Electric Iron	153	47	56
Electric Fans	582	220	252
Wrist Watches	1024	706	734
TV-B&W	312	79	100
Sewing machine	98	54	58
Mixer Grinder	55	12	16
Colour TVs	43	7	10
Two-wheelers (motorised)	49	14	17
Washing machine	12	0	1
Refrigerator	35	4	7

Source: EPW 2001.

reaching poor people depends not only on more spending but on improving the quality of services they receive. Targeting government spending to primary education, reducing communicable diseases, improving water and sanitation, and reducing household insecurity through public works programs would do most to reduce poverty. Effective health programs must complement education in raising the potential productivity of labour to reduce poverty. The economic reform that can expand the quantity, quality, transferencey and accountability in the social sector and that work to eliminate social exclusions based on income, gender or caste. By accelerating economic reforms; redirecting towards infrastructure, health, and basic education the large resources now absorbed by ill-targeted subsidies; and improving the effectiveness and targeting of spending in education, health, and antipoverty programs, India can give its long battle to reduce poverty in coming new era.

Conclusion

Economic reforms without clear rules and polices may not be in the interest of any country, International institutions have to frame such rules and policies and oversee their implementation. Whenever the symptoms of crisis appear in a particular country, immediate steps should be taken for preventing it (Jetro 1999). Government will have to encourage that pattern of growth, which makes productive use of labour the most abundant asset of the poor through market incentives, social and political institution, infrastructure and technology etc. (Evans, 2000). Well-targeted transfers, safety nets, investment in sectors directly relevant for the poor including rural and urban infrastructure, basic education and health, social assistance and micro finance, all have pro-poor effects.

There is urgent need for huge investment; the country should immediately start targeted programmes for the bottom 20 per cent and the worst off amongst these. Government should start more and more programmes which directly benefit to the poor and may also trickle down to the rich (Dhillon and Raikhy 1999) Government has to play crucial role in building market supportive institutions and to enhance opportunities for the poor. People cannot be thrown out of jobs without creating alternative avenues elsewhere in the economy. Economic policy has been oriented towards the better off not infrequently at the expense of the poor.

Therefore, the country requires the policies with "human soul" and not only with "human face". As Gandhi had reminded us, "The earth has enough for everyone's needs, but not for some people's greed".

REFERENCE

1. Bawa, R.S. *"Challenges and Opportunities of Globalisation-Implications of India"*, Presidential Address, 84th Annual Conference, Dec. 28-30, 2001.
2. Dhillon, S.S. and P.S. Raikhy, *"Social Choice Growth and Income Distribution: Theory and Evidence"* In IEA 82nd Annual Conference Volume, Amritsar, 1999.
3. Dunning, J.H. and Khalil A. Hamdani (ed), *"The New Globalism and Developing Countries"*, Bookwell, New Delhi, 1997.
4. *Economic and Political Weekly,* March 24, 2001, pp. 1017.
5. Evans, Alison, *"Poverty Reduction in the 90—An Evaluation of Strategy and Performance"*, World Bank, Washington, 2002.
6. Focus on Poor, *"Government of India"*, 1997.
7. Japan External Trade Organisation (JETRO), *"The Merits and Demertis of Globalisation and the Future of the Asia"*, Tokyo, Februry, 1999.
8. Mabub-ul-Haq, *"Human Development in South Asia"*. 1997.
9. Meier, G.M. and J.E. Stiglitz (ed), *"Frontier of Economic Development"*, Oxford University Press, New York, 2000.
10. NSSO (2000)-*NSS Survey,* 55th Round.

11. NSSO, Government of India, *"Household Consumer Expenditure and Employment Situation in India"*, Round, 50th (1994), 51st (1995), 52nd (1996), 53rd (1997), 54th (1998).

12. Sen, Amartya K, *"Poor, Relatively Speaking"* in Amartya Sen (ed), Resources, Values and Development, Oxford, UK, 1984.

13. Tisdell, Clem, *"Economic Globalisation: Background and an Overview"*, Indian Journal of Quantitative Economics, Vol. 14, No. 1, 1999.

NOTES

1. www.foreigawire.com/india.html
2. www.undp.org.in/news/press/press109.htmdevelopment
3. http://www.worldbank.org/html/exdr/extrme/1963.htm
4. http://wbln1018.worldbank.org/sar/sa.nsf/a22044doc4877a3e852567de0052e0fa/289ea01043987e778525688d006fd5d8?OpenDocument

42

Globalisation, Information Revolution and Women

(Its Dimensions and implications in the context of women in India)

Sushila Jain*

Globalisation: Meaning

The concept of globalisation is one that has become widely used in debates, in politics, business and media over the past few years. A decade ago, the term 'globalisation' was relatively unknown. Today it seems to be on the top of everyone's tongue. Globalisation refers to the fact that we are all increasingly living in 'one world', so that individuals, groups and nations become more interdependent.

Sociologist use the term globalisation to refer to those processes which are intensifying world wide social relations and interdependence. It is a social phenomena with vast implications, it should not be thought of simply as the development of world wide networks-social and economic systems that are remote from our individual concerns. It is a local phenomena too, one that affects all of us in our daily lives. It is changing the way the world looks, and the way we look at the world. By adopting a global outlook, we become more aware of our connections to people in other societies. We also become more conscious of the many problems the world faces at the start of the twenty first century. The global perspective opens our eyes to the fact that our increasing ties with the rest of the world means that our actions have consequences for others and that the world's problems have consequences for us.

* Head and Associate Professor. Department of Sociology, University of Rajasthan.

Anthony Giddens, in a book On the Edge; living with global capitalism identifies many meanings of globalisation: firstly as-

1. The world wide communication revolution.
2. Secondly, he refers to what he terms the "weightless economy". By this he means the new "Knowledge economy" with financial markets at its leading edge.
3. Thirdly, it refers to a post-1989 world, that is, a world after the fall of communism. and,
4. Fourthly, it refers to transformations happening on the level of everyday life.

Globalisation: The Historical Process

The system we are dealing with began with the expansion of western economic interest, western political domination. Economically this was capitalist development, which marked the rise of a new social class in the west bourgeoise, the merchant class. By the end of the 17th century and the beginning of the 18th, it began to exercise political domination. Most of the great corporation that now rule the world began to mushroom from the middle to the end of the 19th century.

Today's globalisation is the third stage of a long historical process, the earlier two being colonialism and imperialism and all these have their roots in capitalism and market economy.

Over the centuries capitalism has changed forms, from mercantile capitalism of the 16th and 17th century to industrial capitalism of the 19th and 20th century to what can now be termed as knowledge capitalism of the new millennium. Along with it has changed the mode of expansion of the markets. Earlier it was the colonisation of the new lands followed by political conquest and empire building. Today it is globalisation backed by communication and information technology which has truly conquered the geographical space and has literally transformed the entire globe into a common market. Thus in laymans language globalisation is understood in terms of compression of distances and intensification about consciousness that there is a global village.

Its Technical Connotation

Its technical connotation is in terms of economic activity i.e. Internationalisation of Economic activity. With the increased scale, diversity and complexity of international business, globalisation conveys the integration of world wide economic activities. "For the first time in human history, anything can be made anywhere and sold every where." Such integration is necessary for businesses to capture expanding market opportunities through coordinating and controlling their operations to maximum effect, but at the same time there is a threat of intensified competition at home. Governments are worried to sustain their national competitiveness and economic growth to minimise the economic dislocation and job losses caused by the defensive restructuring of domestic industries. Both OECD, in Globalisation of industry (1996) and IMF, in Globalisation: Opportunities and Threats (1997) have considered the policy implications of globalisation as the new powerful motor of world wide economic growth.

The current challenge for many countries-in a situation of low economic growth and high unemployment-is to ensure effective adjustment so that the potential welfare and efficiency gains from globalisation are attained (OECD 1996:9) Therefore, national economies are more closely integrated, with greater economic efficiencies and welfare as well as more intense competition, greater need for adjustment and more demands on national and international policy.

Dimensions of Globalisation

The entire process has both positive and negative effects. However, the positive effects are pocketed by a few and the negative effects are suffered by a larger humanity. As a result globalisation increases inequities between nations; between classes, within nations and above all, between men and women-a fact that is often overlooked.

1. Domestic markets are no longer the focus of economic activity and competition, it is competing to world class standards that counts according to Kenneth Ohmae (1989) in "Managing In a Borderless World", Rosabeth Moss Kanter in World Class: Thriving Locally in the Global Economy (1996) identifies four broad processes as aspects of globalisation mobility simultaneity, bypass and pluralism.

2. The electronic movement of capital have vastly increased financial flows which making them more difficult to detect or regulate. The international flow of migrant professionals and knowledge workers has helped to create a global labour market in a growing number of occupations. Ideas move immediately around the world through the global media, CNN and BBC World News is available in 140 countries, the Wall Street-Journal and Financial Times are available in European, Asian and South American editions. High speed information transfer makes place irrelevant.

3. Globalisation means time lags in the introduction of products and services are declining precipitously. Time lags before full international market penetration in consumer electronics have reduced from six years for colour TV to one year for CDs with VCRs different formats have struggled on, but for the fax machine a common standard was adopted universally by 1988. Brand names are travelling the world, creating their own infrastructure or support influencing practices in every country.

4. Cellular and Satellite telecommunication systems bypass land based systems; the Internet bypass established sales channels. New international network provides new opportunities and proliferating choices for consumers.

5. In finance, telecommunications, car manufacture and a range of other industries the traditional centres of control and technology are encountering the growth of multiple centres of innovation and influence. It is the processes of globalisation that make possible the design, production, distribution and consumption of processes, products and services on a world scale, using patents, data based, advanced information, communication and transport technologies and infrastructures. Credit cards are a typical illustration of a global service.

6. There is evidence of increasing unemployment and widening inequality as the world economy develops. In the 1990's unemployment grew to 34 million in the OECD countries, with atleast 80 million unemployed in the developing world and further 600 million underemployed (Buckley 1996).

In the 1980's all of the gains in male-earning went to the top 20% of the work force, and an amasing 64% to top 1%. The pay of the average Fortune 500 CEO goes from 25 to 157 times that of the average production worker. CEO salaries tripled in France, Italy and Britain, and more than doubled in Germany. At no other time since data have been collected have American Median real male wages consistently fallen for a two-decade period of time. Never before have a majority of American workers suffered real wage reduction while the per capita GDP was advancing (Thurow 1996-24-4).

7. As finance, technology, factories and equipment seem to move 'effortlessly across borders' it raises the question Robert Reich has posed; to what extent can a nation continue to be thought of as a society when it no longer has an identifiable national economy. The images of globalisation are so powerful that they are often presented

as dissolving national cultures, national economies and national borders.

'Triadisation' of the world economy concerns scientific power, technological supremacy, economic dominance and cultural hegemony, and therefore the ability to govern the world into the future (Petrella 1996-77). According to Petrella, multinationals, as providers of technology infrastructure, goods and services for the world economy have seised the initiative. Multinational Companies are the only Organisations that have transformed themselves to become 'global' players, and therefore operate at the most influential level of decision making. The world economy gives top priority to technology and to those who research, develop and produce technology, overwhelmingly the multinationals. Multinational companies are considered to be the key actors in the production of wealth, ensuring employment and therefore, individual and collective well being, multinationals stand at the core of globalisation arguments that stress the actions of business and the rise of the markets.

8. Impulses to form international alliances occur as a part of seemingly irresistible pressure towards further globalisation of corporate strategies.

Globalising strategies often gain support from assumptions that they constitute a universal force of unilinear dimensions. Levitt's (1983:77) insistence that 'the worlds' desires have been irrevocably homogenised......no one is exempt and nothing can stop the process is a case in point. If such a proposition were true this homogenisation of taste and consumption would inevitably lead to stand standardisation of products, manufacturing, marketing and trade. This saturation of markets, with a few common products gaining enormous profit, is manifested in the 'Cola Culture'. Coca-Cola is the worlds most famous expression (after OK), has the world most famous brand name and is sold in almost 200 countries. Selling soft drinks requires little capital, produces superb returns, demands minimal reinvestment and yields huge cash flow (the Guardian 8 February, 1997). Another similar example is MacDonalds, which having reached the stage of feeding 0.1% of the U.S. population everyday, sees no reason why it should not feed a similar proportion of the world. However, standardisation has its limits and there are important cultural, political and economic forces for local differentiation that have emerged powerfully in recent years to question the logic of globalisation. In a sense this dilemma is the traditional global/local one facing managers as their enterprises become increasingly international.

The concept of global corporations as roaming stateless organisations, staffed by functionaries who are global citizens, working out of a laptop while living in identical hotel bedrooms in whatever part of the world they happen to be in today, is somewhat wide of the mark. 'Companies can outsource; they can descentralise operations; they can relocate: But when all is said and done, even multinational giants have to put down roots and build strong ties with communities if they expect to excel. (Drache 1996: 57). Understanding that even multinational corporations have a well defined national identity, increase the importance of winning acceptance in foreign markets.

9. A paradoxical consequence of increasing globalisation is the concentration in different local economies around the world of clusters of world class expertise in specialist industries. This significant local dimension of the globalisation phenomena, consists of local economies built upon interlinked networks of relations among firms, universities and other institutions in their local environment (OECD 1996; de Vet 1993; Storper and Scott 1993).

Globalisation increases the competitiveness of these local economies by attracting in international firms with their own specific advantages and enhancing established sourcing and supply relations. Small and medium sised enterprises and globalisation: Globalisation is associated with giant corporations, yet in most industrial countries over the last twenty years the share of small and medium sized (SMEs) has been increasing, as has their general significance to economic activity. SMEs have been more important in generating employment in service such as construction and transport, and in traditional manufacturing industries. Exporting is the way SMEs connect with the international economy, often acting as suppliers and subcontractors for large global companies in the electronics and car industries.

The Limit of Globalisation

1. Rodrick poses the question is social disintegration the price of economic integration (1997). The two primary causalities of globalisation appear to be low skilled workers in traditional manufacturing countries who either see their jobs slip away overseas or experience a painful slide in their wage rates as their employees strive to reduce costs. Secondly, and more seriously, whole countries and regions find they have been sidelined by the forces of international trade and investment, and instead of experiencing a growing involvement and benefit from the global economy, may encounter a greater sense of dependence and isolation. Particularly vulnerable are the relatively unskilled and under educated.

Wood reckons that trade with developing countries has reduced the demand for low skilled workers in rich economies by more than a fifth. It must be recognised that though most jobs are still non tradable sectors (ex truck drivers) more jobs and skills are entering the tradable sector, as the prospects for those without skills diminish, the opportunities for those with highly specialised skills suddenly become global.

Winner take all markets are spreading to more and more occupations, such as lawyers, doctors, bankers, academics and chief executives. In such jobs the market pays individuals not according to their absolute performance, but to their performance relative to others...........what has changed is that new technology and globalisation have expanded the market for skills from a local into a global one, increasing the opportunity for the rich to become ever richer. (Economist 1966 9:33).

2. Global capital market has given poor countries better access to capital, and technology has become more transferable. Information technology allows knowledge to be codified and diffused across borders more rapidly, making it easier for developing countries to catch-up. Intelligent organisation is no longer just the preserve of clever countries.

The growth of information technology and intelligent organisation "allows previously untradable services to be traded just like steel or shoes. This is because the increasing codification of knowledge reduces the need for physical contact between producers and consumers. Routines can be cheapened further by greater routinisation of existing tasks; the engineered tasks can then be moved to places where wages are cheaper, the transaction cost associated with doing so do not appear to be great. Satellites and Computers can ensure virtual linkage....."Firms in the rich world have out sourced all manner of things to developing countries from computer programming and airline revenue accounting to processing hospitals patients records and insurance claims. More than 100 of America's top 500 firms buy software services from firms in India, where programmers are typically paid less than a quarter of the 'American rate' (The Economist 1996 9:34).

3. Serious consequence may result in terms of increased poverty, unemployment, alienation and crime. A new divide in the world appears. Delinking is the process through which some countries and regions are gradually losing their connection with the most economically developed and growing countries and regions of the world.

4. Kenneth Ohmae (1993: 78) insists the nation state has become an unnatural, even dysfunctional unit for organising human activity and

> managing economic endeavour in a borderless world.....it defines no meaningful flows of economic activity. The reasons for this are evident in reasoning triumph of markets over polities: as Drache (1996:32) insists. Efficiency has become the universal belief of all major corporations and most leading industrial powers. In their view, capital has to be free to move across national boundaries. 'The logic of efficiency has to determine the allocation of activity among all trading nations, as defined by Bhagwati (1988: 33). What is in danger of being lost is, in Drache's (1996: 49) words, 'any viable notion of social responsibility-the institutional capacity for the achievement of a more equitable society. Also at risk are those many fibres of a civil society. Its 'social capital', that enable a market economy to operate efficiently.

Thus development has to take place not only in terms of economic growth but also in terms of human development and community or social development i.e. to preserve the social bonds and the social values.

Its Implications in the Context of Women in India

The effect of media globalisation can be seen clearly on women. In the recent years the media landscape has changed profoundly the traditional notions of Indian female as weak, submissive, illiterate and the poorest of poor. Prior to 1980, with high rates of illiteracy and fragile sense of identity. India was dominated by the national T.V. broadcaster, Doordarshan. The Indian government relied on Doordarshan as a way of building national unity, promoting certain 'development' & objectives among the population and educating the Indian citizenry. Although the print media was historically free in India, Doordarshan was tightly controlled and censored. One of the significant turning points in Indian media came under the leadership of late (Mrs.) Indira Gandhi who believed that television was a critical medium for promoting ideas of nation building and upgrading the lifestyles of its people, and thereby opening the doors for foreign media corporations to broadcast programming within a previously closed system. Rapid growth in cable connections and satellite dishes alongwith modern educational facilities, growing and advancing scientific and technological inventions and creative innovations, brought about changing attitude among women folks towards favourable urbanism and urbanisation, better job opportunities, improved life styles and a some what congenial atmosphere for economic and political mobility. Also changing to a large extent the male dominated Indian society to change their traditional outlook, attitudes, traditions & styles towards women in order to blow them to meet the challenging technological advancements and globalisation made them realize that women are not meant to be kept behind the walls but they like male counterparts have to comeforth to realise their inherent capacity, fertile intellect, strong psychological sense of their boldness, enthusiasm and guts, and helped them to come outside of their homes and hamlets to express and expose themselves in the challenging worlds of today and also to fight for their rights.

But this favourable, constructive role of media to bring about constructive change in women's position also brought about its own problems, social evils, corruptions and misdeeds committed against them.

Indecent Exposure of Women in Media and its Social Impacts

Dominance of sexualisation largely in society and particularly in media has led to objectification of women, whereby her body has been converted into a commodity. The studies on women and media during last two decades indicate that media image tended to define women within narrow confines of traditional domestic roles and sexual appeal. This two dimensional image was not sufficiently counteracted by alternative portrayals of women that reflected their significant contribution in contemporary society. The reasons for above mentioned phenomena can be seen in the light of various facts such as men dominating the media scene both as producers and consumers.

In the present scenario efforts are being made to involve women through various schemes, designed to exploit the talent of these women in a big way.

A close look at the portrayals of women both in print as well as visual media will show that women are being treated as commodities for sale and to sell other's products. Even the censor board which used to be vigilant earlier has now shut down its eyes in the wake of the winds of globalisation and liberalisation sweeping the country. The global T.V. channels have brought cheap saleable stuff in developing countries. Instead of projecting democratic norms, notion of justice and equality and other values, which are imitable dimensions of western society, marketing of ignoble things have led to a new and culturally alienated image of women in India.

On one hand outdated cultural practices continue as a part of social structure, while on the other hand the sexual presentation of women reinforce the negative aspects of women's role, status and relationship. Paradoxically even after the great achievements of women, media has failed to highlight this aspect and make concerted efforts to discuss serious issues that concern women and make them play equal and rightful role in society.

The contemporary media does not generally intervene in the field of women's issues and even when they are taken up they generate ambiguity.

Many a times the news items and visuals subvert the very purpose regarding the main issue and instated create a pervert person in the issues. In such a situation one does not really feel concerned after reading a rape news but reads the news about rape or molestation for a perverse delight. There is greater depiction of a women's body and greater sensuousness in the representation of a situation involving men and women in magazines, television and cinema (Singh 2001).

Women in Advertisement

Many studies like Rosemary 1985, report that in fictions and women's magazines, 'sexism in advertising' and to a lesser extent "low portrayal' of women in T.V. has multiplied over years. A study conducted by Indian Institute of mass communication revealed the perception of women as a sex symbol. (Mankikar, 1983). One out of every five advertisements featured women irrespective of her relevance to the product being sold. This itself is a pointer to the ambivalence of viewers about the image of women in society.

Advertising though originally used to market products, now unfortunately it seems to market feelings, sensations and styles of life, an astounding revolution in manners and morals. The emotive attitudinal fixity of women has been reinforced by media. 'She' cries, fears, given in, needs protection, is loving, caring and tender. On the other hand 'He is depicted as 'Macho'. The women is delicate, slim with standards of measurements which prescribes her sizes. The advertisement given messages which set her standards of behaviour, emotive, expressions, gait, speech modulation and the cat walk. (Singhi 2001)

The women in advertisements express tenderness, of applying balm, preparing certain brand of tea for family members, is shown to wait at the during table for family member to serve food cooked in a particular brand of oil or apply a particular cream to be fair and presentable. The other side of women is shown to submit to a male under influence of certain brand of perfume of after shave used by him. Women is either shown as good or bad, she is never depicted to be a normal human being. The above mentioned representations conceal the inner experience of drudgery, routinisation of life and the suppression of potential.

Portrayal of Women in Films

The scenes of molestation, rape and cruelty to women are screened in the most undesirable manner. This gives impetus to the youngesters to follow the same pattern of life. It makes them ill treat all other women folk as presented in the films. Many times such representation given the feeling that women are a toy to be played with. Such negative portrayals of women are responsible for various offenses like kidnapping, abduction, violence eve-teasing and even rape. Women of our society are vulnerable to such crimes and are not bold enough yet to fight with them.

Even the signboards and posters of films are highly objectionable and full of vulgarity. Society is ignoring all this nuisance and government also seems unable to take any strict action against this.

Presentation of women in T.V. Serials

The role of daughter, wife and mother in media is changing but not substantially. There is a great deal of diversity and conflicting messages generated through serials, episodes and programmes.

The serials present life-course events in women's lives, consisting of pre-marital sex, pre marital pregnancy, rape, divorce, familial maladjustment, extra-marital relations, physical liberties, lewd jokes etc.

This portrayal of women in media affects society considerably. A real example of this effect can be seen in a recent news in 'Times of India' 23rd Feb. 2003 about violence against women being a universal phenomena. A middle aged rich executive used to beat his wife because he felt that she will be spoiled by the serials she watches on T.V. showing extra marital affairs.

This example shows that the media has impact on our lives and according to studies by Das & Bishnoi (1996) male viewers are more exposed to the mass media than females: Males prefer watching film songs, films and advertisements which are the focal point of exposure.

Presentation of females in stereotyped roles of good wife, mother and daughter, always looking and behaving charming, with unusual, unnatural temperament is bound to highten expectations of males from their wives, non fulfillment of which results in physical manifestations of violence. Women in print media.

Women in Print Media

As reported by Thakur and Agarwal (1988) the coverpages of many magazines has certain uniformity in them. Each of them featured brightly dressed women or doll, showing some part of her body. Apart from women's looks and dresses there was stress on development of mental faculties and behaviour in a way that they can fit into a male dominated social structure. Pornography is emerging as the biggest centres of indecent exposure; leaving nothing to imagination.

What is needed is a re-imagining of economic structures, and the basic unit of exchange, from its narrow monetary basis i.e. towards an economy of care, based on relationships of mutual respect and responsibility. An example of the politics of mothering under globalisation is even more chilling. The anthropologist Nancy-Scheper-Hughes in her book 'Death without weeping', researched the communities of Alto-de-Cruzeiro in N.E. Brazil, where child death through chains of poverty was the norm.

The way forward must be in making visible the labour which sustains life, and by reconnecting the economy to the foundations of society which promote a culture of peace, non-violence, devoted to the flourishing of all interdependent life forms. This means recognising and valuing the contribution that women make and revaluing the basis of the economy, recognising all the connections with nature, water, trees, seeds, air and its quality.

The economist Amaritya Sen and philosopher Martha Nussbaum say that human rights are insufficient without ensuring proper quality of life. They have suggested the criteria of measure this.

Thus without the revaluing of economic life on the basis of a culture of peace where the poorest of communities not only survive, but are enabled to flourish, where women's work is made visible and valued, without a revaluing of the structures of care and the sacredness of earths resources, the very future of our planet is endangered.

REFERENCES

1. Arthur, B (1996) 'Increasing Returns and the Two Worlds of Business', Harvard Business Review, July.
2. Bambawale Usha; Women's Image as Projected on Screen, Mainstream, 32(5), 26 Feb. 94.
3. Bartlett, C.A. & Ghoshal S (1990) Managing Across Borders: The Transnational Solution, Boston: Harvard Business School Press.
4. Boyer, R & Drache D. (1996) States Against Markets: The Limits of Globalisation, London: Routledge
5. Bradley, S. (1993) Globalisation, Technology and Competition: The fusion of Computers and Telecommunications in the 1990s, Cambridge: Harvard Business School Press.
6. Brain Arthun, 'Increasing Returns and the Two Worlds of Business, Harvard Business Review, July 1996.
7. Buckley, R. (1996) Fairer Global Trade? The Challenge for the WTO, Understanding Global Issues, Cheltenham: Understanding Global Issues Limited 1996/6.
8. Clarke, T. and Bostock, R. (1994) International Corporate Governance: Convergence and Diversity, in Clark T and Monkhouse E, *Rethinking the Company,* London: Financial Times Pitman Press.

9. Clegg, S.R. (1990) Modern Organisations: Organisation Studies in the Postmodern World, London: Sage

10. Cusamano, M.A. and R.W. Selby (1996) Microsoft Secrets-How the worlds's most powerful software company creates technology, shapes markets, and managers people, New York: Harper Collins Business, 1996.

11. Cusumano M.A. and Smith S.A. (1997) Beyond the Waterfall: Software Development at Microsoft, in Yoffie, 374-411.

12. Das, Land Bishnoi I.; Portrayal of Women in Indian Television, Interaction Vol. 14, No 2, 1996.

13. De Vet, J. (1993) 'Globalisation and Local and Regional Competitiveness', STI Review, No. 13, OECD, Paris.

14. Deshpande Anjali; Hypocrisy Over Obscenity. Mainstream, 22(1); 3 Sep. 1983.

15. Doz, Y.L., Barlett, C.A., Prahalad, C.K. (1981) 'Global Competitive Pressures and Host Country Demands': California Management Review, Vol. 223, No 3.

16. Drache, D. (1996) From Keynes to K. Mart: Competitiveness in a Corporate Age, in Boyer and Drache.

17. Dunning, J.H. (1993) multinational Enterprises and the Global Economy, Wokingham: Addison Wesley.

18. Economist, (1996) World Economy Survey, 28 September 1996.

19. Ghoshal, S. and Bartlett C.A. (1998) The Individualised Corporation, London: Heinemann.

20. Giddens A. and Hutton, W. (2000 b). On Edge, London; Jonathan Cape.

21. Hart, S.L. (1997) Strategies for A sustainable World, Harvard Business Review, Jan-Feb.

22. Harvey D (1992) The Condition of Postmodernity, Oxford: Blackwell.

23. Joshi G. Uma: Video film on Images of Women in Indian advertisements and its effectiveness in changing perceptions of college students; Interaction year-1998, Vol. 16, No 1-2.

24. Keohane R. And Ostram, E. (eds). (1995) Local Commons and Global Interdependence: Heterogeneity and Cooperation in Two Domains, London: Sage.

25. Kumar Nirmal: Women Over Doordarshan: Retrospect, Interaction, Vol. 14, No. 1, 1996.

26. Levitt T. (1983) 'The Globalisation of Markets', Harvard Business Review, May-June, 92-102.

27. Lioyd, P.J. (1992) Regionalisation and World Trade, OECD Economic Studies, No. 18, Spring.

28. Mankikar, Purnima: "Advertising and Social Responsibility", Indian Institute of Mass Communication. J.S. Yadav and Abhilasha Mohnet (ed.) 1983, Vol. 2.

29. Mishra S.K., Devi M., Goyal K., Dubey V.K.: Gender Presentation in Indian Print Media, year 1996, No. 2. Vol. 14.

30. Nagori Monika, Effects of the mass media; Ideas and Insights, Vol. 1, No. 1 April 2002.

31. OECD (1989) Information Technology and New Growth Opportunities, Information, Computer and Communications Policy Committee, Paris: OECD.

32. OECD (1992) Technology and the Economy: the Key Relationships, Paris: OECD.

33. OECD (1996) The Knowledge, Based Economy, Organisation for Economic Co-operation and Development.

34. Ohmae K. (1985) Triad Power, New York: Free Press.

35. Ohmae K. (1990) The Borderless World, London: Collins.

36. Ohmae, K. (1989) Managing in a Borderless World, Harvard Business Review.

37. Petrella, R. (1996) Globalisation and Internationalisation: The Dynamics of the Emerging World Order, in Boyer and Drache, 1996.

38. Rosemary J. Harris: "Sex roles within the mass media", (Newsletter) 1985.

39. Singhi N.K.; Gender Construction and Media: Presentation Repression; Nucleus: Vol. 1, No. 1 & 2,2001.

40. Thurow, L. (1992) Who Owns the 21st Century? Sloan Management Review, Spring, 5-17.

41. Thurow, L. (1996) The Future of Capitalism, London: Nicholas Brealey.

43

Challenges of Globalisation on Sustainable Development with Reference to the Developing Countries

M. Rathedi*

Since the late 1980s and with gathering momentum following the collapse of communism, globalisation has become a powerful force in today's world. And there is no doubt that globalisation – the process by which international interactions have increasingly greater importance on decision-making – is transforming the prospects for both achieving sustainable livelihoods among the world's poor and regenerating natural systems for future generations, the core of sustainable development.

Sustainable development is development that meets the needs of the present without compromising the ability of future generations to meet their own needs. It contains with in two key concepts- the concept of 'needs' in particular the essential needs of the world's poor, to which overriding priority should be given; and- the idea of limitations imposed by the state technology and social organisation on the environment's ability to meet present and future needs (World Commission on Environment and Development, 1987). The current view is that sustainable development has three dimensions: social, economic and environment. Sustainable development remains a useful vehicle for furthering the social message of achieving certain important social objectives especially in developing countries.

This chapter focuses on the challenges of globalisation on sustainable development. It identifies the main globalisation trends and the

* Lecturer, Department of Economics, University of Botswana, Gaborone, BOTSWANA.

environmental problems and opportunities these generate, and the implications of these for the poor. It then highlights the important challenges for developing countries.

Trends of Globalisation

Globalisation appears to be built on five important trends, which are mutually reinforcing and subject to increasingly rapid change:

- Economic: The spread of market-oriented approaches to development; withdrawal of state provision; privatisation and deregulation; trade and investment liberalisation; increasing penetration of transnational corporations;
- Technological: Rapid innovation and increasing inter-connectivity, particularly for information and communication services and also biotechnologies; the growing significance of the information economy
- Political: New global institutions like WTO and broad trends such as democratisation and gender equality, changing position of women and assertiveness of civil society;
- Cultural: Increasing homogenisation of lifestyles and aspirations via mass media, films, tourism etc; combined with greater scope for the rapid spread of different views and greater opportunities for marginalised voices to be heard; and
- Environmental: Increasing inter-linkages between ecosystems, accelerating biological invasions; simplification and homogenisation of natural systems; and intensifying pressure on global commons.

How these trends help or hinder progress towards sustainable development is unclear and contested. Globalisation is a double-edged sword, capable of bringing environmental opportunities, for example through increased access to markets, information, capacity sharing and cleaner technologies, but also environmental problems, such as increased consumption of natural resources and generation of waste. These opportunities and problems apply to each of the five trends identified above, as shown with examples in Table 1.

The distribution of these problems and opportunities among the world's population has a crucial bearing on the impact of globalisation on sustainable livelihoods. Globalisation is not neutral in its impacts. Indeed, there appears to be a powerful tendency for current patterns of globalisation to exacerbate inequalities. For those already 'included' in the globalisation process, their access to capital – whether human, financial, technological or natural – tends

Table 1: Globalisation: Environmental Opportunities and Problems.

Globalisation Trends	*Potential opportunities*	*Potential problems*
Economic	• New markets for environmental regulation, e.g. Carbon regeneration; • Development of instruments allowing market differentiation e.g. timber certification	• Deregulated competition leading to a 'race to the bottom' of lower environmental standards; • Spread of unsustainable export•oriented production, e.g. timber from central Africa, shrimps from Asia; • Growth in transport intensity of development
Technological	• Access to cleaner technologies and better information about environmental trends	• Potential adverse impacts of new biotechnologies on biological diversity
Political	• Global institutions allowing collective decision making on environmental issues • Stronger and more vocal local civil society groups challenging globalisation, often in global networks	• Global institutions limiting the autonomy of governments in ways that ignore local needs and preferences
Cultural	• Shared understanding and values with respect to environmental issues	• Loss of cultural diversity and indigenous knowledge; growth of monoculture • Spread of unsustainable lifestyles
Environmental	• More efficient allocation of natural resource use and environmental impacts through specialisation	• Growing scale of damage to the global commons e.g. climate change

to be enhanced. By contrast, it is the 'excluded' that appear most likely to suffer further marginalisation, increased vulnerability and displacement, as well as the effects of intensifying environmental degradation and the erosion of common space.

One powerful insight is the way in which globalisation discriminates against the least mobile and those tied to a particular place – with profound implications for the world's poor and natural resources. Constraints on public spending driven by structural adjustment programmes are also limiting the state's role to regulate the social and environmental impacts of market openings and to provide essential services, such as education, health and sanitation. At the same time, the withdrawal of the state from direct involvement in productive activities has led to both greater efficiency and more open governance.

The result is a widening gap between the two worlds of the 'haves' and the 'have-nots', at local, national, regional and international levels. At present, there is little sign of a coherent strategy at any of these levels for either narrowing this gap or ensuring that the resources of the poor are not appropriated further.

And in pure environmental terms, it is incontestable that globalisation has accelerated in parallel with intensifying environmental stress and the spread of unsustainable production and consumption patterns on a worldwide scale. Indeed, the five-year review of the Earth Summit agreements in 1997 and 2002 concluded that the overall trends for sustainable development are worse today than they were in 1992 (UNEP, 2002).

Challenges

Neither globalisation nor sustainable developments are inevitabilities. Both depend on conscious (and unconscious) choices. The critical question is how can people, communities, companies and countries – particularly in the developing world take action to turn globalisation to the benefit of sustainable development? The key is to generate investment in natural, human, economic and social capitals that drives a 'race to the top' in terms of environmental performance and provision of sustainable livelihoods.

To enable this, three systemic challenges need to be addressed:

- Analytical – we need better understanding of the linkages between globalisation and sustainable development, and to disseminate this information to facilitate awareness of globalisation's impacts and opportunities;
- Capacity – coping with global change requires investments by global institutions, national governments, the private sector and civil society to ensure that this understanding can be put to practical use;
- Governance – the rules of global and local engagement must be redesigned to take account of global interactions.

By addressing these challenges, the natural resources must be properly valued, the benefits of globalisation be equitably shared, and livelihoods be promoted. This process of empowerment is necessary to minimise globalisation's problems to the process of sustainable development, and to maximise the opportunities it provides to enhance livelihoods and environmental quality.

The Analytical Challenge

The twin concepts of globalisation and sustainable development are hard enough to grasp individually. Understanding the linkages between them is even more difficult.

Considerable effort is required to collate and analyse information on global environmental, economic and social trends, the reasons for policy and institutional failures and ways of overcoming these. Issues requiring particular attention include:

- Valuing non-marketed resources of global interest, such as biodiversity, and identifying the links between these resources and the livelihoods of the poor, to inform choices about natural resource use and management, e.g. evaluating the benefits of some of the transnational corporations prospecting in Asia, Africa and Latin American countries and their potential role in biodiversity conservation.
- Identifying the different channels by which macroeconomic policy reforms and liberalisation affect the use of traded natural resources, and measures required to anticipate and mitigate adverse impacts, such as in the industrial and forest sectors (Barbier *et al.*, 1994; Johnstone, 1996a; Reed, 1992; Young and Bishop, 1995);
- Clarifying the potential and the limits of private provision of environmental goods and services, for example the impacts of increased private sector participation in water supply and sanitation on economic efficiency, the environment and the poor, and alternative institutional frameworks for meeting social and environmental goals (Johnstone *et al.*, 1999)
- Defining benchmarks, process standards and management systems in specific sectors that take advantage of market self-regulation where appropriate. This is needed in order to spread the best practice, while retaining the flexibility to cope with diverse local conditions. Such systems would help governments, stock markets and individuals to distinguish the good partners – those companies that integrate sustainable practices into their operations – from the bad. For example, in the forest industry, these could include encouraging the certification of all foreign-owned forestry operations and supporting civil society networks such as Global Forest Watch (Mayers and Bass, 1999).

- Analysing cases where technological change has occurred and identifying the conditions, which promote it, for example the adoption of chlorine-free bleaching in pulp and paper production in Latin American and SE Asia (IIED, 1996).

In many cases, participatory techniques can be used to ensure that information and analysis adequately reflects local perspectives. New approaches must be developed to value traditional knowledge and to enable different stakeholders to articulate existing knowledge, for example, bioquality assessment techniques. As the linkages between globalisation and sustainable development become clearer, this information must be made available to those who could most benefit from it. Dissemination must be clearly targeted to promote accessibility by those who are generally excluded from global decision-making.

The Capacity Challenge

Accelerating globalisation and a declining resource base pose serious challenges for the strengthening of human and institutional capacities needed to produce sustainable outcomes. In particular, the increasing reliance on authoritative global institutions to manage environmental and development issues – such for hazardous waste, biodiversity, climate change and trade – mean that the need to enhance local and national capacity is greater than ever.

- In an increasingly market-oriented world, the public sector needs the capacity to enable smarter regulation of private firms, such as how to manage international timber companies seeking logging concessions in Central Africa (Sizer & Rice, 1995).
- The nation state and civil society require enhanced negotiating capacity in international fora and in their relations with transnational businesses and investors.
- In a world in which knowledge is rewarded, the provision of education becomes increasingly important. Targeting the skills base of the poorest in particular will enable the benefits of globalisation to be shared more equitably. For example, small enterprise development and training can form part of pro -poor strategies aimed at enabling access to markets, adding value and creating linkages between the formal and informal sectors (DFID, 1999).
- Civil society groups and independent researchers based in developing countries have a key role to play in both national and international dialogue on global environmental management. Capacity

strengthening requires support for technical and managerial training, as well as access to global information networks. This can be done in the form of long-term collaborative partnerships with established institutions based in advanced industrialised nations (CREED, 1994).

- With economies of scope and scale rewarding large corporate players based in developed countries, Small and Medium Enterprises (SMEs) in the developing world find it increasingly difficult to compete. Support for research and development targeted at SMEs is needed for development of suitable technologies (Robins and Roberts, 1997).
- Businesses have a crucial role to play in setting standards and building capacity of their stakeholders. Some forward -looking companies have to investigate the ways of developing partnerships along their supply chains (Robins and Roberts, 2000). Corporate responsibility will become increasingly important as a tool for building capacity for sustainable development. This will require new forms of partnerships if it is to be effective (Utting, 2000).

The Governance Challenge

Existing governance systems will need to be reformed and new ones developed to ensure that globalisation produces outcomes that are recognised as fair and just, particularly in the distribution of problems and opportunities. New initiatives are required to tackle free riders and concentrations of market power, and to provide mechanisms that incorporate externalities into decisions on resource use. The present governance gap between policy and practice must be narrowed through innovative models for partnerships between governments, civil society and the private sector.

- As economies are deregulated, transnational business is becoming increasingly powerful relative to the state. In many sectors, the pursuit of economies of scale is leading to ever-greater concentration of ownership. This can be seen as *de facto* vertical integration along whole supply chains, for example in contract farming and export of agricultural produce. This can result in improved economic opportunities for poor countries and for small farmers where there is appropriate government facilitation and farmer organisation. However, it can also put pressure on the incomes of upstream suppliers, particularly those involved in the production of primary commodities. In many cases, low producer prices mean that investment in regenerative practice simply cannot be undertaken, for example in the Ghanaian cocoa industry (Robins and Roberts, 2000).

- Market forces, until now constrained to a greater extent by government intervention, may lead to increased insecurity for weaker stakeholders. For example, uncoordinated expansion of pulp-mill capacity in the globalising forest industry has caused more extreme price fluctuations. New, globally inclusive systems of governance must be designed to mitigate these impacts, or to insure against them.

- Property rights must be clarified and economic incentives introduced to ensure the proper valuation of natural resources and to account for global environmental externalities. This has to be fulfilled while recognising differing local priorities and preferences through certification schemes, intellectual property rules, and other incentive measures.

- The globalisation of brands is fuelling a burgeoning counterfeiting sector in some mass-market consumer goods industries, e.g. garments. The implications of this for property rights and environmental quality standards must be analysed. For this, appropriate mechanisms must be designed to minimise the environmental problems while recognising the need to protect livelihoods.

- Where global markets encourage the use of environmental resources, for example, in cash crop production for export or international trade in waste paper, the wider implications on food security and livelihoods should be addressed (Van Beukering and Sharma, 1996). There may be a role for government to avoid conflicts between areas competing for export contracts.

- At the level of global institutions, there must be policy integration of environment and development issues and enhanced transparency to enable equal access by all countries and communities. The present constraints preventing the poor from contributing to decision-making and to the global economy must be tackled. The legal rights of local groups should be upheld, for example, concerning access to land and ownership of intellectual property rights. Excessive red tapism should be removed to reduce the advantage held by the powerful in international negotiations and to facilitate access to global markets.

Conclusion

For all its potential to act as a driver for sustainable development, globalisation is currently viewed by many to be contributing to the further marginalisation of developing countries and the weakening of their capacity to improve the livelihoods of their people in a sustainable way (UNCTAD, 1999; UNDP, 1999). The failure of the advanced counties to meet the challenges of globalisation on sustainable development has generated widespread distrust across the developing countries of the intentions of the industrialised world in its promotion of further measures to deepen globalisation. Promises made for increased aid to the developing countries to mitigate the problems of globalisation have not been realised. New measures are urgently needed to build confidence and steer global cooperation so that the poor and their environments are seen to benefit.

We have to develop a greater understanding of the links between globalisation and sustainable development by spreading this understanding to all stakeholders. This enhances their capacity to act upon it and creating new systems of governance to cope with global change, the potential environmental benefits from globalisation can be shared more equitably. Through this process of empowerment, the potential risks for disadvantaged groups and the negative impacts on the environment can be identified and minimised. This is the task facing development cooperation in the years ahead.

REFERENCES

1. Barbier, E.B., Burgess, J.C., Bishop, J. and B. Aylward. 1994. *The Economics of the Tropical Timber Trade*. Earthscan: London.
2. CREED 1994. *Collaborative Research in the Economics of Environment and Development: A Programme for Capacity-Strengthening*. Institute for Environmental Studies (Amsterdam) and International Institute for Environment and Development: London.
3. DFID 1999 *Tourism and Poverty Alleviation: Untapped Potential*, Summary paper, Department for International Development, London.
4. IIED 1996. *Towards a Sustainable Paper Cycle*. International Institute for Environment and Development: London.
5. Johnstone, N. 1996a *International Trade and Environmental Change: Evidence and Implications for Developing Countries*. Environmental Economics Working Paper No. 96 - 01. IIED: London.
6. Johnstone, N. 1999 *Environmental Policies and Industrial Competitiveness: The Choice of Instrument*. Environmental Economics Working Paper No. 99 -01. IIED: London.
7. Johnstone, N., Wood, L. and R. Hearne. 1999. *The Regulation of Private Sector Participation in Urban Water Supply and Sanitation: Realising Social and Environmental Objectives in Developing Countries*. Environmental Economics Working Paper No. 99 -01. IIED: London.

8. Mayers, J. and S. Bass 1999. *Policy that Works for Forests and People*, IIED, London.
9. Reed, D. (ed.) 1992. *Structural Adjustment and the Environment*. Earthscan: London.
10. Robins, N. and S. Roberts (eds.) 1997. *Unlocking Trade Opportunities*, IIED, London.
11. Robins, N. and S. Roberts (eds.) 2000. *The Reality of Sustainable Trade*, IIED, London.
12. Sizer, N. and R. Rice 1995. *Backs to the Wall in Suriname: Forest Policy in a Country in Crisis*, World Resources Institute, Washington, DC.
13. UNCTAD, 1999, *Trade and Development Report*, United Nations, Geneva.
14. UNDP, 1999, *Human Development Report*, Oxford University Press.
15. UNEP, 1999, *Global Environment Outlook 2*, Earthscan.
16. Utting, P. 2000. *Business Responsibility for Sustainable Development*, Occasional Paper 2, UNRISD, Geneva.
17. Van Beukering, P. and V. Sharma. 1996. *International Trade and Recycling in Developing Countries: The Case of Waste Paper Trade in India,* CREED, London.
18. Young, C.E.F. and J. Bishop. 1995. *Adjustment Policies and the Environment:.* CREED Working Paper No. 1. IIED: London.
19. WCED, 1987. World Commission on Environment and Development, *Our Common Future*, New York, Oxford University Press, 1987, P. 43.

44

Achieving the Goals of Globalisation Through Regional Economic Integration in Southern Africa

*G. R. Motlaleng**

Introduction

The objective of this paper is to access how the goals of globalisation have been achieved through the arrangement of regional economic integration programmes in Southern Africa. The role and impact of globalisation is accessed though its likely impact on the existing trading arrangements in the Southern African region. Economic policy makers basically view globalisation as an economic phenomenon that involves the increasing free interaction or integration of economic systems through the growth of trade, investment and capital flows. Globalisation refers further to the absence of boarders and barriers to trade between countries and continents at large. This paper therefore reviews the trading arrangements in the Southern African region and access how they are likely to operate under globalisation.

Economic policy makers are of the view that, if the existing regional trading patterns do not change, Southern Africa may become increasingly marginalised in the global economy. Thus, remaining an exporter of primary commodities with low or no value-added, and an importer of manufactured goods whether consumer, intermediate or capital. Lack of a diversified production structure, compounded by the absence of complementarity in the productive base of industries are the structural rigidities to economic integration in Southern Africa.

* Department of Economics, University of Botswana, Private Bag 0022, Gaborone, Botswana. Email: Motlaleg@mopipi.ub.bw

It is therefore argued that, for Southern Africa to be globally competitively it must be integrated to achieve scale economies and other efficiencies. However, the spirit of economic integration has been in progress in Southern Africa. This is demonstrated by the formation of the following trading regional blocs. The establishment of the Southern African Customs Union (SACU) in 1889, the formation of the Southern African Development Community (SADC) in 1992, and that of the Common Market for Eastern and Southern Africa in 1994.

Southern Africa is made up of the following countries; Angola, Botswana, Lesotho, Malawi, Mauritius, Mozambique, Namibia, Republic of South Africa (RSA), Swaziland, Zambia and Zimbabwe. Homogeneous features of these economies are as follows. First, persistent negative resource balances, except for Botswana and the RSA. Second, open but unbalanced trade and capital accounts with the developed world. Third, weak international reserve positions resulting in lack of funds to permit convertibility of foreign exchange, except for Botswana and South Africa and four, high inflation rates and excessive government deficits.

Heterogeneity in the countries of Southern Africa is brought up by a wide dispersion in their populations. It is only South Africa that has a population of over twenty million people. Countries that have populations between five and twenty million are Angola, Malawi, Mozambique, Zambia and Zimbabwe. Botswana, Lesotho, Mauritius, Namibia, and Swaziland have populations of less than two million people (Table 1). The small populations of these economies imply a small market for the region. Therefore, with globalisation we expect an expanded market and economies of scale for firms in Southern Africa. Urbanisation rates range from 12% in Malawi to 50% in Zambia. It is only South Africa and Zambia that have urbanisation rates of more than 50%.

Most countries in Southern Africa are members of the following trading agreements: the Southern African Customs Union Agreement (SACUA), the Southern African Development Community (SADC), and the Lome Convention. A review of these intra and extra trading arrangements in Southern Africa would give us the institutional framework under which trade is conducted in the sub-region. Obstacles and opportunities to economic and trade integration in Southern Africa are also discussed. An analysis of the effects of Free Trade Areas (FTAS) or Regional Economic Partnership Agreements (REPAS) proposed by major trading nations to Southern Africa's existing trading arrangements is also given.

The rest of the chapter is organised as follows, Section 1 gives an overview of the output, income and trade structures of the region. In section 2, Intra and extra regional trading institutions in Southern Africa are discussed in Lastly, Section 3 provides some concluding remarks and policy, implications of the study.

Output, Income and Trade Structure of Southern Africa

Output Structure

The output structure of the regional economies is said to be competitive rather than being complementary. This is due to the fact that these countries mostly produce similar primary products and compete for the export markets. Mayer et al (1997) argues that the lack of a diversified production structure in the region is frequently cited as the main obstacle to successful integration and economic development. For example, in the manufacturing sector the Southern African economies do not produce a diversified range of manufactured products, hence limiting their scope for trade. Lack of export diversity exposes the region to a greater degree of risk in the event of fluctuations in world demand and income. Additionally, vertical production structures in the different branches of production are lacking. For the region as a whole, manufacturers make up more than 70% of total imports, while only 10% is exported.

Most countries are dependent on minerals, raw materials and agriculture. For example, Botswana depends entirely on diamond exports. Countries that have a sizeable manufacturing sector are, Mauritius, Republic of South Africa (RSA), Zambia and Zimbabwe. The industrial output is mainly concentrated in resource-intensive activities. These are usually beverages, foodstuffs, textiles and tobacco and they account for half of the regional manufacturing value-added. The RSA dominates the industrial production in the region. Its manufacturing value-added is more than five times larger than the manufacturing value-added of all other countries in the region. It is also said to be almost fifteen times that of Zimbabwe the second largest manufacturer. Therefore with globalisation it is likely that the RSA's dominance would be undermined, as more goods from various regions would be flowing freely in the region. Major obstacles to trade in the Southern African region are lack of complementarity and underdeveloped production structures. Therefore, regional trade policies must focus on industrial development and diversification in order to improve intra- regional trade and be globally competitive.

Regional Income Levels

The regional economies fall into three distinct income groups of less developing countries (LDCs), developing countries and developed countries.

The LDCs are Angola, Lesotho, Malawi, Mozambique, and Zambia. The developing countries are Botswana, Mauritius, Namibia, Seychelles and Zimbabwe. The African Development Bank (1993) found that the combined GNP of Southern Africa was about US$120 billion or only 70% of that of Belgium that is among the smallest of the OECD economies. The RSA is classified as developed by the WTO and as a country in transition by the European Union. From Table 1 the RSA's GDP accounts for 76.8% of regions GDP and its per capita GDP is also among the highest. But, it has the worst income distribution in the region because economic disparities between black and white South Africans are among the worst in the world (World Bank 1994, Rangasamy 1998). Most countries in the region have small economies in US dollar equivalents. The dominance of the RSA's economic and political power has a profound influence in the extra and intra-regional trading arrangements as would be demonstrated under the Southern African Customs Union, where it can make unilateral decisions without consulting other members. This poses a problem of a narrow market for countries in Southern Africa. Therefore with globalisation countries in this region would have a wide range of markets associated with scale economies, employment and efficiency.

Trade Structure in Southern Africa

Trade statistics suggest that the economies of the region are quiet open. Openness is defined as the sum of exports and imports as a ratio of GNP. It measures the degree of trade dependence and can also capture the welfare effects of trade (Table 1). The smaller the ratio, the lower dependence on trade is the country. Southern African exports are mostly primary commodities and are directed to a small number of OECD countries. Imports also originate from the industrial countries. i.e., trade is characterised by primary exports and manufactured imports. This is an unimpressive economic scenario for Southern Africa because manufacturing is the most dynamic part of the industrial sector necessary to stimulate growth. South Africa is the least open economy. On the other hand, small economies of Botswana, Lesotho, Mauritius, Namibia and Swaziland are the most open economies of the region.

Rangasamy (1998) points out that intra-regional trade in Southern Africa is estimated at only 5% of total trade, while the European Union is the regions largest trading partner and it accounts for 29% of exports and 35% of imports. The SACU members further account for 40% of the RSA's manufactured exports. For the period 1985 to 1992, RSA's exports to SACU members accounted for more than one third of its gross domestic product and

Table 1: Regional Income levels and Trade Ratio- 2000.

Country	*Population Millions*	*GDP $USA billions*	*Per capita GDP $USA*	*HDI*	*HDPI*	*Trade ratio*
Angola	9.70 (7.7)	7.20 (5.7)	610.00	0.14	0.73	n/a
Botswana	1.5 (1.1)	5.29 (2.7)	3434.00	0.55	0.87	1.06
Lesotho	1.90 (1.5)	0.54 (0.4)	590.00	0.43	1.13	1.43
Malawi	9.00 (7.2)	1.67 (1.2)	210.00	0.17	0.88	0.63
Mauritius	1.10 (0.9)	2.57 (1.9)	2700.00	0.79	0.95	1.91
Mozambique	16.50 (13.1)	0.97 (0.7)	60.00	0.15	0.69	0.99
Namibia	1.50 (1.2)	2.11 (1.6)	1610.00	0.29	0.79	1.19
South Africa	39.80 (31.5)	103.65 (76.8)	2670.00	0.67	0.85	0.44
Swaziland	0.80 (0.6)	0.80 (0.6)	900.00	0.46	0.82	1.82
Tanzania	25.90 (20.5)	2.35 (1.7)	110.00	0.27	1.39	0.78
Zambia	8.30 (6.6)	3.83 (2.8)	390.00	0.31	1.63	0.67
Zimbabwe	10.40 (8.2)	5.04 (3.7)	570.00	0.40	1.10	0.75

Source: World Development Report- 2001
HDI = Human development index
HDPI = Human development performance index
() = Percentage of the group.

merchandise exports. All SACU members have trade deficit with the RSA. This low intra-regional trade is due to trading relations that were well established with previous colonial powers. Hence, Rangasamy argues that any attempt to promote intra-regional trade has to contend with this competition, and there is a need for the orientation of production towards the demand of the region. He further argues that identification of niche products for the region should be one of the focal points of entrepreneurial activity.

The obstacles to economic integration in Southern Africa can be summarised as follows. First, there is limited amount of intra-regional trade estimated at 5% per annum due to lack of diversification and complementarity in the productive base of the economies in the region, except in South Africa and Zimbabwe. Second, excess reliance on external funding. Third, there is macroeconomic instability and continued economic stagnation in most of the regional economies. Four, there exist the threat of the polarisation of economic activities due to the economic dominance of the RSA. The opportunities for economic integration for Southern Africa on the other hand are the region's abundance of natural resources and the great potential to expand agricultural output.

Intra and Extra-trading Arrangements in Southern Africa

The Southern African Customs Union (SACU)

This customs union, made up of five countries has been in existence for more than a century. It was established by the territories that currently constitute RSA in 1889 and was extended to Botswana, Lesotho and Swaziland (BLS) by 1895. Namibia joined separately in 1991 after it has been declared an independent state. The SACU can be regarded as the origins of economic integration in Southern Africa. A customs union involves free trade among members, but applies a common external tariff with members ceding sovereignty to a single unified customs administration or applying their own different tariff regimes along side the common external tariff.

The main provisions of the SACU are as follows: Firstly, a common external tariff is the existing phenomenon. Secondly, the duty free movement of goods within the customs area is taking place. Thirdly, the right of transit across the RSA of imported goods consigned to landlocked members. Fourthly, the revenue derived from the common tariff levied on imports to the region were to be shared by members in accordance their respective contributions to total regional imports.

In 1910, a treaty (1910 Customs Union agreement) was signed which allowed the RSA to administer and collect all revenue from customs and excise duties and to allocate it to other members quarterly. It must be noted that the BLS countries did not participate in the negotiations of this treaty but were only represented by Britain[1] . The distribution of revenue to BLS countries was based on proportion to their share of total duties in the customs area. The distribution of revenue in the 1910 customs union agreement in percentages were as follows; the RSA 98.68903%, Lesotho 0.88575%, Botswana 0.27622% and Swaziland 0.14900%.

The BLS countries were dissatisfied with the SACU agreement, and after being granted political independence in the late 1960's they asked for a renegotiation of the SACU agreement. The main dissatisfactions of the BLS about the SACU agreement were as follows. First, the price-raising effects of the common external tariff designed to protect South African producers from international price competition on imports into the BLS countries. Thus, the SACU was designed to suite the RSA's industrial development strategy of import-substitution. Due to the protectionist nature of SACU because of the common external tariff, the BLS countries were disadvantage because they were paying import prices that were above world prices.

Second, the industrial polarisation effect arising from the tendency of industries serving the SACU market to locate in the RSA to the detriment of the BLS counties.

Third, loss of discretionary authority to pursue an independent national fiscal policy (loss of fiscal discretion by the BLS countries), due to the retention by the RSA, acting in consultation with the Board on Tariff and Trade only and not the BLS countries, of the right to set customs and excise duty rates unilaterally for the entire customs union area. The BLS countries were to maintain customs and excise legislation identical to that of the RSA.

Four, the time lag involved in the distribution of shares in the revenue pool, due to the procedures employed in collecting, presenting and agreeing on the pertinent import statistics. This resulted in payments being delayed initially and subject to further adjustment in the following years, thereby in effect granting interest-free loans to the RSA which were further enlarged during periods of growing imports and inflation.

Fifth, limitations on the scope of the BLS countries to provide protection to their infant industries, due to narrowly defined eligibility criteria and other provisions which made this technique of industrial promotion extremely expensive for them.

Sixth, the inadequacy of procedures for consultation on actions by the RSA which the BLS countries found objectionable, and the inadequacy of dispute resolution procedures, and

Seventh is the difficulty with using Article 7, of the SACU agreement to establish new industries in the BLS countries.

The contentious issue in the SACU agreement has been its revenue sharing formula. Due to this, the revenue sharing formula has been amended in 1969 and 1975 in an attempt to compensate the BLS countries for the economic losses for being in the union. The evolution of the SACU sharing formula is in three phases. *Phase one*, the revenue-sharing agreement upon inception of the SACU in 1910, which was in the form of a fixed share of the common revenue pool independently of the BLS counties' share of imports. The respective revenue shares of the SACU members were as follows; RSA *98.68903%*, Lesotho *0.88575%*, Botswana *0.27622%* and Swaziland *0.14900%*. *Phase two*, an introduction of the compensation/an enhancement factor in 1969, which aimed to compensate the BLS countries for the negative economic effects which the membership of the SACU entailed. *Phase three*, an introduction of a stabilisation factor in 1976 to prevent the SACU revenue from the BLS countries from fluctuating too much by keeping it within the range of 17-23% of the value of the imports and excisable production of the BLS countries.

The 1969 Revenue-sharing Formula: The Compensation/Enhancement Factor

Due to the dissatisfaction of the BLS countries about the 1910 customs agreement, the SACU was renegotiated in 1969. The renegotiations led to the incorporation of Articles 13 and 14, which addressed the grievances of the BLS countries over the pool of customs, excise and additional taxes collected within the union. Article 14 in particular deals with the formula for determining the respective shares of the BLS countries in the common revenue pool. The following formula expresses the revenue shares received by the BLS countries.

$$R = \frac{(i+p)*(C+E+S)*1.42}{I+P}$$

R = share accruing to a particular BLS country.

i = total cif value at the border of all imports into BLS country inclusive of customs, excise and sales duties.

I = total cif value at the border of all imports into the customs union area inclusive of customs and sales duties.

p = the total value of dutiable goods produced and consumed in a BLS country inclusive of duties.

P = the total value of dutiable goods produced and consumed in the customs union area inclusive of duties.

C = the total collection of customs duties within the customs union area.

E = the total collection of excise duties within the customs union area.

S = the total collection of sales duties within the customs union area.

1.42 = the enhancement factor.

The 1.42 enhancement factor was introduced to compensate the BLS countries for the adverse effects to their economies for being the SACU members. It was considered to enable the BLS countries to secure an amount from the SACU revenue pool equivalent to 20% of the value of their imports and excisable production.

The RSA's share of the customs revenue is determined as the residual. i.e., its share of the revenue pool is what remains after the BLNS have been paid. The 1969 amendments to the revenue sharing formula resulted in large increased receipts from the revenue pool to the BLS countries. For example, in Botswana the SACU revenue as percentage of total government revenue increased from 20% in 1967 to 50% in 1975.

Despite the fact that the 1969 revenue-sharing formula increased the BLS countries' share of the SACU revenue it has been criticised on the following grounds. First, the RSA has criticised the formula because it compensates the BLS countries for their exports from itself and includes these in the numerator but not the denominator, to South Africa's detriment. Second, the RSA has control over the components of the formula that determine the BLS countries' share of the SACU revenue, over which the BLS countries have no control, while the overall duty rate is determined by the RSA's trade, production and duties.

Therefore, for the BLS countries the revenue sharing formula is flawed because the size of their payments is determined by the RSA's tax and trade policies, which are not inline with theirs. Third, the BLS countries have criticised its practical implementation because their share of the common revenue pool is determined by;1) their level of imports which are subject to fluctuations; 2) the statistics which are used to determine the BLS countries share of the common revenue pool make no provision for under-coverage of goods at border posts; and 3) lack of a clear–cut definition for the calculation of import and export figures has disadvantaged the BLS countries because of double-counting. These criticisms of the revenue sharing formula by the BLS countries has led to its amendment again in 1976 as discussed in the following section.

The 1976 Formula Amendment and the Stabilisation Factor

The fluctuations in the revenue accruing to the BLS countries led to the introduction of the stabilisation factor in 1976. The SACU revenue to the BLS countries was fluctuating around less than 20% of the value of their imports and excisable production. These fluctuations resulted in instability in government revenues for the BLS countries. Therefore, in 1976 it was agreed that, if the revenue calculated with the aid of the original 1969 formula was not equal to 20% of the duty inclusive value of imports and excisable production, a stabilisation factor must be calculated.

The stabilisation factor is equal to 50% of the difference between the amount corresponding to 20% and the amount calculated with the 1969 formula. In case the difference is positive, it is added to the latter amount. If it is negative it is subtracted. However, a lower limit of 17% and upper limit of 23% for the stabilised value were specified. Numerous discussions concerning the revenue sharing formula have been held in resent years but with no optimal solutions or no consensus. This means that SACU is still operating unaltered since the original agreement entered into in 1969 and the marginal amendment of 1976.

The only issue on which the BLNS countries and the RSA agree to be detrimental and unfair to the BLNS countries is the effect of the two-year lag in payment to the BLS countries from the customs revenue pool. The accrued revenue due to the two-year lag is said to exceed the annual cash payments to the BLS countries on average by 27%. This amount can therefore be regarded as an interest-free loan to the RSA by the BLS countries. The enhancement factor is unable to compensate the BLS countries because it is eroded by inflation and the depreciation of the exchange rate. For example, in a static cost-benefit analysis, Leith (1992) found that the loss to Botswana of being a member of SACU was about 3.5% of GDP for the year 1987, half of which was due to the two-year time lag.

Apart from the two-year time lag, there are other adverse effects the SACU have on the BLNS countries[2] . These include negative effects of dumping by the RSA and the loss of sovereignty. The latter is due to the fact that the BLNS countries have to maintain customs duties similar to those of the RSA. The African Development Bank (1993) argues that the net importer position of the BNLS vis-à-vis the RSA suggests that South African industries have effectively been subsidised by the BNLS residents for a long time. Therefore, equitable customs union arrangements would indicate that compensatory transfers should be made from the RSA to the BLNS countries.

The Southern African Development Community-SADC

The SADC is made up of all member states of the Southern African region already outlined. The SADC is the successor of the Southern African Development Coordination Conference-SADCC established in 1980. The SADCC had ten members only, namely, Angola, Botswana, Lesotho, Malawi, Mozambique, Namibia, Swaziland, Tanzania, Zambia and Zimbabwe. Its establishment was the beginning of a process of economic and social development among the majority-ruled states of Southern Africa. The aim of regional economic integration in Southern Africa is the creation of a common market in the long run, characterised by free movement of factors of production, goods and services among member states.

The SADCC had the following goals: First, the reduction of external dependence, especially on the RSA. This is because the SADCC was established during the apartheid white minority regime in South Africa, which, was replaced by a democratic government in April 1994. Second is the creation of operational and equitable regional integration. Third is the mobilisation of domestic and regional resources to carry out national, interstate and regional policies to reduce dependence and build genuine regional coordination. Thus, through regional cooperation, SADC seeks to promote collective self-reliance through economic development and the forging of closer links among its member states to create genuine and equitable regional integration. This highlighted the need to promote and coordinate the economic development of member countries. Four is the joint action to secure international understanding and practical support of the SADCC strategy. The SADCC therefore like SADC was still an economic not a political organisation. The SADCC was transformed into SADC in 1992 through the *SADC Treaty and Declaration of 1992*. The SADC is aimed at deepening and expanding the process of economic coordination and integration in Southern Africa.

There are some differences between the SADCC and the SADC. First, the SADCC was designed to coordinate development in the region, while the SADC was established to promote economic integration in the region in accordance with the 1980 Lagos Plan of Action and the 1991 Abuja Treaty. Second, the SADCC was established by the Lusaka Declaration of 1980, which conferred no legal status on the executive of the SADCC. On the other hand, the SADC was established by the SADC Treaty of 1992 which granted it legal backing to its executive.

Some Initiatives towards Globalisation

Currently, the issue that is of priority in the SADC is the trade and investment protocol adopted by member states in August 1996. Within the WTO framework this trade protocol constitutes what can be defined as an *interim agreement* leading to the establishment of a Free Trade Area. The trade protocol tries to tackle the current problem of inequitable trade relationship in the region by removing obstacles to a free trade area/intra-regional trade. This protocol aims to replace the sectoral cooperation with the process of trade integration among member states.

The trade protocol is regarded as a policy instrument to eliminate the structural problems of lack of diversified and complementary productive structures of the economies of Southern Africa. i.e., the trade protocol is viewed as an instrument to bring about structural change.

The main objectives of the SADC protocol on trade are as follows. First, to further liberalise intra-regional trade in goods and services on the basis of fair, mutually equitable and beneficial trade arrangements complemented by Protocols in other areas. Second, to ensure efficient production within the SADC reflecting the current and dynamic comparative advantages of its Members. Third, To contribute towards the improvement of the climate for domestic, cross-border and foreign investment. Fourth, to enhance the efforts of economic development, diversification and industrialisation of the region. Lastly it is to establish a Free Trade Area in the SADC region (SADC Protocol on Trade, 1996, Article 2; P 4).

A period of eight years has been set by the trade protocol for the elimination of tariff and non-tariff barriers. Article 3:1c, of the trade protocol provides for a flexibility in the reductions of tariffs by arguing that member states who believe they may or may have been adversely affected by the removal of tariff and non-tariff barriers to trade, may upon application to the Committee of Ministers on Trade, be granted a grace period to allow them additional time for the elimination of such tariffs and non-tariff barriers.

Mayer and Thomas (1997) have, however, challenged the SADC protocol on trade by arguing that the removal of barriers to intra-regional trade is a necessary, but not a sufficient condition for regional industrial development. They argue that, in the absence of supporting supply-side measures, member states may not have the ability to exploit opportunities such as economies of scale due to an enlarged market. To them, the critical constraint to intra-regional trade is structural in nature. These structural rigidities are, lack of diversification in all the SADC countries except South Africa and Zimbabwe, and the concomitant lack of complementarity in their productive base. These structural rigidities they argue can be overcome if the region collectively endeavours to foster industrial development.

The following is a systematic critical analysis of the trade protocol by Mayer and Thomas (1997). They further argue that as a trade policy instrument the trade protocol has the following deficiencies. First, it fails to provide for differential treatment for least developed member states. Thus, the trade protocol fails to provide preferential treatment for member states classified by the WTO as least developed countries. By this, the protocol takes away rights granted the least developed countries in terms of international trade laws, and this will work against their economic development and will result in further industrial polarisation in more advanced member states.

Second, it emphasises tariff barriers to trade when they are not the main obstacles to intra-regional trade and economic integration. They argue that the existing schedule of tariffs applies in theory but not in practice, because of ineffective administration of customs at border posts and due to misrepresentation and misclassification in bills of landing for imports. Therefore, the trade protocol's emphasis on tariff barriers and failure to address the elimination of non-tariff barriers to trade in Southern Africa override the objective of removing obstacles to intra-regional trade.

Third, there are no provisions that address supply-side measures, i.e., no provisions are made for supply-side measures to encourage industrial restructuring and diversification. Lastly, provisions to foster equitable industrial development in the region are inadequate and there are no compensatory mechanisms. Thus, the trade protocol does not include measures to compensate member states that may incur costs in the form of de-industrialisation as a result of its implementation, as economic development is likely to be polarised in the more advanced member states of the community. If this scenario comes out, *industrial development*, as the primary rationale for regional integration in developing countries would not be accomplished in Southern Africa.

The Common Market for Eastern and Southern Africa (COMESA).

The Preferential Trade Area for Eastern and Southern Africa (PTA) was the predecessor to COMESA. The PTA was established in 1982, under the auspices of the Lagos Plan of Action, a blue print for economic development in Africa. Member states of the COMESA are from Southern and Eastern Africa and the Indian Ocean states. The COMESA is made up of twenty member states, namely; Angola, Burundi, Comoros, Democratic Republic of Congo, Djibouti, Egypt, Eritrea, Ethiopia, Kenya, Madagascar, Malawi, Mauritius, Namibia, Rwanda, Seychelles, Sudan, Swaziland, Uganda, Zambia, and Zimbabwe. Twelve of which are members of the SADC. Currently, only Botswana and the RSA are the SADC members who are not in the COMESA.

The PTA's objectives were to enhance economic development of member states, enhance intra-regional trade and investment in East and Southern Africa. These objectives were to be achieved through, the promotion of trade liberalisation through the removal of tariffs, the use of local currencies within the PTA through a dedicated clearing house and the harmonisation of monetary policies of member states. In December 1994, the PTA was transformed from a preferential trade area to a common market, COMESA. The aim was to establish a common market in the PTA area by the year 2000. The operations of this common market involve, the establishment of customs unions with free movement of goods internally and a common external tariff within ten years.

The existence of the COMESA can therefore serve to negate the implementation of the SADC trade protocol, since member states of both organisations will be trying to maintain two different trade policies between the same participating countries. For example, the SADC trade protocol envisages a free trade area within eight years, while the COMESA argues for a common market with a common external tariff within ten years. Therefore, these organisation with the aim of enhancing economic development of member states need to be harmonised and probably ultimately merged in the future for them to yield the benefits of economic integration (Mayer and Thomas, 1997).

The European Union-South Africa Trade, Development and Co-operation Agreement (TDCA)

This is a bilateral trade arrangement signed between the RSA and the EU in October 1999. The TDCA is the first fully reciprocal Free Trade Area (FTA or REPA) in Southern Africa and it will be implemented by the year 2010. This bilateral trade arrangement came about because the new the RSA government in 1994 had wanted to secure the Lomé status of free access to the EU market. Currently, the RSA does not benefit from the trade provisions of the Lomé Convention. The EU offered the RSA a Free Trade Area arrangement within the WTO rules that require the elimination of all duties on substantially all trade. *Substantially all trade* is interpreted to mean 86% of current EU exports to the RSA over a ten-year period and 96% of current South African exports to the EU over a twelve year period.

The WTO is said to have been very influential in determining both the decision to adopt an FTA framework to govern the trading relationship between the RSA and the EU and the structure of the FTA itself. By eliminating these duties the RSA-EU Free Trade Area (SEFTA) will be WTO compatible. This trade agreement is designed to integrate South Africa into the world economy by eliminating most tariffs. The SEFTA demonstrates, a case where the WTO rules are used to legitimise the ACP preferential market access on a condition that the ACP developing countries agree to open their markets to all European goods over a 10-12 year period. The creation of free trade areas, which are WTO compatible, and linking Europe with regional groupings of the ACP countries is the EU's favoured trading strategy in the

21st century. For the EU, regionalism is seen as a way to promote trade liberalisation within the ACP regions and which in the long run can lead to their economic integration into the world economy.

The TDCA further demonstrates the RSA's dominance and influence in making unilateral decisions that affect its trading partners. Since the RSA has a Customs Union, the SACU, with the BLNS countries, SEFTA applies de facto to the BNLS countries. The implication is that, the SEFTA is going to be applied to the BNLS states without having been represented during the formulation of the TDCA. Therefore, European goods entering South Africa at duty free rate may have two options. First is to enter the BNLS countries without tariff. This has negative implications for the infant industries in the BNLS countries, since they will face unfair competition from manufactured exports from industrialised nations of Europe. Thus, the enlarged market for the European goods can result in the de-industrialisation of the BNLS countries. Second, intra-SACU customs posts may have to be constructed in order to tax the intra-SACU movement of EU goods (Gibb, 2000). The second option hinders intra-SACU trade and regional economic integration.

The signing of the SEFTA by the EU and South Africa without the BNLS countries' views can be seen as a contravention of one of the provisions of the EU's mandate. The provision states that REPAs will be negotiated with ACP subgroups chosen on the basis of existing regional integration initiatives with the final decision over which regions and countries are included being taken by the ACP countries themselves. The BNLS countries must have been included in the negotiations, because once the REPAS becomes operational, even the less developed countries like Lesotho would loose their non-reciprocal market access. It is argued that less developed countries have greater accesses to the EU market under the super-GSP than under the REPA model.

As already noted, LDC's like Lesotho in the SACU will be forced either to adopt an FTA with the EU, or erect its own customs posts, or leave SACU. In addition, the SEFTA will affect the implementation of the SADC's trade protocol. Policy makers in Southern Africa are left with the question, what impacts will the SEFTA have on regional integration, and in particular, trade and investment flows within the region?

The Lomé Convention[3]

It is a trade, aid and development cooperation agreement between the member states of the European Union (EU) and seventy-one, African, Caribbean and Pacific (ACP) states established in 1975. Lomé IV (1995-2000)[4], expired on February 2000 and was replaced by the Cotonou Partnership Agreement in June 2000. Changes to the Lomé Convention were necessary to make its trading arrangement WTO compatible. At this convention, negotiations centred on free trade agreements between the EU and the ACP countries by 2008. The EU's new trading strategy is committed towards multilateralism, differentiation and regionalism. The EU argues that multilateralism, driven by globalisation and policed by multilateral agencies like the WTO, has served to undermine Lomé. The EU's new trading regime is based on the creation of Regional Economic Partnership Agreements (REPAS) or Free Trade Areas (FTAS) that will link Europe with regional groupings of the ACP states. The EU favours this strategy because it ensures that EU-ACP trading arrangements are WTO rules compliant. It is estimated that REPAS or FTAS will need about 12-15 year transition periods to be fully operational. During this transitional period the EU and the ACP states have asked the WTO for a waiver allowing them to keep the present preferential trading arrangements (Gibb, 2000).

The foundations of the Lomé Convention are premised on the following. First is the discrimination in favour of European ex-colonies. Second, preferential access to the European market by the ACP states via non-reciprocal trade arrangements. Third is the spirit of an equal partnership of two regional groups representing the developed and underdeveloped worlds. Lastly, the political infrastructure and norms used to support and legitimise the ACP group and institutionalise the EU-ACP relationship. The trade provisions of the Lomé Convention are such that exports of the ACP states are accorded the most preferential and favoured terms of access to the EU market. They cover Industrial (100%), processed and agricultural (80%) exports. These preferences are non-reciprocal. It implies that most of the ACP exports are allowed duty free to European market, while the ACP states maintain tariff barriers and quota restrictions against European goods.

There are also four commodity protocols covering beef, sugar, bananas and rum that provide particular ACP countries with quota free access to the EU market. In addition, there is the STABEX, which guarantees certain export earnings from the sales of raw materials and the SYSMIN for minerals. The ACP countries are compensated by these bodies for lower than the expected export earnings when trading with the EU. The objectives of these preferences are to enhance economic development and the gradual integration of the ACP into the world economy.

Currently, the EU is of the view that the twenty-five years old Lomé Convention needs to be renegotiated, restructured or even replaced with an organisation who's trading principles are WTO compliance. First, the non-reciprocal and discriminatory trade policies of the Lomé are not complaint with the WTO multilateral trading regime, which requires trade to be conducted on the basis of non-discrimination. Second, despite the preferential trade arrangements accorded to the ACP states under the Lomé, these countries have failed with a few exceptions to diversify their exports and to be integrated into the world economy. Most of the ACP states are still exporters of primary products and importers of manufactured goods from the industrialised countries. This shows that the Convention has not promoted and expanded trade for the ACP states. Also the EU's decision to expand the non-reciprocal trade preferences to non-ACP states but at the same level of development as the ACP states have further eroded the benefits of this clause. It is further observed that the ACP states have experienced a declining share of world trade. For instance, its share in world trade is said to have dropped from 3% in 1976 to just over 1% in 1997.

In Southern Africa Lomé may be replaced with a minimum of potentially four EU-South Africa preferential trading agreement. First, the SEFTA signed in October 1999. Second is the extension of the SEFTA to the BLNS, perhaps with exemptions and special safeguards. Third is a separate reciprocal REPA agreement, with Zimbabwe, Mauritius and the Seychelles. Four is a Lomé-type non-reciprocal agreement with the SADC LDCs. This multiplicity of EU-Southern Africa trading regimes can result in undermining attempts to promote regional integration.

The Multiplicity of trading arrangements calls for a need to govern intra-SADC trade movements even in the event of a SADC free trade area. i.e., intra-SADC customs posts will have to police the intra-SADC movements of all goods. The proposed trading arrangements (*The post-Lome REPA model*) are said to have a fragmentary impact on economic integration and regionalism in Southern Africa. Critics to the REPA model argue that, REPAs may actually do harm than good to the process of regional integration itself, by fragmenting the regimes applying to imports from the EU and by impending the adoption of common external policies. Thus, to them the new EU's strategy of free trade areas promoting regional integration as a mechanism to achieve trade liberalisation, linking Europe with regional groupings of the ACP states has the potential to damage the cause of regional solidarity among developing countries of Southern Africa (Gibb, 2000).

Conclusions

The following conclusions can be drawn from the preceding discussions. First, lack of a diversified production structure compounded by the absence of complementarity in the productive base of industries is the structural rigidity to economic integration in Southern Africa. Second, the regional economies fall into three distinct income groups of less developing countries, developing countries and developed countries. Third, the Southern African countries mostly produce similar primary products and compete for the export markets. Fourth, the RSA dominates the industrial production in the region. Its manufacturing value-added is said to be more than five times larger than the manufacturing value-added of all other countries in the region. Fifth, the Southern African economies are quiet open, but with unbalanced trade and capital accounts with the developed world. For example, the intra-regional trade in Southern Africa is estimated at only 5% of total trade, while the European Union is the regions largest trading partner and it accounts for 29% of exports and 35% of imports. This implies that the existing regional trading arrangements have not developed enough economic integration. Lastly, the EU's new proposed trading arrangement of REPAS or FTAS are likely to have a fragmentary impact on the existing integration and regionalism in Southern Africa when they are implemented.

REFERENCES

1. African Development Bank (1993), Economic Integration in Southern Africa. Volume I. Oxford, Oxford University Press.
2. African Development Bank, Annual Reports, 1998, 1999 and 2000, Oxford, Oxford University Press.
3. Gibb. R (2000) Post-Lomé: The European Union and the South. *Third World Quarterly, Vol. 21 (3),* pp.457-481.
4. Leith. J. C (1992) The Static Welfare Economics of a Small Developing Country's Membership in a Customs Union: Botswana in the Southern African Customs Union. *World Development, Vol. 20(7),* pp.1021-1028.
5. Mayer. M and Thomas. R. H (1997) Trade integration in the Southern African Development Community: Prospects and Problems, *Development of Southern Africa, Vol. 14(3),* pp.327-353.
6. Rangasamy. L (1998) Regional Economic Development: The case of Southern Africa. Occasional Paper No. 8. University of Cambridge.
7. SADC (1996), The SADC Protocol on Trade, Maseru-Lesotho, August 1996. SADC.

FOOTNOTES

1. The BLS countries were British protectorates until the late 1960's
2. The BNLS are; Botswana, Namibia, Lesotho and Swaziland. Namibia joined independently in 1991. It has been under RSA since 1915.

3. The Cotonou Partnership Agreement in June 2000 replaced Lomé Convention, however the current ACP non-reciprocal tariff preferences will be maintained until December 2007.
4. Lomé I (1976-80), Lomé II (1981-85), Lomé III (1986-90) and Lomé IV, for 10 years (1990-2000), Mid-term review done in 1995.

45

Multinational Marketing Risk and Opportunities

Dr. P.P. Ekerete*

Introduction

The emergence of marketing activities across national borders is one of the major break-through in the competitive world of business today. For this reason, astute marketing, innovative design and good timing are the main stay of multinational marketing.

This growth in multinational marketing activities within the global framework invariably has brought far-reaching economic advancement to both the multinational operations (MNCS) and host countries (Paliwoda, 1997).

Multinational marketing is marketing activities performed across national boundaries, Peter (1998). That is to say, multinational corporations locate their business operations, produce and sell their products or services in many different countries of the world. In other world, their business operations span the globe as a result of their size and strong capital base.

Management of international marketing activities requires a prior understanding of the marketing risks and opportunities implicit in the venture. For our purpose in this research, risk could be defined as external factors that may result in or have resulted in the firm's failure to achieve its objectives. On the other hand, opportunities are external factors and situations that will substantially assist an organisation in its efforts to achieve or exceed its objectives. They are always expressed in terms of market potentials.

* Lecturer in Marketing, Rivers State University of Science and Technology, Box 50, Port Harcourt, Rivers State Nigeria.

A proper grasp of the environment complexities of host countries remain a veritable exercise. Other reason, global marketing strategies will be developed, will corporations' strengths, weaknesses, opportunities and threats (SWOT) will be analyzed.

Given that both risks and opportunities abound in multinational marketing, the question becomes, "how do MNCs adjust to the former (risks) so as to avail of the later (opportunities)". Basically, this is the crux of or discourse in this research work.

Most MNCs are constrained to analyze different environments and determine market potentials risks and opportunities in their countries. This is due to orchestrated environmental peculiarities of host nations. According to Jacoby (1970), what is needed are reasonable and effective coordinating and regulating mechanisms to 'de-politicize' major disparities in national policies which bear on multinational corporations. This shows that multinational marketing risks cut across geo-political dimensions.

Critically, environmental risks that usually influence multinational marketing may be included in the following:

- Cultural forces
- Social forces
- Economic forces
- Technological forces
- Political and legal forces (Catera, 1996).

However, Franco (1978) agrees that MNCs have gained acceptance as they become more sensitive to host nation's environmental risks. Again, their (MNCs) level of involvement in multinational business covers a wide spectrum. That justifies Heenams (1999) claims that South Korean multinationals have paved their way in Nigeria, while Filipino firms operate all over the globe.

In recent years, the attempt to inquire into multinational corporations' indulgence in international marketing has preoccupied researchers. Yet, despite a background of intensive studies on the subject matter, something remains unraveled. Thus, evaluation and analysis of multinational marketing activities, vis-a.vis risks and opportunities remains imperative. Therefore, this research is set out to analyze the multinational marketing risk and opportunities using some selected MNC as case study.

Multinational marketing activities are globally performed and carried across international boundaries. Implicit in this exercise is marketing risks and opportunities. In the light of these; "do the marketing risks out-weigh opportunities and vice-versa?".

The purpose of this study is therefore to identify and analyse possible risks and opportunities faced by MNCs in the course of their global marketing activities. These were investigated using some selected multinational corporations as case study.

Research Hypothesis

The following hypotheses were therefore tested to confirm the data collected.

Ho_1: Multinational marketing does not help in achieving heir organisational goals.

Ho_2: Multinational risks are not challenging to the attainment of marketing goals.

Environmental Complexities In Multinational Marketing

According to Ricks (1993), a detailed analysis of the environment is an absolute necessity before a company enters foreign markets. If a marketing strategy is to be effective across national boundaries, the complexities of all environments must be understood. To this end, we will see how the cultural, social, economic, technological, political and legal forces affect multinational marketing.

By moving from the analysis of individual nation's influence on mulinational marketing, to the more abstract level of institutions, we can better understand foreign markets. Institutions serve as structures for achieving some necessary social goals social intuitions include the family education, institutions, religion, health and recreational systems. Economic institutions are made up of producers, wholesalers, retailers, buyers and other organisations that produced, distributed and purchase products. Political and legal institution included public agencies, laws, courts, legislature and government bureaus.

Concepts, values and tangible items, such as tools, buildings and foods, make up culture. Culture is passed on from one generation to another; in a way, it is the blueprint for acceptable behaviour in a given society. It is the totality of people's way of life (Ekerete, 2000).

When products are introduced into on nation from another, acceptance is far more likely if there are similarities between the two cultures. For example, as Italians cultural value towards weight approach American values, then weight watchers' products will become more successful.

The connotations associated with body motions, greetings, colours, numbers, shapes, sizes and symbols very considerably across cultures. For multinational marketers, these cultural difference have implication that pertain to product development, personal selling, advertising, packaging and pricing, (Johason 1997).

A society's attitude toward the body also effects international marketers. The American custom of patting a child on the head would not be considered and of friendliness the orient, where the heard has been held scared. In contrast, the illustration of feet is regarded as despicable in Thailand.

A multinational marketer also must know a country's customs regarding male-female social interaction. Advertising that is based on the togetherness of married life could backfire in Japan and Western Europe, where husbands and wives often lead separate lives. In Italy, it is unacceptable for a salesman to call on someone's wife if the husband is not at home. In somc parts of Moslem states in Nigeria, television commercials, which portray boy-girl romantic relationships would be unacceptable. In Saudi Arabia, the use of women's photographs in advertisement is strictly prohibited.

Marketing activities are primarily social in purpose; therefore they are structured by the institutions of family, religions, education, health and recreation. In every nation, these social institutions can be identified. By finding major deviations in institutions among nations, one can gain insights into the adaptation of marketing strategy. For example in a Bic pen television commercial in Nigeria, viewers see a mummy break out his sarcophagus (Stone Coffin). Using the pen-the pen keeps on writing. Research indicated that most Nigerian viewers would not believe a serious 'torture' test, so the commercial pokes fun at a test while making a point about durability. Because of different socialisation, Nigerian viewers would probably believe a serious torture test, (Okwandu 1977).

Economic differences dictate many of the adjustments that must be made in marketing across national boundaries. Most prominent are those adjustment caused by standards of living, availability of credit, discretionary buying power, income distribution, national resources, climate and conditions that affect transportation.

In terms of the value of all produced by a nation, the United States has largest GNP in the world. GNP is an overall measure of the nation's economic standing, but it does not take into account the concept of GNP in relationship to population (GNP per-capita). The fact is that knowledge about per capita income, aggregate GNP, credit and distribution of income provides general insights into market potentials, (Litton, 1980).

Opportunities for international marketers are not limited to those countries with the highest incomes. Some nations are progressing at a markedly faster rate they were a few years ago, and these countries especially in Latin America, Africa and the Middle East have tremendous market potential for specific products, (Litton 1980). However, marketers must understand the political and legal environment before they can convert buying power into actual demand for specific products, (Litton 1980). However, marketers must understand the political and legal environment before they can convert buying power into actual demand for specific products. For example, Coca-Cola is boycotted in most of the Middle East for political reasons, but Coke has found a haven in Egypt, where sidewalk peddlers and space-strapped shop owners keep the soft drink in full view, (Thompson 1980).

Much of the marketing technology used in most advanced and industrialised areas may be ill suited for developing countries. Mass marketing techniques, for instance, are too complex and expensive to create the jobs needed to absorb the rapidly expanding labour forces of developing countries, (Jains 1981).

Records show that when supermarkets are introduced in developing countries, they are limited to high-and middle-income areas because there is too little buying power in low-income neighborhoods, therefore they do not create many jobs, (Kingsey, 1988).

A country's political system, national laws, regulatory bodies, national pressure groups, and courts all have great impact on multinational marketing activities. A government's policies toward public versus private enterprise, consumers and foreign firms influence marketing across national boundaries, (Summuel 1998).

Multinational marketing should consider insuring against unexpected acts of a government. For example, Julius Berger company did not find the Dictator's (Abacha) military regime easy in respect of business performance. likewise, when a socialist president was elected in France, many multinationals feared nationalisation. Differences in ethical and governmental ethical standards are illustrated by what they Mexican call 'La Mordida'—the bite. The use of pay—off and bribes is deeply entrenched in many governments. If a country's government trade and corporate policy and laws prevent direct involvement in pay-offs and bribes, most multinational may have hard time competing with other foreign firm that engages in this practice. On refusal to make pay-offs, they will be forced to hire local consultants, public relations firms, or advertising agencies-which results in direct or indirect pay-offs. The ultimate decision about whether to give small tips or gifts where they are customary must be based on a firm's code of conduct; it is illegal for U. S. firms to attempt to make large payments on bribes to influence policy decisions of foreign governments, (Okwandu 1997).

Gains From Multinational Business: Hosts' Perspective

In spite of the many criticism against multinational corporations, host countries derive substantial net gains and benefits from foreign operations in their nation. While some foreign operations are clearly more beneficial to the host country than others, virtually all contribute at least something.

Direct foreign (private) investment by MNCs usually provides desirable risk capital to host countries. Unfortunately, there is no consensus as to what the impact has been or is. It is a fact that MNCs have played an important part in the development of many developing nations. At the same time, there have been economic, social and political consequences, which have given cause for concern, (Cateora, 1996).

Often, These advantages and disadvantages are expressed in an extreme fashion. At one end of the spectrum, the MNC and its supporters have argued that the MNC is essential in the development process since developing countries lack capital and expertise to undertake their own industrialisation. The Multinational corporation brings not only the necessary technology but also a broader package deal of jobs, foreign exchange, entrepreneurship and management and the rest with the result that a multiplier effect is set in motion. At the other extreme, the critics have argued that the MNC is an exploiter and neocolonialist. Originally, investing in extractive type activity in order to acquire raw materials, it kept the developing countries a advantage and dependent. Today, they suggest it has added to its sins by upsetting countries' political, social and cultural fabric, (Kingsey 1988). These impacts would be looked at from the following perspectives:

The multinational and their supporters would argue that they are absolutely essential in a developing country's industrialisation, since first and foremost, they bring the necessary technology, which could not be developed by the host country itself. Proponents of the need for multinationals further argue that they promote an improved manufacturing capacity, and ensure that knowledge and skills (particularly management skills) are transferred, (Okwandu 1997).

Integrated manufacturing by MNCs brings in reasonably sophisticated technology and establishes important industries such as cars and textiles in developing countries.

Finally, since technology involves more than just a production process, the MNC trains manpower and skills can then be diffused.

The benefit the MNC brings to the host nation are jobs. It is associated closely with the issues of entrepreneurial development, competition, complementary activity and management. It is not only that jobs are created directly at both the managerial and blue-collar level, but they are also simulated indirectly.

A Multinational corporation provides training in other that its requirements can be met. Technical, financial and marketing expertise is passed on and confidence is therefore built up in other sectors of the economy. Multinational employees can in time move their own business and other entrepreneurs are stimulated to upgrade their products, expand their market and develop more backward and forward linkages themselves, (Kingsey 1988).

There have been many accounts of such development. Vernon (1971) argued that the Mexican mining and railway building boom of the nineteenth century helped to establish a new entrepreneurial class composed of traders, bankers, provision providers, contractors and small manufacturers. Other have pointed the positive correlation between the growth of an entrepreneurial class and increase in foreign investment in the most successful newly industrialised nations, such as Hong Kong, Malaysia, South Korea and Taiwan.

An oligopolistic market structure may also develop from highly capital intensive multinational activity, for the technology is oriented to high demand and the developing country's domestic market is usually too small to provide this. Multinationals are known to induce competition and encourage entrepreneurial development, since they possess the advantages of superior technology, and more financial resource for advertising.

The next major benefit about MNC is management. This has been said to be absolutely essential to the unlocking of any potential a country possesses and the provision of its organisation. Management techniques are demonstrated, nationals are trained and skills are passed on to sectors of the economy. Before any of the mentioned benefits are maintained, management must be provided and the MNC remains perhaps the most Important factor in introducing it.

Though there is no argument that most developing countries need foreign exchange, there remains controversy over the extent to which MNC activity provides it. However, MNC's impact in this area remains extremely positive. The host country either saves scarce foreign exchange through MNC manufacturing products formerly imported or earns foreign exchange through MNC exporting its manufactured goods. In the course of this, income within nation is raised, which leads to domestic savings which can be ploughed back to generate more income, (Feleye 1993).

Economic development takes off from joint ventures between host countries and MNCs. It may also be a result of the form of expansion of MNCs activities in host countries. There are also cases where MNCs have reinstated abandoned projects in host countries. For instance, in 1994, Fontina-a Brazilian and Japanese MNC- succeeded in bringing back to operation, abandoned steel project in California, (Rourke 1991). In the recent past, a similar effort was made here in Nigeria by those of the Soviet Union (Russia) and France to give operational life to Nigeria's Largest Iron Steel Complex in Ajaokuta. How much success has been achieved is another issue. In the U.S., Honda, Subaru and other Japanese cars now being made under wholly owned subsidiaries. Certainly, this has brought growth and development for the United States of America.

The global outreach of MNCs creates and maintains global economic interdependence among nations. For instance, in 1993, Japan had a total of 16.9 billion-dollar investments in the United States of America. On its part, the US had a total of 53.4 billion-dollar investment in Japan, Economic interdependence means that Japan and the US would not hastily into a state of war. This mutual economic interdependence reinforces more of collaborative tendencies than discord and tension, (Majaro 1977).

The MNC provides the means of introducing the necessary attitudes and consequently reducing the associated non-economic barriers to development. At the same time, because people see what is available and what can be achieved, demand is simulated and a multiplier effect set in motion. The MNC therefore brings in products and processes, which are wanted but would not be available otherwise, (Majaro, 1997).

Multinational corporations (MNCs) are not completely indifferent to the creation of good relationship with the host countries. They extend their goodwill and social/welfare services to the communities where they are based. For instance, they have built schools, hospitals, pipe-borne water, and access roads in local communities of their operations. Oil producing companies in Nigeria have continued to provide educational assistance and scholarship to many Nigerians, (Nhedu 1990).

Losses From Multinational Business: Hosts' Perspective

First, it is often argued that inappropriate technology is implanted. If intermediate technology is used, this may be considered obsolete and a ploy to keep the developing country at a permanent disadvantage. It has also been suggested that labour-intensive practices may not be more economical in some instances. Where skilled labour is scarce. It may be preferable to use capital intensive methods rather than train and supervise labour, however cheap. Conversely, the argument goes, if very sophisticated technology is introduced, employment is not created and the balance of payments worsen because of the need to import expensive capital equipment, (Okwandu 1997).

It has been indicated by many developing countries that technology is never completely transferred, because MNC continually innovates and keeps vital process at home in order to maintain its lead. Indeed, R & D facilities tend to remain in the home country.

Second, it has been argued that MNC brings that wrong type of jobs. Highly capital intensive jobs as well as being inappropriate in some contexts, may also lead to a very small multiplier effect. At the same time, economic and social inequalities may be promoted. Since only a few local people benefit from higher wages and an enclave of wealth among a sea of poverty is said to result. Sometimes, ethnic stratification too is promoted, (Okwandu 1997).

Third, jobs are actually destroyed, since the MNC operating on this basis kills local competition and stifles entrepreneurial development. Since the MNC possess superior technology, the entrepreneur's position is therefore undermined and potential new competitors are discouraged.

Fourth, management is not effectively provided since culture is not sufficiently taken into account. Consequently, inappropriate techniques are introduced and local cultural values are destroyed. These tend to undermine the growth and development of local initiatives entrepreneurship and innovation. To this extent, MNCs are seen as facilitators of underdevelopment.

Fifth, critics argue that financial benefits of MNC are kept at minimum by the former and may even be considered negative if a wider conception of wealth is deceptive. One way through which the MNCs under-develop their host nations is through repatriation of salaries and profits. What the host countries do is to agree on a definite percentage of salaries and profits to be repatriated. In practice, however, what is habitual of MNCs is the evasion of taxes. Their activities are shrouded in secrecy. This explains their unwillingness to disclose or declare the profits made annually to host countries. Consequently, it is difficult to allocate appropriate value of tax that is commensurate with their income. That is even more difficult since developing countries have weak bureaucracy to effectively monitor and control the MNCs.

Sixth, environmental pollution is another area to be viewed very seriously. Pollution is a health hazard. It can take the form of industrial sewage, spillage, toxic waste and gaseous effect. For instance, if we take the activities of the MNCs in Nigeria and Libyan, oil sectors the issues of environmental pollution becomes illustrative. Oil spillage pollutes streams, arable economic lands, crops and even air. The other is that gas flaring has side effects on the inhabitants of the local communities. In the South-South and some parts of the South-eastern part of Nigeria, environmental depletion and pollution occasioned by the ill-regulated activities of oil companies have been a source of tension and conflict.

Finally, MNCs interfere politically in the affairs of the host nation. They are regarded as agents of imperialism; and have been described as a predatory octopus capable of reaching out, through its tentacles, to grasp and swallow a small fish.

The Chilean government under EI Salvador in 1973 was overthrown by the help of ITT. In Nigeria, it was alleged that some oil MNCs had a hand in overthrowing General Murtala Mohammed in 1976. They have also been involved is similar tendencies in Nicaragua, Cuba, Haiti, Libya, Iraq and Panama. MNCs are also ready instruments of parent countries to achieve any desired political and economic goals, be it economic assistance or economic sanction.

Sample Procedure

Nwankwo (1983) views population of a research as the universe of some group of people or objects in which a researcher is interested. Nevertheless, the above view does not guarantee that the researcher can establish the boundary of the conditions that specify who shall be included or excluded from the population.

In the light of the above, researcher identifies the population of this study as all Multinationals Corporations (MNCs) operating in Nigeria. Through a random sampling technique, the sample size for the study was drawn from MNCs operating within Port Harcourt and its immediate environs. The choice of Port Harcourt was born of the fact that as fast growing industrial town, it harbours much of the target population companies that will provide the required data for the study.

Analysis

For this study therefore, 20 multinational companies that had been in operation for more than 20 years are selected for the study out of 62 corporation that met the study requirement. It was also important to know the gains accruable from global operations of MNCs. They are as presented in table 1

Table 1: Gains from Global Operations.

Gains	*No. Of Frequency*	*% Of Responses*
Market Expansion	49	27
Foreign Production Facilities	21	11
Access to Natural Resources	33	18
Economics of Scale	22	12
Profitability	41	22
Personnel	18	10
Total	**184**	**100**

Source: Survey Data, 2003.

In order to elicit data on gains that make most of the MNCs embark on global operations, the above table 1 was drawn. It was shown from the table that the major gain attainable from going international is expansion of market as it had a frequency of 49 respondents. Profitability came next as gain from global operation with a frequency of 41 respondents. Of course, with an enlarged market, profit is expected to be high. Moreso, access to raw materials was also another gains with a frequency of 33. It was observed in this regard that mostly the exploration firm that were concerned in the study saw raw materials as gain. The foreign production facilities, economics of scale and personnel have frequencies of 21, 22 and 18 respectively. We than proceed to know the extent to which global operations help to achieve goals. See table 2.

Table 2: Extent to which Global Operations held MNCs to Achieve Goals.

Responses	*No. of Responses*	*% Of Responses*
Great Extent	26	50
Considerable Extent	18	35
Small Extent	8	15
Not At all	–	–
Total	**52**	**100**

Source: Survey Data, 2003.

The above table 2 was drawn to know the extent to which operating internationally helps the firm to achieve their goals. From the table above, it is observed that global operations help in attainment of a great extent as we had 26 of the respondents in favour of that option which also implies 50% rate of response. The *considerable extent* has 18 respondents and *small extent* also has 8 respondents. It therefore means that operating beyond the shores of the country of the MNCs assist to a great extent in global attainment.

Table 3: Extent to which Business Risks Affects Marketing in the MNCs.

Risks	*Great Extent*	*Considerable Extent*	*Small Extent*	*Not At All*	*Total*
Cultural	–	11(21)	24(46)	17(33)	52
Social	4(8)	27(52)	18(35)	3(7)	52
Economic	38(73)	10(20)	3(6)	1(1)	52
Technological	42(80)	7(13)	2(4)	1(3)	52
Political	9(17)	33(63)	10(20)	-	52
Legal	6(12)	21(40)	22(42)	3(6)	52
Total	**99(32)**	**109(35)**	**79(25)**	**25(8)**	**312**

Source: Survey Data, 2003. (All the figures in Parenthesis are percentage (%) figures.

In order to elicit data on the extent to which various business risk affects marketing activities of the MNCs, the above table 3 was drawn. *Cultural risk* was shown to affect them to a small extent as 24 respondents responded to that option. 17 of the respondents responded that it does not act as risk while 11 agreed that it is to a *considerable extent.*

The *social factor* was seen as marketing risk in a considerable extent since 27(52%) of the respondents respondents responded to it and the small extent has 18 respondents. Further, the *economic risk* was considered affecting marketing to a great extent. This was shown by the response pattern, which has 38 of the respondents responding to that option while 10 were of the opinion that it does to a considerable extent.

Another factor, which was also seen as affecting MNCs to a great extent is the *technology,* 42(80%) of the respondents responded to that option and just 7 felt it is to be considerable extent. Again, the *political risk* was considered as business risk to a considerable extent as it had 33 of the respondents who believed it does, while 10 and 9 of the respondents said it does to a considerable and great extent respectively. As for *Legal factor,* it was shown to have affected to a small extent.

However, it was generally observed that the business risk affects marketing activities of MNCs to considerable extent as the column total of respondents showed 109 frequency and the great extent had 99 frequency. At this juncture, it was necessary to know the extent to which opportunities are available to MNCs.

Table 4: Extent to which Opportunities are Available to MNCs.

Opportunities	*Great Extent*	*Considerable Extent*	*Small Extent*	*Not At All*	*Total*
Technology	24(46)	17(33)	9(17)	2(4)	52
Entrepreneurship	21(40)	12(33)	12(23)	7(14)	52
Management	16(31)	26(33)	10(19)	–	52
Efficiency	8(15)	32(62)	8(15)	4(8)	52
Foreign Exchange	9(17)	14(27)	24(46)	5(10)	52
Personnel	38(73)	12(23)	2(4)	–	52
Business Attitudes	20(38)	16(31)	9(17)	7(4)	52
Demands	15(29)	20(38)	13(25)	4(8)	52
Total	**15(36)**	**149(35)**	**87(21)**	**29(8)**	**416**

Source: Survey Data, 2003. (All the figures in Parenthesis are percentage (%) figures.)

The above table 4, was drawn to know the extent to which each of the listed opportunities is available to MNCs.

Technology an opportunity was said to be available to a great extent with 24 respondents responding to that option. 17 of the respondents said it is to a considerable extent. The small extent and not all have 9 and 2 respondents respectively.

Entrepreneurship was observed to be available to a great extent considering 21 respondents in favour of that option. The considerable and small extent options have 12 respondents each.

As for *Management,* 26(50%) of the respondents responded that it is to be a considerable extent and 16 and 10 respondents favoured great extent respectively. *Foreign Exchange* is however available as an opportunity to a small extent as 24 of the respondents believed and 14 of them said it is to be considerable extent.

Personnel and Business Attitude were seen as available as opportunities to a great extent. For sure, the cream of personnel out together by most of the MNCs, considering their (MNCs) ability to cope with high wages demanded and to achieve competitive advantage made them most times have the best of personnel compared to their indigenous counterparts. 38 and 20 of the respondents responded to the great extent for the opportunities.

Demand for their product as an opportunity was seen to be available up to considerable extent with 20(38%) of the respondents responding to that option. This could be traceable to their quality products. Generally, opportunities were observed to be available to the MNCs to a great extent considering the column sum of 151 frequency. Respondents were however asked on the extent to which opportunities have enhanced goal achievement, see table 5.

Table 5: Extent to which Opportunities Enhance Goal Achievement.

Responses	*No. of Responses*	*% Of Responses*
Great Extent	38	73
Considerable Extent	14	27
Small Extent	–	–
Not at all	–	–
Total	**52**	**100**

Source: Survey Data, 2003.

The researcher sought to know the extent to which opportunities available to MNCs will enhance goal attainment. From the above table 5, it was explicitly revealed that they do to a great extent with 38 respondents which implies 73% responding to that option while the considerable extent had 14 respondents and leaving the other options with no respondents. Apparently, opportunities exist to ensure achievement of the objectives of MNCs for going international.

Hypothesis Testing

Answers to some of our research questions are tested scientifically using the statistical tool of chi-square (X^2). This exercise is done to make such answers not to look like mere assumptions.

In testing, the states hypothesis the chi-square formula is $X^2 = \frac{\Sigma(0-E)^2}{E}$

Globalisation Growth and Poverty

When 0 = observed frequency

E = Expected frequency

The degree of freedom (df) was appropriately located according to the number of rows and column using the formula (R-1) C-1)

All the tests were conducted at 95% confidence interval and 0.05 significance level.

Hypothesis One

$H0_1$ Multinational marketing does not help MNCs in achieving their organisational goals.

The data used in testing the hypothesis were as presented in out table 2.

Contingency Table

Great Extent	*Considerable Extent*	*Small Extent*	*Not At All*	*Total*
26 (13)	18 (13)	8 (13)	– (13)	52

All figures in parenthesis are Expected Frequencies (E)

Calculated $X^2 = 29.84$

At df = 3, 95% confidence interval and significance level of 0.05, Critical X^2=7.81

Decision Rule

- Accept the Null hypothesis (Ho) is calculated X^2 is<critical X^2
- Reject the Null hypothesis (Ho) is calculated X^2 is>critical X^2

From the above statement, the Ho is hereby rejected since the calculated $X^2 = 29.84$ is great than (>) the critical X^2=7.81,

In other words, multinational marketing helps the MNCs in achieving their goals.

Hypothesis Two

Ho_2 Marketing risks are not challenging to the attainment of marketing goals of MNCs. The data used in testing the stated hypothesis were as presented in our table 3

Risks	*Great Extent*	*Considerable Extent*	*Small Extent*	*Not At All*	*Total*
Cultural	-(16.5)	11(18)	24(13)	17(4)	52
Social	4(16.5)	27(18)	18(13)	3(4)	52
Economic	38(16.5)	10(18)	3(13)	1(4)	52
Technological	42(16.5)	7(18)	2(13)	1(4)	52
Political	9(16.5)	33(18)	10(13)	-(4)	52
Legal	6(16.5)	21(18)	22(13)	3(4)	52
Total	**99**	**109**	**79**	**25**	**312**

All figures in parenthesis are Expected Frequencies (E)

Calculated X^2 = 214.79

At df = 15, Critical X^2= 24.99

Decision Rule

Since the calculated X^2 = 214.79 is greater than (>) the critical X^2 = 24.99, the null hypothesis stated is hereby rejected. It therefore means that marketing risks are highly challenging to marketing goal attainment of MNCs.

Summary of Findings

The researcher intends at this juncture to present the cardinal findings of this work in a capsule form. This is to serve an at-a-glance purpose and make for an easy understanding of the issues addressed in our research. They are as follows:-

1. MNCs engage in global operation in order to have an enlarged market share and improvement of profit level. In addition, access to raw materials and economies of scale were also identified as basic reasons and gains for international operations.
2. Multinational marketing helps MNCs to a *great extent* in achieving their marketing objectives since their products are made available in different markets around the globe.
3. Risks, such as economy condition, technology, political and socio-cultural risks have affected the international operation of most MNCs. Culture has left most products to the glare of the producer just as depressed economies has made many willing customers unable to buy.
4. Risks are challenging to the success of marketing activities to a *great extent.* In order words, risk inhibits the attainment of marketing goals of MNCs.
5. MNCs in a bid to be known opportunities and risks that are around their operational environment, very often carry out environmental scanning to identify same.
6. Opportunities like. technology, entrepreneurship, good management, personnel business attitude exists to a *great extent* to help MNCs survive and achieve marketing objectives.
7. MNCs adopts product differentiation, product development, and market niche as cardinal strategies geared towards goal achievement.

These are however subordinated with best-cost provider and promotional strategies.

Conclusion

The study was certainly an exploratory one geared towards identifying the marketing risks and opportunities that are available around the operational landscape of MNCs. It is only through such identification that MNCs can be guided to achieving their desired marketing goals and objectives.

Expediently, in developing economies where the standard of living is low, it is through knowing the opportunities that the right venture can be made and attain sustainable profit level of leaving known the market risks. There are however clear indications that risk abounds for the marketing activity but interesting to note they are surmountable with existing opportunities which can only be known through environmental scanning. We noted that exercise was been done by the MNCs.

Be that as it may, it lies within the ambit of MNCs to strategize accurately and reap the benefits of such opportunities to their advantage. The product differentiation and development characteristically offers much to achieve the marketing objectives of the MNCs.

Recommendations

This study as earlier observed was tailored identifying marketing risks and opportunities of MNCs. Based on our findings on the subject, we recommend as follows:

1. The economic situation of developing nations be brought into focus when depressed economies is so low that they cannot afford some of the products of the multinational firm. In this sense, affordable products sold be encouraged.

2. It will amount wasteful economic venture if products are developed in environments where they are not consumed for cultural reasons. To this end, the cultural milieu must be considered important since most consumers will not be willing consume products that are culturally barred.

3. In order to reduce production cost and make products affordable, the technology of host nations should be jointly improved upon. Efforts should be made by MNCs to assist in developing the technologies of hosts so that they will not necessarily import technology to work in their newly captured markets.

All figures in parenthesis are Expected Frequencies (E)

Calculated $X^2 = 214.79$

At df = 15, Critical $X^2 = 24.99$

Decision Rule

Since the calculated $X^2 = 214.79$ is greater than (>) the critical $X^2 = 24.99$, the null hypothesis stated is hereby rejected. It therefore means that marketing risks are highly challenging to marketing goal attainment of MNCs.

Summary of Findings

The researcher intends at this juncture to present the cardinal findings of this work in a capsule form. This is to serve an at-a-glance purpose and make for an easy understanding of the issues addressed in our research. They are as follows:-

1. MNCs engage in global operation in order to have an enlarged market share and improvement of profit level. In addition, access to raw materials and economies of scale were also identified as basic reasons and gains for international operations.
2. Multinational marketing helps MNCs to a *great extent* in achieving their marketing objectives since their products are made available in different markets around the globe.
3. Risks, such as economy condition, technology, political and socio-cultural risks have affected the international operation of most MNCs. Culture has left most products to the glare of the producer just as depressed economies has made many willing customers unable to buy.
4. Risks are challenging to the success of marketing activities to a *great extent*. In order words, risk inhibits the attainment of marketing goals of MNCs.
5. MNCs in a bid to be known opportunities and risks that are around their operational environment, very often carry out environmental scanning to identify same.
6. Opportunities like. technology, entrepreneurship, good management, personnel business attitude exists to a *great extent* to help MNCs survive and achieve marketing objectives.
7. MNCs adopts product differentiation, product development, and market niche as cardinal strategies geared towards goal achievement.

4. The pricing strategy for MNCs' products should be given attention. Naturally, indigenous products whose prices are far lower than that of MNCs might attract high demand if their products are far higher in price. Prices of products therefore, should be made to reflect home economic worth.

REFERENCES

1. Cateora, Philip R. (1996), Irwin McGraw Hill, International Marketing
2. Ekerete, P.P. 2000, *Consumer Behaviour Theory And Practice,* Springfield Publishers, Owerri, Nigeria.
3. Jains, S.C. (1981) *Marketing Planning Strategy* Cincinnati, Ohio South West Publishing Company
4. Kingsey, J.T. (1988) "Marketing in Lesser Development Countries" *Quarterly Review of Marketing.* Vol. II. No. 2 Autumn
5. Kotler P. (1998), *Marketing Management Planning And Control* Prentice Hall Nuwuechi
6. Kolter, P. (1974) "Marketing During Period of Shortages" *Journal of Marketing.* Vol. 38. No. 11
7. Litton. T. (1980) "Marketing Strategy Under Conditions of Economic Scarcity" *Journal of Marketing* Vol. 39. Pages 63-65
8. Majaro, A.A. (1977) *Marketing Research: A Structure For Decision Making* Adbon-Wesley Publishing Company
9. Nnedu, J (1990) Trade of Analysis of Consumer Values *Journal of Marketing Research.* Vol. 3. No. II
10. Nwankwo, J. I. (19830 *Introduction to Research Operations in Education and The Social Sciences* Izhardons Press Karachi, Pakistan
11. Okwandu, G. A (1992)- International Business Management. *Unpublished Monograph, Rivers States University of Science and Technology, Port Harcourt.*
12. Paliweda (1997) *International Marketing,* Martins The Printers Ltd, reat Britian.
13. Ricks, David A (1993) *Blunder in International Business* Cambridge, Mass Black Publishers.
14. Sammuel, Barbara C (1990) *Managing Rick in Developing Countries National Demands and Multinational Response* New Jersey Prentice University Press.